THE NEW WORLD OF POLITICS:
AN INTRODUCTION TO POLITICAL SCIENCE

FOURTH EDITION

NEAL RIEMER
Drew University

DOUGLAS W. SIMON
Drew University

COLLEGIATE PRESS

Collegiate Press
San Diego, California

Executive editor: Christopher Stanford
Senior editor: Steven Barta
Senior developmental editor: Jackie Estrada
Design and production: John Odam Design Associates
Photo researcher: Susan Holtz
Proofreader: Elaine Kleiss
Cover art: Eldon P. Slick

Copyright © 1997 by Collegiate Press

Library of Congress Catalog Card Number: 96-072188

ISBN: 0-939693-41-0

Printed in the United States of America

10 9 8 7 6 5 4 3 2

To my Riemer siblings and their spouses:
Evelyn and (of blessed memory) Morton
Blanche and Leonard
Arthur and Rhoda

To members of the Simon Clan:
Susan, Darren Donald, and Michele

CONTENTS

ABOUT THE AUTHORS

Neal Riemer is Andrew V. Stout Professor of Political Philosophy, emeritus, of Drew University. He received his B.A. from Clark University in 1943, and—after three years of military service in World War II—his M.A. (1947) and Ph.D. (1949) from Harvard University. He has taught at the Pennsylvania State University, the University of Wisconsin—Milwaukee, and the University of Innsbruck, Austria. His books include *Problems of American Government* (editor), *World Affairs: Problems and Prospects* (co-author), *The Revival of Democratic Theory, The Democratic Experiment, The Future of the Democratic Revolution: Toward a More Prophetic Politics, New Thinking and Developments in International Politics: Opportunities and Dangers* (editor/co-author), *Karl Marx and Prophetic Politics, James Madison: Creating the American Constitution, Creative Breakthroughs in Politics,* and *Let Justice Roll: Prophetic Challenges in Religion, Politics, and Society* (editor/co-author). In 1967–68 he received the Outstanding Professor Award at the University of Wisconsin—Milwaukee, and in 1985 the Distinguished Professor Award from the Graduate School, Drew University. In Spring 1996 he served as Distinguished Visiting Honors Professor at the University of Central Florida.

Douglas W. Simon is a professor of political science at Drew University, specializing in international affairs, United States foreign policy, international organization, and national security. He received his B.A. from Wilamette University in 1963 and his Ph.D. from the University of Oregon in 1971. Prior to entering graduate school, he served in U.S. Air Force Intelligence, including a tour in Vietnam in 1965–66. After arriving at Drew in 1971, he directed the university's Semester on the United Nations for fifteen years and then served a five-year term as Convener of Drew's Masters in International Affairs Program. In 1991 he was the first recipient of Drew's Presidential Distinguished Teaching Award and that same year received the Sears Outstanding Educator Award. In addition to *The New World of Politics*, he is the co-author of *New Thinking and Developments in International Politics: Opportunities and Dangers* and has contributed to such publications as the *Harvard Journal of World Affairs, East Asian Survey, Comparative Political Studies, International Studies Notes, Teaching Political Science,* and *Society.*

ACKNOWLEDGMENTS

We deeply appreciate the keen editorial skills of Jackie Estrada, who has so resourcefully guided the preparation of this fourth edition. It is, indeed, wonderful for authors to have such an intelligent and talented editor with whom to work. We also are indebted to our fine photo researcher, Susan Holtz, whose efforts have served to make this edition more attractive to readers.

We should also like to thank a number of our Drew University colleagues for their helpful counsel in their areas of expertise: David Cowell, Catherine Keyser, Julius Mastro, William Messmer, Hans Morsink, Philip Mundo, Richard Rhone, Paul Wice.

We continue to benefit from the sage advice of David Raphael Riemer on problems of welfare reform and urban politics, of Jeremiah Michael Riemer on European history and politics, and of Seth Daniel Riemer on religion and politics.

Members of Drew University's library staff have again responded helpfully to a number of our bibliographic inquiries: Jody Caldwell, Josepha Cook, Linda Connors, Ruth Friedman, and Juli Johnsen Papp. Neil Clarke and Ray Semiraglio of Drew University's computer center, by performing their magic on disks, were again of great assistance in the preparation of this edition of the book. Renaldo Reyes and Luis Delgadillo at the United Nations kindly assisted with photographs from the U.N.'s photo collection. Peggy Farrell, Thomas Atkinson, and Michael King kindly responded to our many requests to make duplicate copies of chapters. Lydia Feldman, our departmental secretary, cheerfully and efficiently facilitated our work in enumerable ways.

Finally, we thank our respective wives:

To Ruby Riemer for continuing dialogoue on issues relevant to the relationship of politics to philosophy, literature, and women's studies.

To Susan Simon for her patience and common sense about issues of the day.

Neal Riemer
Douglas W. Simon
January 1997

PROLOGUE

In this fourth edition we again seek to introduce students to the challenging discipline of political science by highlighting six cardinal features. We strongly believe that our unique and comprehensive approach, employing those six features, can best equip students of political science to stay abreast of the ever-changing, and ever-challenging, world of politics, a world now on the brink of a soul-searching new millennium. This is still a world in which the issues of peace/war, human rights/tyranny, prosperity/poverty, and ecological balance/malaise still dominate the political agenda.

The key changes and challenges over the three years since the third edition involve a host of significant developments—for example, momentous elections in the United States, Russia, Israel, and South Africa. These changes and challenges require us to reassess the strength and effectiveness of liberal democracy in the United States, to ponder the shaky political evolution of Russia, to assess the fate of the peace process in the Israeli-Arab world, and to examine the possibility of a genuinely democratic multiracial society in South Africa.

However, even as we seek to keep abreast of a new world of politics, we will need, again, to keep our eyes critically focused on the six enduring and interrelated features of our unique approach to the study of politics.

First, and most important, we affirm the importance of addressing the three main concerns of political science: political philosophy and ethics, empirical/behavioral political science, and public policy. We seek to do so by addressing three major and most challenging problems:

1. Can we as citizens as well as political scientists articulate, and defend, a view of the good political life and of other guiding political values?

2. Can we develop a science of politics to help us understand significant political phenomena—the empirical realities of politics?

3. Can we bring political wisdom to bear on judgments about politics and public issues?

These three problems clearly suggest a fourth problem that will also engage our attention:

4. Can we integrate these ethical, empirical, and prudential concerns in a unified field of study?

These problems are challenging because vigorous debate still rages about the meaning of the good political life, about the very possibility of a science of politics, about the likelihood of making wise judgments, and about the difficulties of linking the ethical, social scientific, and prudential concerns of political science. We welcome these challenges and hope that our unique and comprehensive approach will contribute to enlightened dialogue and creative debate. We invite our readers to join in this stimulating dialogue and debate.

Second, we reaffirm our normative preference for politics as a civilizing enterprise, one that enables people in the political community to live better, to grow robustly in mind and spirit, and to find creative fulfillment. This normative premise has guided our choice of topics in this book. This theme of politics as a civilizing enterprise has also provided a standard for exploring the meaning of political well-being, a metaphor for the healthy political community that is able to enhance individual realization within the framework of the common good.

To hold this perspective, however, does not mean ignoring the ugly fact that politics is often not a civilizing enterprise, that politics is sometimes a dirty and unpleasant business. Truth, honor, decency are sometimes casualties in the world of politics. Appreciating the realities of politics clearly requires a keen understanding of war as well as peace, tyranny as well as freedom, injustice as well as justice, ecological malaise as well as ecological health. Political well-being and political disease, as we shall clearly see in the chapters of this book, are intimately related subjects of inquiry. It remains important, however, to see and seek to achieve politics at its best, as well as to recognize how it can degenerate and function at its worst.

Political health, or political well-being—the third cardinal feature of our approach—provides a central concept that integrates the three major concerns of political science. This concept, we believe, is fruitful because it allows us to view political health as an ethical norm—the norm of the good political life. A focus on political well-being also influences the social scientific investigation of politics, an inquiry that centers on empirical hypothesis, evidence, and validation and that may yield a scientific understanding of political health or illness. Finally, ethical inquiry and social scientific investigation can, indeed should, lead logically to wise political judgment—to political healing, to sensible public policies that may improve the well-being of people and political communities.

The fourth cardinal feature of our approach requires us to recognize realistically the ever-changing nature of politics and the tasks that such changes thrust upon the student of politics. These are the tasks of assessing and responding to changing values, changing institutions and behavior, and changing domestic and international politicies. Changes in politics strikingly reinforce in a very significant way the book's major emphasis on the interrelatedness of political values, political realities, and prudent judgment. These changes and tasks also reinforce the continuing need to explore the political health of political communities.

Keeping abreast of the changing nature of politics is, clearly, an imperative of a realistic political science. A realistic political science cannot, however, neglect a thoughtful recognition of the enduring realities of the struggle for power. Current developments and contemporary changes are always best understood in the light of those enduring ethical, empirical, and prudential realities. It is most important, moreover, to appreciate that changes may pose dangers to be avoided as well as opportunities to be seized. Changes may, ironically, usher in the "best of times" or the "worst of times."

Strikingly, political changes all relate significantly to the cardinal values of peace, freedom, economic well-being, and ecological balance stressed in this book. These changes highlight political realities that vitally affect domestic and international politics. Political actors, as they seek to advance their values in the light of the realities of politics, will need to exercise prudent, wise judgment as they respond to the striking changes that have taken place in recent years. The new world of politics calls on political scientists to respond intelligently to the end of the Cold War, to the ongoing problems of liberal democracies, to the continuing plight of developing countries, and to a host of challenging political, economic, religious, scientific, and environmental developments.

Moreover, as political actors and political scientists respond to the opportunities afforded by and the dangers inherent in a significantly changed world of politics, they need to be sensitized to the possibility of our fifth cardinal feature of this book: creative breakthroughs in politics. We argue that political breakthroughs in politics, although rare in history, are possible and that political scientists have a major contribution to make in advancing such breakthroughs. Such breakthroughs are generally prompted by a tough problem that the conventional wisdom says cannot be solved: Can we, for example, really protect against genocide? Can a formerly Communist Russia or a currently Communist China ever achieve constitutional democracy? Will a multiracial South Africa really work? Can Israel and its Arab neighbors really achieve a genuine peace and prosperity? Can the United Nations really fulfill the high-sounding purposes of its creation? Can nations of the Third World achieve political unity, economic prosperity, and constitutional democracy? The exploration of these tough questions constitutes a prominent part of this book. We invite students of political science to respond creatively to the tasks attendant on such exploration.

Finally, and here we come to our sixth cardinal feature of *The New World of Politics: An Introduction to Political Science,* it is important to keep the future in mind—not only the immediate future, but the long-range future. In the prophetic tradition we must carefully scrutinize the future as well as the past and the present. Political scientists need to be trained to use futuristic scenarios, positive and negative, to critically assess the future of politics. Although difficult, it is crucially important to look to that future as best we can. Here students of political science are challenged to explore the future imaginatively.

Consequently, we encourage students (1) to probe the future of political values more clearly, fully, and critically; (2) to seek to grasp the emerging realities of politics more incisively, keenly, and astutely; and (3) to weigh the costs and benefits of future alternative judgments, policies, and actions more prudently, humanely, practically in order to reach wise decisions.

This book seeks to advance the critical exploration of those six cardinal features of *The New World of Politics: An Introduction to Political Science* in its five parts and twenty chapters. Each of these five parts explores a key organizing question.

In Part One—our "Introduction" to the field of political science—we ask this question: How do we understand political science and politics? The four chapters in Part One attempt some answers. To stimulate interest about the nature and challenge of politics, Chapters 1 and 2 use some dramatic "political games" and some crucial choices. For example, Chapter 1 employs four cases drawn from history, literature, and political philosophy to focus on the players, stakes, rules, strategies, and tactics in the "game" of politics. Chapter 2 uses four memorable cases to emphasize the central role of choice in politics. Then, after using these "games" and choices to highlight goals, realities, and judgments in politics, we move on in Chapter 3 to a more systematic way of outlining the major tasks, fields, and controversies of political science. Finally, in Chapter 4, we emphasize how the larger physical, social, and cultural environment affects the discipline and its tasks.

Our guiding question in Part Two, "Political philosophy and Ideology," is: How do political philosophy and ideology illuminate our understanding of politics? In Chapters 5 we discuss the contributions of the great political philosophers, and in Chapters 6, 7, and 8 we examine such political ideologies as liberal democracy, communism, and democratic socialism. In the final chapter in Part Two, Chapter 9, we outline the challenges to these ideologies (or belief systems) posed in different ways by fascism, the Third World, and the political futurists.

In Part Three, "Comparative and World Politics," we consider the question: How far have we come in developing a fruitful science of politics? In Chapter 10 we begin by defining the central features of the scientific method and by considering how these features can be applied to the discipline of political science. In Chapters 11–14 we focus on such significant empirical problems as the gap between the actual and professed values of political actors, and we explore which political patterns are successful in furthering cooperation, advancing accommodation, and handling conflicts in national and international politics. In Chapter 15, on decision-making models in politics, we underscore the important reality that politics inescapably involves judgment and action—a topic that leads logically to a fuller exploration of public policy in Part Four.

In Part Four, "Political Judgment and Public Policy," we focus on the question: How can we sharpen our prudent judgment on key issues of public policy? To probe this question we explore in Chapters 16–19 a number of policy issues of global concern, such as the achievement of a peaceful world order, greater freedom for the "least free," worldwide economic well-being, and a sane ecological balance. The public policy chapters seek to encourage students to articulate their own ethical values, to present and assess significant empirical findings relevant to the problems at hand, and, finally, to balance ethical, empirical, and prudential concerns in reaching sensible political judgments. These chapters seek to engage the active judgmental ability of students on important—and controversial—problems of the day, the decade, and the future.

Finally, in Part Five, our "Conclusion," in Chapter 20, "The Challenging Future of Politics and Political Science," we ask: How will we, in the twenty-first century, carry on the work of politics as a civilizing enterprise? Here we recapitulate the argument of our book and modestly pick up again on the sixth cardinal feature of the book: that concerned with the future of politics and, indirectly, of political science. Consequently, we set forth some scenarios about the future of politics—scenarios involving the character of the political world in the twenty-first century. Our final chapter recognizes that those who read this book will be engaged in the politics of the next century. They will have to be prepared to take charge and to respond intelligently, effectively, and humanely to the political issues of that time. In this book, which seeks to introduce students to political science as a discipline intimately involved with ethics, empirical social scientific inquiry, and public policy, we are endeavoring to help students respond to those future problems with understanding and wisdom.

Lawrence Chang
Kean College of New Jersey
Union, NJ

Bernard Condon
Iona College
New Rochelle, NY

Barbara Conkle
Western Kentucky University
Bowling Green, KY

Allan D. Cooper
Otterbein College
Westerville, OH

Eugene J. Cornacchia
Saint Peters College
Jersey City, NJ

Cindy Courville
Occidental College
Los Angeles, CA

George Cvejanovich
Barry University
Miami Shores, FL

Marlyn Dalsimer
Adelphi University
Garden City, NY

James Delahanty
Mount Saint Marys College
Los Angeles, CA

David R. Eberhardt
University of Colorado at Denver
Denver, CO

E. Joseph Fabyan
Vincennes University
Vincennes, IN

Sam H. Farahani
San Diego Mesa College
San Diego, CA

Tibor Farkas
Marymount Manhattan College
New York, NY

Michael P. Federici
Concord College
Athens, WV

Michael Fischetti
Montgomery College
Rockville, MD

Robert J. Fitrakis
Columbus State Community College
Columbus, OH

James L. Gillespie
Notre Dame College
Cleveland, OH

Yogesh Grover
Winona State University
Winona, MN

Stylianos Hadjiyannis
Shawnee State University
Portsmouth, OH

Joseph Hajda
Kansas State University
Manhattan, KS

Roger Hamburg
Indiana University at South Bend
South Bend, IN

David Hartsfield
Northeast Missouri State University
Kirksville, MO

Professor Heidenreich
Kemper Military School and College
Boonville, MO

Ceferina G. Hess
Lander University
Greenwood, SC

Susan Hunter
West Virginia University
Morgantown, WV

Rathnam Indurtny
McNeese State University
Lake Charles, LA

Jerry D. Johnson
Montana State University
Bozeman, MT

Daniel Jurkovic
Carthage College
Kenosha, WI

Mark Kelso
Saint Francis College
Loretto, PA

Daniel Kumar
Seton Hall University
South Orange, NJ

Perri L. Lampe
Maple Woods Community College
Kansas City, MO

Carolyn Landau
Marist College
Poughkeepsie, NY

Robert W. Lane
Saginaw Valley State University
University Center, MI

James Lea
University of Southern Mississippi
Hattiesburg, MS

Alan T. Leonhard
University of New Orleans
New Orleans, LA

David S. Lindberg
Elmhurst College
Elmhurst, IL

Yu-Long Ling
Franklin College
Franklin, IN

Carl Livingston
Seattle Central Community College
Seattle, WA

Patrizia Longo
Saint Marys College
Moraga, CA

R. Douglas MacPherson
Charleston Southern University
Charleston, SC

John L. Martin
University of Maine
Fort Kent, ME

Krishan Mathur
University of the District of Columbia
Washington, DC

Steve Mazurana
University of Northern Colorado
Greeley, CO

Kelly L. McDaniel
Three Rivers Community College
Poplar Bluff, MO

Christine Miller
Davenport College
Lansing, MI

Ann Nelson
Salve Regina College
Newport, RI

Francis Nyong
Pasadena City College
Pasadena, CA

Edwin A. O'Donnell
Wayne State College
Wayne, NE

Nchor Bichene Okorn
Dillard University
New Orleans, LA

Ebere C. Onwudiwe
Central State University
Wilberforce, OH

Robert Parks
Elmira College
Elmira, NY

Chris Patrinos
Holy Names College
Oakland, CA

Iraj Paydar
Bellevue Community College
Bellevue, WA

William D. Pederson
Louisiana State University
Shreveport, LA

Glenn E. Perry
Indiana State University
Terre Haute, IN

Chau T. Phan
Rider University
Lawrenceville, NJ

Lucille Poirier
North Country Community College
Malone, NY

William Postiglione
Quincy College
Quincy, IL 62301

James Rhoads
Westminster College
New Wilmington, PA

Kenneth Rogers
Arkansas Technical University
Russellville, AR

Robert M. Ruff
Volunteer State Community College
Gallatin, TN

G. Russell
University of Oklahoma
Norman, OK

Don Schmidt
University of Nebraska
Kearney, NE

Seymour J. Schwartz
Daley College
Chicago, IL

Alan Simmons
Chatfield College
Saint Martin, OH

Valerie Simms
Northeastern Illinois University
Chicago, IL

Laura M. Stearns
Southern Seminary College
Buena Vista, VA

James Sundberg
Western Illinois University
Macomb, IL

Thomas T. Sweeney
North Central College
Naperville, IL

Estrella Sybinsky
University of Hawaii
Windward Community College
Kaneohe, HI

C. Stephen Tai
University of Arkansas at Pine Bluff
Pine Bluff, AR

Mehran Tamadonfar
University of Nevada Las Vegas
Las Vegas, NV

Meta Townsend
Wagner College
Staten Island, NY

Ignatius J. H. Ts'ao
SUNY College at Oneonta
Oneonta, NY

Christopher T. Vanneson
Pierce College
Puyallup, WA

Dick Van Tassell
York College
York, PA

Jacqueline Vieceli
Mankato State University
Mankato, MN

Thomas A. Waters
University of Wisconsin
Platteville, WI

Robert A. Wells
Thiel College
Greenville, PA

Majid Yazdi
East Texas State University
Commerce, TX

John Ziegler
Hendrix College
Conway, AR

P   A   R   T   O   N   'E

INTRODUCTION

The chapters in Part I seek to introduce you to politics and to the discipline of political science. They are designed to help you understand the political scientist's tasks, fields of study, and key controversies. You are invited to think critically about politics, especially about the extent to which politics functions as a civilizing activity. Are the tasks we discuss the tasks that political scientists ought to be performing? Do the traditional fields of study do justice to the discipline? The central question that each of these introductory chapters addresses is: *How can we best understand politics and political science?*

Chapters 1 and 2 begin by presenting some "games" that politicians play and by emphasizing the importance of choice. These games and choices highlight differing views of the good political life, of political realities, and of wise judgment. The metaphor of a game calls attention to these crucial features of politics: players, stakes, rules, and behavioral strategy and tactics. Four dramatic models illustrate the way power—a cardinal factor in politics—is used. These sample political games are designed to help you think critically about ends and means in politics. The chapter also highlights the struggle for power in politics—that is, who gets what, when, how, and why. Our presentation builds on your commonsense understanding of power as strength and influence and on your appreciation of the military, political, economic, or ideological aspects of power.

Politics involves grappling with tough problems in an often difficult world. By focusing on four momentous choices in politics, Chapter 2 underscores the relationship between values, behavior, and judgment. These choices highlight the creative challenge involved in reaching wise decisions. Thoughtful investigation of these choices should stimulate you to probe political philosophy and ethics, comparative and world politics, and public policy in the succeeding parts of this book.

Chapters 1 and 2 are designed to engage your interest and to prepare you for a somewhat more systematic presentation of our approach to political science and its main concern: politics.

Chapter 3 defines political science and outlines the conceptual framework for the entire book. Political scientists, we emphasize, explore the good political life, a science of politics, and wise judgment on public policy. Although these interests are evident in the traditional fields of political science, political scientists still argue about which of these concerns should be most prominent and about fitting them into a unified discipline.

Our exposition of the nature of political science assumes some familiarity with our suggested framework. Indeed, you could not have lived seventeen to twenty-one years or more without arriving at some views about the good political life, acquiring some understanding of political realities, and making some judgments about political actors, institutions, and policies. Chapter 3 builds on this awareness.

Chapter 4, the final chapter in Part I, explores how the larger physical, social, and cultural environment influences political values, behavior, and judgment. To understand problems in politics, people need to be aware, for example, of the geographical world they live in, the biological creatures they are, and the social communities they have built. The work of political scientists is thus informed by a variety of scholars, among them historians, economists, geographers, sociologists, anthropologists, psychologists, physicists. Chapter 4 seeks to make students of political science very cognizant of the interdisciplinary setting of politics.

Our four introductory chapters provide you with a framework for a more complete exploration of the nature of politics and political science.

AT ITS BEST, politics can be a civilizing activity. It can preserve the peace, protect human rights, advance economic well-being, and encourage excellence in the arts and sciences. At its worst, however, politics—particularly for those on the losing side of the struggle for power—makes for war, tyranny, economic ruin, and barbarism. Even in democratic and constitutional countries, politics at its worst involves falsehood, deception, meanness. In this chapter we explore politics at its worst and at its best by examining some classic political models from history, literature, and political philosophy. These examples suggest certain patterns that we call "political games."

THE GAME OF POLITICS

Politics is a process, within or among political communities, whereby (1) public values are articulated, debated, and prescribed; (2) diverse political actors (individuals, interest groups, local or regional governments, and nations) cooperate and struggle for power in order to satisfy their vital needs, protect their fundamental interests, and advance their perceived desires; and (3) policy judgments are made and implemented.

Although subject to certain constraints imposed by the larger environment, political actors are still remarkably free to shape their own destiny—for good or ill. They have a creative ability to respond to political problems in diverse ways. The political games we will analyze in this chapter illustrate a variety of responses. Your critical appraisal of these games should advance three of this book's central purposes:

- To deepen your critical appreciation of the good political life
- To enhance your scientific understanding of politics

GAMES POLITICIANS PLAY

• To develop your capacity for wise political judgment

In this introductory chapter our guiding question is, *How can the metaphor of a game serve our understanding of politics?*

We chose the games that follow because they illustrate a wide range of political activity: physical annihilation, the Machiavellian struggle for power, the political strike, and nonviolent civil disobedience. These patterns illustrate various forms of power: military power, political cunning, the withholding of vital services, and the appeal to conscience. Although we do not include the wheeling and dealing of such games as "bargaining"—commonly referred to as the politics of accommodation—this pattern is treated frequently later (for example, in Chapters 2, 6, 7, 12, 13, and 15).

Elements of the Game

The model political games presented in this chapter are both dramatic and educational. As drama they may entertain. As education they may enhance critical intelligence and shape political character and wise judgment. But can such a serious business as politics be called a game? We certainly do not mean to imply a frivolous pastime. We do mean to suggest that all politics is a contest, or a series of contests, usually among identifiable *players*, with certain *stakes* at issue, sometimes pursuant to designated *rules*, and often in accord with appropriate *strategies and tactics.*

A game includes **players**—contestants who win or lose, who compete or cooperate in pursuit of certain goals, who exercise power or will, who enjoy or suffer.

The **stakes** in the game are the goals that can be gained in victory or lost in defeat. The **rules** are the agreed-on procedures that must be followed if the game is to retain its identity; they regulate the conduct of the game.

Finally, games entail strategies and tactics—plans of action, schemes of attack or defense, judgments that bring about victory or defeat.

Thus, one way to look at politics is to see it as a gamelike struggle to fulfill certain purposes; to gain, keep, and use power; and to formulate public policy. By viewing politics in this way, we can better explore its key patterns, particularly with the help of the following questions:

• *Who are the players? Why do they play as they do? What are their strengths and weaknesses?* Answers to these questions can reveal the players' political values, behavior, and judgment.

• *What is the game about?* In politics the stakes may be life or death, freedom or slavery, peace or war. The issues may involve economic prosperity or poverty, order or disorder, civilization or barbarism. A given contest may take the form of an election. In a developing nation, independence and orderly growth may be at stake. Elsewhere the crucial issue may be economic growth, education, or crime. Or it may be increased opportunities for minorities. To explore such contests is to explore political ideals, behavior, and judgment.

• *How is the game ordered—if it is ordered?* Students of political games are vitally interested in what the rules permit and what limits and penalties they impose. Are the rules designed to advance order and fairness? Students of politics are particularly concerned about the existence of an umpire to ensure that the rules are followed. Such considerations also require students to explore ethical, empirical, and prudential questions.

• *Which strategies are wisest?* This question encourages students of political games to distinguish between strategy and tactics, to increase their capacity for wise judgment, and to explore the connections between policy, purpose, and power.

Unfortunately, the games politicians play are more complicated than football or chess. Unlike the contestants in such games, politicians involved in a given battle may not follow the same rules, or even any discernible set of rules. If not all players follow the same rules, the players who have to respond to their opponent's rules are at a serious disadvantage. This creates the kind of confusion and alarm we call the Alice-in-

Wonderland effect. When Alice plays croquet in Wonderland, she is not accustomed to using hedgehogs for croquet balls, flamingos for mallets, and playing-card soldiers for wickets. Nor is she accustomed to a system in which the accused is first beheaded and *then* tried!

To compound the confusion created when there is no agreement on rules, politicians frequently shift from one game to another without warning. Consequently, a participant may not be aware of the decisive game—and its rules—until the contest is over. Politicians may also attempt to play several games simultaneously.

The Destruction-Accommodation-Conversion Continuum

Can we devise a scheme to help us understand the variety of political games? Several classifications are possible. Figure 1.1 offers a scheme in which the games are seen as ranging across a destruction-accommodation-conversion continuum.

At one end of the continuum are games aimed toward complete **destruction** of the opposing player. These games are marked by deadly conflict and war. Violence, including terrorism and torture, is prominent, and political, economic, psychological, and military instruments of force are used to exercise power.

Joseph Stalin's destruction of his "enemies" within the Soviet Union is one infamous example of this strategy. Stalin came to power in the Soviet Union shortly after V. I. Lenin's death in 1924 and ruled with dictatorial power until

his own death in 1953. Through his actions an policies, Stalin destroyed high-ranking political and military leaders, millions of Russian farmers, and millions of people suspected of disloyalty. Many were killed outright; others (for example, rich farmers) died of starvation; still others were broken or died in prison camps.

Adolf Hitler also illustrates a twentieth-century pattern of destruction. He, too, killed high-ranking party members who had helped him come to power. He, too, destroyed all effective political opposition to his rule. His barbaric campaign of destruction led to murderous onslaughts against Germany's neighbors; to slave labor for millions forced to work for the Nazi war machine; to concentration camps and death for millions of Germans and other Europeans; and to the Holocaust (the systematic killing of 6 million Jews).

An even more recent example of the destruction game is the notorious campaign of "ethnic cleansing" carried out in Bosnia-Herzegovina—a former part of Yugoslavia—primarily by Serbs against Muslims. Genocidal killings have also occurred and continue to occur in Rwanda and Burundi in Africa.

In the middle of the continuum are games of **accommodation,** marked by cooperation, bargaining, and balloting. This pattern of politics is characterized by free elections, a two-party or multiparty system, public debate, and constitutional action according to the rule of law. Games of accommodation predominate in liberal democracies and in democratic socialist regimes.

Destruction	**Accommodation**	**Conversion**
Fierce clash and deadly conflict	Compromise	Loving consent and voluntary agreement
Imposed choice	Cooperation Competition	Free choice
War	Bargaining Balloting	Peace
Violence	Rule of law	Nonviolence
Appeal to force	Appeal to public sanction	Appeal to conscience

Figure 1.1
The destruction-accommodation-conversion continuum.

However, variations on these games also occur in authoritarian regimes.

At the other end of the continuum are games characterized by the peaceful **conversion** of the opponent. This pattern of politics emphasizes voluntary agreement and free choice. In this pattern even a majority decision may be ignored if the majority deviates from the claims of conscience. Love, conscience, and reason are the instruments used in games of conversion. If games of destruction rely on arbitrary dictatorial edict and games of accommodation rely on constitutional majority rule, then games of conversion look to unanimous agreement. Players of the game of conversion—for example, religious groups such as the Society of Friends (Quakers)—may seek to exercise influence (a version of power), but such influence is based, they argue, on truth and love rather than on majority rule or physical force.

Thus, the use of **power** to get political actors to do what they would not normally do ranges from overwhelming violence at the extreme pole of destruction to overwhelming charismatic, or spiritual, power—the free appeal, by word and deed, to the mind and heart—at the pole of conversion. Political games, then, may involve fierce clashes and deadly conflicts, mild competition and pacific accommodation, or loving consent and freely given obedience.

Along the continuum, power may be used in many ways other than for destruction or conversion. Power may be used to balance, to seduce, or to support. For example, political actors may use the carrot or the stick to exercise influence: they may promise and deliver a host of benefits (money, goods and services, position, prestige), or they may threaten and retaliate with sanctions (the loss of benefits).

Political behavior is thus often a mixture of bullets and ballots, of arbitrary might and the rule of law, of bullying and encouraging. The character of the game depends significantly on the sanity of the players, the vital interests at stake, the status of rules and law, and judgments about wise policy and strategy.

Now let us turn to some dramatic games drawn from history, literature, and political theory.

"WIPE-OUT": THE POLITICS OF DESTRUCTION

Superficially, **"wipe-out"** is a simple game. One player, insisting on total domination, encounters resistance and uses brute physical force to destroy an opponent. Wipe-out exemplifies the ultimate use of force in the struggle for power. Of course, complications can occur because of the different ways in which power is used, the maneuvers that precede total destruction, and the strange "logic" of a "reason of state" that "justifies" exterminating the opponent. The following classic model of "wipe-out" will help explain some possible complications.

Athens and Melos

In his *History of the Peloponnesian War* the Greek historian Thucydides presents the game with brilliant clarity.[1] The game unfolds at Melos, a Greek island caught in the midst of the savage war between two mortal political enemies: Athens and Sparta. Because the Melians will "not submit to the Athenians like the other islanders," they are forced into a confrontation. In the great struggle between Athens and Sparta for the mastery of greater Greece, the Melians at first remain neutral. But when the Athenians plunder their territory, the Melians assume "an attitude of open hostility." This leads to the brutal confrontation between the Athenians and the Melians.

Initially, the Athenians seek to negotiate the capitulation of Melos without all-out war. They have overwhelming military power and want to press their advantage. Their message is loud and clear: Surrender or be wiped out! They attempt to win the Melians over by appealing to their self-interest. The safety and security—indeed, the very preservation—of Melos requires that the Melians submit to Athens. The Melians must accept the harsh realities of power politics. The Athenians candidly declare: "You know as well as we do that right, as the world goes, is only in question between equals in power. . . . The

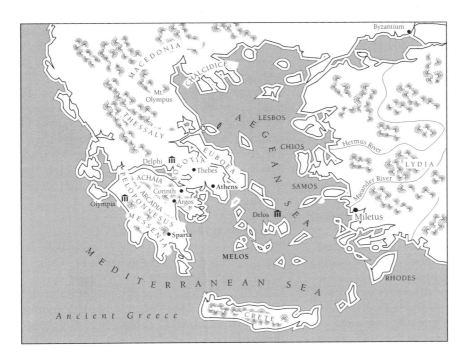

*Figure 1.2
Ancient Greece: Note
the relation of Melos to
Sparta and Athens.*

strong do what they can and the weak suffer what they must." Do not, they urge the Melians, rely on appeals to justice, the gods, or the Spartans. Such appeals will not be answered.

At a serious disadvantage in the contest, the Melians try desperately to shift the game's emphasis from power to **justice**. They plead for the "privilege of being allowed in danger to invoke what is fair and right." They appeal to the gods. They remind Athens of the power of Sparta. They warn Athens of potential dangers. They cling to the idea of heroic resistance: "To submit is to give ourselves over to despair, while action still preserves for us a hope that we may stand erect. . . . We will not in a moment deprive of freedom a city that has been inhabited these seven hundred years . . . and so we will try to save ourselves. Meanwhile we invite you to allow us to be friends to you and foes to neither party."

The Athenians reject the idea of a neutral Melos and reemphasize their earlier arguments. The neutrality of Melos would adversely affect Athenian power, and appeals to justice, the gods, and the Spartans will not be answered, because

gods and men respect power. "Of the gods we believe, and of men we know, that by a necessary law of their nature they rule wherever they can." The Spartans will aid the Melians only when Spartan self-interest is engaged and Spartan power can be mustered without grave risk. Unfortunately for Melos, Sparta's vital interests are not at stake, and its power is not great enough to warrant a challenge to Athens at Melos. And so the Athenians plead with the Melians: Do not be blind. Be prudent. Save yourselves. Do not be led by fear of disgrace into hopeless disaster. Do not hesitate to protect your country and its prosperity. Choose security, not war and ruin.

So the game is played. The Athenians seek domination without war but reserve the power to destroy their opponent. The Melians insist on freedom and independence even at the risk of war, and they hope for the best. Thus, the debate over power and justice, over "reason of state" and enlightened self-interest comes to an end. The war of words, which so candidly reveals the strategy and tactics of the players, ceases. Physical hostilities commence. The Athenians lay siege to the isle of Melos. Pushed beyond endurance, the Melians finally surrender. Thucydides writes that the Athenians "put to death all the grown men whom they took, and sold the children for slaves, and subsequently sent out five hundred colonists and inhabited the place themselves."

This sketch identifies the players, stakes, rules, and strategy of the wipe-out game. The opponents played for varied stakes. Athens sought to dominate Melos. For Melos there were three possible outcomes: (1) life and freedom, at best; (2) submission and domination if Melos agreed to accept Athens's terms; or (3) war, destruction, slavery, and death, at worst.

In examining this game, we discover that there were no agreed-upon rules to protect the Melians. They sought in vain to persuade the Athenians to honor a code of justice and to respect the rules of neutrality. The Melians also failed to convince the Athenians to observe the rule that warns of the penalties for aggression. Such penalties may have to be paid when the aggressor's action engenders countervailing power or when the aggressor loses power.

The Athenians urged the Melians to accept the game of mastery. They urged the Melians to consider the penalties for failing to play the Athenian game: war, destruction, and death.

They urged recognition of the rule that justice is the interest of the stronger party. Superior power, not abstract justice or sentimental good will, is what counts in politics.

Athenian strategy was thus guided by Athens's need to protect its vital interests with superior strength. Such strength could normally convince a rational opponent, who sees self-preservation as the most vital interest, to back down. Melian strategy included an appeal to the gods, to justice, to the Spartans, and to Athenian self-interest.

Relevance to Modern Politics

The pattern of purpose, power, and policy revealed by this game can be illustrated in a host of actions throughout history. We have already referred to the destructive patterns of Stalin and Hitler. The notorious Khmer Rouge Communist regime in Cambodia (Kampuchea) is another illustration of dreadful wipe-out. From 1975 to 1979, according to the U.S. State Department's 1989 *Country Reports on Human Rights Practices,* the Khmer Rouge, led by Pol Pot, compiled one of the worst records of human rights violations in history as a result of a thorough and brutal attempt at restructuring Cambodian society. More than 1 million people, out of a total population of

Young children at the "Killing Fields" memorial, on the outskirts of Phenom Penh. More than 1 million out of a population of 7 million lost their lives during the genocidal regime of the Khmer Rouge in Cambodia (Kampuchea).

approximately 7 million, were killed or died under the Khmer Rouge's genocidal regime.[2]

To Stalin, Hitler, and the Khmer Rouge, we can add thousands of other wipe-outs, such as the "conquests" of native Americans by Spaniards and Anglo-Americans. Communist regimes in North Korea, China, and Cuba have also wiped out their political opponents, sometimes through murder, sometimes through prison or exile. Fascist dictatorships such as Mussolini's in Italy and Franco's in Spain did likewise. Ethnic cleansing in Bosnia illustrates a contemporary pattern of wipe-out.

To understand such political games is not to approve of them, any more than a doctor approves of disease. But in the body politic, as in medicine, diagnosis must precede prognosis. Only with a fuller, more critical understanding of purpose, power, and policy can we begin to explore what leads some political actors to engage in wipe-out. We can then ask a crucial ethical question: What power should be exercised to protect a state's vital interests or a ruler's ideological commitments or positions? We can also ask an important empirical question: Is superior power (understood here as physical force) what counts in politics? And we can ask a troubling prudential question: Is it ever wise to sacrifice freedom to ensure self-preservation?

The relevance of these matters to twentieth-century politics is suggested by the following questions, which illustrate the problematic character of politics:

- In order to protect the lives of American soldiers and to bring World War II to a rapid end, was President Truman justified in ordering the destruction of Hiroshima with the first atomic bomb?
- If the allies had not mustered superior physical force against the Nazis and the Japanese in World War II, would Hitler and the Japanese warlords have triumphed, and with what consequences for freedom?
- Were the Japanese and the Germans wise to accept unconditional surrender—and at least a temporary loss of their freedom—to ensure their self-preservation?

These questions suggest the difficulties inherent in the struggle for power. Next we will examine another political game to illustrate the complexity of that struggle.

"LION AND FOX": THE POLITICS OF THE NATION-STATE

We find the title of our second game in the works of Niccolò Machiavelli, who studied and wrote about the politics of Renaissance Italy.[3] The key players in the game of **"lion and fox"** are the rulers of states. At stake are a state's vital interests: its unity, independence, freedom, security, power, and prosperity. The key rules in this game require leaders to behave realistically, to protect their community's vital interests, and to use both force and craft. Violation of rules will incur severe penalties.

Niccolò Machiavelli (1469–1527), high-level Florentine civil servant, sought to draw maxims for politics from history and experience. He recognized that politics often confronts the politician with a choice between public success and private morality. Realistically aware of politics as a struggle for power, and yet republican in his political philosophy, Machiavelli's thought poses the problem of determining how far political success excuses immoral behavior.

Machiavelli: The End Justifies the Means

If "princes," or rulers, are to win amidst the struggles for power that surround them, they must be adept at the "beastly" game of realistic politics. They cannot survive and prosper if they know or play only the higher human game of morality and law. They must know the game of lion and fox, played primarily with force and craft and, if necessary, unscrupulously. As Machiavelli put it: "A prince being thus obliged to know well how to act as a beast must imitate the fox and the lion, for the lion cannot protect himself from traps, and the fox cannot defend himself from wolves. One must therefore be a fox to recognize traps, and a lion to frighten wolves."

Machiavelli held that a prince is justified in playing the game of lion and fox because "in the actions of men, and especially of princes . . . the end justifies the means." "For," he wrote, "where the very safety of the country depends upon the resolution to be taken, no considerations of justice or injustice, humanity or cruelty, nor of glory or of shame, should be allowed to prevail. But putting all other considerations aside, the only question should be, What course will save the life and liberty of the country." When the occasion demands it, force and craft must be used boldly and shrewdly. On such occasions "good faith" and "integrity" can be sacrificed. The prince (as a lion or a fox) has only "to be a great feigner and dissembler." Machiavelli continued, "Thus it is well to seem merciful, faithful, humane, sincere, religious, and also to be so; but you must have the mind so disposed that when it is needful to be otherwise you may be able to change to the opposite qualities." Hence, "in order to maintain the state," a prince may be obliged "to act against faith, against charity, against humanity, and against religion."

Machiavelli outlined the general strategy of lion and fox with great candor. The prince must act "to secure himself against enemies, to gain friends, to conquer by force or fraud, to make himself beloved and feared by the people, [and] followed and reverenced by . . . [his] soldiers." With a keen regard for circumstances, he must act with Renaissance *virtu*—that is, with resolve and energy. Appreciative of dangers, the prince must be prepared to "destroy those who can injure him." With an eye to power, he must "maintain the friendship of kings and princes in such a way that they are glad to benefit him and fear to injure him." Recognizing the importance of the citizenry, the prince will win and keep widespread popular support and rely on a loyal citizen-army. Above all, he will use muscle power and brainpower, severity and kindness, with discrimination and a shrewd regard for his ends and his power.

Machiavelli did not exclude the rule of law or the influence of traditional Christian morality. But he did assert that in playing the game of lion and fox in a corrupt world, the prince who confuses what ought to be with what is will surely lose. "For how we live is so far removed from how we ought to live, that he who abandons what is done for what ought to be done, will rather learn to bring about his own ruin than his preservation."

The foregoing strategy is prominent in *The Prince*, which Machiavelli wrote as a textbook for statesmen who would establish a state in a world beset by corruption, quarrelsome groups, foreign interference, and external aggression. But even in *The Discourses*, his book on the internal and external affairs of Rome, Machiavelli insisted that those who would rule a republic on the basis of good laws must also be concerned with good arms. Moreover, even in a republic, a high commitment to popular virtue, a balance of social classes, the constitutional competition of parties, and the sound exercise of public opinion must not make the republican ruler forget the beastly game of lion and fox.

Physical power, particularly military strength, is crucial in nation-state politics and must be used, when necessary, effectively. For Machiavelli, military power meant a citizen-army. Good soldiers were the "sinews of war." The prince must be skilled in the organization, discipline, and conduct of war. He must use power to eliminate actual enemies and to paralyze potential enemies. The prince must be wary of helping others to become "powerful." He must avoid making common cause with someone more powerful than himself. He should always use shrewd judgment in exercising power—guarding against false hope, overexpansion, the "insolence of victory," empty threats, and "insulting words."

The prince must be a "ferocious lion" and an "astute fox." He must shrewdly consider the uses of power and the uses of love, fear, hate, cruelty, and magnanimity. Thus, to build a strong internal base for his power, a prudent prince should seek to maintain popular favor, satisfy popular needs, and reward merit and achievement. The prince must artfully seek "to be feared and loved." But since "it is difficult for the two to go together," if he has to choose, he will act on the assumption that "it is much safer to be feared than loved." Moreover, the "prince should make himself feared in such a way that if he does not gain love, he . . . avoids hatred." To this end, a prince should abstain "from interfering with the property of his citizens and subjects or with their women." If he has to take a life, let the reason be clear and the justification convincing.

If possible, villainy and hatred should be avoided, but sometimes circumstances require cruelty. Then, Machiavelli suggests, "the conqueror must arrange to commit all his cruelties at once, so as not to have to recur to them every day, and so as to be able, by not making fresh changes, to reassure people and win them over by benefiting them." Here Machiavelli makes his famous—or infamous—distinction between "well committed" and "ill committed" cruelties: "Well committed may be called those (if it be permissible to use the word well of evil) which are perpetuated for the need of securing one's self, and which afterwards are not persisted in, but are exchanged for measures as useful to the subjects as possible. Cruelties ill committed are those which, although at first few, increase rather than diminish with time." And, of course, the prince should let others handle his cruelties and unpopular duties while he bestows "favors."

Relevance to Modern Politics

Lion and Fox is a difficult and dangerous game that is probably played more frequently throughout the world than most rulers (liberal democrats as well as authoritarians) are willing to admit. The high goals of classical political philosophy and modern constitutional morality are abandoned in this game. Machiavelli was willing to accept less than the best political life because complete justice is not possible for earthly political actors. In the battle between actual power and traditional morality, morality loses.

This game is notorious because of the candor with which Machiavelli laid bare its rules and its strategy. This notoriety should not obscure either the strengths or the weaknesses of the game. Machiavelli sought to achieve unity for Italy in the face of widespread popular corruption, dreadful internal divisions, and despised foreign domination. He held that the philosophy and tactics he advocated would achieve victory. He hoped, of course, that the outcome of the game would be a virtuous republic in which a divisive church, quarreling nobles, numerous principalities, and interfering foreign powers would not prevent the people from enjoying unity, liberty, prosperity, and strength.

But is it possible to find a Great Man—a Machiavellian Prince—able to do the job? The problem haunted Machiavelli in Renaissance Italy:

> And as the reformation of the political condition of a state presupposes a good man, whilst the making of himself prince of a republic by violence naturally presupposes a bad one, it will consequently be exceedingly rare that a good man should be found willing to employ wicked means to become prince, even though his final object be good; or that a bad man, after having become prince, should be willing to labor for good ends, and that it should enter his mind to use for good purposes that authority which he has acquired by evil means.

The problem still haunts us today as we reflect on the careers of Napoleon, Bismarck, Stalin, Hitler, and hundreds of other national leaders, oppressive tyrants, false messiahs.

It is a tribute to Machiavelli's genius that he understood so well what rulers of modern nation-states think they must do. They must protect the state's vital interests. They must be devoted, pragmatically, to success. They must maintain a love affair with power, particularly military power. They must not confuse what ought to be with what is. They must be prepared to operate as both lions and foxes.

Sometimes we may think that lion and fox describes only authoritarian rulers, or such forceful and astute leaders as Otto von Bismarck, the "Iron Chancellor" of nineteenth-century Germany, whose use of military might and diplomatic cunning played a dominant role in unifying his country. Yet rulers of constitutional democracies also play lion and fox in foreign affairs. The Iran-Contra scandal in the Reagan administration is one notorious illustration. This scandal involved secret efforts within the White House to violate federal law by selling arms to Iran to finance Contra forces opposing Nicaragua's Sandinista government.

The game is also evident in U.S. domestic politics. For example, dirty tricks in political campaigns illustrate "foxy" politics in operation. The Watergate scandal is the best known because it reached into the office of the American presidency itself. Watergate is the name given to a series of scandals in President Richard M. Nixon's administration. First, there was an attempted burglary of the Democratic party's national headquarters at the Watergate Hotel in Washington, D.C. in June 1972. Two employees of President Nixon's reelection committee were involved, and Nixon's former attorney general was accused of approving the break-in. Then the president's top advisers and allegedly Nixon himself attempted to cover up the bungled burglary. A number of officials were convicted for their roles in the affair. On August 9, 1974, Richard Nixon resigned his presidency under threat of impeachment.

Leaders in other administrations have also been seen in a Machiavellian light. For example, James McGregor Burns subtitled his sympathetic study of Franklin D. Roosevelt "The Lion and the Fox."

Students of political science must, however, ask critical questions about this game. Should we accept the doctrine that the end justifies the means—no matter what the end or the means? How realistic is Machiavelli's "realism"? Do Machiavellian realists miss important aspects of power because of their narrow understanding of power? Do such realists fail to see that short-range success does not necessarily secure long-range vital interests?

We now turn to another game, concerned with peace and an unorthodox means of achieving it.

"STRIKE": THE POLITICS OF WITHDRAWAL

For our third game, we turn to the comedy of the dramatist Aristophanes. The geographical terrain is once again ancient Greece, and the background is once again the contest between Athens and Sparta.

Lysistrata: *Make Love, Not War*

The game is "**strike**," as sketched with ribald delight in Aristophanes's play *Lysistrata*.[4] In it, the women of Greece are pitted against the men of Greece. Peace or war is the issue. No orthodox set of rules seems to govern this game. But we do encounter a strategy in which one side seeks to paralyze the will and convince the mind of the other side. Here in Aristophanes's bold and blunt play is the first women's strike for peace.

Lysistrata, the Athenian ringleader of the strike, and the other women of Greece are tired of war. They constitute one side in the game. The men of Greece, who have been fighting the Peloponnesian War for twenty-one years, constitute the other side. Lysistrata conceives a masterful plan to end the war. If all the Greek women on both sides of this protracted bloodletting will abstain from sexual relations with their men, the men will be forced to sue for peace. The action is a strike, a true withholding action designed to make the soldiers on both sides see the profitlessness of war. The weapon to be employed is the power of sex.

The game reveals, with startling clarity, the strengths and weaknesses inherent in the game of strike. The strikers must be united and resolute. The activity withdrawn must be an indispensable one. Moreover, once victory is achieved, the strikers must be able to strike again if the other side reneges.

Initially, Lysistrata seeks to unite her forces. She gathers female leaders in Athens and proposes her strategy of total abstinence. There is murmuring in the ranks. Self-denial will affect the women as well as the men, and not all women are prepared to put peace before sex. Lysistrata must assure them that her strategy will be effective. She carries the argument and then moves to unite her forces by a solemn oath:

> I will have naught to do whether with lover or husband. . . . I will live at home in perfect chastity . . . beautifully dressed and wearing a saffron-colored gown . . . to the end that I may inspire my husband with the most ardent longings. . . . Never will I give myself voluntarily . . . and if he has me by force . . . I will be as cold as ice, and never stir a limb . . .

Trouble, however, breaks out in the ranks that Lysistrata has assembled in the Acropolis, the citadel housing the Athenian treasury with which the war is financed. Many women find it too difficult to remain there. They lust after their men and seek to escape. Lysistrata urges them to hold out: "You want your husbands, that's plain enough. But don't you think they want you just as badly? . . . But hold out . . . hold out! A little more patience and the victory will be ours."

Aristophanes used an encounter between Cinesias, an Athenian man, and his wife, Myrrhine, to illustrate the astute strategy in the game. "All afire with the flames of love," Cinesias approaches the group of women and asks for his wife. Lysistrata urges Myrrhine to use her feminine power to force him to capitulate and give up war: "To work then! Be it your task to inflame and torture and torment him. Seductions, caresses, provocations, refusals, try every means! Grant every favor—always excepting what is forbidden by your oath."

The dialogue between Cinesias and Myrrhine

is an intimate and revealing account of one variety of feminine power in this game of strike. At the crucial moment when Cinesias hesitates about voting for peace, Myrrhine runs away. Cinesias, frustrated and tormented, is left to exclaim, "I'm a dead man."

Meanwhile, the Spartan women have been successful with their part of the strike, and the Spartan men are ready to sue for peace. The strike is carried out successfully in all parts of Greece and brings peace to the land. The men of Greece wanted their women more than war. They are enjoined to return to their homes and henceforth make love, not war.

The play's ending has a modern ring. However, its feasibility, except in the imagination of a comic genius like Aristophanes, remains to be tested. Quite clearly, enormous willpower on the part of a united womankind is mandatory. And it is by no means established that women have differed significantly from their men on the great issues of war and peace over the centuries. Nor is it clear that women have greater willpower than men.

Relevance to Modern Politics

The technique of the strike has, of course, been widely used in labor-management disputes, and it figures prominently in Marxist political strategy in capitalist countries. In the United States the strike is a powerful weapon, used by a wide range of workers to accomplish primarily economic objectives such as higher wages, better working conditions, and increased benefits. The strike is a potent weapon in strategic industries such as steel, coal, and railroads. If carried on long enough, strikes in key industries can bring a nation's economy to a halt. Indeed, even certain local strikes—say, of garbage collectors in New York City—can threaten public health. The withdrawal of important services—whether those of factory workers, teachers, telephone employees, or farmhands—can put great pressure on employers and government.

Although strikes in countries such as the United States are not intended to bring down a govern-

The 1968 strike by French students sought to bring pressure on the French government to change its policies that adversely affected students.

ment, they have been used to exact concessions from government, and some have led to changes in public policy. For example, strikes in the auto industry in the mid-1930s led to the passage of the Wagner Act in 1935, which helped ensure labor's right to organize and bargain collectively. In some countries strikes have played a prominent role in bringing down a government or altering its policies.

In Communist countries strikes have been rare. Nonetheless, the activities of the independent labor movement Solidarity in Poland in the 1980s led ultimately (despite repressive efforts) to a major upset of the Polish Communist regime and to a presidential role for Solidarity's leader, Lech Welesa, in the Polish government of the 1990s. Even in the former Soviet Union, strikes (for example, by miners) sometimes led to concessions from the Communist regime.

The use of the strike as a political weapon—as in the case of a "general strike" against a government in power or against particular policies of that government—is rare but not unknown in capitalist countries. The French writer Georges Sorel advocated the general strike as a way to bring about revolutionary change, but such strikes usually fail. Occasionally, student strikes (as in France in 1968 or in the United States during the

Vietnam war) have put pressure on governments to change their policies. Such strikes are effective because they publicize issues, not because the students have withdrawn a vital service.

The political game of strike raises a number of ethical, empirical, and prudential questions. For example, should withdrawing vital services be considered a legitimate means of advancing a political objective? Do strikers have the ability to maintain unity to accomplish legitimate political objectives? Will strikers use their power on behalf of peace, human rights, and ecological health, as well as on behalf of economic prosperity?

"CIVIL DISOBEDIENCE": THE POLITICS OF MORALITY

The game of "**civil disobedience**," which was dramatized by the Greek tragedian Sophocles in *Antigone*, is well known to the modern world. Henry David Thoreau explored the game in a perceptive essay in the nineteenth century. Mohandas Gandhi made civil disobedience popular in India—and the world—in the twentieth century. Norwegians and Danes used it tellingly against the Nazis in World War II. And Martin Luther King, Jr. revealed its capabilities in the United States during his tragically brief but influential life. We have subtitled this game "the politics of morality" because the appeal to conscience, and thus to a higher law, is its central characteristic. In our examination we will use Thoreau's brilliant essay "On Civil Disobedience" as our model.[5]

Thoreau: "On Civil Disobedience"

Who are the players in Thoreau's game? His answer resounds across the century. On one side are people of conscience—people of superior morality and integrity, who are human beings first and subjects second. On the other side are those who lack moral vision or courage—governments, majorities, people blind to the higher law or lacking the courage of their convictions. Specifically for Thoreau, on one side were those who oppose slavery and war; on the other side were the federal and state governments and the spineless multitudes who followed them.

What are the stakes? Nothing more—and nothing less—than the abolition of outrageous moral evil and the return to the commandments of the higher law. In Thoreau's case the evils were slavery and war, and the commandments were freedom and peace. Thoreau insisted, "This people must cease to hold slaves" and cease to "make war on Mexico, though it cost them their existence as a people."

The following rules apply to the people of conscience who play this game. First, the game must be peaceful. To use violence is to break a cardinal rule. Second, the act of disobedience must be selectively aimed at an outrageous moral evil. The protest must not be an indiscriminate one against all authority. Third, those disobedient must be public, not secretive, in their actions. Fourth, the participants must be prepared to pay the price of their disobedience. Thus, Thoreau peacefully went to jail rather than pay taxes to a government that supported slavery and fought the Mexican War. These rules hold only for those who engage in civil disobedience, not for their opponents.

What strategies and tactics guide the players? The disobedient must convert the ruling establishment by dramatizing the evil against which they protest. To do this they must mobilize the sleeping conscience of the political community and destroy support for a government that sanctions immoral acts. This they can do by (1) effectively rallying their own forces, (2) making moral partisans of the neutral and the indifferent, and (3) converting, or weakening the position of, the immoral ruling elite.

According to advocates of civil disobedience, this general strategy can be implemented when people of conscience cease to obey an unjust government. They do so by peacefully withdrawing their support "both in person and in property." They break the law rather than serve as agents of injustice. They may, as in Thoreau's case, refuse to pay taxes and be put in jail. Here their purpose is to clog the courts and the jails.

Henry David Thoreau (1817–1862), New England transcendentalist and radical individualist, wrote "On Civil Disobedience" in 1847. It is a provocative essay on political obligation, powerfully motivated by Thoreau's outrage against slavery and aggressive war.

Consciences throughout the land will be aroused at the sight of just men and women in jail. A chain reaction will set in as conscientious citizens refuse allegiance to, and conscientious officers resign from, the unjust government. Such action will provide the friction essential for stopping the machinery of government. The ruling elite will be divided and thus weakened. When confronted with the possibility of keeping all just people in jail or of giving up war and slavery, the state will abandon its immoral acts. Blood need not be spilled. If it is, however, it will be spilled by a state that has superior physical strength but not superior moral strength. Thus, moral strength will prevail. Civil disobedience is therefore not only desirable but feasible.

Practitioners of civil disobedience are moral crusaders. To rally his own forces, Thoreau declared:

I know this well, that if one thousand, if one hundred, if ten men who I could name,—if ten honest men only,—ay, if one HONEST man, in this state of Massachusetts, ceasing to hold slaves, were actually to withdraw from this copartnership, and be locked up in the county jail . . . it would be the abolition of slavery in America.

To rouse—indeed, to radicalize—the indifferent, Thoreau wrote:

When a sixth of the population of a nation which has undertaken to be a refuge for liberty are slaves, and a whole country is unjustly overrun and conquered by a foreign army, and subjected to military law, I think that it is not too soon for honest men to rebel and revolutionize.

To induce neutral observers to join the cause of the righteous, Thoreau emphasized several crucial arguments. Moral men and women cannot "recognize that political organization" as their government "which is the slaves' government also." They appreciate that under "a government which imprisons any unjustly, the true place for a just man is also a prison."

To undercut the legitimacy of the immoral government, and to convert and weaken the ruling elite, Thoreau appealed to a higher law: "They only can force me who obey a higher law than I."

Thoreau was aware that his opponents would argue that he rejected democratic and constitutional politics. He knew they would contend that civil disobedience illustrates a dogmatic, self-righteous position. He anticipated the criticism that civil disobedience is hostile to the normal give-and-take of democracy and constitutional compromise. Thoreau's critics argued that he refused to recognize that just and brave people may not agree about all moral issues in politics and that civil disobedience is incompatible with democratic accommodation and makes for anarchy.

Thoreau was ready to repel this counterattack. He insisted that it is important to distinguish between minor and major matters in politics. Matters that present no serious moral problem can be handled by majority rule. However, fundamental matters such as slavery cannot be left to the ethical competence of majorities. He was not seeking to destroy all aspects of government. As a good citizen, he was quite prepared to pay his highway tax and to educate his fellow citizens. He was aware of the virtues of obedience to the law, of majority rule, of constitutional debate and decision. But he also recognized that a higher law may have to take precedence over civil law. A constitution that recognized slavery and refused even to receive petitions protesting slavery did not deserve respect. Thoreau did not "wish to quarrel" or "set myself up as better than my neighbors," and he sought to obey the laws of the land. He conceded that "from a lower point

of view, the Constitution, with all its faults, is very good; the laws and the courts are very respectable; even this State and this American government are, in many respects, very admirable, and rare things, to be thankful for." But from the vantage point of a higher law of justice, the Constitution failed.

So Thoreau elaborated the strategy and tactics of civil disobedience. The boldness, as well as the difficulty, of the game is underscored by his basic assumptions: the superior power of conscience in politics, agreement on what is righteous, and the establishment's ultimate benevolence. He assumed there would be no reactionary backlash and that disobedience would not be brutally repressed.

Relevance to Modern Politics

As we noted in discussing the game of lion and fox, Machiavelli challenged most of these assumptions. They are also impugned by wipe-out. Yet, despite the objections of many to Thoreau's assumptions, Martin Luther King, Jr. used civil disobedience successfully in the civil rights movement of the 1960s. When used according to Thoreau's rules, civil disobedience proved an effective weapon for advancing the rights of African Americans. Moreover, an accumulating literature highlights the success of civil disobedience against a wide variety of authoritarian regimes. Indeed, as we will see more fully in Chapter 16, some scholars maintain that the only sane road to peace and human rights in the nuclear age is through nonviolent civilian defense.

Civil disobedience has also been used in relation to another highly controversial issue in American society: the morality, lawfulness, and wisdom of abortion. Anti-abortion advocates have, for example, used civil disobedience in their protests against abortion clinics. This issue pits pro-choice advocates against pro-life advocates. The debate involves judgments on a number of troublesome moral and legal questions: whether a fetus is a person and therefore entitled to moral rights and legal protection; how much control a woman has over her own body; how to balance the competing needs of fetus, mother, and other parties; when a fetus is viable; what to do about life-threatening pregnancies or those caused by rape or incest.

Critical questions must be asked in evaluating civil disobedience. Should people rely mainly on civil disobedience to combat outrageous moral evils? What makes a moral evil outrageous? In the real world of politics, characterized by a struggle for power, is the risk of civil disobedience worth taking?

CONCLUSION

The games presented in this chapter are educational models. As such, they may help us understand (1) the character of the major players in politics, (2) the stakes involved in key political games, (3) the rules of politics, and (4) influential strategies and tactics. These games may suggest other variations, such as *balance of power*—the politics of equilibrium; *class conflict*—the politics of domination; *stake-in-society*—the politics of vested interests; *bargaining*—the politics of accommodation; and *miracle, mystery, and authority*—the politics of benevolent authoritarianism.[6]

These games call attention to a number of important ethical, empirical, and prudential problems in politics. They highlight the clash between power and justice. They force us to look critically at "reason of state"—that rationale that prompts leaders of states to protect their nation's vital interests. They force us to ask whether a ruler must accept the "beastly" character of politics and function both as a ferocious lion and an astute fox to protect the state's vital interests. We must decide whether Machiavelli was right in holding that idealism will lead to ruin. The study of these games also entails a deeper look into the ethics and politics of political means. We have to decide if and when the strike is an effective and wise weapon, and whether civil disobedience is compatible with majority rule, democratic law, and other time-tested constitutional forms.

Today, we desperately need to clarify the purposes of politics, the uses of power, and the wisdom of policies. In recent years the ends of political life and the exercise of power have not been keenly criticized. The result has been failure to devise a prudent way to harness power for just and humane purposes. In Chapter 2 we will investigate additional scenarios in order to focus on the problems of political choice.

ANNOTATED BIBLIOGRAPHY

The following novels and plays present a wide variety of additional games that politicians play:

Bolt, Robert. *A Man for All Seasons*. New York: Random House, 1966. Highlights the clash between loyalty to conscience (and God) and to king (and country). Also reveals the nobility—and weakness—of reliance on the law in the face of a powerful, determined, and unscrupulous ruler.

Dostoevsky, Feodor. "The Legend of the Grand Inquisitor," Book V, Chapter 5, *The Brothers Karamazov*. New York: Random House, Modern Library Edition, 1950. Contains the Grand Inquisitor's brilliant (if perverse) argument that a benevolent authoritarian ruler should relieve inadequate humans of the burden of freedom.

Huxley, Aldous. *Brave New World*. New York: Harper, 1946. Describes an anti-utopian world of the twenty-fifth century.

Ibsen, Henrik. *An Enemy of the People*. R. Sarquharson Sharp, trans. New York: Dutton, 1926. Explores the conflict between a doctor's dedication to public health, truth, and the common good, and a community's interest in profit even at the expense of good health. Raises the question of the wisdom of the majority.

Kafka, Franz. *The Castle*. Willa and Edwin Muir, trans. New York: Knopf, 1930. Addresses the individual's plight in the baffling world of bureaucracy.

Koestler, Arthur. *Darkness at Noon*. Daphne Hardy, trans. New York: Macmillan, 1941. Illuminates the minds and politics of communist revolutionaries out of power and in power.

Naipaul, V. S. *Guerrillas*. New York: Vintage Books, 1980. A cynical exposé of misguided revolutionary idealism in a Third World Caribbean country.

Orwell, George. *1984*. New York: New American Library, 1951. Throws light on the loss of freedom in a totalitarian society.

Paton, Alan. *Cry, the Beloved Country.* New York: Scribner's, 1948. Movingly examines racial tensions in South Africa.

Sartre, Jean-Paul. *Dirty Hands.* New York: Knopf, 1949. Explores the ethics of ends and means in revolutionary politics.

Shakespeare, William. *Richard III*, 1592; *Julius Caesar*, 1599; *Measure for Measure*, 1604; *Macbeth*, 1605; *Antony and Cleopatra*, 1606; *Coriolanus*, 1607. Examines the games politicians play, from the viewpoint of the greatest literary voice in the English language. Highlights political machinations involving the struggle for power and who gets what, when, and how.

Shaw, George Bernard. *Arms and the Man*, 1894; *The Devil's Disciple*, 1897; *Caesar and Cleopatra*, 1899; *Man and Superman*, 1905 (especially that section often produced separately as *Don Juan in Hell*); *Major Barbara*, 1905; *Saint Joan*, 1923. No one play can do justice to Shaw's witty socialist criticism of politics and society. By all means read those magnificent lengthy prefaces, which are also great lectures on modern social science.

Skinner, B. F. *Walden Two.* New York: Macmillan, 1948. Portrays a genuinely utopian community based on scientific principles, especially stimulus, response, and positive reinforcement. Lots of cooperation and accommodation; hardly any conflict!

Sophocles. *Antigone* (c. 441 B.C.). Illustrates the tragic clash between individual conscience (as informed by a higher law) and public order (as dictated by the need for stability and safety in the community). For a dramatic contrast in interpretation, see Jean Anouilh's *Antigone*, 1944. Anouilh sees Antigone as a spoiled child and Creon as a mature and responsible leader.

Warren, Robert Penn. *All the King's Men.* New York: Harcourt, Brace and World, 1946. Describes the rise and fall of a southern-style political boss.

SUGGESTIONS FOR FURTHER READING

The following novels shed additional light on the games that politicians play. Some of these novels, as well as those listed in the Annotated Bibliography, are keenly analyzed in Irving Howe, *Politics and the Novel* (New York: Columbia University Press, 1992).

Adams, Henry. *Democracy*, 1880.

Burdick, Eugene L. *The Ninth Wave*, 1956.

Camus, Albert. *The Rebel*, 1958; *State of Siege*, 1958; *The Just Assassins*, 1958; *The Plague*, 1948.

Dos Passos, John. *U.S.A.*, 1937.

Ellison, Ralph. *Invisible Man*, 1952.

Grass, Gunter. *The Tin Drum*, 1961.

Hugo, Victor. *Les Miserables*, 1862.

Kallenbach, Ernest. *Ecotopia*, 1975.

Le Carré, John. *The Spy Who Came in from the Cold*, 1962.

Le Guin, Ursula K. *The Dispossessed*, 1974.

Malraux, André. *Man's Fate*, 1934; *Man's Hope*, 1938.

Melville, Herman. *Billy Budd*, 1924.

O'Connor, Edwin. *The Last Hurrah*, 1955.

Silone, Ignazio. *Bread and Wine*, 1962.

Snow, C. P. *The Masters*, 1951; *The New Men*, 1954; *Corridors of Power*, 1964; *Last Things*, 1970.

Solzhenitsyn, Aleksandr. *The Gulag Archipelago*, 1974.

Steinbeck, John. *The Grapes of Wrath*, 1939.

Stendhal, Marie Henri Beyle. *The Red and the Black*, 1831.

Swift, Jonathan. *Gulliver's Travels*, 1726.

Tolstoy, Leo. *War and Peace*, 1862-1869.

Zola, Emile. *Germinal*, 1901.

GLOSSARY TERMS

accommodation
civil disobedience
conversion
destruction
justice
lion and fox
players
politics
power
rules
stakes
strike
wipe-out

POLITICS AND CHOICE

THIS CHAPTER focuses on the challenging subject of politics and choice to underscore the intimate connection between values, facts, and judgment. We use four dramatic cases to illustrate the dimensions of choice in politics: (1) Socrates's choice not to flee Athens to avoid an unjust punishment, (2) James Madison's choice of a new political theory to guide the American Constitution of 1787 and the federal republic it created, (3) the choice by German citizens of Nazism and Adolf Hitler in 1932 and 1933, and (4) President John F. Kennedy's choice of a blockade to counter the Soviet Union's placement of offensive nuclear weapons in Cuba in the fall of 1962.

FOUR IMPORTANT THEMES

These cases illustrate that choices in politics can be tragic, creative, burdensome, and perilous. They enable us to see that it is not easy to choose what is right, to break through to a new political understanding, to bear the burden of freedom, or to select the least perilous alternative. As you read these cases, ask yourself what you would have done if you had been Socrates in ancient Greece, James Madison in 1787, a German citizen in 1932–1933, or President Kennedy in 1962:

- What would you do if you had been lawfully sentenced to death on charges you knew to be false and were then offered the opportunity to escape?

- Would you try a new, untested experiment in government in the face of conventional wisdom suggesting that your experiment could never work?

- As a German citizen, would you have supported Adolf Hitler's Nazi party in 1932 and 1933?

- As president of the United States, how would you have responded to the news that the Soviet Union had placed offensive nuclear missiles in Cuba?

Of course, these four cases do not exhaust the category of choices faced by political actors. However, they merit special attention because they invite critical thinking about four important themes in politics today: political obligation, creative political breakthroughs, the responsible exercise of freedom, and constraints on power politics in the nuclear age.

The first case delves into *political obligation*. Why should individuals obey those who demand their allegiance in politics, particularly those who constitute the government?

The second case explores *creativity in politics*. Is it possible, in theory and practice, to achieve a new ethical, empirical, and prudential understanding of politics? More specifically, can we devise new ways to reconcile liberty and authority?

The third case explores the *responsible exercise of freedom*—whether citizens can respond sensibly to social, economic, and political crises. Are people strong enough to bear the burden of freedom? Are they mature enough to exercise freedom responsibly, or do people, under adverse conditions, tend to abandon freedom for authoritarian rule?

The fourth case probes *power politics* in the nuclear age—the difficulty of working out sane, sound strategy and tactics under the threat of nuclear war. In times of crisis, can leaders choose courses of action that preserve the country's vital interests in peace, national security, and freedom?

Elaborating the Themes

Each case in this chapter develops one of these key themes, which recur throughout this book. Socrates, father of political philosophy in the West, initiated the critical examination of **political obligation.** His views present a **counterargument** to those advanced by Thoreau in Chapter 1. And this debate persists whenever

a government's legitimacy is called into question—by American students who protested the Vietnam war, resisted the draft, or fled their country in the late 1960s and early 1970s; by Polish members of Solidarity who protested or resisted martial law in their country or fled to avoid tyranny in 1982; by South Africans opposed to apartheid; by Chinese students in Tiananmen Square in 1989. To explore the question of political obligation is to ask what makes a government legitimate—that is, what makes government lawful and entitled to obedience and respect.

Similarly, James Madison, father of the American Constitution, merits our study. He is America's most seminal political theorist. His ideas help us understand the formation of the American federal republic, now the oldest constitutional democracy in the world—an experiment that is still unfinished. A study of Madison's guiding theory illustrates **political creativity** at its best. The task of reconciling liberty and authority remains today. It is a problem common to all nations, whether rich or poor, developing or developed, liberal democracies, democratic socialist states, or communist states.

We focus on the fateful choices made by German citizens in 1932 and 1933 for several important reasons. Historically, we want to know more about the circumstances that permitted Hitler to attain power and to use that power to unleash World War II and its dreadful consequences. Who voted for Hitler, and why? More generally, we want to know what produces **responsible citizenship** and leadership. Given the freedom to do so, can people really govern themselves successfully, particularly under adverse conditions? This question can be asked about authoritarian regimes on the left or the right, or about nations emerging from authoritarian rule (such as the republics of the former Soviet Union or the Eastern European nations now freed of Communist domination; or Spain, the Philippines, and Chile throwing off right-wing dictatorships). This question can also be asked about the struggling developing nations of

In 1989 Chinese students demonstrated in Tiananmen Square to protest the absence of freedom in China under Communist rule. The students were brutally repressed.

the world, and even about supposedly mature democratic regimes in times of crisis.

Finally, the Cuban missile crisis merits attention because it brilliantly illuminates the character of **power politics** in the twentieth century. In a world of nuclear weapons it is important to understand how in 1962 the leaders of the two military superpowers—the United States and the Soviet Union—responded to political crisis. When political actions reach the stage of big-power confrontation in the nuclear age, the fate of the entire globe is at stake. This chapter provides only a preliminary treatment of these cases and the themes they illustrate; subsequent chapters will develop these matters more fully.

Values, Facts, and Judgment

By exploring these cases and the choices they involved, we discover the intimate relationship of values, facts, and judgment. For example, Socrates's choice is incomprehensible if we do not understand the high value he placed on his birth, education, and citizenship in the Greek *polis* (city-state). Of course, the unacceptable consequences of escape and life in exile also influenced his decision.

The second case shows that Madison's dedication to republican values of popular rule and basic rights, as well as to effective governance, clarified his quest for a breakthrough to our modern federal republic. However, his respect for the seeming "facts"—that liberty is possible only in a small state or that a large country cannot be governed on republican principles—did not prevent him from challenging them and articulating a new empirical theory that enabled Americans to reconcile liberty and authority.

The third case depicts how adverse circumstances led Germans to seek a political change in order to give meaning to values such as order, strength, prestige, and prosperity. Many Germans supported Hitler because they sympathized with Nazi promises to help Germany overcome economic depression, avoid the alleged Communist menace, and recover from defeat in World War I.

Finally, President Kennedy's choice also illustrates the close connection between values, facts, and judgment. His choice in the Cuban missile crisis was dictated by the value of national security; at the same time it was made agonizing by the danger of nuclear holocaust if the Soviet Union refused to back down. Key facts—especially the military estimate that a "surgical" air strike could not guarantee the destruction of all Soviet missiles—led him to endorse a blockade, which permitted a firm response, gave the Soviet Union time to reconsider its bold gamble, and yet held open more militant options if the Soviet Union refused to withdraw its offensive weapons.

Our key question in examining these four cases is, *How does political choice illustrate the intimate connection between values, facts, and judgment?*

SOCRATES AND THE MORAL LIFE: POLITICAL OBLIGATION IN ANCIENT ATHENS

The story of Socrates's life and teachings comes to us primarily in the writings of Plato, Socrates's devoted student. Here we focus on the very end of the great teacher's life.

Socrates's Choice

Socrates has been accused of corrupting the youth of Athens and of not believing in the gods. At his trial, he vigorously denies both charges. He maintains that he is being falsely accused because of his relentless probing of ignorance and pretension among people of repute—particularly rhetoricians, poets, and artisans. This mission, ordained by God, has gotten him into trouble because those who pretend to be wise do not like having their folly exposed.

Socrates sees himself as a "gadfly"—"arousing," "persuading," "reproaching," "exhorting . . . to . . . virtue." He has tried to teach his students to put "virtue and wisdom" before their "private interests." He cannot hold his tongue because "this would be a disobedience to a divine command." And he cannot abandon his mission out of fear of death "or any other fear." He cannot give up teaching about the care of the soul. He has never yielded to injustice in either public or private life. His "only fear was the fear of doing an unrighteous or unholy thing." He has taught virtue for its own sake, not for the sake of money. He believes in a higher divinity: "Men of Athens,

I honor and love you; but I shall obey God rather than you, and while I have life and strength I shall never cease from the practice and teaching of philosophy."[1]

When he is condemned to die by drinking hemlock, a poison, Socrates refuses to bargain for his life or to accept exile or a stiff fine instead. Why should he plead for his life when he cannot be sure that life is better than death? Imprisonment, as a punishment, is intolerable because it is a kind of slavery. He cannot pay a stiff fine because he has no money. Exile, too, is unthinkable: "What a life should I lead at my age, wandering from city to city, living in ever-changing exile, and always being driven out!" On the urging of his friends, he proposes a minuscule fine as punishment.

Socrates does not regret his defense—his "apology." He has avoided unrighteousness. He departs "condemned . . . to suffer the penalty of death." Those who have accused and condemned him to death are themselves "condemned by the truth to suffer the penalty of villainy and wrong."

Crito, one of Socrates's disciples, comes to him in jail with a proposal to bribe the guards and permit him to escape. Crito does not want to lose a dear friend, nor does he want people to think that he did not do enough to save his mentor's life. Appreciative of Socrates's sensibilities, Crito argues that Socrates should not play into the hands of his enemies. Crito points out that people will respect and love Socrates in exile, that he should not betray his own children, who need him for their education, and that escape will not be disgraceful.

Socrates responds to Crito's entreaty by arguing that the key question, "the only question . . . is . . . whether we shall do rightly either in escaping or in suffering others to aid in our escape." He cannot intentionally injure others; he cannot "render evil for evil to any one, whatever evil [he] may have suffered." In escaping, would he desert the just principles by which he has lived?

Socrates puts into the mouths of those who speak for the "laws and the government" the

Jacques Louis David (1748–1825), influential French painter with strong republican sympathies, completed The Death of Socrates in 1787, the same year as the writing of the U.S. Constitution. The painting reveals David's concern for virtue, and also the anguish of Socrates's friends at his refusal to escape from prison. (Courtesy of Metropolitan Museum of Art)

answer to his cardinal question. He cannot be justified in escaping because that action would destroy the laws, the government, and the state. Athens cannot endure if its lawful decisions have no power, if individuals can set them aside at will. Socrates is indebted to his polis—his political community—for birth, for nurture and education, and for fulfillment in citizenship. By his life, growth, and fulfillment in the political community, he has undertaken a contractual agreement that he cannot now violate by escaping. He cannot disobey his parents, "the authors of his education," nor can he disavow his own agreement to obey the commands of the polis— especially when he has not been able to convince the political community that its commands are wrong. He must choose death over banishment; he could not be a "miserable slave," "running away and turning [his] back upon the compacts and agreements [he] made as a citizen." Having been born and having lived and enjoyed citizenship in the political community, Socrates cannot now repudiate that community.

Moreover, his escape would harm his friends and children and bring him no peace in exile. His friends would lose their property and citizenship and would be driven into exile as well. Other good cities would view Socrates as an "enemy," a "subverter of the laws." And he would find no happiness in fleeing from "well-ordered cities and virtuous men." If he lived in disordered cities, could he, having turned his back on his own principles, talk of "virtue and justice and institutions and laws being the best things among men?" Would he deprive his children of Athenian citizenship?

And so Socrates concludes the argument he has made for law-abiding Athenians and against his escape. Law-abiding Athenians will say:

Now you depart in innocence, a sufferer and not a doer of evil; a victim, not of the laws, but of men. But if you go forth, returning evil for evil, and injury for injury, breaking the covenants and agreements which you have made with us, and wronging those whom you ought least to wrong, that is to say, yourself, your friends, your country, and us, we shall be angry with you while you live, and our brothers, the laws in the world below, will receive you as an enemy; for they will know that you have done your best to destroy us.

Socrates's choice not to escape illuminates the problem of political obligation and the key question: Why should people obey the political community that makes claims on their allegiance? Socrates's answer is that because of the contribution that the political community makes to individuals' own lives, growth, and fulfillment, they are required to obey its laws. He argues that if one cannot persuade the political community that its laws are wrong, one is obligated to obey them.

Questioning Socrates's Choice

Socrates's view, of course, is only one way of looking at political obligation. Thoreau's position, discussed in Chapter 1, represents another view. He argued that people have no obligation to obey a government that violates a higher law and engages in outrageously immoral action such as aggressive war or human slavery.

The American revolutionaries of 1776 articulated yet another position on political obligation. They held that when a government violates the trust that brought it into being, when it persistently violates the right to life, liberty, and the pursuit of happiness, when it is not responsive to redress of grievances, then the people have a right to revolt and overthrow such a government and establish a new one, based on their consent and dedicated to the protection of their rights. This position rests on the premise that citizens owe obedience only to governments of their own making that protect their basic rights and, pursuant to their will, advance life, growth, and fulfillment.

Critical minds will raise questions for Socrates (held to be one of the wisest, most just, and best of humans), for Thoreau (as we saw in Chapter 1), and even for the authors of the American Declaration of Independence. For example, do we uncritically accept Socrates's statement that "whether in battle or in a court of law" we "must do" as our country orders? Do we accept that "punishment is to be endured in silence"? Even in battle, following orders is no legitimate excuse for violating international law or for committing genocide, the systematic killing or extermination of a whole people. Moreover, is there no obligation to speak out against unjust punishment? Some would argue (as did Martin Luther

King, Jr. and many others—including Socrates—in a long tradition of obedience to a higher law) that to endure injustice in silence is to perpetuate injustice.

Even the theory of political obligation enshrined in the Declaration of Independence has its difficulties. How do we more precisely define those "unalienable rights to life, liberty, and the pursuit of happiness" that are to be protected by a government? What conditions justify our conclusion that government is destroying those rights? How do we understand the "consent of the governed" from which "just powers" derive?

African Americans were denied liberty, often life, and certainly the pursuit of happiness when they first were enslaved in the United States and then later treated as second-class citizens after emancipation. Even today they may not be treated with genuine equality in all respects. Women in the United States have also been fighting a long battle for genuine equality. Given this record of unequal treatment, do African Americans and women have the same obligation to obey the government as others? What about other mistreated minorities? If we extend our democratic theory of obligation—that is, obedience in return for fulfillment of basic rights—to include the right to education, a job, or adequate health care and housing, then the ignorant, the unemployed, the sick, and the homeless may have less of an obligation to obey government than the educated, wealthy, and well housed. This theory of obligation certainly provides food for thought.

These critical inquiries are disquieting, but they make us see that our judgment about obligation cannot be separated from our evaluation of whether a government is legitimate, whether it honors citizens' rights, and whether it is truly based on the consent of the governed. Depending on their values and their assessment of the facts, different observers may reach different conclusions about political obligation. The young Americans who refused to fight in Vietnam had a different sense of obligation than those who fought. African Americans who refused to accept racial segregation in buses, restaurants, movie theaters, and schools had a different sense of obligation than those who went along with "separate but equal" legislation.

Clearly, an individual's respect for his or her political community—and responsibility to the government—can be interpreted in various ways, and these interpretations are closely related to how the interpreter balances values, ascertains circumstances, and weighs alternatives. James Madison and the constitutional reformers of 1787, for example, felt obligated to disobey the instructions from their states to simply amend the flawed Articles of Confederation that had governed the nation since 1781. In the very interest of improving the young republican union, they drafted a constitution with striking new powers. They undertook what some consider to be a contradiction in terms—a "peaceful revolution."

JAMES MADISON AND THE NEW REPUBLICAN AND FEDERAL THEORY: THE STRUGGLE FOR A CREATIVE BREAKTHROUGH IN MODERN POLITICS

James Madison's choice was not as simple as Socrates's. Madison's choice was a theoretical and practical response to a more complicated problem. Between 1776 and 1783, the Americans had fought a revolution to achieve independence as a new nation. But could the new nation hold together? Could the Articles of Confederation, adopted in 1781, cope with four major difficulties that plagued the infant republic: disunion, large size, faction, and the antirepublican danger?[2] Would it be enough to patch the Articles of Confederation? Or was a more fundamental change required? And how far should radical reform go?[3]

The Problem: Reconciling Liberty and Authority

These questions led Madison to formulate his key problem as follows: How can liberty and authority be reconciled in a large state? This problem would dominate Madison's thinking throughout his life. It occupied his thought and

James Madison (1751–1836) is commonly regarded as father of the American Constitution of 1787, as well as being credited as the author of of the Bill of Rights, and co-author of The Federalist.

action in 1787–1788 as he battled to draft and win support for the U.S. Constitution. It also influenced key decisions he made in the 1790s in his fight against rich, powerful forces that were unsympathetic to popular interests and to a more generous protection of democratic rights. And, finally, it dominated Madison's thinking and writing in the late 1820s and mid-1830s as he fought the growing forces of nullification and secession. These forces held that a state could nullify an act of the national government and could even secede from the Union that was the United States. (As we will see, these battles in the 1790s and later also throw considerable light on the meaning of political obligation.)

Madison's values and the facts of American geography significantly shaped his problem. He was strongly committed to popular government and human freedom in a new and large American nation that required power and authority for survival. Madison's problem was most troublesome because the conventional wisdom—the evidence of history, the testimony of political theorists, the judgment of the political science of his day—declared that it was impossible to reconcile liberty and authority in a large state.

According to conventional wisdom, republican government (based on self-government and liberty) was possible only in a small political community—for example, a city-state such as Athens, Florence, Venice, or Geneva. But the United States of America was large. Moreover, according to the conventional wisdom, a large state could be governed only by a monarch or a despot—a system incompatible with self-government and liberty.

How, then, were Americans to deal with this dilemma? Could American republicans have the best of two seemingly contradictory worlds? Could they have self-government and liberty in a republic and also enjoy legitimate power, order, and security in a country as large as America?

Others had refused to face up to the problem because they believed it to be insoluble. Patrick Henry and the other Anti-Federalists, who were opposed to the new Constitution of 1787, argued that republican government is possible only in a small political community. They did not lift their sights beyond the loose political alliance of the Articles of Confederation. They rejected the possibility—and the desirability—of a greatly strengthened central government. On the other side of the political spectrum, Alexander Hamilton and advocates of "high-toned" government, who supported the movement for a new and stronger constitution, initially maintained that only an empire or a strong central government based on the British model could hold together a political community as large as the new American nation. Confederations, they insisted, were notoriously weak, unstable, and detrimental to the interests of justice. Thus, if Henry and his friends argued that great strength in a central government jeopardized republican self-government and republican liberty, Hamilton and his friends held that in the small political community, **faction** prevailed and jeopardized both the public good and a strong national union.

Neither Henry nor Hamilton challenged the accepted political science of his day or perceived that the traditional understanding of how to reconcile liberty and authority (in the large expanse of the new United States) had to be reexamined. Only Madison challenged the con-

ventional wisdom and was bold enough to look at the problem in a new light and to ask if a new political theory—that of a federal republic—suggested a way out.

Madison's Solution

Madison's theory of the **extensive republic** constituted a breakthrough in political thought because he proposed that Americans could work out a new synthesis. They could have liberty, self-government, and justice at the local level of state government and also have a powerful central government able to protect the common interests of the whole Union—but only by adopting the model of the new Constitution of 1787. This new federal model allowed the states to control their local affairs while giving the new central government authority in matters concerning all members of the Union. For good measure, the new federal republic operated to control the effects of faction. The Constitution of 1787 created a central authority—the new federal government—that rested more legitimately on popular consent and the Union's component states, yet possessed greater strength than any confederation in history.

The features of the American federal republic are well known today, but in 1787 they constituted a **creative breakthrough** in governmental theory and practice. The federal republic had such unique features as the division and sharing of powers among Congress, the president, and the Supreme Court; constitutional limitations on national and state governments; a national government with significant powers operating directly on the people; and a strong chief executive. The breakthroughs, moreover, occurred on three fronts.

Ethically, Madison's theory (particularly as fully developed in the 1790s) included broadened concepts of liberty, self-government, pluralist democracy, and the good political life. More specifically, Madison advocated modern principles of religious liberty; freedom of speech, press, assembly, and other constitutional protections of liberty; an explicit acceptance of interests, parties, and public opinion in the process of self-government; and a more enlightened idea of popular rule, governmental power, and national union.

Empirically, Madison's theory of the extensive republic was designed to explain how Americans could enjoy the best (and escape the worst) of two worlds: how they could enjoy liberty without fear of anarchy and the adverse effects of faction, and how they could enjoy authority without fear of tyranny and the adverse effects of an overpowerful central government. The political community's large size plus its diversity and multiplicity of interests would inhibit the operation of faction and thus ensure greater success for the public good. The existence of many interests in the geographically large political community—farmers, merchants, bankers, and workers—would make it difficult for any one interest to achieve power and work against the public interest.

Representation would also filter the evil effects of faction. People would not determine policy in one great mass meeting (where they might easily be inflamed by demagogues). Rather, they would select leaders to represent them. Presumably, these leaders would be chosen because of their virtue, character, and intelligence, and they would, in turn, meet with other comparably chosen representatives to make law. This process would make it difficult for factional interests—interests opposed to the public good—to prevail.

Constitutional limitations on power and the separation of powers were "auxiliary precautions" that would help reconcile liberty and authority in the new republic. Congress would have broad, but not unlimited, powers to tax and spend, to regulate interstate commerce, and to attend to other designated objectives. But a wide range of powers would remain with the states. Moreover, the power given to the central government would not be concentrated in one organ or person; rather, it would be divided among Congress, the president, and the Supreme Court.

In addition, as Madison was to emphasize in the 1790s (in his battle against the alleged pluto-

cratic, antirepublican policies of the Hamiltonian-led Federalist party), a loyal republican and constitutional opposition party would guard against tyranny at the center. Several factors would protect against the evils of monarchy, plutocracy, and tyranny in the central government and against antirepublicanism and anarchy in the component states: (1) the constitutional operation of majority rule; (2) a sound public opinion, based on a free press; (3) a healthy two-party system; (4) the federal judiciary; and (5) wise statesmanship that could distinguish between usurpation, abuse, and unwise use of constitutional power. Given the assumptions of this theory, the central government could safely exercise generous and necessary republican power.

Prudentially, Madison's theory constituted sound political judgment on a number of crucial matters, not only in 1787 but in the 1790s and later in the 1820s and 1830s. In 1787 Madison saw the need to strengthen the powers of the central government. He wisely insisted on a new federal system that would do a better job of reconciling liberty and authority. He refused to listen to those who denied the possibility of republican government in an extensive country. And he was willing to settle for a central government that was not as strong as he had wanted because he perceived that the Constitution of 1787 was at least a major step in the right direction. Guided by his political theory, Madison articulated key features of the new federal republic in Philadelphia in 1787 and defended the new Constitution effectively in *The Federalist* and at the Virginia Ratifying Convention. After the adoption of the Constitution in 1789, he authored the Bill of Rights and supported other key legislation to shore up the new Constitution. In the 1790s he led a constitutional opposition party when he became unhappy with the Alien and Sedition Acts and other Federalist legislation. Finally, at the end of his long life, he defended the Union against the advocates of nullification and secession.

Madison took issue with the Sedition Act because it labeled as seditious (i.e., stirring up discent, resistance, or rebellion against the government in power) any hard-hitting criticism, in speech or publication, of the government. For Madison, such criticism was essential to republican government—government based on popular consent and the protection of basic rights. Indeed, Madison maintained, criticism was an obligation of good citizenship.

Nullification and secession were different matters. The Union would be destroyed if single states could nullify national legislation or withdraw from the Union at will. Either action would mean the end of republican government. Nullification and secession could only lead to tyranny and anarchy. Such actions would defeat the creative endeavor to reconcile liberty and authority in a large political community. States had an obligation to abide by majority rule in the national government and to use the U.S. Constitution to seek necessary changes.

Continuing Efforts to Reconcile Liberty and Authority

Madison's republican and federal theory of 1787 served as a generally successful guide to prudent action throughout his lifetime. His theory demonstrated that Americans could wisely reconcile liberty and authority in a large state. However, when Americans deviated from this theory, they encountered grave difficulties, the most serious being the Civil War. Madison's theory illustrates great creativity in politics; the American Civil War represents the failure of politics as a civilizing activity.

The search for creative approaches to such persistent problems as the reconciliation of liberty and authority continues, and it occurs all over the globe. This search is apparent in the countries that once made up the Soviet Union. Comparable efforts to reconcile liberty and authority are going on in other Central and Eastern European countries as they painfully attempt to achieve constitutional democracy.

Many developing countries in Asia, Africa, and Latin America also struggle to reconcile liberty and authority, often under adverse circumstances. Such struggles can be seen in a long list of countries, including Lebanon, Liberia, Cambodia (Kampuchea), Nicaragua, El Salvador, South Africa, Indonesia, Nigeria, and the Philippines. Many of these countries have suffered the agonies of civil war or acute internal discord.

Will troubled countries be successful in their efforts to reconcile liberty and authority? Can they achieve breakthroughs in politics comparable to Madison's? Such breakthroughs are rare, but the Madisonian example does hold out hope for such countries, and it may stimulate political scientists in their search for creative breakthroughs in politics.

We now turn to another case, which illuminates the burden of choice under adverse circumstances. If Socrates's decision illustrates the tragedy of choice and Madison's decision illustrates the creative opportunity of choice, then the decision of German citizens in 1932–1933 highlights the burden and disastrous consequences of choice.

THE GERMAN CITIZEN AND THE NAZI REGIME: CAN MODERN CITIZENS BEAR THE BURDEN OF FREEDOM?

Choice presupposes **freedom**. And freedom, to be most defensible, requires responsible judgment. When "the times are out of joint," responsible judgment is not easy. Does the average citizen, especially under difficult circumstances, have the common sense, virtue, wisdom, and strength to choose responsibly? Can the people be trusted to make the right choices?

Plato, Socrates's greatest pupil, would have answered no. After all, the people had condemned his beloved teacher to death. Aristotle was also suspicious of Greek democracy, which he understood as rule by the people in their own selfish interest. He argued that only in a polity (which we translate as a constitutional democracy) would popular rule be safe. A polity, he maintained, would be most secure when it rested on a strong, virtuous, well-educated, prosperous middle class. But what happens when such a middle class does not exist?

Suspicion of the people's judgment has endured. In the nineteenth century, Alexis de Tocqueville saw **democracy** as providential and inevitable. America, he felt, illustrated the future. Yet he worried about democratic despotism. Given a favorable Old World inheritance, a favorable New World environment, and creative statesmanship (illustrated, for example, in the work of people such as James Madison and other Founding Fathers), America might make democracy work. But what of countries that lacked these favorable conditions?

John Stuart Mill in nineteenth-century Great Britain also worried about the tyranny of the majority. However, he maintained that a sound constitutional, representative government—with excellent political and intellectual leadership—could preserve liberty. His fundamental confidence, despite misgivings, was reinforced by a long tradition of British liberty and by Britain's relative stability and prosperity in the nineteenth century. But, again, how would democracy work in the absence of favorable circumstances?

In the case at hand—Germany in 1932–1933— we will focus primarily on the voters who chose the Nazi party and Adolf Hitler. What circumstances led to their choice? How many, in fact, supported the Nazis, and why? We will also ask what other choices—by leaders, voters, and even anti-Nazi forces—contributed to Hitler's triumph. Our treatment will again underscore the interrelationship of values, facts, and judgment.

The Situation in Germany

First, a word about adverse circumstances in Germany. From 1919 to 1932, Germany struggled to make democracy work under the least favorable conditions. In Germany, unlike Great Britain or the United States, constitutional democracy had not put down firm roots before World War I. The new German Republic—known as the Weimar Republic because its constitution had been proclaimed in the city of Weimar in 1919—was ushered into the world under severe difficulties. Germany had lost World War I (1914–1918); 1,744,000 of its soldiers had been killed, and 225,000 of its civilians had died. Economic distress was rampant. Enemies on the Left and the Right sought to overthrow the infant republic. The Weimar Republic struggled in the early and mid-1920s to cope with postwar reparations, inflation, and depression. Its modest successes after 1925 were seriously jeopardized by the Great Depression that began in 1928. Bad times affected almost every segment of German society: industry, small business, labor, agriculture, and civil service. In a nation of 60 million, 6 to 8 million were unemployed. Profits declined and were wiped out. Farmers revolted; small-business owners and craftsmen feared destruction.

The attack on the Weimar Republic intensified in the early 1930s. Nationalists, National Socialists (Nazis), and reactionary liberals attacked from the Right. Communists attacked from the Left. And the Center (the Weimar coalition of the Social Democrats, the Catholic Center party, and the Democratic party) did not hold together. The Democratic party disintegrated. The Catholic Center party governed ineffectively in the crucial years from 1930 to 1932. As one historian noted, the Social Democrats and Communists "devoted far more energy to fighting each other than to the struggle against the growing threat of National Socialism."[4] The Nazis played on the fear of Communists and falsely accused the Social Democrats of being responsible for the defeat of 1918, the Versailles Treaty, inflation, and other German ills. The Nazis condemned the ineffectiveness of the center parties.

Hitler shrewdly took advantage of Germany's disarray to encourage the German people to escape from responsible freedom to a regime of miracle, mystery, and authority. He promised miraculous results that would endure for a thousand years. The German people had only to follow Hitler's authority to see the payoff in jobs for unemployed workers, profits for suffering industrialists, self-respect for an alienated middle class, and power and prestige for a defeated army. The people were not, however, to inquire closely into the mystery whereby the Nazis—the party of the crooked cross—would accomplish the miracle of the thousand-year Reich.

How many Germans actively supported the Nazis? And how did this support contribute to Hitler's ascent to power? In 1928 only 2.6 percent of the total vote went to the Nazi party. This figure rose to 18.3 percent in 1930 and to a high of 37.3 percent in the first 1932 election. In the second 1932 election, which was the last free election under the Weimar Republic, the Nazi vote actually fell to 33.1 percent. However, because the Left was split (the Social Democrats receiving 20.4 percent and the Communists 16.85 percent of the vote), the Nazis emerged with the single largest party vote. The Catholic Center party had maintained its percentage (16.2), but the other middle-class parties had disintegrated. Even after January 30, 1933, when Hitler was appointed chancellor, the Nazi vote in the spring 1933 election came to 43.9 percent, not a clear majority.[5]

Hitler's appeal was reflected in the first 1932 (April) presidential election, when he polled 11,339,446 votes, or 30.1 percent. Paul von Hindenburg, Germany's leading general in World War I, received 18,657,497 votes, or 49.6 percent. The Communist party candidate, Ernst Thaelmann, received 13.2 percent, and Theodore Duesterberg, a right-wing candidate, 6.8 percent. On the second ballot in 1932, candidates received the following percentages of votes: Hindenburg, 53.0 percent; Hitler, 36.8 percent; and Thaelmann, 10.2 percent.[6]

The rise of the Nazis led President Hindenburg, on the advice of right-wing, conservative advisers—especially his former chancellor, Franz von Papen—to offer Hitler the chancellorship. (The chancellor in Weimar Germany was the equivalent of the British prime minister.) Hindenburg and Papen believed that a cabinet of conservatives would be able to control the policies that Hitler would "sell" to the country through his party and its propaganda machine. This decision proved to be a terrible mistake.

But how had Nazi strength increased to the point that President Hindenburg and his advisers felt it necessary to bring Hitler in as chancellor? Why did people vote for the Nazis? The choice of Hitler was fateful; it doomed German democracy (1933–1945), brought on World War II, made the Holocaust possible, and split Germany into two parts from 1945 to 1990.

The Nazi regime used the burning of forbidden books as part of their totalitarian strategy of gleichshaltung, *or enforced conformity.*

"The ideal-typical Nazi voter," wrote Seymour Martin Lipset in *Political Man*, "was a middle-class self-employed Protestant who lived either on a farm or in a small community, and who had previously voted for a centrist or regionalist political party strongly opposed to the power and influence of big business and big labor."[7] Obviously, those who voted for the Nazis had other common characteristics as well. The Nazis drew some support from every large group of voters. They had success with the middle-class unemployed and with conservative and nationalist voters on Germany's eastern borders. The Nazis also received above-average support from male voters and from younger voters. In general, however, according to Lipset, Nazi votes came "disproportionately from the ranks of the center and liberal parties rather than from the conservatives."

The Nazis were weakest among laborers, residents of big cities, Catholics, women, and older voters. Lipset noted: "With the exception of a few isolated individuals, German big business gave Nazism little financial support or other encouragement until it had risen to the status of a major party. . . . On the whole, however, this group remained loyal to the conservative parties, and many gave no money to the Nazis until after the party won power."[8]

So the heart of Nazi strength was the middle class: small businessmen, small farmers, the self-employed, white-collar workers, civil servants, and inhabitants of small towns. These voters were hostile to big industry, big cities, big unions, big banks, as well as to the Treaty of Versailles, Communists, and Jews. Nazi supporters felt threatened by a loss of their status, by liberal values, and by economic depression.[9] They were threatened by key developments of modern society. As David Schoenbaum has noted in *Hitler's Social Revolution,* the Nazis drew on a longing for security, a common hostility to the existing order, and a universal desire for change.

It is extremely important to emphasize that the middle class was not alone in its inability to bear the burden of responsible choice. Choices made by other segments of the German population also paved the way for Hitler. For example, there was the conservatives' disastrous decision to persuade Hindenburg to offer Hitler the chancellorship, and the poor policy choices of the Catholic Center party and its leader, Heinrich Brüning, chancellor from 1930 to 1932. Brüning's deflationary policies (designed to decrease the amount of money in circulation, with a resultant increase in the value of money and a fall in prices) were very unpopular. Many scholars believe that his attempts to govern by decree undermined German democracy. In addition, the Social Democrats were unable to devise a strategy to stop Hitler. German Communists made fateful choices to work against the Social Democrats and thus divided working-class support for the Weimar Republic. Moreover, some army generals (Erich Ludendorff is the most notorious) supported the Nazis early on; others, closing their eyes to Nazi domestic politics and dreaming of the rebirth of German military power, gave their allegiance to Hitler after he became chancellor and then president. Industrialists, fearful of Bolshevism and disorder and longing for profits and prosperity through armament sales, also decided, early or late, to support the Nazis. Thus, in one way or another, many Germans proved unable to exercise freedom responsibly.

Lessons of the Nazi Experience

The Nazi experience illuminates the problem of political obligation and the failure of creativity in politics as well as the difficulty of bearing the burden of freedom under adverse conditions. Too few people in Germany were dedicated strongly enough to the Weimar Republic and to democratic values. The Nazi Right and the Communist Left clearly sought the demise of liberal democracy in Germany. The parties committed to the Weimar Republic—especially the Social Democrats and the Catholic Center—were uncreative and ineffective. Unquestionably, unsettled social and economic conditions led to the poor political decisions that jeopardized German democracy. The Communists hoped that they would come to power with the collapse of the Weimar Republic. The Nazis used the fear of communism to rally support for their cause. Democratic forces were unable to unite effectively and rally the majority of Germans to their side.

The Nazi experience raises this question: Which values, circumstances, and leadership judgments make the responsible exercise of freedom possible—and probable? This question is particularly troubling in many developing nations, especially the younger countries of Asia and Africa. They may despair of finding solutions for internal strife, poverty, unemployment, and loss of self-respect and may look for authoritarian rulers and solutions. They, too, may seek escape to a regime of "miracle, mystery, and authority."

Comparable difficulties also face many Latin American countries. These nations have longer histories of independence but lack the conditions that make for successful democratic and constitutional government. Similarly, the Eastern European nations that emerged in 1989–1990 from the unwanted embrace of the Soviet Union and from imposed Communist regimes face difficult times as they assume the responsibilities of freedom. So, too, do the republics that once constituted the former Soviet Union. Is it possible for such countries to create conditions of peace, human rights, prosperity, and self-esteem that will ease the burden of freedom and facilitate democratic, constitutional, and humane governance?

We now turn to decision making in another period of crisis, which might have been even more momentous than events in the Third Reich.

JOHN F. KENNEDY AND THE CUBAN MISSILE CRISIS: THE PERILS OF CHOICE IN THE NUCLEAR AGE

On Tuesday, October 16, 1962, at 8:45 A.M. McGeorge Bundy, the special assistant for National Security Affairs, informed President John F. Kennedy: "Mr. President, there is now hard photographic evidence . . . that the Russians have offensive missiles in Cuba."[10] This disturb-

ing news presented Kennedy with the most difficult choice of his presidency.

He convened a small group of top-level advisers to help him decide on an appropriate response. The news was especially disturbing because the Soviet Union had previously stated that it would not place offensive nuclear weapons in Cuba and that any weapons supplied to Cuba were defensive. Despite Soviet insistence, there had been rumors and charges that the Soviets were "up to something" unusual in Cuba. And in late August the Central Intelligence Agency had reported that "something new and different" was under way. What did those late-summer Soviet shipments to Cuba indicate?

Although in early September the president did not have hard evidence of offensive weapons in Cuba, he had warned that the "gravest issues would arise" if such evidence were found. At his September 13 press conference, he had declared that new Soviet shipments to Cuba did not constitute a serious threat, but he warned that if Cuba were to "become an offensive military base of significant capacity for the Soviet Union, then this country will do whatever must be done to protect its own security and that of its allies." With evidence of the missiles' arrival, Kennedy felt betrayed. He felt as if his efforts to work toward a more peaceful world had been compromised.

Considering the Alternatives

The Executive Committee of the National Security Council—or ExCom, as the President's group of advisers came to be known—met at 11:45 that Tuesday morning to consider a response. They explored six major alternatives. The United States could (1) do nothing, (2) engage in diplomacy, (3) secretly approach Castro, (4) blockade Cuba, (5) launch a surgical air attack, or (6) invade Cuba. ExCom operated with the knowledge that the Soviet missiles would be on their launch pads and ready for firing within ten days.

"On the first Tuesday morning the choice for a moment seemed to lie between the air strike or acquiescence—and the President had made clear that acquiescence was impossible," historian Arthur Schlesinger observed. The argument for doing nothing was based on the view that the USSR's ability to strike the United States from Cuba made little difference, given America's vulnerability to missiles already stationed in the Soviet Union. Doing nothing would prevent escalation and avert the danger of overreaction and an eventual nuclear catastrophe. Playing it cool would deprive Nikita Khrushchev, the Soviet leader, of any political advantage from his bold stroke.

Opponents of this alternative raised a number of serious objections. Doing nothing would permit the Soviet Union to double its missile capability, to outflank the U.S. early-warning system, and to reverse the strategic balance by installing yet more missiles on a base 90 miles from the American coast. Politically, the "do nothing" option would undermine America's credibility and resolve in the eyes of the world by making the U.S. appear weak.

Diplomatic approaches—through the United Nations, through the Organization of American States, or directly or indirectly to Khrushchev—required time, and the United States did not have much time. The Russians could stall or veto action in the United Nations. While diplomats talked, the missiles would become operational. Approaches to Khrushchev might lead to an unsatisfactory "deal" in the midst of a threatening crisis. A secret approach to Castro overlooked the vital fact that the missiles belonged to the Soviet Union and that the key decision to withdraw them was the Soviets' alone.

So the president was initially drawn to the possibility of a "surgical strike," an air attack confined to the missile bases. But was there no choice between bombing and doing nothing? If successful, an air strike would eliminate the threat to the United States. But could it be successful? Military leaders at the Pentagon concluded that a surgical strike would still leave Cuban airfields and Soviet aircraft operational. Moreover, the Pentagon could not guarantee that the Air Force could destroy all the missiles. A limited strike might expose the United States to nuclear retaliation. It would be prudent, militarily, to opt for a large strike to eliminate all sources of danger. So the surgical strike might have to be replaced by a massive strike; but this could lead to loss of Russian lives and, perhaps, to Russian retaliation in Berlin or Turkey. Moreover, could the president of

President John F. Kennedy and his advisers in the White House, in October 1962, endeavored to respond to the crisis created by the Soviet Union's installation of missiles in Cuba.

the United States, with his memory of Pearl Harbor, order a surprise attack? Was the elimination of the missiles and of Castro worth the cost of a massive strike?

Kennedy's Latin American advisers warned that a massive strike would kill thousands of innocent Cubans and do great permanent damage to the United States in the eyes of Latin Americans. His European advisers warned that the world would regard a surprise attack as an excessive response. And if the Russians moved against Berlin, the United States would be blamed and might have to fight under disadvantageous circumstances.

An invasion was also risky because American troops would be confronting about 20,000 Soviet troops in the first direct conflict between the forces of the world's two great superpowers. Would such an invasion guarantee a Soviet move against Berlin? Would it bring the world closer to World War III?

On the next day, Wednesday, Secretary of Defense Robert McNamara argued strongly on behalf of another alternative: a blockade, which would provide a middle course between doing nothing and engaging in a massive attack. The blockade would require Khrushchev to respond to a firm but not excessive step; he could avoid a military clash by keeping his ships away. The blockade would set up a confrontation in an advantageous location—the Caribbean. This alternative kept open other options, such as diplomacy or other military action, and it averted the confrontation that brought one's "adversary to the choice of either a humiliating defeat or a nuclear war," as President Kennedy noted.

But there were objections to the blockade. A blockade was an act of war and might be deemed a violation of the U.N. Charter or of international law. Even more seriously, would the blockade bring enough pressure on Khrushchev to remove the missiles already in Cuba? Would it stop work on the bases? Opponents of the blockade maintained that it would lead to a Soviet counterblockade of Berlin and to confrontation with the USSR: If Soviet ships did not stop, the

United States would have to fire the first shot, and this might invite Soviet retaliation.

On Thursday evening, President Kennedy met with ExCom. According to Schlesinger's account, the president was leaning toward the blockade:

> He was evidently attracted by the idea of the blockade. It avoided war, preserved flexibility and offered Khrushchev time to reconsider his actions. It could be carried out within the framework of the Organization of American States and the Rio Treaty. Since it could be extended to nonmilitary items as occasion required, it could become an instrument of steadily intensifying pressure. It would avoid the shock effect of a surprise attack, which would hurt us politically through the world and might provoke Moscow to an insensate response against Berlin or the United States itself. If it worked, the Russians could retreat with dignity. If it did not work, the Americans retained the option of military action. In short, the blockade, by enabling us to proceed one step at a time, gave us control over the future. Kennedy accordingly directed that preparations be made to put the weapons blockade into effect on Monday morning.[11]

Making the Choice

The debate between advocates of the blockade and those of the air strike persisted until the formal meeting of the National Security Council on Saturday. After hearing both arguments again, Kennedy endorsed the blockade. But before making his decision final, he wanted one last talk with the Air Force Tactical Bombing Command to satisfy himself that a surgical strike was not feasible. This meeting was held Sunday morning. The Air Force spokesman told the president that the air strike would have to be massive, and even then it would not guarantee the destruction of all Soviet missiles. The president had been worried that the blockade would not remove the missiles; now it was clear that an air attack could not guarantee that result either.

On Monday, October 22, at 7:30 P.M., President Kennedy addressed the nation (which had known nothing of the crisis that had engaged ExCom since October 16) and set forth his choice. He emphasized that the Soviet missile bases provided the USSR with "a nuclear strike capability against the Western Hemisphere." Soviet action constituted "a deliberately provocative

"LET'S GET A LOCK FOR THIS THING"

NUCLEAR WAR

HERBLOCK
©1962 THE WASHINGTON POST Co.

and unjustified change . . . which cannot be accepted by this country, if our courage and our commitments are ever to be trusted again by either friend or foe." The nuclear threat to Americans had to be eliminated. The president then indicated that he had imposed a "quarantine" on all offensive military equipment under shipment to Cuba. Cuba would be kept under intensive surveillance. The president also declared that any missile launched from Cuba would be regarded as an attack by the Soviet Union on the United States and would elicit immediate retaliatory response on the Soviet Union. He called for a meeting of the Organization of American States to consider the threat to the security of the American hemisphere and for an emergency meeting of the U.N. Security Council to consider the threat to world peace. Kennedy also appealed to Khrushchev "to abandon the course of world domination, and to join in an historic effort to end the perilous arms race and to transform the history of man."

So the basic choice was made. But before the crisis was over, Kennedy would have to make other key choices: to interpret the blockade flexibly (rather than rigidly) to give the Russians time to respond to a peaceful solution, and to use diplomacy (rather than force) to accomplish his objective of removing the missiles. By Thursday, Adlai Stevenson, the U.S. ambassador to the United Nations, had effectively destroyed the Soviet argument that the missiles were defensive. After asking the Soviet Ambassador to the U.N., Valerian Zorin, "Do you . . . deny that the USSR has placed and is placing medium- and intermediate-range missiles and sites in Cuba? Yes or no?" Stevenson presented the aerial photographs that revealed Soviet nuclear installations.

The Soviets then probed for a deal, and the Americans responded favorably. The Soviets would remove their missiles under U.N. inspection and the United States would promise publicly not to invade Cuba. On Friday, October 26, Khrushchev cabled Kennedy: "If the United States would give assurances that it would not invade Cuba . . . and if it would recall its fleet from the quarantine, this would immediately change everything." Kennedy responded by indicating that as soon as work stopped on the missile sites and the offensive weapons were rendered inoperable, a settlement along Khrushchev's lines was in order. Robert Kennedy, in delivering his brother's message to the Soviet ambassador to the U.S., Anatoly Dobrynin, indicated that unless the United States received assurances within 24 hours, it would take military action by Tuesday.

Saturday night was a disturbing one for President Kennedy as he waited for Khrushchev's reply. At 9 A.M., Sunday, October 28, Khrushchev's response came in. Work would stop on the missile sites. The arms "which you described as offensive" would be crated and returned to the Soviet Union. Negotiations would start at the United Nations.

And so the two-week crisis—perhaps the closest we have come to World War III—ended. President Kennedy's choices in the Cuban missile crisis underscore the dangers and difficulties of achieving national security in the nuclear age. Presidential choices have become more potent for good or ill. Presidents are forced to recognize that the stakes are higher and that their actions affect not only the vital interests of the United States but also of all humankind. These same thoughts must have troubled the Soviet leaders. This recognition may explain the relative prudence both superpowers demonstrated in respecting each other's vital interests, in achieving arms reduction and arms control agreements, and in limiting the spread of nuclear weapons. Later chapters, particularly Chapters 14 and 16, examine how prudent such policies actually are.

CONCLUSION

Our brief examination of these four cases makes clear that wise choices in politics rest on sound values, an accurate understanding of political phenomena, and astute judgment. These components are closely connected. The four cases also emphasize the importance of addressing the problem of political obligation, striving for creative political breakthroughs, learning to bear the burden of freedom, and responding wisely to the perils of decision making in the nuclear age.

Succeeding chapters reveal a host of other choices. Many are less momentous and less dramatic than those in this chapter. Some are more modest personal choices. All, however, reveal the intimate connection between values, facts, and judgments. A number of decision-making models are, for example, more fully explored in Chapter 15. And the public policy chapters in Part IV illustrate at greater length what contributes to sound judgment on four major issues.

ANNOTATED BIBLIOGRAPHY

Allen, Reginald A. *Socrates and Legal Obligation.* Minneapolis: University of Minnesota Press, 1980. Offers help for those who want to explore more fully the pros and cons of Socrates's choice in Plato's *Apology* and *Crito.*

Allison, Graham T. *Essence of Decision: Explaining the Cuban Missile Crisis.* Boston: Little, Brown, 1971.

Brilliantly analyzes a crucial choice and offers a penetrating exploration of decision making in general.

Anderson, Charles W. *Statecraft: An Introduction to Political Science and Judgment.* New York: Wiley, 1977. Adopts the standpoint of a participant actively involved in making up his or her mind about political problems. A helpful introduction.

Brinton, Crane. *The Anatomy of Revolution.* 1938. Rev. ed. New York: Vintage, 1965. Illuminates judgment and choice in four successful "democratic" revolutions in the West.

Christenson, Ron. *Political Trials: Gordian Knots in the Law.* Brunswick, N.J.: Transaction Books, 1986. Includes a perceptive account of the trial of Socrates and a number of other intriguing trials. Indispensable reading on this subject.

Fromm, Erich. *Escape from Freedom.* New York: Avon, 1965. Explores the factors in the modern world that created the "burden" of freedom and choice and tempted modern people (especially the Germans) to succumb to Nazism.

Gosnell, Harold F. *Truman's Crises: A Political Biography.* Westport, Conn.: Greenwood Press, 1980. Deals with a number of crucial presidential decisions at the end of World War II and in the crucial post–World War II years, including the decision to drop the A-bomb at Hiroshima.

Hamilton, Alexander, Jay, John, and Madison, James. *The Federalist* (1787–1788). Cleveland: World, 1961. Provides persuasive arguments on behalf of the choice of the then new federal Constitution of 1787. Unrivaled in its influence on the fateful choice over 200 years ago.

Kershaw, Ian. *The Nazi Dictatorship: Problems and Perspectives of Interpretation,* 2nd ed. London: Edward Arnold, 1989. Deals with "Historians and the Problem of Explaining Nazism" in Chapter 1.

Riemer, Neal. *James Madison: Creating the American Constitution.* Washington, D.C.: Congressional Quarterly Press, 1986. Highlights Madison's choices as a nationalist, Federalist, empirical political scientist, and democrat. Underscores Madison's theory as a creative breakthrough in politics.

Riemer, Neal. *Creative Breakthroughs in Politics.* Westport, Conn: Praeger, 1996. Explores two genuine and two spurious historical breakthroughs, one contemporary breakthrough-in-process (European Union), and a future breakthrough (protection against genocide).

Riesman, David, Glazer, Norman, and Denney, Reuel. *The Lonely Crowd*. New Haven, Conn.: Yale University Press, 1950. Presents the idea that people are tradition-directed, other-directed, and inner-directed. Underscores the difficulties of rational and ethical choice in the modern world.

Schlesinger, Arthur M., Jr. *A Thousand Days: John F. Kennedy in the White House*. Boston: Houghton Mifflin, 1965. Provides a lucid account by a sympathetic insider. Chapter 30 deals with the Cuban Missile Crisis.

Stone, I. F. *The Trial of Socrates*. Boston: Little, Brown, 1988. Offers a wonderfully refreshing account by a great journalist; much more sympathetic to those who tried Socrates and more critical of Socrates than most accounts.

SUGGESTIONS FOR FURTHER READING

Bracher, Karl D. *The German Dictatorship*. New York: Praeger, 1970.

Broszat, Martin. *Hitler and the Collapse of Weimar Germany*. New York: Berg, 1987.

Garthoff, Raymond L. *Reflections on the Cuban Missile Crisis*. Rev. ed. Washington, D.C.: Brookings, 1989.

Hamilton, Richard F. *Who Voted for Hitler*. Princeton: Princeton University Press, 1982.

Kolb, Eberhard. *The Weimar Republic*. London: Unwin Hyman, 1988.

Lipset, Seymour Martin. *Political Man: The Social Bases of Politics*. Johns Hopkins University Press, 1981.

Medland, William J. *The Cuban Missile Crisis of 1962: Needless or Necessary?* New York: Praeger, 1988.

Ortega y Gasset, Jose. *The Revolt of the Masses*. 1932. Notre Dame, Ind.: University of Notre Dame Press, 1985.

Pateman, Carole. *The Problem of Political Obligation: A Critical Analysis of Liberal Theory*. New York: Wiley, 1979.

Riemer, Neal. *The Democratic Experiment*. Princeton, N.J.: Princeton University Press, 1967.

Sorensen, Theodore. *Decision-Making in the White House: The Olive Branch and the Arrows*. New York: Columbia University Press, 1963.

Wills, Garry. *Explaining America: The Federalist*. New York: Penguin, 1982.

GLOSSARY TERMS

creative breakthrough
democracy
extensive republic
faction
freedom
political creativity
political obligation
power politics
responsible citizenship

HOW CAN WE usefully define the discipline of political science? This basic question is addressed specifically in this chapter and is also explored throughout the book. We begin by focusing on three subjects of great interest to political scientists: political philosophy and ethics, the empirical and behavioral study of politics, and public policy.[1] These subjects suggest a concern for

1. The good political life and the underlying ethical principles of politics
2. A science of politics and an understanding of significant empirical phenomena (facts, circumstances, experiences)
3. Political wisdom and judgment in the arena of citizenship and public policy

And because these three concerns are interrelated, a fourth concern arises:

4. The integration of ethics, science, and statesmanship

The traditional fields of political science (political theory, comparative politics, international politics, American politics, public administration, and public policy) can best be understood in terms of these four concerns. Of course, the emphasis may be different depending on the field. Yet we must pay at least some attention to each concern in all these fields. Indeed, the study of political science would suffer if any one of the four were neglected.

Political scientists who favor the more traditional approaches to their discipline tend to stress the importance of ethics, history, law, constitutions, formal institutions, and citizenship. Less traditional political scientists stress scientific methodology and human behavior.

POLITICAL SCIENCE: COMPONENTS, TASKS, AND CONTROVERSIES

THE THREE MAJOR COMPONENTS OF POLITICAL SCIENCE

The Ethical Component

The Empirical Component

The Prudential Component

THE FOUR MAJOR TASKS OF POLITICAL SCIENCE

Ethical Recommendation

Empirical Understanding

Prudential Judgment

Theoretical Integration

CONTINUING CONTROVERSIES IN POLITICAL SCIENCE

The Quest for the Good Political Life

The Search for a Science of Politics

Helpful Guidance for Leaders of State and Citizens

Toward a Unified Discipline of Political Science

CONCLUSION

They usually draw on psychology, sociology, economics, and mathematics in their investigations. Sometimes they combine political science and a related discipline, as in the subfield of political economy.

The controversies among approaches have centered on arguments about emphasis. Some less traditional political scientists have even argued that instead of focusing on questions about the good life and wise public policy, political science should be made a rigorous empirical science like physics or biology. Others counter that such a move would be false to the nature of politics, which is inevitably concerned with both the good political life and wise action in the political arena.

To highlight another emphasis, radical political scientists have attacked the empirically oriented students of politics for being not only narrowly scientific but also conservative. They argue that empiricists focus too narrowly on dominant power relationships and ignore the poor, the weak, and the maltreated. Empirical political scientists tend to accept what is normal as what should be, whereas radical political scientists, who may be Marxists or critical social theorists, are generally unhappy with the status quo.

Controversies like these suggest the wisdom of a broader approach. They indicate that any definition of political science that rules out political philosophy and ethics, or empirical and behavioral studies, or public policy is inadequate.

With this warning in mind, we can attempt a tentative definition of the field: **Political science** is a field of study characterized by a search for critical understanding of (1) the good political life, (2) significant empirical political phenomena, and (3) wise political and policy judgments. Political science is thus concerned with the search for

meaningful knowledge of the interrelated ethical, empirical, and prudential components of that community concerned with the public life.

The central activity of the political community is, of course, politics. As we saw in Chapter 1, **politics** is a process within or between political communities whereby (1) public values are articulated, debated, and prescribed; (2) diverse political actors (individuals, interest groups, local or regional governments, nations) cooperate and struggle for power in order to satisfy their vital needs, protect their fundamental interests, and advance their perceived desires; and (3) policy judgments are made and implemented. Let us now try to clarify these definitions by addressing the components of political science and the tasks they suggest.

THE THREE MAJOR COMPONENTS OF POLITICAL SCIENCE

Table 3.1 shows the three interrelated components of the study of politics that shape the political scientist's major tasks. By major components we mean the major concerns or parts of political science: ethical, empirical, and prudential. Throughout history, political scientists have been concerned with the study of the good political life, political institutions, behavior, and wise judgment. Until recently, these emphases were linked. In the post–World War II period, some political scientists argued that these components should be separated for study. Others, however, continued to insist on integrating these concerns.

The Ethical Component

The student of politics is concerned with political **ethics,** or what ought to be in politics. Every community adheres to certain values, is inspired by certain purposes, is dedicated to certain goals,

Table 3.1 The Major Components of Political Science

Dimension	I. Ethical	II. Empirical	III. Prudential
Main focus	Political values	Political phenomena	Political judgment
Main question	(What ought to be?)	(What is?)	(What can be?)
Foundation	Philosophy	Science	Public policy

and is committed to certain conceptions of the good life. Critical examination of these norms is a central concern of the political scientist as ethical theorist or political philosopher. For example, the Preamble to the U.S. Constitution expresses the cardinal values of the American political community: "We, the people of the United States, in order to form a more perfect Union, establish justice, insure domestic tranquillity, provide for the common defense, promote the general welfare, and secure the blessings of liberty to ourselves and our posterity, do ordain and establish this Constitution for the United States of America." Other constitutions contain similar statements of goals, purposes, and values.

But what do these values mean? This is a question the political scientist cannot avoid; it is a starting point for his or her critical investigation. Although there is widespread agreement at a general level on such values as life, liberty, peace, justice, and economic well-being, the specific meaning of these concepts in particular circumstances—and their harmony with one another—remains a source of great controversy. Indeed, most political battles center on the meaning given to these values.

Thus, critically examined values provide a *standard for judgment* in politics. This standard permits one to say that a domestic law is good or bad, that a foreign policy is morally right or wrong, that the action of a governmental official, politician, or interest group is desirable or undesirable.

The Empirical Component

Political scientists are also concerned with understanding political phenomena—political realities—in the community: events and their causes, conditions of well-being, patterns of conflict and accommodation, institutions, public policies. In short, they are concerned with political **empiricism**—*what has been, what is, and what will be.* As social scientists, they investigate significant problems related to politics, such as the causes of war and the conditions that make for peace, the factors influencing democratic or undemocratic rule, and the circumstances connected with justice or injustice within a political community. Political scientists are also connected with the behavior of key political actors (such as the president, Congress, the Supreme Court) and with the role of political parties, the media, and interest groups in the political process.

To investigate these questions political scientists rely primarily on the methods of empirical science: observation, description, measurement, inductive generalization, explanation, deductive reasoning, continued testing, correction, corroboration, and carefully qualified prediction.

Empirical investigations are designed to discover who rules and who benefits in politics and why. Indeed, one famous shorthand definition of the empirical approach to political science is found in the title of Harold Lasswell's influential book—*Politics: Who Gets What, When, How.*

Empirical evidence is used to test hypotheses and arrive at supportable generalizations. Do businesspeople, farmers, or factory workers get the biggest "breaks" on income tax legislation in the United States? Is it really true that the "strong do what they can and the weak suffer what they must" in international politics? Is there an "iron law of oligarchy" at work in politics as well as in large organizations—a "law" that a minority of insiders run the show? In their empirical investigations, political scientists explore these and other questions to arrive at meaningful, coherent, and objectively testable generalizations.

The Prudential Component

Political scientists are also concerned with political **prudence**—with what *can be:* workable public policies and a host of practical judgments. The prudential component involves making wise judgments about the practical tasks of politics.[2] How can a political candidate gain enough votes to win an election? How can a nation's leaders most wisely deal with their actual or potential enemies? What actions can a citizen take to influence public officials? How can a nation grapple with problems such as nuclear disarmament, violations of human rights, poverty, unemployment, pollution, crime, drugs? Formulating answers to such questions requires practical judgment, or good sense.

Wise practical judgment must be exercised in making or carrying out public policy and in deciding disputes under the law. But legislators, executives, and judges are not the only political actors who make judgments. Prominent party officials, powerful interest group leaders, and influential members of the media also make key judgments. And beyond even these important decision makers, a variety of economic, social, religious, and educational groups and scores of individuals influence public policy in major or minor ways. Citizens voting in the election booth are making practical judgments. Furthermore, millions of ordinary people are involved in the process of making judgments as they read newspaper stories, listen to political news on their television sets or radios, hear political candidates, and contribute to or work in political campaigns.

We will postpone consideration of how these components interrelate until we have examined the four major tasks they suggest.

THE FOUR MAJOR TASKS OF POLITICAL SCIENCE

The major tasks of political science follow logically from an acceptance of the major components of the discipline we have just examined:

1. The concern for what is right or wrong in politics leads, initially, to the task of ethical recommendation.
2. The concern for political phenomena—facts, circumstances, experiences—leads to the task of empirical understanding.
3. The concern for what can sensibly be done leads to the task of prudential judgment or action.
4. The first three tasks suggest the task of theoretical integration of these ethical, empirical, and prudential concerns.

Let us now examine each task in turn.

Ethical Recommendation

Political scientists have the controversial task of recommending what actions leaders of state, citizens, and all others involved in politics ought to take. They prescribe standards and make critical appraisals that assist political actors to pursue the good political life. This task also

Affirmative action—a policy designed to help overcome discrimination against African Americans, women, and other minorities—has aroused passionate responses, pro and con. Its defenders argue that it is necessary to guard against historical and continuing discrimination. Its opponents label it as "reverse discrimination" and contrary to genuine equality of consideration.

helps political scientists address problems of legitimacy and obligation in politics, such as which governments or actions are legitimate and therefore entitled to public consent and which political rights and responsibilities are citizens obliged to honor.

Political philosophers have been concerned about the ideal regime and the best practical political community since Socrates, Plato, and Aristotle founded systematic philosophy in ancient Greece. But what is "best" calls for critical examination. The definitions of key political values—whether justice or the common good or liberty or order or equality or fraternity—are not self-evident. People in politics dispute their meaning. Moreover, the relationship of one value to another—for example, of justice to order, of liberty to equality—cries out for analysis.

In carrying out such an analysis, political scientists as political philosophers are not completely divorced from the world as it is and as it can be. Their ethical analysis must be compatible with real people, as they now are or as they can sanely become in a real world. Thus, political scientists cannot sensibly recommend political values that are biologically and physically impossible or socially and politically perilous.

Yet political scientists as philosophers are, if not completely unlimited, significantly free to let their imaginations soar. They can raise their ethical sights to discover possibilities undreamed of by pedestrian political actors following the unexamined routes or the bureaucratic ruts carved out by tradition. They are free to articulate political ideas far removed from the current system. They can voice better ways for handling the business of the political community.

They can, for example, imagine a world without war. They can imagine political communities wherein social and economic justice prevails and policies ensure economic well-being for all. And they can imagine a global physical environment in ecological balance. In more concrete terms, they can imagine the reduction and eventual elimination of nuclear arms, poverty, and torture. They can imagine good jobs for all able-bodied

persons, financial security for the aged and ill, pure water, and the end of racism.

Critical analysis of values goes beyond a keen appraisal of *standards* that ought to guide political actors. It includes criticism of *actual* behavior, institutions, and policies in the light of these standards. Is a given country, for example, engaged in a war? Is it oppressing its own people? Is the American presidency, or the Chinese leadership, too powerful—oppressively powerful? Is the United States taking appropriate action to enhance employment, extend health care, reform the welfare system, ensure educational opportunity, and protect the environment? Can the United States reduce, and eventually eliminate, the federal budget deficit?

Finally, such critical analysis involves examination of sensible alternatives for the future. In the near future, should the number of nuclear weapons be reduced to zero? Can the proliferation of nuclear weapons be avoided? How much should conventional armaments be cut?

As political scientists analyze the protection of human rights. they can ask whether "quiet diplomacy" works best or whether violators should face publicity and strong sanctions. Disturbingly, answers depend on whether the violators of human rights are powerful nations such as China or weak nations, "friends" or "foes."

And how should Americans criticize alternatives as they seek to overcome poverty? Should the poor lift themselves by their own bootstraps? Or should the rich nations (mostly located in the Northern Hemisphere) help the poor nations (mostly located in the Southern Hemisphere)? Or should Americans favor a more complex set of policies—self-help, governmental assistance, and salutary international policies of trade and aid?

And how should Americans respond to the ecological alternatives facing the world? Should science and technology be relied on to overcome the dwindling supplies of oil and other precious nonrenewable resources? Or should the focus be on prudently managing natural resources to achieve a "steady-state" society?

These questions underscore the connections between ethical recommendation, empirical understanding, and prudential judgment.

Empirical Understanding

Political scientists seek to understand how political actors carry out their business. What really goes on in politics—and why? Here political scientists are concerned with political realities—with what can be scientifically observed, described, confirmed, and explained. Their concern is with what has been, is, and will be the case in politics. But they seek more than just the bare facts; they seek comprehensive knowledge. Although they may begin with description, they hope to end with explanation.

A number of important empirical questions challenge the political scientist:

- How does the larger environment of politics—the geographical world human beings live in, their biological endowment, economic resources and activity, historical memory, religious beliefs, scientific and technological achievements, social mores—influence their political values, patterns of conflict and accommodation, and decision making?
- Are people's political values rooted in universal human needs or merely the result of the way people carry on their economic life?
- Are people's values influenced primarily by their religious commitments, or are they fashioned by unique historical experiences?[3]
- Do citizens, as creative political actors, make wise decisions?
- What is the state of political health of the world and its nations?
- Why do some political communities succeed better than others at satisfying such values as security, liberty, justice, and welfare?

In attending to these and comparable questions, empirical political scientists attempt to develop a general theory that will aid their efforts to order and explain the complex data of politics. As they develop their theories, they follow, as much as possible, the elements of scientific investigation. Thus, they try to examine the data systematically and critically and to develop fruitful generalizations. Such generalizations enhance the ability of political scientists to grasp connections in the world of political phenomena and even (sometimes) to predict future political events.

This, of course, is an ideal portrayal of the empirical task. In fact, political science is far from reaching this ideal. Nonetheless, the empirically oriented political scientist strives to explain how and why political actors (1) formulate political values, (2) accommodate diverse interests and umpire the struggle for power, and (3) exercise judgment (wisely or foolishly) in grappling with problems, making decisions, and administering public policy.

Thus, the empirically oriented political scientist is still concerned with values and judgment as well as with actual behavior.

Prudential Judgment

Political scientists must also provide sensible guidance in political life. This means using practical wisdom and making decisions in concrete situations. Political scientists may use this capability when they exercise power themselves as politicians or administrators; when they advise leaders of state, legislators, or party officials; when they work as teachers or scholars; or when they function as ordinary citizens.

Initially, we political scientists need to be clearheaded about the values we seek to preserve—for example, peace or prosperity or human rights or clean air. Second, we need to recognize the factors that threaten (or advance) these values. Third, we must identify and debate alternative policies addressed to these problems. Finally, we need to decide on the most desirable and feasible policy. Part IV of this book explores these matters in greater depth.

The task of prudential judgment rests on the tasks of ethical recommendation and empirical understanding. Judgment must be guided by critically examined values (for example, respect for human life and human rights) and must recognize the limitations and opportunities of political reality. Yet prudential judgment differs in important ways from the other tasks.

In contrast to political scientists who make ethical recommendations, those engaged in making wise judgments are limited by the constraints of politics as the art of the possible. They must tailor their judgments to fit a real, rather than an ideal, world. Prudent judgment cannot be falsely utopian. But political scientists do not have to be timid or rigidly conservative. Bold, imaginative judgments that are nonetheless prudent are possible, even though they often have to be made under urgent circumstances. Nonetheless, there always remains a tension in politics between the ethically ideal and the politically feasible.

Although feasibility requires political scientists to respect reality, they are only concerned with that reality as it helps them judge present and future behavior, consequences, and alternatives. Such judgments are not fully scientific because they go beyond knowledge of what is to what can be—to practical wisdom. Practical wisdom calls for judgment in action—judgment that must usually be made in the absence of complete scientific knowledge. Thus, the judgmental process is not fully scientific, and it entails more than science. Science is, however, indispensable in politics.

Ethical and empirical components are integrally connected with prudent judgments. The interrelationship of these three components brings us now to a fourth task—theoretical integration.

Theoretical Integration

Although political scientists may specialize in any one of the three realms we have discussed— ethical, empirical, or prudential—they must still appreciate how these components interrelate in a unified and coherent discipline. Table 3.2 presents one view of their interrelationship.

For example, in this framework, on the issue of ecological health, political philosophers concerned with ethics can ask: Should ecological health be a cardinal value in the political community? Empirical political scientists can ask: Does such a condition of ecological health actually exist? And students of public policy can ask: Is ecological health a value that nations can practically achieve?

Other ties among the components of political science are apparent. Indeed, the history of political science and the very nature of politics call for a unified discipline. The great political philosophers who were the first creative political scientists were very concerned with the relationship of ethics to politics. They also saw that politics embraced both empirical understanding and prudent judgment.

Moreover, as we have tried to emphasize, the nature of politics forbids the separation of tasks. Values guide empirical investigation and inform prudent judgment in public policy. Political values make little sense unless they are in sane accord with actual (or potential) political realities and with creative, but feasible, political decisions. Judgments as to what is feasible influence actual behavior. And judgment not only

Table 3.2 *The Major Components of Political Science and Their Interrelationship*

Dimension	Political Values	Political Phenomena	Political Judgment
Ethical	Which political values should exist?	How should political actors behave?	Which public policies should prevail?
Empirical	Which values actually exist in the political community?	How do political actors actually behave?	Which public policies are actually in existence?
Prudential	Which values can wisely exist in the political community?	How can political actors behave wisely ?	Which public policies can be formulated and sensibly implemented?

is informed by the values that motivate political actors but also is qualified by the realities of political phenomena. Thus, political science is fruitful because political scientists, at the highest level of political theory, grapple critically with the interrelationship among (1) articulated political values, (2) empirical data and theory on the actual behavior of political actors (individuals, interests, political communities), and (3) the creative judgments required in statesmanship. In the political life of the real community, these three components, although partially separable in logic and distinguishable for purposes of specialized research, cannot be treated in isolation. Figure 3.1 illustrates this point.

Some additional illustrations will help clarify this interrelationship. For instance, heightened awareness, over the past several decades, of the meaning of equality in the United States has led to empirical investigation of racial discrimination, poverty, and sexism, as well as to measures to reduce inequalities: a civil rights act, a "War on Poverty," and affirmative action programs. Some programs helped, others worked imperfectly, and still others backfired—that is, they

often resulted in protests against such policies as "forced busing" or "forced integration" or "reverse discrimination." These consequences sometimes led to a reconsideration of the methods used to fight inequality and of the meaning of equality, and thus to new empirical research.[4]

Political Health as an Example of Theoretical Integration—So the tasks of ethical recommendation, empirical understanding, and prudential judgment stimulate political scientists to envisage an ambitious fourth task—integration in the discipline. Such theoretical integration might come with an old or new concept, such as the idea of political health or well-being.

The concept of **political health** would encourage integration because it could enable political scientists to address their three major concerns: ethical, empirical, and prudential. Initially, political scientists could explore political health as a norm or standard of the good life. Theoretically, it is possible to define health in politics as peace and peaceful constitutional change, security, liberty, democratic governance, political and social justice, economic prosperity, and ecological balance.

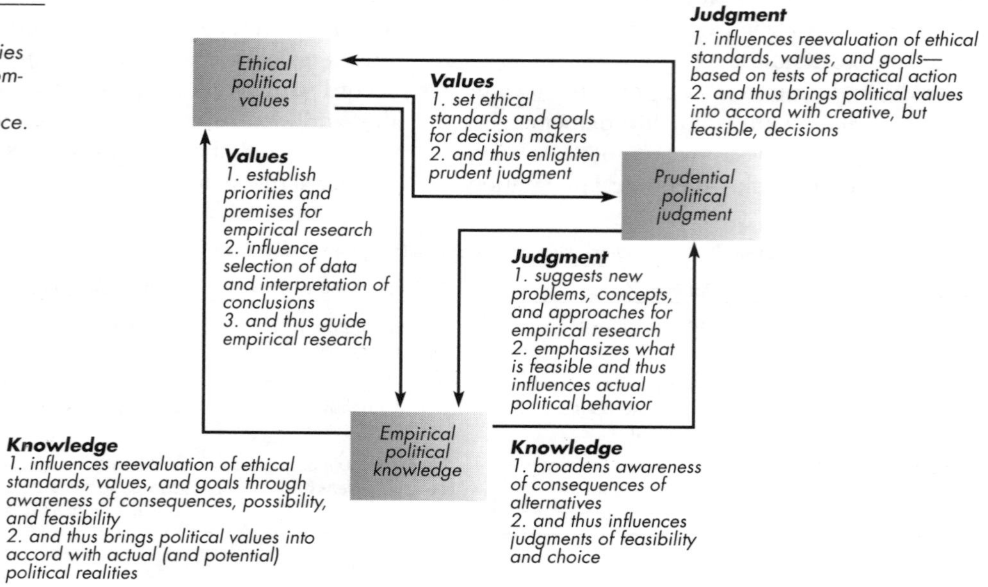

Figure 3.1
The intimate ties among the components of political science.

Judgment
1. influences reevaluation of ethical standards, values, and goals—based on tests of practical action
2. and thus brings political values into accord with creative, but feasible, decisions

Ethical political values

Values
1. set ethical standards and goals for decision makers
2. and thus enlighten prudent judgment

Values
1. establish priorities and premises for empirical research
2. influence selection of data and interpretation of conclusions
3. and thus guide empirical research

Prudential political judgment

Judgment
1. suggests new problems, concepts, and approaches for empirical research
2. emphasizes what is feasible and thus influences actual political behavior

Knowledge
1. influences reevaluation of ethical standards, values, and goals through awareness of consequences, possibility, and feasibility
2. and thus brings political values into accord with actual (and potential) political realities

Empirical political knowledge

Knowledge
1. broadens awareness of consequences of alternatives
2. and thus influences judgments of feasibility and choice

Second, political scientists could investigate political health in a scientific fashion. Are political communities healthy? Why or why not? What evidence supports an empirical conclusion about their well-being? Here we emphasize that political scientists can move beyond symptoms of political well-being or malaise to empirical generalizations and theories about the healthy political community.

Third, political scientists—guided by an ethical norm, and aided by social scientific knowledge—could engage in healing by addressing themselves to wise actions, policies, and judgments designed to maximize political health. They are encouraged as teachers, political advisers, citizens, governmental leaders, or administrators to put their knowledge to work as best they can.

To summarize, the task of theoretical integration involves developing a general theory (say, of political health) that harmoniously relates the discipline's ethical, empirical, and prudential components and ties together its traditional (and nontraditional) fields of study. Ambitious? Yes. Impossible? No, but very difficult!

Historical Theories of Integration—The linkage of political values, social scientific knowledge, and wise action has been noted by key political philosophers—including Plato, Aristotle, James Madison, and Karl Marx—and by twentieth-century political scientists. In ancient Greece, Plato saw no sharp division between fact and value, or between these two and practical wisdom. For Plato, the Good was true, and practical wisdom involved approximating the Good as closely as circumstances permitted. Aristotle took a somewhat different position, but argued on behalf of the intimate connection between ethics and politics; he saw prudence—or practical wisdom—as depending on a good goal pursued sensibly in the light of existing realities.

In the late eighteenth century James Madison clearly saw the importance of making republican values central in his thinking. He also recognized that he must advance those republican values in the light of America's realities—a nation of large size with diverse interests. Prudence dictated the concept of an "extensive republic"—the present U.S. federal republic—as a wise solution to the problem of reconciling republican liberty and large size.

In the nineteenth century Karl Marx sought a unity of theory and practice. It was not enough to understand the social world; one had to change it for the better. For Marx, history was moving toward his preferred values, which would be realized in a communist society.

Of course, not all political scientists accept the theories of integration put forth by Marx and Plato. Few, however, would deny that their ideas have been stimulating. Most political scientists are probably more amenable to the ideas of Aristotle and Madison on the intimate relationship of values, realities, and judgment.

Modern Approaches—In the mid-twentieth century, David Easton used the phrase *political system,* in his highly influential 1953 book by that name, to underscore his commitment to understanding the whole domain of political science. And although his major concern was scientific unity, he understood that ethical values underlie the scientific enterprise and that knowledge cannot be easily separated from action.

Karl Deutsch, another prominent twentieth-century political scientist, wrote:

> We need a cumulative political science where knowledge will grow and clearly improve in scope, amount, and quality, as it has done in so many other fields of human knowledge. Such a cumulative knowledge of what can and what cannot be done in politics under specific conditions should open the way to more effective applications of political science in the service of freedom and peace, within countries and among them. [5]

Other modern political scientists press more frankly for a *holistic* approach, which calls for an appreciation of the whole: concern for the survival of all people on earth, social and political justice, economic interdependence in a global community, and environmental quality of life. They are joined by an array of humanists, who argue that the earth is an interrelated global community and who never worry about separating their ethical beliefs from their empirical observations about the world or from their judgments about wise public policy.

Practical Applications—Political scientists in all the traditional fields undertake the four tasks we have outlined. At first glance, this may not seem to be the case. To the superficial observer, ethical recommendation may seem more immediately visible in the field of political theory, empirical understanding more apparent in comparative politics and American politics, and prudential judgment more central in international politics and in public administration and public policy. However, a more thorough examination of fields reveals that the ethical and prudential approaches are never much below the surface in comparative politics or American politics. Moreover, international politics, public administration, and public policy are clearly guided by ethical norms and must rest on a sound foundation of empirical understanding. And, of course, political theory presupposes both a firm appreciation of political reality and appropriate attention to wise judgment.

The traditional fields of political science—and the several approaches in these fields—are explored more fully later in this book. Political theory is explored in Part II. Comparative politics, American politics, and international politics are explored in Parts III and IV.

Before turning to the fuller exploration of problems in these fields, we must point out that not all political scientists agree on the approach outlined in the previous pages. Controversy persists on the legitimate subject matter of political science, on proper methodology for the discipline, and on approaches to be taken in the several fields of political science.

CONTINUING CONTROVERSIES IN POLITICAL SCIENCE

Controversies center on the priority to be given to (1) the quest for the good political life, (2) the

search for a science of politics, (3) guidance for citizens and leaders of state, and (4) the importance of a unified discipline that can do justice to politics. Moreover, political scientists remain divided on key questions within each area of emphasis.

The Quest for the Good Political Life

Should the ethical quest for the good political life be guided by a philosophic, religious, or scientific concern for the highest truth? Or should it be guided by a quest for the most acceptable opinion? Are philosophic reason, religious revelation, historical experience, human needs, or societal preference the keys to unlock the mysteries of the good political life?

Some political scientists argue that only ethical reasoning can help determine standards for what is right or wrong. Others contend that such norms and standards derive from religious faith and divine revelation as expressed, for example, in the Ten Commandments. Still others look to historical experience—to what Edmund Burke called the prescriptive constitution—for understanding what is good and how to deal with political problems. Still others look to human needs as the root of cardinal values. They insist that humans elevate their needs for food, shelter, sex, expression, companionship, and fulfillment into preferred values and then into human rights— the rights to life, liberty, property, and so on. Finally, some maintain that society strongly influences, if it does not dictate, the ways in which the good political life is understood. For example, in a liberal democratic society with a market economy, a two-party or a multiparty system and private property and enterprise are endorsed and supported; in a communist society with a command economy, the norm has been a single-party system, centralized economic direction, and collective ownership.

The Need for Standards—Leo Strauss, a profound student of classical political philosophy, argued that the quest for the "best political order" must be central in politics. Politics, he maintained, inevitably requires "approval and disapproval," "choice and rejection," "praise and blame." Neutrality is impossible; political matters inevitably "raise a claim to men's obedience, allegiance, decision or judgment." Inescapably, citizens judge political affairs "in terms of goodness or badness, of justice or injustice." Since judgment requires a standard for judgment, and since sound judgment requires sound standards of judgment, citizens seek the best standard for the good political life. Only with such a standard of excellence, of virtue, of the best political order can political leaders umpire the "controversies between groups struggling for power within the political community." Here the tie between ethics and statesmanship becomes explicit. A standard of excellence is necessary if a leader is "to manage well the affairs of his political community as a whole."[6]

Political science, Strauss pointed out, originally meant the skill, art, prudence, and practical wisdom of the excellent leader of state. Such a leader could only shape sound public policy if he or she were knowledgeable about sound political standards and possessed prudential skill. Policies recommended by the philosopher-statesman are normally "a compromise between what he would wish and what circumstances permit. To effect that compromise intelligently, he must first know what . . . would be most desirable in itself." After that, the leader tries prudently to bridge the gap between what is most desirable in itself and what is possible in given circumstances. Those "scientists" and "historicists" who deny the possibility or desirability or primacy of the quest for the good political life are the enemies of a true political science, Strauss says.

Robert Dahl, an outstanding and sophisticated empirical political scientist, also addressed the relationship of ethics to politics. He asked: Can the study of politics be ethically neutral? Should it be? He presented the "value-fact" controversy as seen by empirically oriented political scientists and their opponents. This controversy revolves around the question of whether "ought," or value, propositions differ fundamentally from "is," or empirical, propositions. Empirical theorists, Dahl wrote, hold that a "substantial and important aspect of politics is purely empirical, and that this empirical aspect of politics can be analyzed (in principle at least) neutrally and objectively." And so the battle is joined. Dahl attempted to find common ground between the conflicting schools and to explain and defend the position of a sophisticated empirical political science.[7]

Ethics Versus Positivism—Like Strauss, John H. Hallowell defended the primacy of the ethical approach to politics and attacked positivistic—or empirical—political science. **Positivism** is a philosophy that holds that human beings can know only that which is based on positive, observable, scientific facts, on data derived from sense experience. "Positivism . . . the dominant and most influential perspective within American political science today . . . is reflected in contemporary political science in what has come to be called the behavioral approach to political phenomena." Hallowell was disturbed by two theoretically inconsistent characteristics of this approach: on one hand, "an attempt to avoid all normative judgment," and on the other, a dangerous "conception of politics as a science of social perfection." Hallowell endorsed Thomism (the political philosophy of Thomas Aquinas) as a sound tradition for politics because it "combines the wisdom of the Greeks with the revelation of Christ." Politics is given meaning by a divine order and a natural law that "man can participate in because he is a rational being." Politics "is good only to the extent that it assists human beings to realize their potentialities as persons who belong ultimately to God."[8]

British political theorist Alfred Cobban took his clues from the tradition of political theory as it culminated in the ethics of the Enlightenment. Writing in the 1960s, Cobban was disturbed by the fact that political theory was not used to clarify and prescribe political values in the interest of a sane and humane politics. If such politics is to survive, he said, the political theorist must be concerned primarily with what ought to be, with ethical political preferences, with condemnation, support, or justification of existing institutions, with persuasion on behalf of political change where needed, and with appraisal of and influence on actual political problems. Such activity can help guard against the monstrous cruelty and brutality of modern politics. Genuine public discussion of "the rights and wrongs" of political behavior can reintroduce the sense of ethical purpose and rational direction that Cobban saw as absent. Without this ethical concern, empirical political science would remain a "device, invented by university teachers, for avoiding that dangerous subject politics, without achieving science."[9]

The Search for a Science of Politics

Should the search for an empirical science of politics be based on the models of the physical and biological sciences—or on some other model? Some behavioral political scientists maintain that we will progress in political science only if we recognize that our primary business is to state and test hypotheses about relationships in the world of sense experience. Others may even argue that at the highest level (following the model of physics), political scientists should seek the political science equivalent of Albert Einstein's famous formula $E=mc^2$, a result of his special theory of relativity. Still other political scientists contend that we should follow a biological model, guided by a political science equivalent of Louis Pasteur's germ theory of disease, to explain health or illness in the body politic. Not all empirical political scientists agree on these models. Clearly, we are far from masterful empirical breakthroughs in political science. Quarrels persist on models and methodology, even as empirical political scientists agree in emphasizing the importance of scientific investigation as a way to proceed.

The Behavioralist Approach—The search for an empirical science of politics in modern America has been closely associated with the behavioral emphasis in the discipline. And although not all behavioralists agree, they do seem to share—as David Easton, a leading empirical theorist, pointed out in 1965—a common goal: "A science of politics modeled after the methodological assumptions of the natural sciences." Easton identified eight "intellectual foundation stones" of **behaviorialism:**

1. A belief in *regularities*, "discoverable uniformities in political behavior" that "can be expressed in generalizations or theories with explanatory and predictive value"
2. A commitment to *verification* of such generalizations through testing
3. An experimental attitude toward *techniques*, with the goal of obtaining ever more rigorous means for observing, recording, and analyzing behavior
4. An emphasis on *quantification* where possible, relevant, and meaningful
5. A sophisticated attitude toward *values* and especially a recognition that ethical "valuation and empirical explanation involve two different kinds of propositions that, for the sake of clarity, should be kept analytically distinct"
6. A stress on *systemization*, on the importance of theory in research and in the development of a "coherent and orderly body of knowledge"
7. An acknowledgment of the primacy of *pure science,* as against applied science or practical problem-solving
8. An acceptance of *integration* of the social sciences and the value of interdisciplinary fertilization.

Easton emphasized not only the importance of a unifying empirical theory but also the importance of empirical "units of analysis." These units of analysis provide frameworks for empirical investigation. They are the concepts—such as "power," "group," "decision," "structure and function," message," "system"—that can help political scientists make sense out of the otherwise bewildering data of politics.[10]

The controversy between the behavioralists and their opponents involves a number of points. The more radical behavioralists criticize traditional political scientists for not pushing their discipline toward "a science capable of prediction and explanation." Many behavioralists criticize traditionalists for not limiting political science to a study of phenomena that can actually be observed and for not pushing quantification more rigorously. They also fault them for using unsophisticated methods, for not being interdisciplinary, and for not seeking overarching generalizations about politics. Behavioralists also tend to dismiss the legitimacy of the task of ethical recommendation. They hold that the "truth or falsity of values . . . cannot be established scientifically," and that values "are beyond the scope of legitimate inquiry." They also tend to reject as illegitimate political scientists' engagement in political reform. [11]

Beyond Behavioralism—Not all those who agree that empirical political research is important are convinced of the merits of the research that has been done. For example, Norwegian-born Christian Bay criticized a good deal of the behavioral literature as "pseudopolitical" and pleaded for more genuine political research. Such behavioral research would be done in the light of the "purpose of politics" to "meet human needs and facilitate human development." The common good as well as power would be taken into account. Bay saw no reason for empirically oriented political scientists to abandon the normative commitment to a better life, real satisfaction, the full dignity of democratic citizenship, the stress on reason as a crucial factor in politics, and the belief in a real polity. Research that does not face up to these values may achieve scientific rigor at the price of a divorce from politics. Such research will be not only pseudopolitical but conservative, because it implies that individual neuroses, private advantages, irrational actions, harassed lives, and stultifying pressures "always will be the natural or even the desirable state of affairs in a democracy." [12]

A refugee from Nazi Germany, Hans Morgenthau, another influential student of politics, asked: "What, then, ought a political science be like, which does justice both to its scientific pretense and to its subject matter?" Such a political science will profit from the "valuable insights" of philosophic traditions other than the dominant positivism of contemporary political science. It will appreciate that although these insights are not rigorously scientific, they do illuminate a scientific understanding of politics. Such a political science will maintain "ties with the Western tradition of political thought, its concerns, its accumulation of wisdom and knowledge." It will recognize the identity of political theory and political science. It will hold that a "scientific theory is a system of empirically verifiable, general truths sought for their own sake." Political science will also communicate an "objective and general truth about matters political," a truth that holds "regardless of time and place." Such a political science will be guided by a theory whose purpose, of course, "is to bring order and meaning to a mass of phenomena." Contemporary political scientists will wisely recognize that their task is "to reformulate the perennial truths of politics" in the "light of contemporary experience." Even at the almost certain risk of being controversial, political scientists must grapple with the burning problems and great political issues of society. Here the relevance of political science to statesmanship becomes clear. A "theory of politics presents not only a guide to understanding but also an ideal for action." It maps the political scene "in order to show the shortest and safest road to a given objective." [13]

Helpful Guidance for Leaders of State and Citizens

Is prudential guidance for leaders of state and other political actors influenced primarily by practical wisdom? Is sound judgment based on good character, significant intelligence, common sense, and political intuition? Those concerned with wise judgment and action in politics may concede that there are no scientific answers to the problems that baffle them in politics, yet they seek to enhance the capacity to decide how, for example, to avert devastating wars, to protect human rights, to enhance prosperity, to guard against ecological disasters. They know that a conscious appreciation of key values and realities is crucial in this endeavor.

Take the issue of poverty and welfare reform in the United States. It is relatively easy to affirm the value of a decent income, decent housing, decent health, decent diet, decent education for all Americans. It is also relatively easy to identify the poor and those on welfare (the elderly poor; the disabled, poor, and jobless women and their dependent children; poor and jobless men); the working poor; and the homeless who are destitute and not on welfare. But, it is considerably more difficult, although not beyond current capability, to determine why people are poor and why the welfare system fails. It is also difficult to know which rational policies will turn things around. Is the key to welfare reform private sector or community service jobs for able-bodied men and women now on welfare, plus an income tax credit for the working poor, plus appropriate health insurance and day care for working mothers? Or is it better education and job training? Is it more generous welfare benefits, or perhaps the abolition of the entire welfare system? What will be the costs and benefits of the choices that turn out to be politically feasible? [14]

Clearly, assessing alternatives is central to sound judgment, even though no one can be absolutely sure which alternatives will be the wisest or which specific qualities make for sound judgment.

The senior author of this book, in *The Revival of Democratic Theory,* highlighted the special role of prudent judgment in politics. He defined *prudence* as "practical wisdom or that sound judgment which requires conscious and rational adaptation of means to ends." The ends must be proper ends, or else the judgment is not prudent but simply clever, narrowly expedient, or basely

pragmatic. Prudence requires the ability to judge what is appropriate in a specific situation. It is not to be confused with timidity, priggishness, overcautiousness, weakness, or paralysis. Prudence involves deliberation, awareness of consequences, appreciation of the relationship of means to ends. Moreover, it requires the ability to act in a real world to meet real problems, and the strength to decide in a morally ambiguous world where there are only proximate solutions to insoluble problems; it can provide a bridge between what ought to be and what is. Most important, prudence may enable the political scientist to focus on fundamental political problems as they are currently illustrated in public policy. [15]

In his important article "Political Science and Prevision," French political scientist Bertrand de Jouvenal illustrated in more detail the role of the political scientist in providing prudent guidance for leaders of state. He saw the political scientist as "a teacher of public men in activity." Guidance for leaders of state requires, above all, foresight. The political scientist, he argued, "must therefore develop that skill in himself, and in his pupils, and offer it to statesmen he has to advise." This is one of eight points that de Jouvenal made in this article, which highlighted prudential guidance in domestic and international affairs. [16]

Harold Lasswell also sought to bring political science to bear on problems facing decision makers in politics. The problem-solving approach, he wrote, poses five intellectual tasks: clarifying goals, ascertaining trends, identifying conditioning factors, noting projections, and posing policy alternatives. Political scientists have concentrated on one or more of these tasks throughout the history of their discipline. They will undoubtedly continue to do so as they grapple with unprecedented and far-reaching challenges in the future. Moreover, they will do so in performing their professional roles as teachers, researchers, advisers, managers, and leaders.

Their contribution to what we have loosely referred to as statesmanship and public policy can be more accurately understood in connection with their involvement in every phase of the decision-making process. The phases of the decision-making process, as seen by Harold Lasswell, include: (1) intelligence (political information), (2) recommendation (promotion of policy), (3) prescription (articulation of official norms), (4) invocation (provisional conformity to policy), (5) application ("final" administration of policy), (6) appraisal (assessment of goal, strategy, and results), and (7) termination (settlement of expectations and claims).[17]

Toward a Unified Discipline of Political Science

So the vital questions recur: Is politics to be viewed primarily in terms of ethics? of science? of statesmanship? Some political scientists emphasize politics as the quest for the good political life. Others stress the search for an empirical science of politics. Still others underscore the importance of prudential guidance for leaders of state. But even if we agree on one focus or another, we must still explore the brand of ethics, the kind of science, and the pattern of leadership involved.

Moreover, we still need to know how the three major components of political science are related to one another in a unified discipline. We need to integrate what ought to be, what is, and what can be. We still need to search for a more systematic theory for the discipline's major emphases and its traditional fields: political philosophy, comparative politics, international politics, public administration, and public policy. This theory would relate political norms, empirical generalizations, and public judgments. It would reconcile philosophy, science, and public policy without withdrawing from politics, distorting political phenomena, or making faulty efforts to bridge the gap between aspiration and reality.

David Easton, an early leader of the post–World War II behavioral revolution in political science, advocated greater harmony in the discipline. In "The New Revolution in Political Science,"

Political theorist David Easton, who received his Ph.D. from Harvard in 1947, taught for 35 years at the University of Chicago and then at the University of California, Irvine. Easton was influential both in advocating the need for underlying empirical theory for the political system and later in advocating greater harmony within the discipline.

Easton outlined a "post-behavioral revolution" to help political scientists integrate their tasks. This revolution would move beyond the important work of behavioral political scientists.

Easton called attention to the post-behavioralists' plea for the "constructive development of values" as a key part of the study of politics. Post-behavioralists are calling, too, for realistic and substantively meaningful empirical research— a political science that will "reach out to the real needs of mankind in a time of crisis." They are, finally, endorsing the need "to protect the humane values of civilization" by taking responsible action in reshaping society and by fulfilling their "special obligation" to put their knowledge to work.[18]

In this account of the post-behavioralist revolution, Easton saw a clear relationship between the ethical, empirical, and prudential components of the discipline. The post-behavioralists modestly endorsed the legitimacy of the four major tasks of the discipline. But, clearly, their perspective by no means dominates the field.

The senior author of this book has also strongly emphasized that the integrative challenge involves the search for a concept that ties together the ethical, empirical, and prudential concerns and tasks of the discipline of political science. He has advanced the thesis that the concept of political health, correctly understood, can serve to integrate these concerns and tasks because this concept can serve as a normative political standard, encourage the social scientific search for the necessary and sufficient conditions of political health, and encourage healing public policies:

1. The concept of political health is value laden; it assumes that life, growth, and development are worthwhile. It points toward the significant problems that need to be investigated.
2. The concept of political health permits—indeed encourages—scientific investigation of the necessary and sufficient conditions of civilized life, healthy growth, and creative fulfillment. It sensitizes the empirical political scientist to the gap between prophetic values and existential reality and encourages the search for reasons for this gap.
3. The concept of political health is incomplete unless concerned political scientists move on from health standards and scientific diagnosis to prescription. They are encouraged to recommend political therapy, to undertake wise action, and to pursue prudent policies that might improve the state of our political well-being.

Legitimate doubts, difficulties, and dangers will be encountered in this integrative effort, but these problems do not rule out either the desirability or possibility of using political health as an integrative concept. This concept will be explored throughout this book. [19]

CONCLUSION

Despite the continuing debate about the scope, substance, and methodology of political science, we can confidently affirm the reality of three central concerns: (1) an ethical concern for the good political life, for the best political community; (2) a scientific concern for empirical theory, generalization, and explanation relevant to the business of the political community; and (3) a prudential concern for judgment,

decision making, public policy, and action. With somewhat less confidence, we can also affirm a fourth concern—a theoretical concern for the integration of the normative, empirical, and prudential components that constitute the leading threads in the design of a complete political science.

Each of these concerns underscores significant problems, suggests appropriate methodologies, and leads to fruitful responses, which we explore in succeeding chapters.

ANNOTATED BIBLIOGRAPHY

Almond, Gabriel A. *A Discipline Divided: Schools and Sects in Political Science.* Newbury Park, Calif.: Sage, 1989. Sees some schools of political science ("soft-left," "soft-right," "hard-left," "hard-right") at separate ideological and methodological tables, each with its own conception of political science. Insists that the "overwhelming majority of political scientists" are in the center—"liberal" and moderate in ideology, and eclectic and open to conviction in methodology.

Ball, Terence, Farr, James, and Hanson, Russell L., eds. *Political Innovation and Conceptual Change.* Cambridge: Cambridge University Press, 1989. Explores a number of key concepts: constitution, democracy, state, representation, party, public interest, citizenship, public opinion, rights, property, revolution.

Bluhm, William T. *Theories of the Political System: Classics of Political Thought and Modern Political Analysis,* 3rd ed. Englewood Cliffs, N.J.: Prentice-Hall, 1978. Makes a stimulating effort to compare certain "classical" political philosophers and their modern analogues.

Crotty, William, gen. ed. *Political Science: Looking to the Future.* 4 vols. Evanston, Ill.: Northwestern University Press, 1990. Vol. l: *The Theory and Practice of Political Science.* Vol. 2: *Comparative Politics, Policy, and International Relations.* Vol. 3: *Political Behavior.* Vol. 4: *American Institutions.* Highlights issues, concepts, methodologies, changes, concerns.

Easton, David. *The Political System.* New York: Knopf, 1953. Lays the theoretical foundation for the systems approach that Easton pioneered. Thought provoking.

Easton, David. *A Systems Analysis of Political Life.* New York: Wiley, 1965. Develops the systems approach, which sees the political system embedded in an environment, receiving input (demands and supports) and delivering output (decisions and actions).

Falk, Richard A. *A Study of Future Worlds.* New York: Random House, 1975. Focuses on peace, human rights, economic well-being, ecological balance. Challenges the "realism" of the realists and their alleged narrow interpretation of power. Seeks a global perspective beyond that of a national interest flawed by the gap between standards and performance.

Lasswell, Harold D. *Politics: Who Gets What, When, How.* New York: Meridian, 1965. Presents one of the most popular definitions of politics by one of America's most creative and versatile political scientists.

Morgenthau, Hans J., and Thompson, Kenneth W. *Politics Among Nations: The Struggle for Power and Peace.* New York: McGraw-Hill, 1992. Presents the ideas of prominent realist Morgenthau, who debunked moralists and cynics alike, emphasized the importance of protecting the national interest in the struggle for power, and favored the use of diplomacy to obtain peace through accommodation.

Ricci, David M. *The Tragedy of Political Science: Politics, Scholarship, and Democracy.* New Haven, Conn.: Yale University Press, 1984. Argues that the tragedy of political science lies in the conflict between a commitment to science and a commitment to the good, wise, democratic life.

Riemer, Neal. *The Revival of Democratic Theory.* New York: Appleton-Century-Crofts, 1962. Analyzes the decline of democratic theory and suggests a case for its revival. Argues that political theory must clarify political values, illuminate empirical political reality, facilitate prudent guidance in politics, and unify the discipline of political science.

Riemer, Neal. *The Future of the Democratic Revolution: Toward a More Prophetic Politics.* New York: Praeger, 1984. Analyzes the strengths and weaknesses of Machiavellian politics, utopian politics, and liberal democratic politics, and argues on behalf of the desirability and feasibility of a model of prophetic politics.

Riemer, Neal. *Creative Breakthroughs in Politics.* Westport, Conn.: Praeger, 1996. Examines several historical breakthroughs (Roger Williams and religious liberty; Madison and the federal republic); two spurious breakthroughs (Calhoun and Marx); a contempo-

rary breakthrough–in–progress (European Union); and a proposed future breakthrough (protection against genocide).

Sabine, George H. *A History of Political Theory.* New York: Holt, 1937. Offers a masterful introduction to political theory—scholarly, keen, critical.

Seidelman, Raymond. *Disenchanted Realists: Political Science and the American Crisis.* Albany: State University of New York, 1985. Notes three trends in American thought: institutionalist, democratic-populist, and "liberal political science." A sharp critique of barren professionalism.

SUGGESTIONS FOR FURTHER READING

Almond, Gabriel A., and Verba, Sidney. *The Civic Culture Revisited.* Beverly Hills, Calif.: Sage, 1989.

Ball, Terence. *Reappraising Political Theory.* Oxford: Oxford University Press, 1995. (Especially Chapter 1, "Reappraising Political Theory," and Chapter 2, "Whither Political Theory.")

Ball, Terence. *Transforming Political Discourse: Political Theory and Critical Conceptual History.* Oxford: Basil Blackwell, 1988.

Baer, Michael A., Jewell, Malcolm E., and Sigelman, Lee, eds. *Political Science in America: Oral Histories of a Discipline.* Lexington: University Press of Kentucky, 1991.

Beiner, Ronald. *Political Judgment.* Chicago: University of Chicago Press, 1983.

Crick, Bernard. *The American Science of Politics: Its Origins and Conditions.* Berkeley: University of California Press, 1959.

Finifter, Ada, ed. *Political Science: The State of the Discipline II.* Washington, D.C.: American Political Science Association, 1993.

Gilpin, Robert. *The Political Economy of International Relations.* Princeton: Princeton University Press, 1987.

Lipset, Seymour Martin. *Political Man.* Baltimore: Johns Hopkins University Press, 1981.

Neustadt, Richard E. *Presidential Power.* New York: Wiley, 1976.

Rawls, John. *A Theory of Justice.* Cambridge: Harvard University Press/Belknap Press, 1971.

Riemer, David R. *The Prisoners of Welfare: Liberating America's Poor from Unemployment and Low Wages.* New York: Praeger, 1988.

Simon, Herbert A. *Administrative Behavior: A Study of Decision-Making in Administrative Organizations,* 3rd ed. New York: Free Press, 1976.

Truman, David. *The Governmental Process: Political Interests and Public Opinion*, 2nd rev. ed. Berkeley, Calif: Institute of Governmental Studies, 1993.

Wolin, Sheldon. *Politics and Vision*. Boston: Little, Brown, 1960.

GLOSSARY TERMS

behavioralism
empiricism
ethics
political health
prudence
political science
politics
positivism

THE PHYSICAL, SOCIAL, AND CULTURAL ENVIRONMENT OF POLITICS

POLITICS IS A CREATIVE but not a completely autonomous activity. Although political actors are free to make choices to fulfill their values, they must make these choices in an environment not entirely of their own choosing. Politics—and political decisions—can only be understood in terms of the physical, social, and cultural *environment* in which the community is embedded.

PROPOSITIONS AND CHALLENGES

Communities do not develop in a vacuum. The larger environment significantly influences political actors' values, behavior, and judgment. It establishes limits for politics, illuminates the capabilities of political actors, calls attention to dangers in the community, and clarifies opportunities facing decision makers. In other words, the world itself shapes most political problems and significantly affects the solutions. Over the centuries, physical and biological sciences, the other social sciences, and the humanities have served to help clarify this larger environment.

This brings us to the key question in this chapter: *How does the larger environment influence politics and political science?* Let us first consider some important propositions that reveal the impact of the physical, social, and cultural environment on politics:

1. The physical *coexistence* of all political communities on a single globe in the nuclear age means that we must learn to live together sensibly or we may die together horribly.
2. Our *biological nature* and destiny should inspire respect for our common humanity—our fundamental equality—and the importance of maximizing cooperation, har-

58

PART ONE INTRODUCTION

nessing aggression, and minimizing the conflicts that threaten our biological existence.

3. *Human needs* suggest the origins of values that provide common purposes, goals, and standards for politics.

4. Increasing geographic closeness and economic *interdependence* worldwide—enhanced by the communications revolution—emphasize the inevitability of political, economic, social, and scientific patterns of cooperation.

5. Human *vulnerability to common disasters*—military, physical, and ecological—underscores the need for global agreements to avert war, famine, disease, and ecological damage.

6. The rapid *exhaustion of nonrenewable resources and the growth of population* beyond what existing resources can support highlight the need for political policies that encourage prudent growth of population and management of resources.

7. The *growth of cities* and their suburbs calls attention to a host of problems (inadequate housing, unemployment, poverty, faulty transportation, crime, disease) and thus to the need for prudent policy to maintain our cities as healthy, vital, manageable centers of modern civilization.

8. Modern *economic life*—involving industrialization, gaps between rich and poor, periodic recession, worker alienation—requires policies to ensure full employment, an equitable distribution of income, and a host of services to protect workers and consumers.

9. The worldwide *revolution of rising expectations,* especially in the developing nations, is significantly influenced by modern ideology and technology; this revolution bespeaks the need for wise political balance between hope and possibility.

These propositions highlight a number of political challenges:

1. The very survival of humanity is threatened by nuclear catastrophe. The challenge is to figure out how to control the spread of and ultimately eliminate the nuclear weapons brought into existence by science, technology, and political decisions.

2. A healthy ecological balance is vital; both ecological and political disaster can result from upsetting this balance. The challenge is to move away from policies that threaten disasters and toward prudent management of resources, population, and polluting industries and activities without sacrificing a decent standard of living, human integrity, or employment and profits.

3. Current political behavior is based on historical patterns of behavior. The challenge is to keep what is best in our past while endorsing changes to meet new conditions—changes that help us to turn away, for example, from racism or sexism or poverty through peaceful, constitutional effort.

4. Dominant economic systems have often shaped politics, law, and the distribution of wealth. The challenge is to ensure that the economic system—whether capitalism or socialism or a combination—serves human needs at the least cost to freedom.

5. Politics can be understood in terms of conflict and cooperation among economic, social, ethnic, religious, and political groups. Most often, it is their struggle for power that determines who gets what, when, and how. The challenge is to umpire this struggle in ways compatible with the public interest.

6. Human beings have biological, psychological, and social needs that must be satisfied. Politics can be understood as the effort to work out patterns to meet these needs. These needs suggest values—goals, purposes, policies—in politics and point to action. The challenge is to ensure that the proper patterns are developed.

7. The challenge in connection with a wide range of scientific and technological devel-

opments (space exploration, DNA mapping, new communication modes) is clear: How can public policy wisely harness the powers of science and technology for beneficial human ends?

8. In the cultural domain, which is concerned with the development and refinement of thought, spirit, literature, art, and taste, the challenge is to develop the creative imagination in all realms to foster a guiding vision of human excellence.

In exploring the physical, social, and cultural environment of politics, this chapter sketches some of the factual background to these propositions and challenges. Our treatment must be selective, yet it emphasizes the interdisciplinary setting of politics.

Political scientists must appreciate this interdisciplinary setting, because political science is only one of many social sciences, and the social sciences themselves constitute only one division of human knowledge and experience. In our treatment of the larger environment of politics, we cannot completely separate the physical and social aspects from the cultural aspects. For example, the geographical world can be considered physical or social or both. Anthropology embraces all three worlds—physical, social, and cultural in the larger sense (embodying the concepts, habits, skills, arts, instruments, and institutions of a given people in a given period). Ecology can be considered as a branch of biology that deals with the relations between living organisms and their environment, or as a branch of sociology (human ecology) that deals with the relations between human beings and their environment. Human biology cannot be discussed in isolation from important societal considerations. The religious setting of politics is both cultural and social. History can be viewed as both a social science and a branch of the humanities. Science and technology are usually located in the physical domain, yet they are products of human society and they illustrate culture at work.

THE PHYSICAL WORLD WE LIVE IN

The physical sciences call attention to limits, capabilities, dangers, and opportunities in politics. For example, they stimulate us to ask about the *carrying capacity* of the planet (that is, how much population earth's resources can support). They provide information that enables political scientists to grapple more intelligently with problems.

To the best of current knowledge, the earth is the only habitable planet in our solar system. As far as we know, we are the only sentient beings in the universe, although some astronomers speculate that there must be other planets capable of sustaining creatures like ourselves. Currently, human beings are the dominant species on a 4.5-billion-year-old planet in one modest-sized solar system of a larger universe whose gigantic dimensions we can barely imagine. We have achieved our position as *Homo sapiens*—the knowledgeable human being—after 3.5 billion years of organic evolution, 2 million years of human evolution, and only 5,000 years of historical experience.

The Population Explosion

Currently, our planet supports approximately 5.63 billion people, distributed unevenly (see Figure 4.1). Population estimates run to approximately 7.46 billion for the year 2015 and 9.83 billion by the year 2050. This large population is of relatively recent origin. The rapid escalation began with the Industrial Revolution at the end of the eighteenth century, and population doubled in the twentieth century. This increase poses momentous problems for politics. It requires study of the correlation between a burgeoning population and other significant developments (such as the opening up of new lands in the Americas), and revolutions in industry, transportation, medicine, and agriculture. Figure 4.2 illustrates population growth and its correlation with a number of key events.

Information about national populations, when combined with other data (population density,

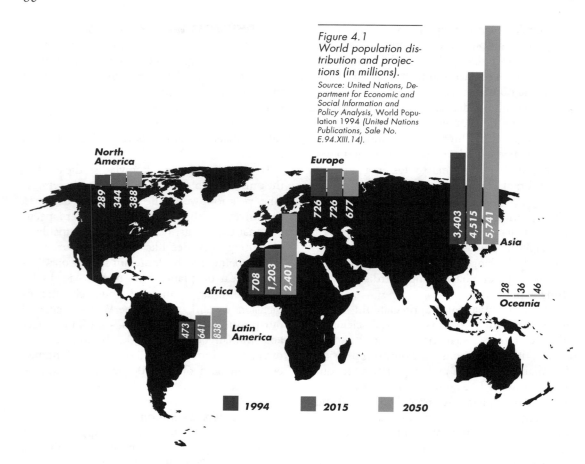

Figure 4.1
World population distribution and projections (in millions).

Source: United Nations, Department for Economic and Social Information and Policy Analysis, World Population 1994 (United Nations Publications, Sale No. E.94.XIII.14).

North America
289 344 388

Europe
726 726 677

Asia
3,403 4,515 5,741

Africa
708 1,203 2,401

Oceania
28 36 46

Latin America
473 641 838

1994   2015   2050

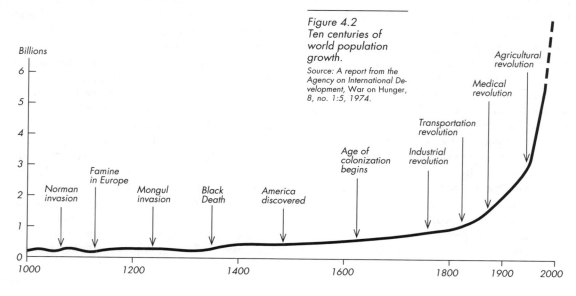

Figure 4.2
Ten centuries of world population growth.

Source: A report from the Agency on International Development, War on Hunger, 8, no. 1:5, 1974.

Billions

6
5
4
3
2
1
0

Norman invasion
Famine in Europe
Mongul invasion
Black Death
America discovered
Age of colonization begins
Industrial revolution
Transportation revolution
Medical revolution
Agricultural revolution

1000   1200   1400   1600   1800   1900   2000

High birth rates place enormous pressure on developing countries.

arable land, material resources, economic resourcefulness, political skill), tells a great deal about nations' political problems, strengths and weaknesses, and potential power.

Approximately one of every five persons on earth today is Chinese. About one of seven lives in India. The United States accounts for about 5 percent of total world population. Table 4.1 lists population by major regions and selected countries and also projects population to the years 2015 and 2050. It is especially significant that three-fourths of the earth's population lives in the less-developed countries.

Finite Resources

The problems for a growing population on a finite earth with finite resources are compounded by the fact that not all land can produce food. For example, approximately 29 percent of the earth's surface is land, but 40 percent of this land is desert or frigid wasteland. Moreover, 33 percent is pasture, forest, marsh, and mountain. Addi-

Table 4.1 *Evolution of the World Population by Main Region and Select Countries (millions)*

	1950	1985	1994	2015	2050
World	2,516	4,837	5,629	7,469	9,833
Developed regions	832	1,174	1,162	1,223	1,207
Developing regions	1,683	3,663	4,467	6,245	8,625
Africa	224	555	708	1,203	2,140
Latin America	165	405	473	641	838
Asia	1,376	2,818	3,403	4,515	5,741
China	555	1,060	1,208	1,441	1,605
India	358	759	918	1,263	1,639
Europe	392	492	726	726	677
United States	180	238	260	309	348

Sources: World Population Prospects, Estimates, and Projections, Sales No. 86.XIII.3 (New York: United Nations, 1986) World Population 1994 (United Nations Department for Economic and Social Information and Policy Analysis, Population Division, 1994).

tional amounts must be subtracted for urban areas, leaving only about 10 percent of the earth's land for producing crops. And of that potential agricultural land, only about 43 percent is in use.

As Table 4.2 reveals, some countries (for example, the Congo, Canada, Argentina, and the United States) have a more favorable population/land ratio (acres of arable land per person) than others. Yet this information must be examined with care. Not all countries with favorable population/land ratios—for example, the Congo—are well developed, and some countries with unfavorable ratios—for example, Japan—are well developed. This suggests that factors other than population and land are important and that we can learn a great deal about the nation's politics and policies by examining such factors.

The United Kingdom and Japan used their human and natural resources to industrialize and to establish global trading networks. Britain's historical devotion to the policy of free trade and freedom of the seas and its longstanding position as a great sea power are intimately connected to its need to import food and raw materials and export finished industrial products. Japan's historical development as a great power, from its opening to the West in the nineteenth century through its defeat in World War II, is closely connected to its unfavorable population/land ratio, its need for raw materials for industry, and its need to import food, as well as to the skill and energy of its people. However, both the United Kingdom and Japan remain vulnerable to a cutoff of food, raw materials, and international trade.

The United States is more favorably endowed, and this is unquestionably a source of its political strength. Yet even the United States may suffer if foreign crude oil cannot be imported cheaply. In 1970 the United States imported approximately 483 million barrels of petroleum. Twenty-four years later, in 1994, the amount was up to 2.56 billion barrels.

Asian nations are among the most disadvantaged in terms of balance between population and food. And many may not be as fortunate as Japan in achieving a healthy economy despite this disadvantage. Although large populations can be a source of political strength, they can contribute to political weakness when nations cannot feed their people because food supplies are inadequate, food cannot be imported, distribution is faulty, or the people have no money. These conditions can lead to economic and political crisis.

A good distribution system and prudent management of other natural resources clearly enhance a nation's strength. Saudi Arabia, for example, was a poor desert country before oil was discovered there. Now oil figures prominently in its economic and political power. The location of key resources (water for irrigation, oil, natural gas, coal, iron ore) tells a great deal about the raw materials of economic, and thus political, power. The locations of some key mineral resources are shown in Table 4.3.

Favorable natural endowments may create difficulties as well as advantages in politics. For example, more powerful nations may covet the natural wealth of weak nations. In the past this situation led to imperialism and colonialism as European countries sought to conquer and colonize South and North America, Asia, and Africa. Today, richly endowed countries such as Saudi

Table 4.2 *Population per Square Mile for Select Countries, 1995*

Country	Population/sq. mile
Canada	8
Congo	19
Argentina	32
United States	75
Egypt	162
Germany	601
United Kingdom	625
India	816
Japan	823
Bangladesh	2,478
Singapore	11,997

Source: Department of Commerce, Statistical Abstract of the United States 1995 (Washington, D.C.: Government Printing Office, 1995) pp. 846–847.

Table 4.3 *Leading Producers of Major Mineral Resources, 1990–1993*

Metals		**Nonmetallic Minerals**	
Aluminum	United States, Russia, Canada	Natural diamonds	Australia, Botswana, Zaire
Bauxite	Australia, Guinea, Jamaica	Nitrogen in ammonia	United States, India, Canada
Copper	Chile, United States, Canada	Phosphate rock	Canada, Germany, Russia
Chromite	Kazakhstan, South Africa, India	Salt	United States, China, Germany
Gold	South Africa, United States, Australia	Sulfur	United States, Canada, China
Iron ore	China, Brazil, Australia		
Lead	Australia, United States, China	**Mineral Fuels**	
Manganese	Ukraine, China, South Africa	Coal	China, United States, Russia
Nickel	Russia, Canada, New Caledonia	Dry natural gas	Russia, United States, Canada
Steel	Japan, United States, China	Natural gas plant liquids	United States, Saudi Arabia, Canada
Tin	China, Brazil, Indonesia	Petroleum, crude	Saudi Arabia, Russia, United States
Zinc	Canada, Brazil, Indonesia	Petroleum, refined	United States, Russia, Japan

Source: U.S. Department of Commerce, Statistical Abstract of the United States 1995 (Washington, D.C.: Government Printing Office, 1995) p. 867.

Arabia, Nigeria, and Venezuela may have trouble absorbing and sensibly using their oil wealth. The wisest use of such wealth requires considerable economic and political skill.

Finally, as discussed in Chapter 19, there is serious concern about humanity's relationship to its global home. In a number of ways we may be irreparably damaging the planet. The ozone layer, which protects the earth from ultraviolet rays, is being destroyed by the release of harmful man-made gases. Massive industrialization is causing the earth to warm at an alarming rate, threatening coastal regions over the next century. Each day 140 plant and animal species become extinct, never to be seen again. Forests are vanishing at an annual rate of 17 million hectares, an area slightly larger than the size of Malaysia, Norway, or Vietnam. The degradation of the earth's environment is critically important.

THE BIOLOGICAL, PHYSIOLOGICAL, PSYCHOLOGICAL, AND SOCIAL CREATURES WE ARE

Our human nature significantly influences our political values, behavior, and judgments. Many political values are rooted in human needs. We do not have to believe that biology is destiny to recognize that cooperation and conflict may have some relation to our human endowment. And certainly some political actors have decided (foolishly) that inequality, whether racial or sexual, is somehow rooted in our genes.

Human beings are highly developed primates. They have a large brain and complex central nervous system with an extraordinary mental capacity. Human beings walk upright and consequently are able to use their arms, hands, and fingers (especially the opposed thumb and forefinger) as remarkably dexterous tools. Humans also live longer than most other animals. Finally, humans have a unique capacity for conceptual thought and articulate speech—making and using words as tools.[1]

These four unique species characteristics— large brain size, upright posture, longevity, and thought—have permitted human beings to develop a complex language, to reason, and to make ingenious tools. Humans have been able to develop a system of communication, gain mastery of their environment, and reshape the natural world.

Human Needs

Although human beings can restructure the natural world, **human needs** (biological, physiological, psychological, social, and cultural) significantly influence their economic and social life and thus their politics.[2] Human beings need to survive, grow, and develop mentally and socially. To survive, they must satisfy certain material needs, such as physiological needs for air, sleep, water, food, and shelter. Heterosexual intercourse is normally necessary to produce children and perpetuate the species. People also need safety and security.

Human beings also have certain social needs: belonging, love, affection, and acceptance. They must also have self-esteem and esteem from others. Deficiencies here can impair both life and development.

In addition, human beings have ethical and cultural needs—a need for love, truth, and service, for justice and perfection, and for aesthetics and meaningfulness. The legitimate satisfaction of these varying needs makes life, growth, and development possible. Satisfying these needs calls for considerable social and political cooperation, which can be richly documented in sociobiology, anthropology, and history.

Cooperation Versus Conflict

How, then, do we explain conflict, aggression, and war? Are conflict and cooperation rooted in our biological nature? Some students of human biology, ethology (the study of animal behavior), and anthropology argue that human beings are aggressive by nature and that war is one outcome of such aggression. They maintain that war could not have existed for hundreds of thousands of years if it did not have roots in the human genetic code. One anthropologist has contended that "fierce war must be attributed to an inborn fierce nature which has developed in tribes long subjected to the rigors of competitive evolution." Such an "inborn competitive . . . nature" has, he insisted, been the "progeny of evolution," an evolution "gone mad."[3] On the basis of their studies of animal behavior, several ethologists,

including Konrad Lorenz and Robert Ardrey, have also posited instinctual human aggression.[4]

However, most biologists, anthropologists, and social psychologists think otherwise. Social psychologists such as Leonard Berkowitz contend that human aggression is learned behavior.[5]

Perhaps Julian S. Huxley best summed up the argument against instinctual aggressiveness when he maintained that "human nature . . . contains no specific war instinct, as does the nature of harvester ants." Huxley wrote,

> There is in man's make-up a general aggressive tendency, but this, like all other human urges, is not a specific and unvarying instinct; it can be molded into the most varied forms. It can be canalized into competitive sports, as in our own society, or as when certain Filipino tribes were induced to substitute football for head-hunting. It can be sublimated into non-competitive sport, like mountain climbing, or into higher types of activity altogether, like exploration or research or social crusades.[6]

Biologists, Huxley declared, can

> say with assurance that war is not a general law of life, but an exceeding rare biological phenomenon. War is not the same thing as conflict or bloodshed. It means something quite definite: an organized physical conflict between groups of one and the same species. Individual disputes between members of the same species are not war, even if they involve bloodshed and death.[7]

However, even if war is not the expression of a biological imperative, it remains, wrote Huxley, an ugly and devastating reality for humankind and especially for political leaders. He emphasized that war is "a biological problem of the broadest scope, for on its abolition may depend life's ability to continue the progress which it has slowly but steadily achieved through more than a thousand million years . . . War is not inevitable for man." But what is imperative is a politics "to make war less likely."[8]

Racism and Sexism

Political battles over slavery, racism, and sexism also require an understanding of human beings as biological creatures. In human history, slavery has been justified on the grounds that some people are slaves by nature. This view has been thoroughly discredited, but slavery still existed legally in some American states through the middle of the nineteenth century; in a few regions of the developing world, it persisted until just a few years ago.

Moreover, racial differences, particularly skin color, remain the actual basis for discrimination almost all over the world, not simply in regimes such as South Africa that practiced separation of the races—apartheid—for decades. Race has figured, and still figures, prominently in U.S. and British politics. **Racism**—the belief that certain races are inferior—explains the brutal treatment of native Americans by the Spanish, the English, and other Americans, and of Africans and Asians by Anglo-Saxons, Portuguese, Belgians, and French. And, of course, racial doctrines based on false science dominated the Nazi regime and guided its extermination of European Jewry.

Although racial discrimination, segregation, and persecution have been repudiated by enlightened public opinion, racism remains a fact of social and political life throughout the world and a continuing problem for public policy. In the United States, for example, immigration policy has historically been prejudiced against Asians and Africans (and even against Caucasians from eastern and southeastern Europe). Battles continue to be fought in American politics over measures to overcome racial discrimination against African Americans, Hispanics, and Native Americans. Arguments continue to rage about such public policies as compulsory busing to overcome racial imbalance in schools and affirmative action programs to ensure equality in employment.

Sexism, usually understood as the doctrine of male superiority and the practice of male dominance, is a worldwide phenomenon. Women have been overwhelmingly subjected to unequal treatment before the law, in economic life, and in politics and society. Only in the twentieth century and in liberal democratic and socialist countries have women achieved legal and political equality in theory. In the United States and Great Britain, for example, such gains came only after political battles to win the right to vote. But even in advanced liberal nations, de facto (actual) discrimination against women persists in the job market, in political life, and in social affairs. In the United States, for example, the political impact of women's fight for equality is dramatized by the controversial, ill-fated struggle to ratify the Equal Rights Amendment to the Constitution during the late 1970s and early 1980s. In politics and in society women have been fighting to overcome the still widespread social conviction, rooted in a narrow view of biology (and religion), that "a woman's place is in the home."

Human biological, psychological, and social characteristics thus strongly influence the development of social communities. In examining these communities we pay particular attention to how they respond to human needs, especially in politics; to how politics affects human tendencies to cooperate and clash; and to political efforts to deal with inequality and equality.

THE SOCIAL COMMUNITIES WE HAVE BUILT

How are the social communities we have built a response to our biological needs and the physical world? How are these communities influenced by psychological needs, by methods of earning a living and carrying out economic relations, by developments in science and technology, and by historical memory? Throughout the following analysis we will emphasize the ways in which the social environment influences politics.

The Sociopsychological Setting of Politics

Material, social, and cultural needs shape values, behavior, and judgment in society and in politics. Social psychologists say these needs include "a frame of orientation and devotion," a sense of roots and of unity, a feeling of "effectiveness," a capacity for "excitation and stimulation," and a guiding "character structure." According to Erich Fromm, these needs can be satisfied in many ways; different political systems represent different modes of satisfaction.[9]

For example, Fromm notes the "need for an object of devotion can be answered by devotion to God, love, and truth—or by idolatry of destructive idols." The adulation of Adolf Hitler was the worship of a destructive idol. Other needs can also be answered in different ways. Thus, says Fromm, the "need for relatedness can be answered by love and kindness—or by dependence, sadism, masochism, destructiveness, and narcissism." Nazism again illustrates the flawed political response. "The need for unity and rootedness can be answered by the passions for solidarity, brotherliness, love, and mystical experience—or by drunkenness, drug addiction, and depersonalization." Drunkenness and drug addiction are clearly social matters that call for a public policy response.

"The need for effectiveness can be answered by love, productive work—or by sadism and destructiveness," says Fromm. The former response enhances political trust and economic prosperity; sadism and destructiveness wreak havoc in the political community. Finally, Fromm says, "The need for stimulation and excitation can be answered by productive interest in man, nature, art, ideas—or by a greedy pursuit of ever-changing pleasures." A thoughtless, pleasure-loving society—heedless of future dangers—bodes ill for ecological and political well-being.

Moreover, the guiding character structure can be principled or unscrupulous, cooperative or combative, altruistic or selfish, democratic or authoritarian. Unscrupulous, combative, selfish, authoritarian people may create political communities that lack agreement on fundamental human rights and are thus prone to exploitation, domination, and war.

Human character can be influenced by historical tradition, coherent inner principles, or the dominant, fickle forces of contemporary society. If people are thoughtlessly directed by tradition, they may not be able to adapt politically. For example, ruling aristocrats who are unwilling to alter their ways may invite disaster for themselves by refusing to admit the middle class into political rule. In turn, the middle class may invite a comparable disaster by refusing to admit the working class. The same risk is taken by whites unwilling to admit African Americans or by men unwilling to admit women.

On the other hand, people with no coherent set of guiding principles will be at the mercy of the latest fad. They will be unable to resist foolish social and political innovations and unable to hang on to what is sound in their constitutional tradition. So we see that human needs—in society and in politics—can be satisfied in a number of ways: traditional or nontraditional, democratic or authoritarian.

The Economic Environment of Politics

People's method of earning a living (whether as laborers, businesspeople, or professionals) has always crucially influenced political life. Moreover, the larger economic relationships of society have an enormous impact on politics and public policy. People seek to protect their economic interests, which leads almost inevitably to politics. The economic influence on politics has been demonstrated by a number of perceptive observers.

Aristotle, for example, saw politics in ancient Greece in terms of the struggle between the few rich and the many poor, with the poor often battling to secure a more equitable distribution of wealth and the rich battling to secure their larger slice of wealth and power.

In seventeenth-century England, James Harrington argued that political power rested on economic power; specifically, he maintained that political power is influenced by the distribution of land. Harrington held that if one man is the sole landlord or if he dominates the people, the result is "absolute monarchy." If a few—the nobility or the nobility and the clergy—own the land or dominate the people, then the result is a mixed monarchy, or what we would call an aristocracy. But when the people are the landlords or there is a wide distribution of land, the outcome is a commonwealth, a republic, a government of laws and not of men. Although Harrington's understanding of economic power was somewhat limited, he nonetheless perceived that military and political power were clearly related to ownership of land, an important component of economic power in his day.

The importance of economics to politics was almost a political truism at the birth of the American Republic. America's Founding Fathers understood that British economic policy had triggered the American Revolution. James Madison held that "the principal task of modern legislation" was to regulate key interests—including those with and those without property, creditors, debtors, manufacturers, merchants, and bankers.

Karl Marx, in nineteenth-century Europe, articulated an even more sweeping view. He held that a society's economic structure, especially its system of economic production, was the real foundation on which the political superstructure and other aspects of the superstructure—religion, art, ethics—rested. For Marx, the power of the ruling class came from its control of economic life. In the nineteenth century this ruling class was the bourgeoisie (the property owners and capitalists in general). As Marx described it, "The executive of the modern state is but a committee for managing the common affairs of the whole bourgeoisie."

A political scientist need not be a Marxist to recognize the influence of economics. This influence manifests itself in the varying ways that powerful economic interests (for example, farmers, workers, and industrialists) seek to shape public policy at home and abroad through favorable legislative, administrative, or judicial decisions. Such interests, of course, may favor inaction as well as action in the political sphere.

Economics, as well as biology, throws light on equality and inequality, values always at the heart of the struggle for power that is politics. Students of political science must always remember that some nations are rich and developed and others are poor and developing—or less developed—and that great disparities exist between the rich and the poor within both developed and developing nations. Table 4.4

Table 4.4 *The Development Gap: Developed and Developing Nations, 1993*

	Low-Income Developing Countries	High-Income Developed Countries
Life expectancy (years)	62	77
Infant mortality rate (per 1000 live births)	64	7
GNP per capita (dollars)	380	23,090
Adult literacy rate (%)	41	<5

Source: World Development Report 1995 (Oxford University Press, published for the World Bank, 1995).

Figure 4.3
Infant mortality rate, 1993 (per 1,000 live births).
Source: World Development Report 1995 (Oxford University Press, published for the World Bank, 1995).

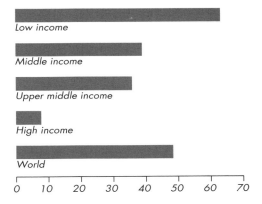

and Figures 4.3 and 4.4 dramatically illustrate these gaps.

The rich-poor gap, within and between nations, is an actual and potential source of troublesome conflict and a major challenge to political leaders. Poverty has political consequences. The fact that millions of people live at a bare subsistence level creates severe political problems. These problems arise from the nations' attempts to feed their people, accumulate capital for development, balance needs for defense against those for development and consumers, and, in general, respond to their people's aspirations for a better life. When circumstances are right, poverty can lead to riots. By intensifying people's sense of injustice, pov-

68

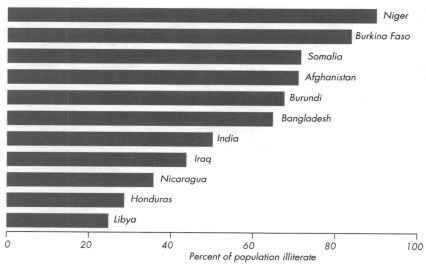

Figure 4.4
Severe national
illiteracy in selected developing countries, 1995.
Source: UNESCO, UNESCO Statistics Yearbook 1995 (Bertram Press,
1995).

Percent of population illiterate

erty can make poor people and those attracted to their cause more sympathetic to radical political ideologies and solutions.

Economic and related social problems are particularly acute in less-developed countries. The lack of nutritious food, pure water, good health care, and adequate income seriously threatens human life and decency in many rural areas of these countries. Also, rapid urban growth creates economic, social, and political problems by straining the economies and exerting extreme pressure for jobs, decent food, water, health care, and housing for millions of often unprepared urban dwellers. Table 4.5 illustrates the recent and projected rapid urbanization of some cities in developing countries.

Our consideration of the economic environment of politics has already overlapped its sociological setting, which is the subject of the next section.

The Sociological Setting of Politics

Economic interests are not the only powerful influences in society and therefore in politics. Other groups—social, ethnic, racial, religious— are also at work, and their efforts to protect their vital interests also impinge on politics. Indeed, all these groups are central to politics, because

public policy often results from their activities. But how else do noneconomic groups influence society? Let us first look at the role of religion in politics.

Religion—Since the Protestant Reformation, battles between Catholics and Protestants in Western Europe have divided nations and led to civil wars. Religious persecution was a factor in the settlement of America. The multiplicity and diversity of religious groups in the United States made for religious freedom. Yet, despite separation of church and state, religious groups have exerted much political influence. For example, they influenced the movement to abolish slavery, although Northern and Southern churches split along regional lines. Protestants, especially Methodists, were active in the Anti-Saloon League, which worked successfully for the 1919 Prohibition Amendment to the Constitution, which outlawed the manufacture, sale, or transportation of intoxicating liquors in the United States. The Catholic Church has taken a strong stand against abortion and on behalf of protecting the needy. American Jews are strongly pro-Israel. The Christian Right plays an important part in contemporary U.S. politics, particularly within the Republican party.

THE PHYSICAL, SOCIAL, AND CULTURAL ENVIRONMENT OF POLITICS

Urbanization, and especially the tragedy of urban squalor, creates difficult problems for modern politics.

Table 4.5 *Urbanization in Selected Third World Cities (millions)*

	Population 1994	Population 2015
Sao Paolo, Brazil	16.1	20.8
Mexico City, Mexico	15.5	18.8
Bombay, India	14.5	27.4
Calcutta, India	11.5	17.6
Jakarta, Indonesia	11.0	21.2
Lagos, Nigeria	9.8	24.4

Source: Concise Report on the World Population Situation in 1995 (United Nations Department for Economic and Social Information and Policy Analysis, Population Division, 1995, p. 28.

Conflicts between Protestants and Catholics in Northern Ireland continue to trouble that unhappy part of the British Isles. Israeli and Islamic claims on the city of Jerusalem add a religious dimension to complicated nationalistic and political rivalries in the Middle East. The Iranian revolution of 1979 that toppled the shah demonstrated the power of a strong-minded Shiite Islamic leader, the Ayatollah Khomeini, to rally religious and nationalist forces to over-throw a long-entrenched ruler and establish an Islamic republic. A host of other religious con-flicts figure prominently in politics: Christians versus Muslims in Lebanon, Muslims versus Hindus in India and Pakistan. Muslims were the victims of "ethnic cleansing" in Bosnia, a prov-ince of the former state of Yugoslavia. Members of Muslim fundamentalist groups were respon-sible for the assassination of President Anwar el-Sadat of Egypt in 1981 and the taking of American and European hostages in Lebanon throughout the 1980s. Religious forces are thus often crucial keys to understanding political values and behavior.

Race and Ethnicity—Race and ethnicity also fig-ure prominently in politics. Battles over slavery, emancipation, reconstruction, integration, and affirmative action have characterized U.S. poli-tics. Discrimination against various ethnic groups—Irish, Chinese, Japanese, Jews, Italians, Poles, Hispanics—has echoed and re-echoed in American politics. The ascent of many eth-nic groups to political power is reflected in the effort (not always successful) to achieve a "bal-anced" political ticket in such large multicultural cities as New York. Race, ethnic background, and class influence politics in particular ways. For example, African Americans often belong to the working class. Since 1933 they have tended to support the Democratic party. Social patterns persist, even with upwardly mobile groups. Jews, Irish Catholics, and African Ameri-cans have continued to support the welfare state even as they have moved up the socioeconomic scale.

Ethnic minorities in political communities create both dangers and opportunities. The dangers are usually most prominent. The dominant ethnic majority often finds the ethnic minority a thorn in its side; the ethnic minority, which often subscribes to a different religion and may also speak a different language than the dominant majority, seeks to preserve its ways and enhance its power. Thus a significant percentage of French-speaking Canadians, particularly in the province of Quebec, do not want to be absorbed into an Anglo-Saxon Canada. Their desire for power in Quebec—and perhaps for independence from Canada—is a thorny problem for Canadians. Sizable Muslim populations in India, Kurds in Iran and Iraq, Arabs in Israel, Chinese in Malaysia, Basques in Spain, and Ibos in Nigeria pose comparable problems. Lithuanians, Latvians, Estonians, Georgians, and Ukrainians—once part of the Soviet Union—finally gained their independent statehood, but now, ironically, Russians are ethnic minorities in these newly independent states. Moreover, Russia faces national and ethnic tensions amounting to regional civil wars in such parts of Russia as Chechnya. In the former state of Yugoslavia, violent conflict erupted between Serbs and Croats, and Bosnian Muslims, creating the worst warfare in Europe since World War II.

Countries often overlook the opportunities that ethnic minorities offer. The key opportunity is to fashion a successful multiethnic society in which groups can preserve their customs, characteristics, languages, and religions in a diverse and pluralistic society; where political power can be shared; and where social trust can ensure peace and constitutionality. Despite its sometimes deplorable historical record with many ethnic groups, the United States has at times attempted to seize this opportunity. But a truly multiethnic society is more often myth than reality.

Class—Although anti-Marxists claim it is a myth, the influence of **class** on politics is a reality that political scientists and sociologists must criti-cally explore. Marxists make class struggle, which for them is rooted in economics, the key to their analysis of society and politics. They see a working class and a capitalist class (owners of the means of production and exchange) competing for power. This struggle, Marxists believe, has universal application: it can be seen in both developed and developing countries. A study of class struggle identifies the forces contending for power, their basic interests, their values, their economic, social, and political behavior, and their contending public policies.

Some Marxists have even used class analysis to critically examine Communist countries such as the former Soviet Union or Yugoslavia. For example, they have criticized the emergence in such countries of a "new class" of elite rulers in defiance of the orthodox Marxist view of a classless society. Indeed, the 1989 dismantling of Communist power in Eastern Europe revealed that Communist officials in country after country had lived isolated lives of privilege while the economies they were charged with running collapsed around them.

Some social scientists maintain that class analysis is too limited—that it focuses too sharply on one factor. Other social scientists argue that class analysis has been neglected by most American social scientists. Nevertheless, it should be clear that the Marxist approach to class is only one of several approaches, albeit one of the most powerful.

The Scientific and Technological Environment of Politics

Modern science and technology, themselves products of social capabilities, have significantly affected the world we live in. They have facilitated industrialization and urbanization. They have brought people and goods closer together through rapid transportation and communication. They have increased our economic interdependence. They have led to the development of modern machinery and fertilizers that enable a tiny farm population in a developed country to produce enough food for a huge nation. Through modern medicine,

Figure 4.5
Comparison of areas of destruction and destructive energy released.
Source: Ruth Leger Sivard, World Military and Social Expenditures 1979 (Washington, D.C.: World Priorities, 1979).

	Kilotons
Chernobyl blast	0.1
Largest World War II conventional bomb	1.2
Hiroshima bomb	15.0
MX missile	5,000.0
All World War II bombs combined	6,000.0
All nuclear weapons (1989)	18,000,000,000.0

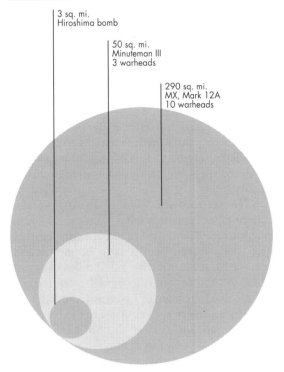

3 sq. mi.
Hiroshima bomb

50 sq. mi.
Minuteman III
3 warheads

290 sq. mi.
MX, Mark 12A
10 warheads

science and technology have assured the growth of population. Most dramatically, they have intensified war's destructive powers. As science and technology have altered our world, they have both created problems for politics and helped policymakers solve problems. A number of key problems cannot even be understood without the help of scientists. For example, they point out the enormous destructive power of nuclear weapons (Figure 4.5). Scientists also warn that the planet can sustain only a certain level of population with current resources, but they hold open the possibility that key ecological problems can be dealt with by developing solar power, prudently limiting population, and increasing the food supply.

The advance of scientific knowledge and technology has had paradoxical results for society and politics. On the one hand, science and technology have encouraged democratic achievements and a **revolution of rising expectations**. The burst of scientific accomplishments in the nineteenth and twentieth centuries coincided with the advent of liberal democracy in the Western world and with significant efforts to overcome backbreaking handwork, illiteracy, disease, and famine. On the other hand, science and technology have made possible the totalitarian state and the potential suicide of the human race through nuclear holocaust. Great scientific advances in the nineteenth and twentieth centuries also coincided with an often virulent nationalism and with dreadful patterns of exploitation, mind control, degradation, and death.

The advent of atomic weapons significantly altered the nature and conduct of modern politics.

Limited scientific knowledge and primitive technologies were generally accompanied by limited aspirations and limited politics. Paradoxically, the advance of science and technology creates both democratic and totalitarian possibilities and produces both benefits and damages. Science and technology can be tremendous forces for good in the world and in politics. The masterful achievements in sending rockets into space, the discovery of the genetic code in DNA, and the possibilities for gene splicing could be a preview of the use of science and technology to overcome war, disease, famine, adverse weather, scarce resources, pollution, and ignorance. Science and technology can open up a bright world for people everywhere.

Yet political leaders have to guard against the pride—the hubris—and the conceit that scientific mastery can create a technological fix for all our problems. The atomic bomb may kill as well as protect. Missiles may destroy cities or help unravel the mysteries of the solar system. Nuclear plants may create dangerous radioactivity or provide an alternative to expensive oil. Gene splicing (recombinant DNA) may unleash new, virulent microbes or lead to a cure for cancer. Modern drugs can be used to brainwash dissidents in a totalitarian state or relieve heart attacks. Modern methods of communication may increase the ability of a dictator or an authoritarian state to control thought or permit oppressed people to acquire outside information. New electronic toys may dull our critical senses or open up avenues of excellence in the arts, education, sports, and politics. Clearly, science and technology create problems that impinge directly on politics and call for difficult decisions to balance benefits and risks. These problems have become an inevitable part of the social and political environment.

The Historical Setting of Politics

An old adage holds that "Political science without history has no root; history without political science has no fruit." Historical roots nourish the societal tree and its political fruits. Historical

memory, for example, plays a vital role in social and political communities. A nation's **prescriptive constitution**—that is, its traditional way of conducting social, economic, and political business—originates in the community's history. This history shapes key principles: respect for private property or a reliance on public ownership, a belief in separation of church and state or their connection, a primary emphasis on liberty or on equality. These principles often become associated with national patriotism and generate powerful emotions that influence political values and behavior.

Our current social and political environment is an inheritance. To understand that historical inheritance is to understand key forces still influencing the present. Alexis de Tocqueville, French author of the perceptive nineteenth-century study of the United States *Democracy in America* (1835), understood this point well. In seeking to explain American society and politics, he called attention to several important factors. He noted the significance of a unique American history, relatively free of aristocracy and feudalism. He stressed the value of an Anglo-Saxon inheritance of constitutional liberty and a sound religious tradition. And he thoroughly appreciated the strategic worth of a bountiful land removed from Europe by 3,000 miles of ocean. These factors, Tocqueville argued, made it easier for creative statesmen to advance democracy and equality in America. In contrast to the French in 1789, Americans in 1776 did not have to concentrate great power in a central government to overthrow a monarchy, a nobility, and an established Church in order to assure equality and freedom. Americans, Tocqueville contended, had been "born equal." They had already established vital institutions of freedom. This history, he argued, moved Americans toward a more egalitarian democracy. They faced challenges to freedom, but their history promoted the success of their democratic experiment.

The study of history helps students of political science appreciate both change and continuity in politics. Traditions persist, but change and revolution may also occur. Both peaceful change and more violent transformation may be part of a nation's heritage and may influence its politics. Today, for example, the United States, France, and the United Kingdom are devoted to peaceful constitutional change, but each experienced important revolutions that significantly affected their current politics. The ideological forebears of today's political conservatives were often political radicals.

History shows that nations wax and wane in power. Empires rise and fall, as do civilizations. These are the truisms of history; yet they may stimulate political scientists to ask about the dynamics of social and political change. For example, does the study of history help us understand the nature of revolution in general and of specific revolutions? Historian Crane Brinton's *Anatomy of Revolution* points toward certain stages that apply to successful democratic revolutions other than the four he studied (the British civil war in the seventeenth century, the American and French revolutions in the late eighteenth century, and the Russian revolution of the twentieth century). Brinton saw revolution characterized by

1. Economic difficulties and the desertion of the intellectuals from existing values
2. A failure on the part of the existing government to maintain its legitimacy, affirm its power, and crush the rebels
3. The achievement of power by the revolutionaries, with the moderates initially in power
4. The displacement of the moderates by more radical revolutionaries who undertake a reign of terror
5. And then a return to more normal, and perhaps even reactionary, behavior after the fires of revolution die down.

Not all scholars agree with Brinton, but his investigation stimulates questions about how such historical studies can illuminate past and present revolutions.

History also shows that views of peoples and nations change over time. So, too, does the **civic culture**—that set of attitudes toward citizenship and politics—that helps sustain a democratic, stable, and effective nation. Germany is a good case in point. There was no state called Germany before the nineteenth century. As late as the eighteenth century, or even the early nineteenth, German-speaking people were often viewed as easygoing, pacific, and sometimes ignorant and uncultured. They lived in a number of separate states in Central Europe. However, by the late nineteenth century, under Prussian domination, a German state had emerged, and Germans were frequently looked on as energetic, militant, intelligent, and cultured. Then, with Hitler's dictatorship (1933–1945) still another transformation took place. German leaders and many German people were characterized as savage, brutal, and sadistic.

After World War II the Federal Republic of West Germany emerged, strongly committed to constitutional democracy. But German citizens did not yet illustrate civic culture at its best. German voters seemed "relatively passive," politically detached, and cynical; hostility between the supporters of West Germany's two largest parties was high and not "tempered by any general social norms of trust and confidence." In 1963 Gabriel Almond and Sidney Verba, two students of civic culture, attempted to explain the attitudes of German citizens by noting Germany's "bitter and traumatic political history," its terrible disillusionment with Nazi politics, and "the intense commitment to political movements that characterized Germany under Weimar [the Weimar Republic, after the end of World War I and before the advent of Hitler] and the Nazi era."[10]

Yet in a follow-up study on Germans and civic culture published in 1980, David Conradt demonstrated how recent history had changed German attitudes, indicating that the portrait of the German political culture painted less than two decades earlier had "changed in every important respect." By the mid-1970s, Conradt observed, "Germans had greater feelings of trust in government and were more supportive of their political system than mass publics in Britain." (In 1963 Almond and Verba had found the United States and Britain to be exemplars of the civic culture.) Conradt held that the Almond-Verba study was a "dated . . . snapshot of a political culture being remade." Conradt saw signs of a healthy, vital, democratic order and concluded that four historical events accounted for these key changes among German voters: (1) postwar socialization, (2) the absence of any credible alternative to liberal democracy, (3) postwar socioeconomic modernization, and (4) system performance.[11]

The historical setting of politics thus enables us to see how tradition influences political values, behavior, and judgment and to understand political problems. Our study of history helps us, as political scientists, to appreciate both continuity and change.

THE CULTURAL UNIVERSE WE HAVE CREATED

In politics, as in other arenas of human endeavor, a people without a vision will perish. This vision of a life to lead—of the good, the true, and the beautiful—comes to all people, including political actors, from a part of our culture understood here as high culture. We distinguish high culture to emphasize the development and refinement of thought, spirit, literature, art, and taste. Thus, our concern is with how philosophy, religion, literature, and art provide insights into human life and creativity. These disciplines call attention to the larger meaning of our world. They underscore the complexity and ambiguity of politics and the wide range and subtlety of human behavior. High culture depicts both the joy and despair of judgment in human and political life and adds a rich texture to the fabric of societal life and to politics.

The Culture of the Enlightenment

Culturally and politically, Westerners are still the children of the **Enlightenment**—the way of thought and life that emerged most clearly in

the late eighteenth century, the century of both the American and French revolutions. Despite the cataclysmic events of the twentieth century, most Westerners still share the outlook of the Enlightenment: a strong commitment to freedom, reason, and progress. We still condemn the follies and barbarities of an oppressive and ignorant past characterized by religious intolerance, violations of due process of law, and a rigid class structure. Westerners also look forward to the earthly emancipation of all human beings. The outlook of the Enlightenment has shaped the political philosophy of liberal democracy, democratic socialism, and communism. And despite the hold of traditional cultures in developing countries, this outlook has influenced the viewpoint of intellectuals and leaders in most Asian and African nations.

But the culture of the Enlightenment is not without its critics, who assail it as naive and unrealistic and who point out the shortcomings of faith in reason, freedom, and progress. The culture of the Enlightenment, they argue, has refused to face up to human irrationality, the denial of freedom, and political retrogression. They call attention, for example, to the decline of belief in eternal truths such as liberty, equality, and fraternity. Looking especially to modern totalitarian regimes, they note that the tradition of civility has been badly wounded in the modern world. They emphasize that the prerequisites for a genuinely democratic society are weak even in developed nations and often nonexistent in others. These critics underscore the failures of both liberalism and communism, pointing out that neither old nor new nations can overcome strife, hatred, poverty, and ignorance. The dreadful years of instability, war, authoritarianism, and totalitarianism of the twentieth century should refute those who continue to believe in progress, ever upward and onward. Unrelenting in their attack, the critics insist that the easy faith of the Enlightenment cannot be sustained in the light of the disillusioning lessons of modern psychology, which reveal people's irrational and childish urges, or in the light of the disheartening data about political behavior and institutions that expose incredible greed and venality and flagrant abuse of power.

Striking a Cultural Balance

Political thinkers seem to be striking a balance between the adulation of Enlightenment culture and harsh criticism of it. That balance has produced a much more sober and prudent— yet still affirmative—assessment of reason, freedom, and progress than previously existed. In striking that balance, these political thinkers have become conscious of the need to limit the power of political actors, including those with good intentions. They have come to see the dangers that people may face even from those who would usher in a just and peaceful world. The new balance is leading to a keener assessment of citizens' political capabilities—what people can and cannot do—and it is challenging individuals to seize real opportunities for greater control of their destiny. For example, human beings may not be able to end all conflicts, perhaps not even all warfare, but they may be able to abolish nuclear warfare. Similarly, we cannot eliminate all violations of civil liberties, but we may significantly reduce flagrant and persistent violations, especially genocide. It may be utopian to believe that we can rid the world of poverty and disease, but we can overcome chronic hunger and starvation and we can prevent a good many afflictions. Overcoming all pollution may be out of the question, but cleaner air and purer water are attainable.

Some students of religion maintain that religion may play a key role in striking a cultural balance. Are they correct? And what can we say about the way in which religion, as a vital part of our culture, influences politics?

Students of religion and politics argue that too often the religious influences on politics are overlooked. They emphasize that people's basic philosophy, deepest aspirations, and daily commitments have been vitally affected by religion. Often religious tradition—whether people are orthodox believers, deists, agnostics, or athe-

ists—has shaped their ideas and practices with regard to birth, education, marriage, and death. Students of religion insist that religion influences human understanding of love, compassion, faith, righteousness, charity, and friendship, as well as notions of peace, liberty, equality, fraternity, and justice. Certainly, they maintain, Judeo-Christian religious conceptions—whether of the covenant or of the biblical commandments—have influenced ideas of constitution and law in the Western world. A comparable account of Islam and other great religions would reveal the political importance of those religious outlooks. For good or ill, the world's great religions have provided a vision for society and politics.

Culture shapes and is shaped by politics. On one hand, religion, literature, and art can influence political values and behavior. On the other hand, what happens in politics and in society is expressed in religion, literature, and art. These forms thus reveal the creative imagination at work and show integration and disintegration, harmony and alienation, peace and war—among nations, within society, and in the human mind. We can profitably turn to great literary figures— Sophocles, Aristophanes, Dante, Cervantes, Shakespeare, Goethe, Dostoevsky, or Tolstoy— for deeper understanding of people, politics and society. Novelists such as Charles Dickens, Emile Zola, Charlotte and Emily Brontë, George Eliot, John Steinbeck, Sinclair Lewis, and Virginia Woolf have successfully popularized a host of social issues.

Great religious leaders and some students of religion have also profoundly influenced politics. A few examples include Moses, Jesus, Saint Paul, Confucius, and Mohammed; reforming popes such as John XXIII; inspiring women such Mother Theresa; great religious leaders from the developing world such as Mohandas Gandhi; influential black religious leaders such as Martin Luther King, Jr.; and modern students of religion, society, and politics such Reinhold Niebuhr. Of course, the creators of great world religions stand in a class by themselves, as do the great

Reinhold Niebuhr (1892–1971) was a distinguished and highly influential religious, social, and political thinker who advocated a tough-minded liberalism in domestic affairs and a tough-minded realism in international affairs.

Protestant reformers Martin Luther and John Calvin. Yet the interpretation of religion—and its impact on politics—goes on. The reforms set in motion by Pope John XXIII breathed new life and vitality into the Catholic Church and helped address a number of religious, social, and political issues. Martin Luther King, Jr. helped lead African Americans into a new day of freedom. And Reinhold Niebuhr developed a position of political realism that influenced the thinking of a generation of U.S. social scientists.

Niebuhr's Political Realism

Niebuhr emphasized that social scientists must recognize that the morality of the individual will not operate in larger social organizations, especially nations. He called attention to the will to dominate as well as the will to achieve a good life. He underscored the importance of the need for power to cope with power. He criticized naive liberals and pacifists who ignored the dark side of human nature—evil, pride, and irrationality.

For domestic affairs, Niebuhr advocated a tough-minded liberalism that was sympathetic to the rights of working people, African Americans, and other disadvantaged minorities and to the need for government regulation of capitalistic abuses. In foreign affairs he saw the need to resist Nazi power in Europe and to contain communist expansionism after World War II. At the end of his life, he again endorsed the civil rights movement and opposed America's ill-fated intervention in Vietnam.

Niebuhr constantly reminded his readers of his religious perspective—informed by St. Augustine—which insisted that there can be no perfect justice in this world; in politics there are only proximate solutions to insoluble problems. Yet, within these limitations, Niebuhr urged that people fight valiantly to achieve significant reforms in society and politics. Of course, he is only one philosopher whose religious perspective has helped illuminate modern politics. Yves Simon and Jacques Maritain are other such writers.

Along with creative intellectuals in the social and physical sciences, culturally creative individuals see the possibility of creative breakthroughs to a new ethical understanding of the good political life, to a new empirical understanding of what really goes on in politics, and to a new prudential understanding of what can or cannot be done in the domain of public policy. These breakthroughs point toward a vision of diversity in human life. They emphasize that the good life in politics must be carried beyond peace, civil liberty, social justice, and ecological balance to a vision of human excellence in all domains. By advancing such a vision of excellence, a society's culture encourages politicians to view their calling as a civilizing enterprise.

CONCLUSION

Politics and political science cannot be understood in a vacuum. The activity that is politics and the discipline that is political science exist in a larger world and are affected by a larger environment. In important ways that larger environment—physical, social, cultural—influences political values, behavior, and judgment and sets the stage on which the political play proceeds. The larger environment calls attention to limits, capabilities, dangers, and opportunities that are the central concerns of political scientists.

We gain a fuller appreciation of the larger environment of politics from other academic disciplines, ranging from history and physics to literature and art. These disciplines suggest theories, generalizations, models, methods, and insights that help political scientists address their own significant problems.

For purposes of specialization, we have separated political science from the other social sciences, yet this division is arbitrary and often severs connections that cannot be severed in the real world. Academic disciplines overlap, just as politics overlaps economics and other human activities. As we come to understand the interdisciplinary setting of politics, we can also understand the importance of focusing on our public life and values, on the struggle for power and patterns of accommodation in the political community, and on public policy judgments.

ANNOTATED BIBLIOGRAPHY

Barber, Benjamin. *Jihad vs. McWorld*. New York: Times Books, 1995. Thought provokingly posits conflict between two powerful forces: an integrative capitalist global economy and the return of fragmentary ethnic and religious movements.

Brown, Lester R. *State of the World 1996*. New York: Norton, 1996. Contains informative articles on the ecological state of the planet.

Foreman–Peck, James. *A History of the World Economy: International Economic Relations Since 1850*. Totowa, N.J.: Barnes & Noble Books, 1983. As title indicates, provides history of the world economy over the last century and a half. Many scholars consider this the best overview of world economy of the past two centuries.

Gilpin, Robert. *The Political Economy of International Relations*. Princeton, N.J.: Princeton University Press, 1987. Examines the impact of economic forces on global politics.

Gore, Al. *Earth in the Balance: Ecology and the Human Spirit*. New York: Houghton Mifflin, 1992. Sets out an environmental action agenda. A best-selling treatise on the ecological problems facing the world as we move toward the twenty-first century.

Kennedy, Paul. *Preparing for the Twenty-First Century*. New York: Random House, 1993. Analyzes the challenges facing the world—demographic, technological, and ecological. Perhaps stronger in identifying problems than in proposing solutions; nevertheless, a significant work.

Maslow, Abraham. *Motivation and Personality*. New York: Harper, 1970. Outlines Maslow's highly influential hierarchy-of-needs theory that throws a great deal of light on political values and behavior. See also *The Farther Reaches of Human Nature* (New York: Penguin, 1976); *The Farthest Reaches of Human Nature* (New York: Peter Smith, 1977).

Naisbitt, John, and Aburdence, Patricia. *Megatrends 2000: Ten New Directions for the 1990s*. New York: Avon Books, 1991. Attempts to define the major economic, social, and political trends of the decade.

Poulsen, Thomas. *Nations and States: A Geographic Background to World Affairs*. Englewood Cliffs, N.J.: Prentice-Hall, 1995. Provides an excellent, thorough introduction to political geography.

Riemer, Neal, ed. *Let Justice Roll: Prophetic Challenges in Religion, Politics and Society*. Lanham, Md.: Rowman & Littlefield, 1996. Explores the biblical roots, historical development, and contemporary relevance of the prophetic in the domains of religion, politics, and society. Brings to bear the insights and understanding—ethical, empirical, and prudential—of the prophetic mode on contemporary problems.

Sivard, Ruth Leger. *World Military and Social Expenditures*. Washington, D.C.: World Priorities, 1996. Presents a valuable annual report on significant social indicators, accompanied by excellent charts. Emphasizes the unhappy consequences of distorted national priorities.

United Nations Development Program. *Human Development Report 1996*. New York: Oxford University Press, 1996. Produced annually, offers an excellent narrative and statistical summary of the conditions under which human beings around the world live.

Yergin, Daniel. *The Prize: The Epic Quest for Oil, Money and Power*. New York: Simon & Schuster, 1991. Pulitzer prize-winning history of oil and its role in international politics. Sweeping in scope and very readable.

SUGGESTIONS FOR FURTHER READING

Cleveland, Harlan. *Birth of a New World*. San Francisco: Jossey-Bass, 1993.

Fromm, Erich. *Escape from Freedom*. New York: Rinehart, 1941.

Fromm, Erich. *The Anatomy of Human Destructiveness.* New York: Holt, Rinehart & Winston, 1973.

Gurr, Ted Robert, and Harff, Barbara. *Ethnic Conflict in World Politics.* Boulder, Colo.: Westview Press, 1994.

Kennedy, Paul. *The Rise and Fall of the Great Powers: Economic Change and Military Conflict from 1500 to 2000.* New York: Random House, 1987.

Mueller, John. *Quiet Cataclysm: Reflections on the Recent Transformation of World Politics.* New York: Harper Collins, 1995.

Neustadt, Richard, and May, Ernest R. *Thinking in Time: The Uses of History for Decision Makers.* New York: Free Press, 1986.

Riemer, Neal. *The Democratic Experiment.* Princeton, N.J.: Van Nostrand, 1967.

Toffler, Alvin and Toffler, Heidi. *Creating a New Civilization: The Politics of the Third Wave.* Atlanta: Turner Publishing, 1995.

GLOSSARY TERMS

civic culture
class
Enlightenment
human needs
prescriptive constitution
racism
revolution of rising expectations
sexism

P   A   R   T   T   W   O

POLITICAL PHILOSOPHY AND IDEOLOGY

The five chapters that constitute Part II begin a fuller exploration of the ethical task in political science. Our guiding question is: *How do political philosophy and ideology illuminate our understanding of politics?* By *political philosophy* we mean a critically examined understanding of the values, realities, and judgments of politics—an understanding that is essential to the search for excellence and fulfillment in a just community. By *political ideology* we mean those beliefs, or operative ideals, that guide political actors in a given community and the justification of those guiding beliefs.

Chapter 5 presents the contributions of some outstanding Western political philosophers to the difficult quest for the good political life and a fuller understanding of politics. Although there is more to political philosophy than the quest for the good political life, there is justification for focusing, at least initially, on this quest. This quest leads to a conscious appreciation of the importance of ethical standards for politics, dictates an empirical search for the necessary and sufficient conditions of the good political life, and encourages students of politics to search for wise public policies.

Questions of the good life are central to politics because they lead to critically examined standards for evaluation. These standards then make it possible to say that a value, a political actor, an institution, an action, or a policy is good or bad; that an empirical problem is significant or insignificant; and that a judgment is wise or foolish.

Moreover, these questions lead to a critical examination of the great political issues. Here we must confront the nature of human beings, the character of community, and the meaning of human destiny. We must probe frequent conflicts between justice and power, liberty and authority, and individual interest and the public interest. We must ask about the relationship between means and ends, a higher law and human law, and personal realization and the common good. Intrigued by the elusive character of the good life, we seek to understand the constitutional order, a nation's vital interests, and political obligation, and we try to assess the reality of human fulfillment and the pros and cons of evolutionary versus revolutionary change. In brief, we seek to uncover the meaning—and the necessary and sufficient conditions—of political health.

The brief review in Chapter 5 of how outstanding Western political philosophers have responded to fundamental issues will help you assess the strengths and weaknesses of liberal democracy, democratic socialism, communism, and other alternative outlooks. Chapters 6, 7, 8, and 9 focus on a number of these contemporary ideologies and also on past, present, and future challenges to these dominant belief systems.

The ethical task of political science, which is the primary concern of this section of the book, does not stop with an exploration of the good political life, the use and abuse of power, or contending ideologies. This task requires concern for a rich science of politics that can help us understand how political actors carry on their business: what values they hold; what patterns of cooperation, accommodation, and conflict prevail; and what decision-making processes exist. By sharpening our sensitivity to what is significant and meaningful, the ethical task helps us deal with significant empirical problems, meaningful hypotheses, data, theories, and explanations in politics. Moreover, the ethical task prepares us not only for the empirical task in Part III but also for the prudential task of Part IV. We should keep in mind the logic of our approach to political science as philosophy, social science, and public policy as we turn to Chapter 5.

THE QUEST FOR THE GOOD POLITICAL LIFE

THE INQUIRY that will guide us in this chapter is, *How have the great political philosophers contributed to defining the difficult quest for the good political life and a fuller understanding of politics?* Our selective examination will address: (1) the problem that prompted their exploration of the good life, (2) their "solution" and their defense or argument on behalf of their position, and (3) the heritage they bequeath to us. Although this brief treatment cannot do full justice to the richness, complexity, and subtlety of these philosophers' thoughts, it may open the door to deeper study.

CLASSICAL GREEK THOUGHT: THE SEARCH FOR POLITICAL EXCELLENCE

Socrates, one of the world's most creative and stimulating teachers, founded Greek political philosophy. Using the *dialogue*, a question-and-answer technique, he sought to explore the nature of the Good, the True, and the Beautiful. Socrates placed the Greek ideal of **arèté**, or excellence, which the Greeks sought to fulfill in all fields of human activity, at the center of thinking and action in the political community. He gathered around him a number of pupils, the most brilliant of whom was Plato, and through relentless examination probed the character of moral life, which was for him the heart of both human and communal life. Socrates's passion for excellence in the political community—a concern that required him to articulate an ethical standard, probe political behavior, and seek the wise course of action—remained a central motif in the political philosophy of Plato and Aristotle.

Plato: Justice as the Harmony of Classes and Rule by Philosopher-Kings

Plato's problem in the *Republic* can be stated simply: What is justice? Plato sought to rationalize, spiritualize, and universalize the ideal life for the **polis**, the Greek city-state.[1] He sought to establish the polis on sound principles, suffuse it with excellence, and help it endure. *Justice*, Plato argued, is the harmonious ordering of the functional classes in the polis: philosophers ruling, soldiers defending, and farmers and artisans providing the necessary food, clothing, and utensils for everyday life. In this fashion, the wise would rule, the brave would defend, and those with earthly appetites and talents would sustain the polis with their labor. Plato believed that the philosopher-kings should order the life of the polis according to a vision of the Good that their superior intellect allows them to perceive. This intellect permits them to grasp the truth of reality. Because of this intelligence—ensured by education and strengthened by the critical examination of ideas—they would govern wisely and ensure excellence. And because each class would do that which it is best endowed by nature to do, each class would receive its due. Conflict would be overcome; justice, or harmony, would prevail.

Plato's preference for the Good, for the enduring truth that lies beyond mere appearances, for excellence, for the rational, for the order that is justice, is very clear. In one bold stroke he solved the problem of the clash between justice and power by making the just powerful. Philosophers are entitled to their power because of their knowledge of the Good and the supreme truth.

The Greek philosopher Plato (427?–347 B.C.) was a pupil and friend of Socrates. Plato's writings—in the forms of dialogues, or conversations—and his concern for the "Good" have been extraordinarily influential in Western thought.

Justice cannot be the interest of the stronger, because might does not make right. Justice cannot be expediency, because it must rest on something more enduring than immediate satisfaction or personal advantage. So the just society must rest on a deeper and more fundamental truth than brute physical power or expedient advantage. That deeper truth—the idea of the Good—provides the proper standard in politics. That truth is illuminated by Plato's theory that ideas—the true "forms"—are the true realities. And, naturally, those in touch with the higher truth those who have ascended the ladder of truth to grasp the idea of the Good may wisely guide others in political life.

To the extent that other forms of government move away from the harmony of classes and the rule by philosopher-kings, they are deficient. Plato identified these deficient forms of government as timocracy, oligarchy, democracy, and tyranny. They reveal what the good political life is not. They represent a progressive falling away from **aristocracy**, which is government by the best. **Timocracy** is government by people of honor and ambition. As aristocracy degenerates into timocracy, so timocracy degenerates into **oligarchy**—government by the rich and lovers of money (what today we would call plutocracy). Oligarchy in turn degenerates into what Plato called **democracy**, government by the many poor. In his view, however, democracy emerges "after the poor have conquered their [oligarchic] opponents." Democracy is based on people having "an equal share of freedom and power." Democracy, however, is also unstable. Plato felt that it degenerates into tyranny when democratic men, preoccupied with "liberty and equality," lose a sense of law and order, a sense of discrimination, and turn to a "champion" to protect them against the rich. **Tyranny,** the lawless rule of one man, is the worst form of government. The lawless tyrant received Plato's harshest criticism.

Plato bequeathed a heritage of rule by natural aristocrats in accord with the Good. That heritage includes the definition of **justice** as the natural harmony of the classes that make up the political community. Plato's method—the dialectical examination of ideas—is part of that heritage. Asking questions, critically examining responses, and achieving truth by eliminating weak or false propositions constitute the dialectic method. In his other political dialogues (such as *Laws and Statesman*), Plato advanced a less exalted theory that makes room for the rule of good law instead of the rule of good men and that permits rulers to prudently adjust decisions to political circumstances. Despite these concessions, however, Plato remained devoted to his aristocratic ideal.

Plato's critics have attacked him as an enemy of the open society: hostile to democracy, a proponent of censorship, and an advocate of a rigid class society. His supporters have defended his commitment to rule by wise people (including women), his affirmation of a standard of a good life as a guide in politics, his dedication to reasoned examination of arguments, and his insistence on moving from opinion to knowledge. Among his critics was Aristotle, his most illustrious student, who, despite differences with Plato, remained indebted to him for many of his own ideas.

Aristotle: Constitutional Government and Rule by the Middle Class

Aristotle reacted strongly against Plato's political ideal. He criticized key features of Plato's *Republic* as unrealistic—especially his advocacy of communism for his class of philosopher-kings. Plato favored this system because public ownership would remove a real source of contention—conflicts over private property—among the members of this class. Aristotle thought such a system unrealistic and incompatible with human nature.

Aristotle sought to adjust Plato's severely aristocratic principles to the actualities of life in Greek political communities. But even as he did so, he endorsed the need to understand the ideally best regime, to relate ethics to politics, and to come as close to the best regime as human nature and political experience permit. Aristotle never lost sight of the anthropological principles that held that the family, the economy, and the local village come into existence to satisfy the bare needs of life, as well as the aristocratic principles that held that the polis then goes on to make the good life possible. The fulfillment of human beings in the political community remains a basic principle. But what was Aristotle's understanding of the best practicable good life?

His answer was the **polity,** or constitutional government—a mixture of democracy and oligarchy. Such a government is based on the many and seeks to respect the common good. Polity seeks to unite the freedom of the many poor with the wealth of the few rich. It heeds the legitimate interests of the many and is respectful of law. This type of government rests most securely on the existence of a well-educated, reasonably virtuous, sufficiently wealthy, moderate middle class. Such a class represents a golden mean between poverty and riches. It would not be envied by the poor or feared by the rich. Members of this class would be interested in politics and good government but would not be overly ambitious. Moreover, the middle class would be able to maintain the rule of law and justice.

Polity, however, was not Aristotle's ideal choice. He preferred monarchy and then aristocracy to polity (the best practicable). Nonetheless, he considered all three preferable to democracy (the most tolerable of the three perverted forms of government), oligarchy (a little better than tyranny), and tyranny (the worst of all). Aristotle recognized, however, that "the best is often unattainable, and therefore the true legislator and statesman ought to be acquainted, not only with (1) that which is best in the abstract, but also with (2) that which is best relative to circumstances."[2] Aristotle's famous classification of governments is presented in Table 5.1.

Aristotle favored the polity, in which the middle class is dominant, because such a government would be well administered, would prevent extremism in politics, would be freer of "factions and dissensions," and would be reasonably stable. Aristotle still hoped, however, that his polity

Table 5.1 Aristotle's Classification of Governments

Number Ruling	Rule in Accord with the Common Good	Rule Motivated by Individual or Class Self-Interest
One	Monarchy (Government by a virtuous ruler)	Tyranny (Government by one lawless person)
A few	Aristocracy (Government by the virtuous few)	Oligarchy (Government by the rich and noble)
The many	Polity (Constitutional government—a mixture of democracy and oligarchy)	Democracy (Government by the poor and free)

would approach his ideal state as closely as circumstances permit. The polis should be small but not too small. Its territory and resources should permit its citizens to live liberally and with abundant leisure. Citizens should be educated, dedicated to wisdom and virtue, and active in the life of the polis.

The Aristotelian heritage is the mixed constitution: respectful of the common good and the rule of law, and aristocratic in the best sense but willing to come to terms with the legitimate claims of the many poor and the few rich. Yet Aristotle's clear bias against "mechanics" and "tradesmen" and farmers, his justification of slavery, and his exclusion of women from the political process led modern democrats to challenge those aspects of his heritage.

CHRISTIANITY AND THE GOOD POLITICAL LIFE

As we pointed out in Chapter 4, religion has significantly influenced our understanding of human values, behavior, and judgment. When Christianity became tolerated in the Roman Empire early in the fourth century, its impact was widely felt in the Western world. Christianity's influence grew as it became the empire's favored religion.

St. Augustine: Incomplete Worldly Peace, Order, and Justice

St. Augustine (354–430) wrote *The City of God* to defend Christianity against the charge, leveled by pagan Romans, that Christianity caused the fall of Rome in A.D. 410. He denied the charge,

arguing that Roman vice, not Christian virtue, was responsible. In the course of his argument, Augustine wrote of two cities—the City of God (the heavenly city) and the City of Man (the earthly city)—that provide two influential standards for judgment, one positive and one negative. Before considering their relevance for the good political life, we must clarify their meaning.

The City of God Versus the City of Man—The heavenly city is formed "by the love of God," whereas the earthly city is formed "by the love of self, even to the contempt of God.[3] The City of God is the kingdom of Christ. In this kingdom, composed of the elect, people live according to God in the hope of everlasting happiness. In Augustine's view, perfect love, peace, justice, freedom, and fulfillment are possible only in the immortal life of the heavenly city.

The earthly city is the kingdom of Satan. In this city, made up of the damned, people live according to human appetites and seek earthly happiness. Perfect love, peace, justice, freedom, and fulfillment are not possible in this world; indeed, the earthly city is characterized by conflict, injustice, and war. It is a hell on earth.

Augustine maintained that the City of God is not coextensive with the Church, even though the Church may represent the heavenly city. Church leaders and church members are not necessarily among the elect. Similarly, the earthly city cannot be absolutely equated with Rome or any actual state. Some members of actual states are also citizens of the heavenly city; they are pilgrims sojourning on earth while awaiting heavenly salvation. On the whole, although both cities are commingled in any historical state, any actual political community is closer to the City of Man than to the City of God.

Human history reveals the clash between the two cities and the ultimate triumph of the City of God. That triumph will not take place in this world but in the heavenly one hereafter. The best regime, as the City of God, will emerge only after the end of history. From God's creation of the world and of people, through the Fall (people's turning away from God) and the advent of Christ (offering hope for salvation in God's grace), to the ultimate triumph of the City of God, we can discern God's providence.

The Christian Commonwealth—But how does this outlook clarify our understanding of the good political life? Augustine's philosophy of history, his idea of human nature, and his view of the two mystical cities leads to a modest view of the good political life on earth. Perfection is out of the question. True love—of God and of neighbor—must be professed but cannot be perfectly fulfilled. Justice—which means giving God his due—cannot be realized completely in this world. The Christian commonwealth, in which the one true God is recognized, is Augustine's ideal regime, but it is possible only in the immortal, heavenly city, not in any earthly community. Similarly, perfect peace is not possible on earth. The good political life in any community is inevitably incomplete. Human nature after the Fall reveals self-love, cupidity, domination, and concupiscence (fleshly lust). Egotism, pride, and lust for money and power lead to dissatisfaction, strife, misery, and war. Even the elect who are intermingled with the damned in this world cannot fully escape the evil consequences of the world of flesh.

According to Augustine's perspective, the best that people in any earthly political community can hope for is an incomplete, although still beneficial, peace and order. The state and its rulers are God's instruments to maintain peace and justice. The political and legal order must

St. Augustine (354–430), a cardinal founder of Christian theology, produced a number of influential works, including The City of God, a powerful defense of Christianity against its pagan critics and a uniquely Christian view of history.

restrain human appetites and passions—especially the lust for riches and power—and guide behavior through law and punishment. Political authority is a gift from God to fallen human beings. Even evil rulers must be seen as divinely appointed instruments to govern people after the Fall. Subjects must obey the powers that be. The state's coercive powers are necessary to restrain prideful appetites and conflicts among sinful human beings. Rulers should be resisted only if they command what God's ordinances forbid, and even then resisters must accept punishment.

Citizens in the political community—including the elect on pilgrimage to the heavenly city—see the value of even this incomplete peace, order, and justice. They see the value of law and of ensuring the necessities of human life. Augustine does not ignore the worth of such temporal blessings as health, material possessions, honor, friends, home, and family, but he does insist that they are always subordinate to the blessings of the heavenly city.

A political and social quietism pervades Augustine's political outlook:

There is little room in his thought for the idea that power may be used to improve the lot of man on earth or to lessen his misery, and certainly no room at all for the view that one form of government should be abolished or a particular ruler replaced so that a better social and political order may be instituted. A relatively peaceful society and good ruler are gifts of God to men; social disturbances, cruel and tyrannous rulers, and civil and foreign wars are punishments that He visits upon men when He sees that they require such chastisements. Since everything that takes place, whether "good" or "bad," is part of God's plan for the world and is, therefore, ultimately good, there is little or no impulse toward social or political reconstruction or amelioration.[4]

Augustine leaves a heritage of political realism. Given the nature of human beings—their pride, egotism, cupidity, and lust for power—our efforts to achieve perfect peace or justice in this world cannot succeed. Nevertheless, in the need for peace, order, security, and justice—however incomplete—people can look to government to help maintain a minimum level of civilization. But is Augustine's realism too pessimistic? And can his optimistic faith in God's providence be interpreted differently? Another Christian perspective on politics may provide answers.

St. Thomas Aquinas: Constitution, Law, Common Good, and Reason

St. Thomas Aquinas (1225–1274) viewed the political community (and its possibilities for human fulfillment) more positively than Augustine. Aquinas, like Augustine, endorsed the surpassing importance of eternal salvation and other key Christian concepts, but he was more inclined to see the political community as an arena for human development. Following Aristotle, Thomas Aquinas held that society and government are natural and arise out of human needs. The political community is necessary to fulfill human nature:

Life in a community . . . enables man . . . to achieve a plenitude of life; not merely to exist, but to live fully, with all that is necessary to well-being. In this sense the political community, of which man forms a part, assists him not merely to obtain material comforts, such as are produced by the many diverse industries of a state, but also spiritual well-being.[5]

Of course, complete spiritual fulfillment is possible only through eternal salvation beyond this mortal life. But the Church must do preparatory work in this world, in partnership with the state. Church and state play complementary roles in advancing human fulfillment. The church

is primarily concerned with ordering religious life; the state deals with secular life. Both operate within a framework of law: eternal law, natural law, human law, and divine law. For Aquinas, **law** was "an ordinance of reason for the common good, promulgated by him who has the care of the community."[6]

Eternal law refers to the reason of God ("God's grand design") by which the universe and all things in it are governed. As rational creatures, human beings are able to participate in eternal law through the light of natural reason and to discern what is good and what is evil. Thus **natural law** is that part of the eternal law known through reason. **Human law** is the application, in specific circumstances, of natural law in earthly affairs. **Divine law**, revealed by God and found in the scriptures, helps human beings understand natural law while guiding them toward their supernatural end.

The good political life calls for peace, right action, and life-sustaining necessities. According to Aquinas,

Therefore to establish the good life for a multitude, three things are required: first, that the multitude should be brought into the unity of peace; secondly, that the multitude, having been united by the bond of peace, should be directed to good action . . . ; thirdly, that through the care of the ruler there should be provided a sufficient supply of the necessaries for good living.[7]

Adherence to virtue, the common good, a constitutional regime, and the reign of law would lead to peace, right action, and life-sustaining goods. Aquinas's ideal political regime was **monarchy**, which requires virtue in rulers and ruled. His best practicable regime was a mixture of monarchy, aristocracy, and democracy. This regime combines a preeminently virtuous ruler, a virtuous governing elite under the ruler, and shared rule. Aquinas held that "a government of this kind is shared by all, both because all are eligible to govern and because the rulers are chosen by all." This form of mixed government is "the best form of polity." As Aquinas pointed out in *Summa Theologica,* it is "partly kingdom, since there is one at the head of all; partly aristocracy, insofar as a number of persons are set in authority; partly democracy, i.e., government by the people, insofar as the rulers can be chosen from the people and the people have the right to choose their rulers."

Constitution, law, common good, and reason are inseparable in Aquinas's conception of the good political life. Those who exercise power must do so constitutionally—within limits ordained by law. Such law—whether natural, divine, or human—protects against the arbitrary use of power. Rulers are thus bound up in a system of law. Power is justified only insofar as it serves the common good. Authority is legitimate because it is reasonable and right. Aquinas defined *law* as "an ordinance of reason for the common good, promulgated by him who has the care of the community." Thus unlawful rulers are rebels against God's divine system. In extreme cases, when constitutional redress has been tried and failed, tyrants can be resisted.

For Aquinas, then, the true end for a human being in the political community is a happy and virtuous life. Such a life contributes to the heavenly life. In a partnership guided by the spiritual leadership of the Church, church and state can work together toward human fulfillment in this world and in the next.

Aquinas's synthesis of faith and reason, of Christianity and Aristotle, became a mighty resource for modern constitutionalism. His belief in a higher law, a common good, the power of reason, and the importance of earthly (as well as heavenly) fulfillment reinforces modern efforts to overcome arbitrary power and to make government limited and responsible. His appreciation of the need, in politics, to apply sound principles to specific circumstances ensures his continued appeal to the modern mind. Critics of the "Angelic Doctor" (as Aquinas is known) question what remains of his political philosophy if one lacks his faith in God and his belief in reason. Such skepticism, they argue, undermines the constitutional system Aquinas created. Machiavelli lacked Aquinas's faith and subscribed to another line of reasoning in quest of a virtuous republic.

THE RENAISSANCE: NICCOLÒ MACHIAVELLI AND THE QUEST FOR A VIRTUOUS REPUBLIC

It is difficult to understand Niccolò Machiavelli without knowing a bit about Renaissance politics in his country. At that time, Italy was divided among a number of often warring states. The papacy was both a religious and a political power. France dominated parts of Italy. Moreover, the Renaissance gave birth to a new secular spirit, which manifested itself in creative activity in literature, art, and architecture and bubbled over into politics, calling traditional religious views into question and inviting bold leaders to demonstrate their talents. Machiavelli, an experienced and resourceful Florentine civil servant, was unquestionably influenced by the energetic mood of the Renaissance as he endeavored to articulate a creative approach to politics.

The Virtuous Republic

It may seem paradoxical to consider Machiavelli's views on the good political life, given the nature of his "lion and fox" philosophy (described in Chapter 1), which had caused the Roman Catholic Church to condemn his book *The Prince*. Yet there is another side to Machiavelli—a republican side. The quest for a virtuous republic was the second part of a twofold problem facing Machiavelli in the tumultuous early sixteenth century. He was first concerned with how to achieve national unity in an Italy characterized by a corrupt people, foreign domination, and internal division caused by the Catholic Church and quarreling nobles. This question elicited his lion-and-fox philosophy. The second problem that Machiavelli addressed—how to maintain a virtuous republic—is often overlooked, but it can help us understand his conception of the good political life.

Machiavelli was convinced that the political community's vital interests—liberty, independence, self-government, unity, security, power, prosperity, and glory—can best be protected, once national unity has been achieved, in a virtuous republic. His virtuous republic was characterized by civic virtue and by Renaissance *virtu* (energy, will), not by the Christian love of God or by the Greek devotion to justice. Although Machiavelli questioned the existence of an ultimate standard that people of reason or faith can know and that might guide them in politics, he still affirmed a view of political ends and means that can sensibly guide republics. The means to succeed in protecting the political community's vital interests in a virtuous republic include:

1. *Virtuous people.* A republican government, one that gives the people a significant role in governing themselves, requires a virtuous people. They must possess civic virtue: probity, integrity, love of liberty, patriotism, concern for the political community, trustworthiness, and good sense. A virtuous people must be intelligent, confident about public affairs, disciplined, and concerned about the welfare of the republic. The voice of such a people is, indeed, the voice of God.

2. A *mixed and balanced constitution.* The equilibrium must be political, economic, and social. The people must exercise control in policymaking and share governance with nobles under a wise ruler. The balance of people and nobles will contribute to the public good, prevent domination by a single interest, limit power, and keep political actors responsive.

3. A *government under good laws.* Good laws are crucial to good republican government. A prince might be superior in making laws, but "the people are superior in maintaining" the laws. With such good laws, the government will be stable and prudent.

4. *Public opinion and popular participation.* Freedom to debate and to propose measures for the public good is most important. It "cannot be wrong to defend one's opinions with arguments founded upon reason, without employing force or authority." Elections give people the chance to choose good,

capable rulers and to keep those who hold office responsible. Debate and elections allow grievances to be aired and conflicts to be settled peacefully.

5. *The healthy competition of parties.* In republican Rome, Machiavelli noted, all the laws that were favorable to liberty resulted from the opposition of the parties (the nobles and the people) to each other.

6. *A citizen army.* People who fight for their own country, government, security, family, and property will be a reliable bulwark for the republic. When they share power in the republic, they will stoutly defend it.

7. *Strong and wise leadership.* The leadership provided by a public-spirited elite and a virtuous ruler will enlighten and guide public opinion. The ruler must be a person of energy, resolve, foresight, and courage, who—along with the elite—will enhance governmental competence and executive vigor.[8]

Machiavelli's Influence

Machiavelli's republican heritage has often been overlooked by those scandalized by his more notorious call for a lion-and-fox prince. Yet, directly and indirectly, his republican vision has influenced modern liberal democratic societies, especially through his argument for a virtuous people, a balanced and mixed constitution, liberty under law, the competition of parties, and creative leadership. Machiavelli's skepticism about absolute truth (whether classical or Christian), his realistic observation of politics, and his Renaissance commitment to will (energetic activity and hard work) contribute to modern toleration, pluralism, and wise and bold efforts to protect our vital interests as best we can in this nonheavenly city. But are the people virtuous enough to govern themselves? Thomas Hobbes, the next political philosopher to be discussed, did not think so.

MODERN POLITICAL THOUGHT

We may consider the seventeenth century as the beginning of modernity in political thought. It was then that key modern themes, especially constitutionalism, individualism, and sovereignty, were sounded by philosophers and affirmed in practice. These themes gained even more prominence in succeeding centuries. Constitutional ideas precede modern times, of course, yet their effective practice had to wait until the late seventeenth century (when Britain's Glorious Revolution of 1688–1689 occurred) and the eighteenth century (when the American and French revolutions took place).

Thomas Hobbes, the first modern philosopher we discuss, did not live to see the British Parliament triumph in the Glorious Revolution, but he did live through Parliament's successful battles to affirm its constitutional claims. Hobbes, John Locke, and subsequent writers focused their political philosophy on the individual. This emphasis, strongly reaffirmed in the democratic revolutions of 1776 and 1789, flowered in the nineteenth and twentieth centuries.

Thomas Hobbes: The Need for a Supreme Sovereign Power

Thomas Hobbes, born in the momentous year (1588) that the Spanish Armada invaded the British Isles, experienced the troubled birth pangs of modern constitutionalism. He lived through a civil war (1642–1648); the execution of Charles I (1649); Britain's experiment with a republican government (the Commonwealth of 1649–1653); the Protectorate of Oliver Cromwell (1653–1658), a military dictatorship; and the restoration of the monarchy with Charles II in 1660. He died in 1679, a decade before Britain's Glorious Revolution. Little wonder that he was driven to ask: How can one obtain peace and maintain civilization in a troubled time? This question recurs throughout human history and politics. Certainly it was Hobbes's central problem in mid-seventeenth-century England, wracked as it was by civil war.

To appreciate Hobbes's response, we have to understand what disturbed him. He was deeply upset by civil war and the disorder it created. His image for the unhappy condition of humankind was that of a state of nature, a state prior to society and government, wherein people lived "without a common power to keep them all in awe." Such a state of nature was a state of war "of every man . . . against every man." Hobbes saw human beings as selfish, self-seeking, materialistic animals. It is no wonder, then, he believed that, in the state of nature:

> There is no place for Industry; because the fruit thereof is uncertain; and consequently no Culture of the Earth, no Navigation, nor use of the commodities that may be imported by Sea; no commodious Building; no Instruments of moving, and removing such things as require much force; no Knowledge of the face of the earth; no account of Time; no Arts; no Letters; no Society; and which is worst of all, continuall feare, and danger of violent death; And the life of man, solitary, poore, nasty, brutish, and short.[9]

In such a world, which lacks sovereign authority, the "notions of Right and Wrong, Justice and Injustice have there no place."

By contrast, the good political life calls for peace and a sovereign power, a "Mortall God." Only such a sovereign could maintain peace and order, law and justice. Only such a sovereign could ensure a civilization of industry, agriculture, science, arts, letters, and commodious living. But how could one move from the state of nature into civilized society under the protection of a sovereign power? Hobbes's answer was a particular kind of *social contract* that people could make because they possessed reason, which urged them to seek peace and their own self-preservation. Consequently, they contracted with each other to give the sovereign the power to make law, ensure justice, and advance civilization.

However, this sovereign would not be limited by the people who had contracted with each other (but not with the sovereign) to grant supreme power. Moreover, Hobbes's sovereign would not be limited by *divine law,* since the sovereign determined the meaning of divine law. The sovereign would also not be limited by *natural law,* because the reason of natural law had led to the social contract in the first place. Nor would the sovereign be limited by *civil law,* which is the sovereign's own command. Finally, the sovereign would not be limited by *common law,* or custom, since the sovereign assents to common law by his or her silence and also determines the civil law that overrides the common law. Hobbes's logic was based on the principle that to limit the sovereign would be to limit the ability to maintain the very peace and order that the people contracted to obtain.

Of course, the sovereign's common sense would ensure that property and liberty are respected, but only within a framework of peace and order. Beyond the maintenance of peace and order, justice, and national defense, the sovereign need not choose to exercise power. People, therefore, are at liberty "to buy and sell, and otherwise contract with one another; to choose their own aboad [abode], their own diet, their own trade of life, and [to] institute [rear] their children as they themselves see fit."

Hobbes's sovereign may be one person, a monarch (Hobbes's personal preference), or a parliament. What was crucial to him was not the form of government, but that there be a sovereign power to overcome the "perpetuall war" of "masterlesse men," which jeopardizes security, property, justice, and civilization.

The Hobbesian heritage is mixed. Those interested in peace, law, and order see the logic of a supreme authority that can overcome the war "of every man . . . against every man," which can also be the war of every nation against every nation. Many will see the logic of giving power to an agreed-on authority to protect people from their own self-destructive appetites and egoistic liberties. Others, however, object to Hobbes's unlimited sovereign power and—like John Locke, our next political philosopher—call for another kind of contract to reach most of Hobbes's objectives. Locke saw more virtue and a different kind of reason in people.

John Locke: Popular, Limited, Responsible, Representative Government

If Hobbes saw the need for a sovereign—a "Leviathan" or "Mortall God"—to maintain peace and order, John Locke worried about the ab-

sence of limitations on sovereign authority. Hobbes wrote during the turmoil of the British civil war in the mid-seventeenth century. Locke was unhappy about the monarch's constitutional violations of liberty toward the end of the seventeenth century. Is it possible to reconcile liberty and authority? Can one devise a political system to give sovereign authority legitimate power without sacrificing constitutional liberty? Locke's answer was yes, but only if one opts for a governmental system that is popular, limited, responsible, and representative.[10]

Locke held that people in the state of nature (a presocietal state) enjoy certain natural, inalienable rights, especially the rights to life, liberty, and property. However, these rights are not fully secure. Unfortunately, there is in the state of nature no common superior person (or law), no common judge, no common executive. There is no established, settled, known rule based on common consent; no known and impartial judge to decide disputes; and no fair, impartial organ to execute the laws. Consequently, people—being moral and rational, possessing common sense and good will—recognize the desirability of moving out of the insecure and inconvenient state of nature into a state of civil society where they can enjoy their inalienable rights more fully. They do this by means of a **social contract** whereby any number of people (capable of abiding by majority rule) unanimously unite to effect their common purposes. They thus establish a society and a body politic. They create governmental organs to make law, resolve disputes, and execute the law. The common legislative and executive power is thus directed toward peace, safety, and the public good. Thus, in Locke's view a legitimate government has four characteristics:

1. It is based on *popular consent.* The legislature is the supreme power in the commonwealth because the people consent, via the contract, to put trust in the legislature.
2. It is *limited* by the very nature of the contract. Neither the legislature nor the

John Locke's writings on natural rights, constitutionalism, and toleration significantly influenced both the American and French revolutions.

king can act arbitrarily. Both are required to act within constitutional limits. The legislature, for example, cannot take a person's property without that person's consent or the consent of his or her representatives. The king cannot hinder the legislature from assembling or acting freely pursuant to its constitutional powers.

3. It is is *responsible* to the people. It must honor the terms of the social contract that empowers it, terms that obligate it to protect life, liberty, and property.

4. It is *representative*; the people are to judge whether their representatives in the legislature (parliament) and their executive (king) act in accord with their trust.

Revolution is the people's ultimate weapon if government becomes tyrannical and violates the social contract—if it arbitrarily deprives people of life, liberty, and property. The people will, of course, invoke this right of revolution only when the government's violation of its trust is clear to a majority and persists, when all other constitutional attempts to redress grievances have been tried and have failed.

Locke has been both hailed and condemned as the father of liberal democracy. His supporters argue that liberal democracy rests on the constitutional protection of life, liberty, and property by a government that is popular, limited, responsible, and representative. They maintain that Locke successfully reconciled liberty and

authority. Locke's critics attack the conservative implications of his defense of property, saying it leads to inequality of wealth and power and reinforces what one critic has called Locke's theory of "possessive individualism." His critics believe that his theory perpetuates dominance by the capitalistic bourgeoisie.

Jean Jacques Rousseau: Popular Sovereignty via the General Will

Jean Jacques Rousseau (1712–1778) was critical of Locke's political philosophy. Rousseau continued to probe the problem of political obligation and to seek a more democratic solution. He asked, What principles of political right make government legitimate, "men being taken as they are and laws as they might be?"[11] "The problem," as he saw it, "is to find a form of association which will defend and protect with the whole common force the person and goods of each associate, and in which each, while uniting himself with all, may still obey himself alone, and remain as free, as before."

Rousseau's solution was yet another version of the social contract: a unanimous agreement to associate under the **general will.** "Each of us puts his person and all his power under the supreme direction of the general will, and, in our corporate capacity, we receive each member as an indivisible part of the whole." This social contract also removes people from an inconvenient and inadequate state of nature (where they enjoy only natural liberty) and creates a moral civil society with a unity, identity, life, and will of its own. In this society people have civil and moral liberty and better opportunity to fulfill themselves. The general will that guides their development is the constant will—the best, long-range will—of the sovereign people; it is the public good or public interest, and it is always right. In this way sovereign authority becomes (1) *legitimate* because it is based on unanimous agreement, not on force; (2) *equitable* because it is common to all; (3) *useful* because sovereign authority can have no other object than the common good; and (4) *stable* because it is guaranteed by the public force and supreme power in the political community.

According to Rousseau, the general will works to the public advantage and is the public's best long-range interest. The general will does not include selfish private interests. It resides in the majority, yet it is not necessarily identical with majority rule. It may be found by counting votes, yet it is not the will of all. The people are sovereign under the direction of the general will. Sovereignty is inalienable and indivisible, and it cannot be represented. Thus, the people cannot be separated from their sovereign power, they cannot share it, and they cannot allow representatives to make policy on their behalf. The sovereign people control their government's policy and personnel, its form, and its membership. The government merely executes the people's will. In this way the people remain free because obedience to self-prescribed law is liberty. Thus, Rousseau "rediscovered" the democratic political community and its role in advancing the fuller civil and moral liberty of those in the community. Only such a community, he felt, is capable of the good political life.

Rousseau's political philosophy, too, has its proponents and opponents. Democrats applaud his endorsement of popular sovereignty and a fuller democracy. Advocates of the common good praise his conception of the general will as an idea that can transcend selfish, shortsighted interest and can bind people together in recognition of a public interest that makes fulfillment possible. Libertarians, on the other hand, question Rousseau's argument that people can be "forced to be free," that they can be required, under law, to do what is right. Libertarians see Rousseau opening the door to dictatorship or to "totalitarian democracy." Political realists doubt whether Rousseau's concept of direct democracy is either desirable or feasible. Still others wonder whether the good political life can be based on so nebulous a standard as the "general will." Edmund Burke, although he had a strong sense of community, did not share Rousseau's radical outlook.

Edmund Burke: Prescriptive Constitutional Government

Edmund Burke (1729–1797) asked whether a prescriptive or historical constitution, prudently interpreted, is the best means to a sane balance that will preserve the right values, principles, and institutions for the political community.[12] This was Burke's central question in the last quarter of the eighteenth century, a period that witnessed the outbreak of two great democratic revolutions: the American Revolution in 1775 and the French Revolution in 1789. Burke's "Old Whig" answer was a resounding yes. But to understand his answer (and his support of the American colonists, his hostility to the French Revolution, and his mixed attitude toward reform in Britain), it is necessary to understand what he meant by "prescriptive constitution," "balance," "political community," and "prudence."

By **prescriptive constitution** Burke meant a constitution—or way of political life—that is the historical choice of successive generations, the successful inheritance of those who have gone before, and the embodiment of the wisdom of the species over time. Such a prescriptive constitution has passed the "solid test of long experience." The British Constitution is one such constitution, which Burke saw as a fortress of genuine natural rights. Justice, private property, instruction in life, and consolation in death are the rights of human beings in and under a prescriptive constitution. Burke contrasted such real rights with the theoretical, abstract Rights of Man, such as liberty, equality, and fraternity. These abstract Rights of Man did not take sound tradition into account. Such abstract rights ignored other values in society—peace and order, morality and religion, civil and social manners, the need for a police power and for an effective and well-distributed revenue.

Burke saw the British Constitution as a *balance* of principles—monarchic, aristocratic, and democratic. He viewed the British Constitution as "a monarchy directed by laws," balanced by an aristocracy (which encompassed the nation's great hereditary wealth, dignity, and leadership) and controlled by the democracy, the "people at large" (in the House of Commons). Burke saw the British Constitution as a successful attempt "to unite private and public liberty with public force, order, peace, justice, and above all, the institutions formed for bestowing permanence and stability" on the nation through the ages. Balance, of course, does not rule out necessary change. Indeed, the British Constitution is based on the principle of progressive inclusion of all politically minded people in the life of the state and on the enlargement of liberty. Only radical innovation is to be avoided.

Burke viewed the state—the political community—as a high and noble association. It is not to be seen as temporary, perishable, or crassly utilitarian. Such a state deserves to be approached with reverence; even its defects should be viewed with awe and caution. In Burke's words, "It is a partnership in all science; a partnership in all art; a partnership in every virtue, and in all perfection." The state is "a partnership not only between those who are living, but between those who are living, those who are dead, and those who are to be born."[13]

But the people must interpret the prescriptive constitution prudently if they wish to achieve the good political life. **Prudence** means giving attention to sound principles as well as to circumstances. The people must understand political actualities thoroughly and avoid dogmatic, abstract theorizing. They must exercise foresight. Although they reject radical innovations, prudent people see the need for sensible change. In the case of the American colonies, for example, Burke was convinced that the abstract principle of parliamentary supremacy should not prevent Britain from conceding autonomous home rule to the colonies, thereby creating practical independence within the British Empire. This wise course of action was suggested both by his interpretation of the British Constitution and by specific circumstances: the Atlantic Ocean that separated Britain from its American colonies; 2 million colonists of European descent; a nourishing Anglo-American trade; and America's "fierce

spirit of liberty" (rooted in British notions of liberty, in popular colonial governments, and in the colonialists' "republican religion"). If Burke opposed the French Revolution, it was because he thought the French revolutionaries to be extremists in rejecting the old French Constitution and in ignoring the mandate of prudent statesmanship to combine "an ability to improve" with a "disposition to preserve."

Burke can be viewed as the father of enlightened constitutional conservatism or as an "Old Whig" opponent of radical democracy. He made a powerful case for the prescriptive constitution and for prudent statesmanship. His criticism of radical democratic theory was hard-hitting. However, his political philosophy may seem too respectful of the status quo, not sufficiently aware of the need for more fundamental and speedy change in the interest of constitutional equality, fraternity, and liberty. A political philosopher more open to change was John Stuart Mill.

John Stuart Mill: Utilitarianism and Liberty

What principles of liberty and authority best guide the individual's and society's quest for happiness through fulfillment? John Stuart Mill's answer provides one influential response. Mill based his liberal political philosophy on (1) an enlightened utilitarianism; (2) convictions about representative, constitutional government; (3) a powerful argument on behalf of liberty; (4) a modified laissez-faire political economy; and (5) strong convictions about the liberation of women.

Despite recognizing the weaknesses of **utilitarianism**, Mill still adhered to the "creed which accepts as the foundation of morals 'utility' or the 'greatest happiness principle.'" This creed "holds that actions are right in proportion as they tend to promote happiness; wrong as they tend to produce the reverse of happiness. By happiness is intended pleasure and the absence of pain; by unhappiness, pain and the privation of pleasure."[14]

However, Mill insisted on a noble interpretation of the utilitarian standard. He recognized a hierarchy of pleasures and absorbed traditional concepts of justice and virtue. According to Mill, "pleasures of the intellect, of the feeling and imagination, and of the moral sentiments" rate more highly than mere sensation or "the animal appetites": "It is better to be a human being dissatisfied than a pig satisfied; better to be Socrates dissatisfied than a fool satisfied." Superior pleasures should be determined on the basis of the "decided preference" of knowledgeable people of taste and discernment. Mill clearly preferred the pleasures of the cultivated mind interested in science, art, poetry, history, and social science. He saw humankind slowly progressing in its battle against the "positive evils of life"—indigence, disease, unkindness, and worthlessness. He saw a harmony between the individual's interest and the public interest. He was convinced that the utilitarian standard would, in time, discredit the false "aristocracies of color, race, and sex," as it had already discredited the "injustice and tyranny" of slavery and serfdom.

Mill endorsed *representative, constitutional government* because of the way it melds liberty and authority. Such a government would permit popular control of the legislature, legislative (or parliamentary) control of the executive, and strong and skilled executive leadership. Mill favored as much popular participation as possible. "But since all cannot, in a community exceeding a single small town, participate personally in any but some very minor portions of the public

British philosopher, political economist, civil servant, and Member of Parliament John Stuart Mill was a dominant figure in the history of liberalism.

business, it follows that the ideal type of a perfect government must be representative."[15] The educated and publicly spirited minority should be given a prominent voice in Parliament through a system of proportional representation and plural voting.

Liberty, for Mill, was the means to happiness through fulfillment. It is not accidental that he chose the following quotation from Wilhelm von Humboldt to preface his famous essay *On Liberty:* "The grand leading principle towards which every argument unfolded in these pages directly converges, is the absolute and essential importance of human development in its richest diversity." In *On Liberty* Mill explored the nature and limits of power—particularly the power that society can legitimately exercise over the individual. His key principle was "that the sole end for which mankind are warranted, individually or collectively, in interfering with the liberty of action of any of their number is self-protection." Mill maintained that "the only purpose for which power can be rightfully exercised over any member of a civilized community, against his will, is to prevent harm to others."

Mill was not convinced that an individual's "own good, either physical or moral," is a sufficient reason for interfering with his or her liberty. In brief, a person is to be free in connection with his or her "self-regarding action." Society can interfere only when the individual's action is harmfully "other-regarding." Consequently, Mill defined the sphere of human liberty as that sphere wherein society, as distinct from the individual, has only an indirect interest. He singled out three fields of human liberty: (a) "the inward domain of consciousness" (liberty of belief, thought, and feeling and freedom of speech, press, and opinion); (b) "liberty of tastes and pursuits"; and (c) "liberty of combinations" (or associations).

Mill was particularly concerned with liberty of thought and discussion. Mental well-being, the basis for all humankind's well-being, necessitates freedom of opinion and expression. Such well-being and freedom rest on four grounds:

First, if any opinion is compelled to silence, that opinion may, for aught we can certainly know, be true. To deny this is to assume our own infallibility. . . . Secondly, though the silenced opinion be an error it may, and very commonly does, contain a portion of the truth; and since the general or prevailing opinion on any subject is rarely or never the whole truth, it is only by the collision of adverse opinions that the remainder of the truth has any chance of being supplied. . . . Thirdly, even if the received opinion be not only true, but the whole truth; unless it is suffered to be, and actually is, vigorously and earnestly contested, it will, by most of those who receive it, be held in the manner of a prejudice, with little comprehension or feeling of its rational grounds. And not only this, but fourthly, the meaning of the doctrine itself will be in danger of being lost, or enfeebled, and deprived of its vital effect on the character and conduct; the dogma becoming a mere formal profession, inefficacious for good, but cumbering the ground, and preventing the growth of any real and heartfelt conviction, from reason or personal experience.[16]

Mill sought a modified *laissez-faire political economy* that is compatible with liberty, the satisfaction of human needs, and the advancement of individual and social happiness. He opposed monopoly and disliked governmental interference. But he was not blind to the need for sensible regulation of industry to protect workers' health, safety, and welfare. (Here, Mill partly opened the door to the modern welfare state.) In successive editions of *On Political Economy*, he became more willing to modify a strict laissez-faire economic system. He moved toward allowing workers greater voice and control, especially through cooperative ventures. (Here he opened the door slightly to a modest variety of democratic socialism.)

Mill was by no means a radical democrat. He opposed giving the suffrage to the "poorest and rudest class of labourers." Nonetheless, in *The Subjection of Women* (strongly influenced by his wife, Harriet Taylor Mill), he wrote a powerful essay on behalf of *greater freedom for women*. Indeed, Mill can fairly be called one of the most eloquent nineteenth-century sponsors of women's liberation. He argued that happiness for individual women cannot be achieved unless they are given greater opportunity, equality, and recognition. He argued

strongly for suffrage and equal education for women. The happiness of society depends on women's being more fully admitted into the life of the nation. Mill emphatically insisted "that the principle which regulates the existing social relations between the two sexes"—the legal subordination of one sex to the other—is wrong in itself, and now one of the chief hindrances to human improvement; and that it ought to be replaced by a principle of perfect equality, admitting no power or privilege on the one side, nor disability on the other."[17]

Modern liberal democracy embodies a great many of Mill's principles: his powerful argument on behalf of liberty of thought and discussion, his utilitarian concern for happiness, his preference for representative government, his growing attention to the welfare of workers, and his bold advocacy of women's liberation. Yet his political philosophy still provokes a number of disturbing questions. Is utilitarianism strong enough to protect constitutional democracy, human liberty, and the least free? Is Mill's position too elitist, too aristocratic for the modern world? Does his approach really come to grips with worker alienation and capitalist abuses? For more radical ideas about liberty and emancipation, we turn to Karl Marx.

Karl Marx: Universal Human Emancipation via Communism

How can universal human emancipation be achieved? This was Karl Marx's radical question. His answer was no less radical: via the proletarian—communist—revolution. To understand both question and answer, we must set forth (1) Marx's vision for humanity, (2) his "ruthless criticism" of the existing bourgeois capitalist order, and (3) his revolutionary strategy.[18] These illuminate his understanding of the good political life to be sought, the alienated (or estranged) and exploited life to be overcome, and the revolutionary costs.

Marx's Vision for Humanity—Marx's vision for humanity encompassed several interrelated val-

German social scientist and revolutionary Karl Marx has been a dominant figure in modern socialism and was the intellectual fountainhead of modern communism.

ues: universal human freedom; integration, harmony, and peace; true humanity and community; and rich human and social development. Universal human freedom means freedom for all, but especially liberation of the most oppressed class—the working class, or the **proletariat**. It means more than political freedom; it means economic freedom—worker control of the means of production and exchange. Freedom will not be complete until the most alienated and oppressed people (workers) have overthrown "*all those conditions*" that keep people "abased, enslaved, abandoned, contemptible." As Marx argued in *The Economic and Philosophic Manuscripts*, workers will not be free until their alienation is overcome. They are estranged from what they produce, from their work, from their own humanity, and from their fellow human beings.

Overcoming estrangement and exploitation means integration, harmony, and peace. Conflicts, especially class conflict and national conflict, said Marx, will disappear. Other divisions—the division of labor, the division between town and country, the division between workers, the division between civil society and politics, and the division between the egoistic individual and the community—will also be overcome.

Freedom and integration will give rise to truly human beings and an authentic human community: human beings controlling their work-product, enjoying their working hours, regaining their humanity, and participating in a genuine community. Here a human being's real

human needs—sensuous and mental—will be satisfied.

Rich human and social development on this earth was Marx's goal. He believed that abundant cooperative wealth, the satisfaction of human needs, and the full development of the individual would go together.

Marx's Criticism of the Bourgeois Capitalist Order — Marx's criticism of the capitalist order centered on the assumption that this order prevents the fulfillment of his values. He criticized both the economic foundation of bourgeois capitalism and the superstructure of civil society, state, education, religion, law, ethics, and art that rests on that foundation. Marx used the same concepts to sum up the condition of workers under capitalism and his indictment of capitalism: wage slavery, despotism, alienation, exploitation, dehumanization, and stunted development. The society that produces such misery for the proletariat is evil. Bourgeois society, state, law, politics, religion, education, ethics, and ideology perpetuate the workers' unhappy lot under capitalism, Marx said. The key ideas of bourgeois liberalism—private property, family, religion, order—sustain capitalism, the bourgeois state, bourgeois law, the hypocritical bourgeois marriage and family, and a religion that dulls the workers' human consciousness by drugging them with false hopes of a heavenly existence. Marx was persuaded that capitalism's own weaknesses—its lust for profit at the expense of the worker and its vulnerability to economic crisis—create the conditions for its inevitable downfall.

Marx's Revolutionary Strategy—To achieve the good communist society, Marx felt a revolutionary reconstruction of society is necessary. The old bourgeois capitalist order must be destroyed and replaced by a communist order based on worker control of the means of production and exchange. Capitalism's own weaknesses set the stage for the revolution. Capitalism has called the revolutionary proletariat into existence. Capitalism is both oppressive and unstable. Forcible overthrow will probably be required because the forces of capitalism will not give up without a violent struggle. Only in certain advanced democratic capitalist countries may the peaceful transition to socialism, and then to communism, be possible. The revolution will occur in stages: First, the revolutionary overthrow of capitalism; then, the interim, "democratic," dictatorship of the proletariat (the stage of socialism); and finally, communism.

Peaceful, gradual, piecemeal reform will not normally do the job, Marx felt. Presumably, the **dictatorship of the proletariat**—the exercise of power by the majority of workers—will be democratic. Universal suffrage will prevail. A people's army will replace the bourgeois army and police. The people's representatives will be responsible to those who elected them and will hold office for short terms. Power in the hands of legislatures, judges, and police will be revocable. Churches will be disestablished. Education will be free. The parasitic bureaucracy of the old regime will be destroyed. As Marx emphasized in *The Civil War in France,* the new workers' regime will destroy, weaken, and transform the old "centralized State power, with its ubiquitous organs of standing army, policy, bureaucracy, clergy, and judicature." The commune—a model for the dictatorship of the proletariat—points toward a system of "cooperative production," of "united cooperative societies" able "to regulate national production upon a common plan, thus taking it under their own control, and putting an end to the constant anarchy and periodical convulsions which are the fatality of Capitalist production." Workers will lead the revolution, but they will draw support from tradespeople and peasants. The revolution will require a popular exercise of armed power, the destruction of repressive forces, and the construction of new democratic forces.

Marx said very little about the ultimate communist society. It will, of course, be classless and without exploitation. As he pointed out in the *Manifesto of the Communist Party,* all production will be "concentrated in the hands of a vast association of the whole nation." Coercive use of power will have disappeared. "In place of the old bourgeois society with its classes and class antagonisms, we shall have an association, in which the free development of each is the condition for the free development of all." At this time society will move beyond the socialist principle of equal pay for equal work. As Marx reminded his readers in the *Critique of the Gotha Program,* in the higher phase of communist society—and after productive forces have increased with the all-around development of the individual and wealth flows more abundantly—bourgeois right can be transcended and society can inscribe on its banner: "From each according to his ability, to each according to his needs!"

Worker control of production, of course, remains the key to communist society. War between nations and exploitation of one nation by another will disappear. Diversity will characterize human activity. Workers will perform necessary labor, under the most favorable conditions, "with a willing hand, a ready mind, and a joyous heart." Real freedom—which begins only where necessary labor ends—will be maximized.

Marx's Legacy—Marx bequeathed to the modern world: (a) a vision of a better world, (b) a philosophy of history (of inevitable movement from feudalism to capitalism to communism), (c) a systematic criticism of capitalism, and (d) a strategy of revolutionary action. How each of these inheritances is appraised depends on whether Marx is seen as a true or false prophet.[19] Is Marx's materialist conception of history and social change acceptable? Is his analysis of capitalism's exploitation of workers and of capitalism's weaknesses convincing? What about his call for a revolutionary overthrow of the bourgeois capitalist order?

Certainly Marx forced those who study him to confront the presence or absence of freedom, peace, well-being, and community for all people and the reasons for our condition. Certainly Marx made it impossible for social scientists to ignore the economic influences that shape modern society and influence social change. He also forced a major appraisal of capitalism as a powerful economic order and of the worker's role in that order. Finally, Marx called attention to a strategy for change that, whether as evolutionary or revolutionary socialism, has significantly affected modern politics.

Others, however, see Marx as a false prophet who based his case on dangerous utopian assumptions of earthly harmony and fulfillment. They see his call for a classless society as part of that mistaken utopianism. They reject Marx's **materialism**—the view that the way people earn their living, arrange the economic relations of production, and satisfy their material needs influences their political, social, and cultural ideas and institutions. The critics maintain that such a materialistic philosophy leaves no place for the transcendent—God, spirit—in history. They underscore Marx's failure (despite his admiration for capitalism's achievements) to appreciate capitalism's potential for reform and adaptation, its virtues, and its staying power. They reject Marx's primary emphasis on violent overthrow (when conditions are ripe); they reject, as undemocratic, his call for a dictatorship of the proletariat in the interim between capitalism and communism; and they note the absence of a clearly defined constitutional regime in his communist society.

CONTEMPORARY POLITICAL PHILOSOPHY

Contemporary political philosophy, as it becomes intertwined with political ideology, is examined more fully in the next four chapters. Here only a few preliminary observations are in order.

First, contemporary political philosophy can only be understood as an outgrowth of the great tradition that we have attempted to sample in the preceding pages.[20] Contemporary political philosophers are deeply versed in the classic tradition. In addressing modern problems and circumstances, they draw inspiration from that tradition. In doing so they often attempt to present a vision of the good political life that, as

we have tried to suggest, must deal with political actualities and prudential judgments as well as with ideals.

Second, the great tradition of political philosophy has clearly influenced not only political philosophers but also those who are called political scientists. William T. Bluhm has persuasively argued that "the classic theories furnish the foundations of nearly all the work which is being done today in the field of politics, work which is as vital and varied as the constellation of the classics."[21] And so he sees ties not only between Thomas Aquinas and Jacques Maritain, or Jean Jacques Rousseau and Carl Friedrich, or Edmund Burke and Walter Lippmann, but also between Aristotle, Seymour Martin Lipset, and Gabriel Almond, between Niccolò Machiavelli and Richard Neustadt, between Thomas Hobbes, Anthony Downs, and William Riker, and between John Stuart Mill and Christian Bay. "To an extraordinary extent, modern political analysis restates and develops the great theories."[22]

Third, even the analytical political philosophers, some of whom have given up the search for the good political life, continue the dialogue on a good political life. Even as they reject key aspects of the great tradition, they articulate their own conception of a good political life, a position that may owe much to the insights of certain political philosophers. They may, for example, reject Plato or Aquinas and yet accept Burke or Mill.

Fourth, new and creative voices in political philosophy must always be heard. Political philosophers may try to retain the best in the classical and modern tradition while they address the unique problems of the twentieth century. Some of these critics can be called futurists. They ask, Which values must be adopted to ensure a bright future for humankind? They respond with the interrelated values of life, peace, democracy, economic well-being, ecological health, and human excellence. Their vision of a bright future is motivated by their effort to overcome six factors that mitigate against it:

1. Humanity is afflicted by a strange attraction to death, destruction, and despair symbolized by the concentration camp and the atomic bomb.
2. Humanity is plagued by a war system rooted in a state system in which powerful sovereign nations possess nuclear weapons capable of mass annihilation.
3. Most of the world is still ruled by elitist, oligarchic, tyrannical forces convinced that democracy is a dangerous illusion.
4. Poverty, inequality, alienation, and waste characterize capitalistic and communist economies, "developed" and "developing" countries.
5. Ecological degradation and imbalance are worldwide.
6. Powerful social, economic, political, and ideological forces militate against cultural excellence and a decent quality of life.[23]

These six factors threaten global survival, healthy growth, and mature fulfillment. The dangers are, of course, interrelated. The puzzling passion for death supports the war system. War and often the sovereign nation-state system mitigate against democracy, a global constitution, the satisfaction of human needs, and ecological health. Undemocratic rule characterizes economics as well as politics. The imprudent use of resources creates economic and ecological disaster. The quality of life is corrupted by war, tyranny, poverty, and pollution.

The great political philosophers most often wrote in the heat of crisis. Creative political philosophy was born out of real difficulties faced by real political actors and communities. As we assess the contemporary scene, we should be open to the creative work of today's political philosophers and their efforts to address our difficult problems in the light of a great tradition.

CONCLUSION

And so we return to our guiding question in this chapter: How have the great political philosophers contributed to our definition of the quest for the good life and a fuller understanding of politics? They have offered critically examined visions of the good life. They have forced us, whether we agree or disagree, to confront political ideals, political actualities, and prudent judgments. They have required us to think through the standards we would use: justice, the common good, order, happiness, individual fulfillment, liberty, equality, and fraternity.

These political standards are also significant for empirical inquiry. They lead us to examine the use and abuse of power, the proper functioning of institutions, and the consequences of operative ideals. They encourage us to give normative meaning to empirical measurements so that, by assessing relevant facts, we can conclude that we are politically healthy. In this way we can sensibly appraise data about war and peace, poverty and prosperity, slavery and freedom, and inequality and equality.

Finally, determining standards for the good political life leads to prudent judgment. Means can be truly prudent only if they are humanely and rationally calculated to achieve good ends. Guided by critically understood standards of the good political life, we can assess the character of political behavior, politics, and institutions and determine whether they are wise or foolish, feasible or unfeasible. The political philosopher, in exploring the good political life, thus facilitates the political scientist's three major tasks: normative recommendation, empirical inquiry, and prudential judgment.

ANNOTATED BIBLIOGRAPHY

To explore the contributions of the great political philosophers to the good life and to a fuller understanding of politics, there is absolutely no substitute for reading their original writings. They have endured for good reasons.

Ball, Terence. *Reappraising Political Theory: Revisionist Studies in the History of Political Thought.* New York: Oxford University Press, 1995. Offers a keen reappraisal of such thinkers as Machiavelli, Hobbes, Rousseau, Bentham, and Marx.

Barker, Ernest. *Principles of Social and Political Theory.*

Oxford: Oxford University Press, 1951. Argues on behalf of justice as the concept that balances liberty, equality, and fraternity. Mature reflections of a distinguished student of political thought.

Bernstein, Richard J. *The Restructuring of Social and Political Theory.* New York: Harcourt Brace Jovanovich, 1976. Maintains, in agreement with Jurgen Habermas, that the primary task of "critical theory" today "is the reconciliation of the classical aim of politics to enable human beings to live good and just lives in a political community with the modern demand of social thought, which is to achieve scientific knowledge of the workings of society."

Bluhm, William T. *Theories of the Political System,* 3rd ed. Englewood Cliffs, N.J.: Prentice-Hall, 1978. Compares certain classical political philosophers with their modern analogues.

Brecht, Arnold. *Political Theory: The Foundations of Twentieth-Century Political Thought.* Princeton, N.J.: Princeton University Press, 1959. Holds that scientific political theory can contribute to the defense of the good life, enlarge our knowledge of politics, and deepen our "wisdom-of-action" in political affairs, but can't establish the absolute validity of ultimate standards.

Flathman, Richard, ed. *Concepts in Social and Political Theory.* New York: Macmillan, 1973. Provides a helpful, intelligent introduction to the analytic, linguistic, conceptual approach to political and social philosophy.

Rawls, John. *A Theory of Justice.* Cambridge, Mass.: Harvard University Press, 1971. A highly influential argument on behalf of justice as fairness.

Riemer, Neal. *The Revival of Democratic Theory.* New York: Appleton-Century-Crofts, 1962. Emphasizes the importance of a democratic theory that is desirable, realistic, and feasible.

Riemer, Neal. *The Future of the Democratic Revolution: Toward a More Prophetic Politics.* New York: Praeger, 1984. Argues on behalf of a model of prophetic politics committed to prophetic values, to a critique of existing political orders, to creative breakthroughs that will narrow the gap between ideal and reality, and to futuristic scrutiny and projection. Analyzes and criticizes three other models: Machiavellian, utopian, and liberal democratic politics.

Riemer, Neal. *Karl Marx and Prophetic Politics.* New York: Praeger, 1987. Examines Marx's values, radi-

cal social scientific critique, and theory of revolutionary action. Uses a model of the just revolution to appraise Marx's revolutionary theory. Highlights Marx's insights and his failures. Concludes that Marx is not a true, but also not a completely false, secular prophet.

Sabine, George. *A History of Political Theory.* New York: Holt, 1937. Provides a balanced, critical, and humane history, even though written from the perspective of "social relativism."

Tinder, Glenn. *The Political Meaning of Christianity: An Interpretation.* Baton Rouge: Louisiana State University Press, 1989. Examines Christianity's contribution to civility via the exaltation of the individual, agapé, prophetic hope, liberty, and social transformation.

Weldon, T. D. *States and Morals,* New York: McGraw-Hill, 1947; The *Vocabulary of Politics,* Baltimore: Penguin Books, 1953. Rejects the metaphysical search for moral foundations and emphasizes the importance of precision of meaning, logical consistency, and empirical verification. Insists, however, that there are empirical tests for political appraisal. Skeptical of the ability of political philosophers to demonstrate the superiority of political values. Suspicious of philosopher-kings.

Wolin, Sheldon. *Politics and Vision.* Boston: Little, Brown, 1960. Offers a fresh look at the great tradition of political theory and its relevance to contemporary concerns.

SUGGESTIONS FOR FURTHER READING

Auerbach, Bruce E. *Unto the Thousandth Generation: Conceptualizing Intergenerational Justice.* New York: Peter Lang, 1994.

Ball, Terence. *Transforming Political Discourse.* Oxford: Blackwell, 1988.

Coole, Diana H. *Women in Political Theory: From Ancient Misogyny to Contemporary Feminism.* Boulder, Colo.: Lynne Rienner, 1988.

Elshtain, Jean Bethke. *Public Man, Private Woman: Women in Social and Political Thought.* Princeton, N.J.: Princeton University Press, 1981.

Hartz, Louis. *The Liberal Tradition in America.* New York: Harcourt Brace, 1955.

Jaggar, Alison M. *Feminist Policies and Human Nature.* Brighton, Sussex: Harvester Press, 1983.

Jordan, Bill. *The Common Good: Citizenship, Morality and Self-Interest.* Oxford: Basil Blackwell, 1989.

MacIntyre, Alasdair. *After Virtue: A Study in Moral*

Theory, 2nd ed. Notre Dame, Ind.: University of Notre Dame Press, 1984.

MacIntyre, Alasdair. *Whose Justice? Which Rationality?* Notre Dame, Ind.: University of Notre Dame Press, 1988.

Purcell, Edward A., Jr. *The Crisis of Democratic Theory*. Lexington: University Press of Kentucky, 1973.

Riemer, Neal, ed. *Let Justice Roll: Prophetic Challenges in Religion, Politics, and Society*. Lanham, Md.: Rowman and Littlefield, 1996.

Talmon, A. J. *The Origins of Totalitarian Democracy*. London: Secker & Warburg, 1952.

Walzer, Michael. *Interpretation and Social Criticism*. Cambridge, Mass.: Harvard University Press, 1987.

Walzer, Michael. *The Company of Critics: Social Criticism and Political Commitment in the Twentieth Century*. New York: Basic Books, 1988.

Zuckert, Catherine H., ed. *Understanding the Political Spirit: Philosophical Investigations from Socrates to Nietzsche*. New Haven, Conn.: Yale University Press, 1988.

GLOSSARY TERMS

arèté
aristocracy
autocracy
democracy
dictatorship of the proletariat
divine law
eternal law
general will
human law
justice
laissez-faire
law
materialism
monarchy
natural law
oligarchy
polis
polity
prescriptive constitution
proletariat
prudence
social contract
timocracy
tyranny
utilitarianism

LIBERAL DEMOCRACY

BEGINNING WITH THIS chapter and continuing through the next three, we will try to clarify the operative ideals of a number of twentieth-century political communities. We thus shift from the classical political philosophers and their conceptions of the good political life to modern politics and its guiding views of the good life in the contemporary world. Because the nation-state is the dominant political community in the twentieth century, we will focus on the guiding vision, the cardinal operative ideals, and (less fully) the illustrative policies of such political communities as the United States, the United Kingdom (Great Britain), China, and several additional European, Asian, Latin American, and African countries. We will also comment on the failure of communism in the former Soviet Union and its diminishing appeal elsewhere in the world.

This examination will involve political ideology and philosophy. **Political ideologies** are the beliefs and practices that guide political actors in real political communities. **Operative ideals** constitute the animating vision of political actors; studying these ideals often illuminates operational practice. Of course, these ideals are not always fully operative, but they help explain the purposes, principles, and rules of the game. By studying operative ideals we pay attention both to what political actors say they ought to do and to what in fact they do. We will also look at how political actors justify beliefs and practices.

How fully and completely these guiding beliefs and practices advance the good political life is a question best addressed by political philosophy. As we assess the strengths and weaknesses of political ideologies such as liberal democracy or communism or democratic socialism or fascism, we can move beyond mere description and justification of operative ideals to critical appraisal.

Chapters 6 through 9 will help readers (1) critically explore the good political life in contemporary politics; (2) locate themselves on the modern political spectrum (left, center, right; radical, liberal, populist, libertarian, conservative, reactionary); (3) understand the reasons for their political positions; (4) examine the standards they bring to politics; and (5) set the stage, through a critical exploration of the meaning of the good political life, for the fuller scientific analysis of comparative politics in Part III and for the more thorough considerations of public policy in Part IV.

The central question in this chapter is, *What are the strengths and weaknesses of liberal democracy?* We will focus primarily on the United States. We begin by examining the roots and evolution of liberal democracy, its major operative ideals, and its liberal and conservative variations.

THE SOURCES OF LIBERAL DEMOCRACY

Political ideologies have a historical life, growth, and development, and political ideals and their implementation are significantly influenced by events. Contemporary conceptions of the good life do not emerge full-blown. Many strands have contributed to the political ideology known as liberal democracy. Although its roots—in theory and practice—are old, its flowering (despite great growth in the late eighteenth and nineteenth centuries) is a mid-twentieth-century phenomenon. For our purposes, we define **liberal democracy** briefly as that philosophy of constitutional governance characterized by commitments to popular rule and protection of basic rights.[1]

The Greek Heritage of Democracy

The word *democracy* comes from the Greek: *demos* means "people," and *ocracy* means "government" or "rule." Hence, **democracy** means "people's rule." Aristotle saw democracy as government by the many poor, who governed in their own class interest and favored freedom and equality. Democracy meant the rule of the less wealthy

and less educated citizen-masses in contrast to that of the plutocratic and aristocratic classes. But democracy in the Greek sense was not constitutional in the modern sense: it lacked effective and regularized restraints on those who wielded power. Moreover, Greek democracy excluded women and slaves from the suffrage. Nonetheless, the Greek democratic ideal did eventually stimulate the imagination of Western Europe. Best put by Pericles, a popular Athenian leader, in his great "Funeral Oration," this ideal stressed rule by the many, "equal justice," excellence, opportunity, public reverence for the laws, citizen involvement in public affairs, and sound democratic judgment. Although incomplete and short-lived in reality, Pericles's conception perpetuated a noble ideal.

Christian Theology and Roman Republicanism

By insisting on absolute freedom to worship God, Christians began a development that was to culminate, first theoretically and later practically, in constitutional protections against governmental interference with religious worship and in constitutional limitations on arbitrary political power. People must be free to worship God. Moreover, all men and women are equal under God; they are brothers and sisters under a common deity. Christian theology also emphasized equality, another concept crucial to liberal democracy. However, it took a long time for moral equality to become translated into political, social, and economic equality. Slavery characterized the Roman period and was not abolished in the United States until 1865.

The Romans made a twofold contribution. They helped keep alive, at least in theory, the concept of popular sovereignty (republican, or popular, rule), and they broadened the concept of citizenship. For the Greeks, all foreigners were barbarians and were excluded from citizenship. The Romans, however, extended citizenship, which brought with it the protection of Roman law, to all who came within the jurisdiction of their empire, whether they be Roman, Greek, Christian, or Jewish.

Medieval Europe

Constitutional ideas, crucial to the evolution of liberal democracy, were current in medieval political theory. Almost all theorists contended that political rule must be just and in the interest of the people. No earthly ruler was absolute. The theorists insisted that princes (rulers) follow the precepts of a higher law: God's law or natural (moral) law, which could be known by humans possessed of "right reason." Of course, political practice in the medieval world fell considerably short of modern canons of democratic and constitutional governance.

The Protestant Reformation

Martin Luther and John Calvin, the great Protestant reformers, were not modern liberal democrats. In most respects they shared a medieval Christian outlook about politics. Although they believed in a higher law, they still took a dim view of popular resistance against political tyrants. Nonetheless, their revolt against the Roman Catholic Church, and some of their ideas, set the political and intellectual scene for the emergence of constitutional ideas crucial to liberal democracy. Of special importance were Luther's idea of the freedom of individuals to find God on their own and Calvin's idea of the legitimacy, in very limited cases, of resistance to political rulers by certain "magistrates."

The Republican and Constitutional Tradition in the Modern World

Republican rule—constitutional rule by the many—had roots in Rome. As we noted in Chapter 5, Niccolò Machiavelli, in Renaissance Italy, endorsed republican rule. In the mid-seventeenth century in England, James Harrington advocated a variety of **republicanism**, an "empire of laws, and not of men." His commonwealth was a blend of popular and aristocratic rule, a republic based on a widespread distribution of property in the form of land. But Harrington's republican commonwealth did not emerge in England. Instead, a constitutional monarchy embodying John Locke's principles of limited,

responsible, representative, popular government was born.

Great Britain led the way in developing modern concepts of constitutional and representative government and in protecting certain basic rights. It was no accident, therefore, that when the American colonies, nurtured in the British tradition, joined together (1776–1787) to form the first major state in the modern world with a republican form of government, their leaders attempted to build on both Harrington and Locke. Earlier republican ideas had assumed that suffrage should be limited to men of property, and this assumption carried over to the new American nation.

The American Republic: The First Great Democratic Experiment

The American Revolution ushered in the world's first large modern republic. Building on Lockean constitutional principles, on colonial experience in self-government, and on a physical environment that favored widespread possession of property, the Americans made republicanism a kind of secular religion. Despite the relatively modest property qualifications that prevailed in most states in 1787 (when the infant republic was put on firmer foundations) and despite the fact that African Americans, native Americans, and women were excluded from the ballot and denied other freedoms, the Americans affirmed their belief in popular rule and the protection of basic rights.

Both the logic of republican, or democratic, theory and the pressure of disenfranchised groups contributed to a growing movement to enlarge the suffrage and expand basic freedoms. In time the commitment to liberty and equality made slavery an anomaly, revealed the racist treatment of native Americans, and highlighted sexist discrimination against women. In addition, it underscored the exploitation of workers, the often perilous economic situation of farmers, and the miserable lot of the poor. Of course, battles had to be fought to expand popular rule and human freedom—mostly with ballots and other peaceful means, sometimes with bullets and other coercive techniques—but almost all were fought to fulfill the American people's understanding of a democratic constitution.

The French Revolution of 1789 and Liberal Democracy in Europe

Although the British had pioneered constitutional and representative government, it was the French Revolution of 1789 that most dramatically challenged political absolutism and popularized democratic ideas throughout the continent. The inspiring motto of the French Revolution, "Liberty, Equality, Fraternity," became the political watchword of European liberal democracy in the nineteenth century.

Nationalism and liberalism joined in a powerful movement against absolutist governments. For a number of countries this led to national independence, greater political freedom, and more popular rule. Increasingly, more liberal laws and constitutions (guaranteeing basic rights, enfranchising more groups, and providing for greater popular control of government) were secured. However, setbacks for liberal democracy (Napoleon's dictatorship in France, the defeat of liberal forces in the several 1848 revolutions, and battles against such "iron" chancellors as Germany's Bismarck) emphasized that liberal democratic forces on the European continent were incomplete and shaky.

LIBERALISM, CAPITALISM, AND DEMOCRACY

Liberalism began as a movement for political, economic, social, and cultural freedom. It was strongly endorsed by the growing middle class and its allies, because such freedom protected and advanced their vital interests. These interests included a stronger role in government; safeguards for religion, speech, press, assembly, and due process; freedom from adverse governmental actions in the economic domain (that is, governmental monopolies, economic regulations and restrictions); and the opportunity for freer choices in politics, economics, and society.

The French Revolution, more dramatically than the American, symbolized the triumph of the middle class—the bourgeoisie—over a royal monarchy, a feudal aristocracy, and an estab-

This painting of the French Revolution, Liberty at the Barricades, *by French artist Eugene Delacroix (1798–1863) romanticizes the revolution, which played a significant role in introducing such liberal ideas as "Liberty, Equality, and Fraternity" throughout the European continent.*

lished church. The French Revolution was not only a political triumph of republicanism over monarchy and of more genuinely constitutional government over autocracy; it was also an economic triumph of the middle class over the feudal aristocracy. Further, the revolution was a social triumph of the middle class and its allies among peasants and workers over feudal and church privilege. It was also a cultural and intellectual triumph of largely middle-class writers, artists, and thinkers over monarchical and religious censorship and oppression.

The coincidence of the American and French revolutions with the Industrial Revolution (which signaled the advent of industrial capitalism) is not accidental. The year 1776 saw both the American Declaration of Independence and the publication of *The Wealth of Nations.* This book by the Scottish economist Adam Smith was to become the bible for the nineteenth-century liberal philosophy of laissez-faire capitalism, the policy restricting governmental interference in economic matters. The new capitalists favored a hands-off policy in the economy, except where it would benefit their enterprise. They wanted governmental policy to favor private enterprise.

The links between liberalism and capitalism, and between liberalism and democracy, are a little clearer than the connection between democracy and capitalism. For example, liberalism and capitalism share a common interest in economic freedom. Similarly, liberalism and democracy share a common interest in freedom, including economic freedom. Of course, capitalists and other members of the middle class share a democratic interest in popular rule and the protection of basic rights, especially when suffrage is limited to people of property and when governmental policy does not interfere with capitalistic enterprise. However, an expanded franchise may lead to policies to protect workers and their needs, and such policies may cut into the power and profits of capitalists. Moreover, capitalists and democrats may disagree on which basic rights to protect and how to protect them. Especially in America, middle-class liberals dedicated

to freedom, including economic freedom, may join with working-class men and women to fight capitalistic abuses that threaten freedom and jeopardize the fulfillment of human needs.

However, we cannot deny that modern democracy emerged and grew up alongside the economic system of **capitalism.** Indeed, private ownership of the means of production and exchange, a market economy, economic competition, free trade, and consumer sovereignty in the marketplace still command widespread popular support in America. Historically, there can be little doubt that liberal democracy—committed to each person's political, economic, social, and cultural freedom—forged ahead with the growth of an essentially capitalistic middle class. Certainly in Europe, the new middle class used liberal democratic principles to gain greater economic, political, and social powers at the expense of absolutist governments and feudal aristocracies. In America, where there was no significant feudal aristocracy to overthrow and where the abundant riches of the frontier beckoned, free and enterprising Americans welcomed the opportunities to advance their economic status in a political economy free of government's interfering hand.

The Changing Character of Liberalism

Liberalism changed significantly between the nineteenth and twentieth centuries. Many nineteenth-century liberals, originally committed to laissez faire in the tradition of Adam Smith, began to believe in the value of more government intervention in economic and social life. Such liberals made this shift, which became more obvious in their commitment to a wide range of reform measures in the twentieth century, in pragmatic response to capitalistic abuses that hurt farmers, small-business owners, workers, and consumers. Those who were hurt protested private monopolies, unfair trade practices, tight money, low farm prices, low wages, bad working conditions, and adulterated food. These protests were heard particularly in bad economic times. Legislation to regulate trusts and railroads came at the federal level as early as 1887. Other key legislation—involving, for example, banks and impure food and drugs—came after the turn of the century. But the new twentieth-century liberalism did not fully emerge until the advent of the New Deal. Reforms came in response to the Great Depression that began in 1928 and that created great economic and social distress in the early and mid-1930s.

The New Deal ushered in a government strongly dedicated to the general welfare. Government responded to popular cries to stabilize prices, provide jobs, stimulate the economy, regulate banking, strengthen labor's right to organize and bargain collectively, provide for unemployment compensation, ensure a fair minimum wage, guarantee a decent retirement income, and provide cheaper electric power. Subsequent reforms opened doors to better education, health, housing, and food; provided more generously for those in need; ensured the right to vote for African Americans; enhanced cultural opportunities; and protected the environment.

The Changing Character of Democracy

Democracy in America has changed significantly in the last two hundred years. Although the American Founding Fathers looked on themselves as republicans, they did not extend the right to vote to poor white men or to women and, with few exceptions, they kept blacks as slaves. They adhered in theory to what we today call democratic principles: rule by the people, through majority decision, in a representative and constitutional system that protects individual and group rights and the freedoms of both majority and minority. But in practice their conception of popular rule and basic rights—although remarkably advanced for their day—was not democratic by modern standards.

Although the old fear of democracy as rule by the many poor and ignorant (the classic Greek model described by Aristotle) had not been overcome by the early nineteenth century in the United States, the republican-democratic demand that suffrage be extended was not to be

denied. Moreover, the word *democracy* began to replace *republicanism* as the key concept characterizing the American republic. As stalwart republicans, Thomas Jefferson and James Madison called their popular party the Democratic party when they created it in the 1790s; it is now the world's oldest political party in continuous existence. In 1835, when Alexis de Tocqueville searched for a title for his perceptive study of the young United States, he chose *Democracy in America*. The fact that he almost decided on "Equality in America" was a measure of the significant shift toward equality in the United States, a shift characterized by the extension of suffrage. Abraham Lincoln also recognized democracy as popular government in his memorable phrase in the Gettysburg Address: "government of the people, by the people, and for the people." Lincoln was the first president elected on the ticket of the new Republican party.

Yet the wider use of the term *democracy* and a truly universal suffrage had to await the twentieth century. Woodrow Wilson, during his two terms as president (1913–1921), was responsible for increasing the term's popularity and prestige in the United States and throughout the world. Practical and legal obstacles to universal suffrage were not fully overcome until fairly late in the century. Nationwide, women did not gain the right to vote until the passage of the Nineteenth Amendment in 1920: "The right of citizens of the United States to vote shall not be denied or abridged by the United States or by any state on account of sex." And the poll tax was not outlawed in federal elections until the passage of the Twenty-Fourth Amendment in 1964! (A poll tax is a fixed amount for all adults, and its payment is usually a requirement for voting.)

As people—regardless of race, sex, or property holdings—acquired the right to vote, they also theoretically acquired the power to protect their needs and their welfare within a constitutional system. They have not used this power to destroy constitutional government, the rule of law, minority rights, or private property, but they have used their political power to address the content of legislation. They have become increasingly concerned with social and economic laws to advance the fuller life of the many.

With these roots and this evolution in mind, we are in a better position to outline and understand the operative ideals of liberal democracy in the United States today.

THE OPERATIVE IDEALS OF LIBERAL DEMOCRACY IN THE UNITED STATES

The operative ideals of liberal democracy have been characterized by both continuity and change. The *democratic* ingredients in liberal democracy that have persisted include (1) popular rule, (2) freedom, and (3) equality. These remain cardinal ingredients even though today we do not accept (as many of our nineteenth-century ancestors did) slavery, sexist discrimination, or property qualifications for voting. Class rule by the many poor was never part of liberal democracy. The call for greater popular participation in politics remains an old/new cry of radical liberal democrats. It is highly unlikely that Americans will move toward proletarian democracy (communist style) or more direct democracy (on the model of the New England town meeting). It is almost certain that they will not abandon representative government.

The *liberal* ingredients in liberal democracy that have persisted include (1) constitutionalism, (2) protection of basic rights, including the right of private property, (3) political and economic competition, and (4) free choice both at the ballot box and in the marketplace. But, as we have seen, liberalism has changed from a laissez-faire position to one that favors government intervention in the interest of public welfare, social justice, and fair play. The U.S. Constitution has been liberally interpreted to permit these changes. Of course, liberalism has also always recognized a **common good.** What was at issue in the nineteenth-century debate, and is still at issue today, is the meaning of that common good and the wisdom of the means to achieve it. Such debate will unquestionably continue.

The Guiding Liberal Democratic Vision

Simply put, the guiding liberal democratic vision is the freest and fullest possible realization of the individual personality within the framework of the common good. Individuals must have the opportunity, within justifiable limitations, to develop the best in themselves. The Preamble to the U.S. Constitution captures the objectives of "a more perfect Union" that will facilitate individual and social development. It is a union that will "establish justice, insure domestic tranquillity, provide for the common defense, promote the general welfare, and secure the blessings of liberty." The liberal democratic vision is not a "single vision"; it is a pluralistic vision providing for justice as well as order and for the general welfare as well as liberty. Because many persons, groups, and interests seek fulfillment, a balance must be struck.

The most influential school of liberal democratic thought in contemporary America—the pluralist—maintains that this balance can best be achieved (1) through a constitutional system of representative democracy, (2) with the help of skillful leaders and resourceful political parties, (3) on the recognition that a rough approximation of the public interest emerges from the clash of contending interests, and (4) in accord with policies that advance the general welfare.

Cardinal Operative Ideals

Liberal democrats want their political ideals to be operative and not utopian. They want to ensure that their principles function in a real political world. They endorse **pluralism**—the view that in society many interests seek to protect and advance themselves and that the struggles of these contending interests constitute the raw material of politics. Struggles are inevitable because they are rooted in liberty and diversity. Government regulates these struggles on behalf of freedom and the common good.

But, liberal democrats insist, government itself must be controlled and politics kept honest, and the struggle for power must be kept within bounds. This struggle must be consistent with justice, domestic tranquillity, the common defense, the general welfare, and liberty. The struggle for power must be civilized. Politics contributes to this civilizing process, which—at the highest level—allows fuller individual realization. The civilizing process requires decent rules and decent results in politics. Contending interests must accommodate each other. Basic human needs must be satisfied, and opportunities must exist for social, economic, aesthetic, and spiritual enrichment. To advance their vision, liberal democrats support and justify a government that is (1) popular, (2) respectful of human rights, (3) constitutional, (4) representative, (5) responsible, and (6) dedicated to human welfare. Advocates of liberal democracy favor the following operative ideals and justify them as contributing to the good life.

Popular Government—Popular rule requires the people to judge. They must be free to debate and to select among competing leaders, parties, and broad policies.

To make choices, the people must enjoy civil liberties that permit them to evaluate how the government operates to achieve the "more per-

fect Union." They must be able, especially, to assess the character and performance of parties and political leaders. Thus, the liberal democratic system is committed to civil liberties, including universal suffrage and robust debate. The system is also committed to an informed and vigilant public opinion, to a diligent and responsible press, to a plurality of contending interests able to articulate and press their claims, and to competitive parties. Such elements protect the people's vital interests and help fulfill their needs and aspirations. Popular government is thus inescapably intertwined with the protection of basic rights and with constitutional, representative, responsible government.

Rights-Respecting Government—Basic democratic rights are both political and nonpolitical. As we have seen, the freedoms of speech, press, and assembly, as well as the right to vote, are clearly political and are intimately related to popular rule. People cannot shape public policy unless they can speak, read, and write about public issues; assemble and organize in political parties or other interest groups; and exert political pressure and vote for or against candidates, parties,

Democratic movements swept through much of the developing world during the late 1980s, with some people voting for the first time.

and measures. They need these rights to rule indirectly and to control the government.

Other freedoms and basic rights are nonpolitical, but they are equally vital to liberal democracy. These religious, cultural, economic, and social rights include, for example, the right to worship according to the dictates of conscience; the right to think one's own thoughts; the right to express one's intellectual, artistic, and scientific ideas; the right to own property; the right to find a job of one's choice; and the right to marry and have children. There is, then, a realm of activity that must be beyond governmental reach and should be safeguarded by a constitutional government that grants, prohibits, and restricts power.

Constitutional Government—In the liberal democrat's preferred system of constitutional politics, power is granted, prohibited, and restricted in the interest of delineating and legitimizing the role of government and its key organs and actors. Thus the constitutional rules of the game establish what government can and cannot do and how those with power are to act.

Some powers, such as the powers to tax, to spend on behalf of the general welfare, and to regulate commerce, may be expressly granted. Other powers may be granted if necessary and proper to carry out expressly granted power. Limits on governmental power—explicit prohibitions—exclude government from entering areas such as religion and thought. But, even when exercising its legitimate powers, government cannot act arbitrarily; it must follow due process to ensure the protection of life, liberty, and property.

Moreover, because of the fear of unrestrained and arbitrary power in the United States, power is divided and shared. The American operative ideal of constitutional government puts the concept of balance to work in several ways: (1) a balance of governmental organs (in the national government): two branches of Congress, a president, a Supreme Court; (2) a balance of geographical units (assured by federalism): the

national government and the fifty states; and (3) a balance of social, economic, and political forces.

Representative Government—Liberal democrats favor representative government because they believe it is the realistic way for the people to govern. Direct democracy—direct rule by the people—is not feasible. In a democratic and constitutional system, the electorate usually chooses representatives with the organizing help of political parties. Government leadership is determined, directly or indirectly, by majority or plurality decision.

But what does representative government really mean in liberal democratic theory? Liberal democrats do not agree on the meaning. They answer the question of who the representative should and can wisely represent in at least four ways.[2] Each position illustrates an aspect of the liberal democratic theory of representation, and each position creates difficulties.

1. Some liberal democrats believe that representatives should be *delegates,* democratically representing primarily (if not solely) the will of the majority of the people who elected them. Other liberal democrats object. They argue that it is not easy to know the will of the majority. They also contend that elections rest on powerful political and economic interests in the constituency rather than on the hard-to-recognize and transient majority.

2. Some liberal democrats argue that the representatives should be *partisans,* at least on key issues; they contend that political parties make modern democratic and constitutional government free, possible, and responsible. Thus, representatives should seek to fulfill the party's platform, which they presumably ran on and share. Other liberal democratic critics question this understanding of representation. They point out that an American political party may not have a coherent guiding platform or

philosophy. Even if it does, representatives often ignore it. In addition, the party may not publicize its real guiding political philosophy but may express the concealed interests of certain political, economic, and social forces.

3. Still other liberal democrats look on representatives as *trustees* who, once elected, act on behalf of the higher interests of the whole political community (past, present, and future), following their perception of the nation's good. But some critics, objecting to this view, hold that representatives were elected by the people and should represent the people and not their own consciences; others say that they were elected as members of a political party and should represent the party and not their own conceptions of the public interest.

4. Finally, some liberal democrats believe that representatives should be *politicians,* who attempt (even more than delegates, partisans, or trustees) the difficult job of balancing the varying claims on their judgment—nation, constituency, interest groups, party, supporters, self-interest, and conscience. Supporters of the other three positions, of course, challenge this. They maintain that such politicians are unprincipled and unable to act responsibly.

These four perspectives suggest that no one view of representative government monopolizes the field and that considerable balancing goes on. Pluralists would argue that such balancing is desirable, realistic, and defensible.

Responsible Government—Responsibility in a liberal democracy also has several interrelated meanings:

1. Liberal democratic government should be accountable to the people from whom it derives its power. More accurately, in the United States the government must be answerable to the electorate or to a majority or plurality within the electorate. (By way of contrast, in Great Britain the government is directly answerable to a majority party or a coalition of parties in the House of Commons and indirectly answerable to an electoral majority or plurality in the country.)

2. Liberal democratic government should be responsible to the political party that puts candidates and choices before the people, helps elect a president, ensures a majority in Congress, and in general facilitates decision making and public policy.

3. Liberal democratic government should be responsible to the Constitution and to the laws and regulations made under the Constitution. Government may be called to account if it violates its own operating rules.

4. Liberal democratic government should be answerable to an authority higher than the people or the Constitution. Government may be answerable to God, or to natural law, or to conscience (as it reflects a higher authority).

5. Finally, those in government—whether the president, members of Congress, members of the Supreme Court, or millions of bureaucrats—should be responsible to professional standards of conduct and administration established by their peers, past or present, in or out of government.

In liberal democratic politics the effort is made to ensure governmental responsibility to "rules of the game" through various means of accountability: elections, public opinion, a free press, party discipline, interest group pressures, an independent judiciary, legislative and administrative investigation, impeachment, administrative supervision, and peer evaluation.

General Welfare Government—Modern government in the United States is clearly committed to the idea of advancing the general welfare. As a liberal democratic operative ideal, this means that minimal needs—safety, civil liberties, income, food, housing, health, education—should be satisfied through the democratic process and in a caring and compassionate community. The liberal democratic nation stands ready to protect these needs, indirectly and directly, when private organs (the family, the church, and charitable organizations) and state and local governments cannot do so. Debate rages, however, on the desirable extent and character of such help.

When Is a Country a Liberal Democracy?

We should be able to use the foregoing operative ideals to determine whether a nation is a liberal democracy. Affirmative answers to the following questions will characterize a liberal democracy:

1. Do most people really have the opportunity, by means of genuinely free elections, to select the people and policies that will govern the nation? (In other words, is the government truly based on the consent of the governed?)

2. Do the people enjoy the right to speak, write, publish, and assemble freely in order to criticize the government and parties and leaders in power? And can the people turn these leaders and parties out peacefully at the ballot box or through other constitutional means?

3. Is there at least one independent opposition political party or coalition that is ready, willing, and able to supplant the governing leadership, if, in a free election, the people turn the incumbents out?

4. Do the people enjoy the right to worship as their consciences dictate, participate in religious or spiritual life through a free organization (church, synagogue, mosque, or meeting) of their own choice, and pay allegiance to a higher power than the secular state? Do they have the right to refrain from worship?

5. Are people protected against the kind of arbitrary and unreasonable action by government that would deprive them of life, liberty, and property without due process of law? (**Due process** is here understood to

forbid two kinds of governmental action: action such as the systematic destruction of a religious group, race, or class, or spuriously "legal" action such as a trial based on false evidence or coerced confession. The first action should be beyond the power of government in a liberal democracy. The second action is flawed because false evidence and coerced confessions violate proper legal conduct.)

6. Is the state's role limited to certain legitimate and necessary public functions, or does the state dominate the cultural and social life of the community? Is the state, for example, forbidden to dictate which books to read, which plays to see, which radio and television programs to tune in, and which clubs and organizations to join?

7. Is the state prevented from becoming so economically powerful that it not only controls the modes of production and exchange (and the livelihood of all citizens) but also uses its economic power to nullify political freedom and dominate other aspects of society such as church, press, and education?

8. Is the state willing and able, if necessary, to enhance the physical and environmental safety of its citizens, guard their civil liberties, ensure their minimal income, assist the unemployed, feed and house the needy, enhance health care, and facilitate education? (In other words, is the state willing to advance its people's minimal welfare needs?)

With this fuller characterization of the operative ideals of liberal democracy, we are better prepared to examine variations on the liberal democratic theme in the United States.

VARIATIONS ON THE LIBERAL DEMOCRATIC THEME

We will focus here on the four major ideological groups within American democracy: liberals, conservatives, populists, and libertarians.[3] We will also describe the left and right wings of

American politics, which we call radical and reactionary. Generally, American liberals, conservatives, populists, and libertarians endorse the major operative ideals we have outlined—popular, rights-respecting, constitutional, representative, and responsible government, and even the concept of government dedicated to the general welfare. Of course, they may interpret these operative ideals differently. Thus, American **liberals** see themselves as more tolerant, generous, willing to experiment, and progressive than conservatives. American **conservatives** see themselves as more respectful of traditional values and institutions (private property and enterprise, family, church, and established governmental authority) than liberals; they may favor liberty over equality on some issues (for example, affirmative action) when these two ideals clash; they see themselves as preserving responsible initiative, a richly textured community life, and standards of excellence in a world driven toward uniformity, novelty, and crass individualism. American **populists** generally tend to favor government intervention in economic affairs and tend to oppose expansion of some "liberal" personal freedoms (such as legalization of marijuana, for example). American **libertarians** rather consistently oppose government intervention in economic affairs and favor expansion of personal freedoms.

As this fourfold classification suggests, liberals and populists are likely to agree with each other that government should act in the economic realm to aid the least powerful, while conservatives and libertarians are likely to oppose such government actions. At the same time, liberals and libertarians are likely to agree with each

other that personal choice rather than government regulation should guide behavior in the private realm. Coversely, conservatives and populists are likely to agree that goverment should regulate some areas of personal and social morality. Figure 6.1 highlights the cardinal features of this fourfold classification.

So American liberals, conservatives, populists, and libertarians differ on how to safeguard democratic ideals and on the guiding vision of human realization in the American republic. They differ, especially, on three interrelated points: (1) their concern for the "least free," (2) their view of the role of government, and (3) their attitude toward change. We will here concentrate on the perspectives of American liberals and American conservatives, indicating where they agree or disagree with populists and libertarians.

American Liberals

Generally, American liberals favor a greater concern for the "least free" and the least powerful in society: poor people, ethnic minorities, women, working people, small farmers, the small-business owner, and consumers. Like populists, they seek to expand popular power and overcome abuses of economic, social, and political power. American liberals seek to end oppression, injustice, poverty, and inequality. In comparison, libertarians are most concerned with protecting individual freedom, whether of the rich or the poor.

Second, American liberals are generally willing to use the power of government, especially the national government, to seek changes on behalf of fair play for the "least free" and the least

Figure 6.1
Issue dimensions and ideological categories.

Source: William S. Maddox and Stuart A. Lilie, Beyond Liberal and Conservative: Reassessing the Political Spectrum (Washington, D.C.: Cato Institute, 1984, 1987), p. 5.

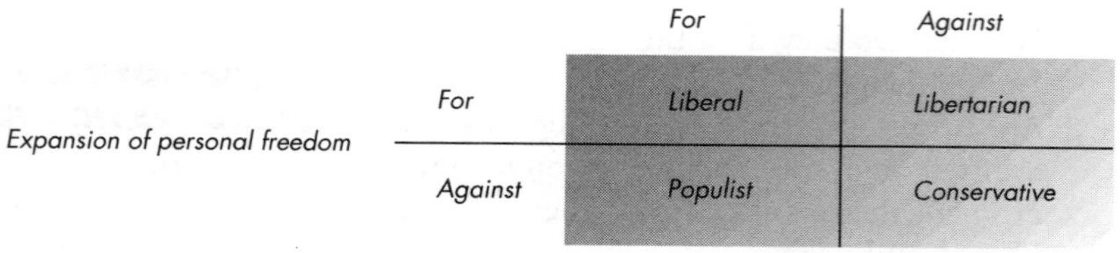

Expansion of personal freedom

	For	Against
For	Liberal	Libertarian
Against	Populist	Conservative

powerful. Populists, too, favor government action to protect groups like farmers or workers or small investors from what they deem the unjust or oppressive action of railroads, corporations, or banks. American liberals favor broader measures to advance the general welfare. Libertarians are generally opposed to any kind of government intervention in either economic or social affairs.

Third, American liberals are more favorably disposed to political, economic, and social change to accomplish the objectives mentioned in the preceding paragraphs. They are not afraid to alter the status quo to permit a liberal democratic society to live up to its own ideals. On some economic issues, populists may share with liberals this more favorable attitude to change. Libertarians, as we have noted, take a dim view of government initiating changes that affect people's lives.

American Conservatives

Generally, American conservatives endorse the interests of the people Alexander Hamilton called the "rich and well born." Given their (usually) greater wealth, education, social position, and power, American conservatives are often less sensitive to the plight of the "least free" than liberals are. Of course, conservatives will not eliminate the safety net for the genuinely needy, but they may differ with liberals as to what constitutes "genuine need."

Second, American conservatives generally endorse a laissez-faire position; they are opposed to adverse government interference in their economic, political, and social affairs; however, conservatives do think government should act on some "moral" issues, such as pornography, drug use, and "deviant" sexual behaviors. Libertarians, more consistently than conservatives, hold to a laissez-faire position, opposing government regulation in the personal and social realms as well as in economic affairs. Conservatives do not object when government acts to support private enterprise and profit, which they see as crucial to freedom and prosperity, or when government action regulates personal choice in support

of traditional social arrangements and values. But conservatives are suspicious of intervention on behalf of the "least free" (whether in the form of school busing to overcome segregation or of affirmative action programs, which they see as reverse discrimination), and they decry abuses and waste in the welfare state. Conservatives normally favor a strong defense establishment and a balanced budget.

Third, American conservatives seek to maintain the existing economic, political, and social scheme of things. They are reluctant to abandon that which is tried and true and of proven value. They may, however, endorse changes that favor traditional values and institutions. Libertarians take a more consistent position in opposing government economic and social regulations affecting individual or corporate freedom.

Let us now see how American radicals and reactionaries fit into the American political spectrum.

American Radicals and Reactionaries

Ideologically, most Americans tend to be somewhat conservative in their ideological theory and somewhat liberal in their operational practice. Only a small minority are radicals or reactionaries.

American **radicals,** in the liberal democratic tradition, are generally more disturbed about the plight of the "least free" than liberals are, more eager to remedy that plight, and more agreeable to speedier and more far-reaching governmental action for economic, political, and social justice. Their differences with liberals tend to be differences of degree, although sometimes they may differ on such substantive issues as disarmament or pollution. Radicals tend to be at the cutting edge of liberal change in modern American society.[4] However, sometimes the unhappiness of radicals with the status quo may lead them outside the democratic framework.

American **reactionaries** generally seek to turn the clock back to recapture what they perceive as a more desirable past. This might be a laissez-faire past or a white supremacist past or a Protestant American past or a law-and-order past. They continue to resist the reforms that constituted the New Deal, Fair Deal, New Frontier, and Great Society. They are often fearful of alleged un-American influences and tend to be rabidly anticommunist and hostile to African Americans, Jews, Catholics, and other "alien" forces in American life. Their substantive differences with conservatives, liberals, populists, and libertarians on key issues may even place them outside the liberal democratic fold.[5]

More liberals tend to inhabit the Democratic party, and more conservatives the Republican party. Yet a more careful examination reveals that both major American parties—the Democratic and Republican—include individuals who see themselves as liberals, conservatives, populists, and libertarians of various hues. Only a tiny sprinkling of radicals and reactionaries can be found in each of the major parties. A wide variety of combinations within each major party is also prevalent. Thus, there may be some neo-conservatives, populists, and libertarians within the Democratic party, and some neoliberals, populists, and libertarians within the Republican party.

LIBERAL DEMOCRACY: DEFENSE AND ATTACK, STRENGTHS AND WEAKNESSES

To fully understand the strengths and weaknesses of liberal democracy, we should examine its responses to a variety of critics.[6] Sympathetic critics, such as Alexis de Tocqueville in the nineteenth century, worried about the tyranny of the majority; in the twentieth century, Reinhold Niebuhr encouraged liberal democrats to overcome their naiveté about human nature, evil, and the struggle for power. Other critics highlighted democracy's failings during the Great Depression and its inability to curb fascist aggression. Fascist critics condemned democracy's devotion to equality, civil liberties, and popular rule and its inability to provide strong leadership. Communist critics attacked liberal democracy's marriage to capitalism and its failure to satisfy workers' needs. Many criticisms were silenced during World War II and the immediate postwar period, but a new round of criticism surfaced with the civil rights movement and the protests against the Vietnam war. Recently, especially with the end of the Cold

Elements within the major political parties represent a wide range of opinion.

War and the demise of communism in the former Soviet Union, liberal democracy has become more attractive throughout the world. Nonetheless, ideological and partisan conflicts and presidential-congressional deadlocks in the United States renew criticisms of the true meaning and smooth functioning of liberal democracy.

Let us first examine the arguments that democracy's defenders advanced to counter the complaints of pre–World War II critics. Then we will address the more contemporary attack on liberal democracy. Our primary focus will be the American scene.

The Defense of Liberal Democracy

Liberal democracy's defenders argue that its guiding vision and operative ideals have enabled Americans to achieve a greater measure of civilized life, healthy growth, and creative fulfillment than is possible under any other political ideology. They maintain that more people enjoy more freedom, equality, and prosperity under liberal democratic regimes.

Democracy's defenders acknowledge its historic and contemporary shortcomings but point out that over time the United States moved successfully toward universal suffrage, abolished slavery, and checked plutocratic abuses of economic and political power. Despite severe trials, democratic institutions demonstrated a remarkable ability to cope with great difficulties. For example, Americans were able to respond to the worst effects of the Great Depression by shaping a state judiciously balanced between liberty and equality, freedom and security.

Responding to friendly critics such as Reinhold Niebuhr, who urged liberals to face the harsh realities of evil and power, Americans learned to mobilize countervailing power against abusive forces at home and abroad. For example, laborers formed unions to protect their interests. Demonstrating the organizational ability of a free people in an open society, the United States mobilized to defeat German fascism and Japanese militarism in World War II, a mighty feat of skill and courage. Then with great imagination,

the United States helped western Europe and Japan recover from the ravages of war with remarkable speed.

In peace and war, in domestic and international politics, the United States demonstrated that liberal democratic ideas and institutions were strong and vital and that its people had the will and resourcefulness to advance the causes of security, liberty, justice, and welfare. America's foreign policy achievements included establishing the United Nations, the Marshall Plan to reconstruct war-torn Europe, and the North Atlantic Treaty Organization (NATO) to protect Western Europe against Soviet aggression. Significant domestic advances were also made to extend democracy by ensuring African Americans an effective vote and by integrating disadvantaged minorities into the educational, economic, and social system. Some shortcomings remained, but liberal democrats maintained that an open and self-correcting system could handle these problems as it had, historically, responded to others. Liberal democracy, in brief, had demonstrated the vitality of free institutions and a remarkable ability to advance key ideas in a realistic way.

By the mid-1960s, the most optimistic liberal democrats announced the end of ideological battles. They declared that the United States had achieved the "good society." This announcement, however, proved premature, as the late 1960s demonstrated. The sharp criticism that had arisen during the depths of the Great Depression revived. This criticism was nourished by the civil rights movement and by opposition to American involvement in the Vietnam war. It was also stimulated by charges of American "imperialism" in world affairs and by a deep-seated fear of nuclear war. This often radical criticism, coming from the left side of the democratic spectrum, fostered a more articulate conservative criticism on the right, which focused on alleged abuses of the welfare state, on distrust of big government and government intervention, and on fears of communism. Nevertheless, this criticism, unlike fascist and communist criticism, did not touch the heart of the liberal democratic commitment to constitutional government.

Liberal democrats also point to the collapse of communism in the former Soviet Union, and the attractiveness of certain democratic ideals in countries formerly under Communist rule, as signs of liberal democracy's continued appeal. Especially important here is renewed respect for human rights, constitutional governance, and a market economy.

Current American administrations will certainly test liberal democracy's ability to respond to some still troubling problems confronting the United States: a huge and costly deficit that constitutes a grave burden for future generations; a disturbing gap between rich and poor in a generally prosperous America; welfare reform on trial; the absence of universal health care; persisting weaknesses in the U.S. educational system; the criminal justice system; responsible family life; and cultural malaise.

The Attack on Liberal Democracy: Left and Right

Radical, democratic, communitarian, and socialist critics on the left contend that American liberal democracy has failed to fulfill its own promise. These critics are concerned that not enough people participate in the modern democratic state. They protest that individuals are not really free but are confined in an exploitive economic and social system characterized by inequality, nourished by racism and sexism, and magnified by a lack of genuine concern for the "least free." While seeking to protect and expand civil liberties, these critics advocate using the state's powers to advance greater social and economic justice. They are unhappy about a still largely laissez-faire economy and about the persistence of the "vandal ideology of liberalism" (an ideology of reckless waste) and the "theory of possessive individualism" (a theory of selfish individualism). They argue that Americans worship private property, profits, and "free enterprise" at the expense of a healthy society, a meaningful

community, and the common good. They see America as an affluent, largely white, democratic nation-state in a globe that is poor, mostly nonwhite, and either unprepared for or hostile to liberal democracy.

Aristocratic, individualistic, and capitalist critics on the right worry that liberal democracy has degenerated into mobocracy, serfdom, and socialism. They worry about the threat to such liberal democratic principles as representative democracy and equality of opportunity. They see dangers in participatory democracy: the decline of prudent judgment, submission to the ignorant, and the loss of quality. They worry about replacing equality of opportunity with a doctrine of equality of results, about reverse discrimination and other programs of preferential treatment. They worry, too, about the triumph of vulgarity, meanness, and mediocrity in our social and cultural lives. They bemoan the loss of individual moral character and responsibility. They fear that the state's growing bureaucratic power to regulate economic affairs will undermine private property and enterprise as bastions of freedom. These critics deplore governmental controls and the encroachment of centralized state power.

Of course, varying combinations and permutations of these two attacks—one from the left, one from the right—are possible. The analyst's task is to arrive at a just appraisal of liberal democracy. Are these criticisms cosmetic or deepseated? Do they call for minor modifications or fundamental changes? We will now assess the strengths and weaknesses of liberal democracy to see what kind of balance we can strike.

The Strengths of Liberal Democracy

Defenders of liberal democracy highlight its ethical, empirical, and prudential strengths. They argue that it is a great historical achievement, a landmark in the evolution of human civilization. It has largely worked out the rules of the political game to strike the proper balance between individual freedom and the common good. It protects individual rights yet legitimizes generous power.

Effective restraints on the exercise of power have been established and maintained, and arbitrary power has been proscribed. Government is responsible to the people's representatives, and representatives are responsible to the people. Citizens neither idolize the state nor expect the reign of earthly perfection. Liberal democratic politics, it would seem, avoids the worst features of both "lion and fox" and utopian politics while realistically safeguarding vital community interests and promoting the "more perfect Union." Liberal democracy seems to have built into itself a realistic sense of the strengths and weaknesses of self-interest and an ability to ensure both justice and order.

Some political scientists sympathetic to liberal democracy would revise its ideology to make it more politically realistic. Such revisions, they contend, would strengthen liberal democracy. They call for a more realistic assessment of leaders and the led—a recognition of citizens' shortcomings as well as their capabilities, and a recognition, especially, of the need for strong but democratic leadership. They endorse the realistic proposition that public policy is, and wisely can be, the result of group pressures and democratic compromise. Finally, they emphasize that it is indeed possible to achieve both stability and welfare in a "mixed economy"— that is, a system of regulated capitalism.

In accord with their generally pluralist political philosophy, such political scientists reject unrealistic expectations about full popular participation. They insist that leaders in a democratic state are inevitable but can be held responsible through the competition of elites, parties, and elections. These political scientists hold that messianic illusions about an ideal common good on this earth must be abandoned in favor of the sensible effort to ensure a public policy agreeable to the many key interests in a democratic society.

Political scientists who favor these strengthening revisions of liberal democratic ideology maintain that a pluralistic balance of power contributes to social, economic, and political justice. They see the existing liberal democratic state as a model for the good political life. What some people call vices, they consider virtues: for example, the lack of full and intense popular participation is seen as enhancing stability. Rule by a few is compatible with effective and responsible democratic leadership. Fear of elite rule is off the mark because no monolithic elite rules consistently on all the issues, and elections, the press, and public opinion guard against abuse of power. The inability to perfectly identify or pursue the common good produces a sane tolerance for the many interests contending for power and advantage. And the resulting public policy— especially as it is expressed in a stable democratic welfare state—is considered the best approximation to justice in an imperfect world.

Not all defenders of liberal democracy, of course, share the views of the liberal democratic pluralists outlined in the preceding three paragraphs or believe that such "realistic" views strengthen liberal democracy. These stalwart defenders of liberal democracy insist that liberal democratic ideals can best be fulfilled if Americans remain committed to virtue and education, more (not less) citizen involvement in politics, truly responsible political parties, wise choice of genuinely democratic leaders, careful scrutiny of interest groups, and a spirited defense of the public interest.

The Weaknesses of Liberal Democracy
Certain weaknesses in liberal democracy, according to other critics, need attention and correction: a faulty ethical vision, a deficient empirical understanding, and a timid prudential assessment. These critics do not share the more accepting "realistic" perspective of those pluralists set forth above.

Faulty Ethical Vision—Ethically, according to these critics, the vision of liberal democratic politics is faulty. The liberal democratic understanding of American politics has historically excluded native Americans, African Americans, women, and the poor. Recent efforts to correct this faulty vision are incomplete. Although working people have fared reasonably well, Americans have never forthrightly faced the problem of worker alienation and democratic direction of the economy. Unemployment continues to plague too high a percentage of the working force, with the unemployment rate among young African Americans double or triple the figure for adult whites. As a people, Americans have been profligate with their natural resources of land, water, timber, and minerals and have demonstrated a shocking disregard for ecological health. Americans may have limited the tyrannical power of government, but they have not seriously questioned abuse of human and natural resources. Americans have not adequately protected against the "vandal" aspects of liberal ideology.

The American sense of responsibility for the "least free," for the environment, and for the future is weak. Politicians have too frequently been the rich and the powerful. They have lacked concern for the quality of the American union, for a just and caring community. Proponents of liberal democracy have been complacent in appraising it. Americans have been too tolerant of existing evils and have lacked a firm conviction of a common good that would ensure a more desirable political order.

So liberal democratic politics today suffers from a too easy acceptance of the status quo and the prescriptive constitution. Americans too often act as if they have reached the pinnacle of wise political evolution. They tend to accept the rhetoric of liberal democratic ideals as reality and to close their eyes to ugly truths. Liberal democratic politics is not heartless, but it can too easily neglect and become accustomed to the difficult-to-deal-with evils of society. Those who support liberal democratic politics may forget to dream. Unless prodded, liberal democratic politicians may lose a passionate and imaginative commitment to a better future.

Deficient Empirical Understanding—Empirically, the ideology of liberal democracy is deficient. It has refused to examine how ethics, economics, and ecology influence politics. It has not properly studied how group pressures affect public policy. It has been blind to the reckless and wasteful aspects of liberalism. By focusing too sharply on the status quo, it has neglected the weak and the poor and the oppressed. It has ignored underlying forces that will become dominant. It has overlooked new possibilities. It has never fully explored the relationship between a capitalistic economic system and a democratic order. Its commitment to incremental change has prevented more radical criticism. It has often failed to acknowledge the gulf between the principles and the practice of liberal democracy.

A powerful existing system often conceals important political forces, "invisible" forces that do not come to our attention except in periods of crisis, riot, and revolution. To miss the underlying forces of today that will dominate tomorrow is to miss future possibilities and actualities. This

The presidents appearing on Mount Rushmore— Washington, Jefferson, Theodore Roosevelt, and Lincoln—are shown here saddened and dismayed over the Watergate scandal during the Nixon administration. But they could as well be dismayed over many of the other weaknesses and scandals of liberal democracy.

deficient empirical understanding is manifested in a wrongheaded view of change. Politics is too often seen in terms of balance and hence in terms of maintaining the status quo. Politics based on progressive change does not allow for radical and rapid change—the kind that may sometimes be needed to handle some crucial contemporary problems.

These generalizations come to life most dramatically in the neglect of African Americans, women, and the poor in an often racist, sexist, and blindly affluent society. Liberal democratic politics also seems congenitally unable to promote satisfaction and creativity in work—human beings' most basic life activity.

Timid Prudential Assessment—Prudentially, liberal democratic ideology is too timid. It is often wrongly conservative instead of rightly conservative; for example, it preserves racism and sexism and prefers property rights to human rights. It is often too hesitant. Liberal democrats are often unwilling to try bold new economic, social, and political experiments. Too often they prefer stability over change, the known over the unknown. They may, for example, have waited too long to clean up the environment and to revive mass transportation. Guided by a timid ideology, liberal democrats have been too slow to attack admitted evils such as the drug problem, homelessness, and the current burden of debt that will weigh heavily on future generations.

Liberal democratic politicians may lack the passion and the vision to act wisely. They may be wrongly convinced that most of the ways ordained by the prescriptive U.S. Constitution are sound for the present and future. Consequently, they will be unreceptive to creative political breakthroughs that could, for example, significantly reduce crime, drug abuse, pollution, and cancer and assure adequate employment, health care, and housing for all Americans.

Unfortunately, the motto of the liberal democratic politician—"to get along one must go along"—often transforms genuine prudence into weak-kneed timidity and makes bold political

action impossible. And so a desirable tension between what ought to be and what is—a tension that nourishes courageous judgment in politics—disappears. Modern "realistic" revisions of liberal democratic ideology have hastened the disappearance of this tension. These revisions mistakenly reflect a lack of faith in the intelligence and capability of the common people, in the possibility of identifying a common good, and in more radical alternatives to the status quo. These revisions call for democratic elitism (leadership by an elite responsible to competing political parties), acceptance of the approximate justice in a public policy hammered out by contending interests, and a complacent appreciation of life in a welfare state.

There are good reasons to critically analyze these revisions. For example, the judgment of the "best and the brightest" turned out to be defective in the Vietnam war. The governing elite's temptation to guard state security by fair means or foul reveals a failure of leadership. Vietnam, the Watergate and Iran-Contra scandals, and the foolish coddling of Iraq before the Gulf War illustrate the persistence of questionable "lion and fox" politics in the liberal democratic state.

Seeing public policy as a result of group pressures frequently leads politicians to endorse the order imposed by the powerful. Such an order may benefit the powerful—whether corporations, farmers, or labor organizations—but does it benefit weaker forces in society? We must ask how it helps the larger public made up of unorganized consumers.

These critical inquiries suggest a need for the bolder judgments that are the very stuff of creative breakthroughs in politics. We are challenged to explore those bold judgments that might enhance the vitality of liberal democratic politics.

CONCLUSION

In our presentation of liberal democracy we deliberately stressed the importance of democratic and constitutional principles. Constitutional principles preceded the liberal democratic state and were incorporated into its politics. These principles will, and must, endure in any future democratic political order.

But if the self-interest of the bourgeoisie led them to advance the cause of constitutional and popular rule, the self-interest of groups such as workers, consumers, African Americans, women, environmentalists, and peace advocates may lead them to use the same constitutional and democratic principles on their own behalf. Moreover, they may use such principles on behalf of a common good that transcends all classes—capitalist or working class, white or African American, male or female. Historically, excluded groups have broadened both constitutionalism and democracy by demanding inclusion. In spite of being self-interested, these claims enhanced society's understanding of the common good, of legitimate human interests and needs, and of the link between democratic power and constitutional protection.

Any guiding pattern of politics for the twenty-first century must remain committed to the progressive flowering of soundly prescriptive principles. Despite its weaknesses, those guided by this pattern have learned to deal with the harsh realities of "lion and fox" politics without sacrificing too much of a higher political ethic. Important vital interests have been protected, though not always adequately. Representatives of religious, economic, and political interests did not idolize the state. Leaders were limited and made accountable. The beastly world of "lion and fox" politics was, generally, made less beastly and somewhat more human.

The practitioners of liberal democratic politics have been more successful in avoiding the weakness of utopian politics than in incorporating its strengths. Guided by the cautionary Niebuhrian judgment that in politics we can seek only proximate solutions to insoluble problems, these politicians have resisted falsely messianic passions for earthly paradise. Yet they have been able to move toward some semiutopian approximations of justice, security, general welfare, liberty, equality, and fraternity. Certainly, ordinary citizens have improved their lot in the modern democratic and constitutional state.

The weaknesses of liberal democratic politics suggest that Americans can do better, and they indicate where improvements can be made. The weaknesses are significant, but they must not be exaggerated. Americans must be careful not to reject vital principles because they are unhappy with particular ideas and practices. On the other hand, a misguided complacency, a thoughtless tolerance, or a restricted vision can threaten liberal democracy.

The task is to build on the strengths, while overcoming the weaknesses, of liberal democracy. It remains to be seen whether current American administrations can demonstrate the renewed vitality and creativity of liberal democracy in the United States.

ANNOTATED BIBLIOGRAPHY

Dahl, Robert. *Democracy and Its Critics*. New Haven, Conn.: Yale University Press, 1989. Richly explores democracy's meaning, flaws, alternatives, defense, and required reforms. Asks whether we are on the threshold of a third democratic transformation. Sees challenges to such transformation in inequalities related to violent coercion, lack of economic democracy, and rule by experts. Mature and rewarding. Compare and contrast the earlier "pluralist" Dahl.

Glassman, Ronald M. *Democracy and Equality: Theories and Programs for the Modern World*. New York: Praeger, 1989. Argues that achievement of democracy and equality requires Americans to build on but find correctives for liberal democracy. Finds correctives for liberal democracy and capitalism in Aristotle, Keynes, and Rawls.

Hartz, Louis. *The Liberal Tradition in America*. New York: Harcourt Brace, 1955. Builds on Alexis de Tocqueville's brilliant *Democracy in America* (1835), emphasizes why and how the United States has avoided the extremes of left and right and adhered most often to the vital center.

Levin, Michael. *Marx, Engels and Liberal Democracy*. New York: St. Martin's Press, 1989. Investigates the uneasy relationship between Marx/Engels and liberal democracy. Although sympathetic to universal suffrage, popular rule, and freedom of speech and press, Marx and Engels were critical of the betrayals and flaws of bourgeois democracy.

Lindsay, A. D. *The Modern Democratic State.* New York: Oxford University Press, 1947. By exploring democracy's operative ideals, helps link democratic theory and practice.

Lowi, Theodore J. *The End of the Republican Era.* Norman: University of Oklahoma Press, 1995. Provocatively explores the topics of the "End of Liberalism," the "Republican Era," the "Conservative Era," the "End of Conservatism," and "Restoring the Liberal Republic." See also his earlier *The End of Liberalism* (1969)—a critique of interest group liberalism and a plea for the rule of law—and Theodore J. Lowi and Benjamin Ginsberg, *Embattled Democracy: Politics and Policy in the Clinton Era* (1995).

Macpherson, C. B. *The Real World of Democracy.* London: Oxford University Press, 1966. Points out that liberal democracy has no monopoly on democracy. Analyzes and criticizes the communist and underdeveloped variants of nonliberal democracy along with liberal democracy.

Maddox, William S., and Lilie, Stuart A. *Beyond Liberal and Conservative: Reassessing the Political Spectrum.* Washington, D.C.: Cato Institute, 1984. Convincingly argues on behalf of broadening the ideological categories of liberal democracy to provide room for populists and libertarians as well as liberals and conservatives, with each being defined by their views on government intervention in economic affairs and on expansion of personal freedoms.

Niebuhr, Reinhold. *The Children of Light and the Children of Darkness.* New York: Scribner's, 1944. Presents an unflattering critique of soft-headed idealists, moralists, and pacifists, and a resounding defense of democratic realism. Provocative.

Parenti, Michael. *Democracy for the Few,* 6th ed. New York: St. Martin's Press, 1994. Offers a sharp, hard-hitting criticism of American politics and society as benefiting primarily the rich and the powerful, the greedy rather than the needy.

Pennock, J. Roland. *Liberal Democracy: Its Merits and Prospects.* New York: Rinehart, 1950. Provides a balanced, but fundamentally favorable, analysis.

Riemer, Neal. *The Revival of Democratic Theory.* New York: Appleton-Century-Crofts, 1962. Bases his case for a reinvigorated democratic theory on eight orienting concepts: political theory as a prudent guide to action; individual realization within the framework of the common good; sensible dimen-

sions of maneuver; the prudential logic of realization; democratic and constitutional accommodation; majority rule; pluralistic and conditional obligation; and constant rescrutiny of democracy's well-calculated risks.

Riemer, Neal. *The Democratic Experiment.* Princeton, N.J.: Van Nostrand, 1967. Emphasizes the creative role of American leaders in reconciling liberty and authority in a large state.

Riemer, Neal. *The Future of the Democratic Revolution: Toward a More Prophetic Politics.* New York: Praeger, 1984. In Chapter 4, assesses the strengths and weaknesses of liberal democracy from the perspective of a model of prophetic politics.

Slater, Philip. *A Dream Deferred: America's Discontent and the Search for a New Democratic Ideal.* Boston: Beacon Press, 1991. Contends that the democratic megaculture requires the complete rout of authoritarianism—military, political, economic, social, religious, educational, medical, psychological.

Spitz, David. *Patterns of Anti-Democratic Thought.* New York: Macmillan, 1949. Provides a keenly reasoned defense of democracy against a wide variety of critics.

SUGGESTIONS FOR FURTHER READING

Anderson, Charles W. *Pragmatic Liberalism.* Chicago: University of Chicago Press, 1990.

Barber, Benjamin. *The Conquest of Politics: Liberal Philosophy in Democratic Times.* Princeton, N.J.: Princeton University Press, 1988.

Bobbio, Norberto. *The Future of Democracy: A Defense of the Rules of the Game.* Minneapolis: University of Minnesota Press, 1987.

Burns, James MacGregor. *Cobblestone Leadership: Majority Rule, Minority Power.* Norman: University of Oklahoma Press, 1990.

Ceaser, James W. *Liberal Democracy and Political Science.* Baltimore: Johns Hopkins University Press, 1990.

Deutsch, Kenneth L., and Soffer, Walter, eds. *The Crisis of Liberal Democracy: A Straussian Perspective.* Albany: State University of New York Press, 1987.

Diamond, Sara. *Roads to Dominion: Right-Wing Movements and Political Power in the United States.* New York: Guilford, 1995.

Dunn, Charles W., and Woodward, J. David. *The Conservative Tradition in America.* Latham, Md.: Rowman and Littlefield, 1996.

Elshtain, Jean Bethke. *Democracy on Trial.* New York: Basic Books, 1995.

Etzioni, Amitai. *Rights and the Common Good: The Communitarian Perspective.* New York: St. Martin's, 1995.

Fishkin, James S. *Justice, Equal Opportunity, and the Family.* New Haven, Conn.: Yale University Press, 1983.

Gilbert, Alan. *Democratic Individuality.* Cambridge: Cambridge University Press, 1990.

Green, Philip. *Retrieving Democracy: In Search of Equality.* Totowa, N.J.: Rowman & Allanheld, 1985.

Huntington, Samuel P. *The Third Wave: Democratization in the Late Twentieth Century.* Norman: University of Oklahoma Press, 1991.

Johnston, David. *The Ideal of a Liberal Theory: A Critique and Reconstruction.* Princeton, N.J.: Princeton University Press, 1995.

Kautz, Steven. *Liberalism and Community.* Ithaca, N.Y.: Cornell University Press, 1995.

Levine, Andrew. *Liberal Democracy: A Critique of Its Theory.* New York: Columbia University Press, 1981.

Nisbet, Robert A. *Conservatism: Dream and Reality.* Minneapolis: University of Minnesota Press, 1986.

Pangle, Thomas L. *The Enobling of Democracy: The Challenge of the Post-Modern Age.* Baltimore: Johns Hopkins University Press, 1992.

Rawls, John. *Political Liberalism.* New York: Columbia University Press, 1996.

Rosenblum, Nancy L. *Another Liberalism: Romanticism and the Reconstruction of Liberal Thought.* Cambridge, Mass.: Harvard University Press, 1987.

Sandel, Michael J. *Liberalism and the Limits of Justice.* Cambridge, Mass.: Cambridge University Press, 1982.

Sandel, Michael J. *Democracy's Discontent.* Cambridge, Mass.: Harvard University Press, 1996.

Schwartz, Joseph M. *The Permanence of the Political: A Democratic Critique of the Radical Impulse to Transcend Politics.* Princeton, N.J.: Princeton University Press, 1995.

Shapiro, Ian, ed. *Power, Inequality, and Democratic Politics.* Boulder, Colo.: Westview Press, 1988.

Spitz, David. *The Real World of Liberalism.* Chicago: University of Chicago Press, 1982.

Walzer, Michael. *Spheres of Justice: A Defense of Pluralism and Equality.* New York: Basic Books, 1983.

Yack, Bernard, ed. *Liberalism Without Illusions.* Chicago: University of Chicago Press, 1996.

GLOSSARY TERMS
capitalism
common good
conservatives
democracy
due process
liberal democracy
liberalism
liberals
libertarians
operative ideals
pluralism
political ideologies
populists
radicals
reactionaries
republicanism

THE EXTRAORDINARY COLLAPSE of communism in the Soviet Union and the breakup of the first communist state in history are momentous events that have dramatically influenced the new world of politics. Although some political scientists in the post–World War II period foresaw trouble for both communism and the Soviet Union, surprisingly few predicted the rapid breakup of the Union of Soviet Socialist Republics that occurred in 1991.

In a famous 1947 essay in *Foreign Affairs*, "The Sources of Soviet Conduct," George Kennan argued that a policy of containing the Soviet Union would in time "promote tendencies which must eventually find their outlet in either the breakup or the gradual mellowing of Soviet power."

More recently, some scholars—notably Zbigniew Brzezinski and Adam Ulam—underscored the ideological, political, and economic weaknesses of both Soviet communism and the Soviet state.[1] In 1989 Brzezinski anticipated the demise of Soviet communism and hinted at the breakup of the Soviet Union. In 1992 (in a book started before the end of Soviet communism and finished shortly after the failed August 1991 coup that was to bring down the USSR) Ulam set forth the reasons for the "simultaneous collapse of an empire and the ideology that engendered it." Yet most political scientists were surprised by the sudden collapse of a regime that had been in power for almost three-quarters of a century (1917–1991).

How can we explain these astonishing events? How do they help us understand communism as an ideology that served as the operative ideal of the Soviet Union, the first communist state? What light does the collapse of communism in what was once the powerful Soviet Union throw on the remaining great communist power in the

COMMUNISM

THE MEANING OF COMMUNISM

THE SOURCES OF COMMUNISM
Karl Marx: Master Theoretician
V. I. Lenin: Master Revolutionary Strategist and Tactician
Joseph Stalin: Master Builder of Soviet Power
Mao Zedong: Founding Father of Chinese Communism

THE OPERATIVE IDEALS OF COMMUNISM TODAY
Communism as a Humanist Philosophy/Ideology
Communism as a Scientific Philosophy/Ideology
Communism as a Revolutionary Philosophy/Ideology

COMMUNISM: PAST, PRESENT, AND FUTURE
The Unraveling of the Soviet Communist Revolution
China After Mao

VARIATIONS ON THE COMMUNIST THEME

COMMUNISM: DEFENSE AND ATTACK, STRENGTHS AND WEAKNESSES
The Attack on Communism
The Defense of Communism
Communist Strengths and Weaknesses

CONCLUSION

world, China? And how are we to assess communism as an ideology elsewhere in the world whether in Europe or in the nations of the Third World?

In this chapter we will focus on communism as a set of beliefs, or operative ideals, that once guided the Soviet Union, that struck fear into noncommunists all over the world, that influenced the thinking of Communist parties around the globe, and that is still the official ideology of the world's most populous state, China. As in Chapter 6, we will try to remedy the political ideologist's shortcomings by critically assessing the communist outlook. Our guiding question is, *How do we appraise the strengths and weaknesses of communism?*

THE MEANING OF COMMUNISM

Historically, the appeal of communist ideas builds on the Marxist heritage that we outlined in Chapter 5. But what exactly is **communism?**

Theoretically, communism is a vision of a better world. Communist doctrine holds out to all peoples a vision of an earthly paradise in which freedom, peace, abundance, community, and fulfillment prevail for all, regardless of race, color, or sex. Communism appeals most pointedly to the oppressed worker. For the exploited, the abused, and the lowly, it promises justice on this earth.

Communism is also a philosophy of history. Communism purports to explain the evolution and structure of human society. It describes historical development in terms of clashing material forces related to how people earn a living and conduct their economic activities. Communist philosophy emphasizes that human ideas and behavior are significantly influenced by the material environment. The present period of history outside communist lands is understood in terms of the clash between capitalists and workers, a clash predicted to end in the worldwide defeat of capitalism and the eventual establishment of communism and a higher freedom.

Communism is, additionally, a critique of capitalism and imperialism and a justification of the new communist order and the "new person" who will live

under it. Communism condemns the exploitation of workers that is allegedly inherent in a system of private ownership and exchange. It views capitalism and imperialism as inseparable phenomena of the modern world, and it castigates what it contends are the consequences of capitalism and imperialism: the misery of workers, colonialism, and war. Communism offers a new order based on worker control of the means of production, the satisfaction of real human needs, and an altruistic pattern of cooperation and development. It has been particularly appealing to radical leaders in poor, formerly colonial nations that seek a rapid path to modernization.

Finally, communism is a strategy of revolutionary action for overthrowing capitalist society and enabling the world's workers to establish the inevitable communist society.

Our attempt to clarify the meaning of communism will involve four steps: (1) outlining the historical roots and evolution of communism; (2) focusing on its operative ideals, as they manifested themselves in the first communist state, the Soviet Union, and as they have influenced China; (3) noting the several variations on the communist theme; and (4) attempting to assess—in the critical spirit of political philosophy—communism's strengths and weaknesses. This assessment is particularly important in light of the demise of communism in the Soviet Union and the evolution of communism in China.

THE SOURCES OF COMMUNISM

We start our fuller exploration of communism with Karl Marx. We will then highlight the contributions of Lenin (the first leader of the first communist state, the Soviet Union), and of Stalin (who dominated the Soviet Union and world communism for over a quarter of a century). We will then note the contributions of Mao Zedong, who played a crucial role in raising a communist regime in China.

Karl Marx: Master Theoretician

V. I. Lenin, in his 1913 essay "The Three Sources and Three Component Parts of Marxism," noted that Germany made Karl Marx a philosopher, France made him a socialist revolutionary, and England made him a political economist.[2] What Lenin neglected to add was that the Western European Enlightenment—which informed German philosophy, French revolutionary theory, and British political economy—made Marx a prophet of the new communist world. Whether he was a true or false prophet is a question that each reader will have to grapple with in this chapter.[3]

The **Enlightenment** was a complex and influential movement that dominated Western thought in the eighteenth century, the century of the American and French revolutions. Many of the *philosophes*—the enlightened ones—condemned the follies and barbarities of an oppressive and ignorant past and looked forward to the emancipation of humanity. Believing in reason, freedom, and progress, they appealed to reasonable people, extolled liberty, and hailed the march of humankind toward a better world. Marx attempted to carry the Enlightenment to what he thought was its logical conclusion: real freedom for all, which for him meant freedom in a classless communist society.

Marx derived important philosophical ideas from two German philosophers, Georg Hegel and Ludwig Feuerbach. From Hegel, Marx borrowed the concept of the **dialectic** (or the clash of ideas) for interpreting historical evolution. According to Hegel, the principal clue to historical development lay in the clash of opposing ideas. Marx was impressed with Hegel's concept of the dialectic but disagreed about the opposing forces. Hegel had argued that ideas are the opposing forces, but Marx concluded that material forces—economic classes—rather than ideas explained evolution in history.

From Feuerbach, Marx derived a philosophic **materialism** (a belief that matter is the ultimate reality) and a radical critique of religion. Both ideas helped him formulate communism. Marx agreed with Feuerbach that religion is an illusion that prevents human beings from focusing on their needs in this world. He also agreed that the

critique of religion leads to a critique of society. But, Marx held, Feuerbach's materialism was inadequate. One must move beyond an understanding of the material world to an effort to change that world. As Marx said in his critique of Feuerbach: "The philosophers have only interpreted the world, in various ways; the point, however, is to change it."[4] It was true, as materialist doctrine held, "that men are products of [material] circumstances," but materialists forget "that it is men who change circumstances." The interrelation of objective, material forces and of human thought and action troubled both Marx and those who followed him.

Marx drew heavily on French socialist literature, revolutionary theory, and experience. He was influenced, for example, by such French Socialist philosophers as Claude Henri Saint-Simon and by such theorists of the French Revolution as Augustine Thierry, who Marx regarded as the father of the class struggle in French historical writing. The French Socialists were disturbed about what the capitalist economy was doing, particularly to workers.[5]

Marx was influenced not only by French Socialists but also by the French revolutions of 1789, 1848, and 1871. Marx saw the revolution of 1789 as the triumph of the French bourgeoisie; the revolution of 1848 as the failure of the bourgeoisie when they had to choose between liberty and property, family, and order; and the revolution of 1871—the short-lived workers' commune in Paris—as a model of the workers' revolution and the dictatorship of the proletariat. Never satisfied with mere intellectualizing, Marx sought to grasp the relationship between theory and practice in order to change the world in a communist direction.

Marx's stay in England and his wide reading of such British political economists as Adam Smith and David Ricardo made him a well-informed political economist. Friedrich Engels's firsthand study of British labor conditions, published in 1845 as *Conditions of the Working Class in England*, stimulated Marx's interest in the actual working of industrialism in the most advanced capitalistic country in the world. Marx spent long hours in the library of the British Museum to explore and document ideas about capitalism that he had begun to develop (1857–1858) in a vast outline called the *Grundriss*, or *Foundations of the Critique of Political Economy*. A part of this research was published as *Capital* (*Das Kapital*) in three volumes.

Thus, the basic theoretical outlook of communism remains that of Karl Marx. Friedrich Engels, Marx's close friend and collaborator, freely acknowledged Marx's primary contribution to communist theory. During a graveside ceremony three days after Marx's death on March 14, 1883, Engels emphasized Marx's achievements as scientist and revolutionary: (1) his materialist conception of history; (2) his theory of surplus value, which illuminated the functioning and fate of capitalist production; and (3) his contribution to the overthrow of capitalism—society and state—and to the "liberation of the modern proletariat which he was the first to make conscious of its own position and its needs, conscious of the conditions of its emancipation."

Although he expected communism to triumph in the advanced industrial nations of Western Europe, Marx did not live to see it prevail in any European country. Communism came to power first in a relatively backward industrial nation in Eastern Europe. The next section focuses on the leader of that extraordinary Russian Revolution, V. I. Lenin, and on the shaping of communism as Marxism-Leninism.

V. I. Lenin: Master Revolutionary Strategist and Tactician

Lenin's modifications of Marxist doctrine became fundamental parts of communist strategy and tactics in his home country of Russia, a land whose history made it strangely receptive to many communist ideas.[6] Thus, Lenin's contributions must be viewed in the context of that politically autocratic, economically backward state. The bourgeoisie were weak in czarist Russia, and the industrial proletariat were few, especially compared to the peasantry. Marx had

generally assumed that bourgeois capitalism would prepare the way for the communist revolution. Lenin perceived the need to speed up the revolution by using a revolutionary Communist party, taking advantage of World War I, winning allies among the peasants, and adopting a revolutionary interpretation of Marx. The autocratic and repressive environment of czarist Russia unquestionably made Lenin's communist strategy sharply revolutionary, conspiratorial, and dictatorial instead of evolutionary, open, and democratic. World War I, especially, gave Lenin a unique opportunity to apply his revolutionary program. Losses on the battlefield and widespread discontent on farms and factories made Russia ripe for revolution.

Lenin shrewdly addressed the disaffected elements in Russia. To all, particularly the soldiers, he promised peace; to the city workers, jobs and bread; and to the millions of land-hungry peasants, land. When convenient, his slogan was: "All power to the Soviets" (councils of workers). Revolutionary councils were set up in principal cities and factories and within the army. The February (or March[7]) 1917 Revolution had been successful in overthrowing the czar. He had abdicated and had been replaced by a provisional government interested in establishing liberal, democratic institutions. Eight months later, when

Vladimir I. Lenin (1870–1924), Marxist theorist and Communist party organizer, was the first leader of the Soviet state.

the time seemed ripe, the Lenin-led Communists overthrew the provisional government and seized power (the October Revolution). The Communist party had indeed speeded up the bourgeois revolution.

Lenin was not afraid to adapt Marx to the revolutionary circumstances of Russia. He used the Communist party to lead the revolution; he used a minority (party and industrial workers) to lead the majority (who were peasants and not communists); and he attempted the proletarian revolution in a country that had not really known a successful bourgeois revolution and was not an advanced industrial nation. Once in power, Lenin did not hesitate to slow up nationalization and encourage small capitalistic undertakings in agriculture and retail trade when the speed of the communist experiment threatened the regime's existence.

Joseph Stalin: Master Builder of Soviet Power

If "Leninism is Marxism in the epoch of imperialism and of the proletarian revolution" (as Stalin once remarked), Stalinism is Leninism in the epoch of the building of Soviet power. Lenin had appreciated the importance of consolidating the Bolshevik Revolution in Russia. Thus Stalin could cite Lenin's action to justify his own emphasis on "socialism in one country" when he was accused of giving up on world revolution and of assuming that the Soviet Union could survive in a world without immediate communist revolutions in the advanced industrial nations.

As Lenin built on and altered Marx, so Stalin built on and altered Lenin. He took from Marx and Lenin those ideas that harmonized with his program and his sense of Russian and world realities, and he abandoned ideas that did not fit. But the single most important clue to understanding Stalin's contribution to, and influence on, communist theory and strategy is the priority that he gave to consolidating communist power within the Soviet Union.

This consolidation was intimately related to the consolidation of personal power, which began with Lenin's untimely death in 1924 and

with Stalin's emergence as the General Secretary of the Communist party and therefore master of the party apparatus.

Indictment of Stalin's ruthless regime came from Nikita S. Khrushchev, who after a power struggle became first secretary of the Soviet Communist party, and then premier of the Soviet Union in 1958. In 1956, three years after Stalin's death, Khrushchev denounced Stalin's use of terror and his fostering of the "cult of personality," a doctrine that makes a "particular leader a hero and miracle worker." These evils, Khrushchev stated, were alien to Marxism-Leninism. This adverse criticism of Stalin was continued by Mikhail Gorbachev.

The cost of Stalin's leadership was high. It involved not only the deaths of those Khrushchev called good Communist party members but also the deaths of millions of kulaks (land-owning or relatively better-off peasants), who were liquidated to achieve collectivization of agriculture. Other segments of Soviet society were also sacrificed; millions of people suffered. Apparently, Stalin viewed these costs as "absolutely necessary."[8]

Stalin believed that state power must grow mightily before it would ultimately cease to be necessary. Consequently, he applied state power to socialize the nation's farms and factories, to create and expand heavy industries, and to organize and equip a mighty army. He permitted no opposition to this course. In fact, he used terror to eliminate real or imaginary opposition. Finally, the cause of world revolution remained subservient to the interest of Soviet national security.

To Stalin and to Stalinists these policies were vindicated by the USSR's success, after enormous losses, in defeating Nazi Germany on the Eastern Front in World War II and by Communist "triumphs" in the postwar period in Central and Eastern Europe. Stalinists ignored Stalin's contribution to the disasters suffered after Hitler invaded the Soviet Union: weakening of Soviet military leadership, Soviet military unpreparedness, and (arguably) devious diplomacy. Stalinists also closed their eyes to the imposition of Communist rule on the countries of Central and Eastern Europe.

Mao Zedong: Founding Father of Chinese Communism

Mao Zedong's main contribution to communism stems from his view of how to achieve power in China and from his concept of the continuing revolution. His primary goal was a united, strong, prosperous, and egalitarian China.[9] He was guided by these objectives: China must not only repel foreign invaders (such as Japan in World War II) but must also defeat reactionary forces (such as the nationalist forces of Chiang Kai-shek and China's warlords) that oppressed and divided the country. China must be strong to prevent future humiliation by foreign powers. China must move out of poverty and into a modern, prosperous economy. And China must achieve a more egalitarian society. These objectives, Mao held, could be achieved only by a communism adapted to China's history and conditions.

Although Lenin had recognized the need to forge an alliance between urban workers and rural peasants, he was sufficiently within the orthodox Marxist tradition to rely on the urban proletariat to make the Soviet revolution. Such a strategy did not make sense to Mao Zedong.

Mao Zedong (1893–1976) was the founding father of the People's Republic of China. As leader of the Chinese Communist party, he came to power in 1949. Mao's controversial efforts to revitalize communism in China included the Great Leap Forward (launched in 1958) and the Cultural Revolution (1966–1969).

China's economy, Mao recognized, was even more agricultural than that of the Soviet Union. The urban workers' movement in China was small. Moreover, Chinese nationalist leader Chiang Kai-shek had crushed the power of the Chinese Communists in the cities at an early stage. Consequently, Mao held that Chinese Communists must build their strength among the peasants and in the countryside of northwest China rather than in the cities and among industrial workers. Aided by the Japanese attack on China before and during World War II, which weakened Chiang Kai-shek's nationalist regime, Mao and the Chinese Communists proceeded—after World War II was over—from their rural base to conquer the cities by military might. Mao successfully used guerrilla warfare to maintain his strength until he could muster superior force against the nationalist regime.

Although the Chinese Communists took over the economy when they seized power in 1949, they did not immediately expropriate all private property. Subsequently, however, following Mao's philosophy of the continuing communist revolution, the government moved to exert greater control over the economy, to collectivize agriculture, and to industrialize.

One important ideological difference from classical Marxian theory emerged as Mao began the transition to communism. Mao sought to abbreviate the period of socialism and move more rapidly toward communism (in the Great Leap Forward, launched in 1958) by introducing **communes**—economic and governmental units for both agricultural and nonagricultural work.

Later, in 1966–1969, Mao attempted a Cultural Revolution to renew revolutionary vigor, speed up the revolutionary process, avoid bureaucracy, and enhance egalitarianism. Even more clearly than Mao's earlier emphasis on a protracted and uninterrupted revolution, the Cultural Revolution illustrates his theory of continuing the revolution under the dictatorship of the people. The Cultural Revolution, which had catastrophic political, economic, and social results, was Mao's effort to continue the communist revolution by resolving the contradictions that he saw in Chinese society: between tradition and modernity, between technical expertise and politics, between town and country. The Cultural Revolution was seen as an effort, by societal upheaval and renewal, to move toward an egalitarian, classless society. The Cultural Revolution was characterized by direct popular action, attempted radical communist changes, and attack on allegedly corrupt power holders. The Cultural Revolution used periodic shakeups to ensure that communism would stay true to its developmental goals.[10]

THE OPERATIVE IDEALS OF COMMUNISM TODAY

Let us now look at the operative ideals of communism today, as they are illuminated by the sources we have just examined, as they played out in the Soviet Union, and as they still influence Communist China. We should constantly ask whether these ideals are indeed operative and to what extent they have been abandoned or replaced. In this examination, we must understand the changes that have occurred in communist theory and practice.

Communism as a Humanist Philosophy/Ideology

Theoretically, communists still adhere to Marx's vision of freedom, peace, abundance, humanity, community, and development. This philosophy is humanist in the sense that it centers on human beings and their development. The creation of the "new Soviet Man" was the goal of Soviet society. This vision remains the vision of Chinese Communists.

Communists claim to stand for freedom as opposed to "slavery"—that is, wage servitude, political oppression, and social subjugation. They envision a cooperative and altruistic community struggling against an individualistic doctrine of profit making, "speculation," and selfishness; a community of real equality and fraternity as contrasted with inequality, sham equality, and racial injustice. Their ultimate goal is the free

and voluntary acceptance by all individuals and groups of society's necessary rules. In the final communist society, coercion and brutal oppression by the government, law, police, and army will no longer exist.

The triumph of the proletariat would not only usher in a classless and conflictless society within a nation but would also overcome hostility between nations. Moreover, the triumph of communism would ensure economic abundance and individual development. In the "higher phase of communist society," Marx said, "the springs of cooperative wealth" will "flow more abundantly." Such a society will realize the communist motto: "From each according to his ability, to each according to his needs." In such a society the all-around development of the individual will be possible.[11]

After World War II, this communist vision was held out to developing nations. In many of these lands the communists draw an even more dramatic contrast between a colonial past of political subjugation, economic exploitation, and racial inequality and the communist promise of political freedom and independence, economic well-being and progress, and genuine equality.

The collapse of communism in the Soviet Union dramatically underscored the failure to deliver freedom, peace, abundance, community, and development. Communist China under a post-Maoist leadership has struggled, unsuccessfully, to reconcile modern economic development with human freedom.

But is the communist vision of a better world a mere utopian dream? Or is it, as communists claim, based on a scientific view of history, economics, society, and politics that assures either its present or future realization? As the next section emphasizes, communists believe that the communist vision is not utopian but scientific.

Communism as a Scientific Philosophy/Ideology

In exploring communism as a scientific philosophy/ideology, we recap the general communist outlook, highlight Marx's materialist concept of history, and emphasize Lenin's critique of capitalism and imperialism.

The Communist Outlook—Communism sees history moving toward a classless society in which the means of production, distribution, and exchange will be owned by the community. In this final communist community, the state (understood as an instrument of coercion and oppression) will have disappeared. Between the revolution, which abolishes the capitalist order, and this communist society lies a transitional period, known as the **dictatorship of the proletariat**—rule (which may sometimes be coercive) by the overwhelming majority of workers in their own interest. This is the period of socialism, or the first stage of communism. When full communism finally arrives, the oppressive state will disappear, and there will be complete freedom in economic abundance. Marx articulated this view, and Lenin shared it.

Marx's Materialist Conception of History—Marx's conception of history is based on three factors: (1) materialism, (2) class struggle, and (3) dialectical change.

1. *Materialism.* For Marx, "life involves before everything else eating and drinking, a habitation, clothing and many other things." History, therefore, first requires the production of the means to satisfy these material needs.[12] The economic structure of society, which is shaped by the prevailing mode of production, constitutes the society's real foundation, upon which the superstructure of law, politics, ethics, religion, philosophy, ideology, and art is built.
2. *Class struggle.* History is dynamic. Economic forces conflict. Economic developments cause forward movement. Marx and Engels saw all history as the result of **class struggles**. Earlier the struggle was between "freeman and slave, patrician and plebian, lord and serf, guildmaster and journeyman, in a word,

oppressor and oppressed." In the modern period the struggle is between the **bourgeoisie** (the oppressor) and the **proletariat** (the oppressed)."By bourgeoisie is meant the class of modern Capitalists, owners of the means of social production and employers of wage-labor. By proletariat, the class of modern wage laborers who, having no means of production of their own, are reduced to selling their labor-power in order to live."[13] Communists believe that just as feudalism broke down and was replaced by capitalism, so capitalism will break down and be replaced by communism.

3. *Dialectical change in history.* Marx never used the rigid dialectical formula of "thesis," "antithesis," and "synthesis" to explain movement in history. He did underscore the importance of contradictions in a given economic system (whether feudalism or capitalism) that will generate dialectical change in that system. For example, the contradictions or challenges that led to the breakdown of feudalism involved new inventions and discoveries that stimulated commercial and industrial production (capitalism) and made individual workshops and the guild economy obsolete. In like manner, the contradictions in the capitalist system will cause its demise. But what are those contradictions? Marx emphasized two contradictions, and Lenin highlighted a third: (1) Capitalism creates a large class of terribly exploited workers whose labor makes profits for capitalists; these workers become conscious of their exploitation, band together to defend themselves, and eventually overthrow their exploiters. (2) Capitalism operates in a faulty, uneven way because it produces periodic catastrophic depressions. (3) Modern imperialistic wars among capitalistic states weaken them at home and facilitate revolution within their colonies.[14]

The Chinese communists generally accepted this Marxist-Leninist outlook. But they placed a greater emphasis on the peasant's role in the class struggle and endorsed perhaps even more emphatically than Lenin or Stalin the need for Promethean effort in the revolutionary struggle to achieve power and restructure society.

Neither Marx nor Lenin spelled out a complete picture of the communist society toward which history is inevitably moving. It will emerge, they insisted, out of the revolutionary struggle.

Communism as a Revolutionary Philosophy/Ideology

In setting forth communist revolutionary theory, as understood historically in the former Soviet Union and today in China, it will again be helpful to review Marx's general orientation—a starting point for Lenin, Stalin, and Mao. We can then examine Lenin's modifications of Marx, and Stalin's modifications of both Marx and Lenin. Then we can highlight Mao's responses to Marxism-Leninism in the light of the situation he encountered in China.

Marx's General Orientation—According to Marx, the communist revolution would occur in three stages: (1) the overthrow of capitalism, (2) the revolutionary dictatorship of the proletariat, and (3) communism. Capitalism would give birth to the proletarian revolution only after capitalistic society had developed the material conditions to sustain the revolution. A feudal society could not normally jump to a communist economy without passing through the stage of capitalist development. Under capitalism, Marx argued, workers must get ready and get set before they can go.

Workers would *get ready* by understanding the march of history (from feudalism to capitalism to communism), their own exploitation under capitalism, the weaknesses of capitalism, the weapons that capitalism has placed in their hands, and the nature of class struggle.

Workers would *get set* by organizing and unionizing, working with progressive and democratic forces, arming themselves, and adopting an independent and militant stance on revolution.

They would have to avoid being deceived by utopian socialists, bourgeois reformers, or even democratic socialist reformers. They could never lose sight of the need to overthrow capitalism with force. The communist revolution must be "permanent" in that it could not merely patch up the bourgeois capitalist order; it must give workers control of production and put state power in proletarian hands.

When the revolutionary situation was ripe, overthrow could take place. Strategy would vary with the character of the bourgeois regime in question and the stage of capitalist development. In 1872 Marx said that in advanced bourgeois democratic countries such as America and England, workers might be able to "attain their goal by peaceful means." But, he went on, "in most countries on the Continent the lever of our revolution must be force."[15] Marx saw the seizure of power by Parisian workers in 1871 as a model of a proletarian revolution as well as a model of the dictatorship of the proletariat.

The Crucial Role of the Communist Party—Marx and Engels argued in the *Manifesto of the Communist Party* that communists are leaders in the working class struggle and "theoretically . . . have over the great mass of the proletariat the advantage of clearly understanding the line of march, the conditions, and the ultimate general results of the proletariat movement." But they also specifically asserted that communists should "not form a separate party opposed to other working-class parties."

Lenin, however, maintained that, left alone, workers would never advance beyond a trade union consciousness, would never become revolutionary. Consequently, as early as 1902 in *What Is to Be Done?* he advocated a Communist party to lead the revolution. Only a revolutionary party—equipped, of course, with "an advanced revolutionary theory"—could educate and lead the masses to victory. Here Lenin articulated the concept of the Communist party as leader of the proletarian revolution, a party that would monopolize political power.

Lenin argued that the revolutionary party must also be united, ideologically homogeneous, limited in membership, strong, and disciplined. Such a party must be directed by a central leadership with power to purge itself of unreliable members. Lenin advocated the principle of "democratic centralism," which called for intra-party democracy at the top level of leadership and subordination of the minority and lower organs to the party's majority and its higher organs. Lenin's views on the crucial role of the Communist party clearly led to the one-party state. The leadership of the party and its Central Committee also led to the leadership of the Politburo (the highest organ of the party) and, as we shall see when we turn to Stalin, to the dictatorship of the party leader.

Lenin on Revolution and the Dictatorship of the Proletariat—In his famous pamphlet, *The State and Revolution*, written on the eve of the Bolshevik Revolution of 1917, Lenin developed ideas that significantly influenced the course of the Russian Revolution and modern communism.[16] He had already urged an alliance of proletariat and peasantry under the leadership of a revolutionary Communist party. Given this alliance and leadership, given the weakening of Russian capitalism in what Lenin called an "imperialist" war, and given the weakness of the bourgeoisie in Russian politics, the communist revolution in industrially backward and undemocratic Russia could take place.

In *The State and Revolution* Lenin justified his theory of violent revolution and dictatorial use of state power. He defended his views against the attacks of two other revolutionary groups: the moderate socialists, who thought socialism could be established by democratic and parliamentary methods, and the anarchists, who imagined that the oppressive state would wither away as soon as the proletariat overthrew the bourgeoisie.

Lenin argued that there can be no liberation of the oppressed proletarian class without violent revolution. The workers cannot be free until they destroy the apparatus of state power as built

and operated by the ruling class. He insisted that bourgeois state power must be smashed, not merely taken over—destroyed, not perfected. He clearly rejected the possibility of peaceful revolution. He attacked the advocates of gradual reform, who maintained that it is possible to evolve peacefully to socialism.

The armed working class will smash the bourgeois state, but destruction does not mean abolition. The state, as a repressive agency, must still be used temporarily (now by the proletariat) to wipe out all vestiges of capitalism. Here, Lenin attacks the anarchists who maintain that, with the overthrow of the bourgeois state, coercive power would cease to exist. Lenin holds that the "withering away of the state" does not refer to this stage of the revolution.

What is to supersede the smashed bourgeois state? Superficially, Lenin's answer was Marx's answer: the dictatorship of the proletariat. Marx contrasted his dictatorship of the proletariat with the dictatorship of the bourgeoisie, not with democracy. Marx assumed that workers constituted the majority in such countries as Great Britain and would in time become the majority in France and Germany. Lenin assumed, incorrectly, that the Communist party stood for the overwhelming majority of workers and people in 1917. Given his assumption, Lenin could write in *The State and Revolution*: "Democracy for the vast majority of the people and suppression by force, i.e., exclusion from democracy of the exploiters and oppressors of the people—this is the change democracy undergoes during the transition from capitalism to communism."

During the dictatorship of the proletariat, the liquidation of the bourgeois state and of bourgeois society will continue until completed. Private ownership of the means of production will be abolished, and, with public ownership of these means, the old exploitation of the worker will end. Other key changes will take place. The armed people will replace the standing army and police. The old administrative machinery will be replaced by a new one, drawn from the people. Government will revert to a simple and easy form to enable everyone to discharge state functions.

However, during this period—economically the period of **socialism**—all vestiges of bourgeois society will not immediately disappear. Since socialism cannot immediately create an economy of abundance, goods will continue to be distributed according to the amount of work each person does. The socialist motto is "From each according to his ability; to each according to his work." Workers will thus be paid equal wages for equal work, as under capitalism; this would not be communist equality, because it does not take the workers' needs into account. Here Lenin followed Marx.

The communist motto is "From each according to his ability; to each according to his needs." This is true communist equality: some workers might get more than others for the same amount of work because they might need more (to provide for families, for example). This genuine equality will be possible because communist production and principles ensure both an economy of abundance and the satisfaction of real human needs.

Communism will transform society completely, from the economic substructure through the political, legal, and cultural superstructure. All capitalist elements will have been purged and class oppression eliminated. Since everyone's real needs will be satisfied, there will be no reason for antisocial behavior. The causes of violence, coercion, and subjugation will disappear. As Lenin contended in *The State and Revolution*, "the people will have become accustomed to observing the elementary conditions of social life without force and without subordination." This will be the outcome of a new generation, brought up under the new and free conditions of socialism. At this point, the state as a coercive power will "wither away."

Stalinism: Fulfillment or Perversion of Marxism-Leninism?—Stalin's interpretation of revolutionary communism was significantly influenced by three considerations: (1) the need to create a socialist

Joseph Stalin was dictator of the Soviet Union from 1928 until his death in 1953. While he oversaw the country's rise to a modern industrial and military power, he ruled principally by terror.

society in one nation, (2) the need to use state power to build socialism, and (3) the need to subordinate the world revolution to the security of the Soviet Union.[17]

Despite his attention to the success of the Russian Revolution, Lenin assumed that the communist revolution in the Soviet Union would not be secure unless followed by communist revolutions in the advanced industrial countries of Europe. By the time Lenin died in 1924, it was evident that communism would not break out in other countries. Against Leon Trotsky, Joseph Stalin argued that a socialist society could be built in one country, the Soviet Union, by its own efforts, despite that country's lack of industrial maturity and without proletarian revolutions in other key countries. Theoretically, Stalin did not admit that the Soviet Union was abandoning the cause of world revolution, but practically he sought to build socialism in the Soviet Union and to subordinate world revolution to the security of the Soviet state.

Stalin did not hesitate to use the power of the Soviet state to build socialism. In several five-year plans he accelerated industrialization and placed the demands of heavy industry ahead of demands for consumer goods. Similarly, and perhaps contrary to Lenin's early admonitions against coercing the peasants, Stalin ruthlessly began the collectivization of agriculture in 1929.

He defended his use of state power (which his critics contended was "totalitarian") by arguing (1) that the mightiest and strongest form of state power must be developed "in order to prepare the conditions for the withering away of state power" and (2) that the state cannot wither away as long as the Soviet Union is "surrounded by the capitalist world [and] is subject to the menace of foreign military attack."

Stalin's tyrannical dictatorship—recognized as such by both anticommunist critics and top Soviet leaders such as Khrushchev and Gorbachev—has been amply documented. In consolidating his position as supreme leader, he ruthlessly wiped out his Communist opponents, millions of lesser Communist leaders and members of the Communist party, and millions of kulaks (land-owning peasants). He instituted a brutal reign of terror through party purges, phony trials, jailings, executions, suppression of dissent, and forced collectivization of agriculture.

Despite the fact that the Bolsheviks had seized power without majority support, Lenin maintained that Communist parties could achieve a victorious revolution throughout the world only if they secured mass support. Such support could not be gained if Communist parties isolated themselves from power. He insisted that power could be attained only if Communists worked within governments, trade unions, and other mass movements controlled by their opponents. They must combine complete loyalty to the ideas of communism with a facility for practical compromises. Their objective, however, would remain the seizure of power when the time was ripe.

Stalin built on this general strategy but did not hesitate to subordinate all Communist parties outside the Soviet Union to the hegemony of the Soviet Union. Stalin's goal was to maintain Soviet power, even though these parties were the main hope of proletarian revolution in other countries.

Mao: Guerrilla Revolutionary Strategy and Continuing Revolution—We have already noted that Mao relied on the peasantry and guerrilla warfare in order to achieve power in China. This successful strategy heartened communists in poor, largely rural, undeveloped countries, who seized upon the Maoist model of revolution. Radical revolutionaries were also heartened by Mao's criticisms of the more conservative Soviet position, his support of Third World revolutionaries, his early disregard of the dangers of nuclear warfare, and his disdain for peaceful coexistence.[18]

However, Mao's philosophy of the continuing, or permanent, communist revolution—as illustrated most dramatically in the Cultural Revolution—proved troublesome for the post-Maoist leadership in China. This leadership—as we shall discuss in a later section—moved away from Mao's more radical revolutionary ideas.

COMMUNISM: PAST, PRESENT, AND FUTURE

In this section we shall explore the demise of Soviet communism and examine the operative policies of Chinese communism today.

The Unraveling of the Soviet Communist Revolution

Even before Mikhail Gorbachev came to power as General Secretary of the Communist party in 1985, Nikita Khrushchev had made efforts to reform the communist system in the USSR. As early as 1956 Khrushchev confronted two disturbing realities and cited what he thought were two favorable developments. The disturbing realities were Stalin's terrorist rule and the advent of nuclear weapons. The supposedly favorable developments were the existence of communist states outside the Soviet Union and the emergence of new nations from among the former colonies of the great powers. In facing up to these developments, Khrushchev attempted (1) to "liberalize" the Soviet Union in various ways, (2) to argue against the "fatal inevitability of war" and for peaceful coexistence, (3) to highlight "the emergence of socialism from the confines of one country and its transformation into a world system," and (4) to emphasize the possibility of

Mikhail Gorbachev became the leader of the Soviety Union (as General-Secretary of the Central Committee of the Communist party) in 1985. He also served as president of the Soviet Union until its breakup in 1991. His policies of glasnost (openness), perestroika (restructuring) and uskorenie (acceleration) were belated attempts to reform the Soviet communist system.

peaceful, parliamentary socialism and communism in the new states of the formerly colonial world as well as in the capitalist world. Gorbachev attempted to follow through on the first, second, and fourth points.

Gorbachev's "new thinking" rested on policies of *glasnost* (openness) and *perestroika* (restructuring) designed to achieve at home and abroad something akin to communism with a human face.[19] Gorbachev also stressed the importance of *uskorenie*—the acceleration of reforms in the Soviet communist system. There is little doubt that Soviet domestic and foreign policies underwent a significant change between 1985 and 1990. Domestically, Gorbachev sought to move the Soviet Union toward greater respect for the rule of law and other basic freedoms, to reform the distressed economy by opting for "market socialism" (away from a centralized, command economy and toward a decentralized market economy), and to reinvigorate the Communist party as well as political, economic, and social life. In foreign policy, Gorbachev sought to end the Cold War, to reduce arms, to allow the formerly Communist regimes of Eastern Europe to go their own ways, and to bring the Soviet Union into a common European home.

Ironically, Gorbachev's efforts at reform placed him in the position of the sorcerer's apprentice, who could not stop the actions he had started. The loss of Soviet preeminence in the international communist movement, the end of Soviet dominance in Eastern Europe, a failing and seriously flawed agricultural and industrial economy, and greater freedom for Soviet citizens all contributed to the unraveling of both communism and the Soviet state itself.

The breakup of the Soviet Union—marked by a failed plot to depose Gorbachev and return to a hard-line communist USSR—led to the emergence of a loose Commonwealth of Independent States in which Russia, under the leadership of Boris Yeltsin, assumed a dominant role. In 1996 Yeltsin was, in a democratic election, chosen president of a Russia struggling with great difficulty to move toward constitutional democracy, a multiparty system, a market economy.

China After Mao

After Mao's death in 1976, and under the leadership of Deng Xiaoping, efforts were made, in both domestic and international affairs, to pursue policies different from those pursuded under Mao.

In domestic affairs, the new leadership under Deng Xiaoping sought to accept the realities of a market economy and to bring China into a more modern, free, and open world. Deng continued to adhere to the famous four principles of Chinese communism: "upholding the socialist road," dictatorship of the proletariat, leadership of the Communist party, and what was called Marxism–Leninism–Mao Zedong thought. However, Deng interpreted these principles pragmatically so that they would not interfere with his ideas for the Four Modernizations: in agriculture, industry, science, and defense. Revolutionary class struggle must not interfere with sensible economic reform. The Communist party, of course, would retain control of policy. The Leninist principle of democratic centralism would prevail. But China would move toward a less centralized, less collectivistic, and less bureaucratic communism.

Ideologically, Deng's approach involved a reinterpretation of communism that focused on moving through the bourgeois, capitalist state rather than skipping it, as Mao had tried to do. Party theoreticians now recognize that China could be in this stage—the capitalist, bourgeois stage—for many years to come, and they had to act accordingly.

Deng's position would thus keep China focused on a central point: economic development. This called for persevering in economic reform and opening up to the outside world. Economic reform meant "maintaining the system of private agriculture that replaced collective farms, dismantling central planning generally in favor of private entrepreneurship and the market, and fully integrating China into the global economy."[20] What is being sought is "socialism with Chinese characteristics."

China's change in foreign affairs was also significant. Earlier, Chinese fears of the Soviet Union's hegemony had greatly influenced Chinese Communist theory and practice. The Chinese refused to be treated as a Soviet Communist satellite, even if their independence would cost them Soviet aid. Initially, in reacting against the USSR, the Chinese Communists took a radical line in international politics, accusing the Soviet Union of being "revisionist"—that is, of soft-pedaling revolution. They condemned both the Soviet Union and the United States. They saw themselves as the leading advocate for the world's developing nations. Howver, over time the Chinese interest both in national security and in economic modernization began to exert a more powerful influence on policy than orthodox ideological considerations.

Strikingly, the fear of Soviet hegemony proved stronger than hostility to alleged American imperialism, particularly when the Vietnam war ended in 1975. China began opening to the United States in 1972, four years before Mao's death. Since his death, and under the leadership of Deng Xiaoping, China's efforts to modernize and to enter into the international economy have accelerated. These changes have come at the expense of some values that Mao had emphasized during the cultural revolution, including egalitarianism, self-reliance, and rhetorical leadership in the revolutionary struggle around the world, particularly in developing countries. Moreover, China's relationship to the post-Soviet Russia has softened considerably. China and Russia have now developed a solid trade relationship.

However, domestic economic reform and a less radical foreign posture did not mean political reform in the liberal democratic tradition. The crushing of the remakable pro-democracy student demonstrations in Tiananmen Square in 1989 clearly demonstrated that there were limits to the "liberalization" of Chinese communism. After tolerating the demonstrations, the Chinese government brutally squelched them and then conducted a campaign of arrests and repression designed to punish the pro-democracy movement and its supporters.

The ideological future of "socialism with Chinese characteristics" is uncertain. What is particularly uncertain is whether China can modernize economically while resisting political reform (and freedom), and while keeping the Communist party as the only center of political power.

VARIATIONS ON THE COMMUNIST THEME

The philosophy of **Eurocommunism** merits mention because it indicates some significant departures by Communist parties in Italy, Spain, and France from classic Marxist-Leninist doctrine.[21] Eurocommunists have abandoned the Leninist concepts of violent revolution as the way to achieve power and of the dictatorship of the proletariat as the way to wield power after the revolution. Instead they have opted for a parliamentary pattern. Many have dropped the Communist party label. They have agreed to compete peacefully and democratically for power, to share in governing coalitions, and to accept being voted out of office if they had gained power in free and open elections. They have also accepted key aspects of capitalism and the market economy; at least they are no longer dedicated to the wholesale elimination of private ownership in favor of public ownership and a centralized economy. Communists have sometimes, if not frequently, shared power with governing coalitions in Italy and France; and they have had considerable success in governing several Italian cities.

Other variations on communism can be found in such countries as North Korea, Vietnam, and Cuba. The classical operative ideals of communism endure in these countries: a single-party system, dictatorship of proletariat-party-Politburo-leader, destruction of the old bourgeois ruling class, and socialized means of production and exchange instead of the capitalist free market economy.

How long these Communist regimes can hang on to power is another question. Economic troubles beset Cuba, Vietnam, and North Korea. The loss of Soviet economic and political support is particularly serious.

COMMUNISM: DEFENSE AND ATTACK, STRENGTHS AND WEAKNESSES

In this section we assess the strengths and weaknesses of communism by first noting criticisms and then examining the response of communism's defenders. The collapse of the Soviet Union has obviously given ample ammunition to critics. We must, however, remember that the world's most populous nation—China—remains under Communist rule; that Communist regimes still exist in North Korea, Vietnam, and Cuba; and that key aspects of the communist system still exist in the countries that once made up the Soviet Union.

The Attack on Communism

Communism, as a set of ideas, has been attacked (1) as utopian in theory and (2) as totalitarian and Machiavellian (that is, committed to a strategy of "lion and fox") in practice. Moreover, communism's critics argue that (3) it has failed as an economic system because it cannot produce goods efficiently and abundantly. These critics find confirmation in the theory and practice of Marxism-Leninism-Stalinism and in the failure of communism in the Soviet Union.

Unrealistically Utopian—Communism is *utopian* because it rests, theoretically, on the unrealistic premise of a classless, conflictless society. No such harmonious society is possible, given human fallibility, liberty, and diversity. The quest for a society that will achieve universal freedom, abundance, and virtue and will banish alienation is a utopian dream. This dream led Communists in the now defunct Soviet Union to try the impossible and to be willing (especially but not exclusively under Stalin) to pay a terrible price in human freedom and sacrifice to achieve their goals. People in China and in other Communist countries continue to pay a heavy price for communism's unrealistic aspirations.

Totalitarian and Machiavellian—Communist theory contains elements that can lead to a **totalitarian** dictatorship or severely repressive **authoritarian** rule. Marx's division of the world into an oppressed proletariat and an oppressive capitalist class is the first step toward totalitarianism. The historical communist commitment to a (generally) violent revolution to overthrow capitalism and establish a dictatorship of the proletariat is an important second step. Lenin's emphasis on the crucial role of the Communist party is a third step. The momentum of the communist revolution then moves from the dictatorship of the proletariat to the dictatorship of the party (with Lenin) to the dictatorship of the party leadership (the Politburo) to the dictatorship of the key party leader (Stalin). Moreover, given the fear of internal and external enemies, and the herculean job of building socialism, the growth and use of state power seem inevitable.

And so the totalitarian state emerges (a) resting on a comprehensive ideology (which has illuminated the true course of history); (b) based on a single party, with top leadership resting ultimately in one person—the dictator; (c) using the state's coercive powers, including terror, secret police, purges, assassinations, and slave-labor camps, to accomplish the party leader's purposes; (d) enjoying a monopoly of weapons; (e) taking full advantage of a communications monopoly; and (f) using a centrally directed economy to carry out plans for development. Although the Soviet Union after Stalin and China today cannot be called fully totalitarian, the Soviet Union was clearly authoritarian, and China is so today.

Critics also charge that communism is *Machiavellian*. To accomplish their central objective—the worldwide triumph of communism—Communists, whether in Russia or China or elsewhere, will not hesitate to use both craft and force. They are clever in being able to zig and zag to accomplish their central objective. For example, they will play the game of peaceful coexistence until they are ready to seize power either peacefully if they can or violently if they must. The Soviet Union, for example, did not hesitate to forcefully put down the "liberal" communist revolution against rigid rule in Hungary in 1956; to send tanks into Prague in 1968 to overthrow the "liberal" Dubcek government when it sought to develop a more democratic, open variety of communism; or to invade Afghanistan in 1979 to prop up a troubled and faltering Communist regime.

Failure of Communism as a Political System—The failure of communism as a political, economic, and social system is clear. This failure is illustrated by the collapse of Communism in the Soviet Union and the USSR's disintegration. The repudiation in free elections of authoritarian Communist rulers and regimes in Eastern Europe is additional evidence of communism's failure. The attempt by Chinese rulers to liberalize their economy is further evidence that communist economic ideas do not work. Moreover, political discontent with China's authoritarian political system—as illustrated by the 1989 protest in Beijing's Tiananmen Square—indicates that many Chinese long for greater freedom.

The Defense of Communism

Communism's beleaguered defenders still maintain that it is a liberating revolutionary philosophy, truly democratic and peaceful, guided by consistent principles, and able to reform itself.

A troubling, unanswered question facing the leaders who have followed Mao in China and Stalin in the Soviet Union is this: Will freedom and democracy eventually emerge in countries under Communist rule?

A Liberating Philosophy—Communism, its true believers insist, remains a liberating philosophy. As Marx pointed out, communism stands for universal human emancipation. In advanced countries where capitalism is overthrown, workers will finally gain control of their economic, social, and political lives and will be able to satisfy their needs in the realms of work, education, health, housing, and culture. In new nations, as Lenin anticipated, former colonial subjects will manage their own destinies and, by following the socialist path of development, will lift themselves into the modern world.[22]

Democratic and Peaceful—Communism is committed to democratic, peaceful policies. Communism is democratic in that it seeks rule by the overwhelming majority of workers in their own interest. The dictatorship of the proletariat is democratic (the majority exercises power) as opposed to the undemocratic dictatorship of the bourgeoisie (the minority acts in the interest of capitalist exploiters). The use of force and violence in the communist revolution depends on the resistance of those who oppose it.

Wise, Consistent Principles—Wise Marxist-Leninist principles can still consistently guide communist theory and practice. According to communists, these principles make it clear that the communist victory is inevitable but that circumstances must be considered in moving toward that victory. These circumstances include, for example, a country's stage of economic, social, and political development. Communists maintain that in light of the dangers of nuclear war, **peaceful coexistence** is the only sane policy. Peaceful coexistence does not, however, bar ideological, economic, and political competition.

Capable of Self-Reform—The reform possibilities of communism, its true believers maintain, were tragically cut short in Gorbachev's Soviet Union. China, however, as it liberalizes its economy, demonstrates the viability of communist reform.

Communist Strengths and Weaknesses

Assessing the strengths and weaknesses of communism as a set of ideas is difficult because judgments have to be made about communism in four different stages of development: (1) under capitalism, (2) during the proletarian revolution that overthrows capitalism, (3) in the period of the dictatorship of the proletariat (socialism), and (4) in maturity. For Communists, different operative ideals are relevant to each stage.

Under Capitalism—Communists are critical of capitalism precisely because values such peace, freedom, justice, and prosperity are not being fulfilled for the great majority of people. This claim seems less valid today for the advanced industrial liberal democratic countries but more valid for other countries that are capitalistic but not liberal democratic, such as right-wing developing nations in Africa, Asia, and Latin America. Communists, of course, are also critical of advanced capitalist countries for their failure to do justice to their own still-oppressed workers and for their continued "imperialistic exploitation." In fact, workers in liberal democratic nations have significantly improved their lives. But even though old-style colonial exploitation is mostly a thing of the past, a new variety of exploitation —often via profit-hungry multinational corporations—merits careful study.

Even if the communist criticism of capitalist and imperialist abuses is morally justified in part, it is by no means clear that this criticism is scientifically sound. Capitalism has not withered away and died. It has demonstrated a tenacious staying power—an ability to adjust to changing conditions, a democratic political order, a welfare state, and economic regulations in the public interest.

Under the Proletarian Revolution—Assessment of the proletarian revolution depends on whether it will go forward peacefully or will be achieved only by violence and, if violent, whether it can be defended as a just revolution.[23] The main Marxist-Leninist position endorses the need for force and violence to overthrow capitalism (because capitalists will not permit a peaceful revolution). Marx and Lenin were so strongly convinced of the evils of capitalism that they were willing to pay the price of violent revolution. Such a revolution, nonetheless, violates a humane commitment to peace and constitutional change. Clearly, during a militant proletarian revolution, the lives, rights, and well-being of its opponents—capitalists and others opposed to communism of the Leninist variety—will be jeopardized. In light of the Russian and Chinese experiences, it is difficult to justify the costs of the communist revolution according to the calculus of the just revolution.

In the last years of the Soviet Union, a peaceful parliamentary path to communism was recognized by Soviet Communist leaders. This path is a possibility, they affirmed, for certain advanced industrial and democratic nations with strong working-class movements and a progressive socialist tradition. France and Italy were usually nominated as candidates for such a peaceful revolution. But communism's declining popularity makes it unlikely that a peaceful Communist party victory in France or Italy will occur.

The historical record of a peaceful parliamentary path to communism is not promising. The Bolsheviks fought a revolution to come to power in the Soviet Union. Current communist regimes (China, North Korea, Vietnam, Cuba) also achieved power through armed revolution. In the post–World War II period Communist regimes arose in Eastern Europe through the leadership of a minority Communist party backed by the Red Army (Poland, East Germany, Hungary, Romania, Bulgaria, and Czechoslovakia). With one possible, and somewhat dubious, exception (the former Yugoslavia), no Communist regime has ever come to power by peaceful means or through the free electoral choice of its people.

Under Socialism—Communist theory on the dictatorship of the proletariat has been significantly influenced by the Soviet and especially the Stalinist example. Here the record is mixed but still disturbing. Millions of lives were lost during the Soviet Union's dictatorship of the proletariat, which really was Stalin's personal dictatorship. The victims were not only capitalists or supporters of the czar; liberals and democratic socialists

Fidel Castro has been the premier of Communist Cuba since he and his supporters overthrew the Batista dictatorship in 1959. Castro's totalitarian regime has managed to survive a host of adverse conditions, including the rupture of diplomatic and economic relations with the United States, disastrous economic conditions, and the collapse of the Communist Soviet Union.

also died. Millions of peasants were liquidated, and huge numbers of Communists were purged. It is easy to blame these excesses on a cruel, despotic, paranoid Stalin. But the theory of the dictatorship of the proletariat itself cannot be exempt from criticism, especially as it leads, partly in communist theory and certainly in Russian practice, to the dictatorship of the party, the Politburo, and finally to one man: Stalin.

Unquestionably, the dictatorship of the proletariat provided a rationale for the USSR's economic development via industrialization, reliance on heavy industry (for example, steel), forced collectivization of agriculture, and creation of a powerful (and costly) Red Army. Under Stalin, one variety of socialism was indeed built in the Soviet Union, and its industrial, military, and scientific record is, in some respects, impressive. Yet a heavy price was paid—for example, in the suffering and death of millions of farmers and other Soviet citizens, in the lack of agricultural productivity, in industrial inefficiencies, in the shortage of consumer goods, and in inadequate housing. Moreover, despite some impressive scientific and military achievements, Stalin's successors were not able to deliver either economic abundance or genuine political freedom.

Communism, in countries such as the former Soviet Union, made its best record in addressing certain aspects of the average citizen's well-being. The Soviet Union probably made its greatest progress in education. Illiteracy was virtually eliminated, and a complete educational system guided millions of citizens into the nation's scientific, technological, social, and cultural life. The average Soviet citizen's basic economic needs were minimally addressed, if not fully met. People did not starve to death in the Soviet Union, even if they did not eat well according to American standards. Medical care addressed fundamental health problems. Housing remained in relatively short supply, bedeviled by long waiting lists, and was not satisfactory by Western standards; but people, even if cramped in city apartments, had at least minimal accommodations.

The Soviet record in protecting civil liberties and human rights was seriously deficient, although it improved under Gorbachev. Stalin's death ended the worst violations by the secret police and the government. Although considerable movement was made toward freedom of religion, speech, press, assembly, and due process of law—as understood in liberal democratic countries in the West—Soviet citizens were still limited in the exercise of many of these freedoms by the prevalent apparatus of a formerly authoritarian state. Greater freedom, for example, to criticize the government holding power and to seek changes in policy was visible under Gorbachev. But despite significant movement toward greater freedom (of speech, press, elections), the Soviet Union in its last years had not fully arrived at a multiparty system, an effective nonparty press, and genuinely competitive elections at all levels.

In international affairs, Soviet communism finally opted for a policy of peaceful coexistence. Such a policy certainly made sense in the age of nuclear weapons. Some reassuring actions were evident in Soviet foreign affairs. For example, the Soviet withdrawal from Afghanistan—and the candid admission by the Gorbachev government that the invasion had been a mistake—was reassuring. The decision under Gorbachev to allow Eastern and Central European nations once under Communist regimes to pursue their own destinies was also reassuring. The Soviet Union also withdrew its earlier active support for wars of liberation in certain developing nations.

The Chinese record has not been so reassuring. Destroying enemies of the communist revolution was excessively costly. Mao's Great Leap Forward and Cultural Revolution were economic, political, and social disasters, causing death for millions of peasants and dislocation, violence, and famine in the Great Leap Forward and purges, mass killings, and imprisonment during the Cultural Revolution. Only after Mao's death was a more moderate domestic course charted. This provided for considerable economic liberalization but did not signify the end of authoritarian political rule or the advent of freedom.

The authoritarian record under other Communist regimes—whether in North Korea, Cuba, or Vietnam—does not even begin to fulfill the Marxist promise of freedom and abundance.

In the Mature Communist Stage—Because no nation has yet moved to a mature stage of communism, it is difficult to compare theory to actual practice; it is impossible to determine what mature communism actually means. Communist theory is deficient in that it does not spell out a democratic and constitutional theory for mature communism. Marx thought it foolishly utopian to describe the details of the full-fledged communist society, so he did not address problems of freedom, integration, abundance, community, and development in the achieved communist society. Rather, he assumed—naively, we believe—that these problems would not be serious ones in the classless, conflictless, harmonious communist society. He did not address the problems of how policy would be made; of relations between people, party, and government; of possible conflicts between different economic, political, and social claimants for power; of the actual operation of a communist economy. Marx apparently believed these matters would take care of themselves because society would be based on worker control of the means of production and exchange, because workers would have achieved communist abundance, because workers would have made the leap from the realm of necessity to the realm of freedom, and because the communist motto would be fulfilled: "From each according to his ability; to each according to his needs."

These Marxist assumptions about mature communism must be seriously challenged. Other orthodox communist theoreticians have done little to clarify the principles, the functioning, and the problems of the mature communist society. More help on these matters has come from some students of Marx and from Marxists of a democratic socialist persuasion.[24]

CONCLUSION

We have attempted in this chapter to outline the historical roots and evolution of communism; to clarify its operative ideals (as they influenced the first communist state—the Soviet Union—and as they now influence China); to call attention to variations on the communist theme; and to assess communism's strengths and weaknesses.

Our emphasis on the relationship of theory and practice is particularly appropriate because communist theory values such a relationship. Our approach does, however, present difficulties. For example, disengaging communism as a set of ideas from the practical concerns of communist states is difficult. Sometimes traditional communist theory and actual practice may harmonize, but very often they do not. When they do not, traditional communist theory may be altered until it fits actual practice. Often this has meant major revisions of Marxism-Leninism.

Political ideology and philosophy help us understand the outlook of a historical communist state such as the Soviet Union. They also help us understand the outlook of China, of other Marxist regimes, and of the Eurocommunist parties of Western Europe. It is important, however, to distinguish between theory and practice, rhetoric and reality. It is important as well to understand how communist ideology and philosophy may change as circumstances change in the world and in the nations that profess to adhere to communism.

In Chapter 8 we examine another interpretation of socialism: democratic socialism.

ANNOTATED BIBLIOGRAPHY

Arendt, Hannah. *The Origins of Totalitarianism*. New York: Meridian Books, 1958. Presents a path-finding, provocative study of totalitarianism. Better on nazism than communism but provides a basis for comparing Stalin's Russia and Hitler's Germany.

Berlin, Isaiah. *Karl Marx: His Life and Environment*, 3rd ed. Oxford: Oxford University Press, 1973. Provides an excellent brief biography of Marx.

Brzezinski, Zbigniew. *The Grand Failure: The Birth and Death of Communism*. New York: Macmillan, 1990. Explores the agony of Soviet communism, the difficulties of international communism, and China's move toward "commercial communism." Concludes that democracy, not communism, will dominate in the twenty-first century.

Gorbachev, Mikhail. *Perestroika: New Thinking for Our Country and the World.* New York: Harper & Row, 1988. Recommended for the remarkable thought of this extraordinary, if tragically flawed, Soviet leader.

Kolakowski, Leszek. *Main Currents of Marxism.* 3 vols. New York: Oxford University Press, 1978. Volume I, *The Founders,* explores Marxism's origins, other socialist ideas, along with the writings of Marx and Engels. Volume II, *The Golden Age,* deals with Marxists such as Karl Kautsky, Rosa Luxemburg, Eduard Bernstein, Jean Jaures, Georges Sorel, George V. Plekhanov, and V. I. Lenin. Volume III, *The Breakdown,* treats the evolution of Marxism in the last half-century and Joseph Stalin, Leon Trotsky, and Gyorgy Lukacs, and key figures in the Frankfurt School, Herbert Marcuse and Ernest Bloch. A very rich history and analysis by a Polish scholar sympathetic to Marxist humanism.

McLellan, David. *Karl Marx: His Life and Thought.* New York: Harper & Row, 1973. Contains good summaries of Marx's writings. The fuller authoritative biography.

Riemer, Neal. *Karl Marx and Prophetic Politics.* New York: Praeger, 1987. Assesses Marx according to the standard of prophetic politics.

Schram, Stuart. *The Thought of Mao Tse-tung.* Cambridge: Cambridge University Press, 1989. A balanced, scholarly, presentation and assessment of Mao's developing ideas.

Terril, Ross. *China in Our Time.* New York: Simon & Schuster, 1992. Presents a revealing account of China under Mao and Deng. Notes that although communism as an idea may be dying, the Communist party is growing stronger.

Townsend, James R., and Womack, Brantly. *Politics in China.* Boston: Little, Brown, 1986. See, particularly, Chapter 4, "The Communist System: Ideology and Change," and Chapter 8, "From Maoism to Modernization: Socialism with Chinese Characteristics."

Tucker, Robert C. *The Marx-Engels Reader,* 2nd ed. New York: Norton, 1978. Offers an excellent, handy collection of readings. See also Tucker's helpful *The Lenin Anthology* (New York: Norton, 1975) and his comparable collection of Stalin's key writings.

Ulam, Adam. *The Communists: The Story of Power and Lost Illusions.* New York: Scribner's, 1992. Presents an incisive account of the simultaneous, and unprecedented, collapse of an empire and its ideology.

Waldor, Andrew G., ed. *The Waning of the Communist State: Economic Origins of Political Decline—China and Hungary.* Los Angeles: University of California Press, 1996. Explores the weakening of Communist parties attributable, ironically, to their efforts to improve economic performance by loosening the reins of centralized economic planning.

SUGGESTIONS FOR FURTHER READING

Aronowitz, Stanley. *The Crisis in Historical Materialism: Class, Politics, and Culture in Marxist Theory,* 2nd ed. Minneapolis: University of Minnesota Press, 1990.

Blackburn, Robin, ed. *After the Fall: The Failure of Communism and the Future of Socialism.* New York: Routledge, 1992.

Brugger, Bill, and Kelly, David. *Chinese Marxism in the Post-Mao Era.* Stanford, Calif.: Stanford University Press, 1990.

Chirot, Daniel, ed. *The Crisis of Leninism and the Decline of the Left.* Seattle: University of Washington Press, 1991.

Cunningham, Frank. *Democratic Theory and Socialism.* Cambridge: Cambridge University Press, 1987.

Johnpoll, Bernard K. *A Documentary History of the Communist Party of the United States.* 8 vols. Westport, Conn.: Greenwood Press, 1994.

Laqueur, Walter. *The Dream That Failed: Reflection on the Soviet Union.* New York: Oxford University Press, 1994.

Levin, Michael. *Marx, Engels and Liberal Democracy.* New York: St. Martin's Press, 1989.

Lukes, Steven. *Marxism and Morality.* Oxford: Oxford University Press, 1988.

Matlock, Jack. *Autopsy on an Empire: The American Ambassador's Account of the Collapse of the Soviet Union.* New York: Random House, 1995.

Michael, Franz, Linden, Carl, Prybyla, Jan, and Domes, Jurgen. *China and the Crisis of Marxism-Leninism.* Boulder: Westview, 1990.

Roeder, Philip. *Red Sunset: The Failure of Soviet Politics.* Princeton, N.J.: Princeton University Press, 1993.

Ruan, Ming. *Deng Xiaoping: Chronicle of an Empire.* Boulder, Colo.: Westview Press, 1994.

Scalapino, Robert. *The Last Leninists: The Uncertain*

Fate of Asia's Communist States. Washington, D.C.: Center for Strategic and International Studies, 1992.

Sun, Yan. *The Chinese Reassessment of Socialism, 1976–1992.* Princeton, N.J.: Princeton University Press, 1995.

Talmon, A. J. *The Origins of Totalitarian Democracy.* London: Secker and Warburg, 1952.

Talmon, A. J. *Political Messianism: The Romantic Phase.* London: Secker & Warburg, 1960.

Walker, Angus. *Marx: His Theory and its Context.* London: Longmans, 1978.

GLOSSARY TERMS

authoritarian
bourgeoisie
class struggle
communes
communism
dialectic
dialectical change
dictatorship of the proletariat
Enlightenment
Eurocommunism
glasnost
materialism
peaceful coexistence
perestroika
proletariat
socialism
totalitarianism
uskorenie

DEMOCRATIC SOCIALISM

IN MANY WESTERN European countries, including the United Kingdom (Great Britain), Germany, France, and Sweden, democratic socialism is the political ideology that guides either the dominant governing party or the major opposition. In the United Kingdom, the democratic socialist British Labour Party, which has been out of power for a number of years, holds a significant lead in public opinion polls and is currently the party favored to win the next British election. In France, Socialist Francois Mitterrand was elected president in 1981 by a slim margin and won reelection in 1988 by 54 percent of the vote. In 1995, although Jacques Chirac, a member of the R.P.R. (Rally for the Republic) party, defeated the Socialist candidate for the French presidency, the victory was by a narrow margin. A democratic socialist party has been the dominant ruling party in Sweden during most of the years since 1932. A democratic socialist party is the main opposition party in the national government in Germany and is in power in many of the German *laender,* or states. Democratic socialist parties have also led governments in Belgium, Holland, Austria, Norway, Denmark, and Greece.

The democratic socialists emerged as a major political force in Portugal after a longstanding dictatorship was overthrown in 1974. Mario Soares stepped down as president after serving two five-year terms, and was replaced in 1996 by another socialist candidate, Jorge Sampaio. Currently, Portugal has both a socialist president and premier. In 1982 the Socialists won an overwhelming victory in Spain and remained in power until 1996, when Prime Minister Felipe Gonzalez, a four-term winner, was narrowly defeated. Outside of Europe, democratic socialist regimes have led governments in Australia,

New Zealand, and Israel. And the philosophy of democratic socialism has also guided a number of developing countries.

But what is the character of democratic socialism? How does it relate to liberal democracy? to communism? What are its strengths and weaknesses? What can we say about its past, present, and future?

Our exploration of the historical roots and evolution of democratic socialism will concentrate on Western Europe, focusing most sharply on Great Britain. For variations on the theme, we will also look at the democratic socialist experience in Germany, France, and Sweden.

THE HISTORICAL ROOTS AND EVOLUTION OF DEMOCRATIC SOCIALISM

In this section we will define democratic socialism, examine its sources, and trace its evolution as a political ideology.

Toward a Tentative Definition of Democratic Socialism

Democratic socialism combines democracy and socialism. But because there are many varieties of both democracy and socialism, it is not easy to define democratic socialism. Nevertheless, it is possible to distinguish liberal democracy from other varieties of democracy (see Chapter 6) and to distinguish democratic socialism from the Leninist-Stalinist version of communism (as this chapter, which builds on Chapters 6 and 7, will do). We will also raise the question of whether the governing ideology painfully emerging in Russia—after the collapse of communism in the former Soviet Union—will be a variety of democratic socialism.

Democratic socialism combines several ideas. *Politically,* it involves a commitment to popular, constitutional rule and the protection of basic rights. *Economically,* democratic socialists maintain that key aspects of economic life must be publicly owned, or socially controlled, to ensure an equitable distribution of the community's wealth. Democratic socialists are especially con-cerned that workers have a voice in their economic (and political and social) destiny and that human needs (particularly those of the "least free") are adequately satisfied. *Socially,* democratic socialists believe that all human beings in a cooperative community should have the opportunity to fulfill their good and creative potential.

We will discuss the ethical, political, economic, and social aspects of democratic socialism as we explore its roots and evolution.

The Sources of Democratic Socialism

Because democratic socialism shares roots with both liberal democracy and Marxism, you may want to review Chapters 6 and 7. Particularly important are the ideas of popular rule and human rights that led to constitutional democracy, and the circumstances (such as capitalism's malfunctioning and exploitation of workers) that led to socialism as an economic system. The democratic emphasis—in liberal democracy and in the early socialist movement—on extending the meaning of the watchwords of the French Revolution (liberty, equality, fraternity) is also noteworthy. Finally, special attention should be given to the importance, in both the democratic and socialist traditions, of extending popular rule and basic rights from the political sphere into the economic and social spheres in the interest of greater social justice.

Our review of democratic socialism's roots and evolution is selective. It emphasizes how modern democratic socialism drew on the early liberal democratic and socialist traditions for its own synthesis. In highlighting democratic socialism's fundamental aspects, we will draw particularly on its religious, utopian, Marxist, revisionist, Fabian, trade unionist, and reformist roots. We will focus especially on how these roots contribute to social justice, democracy, public ownership, and the cooperative commonwealth. We will be concerned with how these influences contributed to a growing criticism of the capitalist, industrial order and to a growing demand for a new order that would be both democratic and socialist.

Before beginning this selective review, however, we must keep in mind that ideas alone did not produce democratic socialism. Economic, social, and political developments first created an environment receptive to new ideas. Capitalism and modern industrialism created the setting for democratic socialism. Capitalism was sympathetic to liberal democracy and to greater economic, political, and social freedom for the middle class. European radicals on the left wing of the democratic movement engendered by the French Revolution sought to extend this freedom to workers and to the people. They generated socialist ideas to support this extension. Capitalism and industrialism helped by creating the modern working class and trade unions. The lot of workers in modern industrial societies produced many critics whose attacks on capitalism significantly shaped intellectual and political opinion and opened people to socialist ideas. The advance of suffrage, made inevitable by liberal democracy, gave workers and their allies political leverage. The institutions of liberal democracy made it possible for democratic socialists in time, and after many hard-fought battles, to take over the reins of political power. Thus, a number of forces converged to develop a philosophy of democratic socialism and to bring democratic socialists to power: the Industrial Revolution and capitalism, the French Revolution and liberal democracy, socialist ideas, working-class consciousness and trade unions, and labor party organization.

The following sections concentrate on the origins of the democratic socialists' philosophy of the good political life.

Religious Roots—The Judeo-Christian prophetic tradition is one source of democratic socialism's ethical ideal. The prophetic emphasis on justice and peace sustained the vision of human beings of integrity joined in a cooperative community where care for the "least free"—the poor, widows, and orphans—fulfilled God's commandments. This emphasis, reinforced by the primitive communalism of early Christianity, has echoed throughout the history of Christianity. It was reflected in the conviction, during the Middle Ages, that covetousness and greed lead to evil and that common ownership is preferable to private ownership, which leads to conflict, exploitation, and inequality. Religious influences manifested themselves in Christian Socialists such as Charles Kingsley and in British Labour party leaders such as George Lansbury and Clement Atlee. "Socialism," Lansbury wrote in 1934, "which means love, cooperation, and brotherhood in every department of human affairs, is the only outward expression of a Christian's faith."

In Great Britain the nonconformist tradition in religion was intimately associated with the articulation, spread, and triumph of a more democratic political order. As religious nonconformists sought freedom in religious matters from the established church, they also sought greater political freedom. They cherished freedom of conscience, which most often meant freedom to challenge dominant political, economic, and social arrangements. This democratic emphasis had emerged as early as the British civil war in the seventeenth century. It continued with the battle of the Chartists (political reformers in the nineteenth century) for universal manhood suffrage. In the seventeenth century the Levellers (who were really radical middle-class democrats) articulated the fundamental argument for universal suffrage that the Chartists and others battling for the vote were to repeat in later centuries. As John Lilburne, a key leader of the Levellers, put it: People are "by nature all equal and alike in power, dignity, and majesty," and consequently civil authority is to be exercised by "mutual agreement and consent." A soldier in Oliver Cromwell's army made the same argument even more eloquently:

Really I think that the poorest he that is in England hath a life to live as the greatest he; and therefore truly, Sir, I think it's clear, that every man that is to live under a government ought first by his own consent to put himself under that government; and I do think that the poorest man in England is not at all bound in a strict sense to that government that he hath not had a voice to put himself under.[1]

The modern **welfare state** (a phrase much abused in American partisan debate) also has deep roots in the Judeo-Christian tradition's concern for the poor and the needy, its preference for a more cooperative commonwealth, its insistence on fair and just economic rules, and its belief in dignified human life. It should, therefore, not be too surprising that nonconformists such as the Diggers (or "true-Levellers") would surface in Britain's seventeenth-century civil war to advocate a primitive communism. Their most prominent spokesperson, Gerrard Winstanley, understood the law of nature as a communal right to the means of subsistence: individuals have an equal right to use and enjoy the earth and its fruits, and people should be free to draw on the common land and the common produce according to their needs. These compassionate and egalitarian ideas continued to find expression in those in the Judeo-Christian religious tradition with a socialist orientation.

The religious socialists consistently held up a vision of brotherhood and sisterhood: all human beings are equal before God. They sought a society in which the gospel principles of love could be more fully realized. They preached cooperation and opposed conflict. They worked to elevate the spiritual character of social life. They emphasized humanity's obligation to the "least free." They took seriously the social gospel and envisioned a socialist society that would fulfill their religious vision of a genuine community.

Utopian Roots—Utopians have always cherished the concepts of justice and communal life and have valued education and cooperation. Although no democrat, Plato did make justice the central concern of his *Republic,* and, of course, education for the harmonious life was crucial to his political community. Moreover, he advocated communism for his philosopher-rulers.

Some of these same themes have echoed throughout the history of utopian thought. For example, a more just ordering of society was the major concern of Sir Thomas More, who, in his work *Utopia* (1516), coined the word that (as *utopia*)

means "no place" but that (as *eutopia*) means "good place." The term **utopia** has come to stand for the perfect political and social order.

A more just, communal society dominated the thinking of the **utopian socialists,** as Marx and Engels called them. The utopian socialists stressed cooperation and underscored the possibilities of using education to change the social and economic environment. Frequently, the utopian socialists concentrated on building self-sufficient communities, divorced from the main political stream. Although the utopians often called for elite leadership to create such communities, democratic principles frequently prevailed in the communities. Henri Claude Saint-Simon, Robert Owen, and Charles Fourier represent the variety of influential utopian socialists.

Although it is by no means clear that Saint-Simon was either a utopian, a socialist, or a democrat, his ideas about the emerging industrial society did influence socialism. He emphasized that "industry cannot be fully efficient, nor its products justly distributed, unless it is socially controlled." Saint-Simon had an uncanny insight into the future of the new industrial society and a "vision of the good society, a social order administered by working industrialists, scientists, and engineers, all in the service, not of the state, but of "the most numerous and the poorest classes."[2] He favored leadership by an industrial elite to advance the cause of the masses.

In *A New View of Society* (1813) Robert Owen looked to a cooperative and integrated agricultural-industrial community to overcome the evils of modern industrial society. Owen favored "villages of cooperation" as models for the new social order. Such planned villages would relieve unemployment by enabling the unemployed to grow their own food. Industrial production, as well as farming, would be communal. Owen's communities would be attractive and would eliminate the squalor of modern industrialism. Good working conditions would prevail. Owen's ideas stimulated his followers to raise and debate a number of questions important for socialism, such as whether human nature was compatible with the egalitarian system Owen was trying to

Title page of "The Crisis, or the Change from Error and Misery, to Truth and Happiness" by Robert Owen and his son Robert Dale Owen, nineteenth-century pioneers of cooperative communities and founders of New Harmony Community in Indiana.

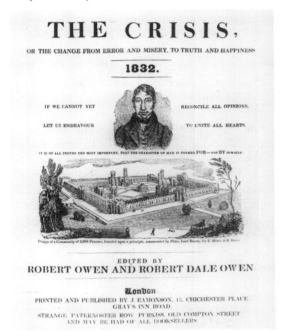

establish in his model factory community. They also asked, "Why are working people poor and wretched?" and "Is the laborer entitled to the whole produce of his labor?"

Owen was a remarkable socialist pioneer with a tremendous faith in the power of education and reform. As early as 1834 he tried, without success, to form a national trade union organization, an "attempt to assemble the entire working class under socialist leadership." He saw his Grand National Union as the means to socialize the economy. Owen also fathered the **cooperative movement** in Britain—the idea of mutually owned stores selling industrial goods for the benefit of their members. Owen also emphasized the importance of education in shaping people and society. The cardinal premise of his social philosophy was the right environment. "Any general character," he wrote, "from the best to the worst, from the most ignorant to the most

enlightened, may be given to any community, even to the world at large, by the application of the proper means; which means are to a great extent at the command and under the control, or easily made so, of those who possess the government of nations."[3]

Another communal model was offered by Saint-Simon's fellow countryman, Charles Fourier. Fourier favored a small agricultural community (the *phalanstère,* in French)—voluntary, self-sufficient, combining a "minimum of public regulation with a maximum of individual freedom."[4] His community anticipated the 1960s commune in America and was a model for Brook Farm, an American nineteenth-century utopian experiment. Fourier would guarantee everyone a livelihood. In his communal association the harmonious economy blended with the harmonious society. Fourier also expressed a number of themes that came to characterize modern democratic socialism. He sought to create a working and living environment free from coercion and arbitrary conventions. His writings illustrate a strong humanitarian, profeminist concern and a strong feeling for society's outcasts.

Marxist Roots—Karl Marx was more influential in the development of European socialism than in British socialism. But his ethical concerns—for universal freedom, peace and harmony, a more genuine community, and rich human development—were widely shared by all socialists. As we saw in Chapters 5 and 7, Marx's dream of worker control over the major means of production and exchange was central to his conception of freedom, especially for the oppressed proletariat. His just society was to be a classless society—one that would overcome alienation and exploitation. It was to be a community in which people would be authentic human beings, their needs richly satisfied and their talents fulfilled. Marx differed from many other socialists in his attempt to establish a more rational, comprehensive, and scientific framework for socialism.

Marx's relationship to democratic socialism is controversial largely because his own position on key political questions is not entirely clear. The most important question is whether socialism can be achieved and fulfilled peacefully and by democratic and constitutional means. In Marxist circles controversy surrounded the debate on whether violent revolution is inevitable and peaceful change possible and whether capitalism must be completely overthrown and destroyed. Marx's ambiguous position leaves us uncertain about whether the state, as a coercive organ, will really wither away and whether socialism will in fact lead to communism and the classless society. The history of communism in the former Soviet Union, in China, and in other countries still under Communist rule leads to skepticism about whether a classless, coercion-free society can actually be achieved.

It is clear that Marx favored extending suffrage and political rights to working people; he endorsed the need to win the battle for democracy; he also held open the possibility, for certain advanced democratic countries, of a peaceful parliamentary path to socialism. But he never ruled out a violent revolution by the majority against a capitalist minority who brutally oppose a peaceful democratic victory. On certain matters, Marx's socialist convictions remained unaltered: He envisaged that, under proletarian rule, state power would expand to achieve public ownership of the means of production and exchange, as well as other socialist objectives in the interest of working people. He was vague or silent on the question of minority rights for those opposed to socialist rule. For example, he never clearly addressed the question of socialists being voted out of office in a free election. Apparently, these matters did not bother Marx, because he held that the state (as a coercive organ) would wither away and that a classless society would emerge under communism. Our discussion of the revisionists (Marxists who sought to revise Marx) in the next section will show that they sought to clear up disturbing questions in Marxism by opting for democratic principles.

Marx's economic contribution to democratic socialism lies more in his systematic analysis of capitalism than in his socialist prescription. He argued that the exploitation of workers is inherent in a system of private ownership and that workers will not be free until they control the means of production, are in charge of the economic system, and use it to create and enjoy the common wealth. In his view, only socialism can overcome the contradictions of capitalism that produce depression and unemployment. Only socialism can achieve abundance and use it to satisfy human needs. Marx clearly saw the economic and political importance of the trade union movement. He strongly supported such economic reforms as reducing the work day to ten hours. Again, his economic analysis was more influential in Europe than in Great Britain. But even on the Continent the revisionists, although powerfully influenced by Marx's perspective, felt the need to adjust his analysis to the realities of economic life.

Marx's social views were presented in Chapter 7. He shared the concern of other socialists for a more genuine community, in which individuals have regained contact with their essential humanity. Marx's utopian commitment to a classless society offers hope for the end of bitter class conflict and the advent of social harmony and integration. For Marx, communism was not really the end of the revolutionary process: freedom and individual development were. Abundant production, under communism, would satisfy basic needs and thus free people to lead richer lives.

Revisionist Roots—The **revisionists** shared Marx's general outlook but differed with his economic and political diagnosis. They felt Marx had to be revised in order to advance socialist goals. This section focuses on one important revisionist, the German Eduard Bernstein, a social democrat who spent many years of exile in England and whose views reflect the pragmatic and constitutional British tradition.[5]

Bernstein shared the socialist dream of social justice but emphasized the importance of a peaceful and parliamentary transition to socialism. He

Eduard Bernstein (1850–1932), a German-born socialist who was critical of orthodox Marxism, developed some of the cardinal ideas of an evolutionary, peaceful democratic socialism.

was more influenced by Immanuel Kant, the great idealist German philosopher, than by Georg Hegel, Marx's philosophical mentor. Philosophically, Bernstein, if he did not fully understand Kant, was sympathetic to his critical spirit and was encouraged to affirm (in Peter Gay's words) that without "idealism and without criticism there can be no socialism." For Bernstein, violent revolution and the dictatorship of the proletariat were doctrinaire ideas out of touch with political realities. Ideals had an important role to play in socialism. For Bernstein, socialism was not inevitable, but it was supremely desirable.

It is not clear that Bernstein went as far as the German Kantian philosopher Hermann Cohen, who maintained that Kant's ethical postulates made Kant "the true and actual founder of German Socialism." Cohen had in mind Kant's second formulation of the categorical imperative: "Act so as to treat man, in your own person as well as in that of anyone else, always as an end, never merely as a means." Cohen believed that this ethical maxim could lead only to socialism. Bernstein's ethical position reflected this perspective and marked a break with Marx's materialistic outlook.

Politically, Bernstein broke sharply with the revolutionary Marxists, opting clearly for the peaceful, evolutionary path to socialism. He accepted the constitutional rules of the game of liberal democracy, although he differed with

liberal democrats on how far a democratic state could intervene in the economy. Bernstein rejected the dictatorship of the proletariat as a barbaric idea incompatible with democracy. He knew that workers needed allies, and he held that it would be counterproductive to adopt a philosophy that affirmed: "We want to help you to swallow the enemy, and right afterwards we shall swallow you." He maintained that "in our era there is almost complete assurance that the majority of a democratic community will not make laws which will permanently interfere with personal liberties." He recognized that "the majority of today may always become the minority of tomorrow." Mature democratic states respected minority rights.

Democracy—understood as popular rule and protection of basic rights—was crucial to Bernstein's political philosophy. Universal suffrage for workers was so crucial that Bernstein was willing to endorse using a general strike to obtain the ballot or guard it against attack. However, once real political democracy had been obtained, he felt, the political strike would become obsolete. Bernstein's political strategy rested on building a broad coalition of Socialist party members, trade unions, cooperatives, and radical bourgeoisie. Such a broad electoral base must rest on democratic principles, class cooperation, and mutual trust.

Bernstein also took issue with the Marxist view that the state is purely repressive. He held that under democratic auspices the state is capable of great accomplishments on behalf of working people. Bernstein would use a democratic suffrage to gain control of the state and then use its powers for democratic and socialist ends. This led him to conclude that the "withering away of the state" is a foolish, utopian idea.

Bernstein took issue with key aspects of Marx's economic analysis and adopted an economic philosophy that called for the coexistence of socialism and capitalism in a **mixed economy**, not for capitalism's complete destruction. The evidence had not persuaded Bernstein that capitalism was going to die, that the middle class was disappearing, or that the workers' lot was becoming ever more miserable. He noted the rising standard of living. He recognized the continued vitality and viability of capitalism—its economic strengths, changing character, and susceptibility to democratic reform. Bernstein wanted a more genuine socialist society, but he was content to move gradually toward public ownership and control of the commanding heights of the economy; to favor a mixed economy (partly public, partly private); to endorse government regulation where public ownership was not feasible; and to accept what we today call a welfare state, one that provides key social services for its citizens. Bernstein rejected the complete socialist revolution that meant the abolition of private property and the total destruction of the social privileges and the economic, political, and military power of the bourgeoisie.

He thus opted for the reformist posture of class cooperation on the peaceful road to socialism. He saw democracy as the "absence of class rule." Greater social and economic equality would come with key social policies such as nationalization of basic industries, social insurance, better housing, and food programs.

Fabian Roots—The **Fabians** were a group of intellectuals committed to the gradual achievement of socialism. Their numbers included such luminaries as George Bernard Shaw and H. G. Wells, as well as social scientists such as Sidney and Beatrice Webb. The Fabians were strongly motivated to overcome the injustices of modern industrial society. This ethical indignation unquestionably motivated their criticism of capitalism. Their investigation uncovered a host of problems involving working people and the maldistribution of wealth and social services. The Fabian Society, which came into being in 1883, grew out of an ethical society called the Fellowship of the True Life.

If the revisionists sought to revise Marx in a more liberal direction, the Fabians sought to revise British liberalism in a more radical direction. Convinced of the importance of constitutional and parliamentary government, the Fabians ad-

vocated a moderate, pragmatic nondoctrinaire variety of socialism to be achieved gradually, step by step. There was no need for violent revolution. Through their research, writing, and powers of persuasion, the Fabians sought to educate the leaders of the British middle and upper classes and to provide intellectual leadership for the emerging British Labour party, which was founded in 1901. They sought practical solutions for practical problems: public control of municipal transport, decent labor conditions in laundries, health regulations in the milk industry, and liquor licensing. Utilitarian, empirical, and hardheaded in their approach, Fabians sought to permeate liberalism with socialism. They constituted an influential lobby on behalf of social reform and planning. Municipal socialism would lead to government ownership of basic industries. Specific social and economic reforms would create a climate of opinion for broader reforms. Fabians called for reform of the educational system to eliminate social privilege and overcome social inequality. They would build new towns with better housing and amenities for workers.

Trade Union Roots—Democratic socialism is, of course, impossible without popular support. Working people provided the bulk of that mass support. One student of British socialism, C. A. R. Crosland, has emphasized the importance of the generous ideals of brotherhood, fellowship, service, and altruism in the Independent Labour party, which anticipated the modern British Labour party. Members were concerned with working people at the economic bottom of society. This concern for social justice appealed strongly to members of the labor movement. A similar concern, in addition to economic self-interest, motivated the millions of workers who joined trade unions and labor parties in other European countries.

In Britain the political role of workers and trade unions had received a setback with the defeat of the Chartist movement (1838–1848) for universal suffrage and other reforms. Leaders of the working class turned away from political action and began building a strong trade union movement. They did not return to politics for several decades. The Independent Labour party was not formed until 1893, and the present British Labour party not until 1901.

Once formed, the British Labour party, with strong trade union support, began building an electoral following. In several decades it came to challenge, and then replace, the Liberal party as the country's second major party. The British Labour party did not adopt a clearly socialist ideology until 1918, however. Trade unions remain a major source of strength of democratic socialism in Great Britain. Their battles for economic, political, and social reform have been central to democratic socialism.

Reformist Roots—No account of the roots and evolution of democratic socialism would be adequate if it ignored a miscellaneous group of reformers—from Jeremy Bentham and John Stuart Mill to R. H. Tawney, John Maynard Keynes, and William H. Beveridge—whose ideas and actions helped set the stage for democratic and socialist victories. Some reformers protested the adverse consequences of the Industrial Revolution, particularly its dreadful effects on workers. Some reformers maintained that laborers produced value and were not getting their fair share of what they produced. Some protested inequities in the way wealth was obtained and distributed. Some pressed for universal suffrage. Some argued on behalf of better working conditions and a shorter workday. Others advocated governmental intervention in the economy to counter depression. Reformers called for social services on behalf of the needy. They emphasized the importance of a better quality of life—a more attractive setting for work and play. They helped to radicalize elements of the middle class and to unite them with working-class people.

Slow Evolution

In concluding this examination of some of the roots of democratic socialism, we must emphasize again that it took a long time to bring together democratic socialist ideas and mass electoral support. For example, the first socialist party in Europe (the German Social Democratic party) was founded in 1875. And it was not until 1918 that the British Labour party become explicitly socialist. Even though, by 1914, socialism had become the most important political force on the European continent, no democratic socialist party came to power until after World War I. The German Social Democratic party came to power in 1918 and again in 1928, in the Weimar Republic. The British Labour party entered the government in 1924 and in 1929. In both Germany and Britain, they came to power briefly and with the support of other parties.

After World War I, circumstances were not favorable. The Bolshevik Revolution in Russia in 1917 created a revolutionary communist left that bitterly opposed (and was opposed by) democratic socialism. Economic depression, particularly severe after 1928 (the year the Great Depression began), afflicted all Europe. Germany suffered from the stigma of defeat, postwar insecurity, inflation, and unemployment. Nazism rallied the forces of the right against democratic socialism. During the depression, democratic socialists could not develop constructive ideas to cope with unemployment, depressed prices, falling profits, and inadequate income. Democratic socialist parties were wiped out by Mussolini in Italy, by Hitler in Germany, and by Dollfuss in Austria.

Before World War II, only one major European country, France, experienced a brief socialist success. In 1936 a democratic socialist party led by Leon Blum came to power in a coalition called The Popular Front. It succeeded in carrying out some significant reforms, often called a French New Deal. Trade unions were given collective bargaining rights; a social insurance system was established; a public works program was instituted to aid the unemployed; and workers' wages were raised in an effort to increase purchasing power and advance prosperity. Blum, however, was unable to carry out fuller economic planning, and his government collapsed after a few years in office. Democratic socialists had to wait until the 1980s to elect a president in France, become a more powerful party, and enact more socialist legislation.

Among the smaller European nations, Sweden had the earliest, most sustained success with socialism. The Swedish Social Democratic Workers' Party (founded in 1889, and since 1917 Sweden's largest party) first came to power in 1932. It adopted policies calling for government intervention in the economy and, by means of economic expansion, managed to wipe out unemployment by 1938. The innovative Swedes established policies that other countries have adopted. Sweden has perhaps the most advanced democratic socialist system in the world today. Its policies involve economic and social security, equal opportunity, full employment, extension of worker rights, national health insurance, and educational reform.

In general, however, and in the world's larger countries, democratic socialism is largely a post–World War II phenomenon. The British Labour party first came to power in its own right with a stunning victory in 1945, at the very end of the war. The Social Democratic party in West Germany emerged only after World War II, did not share power with the dominant Christian Democratic party until 1966, and became the dominant partner in a governmental coalition with the Free Democratic party in 1969. It wasn't until 1982

that the German Social Democrats fell from power. Democratic socialists came to power in Portugal and Spain after the post–World War II demise of dictatorships. Only in 1996 did the Democratic Socialists fall from power in Spain. In Greece the socialists gathered strength after World War II, exercised power under Prime Minister Andreas Papandreou from 1981 to 1989, and again returned to power in 1993. Because of illness, Papandreou was succeeded by another socialist, Konstantinos Simitis, in 1996.

Our examination of the roots and evolution of democratic socialism should help clarify its operative ideals.

THE OPERATIVE IDEALS OF DEMOCRATIC SOCIALISM

In this section we discuss changes that have occurred in democratic socialism, its guiding vision, and its cardinal operative ideals. The section ends with a look at how democratic socialism differs from liberal democracy and communism.

Continuity and Change

Democratic socialists remain committed to popular rule based on universal suffrage and parliamentary institutions, and to the protection of basic rights, including an opposition party's right to replace the governing party in a free election.

Goran Persson is prime minister of Sweden, a country that has been a leader in advancing the welfare state approach in the democratic socialist tradition.

They remain dedicated to the peaceful and gradual achievement of socialism as well as to a mixed economy and the welfare state.

Democratic socialists have, however, changed their position on extending public ownership to key aspects of economic life. They have also altered their stance on other issues. For example, they have been open to new tax and income policies as ways to a more equitable sharing of community wealth. They have explored alternative methods for enlarging workers' roles in economic enterprise. And they have investigated new policies for helping the needy and creating a cooperative community that enhances individual development and quality of life.

Guiding Vision and Cardinal Operative Ideals

Social justice remains the guiding vision for democratic socialists. A strong sense of "fair shares," especially for working people—a desire to more fairly distribute the common wealth, so that all people can develop their personalities—underlies the interrelated operative ideals of democratic socialism. These operative ideals include (1) a more generous extension of democracy; (2) public ownership of key aspects of the economy in the interest of public well-being; (3) a mixed economy—partly public, mostly private—that includes governmental intervention in, and regulation and control of, the economy on behalf of full employment, economic productivity, and prosperity; decent conditions of work; and a more equitable sharing of the common wealth; (4) a welfare state that provides social services to ensure better family life, health, and housing, protection against unemployment, and security in old age; (5) a strong concern for international freedom, unity, and peace; and (6) a strong emphasis on an improved quality of life in a more cooperative community.

Let us examine these operative ideals as they can be found at work in the British Labour party.

Extension of Democracy—Democratic socialists favor the extension of democracy in the political, economic, and social spheres. They adhere to

tenets of liberal democracy such as popular rule and protection of basic rights—the very basis for their gaining power. They thus fully accept the principles of parliamentary government, majority decision, and peaceful constitutional change. And here, of course, the British Labour party is not at odds with the British Conservative party. Questions of how far political democracy should be extended—for example, whether to abolish the British House of Lords—may point out a theoretical difference between some socialists and conservatives, but (except for left-wing members of the Labour party) this is not a burning issue in British politics.

Traditionally, democratic socialists have sought to advance the cause of economic democracy in a number of ways: by strengthening trade unions, passing laws to protect labor, advancing worker voice and control in industry, and encouraging cooperative societies. But there is no unanimous, single policy to expand economic democracy.

The extension of social democracy involves a continuing battle against social privilege, whether related to a snobbish and limiting educational system or to social inequalities produced by unearned wealth. The battle is for greater social equality, which fosters real equality of opportunity and individual fulfillment.

Public Ownership of Key Industries—Most British democratic socialists adhere to a belief in public ownership of key aspects of the economy, a traditional democratic socialist ideal. Although this ideal has been challenged in Britain by more "conservative" members of the British Labour party, most British socialists would not agree to denationalize key industries. And although most British socialists have either abandoned or ignored (if they ever believed in) the principles of full-scale, complete nationalization of all major industries, the rationale for public ownership of key industries still guides socialist thinking to a considerable extent.

The general rationale for "common ownership of the means of production, distribution, and exchange" (Clause IV of the British Labour party constitution) is that there should be collective enjoyment of the fruits of labor. The case is strongest in those industries at the commanding heights of the economy. Monopolistic, "sick," and strategic industries provide additional reasons for nationalization. Industries that are monopolies—public utilities such as railroads or electric companies—should be nationalized to serve the community. Industries that are vital to the economy but that have been "sick" in private hands (for example, coal) should also be nationalized. Other strategic industries (steel or aircraft) should be nationalized because of their intimate relationship to the economy or to national defense.

Mixed Economy—If a mixed economy—a combination of public and private ownership—makes sense, there is no good reason the government cannot intervene in the private sector, as well as in the public sector, to ensure a high level of employment, encourage productivity and prosperity, mandate wage and hour legislation and safe working conditions, and—through appropriate public policies—ensure a more equitable sharing of the wealth.

Democratic socialists who advocate a mixed economy are quite willing to let public enterprises compete with private enterprises in some areas. Such public enterprises can serve as a yardstick to measure the performance and profits of the private enterprise. Total control of the economy is less important than an economic system that enables people to work and that is productive, efficient, prosperous, and fair.

Welfare State—Democratic socialists are committed to a welfare state that provides a range of social services designed to ensure adequate income (for the needy), health care, housing, education, unemployment benefits, retirement benefits, and the like. These services, which also include accident insurance, death benefits, and maternity benefits, are part of a socialist plan for social security. They are intended to protect citizens, literally from the womb to the tomb, and to address the realities of poverty, unemployment, illness, a class system of education, poor housing, and old age.

International Unity, Freedom, and Peace—Democratic socialists have also been committed to the unity of all workers around the globe, to freedom from imperialism and colonialism, and to world peace. Here, however, nationalism and socialism have often been at odds. Yet the British Labour party in power after World War II (1945–1951, 1964–1970, and 1974–1979) did grant independence to a number of colonies, including India. Both Labour and Conservative governments in the first few decades after World War II perceived a Soviet threat to British security in Europe, so there was no significant difference between the parties on British participation in the North Atlantic Treaty Organization.

Quality of Life—Democracy, public ownership of the means of production, government regulation, the welfare state, and international unity and peace are designed to enhance the quality of life in a more cooperative community. Democratic socialists are thus concerned with greater equality of individuals on the one hand and greater quality of life on the other. These socialist ideas have roots in the egalitarian, libertarian, and aesthetic traditions of socialism. Socialists have attacked privilege and favored education reforms to open doors formerly closed to individual fulfillment. They have favored greater intellectual and moral freedom and a relaxation of harsh societal restraints. They have sought to overcome social barriers and to bring people closer together. These concerns—only partly fulfilled by current attention to the aesthetics of new towns and to support of the arts—are gaining prominence in the thinking of socialist critics who look beyond material fulfillment toward a world of greater aesthetic and spiritual attractiveness.

Out of office in the 1980s and most of the 1990s, the British Labour party has been split on issues involving nuclear disarmament, British participation in the European Union, and nationalization policies. The end of the Cold War, a more moderate and pragmatic Labour Party leadership, and the real possibility of a Labour Party return to power may serve to bring the Labour party's left and right wings closer together. How a new Labour party government will interpret its operative ideals in power remains to be seen. The likelihood is strong that a Labour party government will move, as the Labour party leader Tony Blair has indicated, in a more moderate direction, even favoring such ideas as controls on public spending, lower taxes, and free trade.

Democratic Socialism, Liberal Democracy, and Communism

The operative ideals of democratic socialism raise the question of how democratic socialism today differs from liberal democracy or from communism.

Politically, there are no essential disagreements between democratic socialists and liberal democrats. They both believe in free elections, a two-party or multiparty system, majority rule, parliamentary governance, the protection of basic rights, and the opposition's right to come to power peacefully and constitutionally. Both these ideologies differ on all these points from communism as practiced, for example, in China, North Korea, and Cuba.

Economically, democratic socialists and liberal democrats differ on the extent to which democracy, public ownership, government regulation, and the welfare state should be pushed. Democratic socialists are generally more persuaded of the need for greater industrial democracy, more public ownership, fuller governmental intervention in the economy, and a more generous welfare state. But the difference is only a matter of degree. Left-wing liberal democrats and right-wing democratic socialists are often closer to each other than they are to those on the right or left of their own camps. Democratic socialists tend to be more sympathetic to equality of results, and liberal democrats to equality of

opportunity. Democratic socialists tend to favor a greater transfer of community wealth toward working people.

Democratic socialists, in contrast to orthodox communists, usually reject complete national or public ownership of the means of production and exchange. They are more favorably disposed to an economy that mixes public and private ownership. They are willing to leave in private hands much of the capitalist economy: agriculture, most small-scale industries, and almost all retail business. Some democratic socialists even make a strong case for what they call "market socialism."

VARIATIONS ON THE DEMOCRATIC SOCIALIST THEME

Generally, adherents of the democratic socialist left would push more vigorously to achieve social justice, advance industrial democracy, extend public ownership, and expand social services. They seek to diminish the income gap and to create a more cooperative community. Suspicious of nuclear weapons, they favor forthright initiatives for peace, including—sometimes—a call for unilateral nuclear disarmament.

Members of the democratic socialist right, on the other hand, while still committed to greater social justice and a more egalitarian society, take a more conservative stance. They are hesitant about extending public ownership and public services. They recognize that they lack overwhelming popular support, even when they are victorious at the polls and are able to form a government; consequently, they are sensitive to the danger of alienating middle-class support. Members of the democratic socialist right are also more convinced of the virtues of a mixed economy and less apt to press for nuclear disarmament. They may place a higher priority on improving the cultural quality of life than do their colleagues on the left.

Generally, democratic socialist parties tend to be more radical and innovative when they are out of power. This seemingly derives from pragmatic recognition: When they hold power, they cannot risk losing middle-class support for their programs.

To assess variations, let us now examine a few European countries with strong democratic socialist parties.

A democratic socialist party has ruled in Sweden for a longer period than anywhere else in the world. In 1991 the party was ousted from power, only to return in 1994. Several features of Sweden's socialist program are noteworthy. First, socialist cooperatives play a large part in the economy, handling 30 percent of Sweden's retail trade and 10 percent of its wholesale trade. Second, public and private enterprises compete in fields such as housing, logging, mining, power, and transport. State-owned monopolies include radio networks and liquor and tobacco sales. Sweden has been praised as illustrating a "middle way" between capitalism and communism; at the same time it has been blamed for creating an overregulated, drab, and highly taxed society.

West German socialism provides an interesting comparison to democratic socialism in Britain. In the Bad Godesberg declaration of 1959, the German Social Democratic party (SPD) outlined a position on the relation of public and private sectors in the economy that revealed how far the party had come from more rigidly ideological patterns of the past. The SPD stated that private ownership of the means of production was entitled to "protection and promotion" as long as it did not hinder an equitable social order. The German Social Democrats rejected the "idea of subjecting the entire economy to central planning." They accepted "the free market" wherever "there is real competition." They enunciated their basic formula as follows: "As much competition as possible—as much planning as necessary."

In Germany, certain basic industries are nationalized—railroads, air transport, and public utilities such as electricity, gas, and municipal buses. The government has a strong role in certain other basic industries, particularly coal and steel, and a significant role in the Volkswagen auto works. **Codetermination** (that is, worker representation on the directing board of industrial firms) gives workers a modest voice in setting company policy. The government plays a strong role in maintaining employment and prosperity by using various fiscal and monetary tools

Willy Brandt (1913–1992) shown at Berlin's Brandenburg Gate. Social Democratic chancellor of West Germany from 1969 to 1974, Brandt received the Nobel Peace Prize in 1971 for his efforts to reduce tensions between Communist and non-Communist nations.

to speed up or slow down the economy. A wide range of social services are available to help the unemployed and retirees and to provide medical care, housing, and other benefits. Agriculture, in Germany as in Great Britain, is still in private hands.

The French Socialists came to power in 1981 after many years in the political wilderness. The French elected Socialist Francois Mitterrand president of the Republic for a seven-year term. He was reelected in 1988, this time by an even larger percentage of the popular vote. In 1981 the French electorate also gave the Socialist party a majority in the Chamber of Deputies. Pursuant to their electoral campaign promises, the French Socialists nationalized additional business enterprises and virtually all banks, reduced the work week to thirty-nine hours, decreed a five-week paid vacation for workers, and decentralized parts of the French bureaucracy. However, the socialist experiment was halted in 1986 when Socialists lost support and when certain industries, banks, and insurance companies were denationalized. In 1987 three television stations were privatized. The trend away from democratic socialist leaders and policies continued with the election of Jacques Chirac in 1995 as president of France. Currently, Alain Juppe, a member of Chirac's R.P.R. (Rally for the Republic) party, is prime minister, and the R.P.R. party with its allies controls a majority in the French parliament.

DEMOCRATIC SOCIALISM AS POLITICAL IDEOLOGY: PRO AND CON

This section outlines both attacks on democratic socialism and its supporters' defense, then assesses its strengths and weaknesses.

The Attack on Democratic Socialism

Critics of democratic socialism attack it from several directions. Some argue that sooner or later socialism will lead to the loss of liberty. They insist that democratic socialism is a contradiction in terms. Socialism, they maintain, gives the government too much power, and such great

power is the enemy of liberty. These critics associate private enterprise with freedom and see limitations on private enterprise as destroying freedom. They also argue that socialism is inefficient and that it crushes incentive, daring, and flexibility. Production is bound to lag in socialized enterprises. Services are bound to deteriorate. Socialism is bound to fail because it kills the goose (capitalism) that lays the golden egg (a prosperous economy). Furthermore, by interfering in the market economy, socialism does not allow full consumer choice in the marketplace.

Orthodox communists may attack democratic socialism from another perspective. They contend that by coexisting with capitalism, democratic socialists have failed to carry out the revolution. Socialist values can be achieved only if capitalist power—economic, political, and social—is destroyed. Under democratic socialism workers cannot be emancipated, and the fruits of collective labor cannot be fairly shared. Bourgeois power, values, and policies will still prevail under democratic socialism. It is the case, however (as we learned in Chapter 7) that China's Communist rulers have adopted a more pragmatic attitude toward the economy—one more favorable to limited private enterprise and a limited market economy.

Left-wing democratic socialists tend to criticize the practices of moderate democratic socialists as too timid. Although these critics do not endorse an orthodox communist perspective, they do insist that ruling democratic socialist parties have not gone as far as they should and can go.

The Defense of Democratic Socialism

Defenders of democratic socialism argue that it offers a sane middle ground between capitalism and communism. They insist that freedom and economic well-being can come together under democratic socialism. They note that democratic socialist programs have overcome the worst abuses of an unregulated capitalism, have transferred wealth to workers and the needy, and have made life more attractive for the mass of people.

The Strengths and Weaknesses of Democratic Socialism

Democratic socialism has many strengths:

1. It is a brave attempt to advance social justice for those who have traditionally been the least free in society (workers and the needy), especially through the services offered by a socialist welfare state.
2. It is a constructive effort to eliminate the worst consequences of industrialization and to control a wide range of capitalist abuses of power.
3. It has pushed for a more genuinely democratic society in all spheres of modern life (industry, politics, and society) through a strong trade union movement, a labor party, and social legislation in fields such as education.
4. It has advanced the principle of fair shares by modestly redistributing wealth in the direction of a more egalitarian society.
5. It still holds up before all humankind a vision of international freedom, unity, and peace.

Democratic socialism also has its weaknesses:

1. The experience of regimes in power suggests that there are limits on how far democratic socialists can move toward their vision of social justice—of greater democracy, equality, and social welfare. Spending for generous health, retirement, unemployment, and other benefits produces budget deficits and conservative cries for the reduction of such benefits.
2. Democratic socialists have not been able to overcome many of the problems of modern industrial society: recession or depression, business failures, unemployment, and loss of worker income and management profits; troublesome inflation; declining productivity (and loss of competitiveness) in many segments of the economy; and worker alienation and social malaise.
3. Democratic socialists are still struggling with the problems of bureaucracy that plague all large governments, socialist and nonsocialist alike.
4. Democratic socialists face a political dilemma: If they are too radical, they will lose, or not gain, power; if they are not radical enough, they will be indistinguishable from their liberal democratic opponents.
5. Democratic socialists have been no more successful than nonsocialists in achieving their dreams of world peace and brotherhood, of justice and prosperity for the world's least free, of clean air and pure water, and of a global society with a superior quality of life.

Democratic Socialism in the United States

Why has democratic socialism never been a major force in American national politics?[6] Several answers, some of which highlight the uniqueness of the American experience, suggest themselves. For example, some scholars highlight the influence of America's rich natural endowment, its open and beckoning frontier, its strong egalitarian tradition, the absence of an entrenched aristocracy or rigid class structure as explanatory factors. They note that these factors created relatively good opportunities for economic advance and social recognition. Other scholars call attention to the operation of majority rule and a presidential election system as factors that mitigated against minority (here democratic socialist) candidates and parties; to the existence of a moderate American labor movement; and to significant liberal democratic reforms (such as the New Deal) that stole the thunder of the democratic socialists in the United States.

CONCLUSION

Even if not a political force in the United States, democratic socialist parties are a powerful influence in Europe and elsewhere in the world. The values of social justice, greater democracy, public ownership, a mixed economy, a welfare state, a cooperative community, international freedom, unity, peace, and excellence have a deep hold on modern voters in Europe—and, indeed, on other peoples throughout the world. The democratic socialist commitment to democracy links it to liberal democracy. Its commitment to public ownership links it, in part, to communism. From the perspective of a liberal democrat attuned to capitalism, democratic socialists go too far in the economic sphere; from the perspective of orthodox Communists, they do not go far enough. But have they struck the right middle ground in their understanding of the good political life?

Given their relatively short tenure in power, mostly since World War II, it is often difficult to compare their professed values with their actual behavior. In general, however, democratic socialists have remained true to political democracy. They have modestly moved in the direction of greater social justice and a more equitable distribution of wealth. They seem to have accepted a socialist version of the welfare state and the mixed economy, and to have backed away from more complete nationalization or public ownership. Through educational reform, they have attempted to enlarge opportunities for the less privileged. But they have not been able to overcome (though they have managed to alleviate) a number of key economic problems of modern industrial society: periodic recession or depression, persistent unemployment (particularly among those at the low end of the economic and social ladder), worker alienation. The golden dream of industrial democracy in a cooperative society has not been fulfilled. Nor have dreams of international freedom, unity, and peace.

Yet democratic socialists have unquestionably made life better for working people and the needy. They have helped tame and harness modern capitalism. And they have kept the costs reasonable.

Nonetheless, they still face a dilemma in fulfilling their historic mission. If they are too radical, they will frighten off the middle-class support they need for gaining and wielding power. If they are too conservative, their philosophy and programs will be indistinguishable from those of their political rivals. Moreover, democratic socialists face the same problem that liberal democrats face: how to deal with an industrial society characterized by periodic recession, serious unemployment, painful disparities of income (particularly between the rich and poor), worker alienation, environmental pollution, urban malaise, crime, and materialistic values, and strains on the national budget. Democratic socialists must still develop effective, humane ways to advance social justice, democracy, the satisfaction of human needs, a cooperative community, and human excellence.

Which of the political outlooks we have considered thus far—liberal democracy, communism, and democratic socialism—appeals most to the developing countries of Asia, Africa, and Latin America? Are these nations developing political ideologies that are suited to their own histories and conditions? And what of other ideologies—past, present, and future? We turn to these questions as we round out Part II of this volume and our exploration of the search for the good political life.

ANNOTATED BIBLIOGRAPHY

Braunthal, Gerard. *The West German Social Democrats, 1969–1982: Profile of a Party in Power.* Boulder, Colo.: Westview Press, 1983. Offers an able review of a resourceful social democratic party, whose pragmatic tactics and popular appeal will be tested in future German elections. See also his update in *Parties and Politics in Modern Germany* (1996).

Cole, G. D. H. *A History of Socialist Thought.* 5 vols. New York: St. Martin's Press, 1953–1960. Presents the richest, most comprehensive account of the roots and evolution of socialism.

Cunningham, Frank. *Democratic Theory and Socialism.* Cambridge: Cambridge University Press, 1987. Seeks to make a case for the desirability and feasibility of democratic socialism. Sees socialism as necessary to make possible and preserve democratic advances; criticizes capitalism because it severely restricts democracy; holds that democracy expands human freedom.

Dunn, John. *The Politics of Socialism: An Essay in Political Theory.* Cambridge: Cambridge University Press, 1984. Critiques the normative, empirical, and prudential understanding of democratic socialism, in theory and practice. Reflects disappointment with British socialism on the part of the author, who is sympathetic to a rational "true socialism."

Einhorn, Eric S., and Logue, John. *Modern Welfare States: Politics and Policy in Social Democratic Scandinavia.* New York: Praeger, 1989. Sheds up-to-date light on some classic democratic socialist regimes and their problems.

Gay, Peter. *The Dilemma of Democratic Socialism: Eduard Bernstein's Challenge to Marx.* New York: Collier-Macmillan, 1962. Provides an illuminating study of one of the most important revisionists and democratic socialists.

Hamilton, Malcolm. *Democratic Socialism in Britain and Sweden.* London: Macmillan, 1988. Presents a helpful comparison of the two systems.

Hancock, M. Donald, Conradt, David P., Peters, B. Guy, Safran, William, and Zariski, Raphael. *Politics in Western Europe,* 2nd ed. Chatham, N.J.: Chatham House Publishers, 1997. Provides comparative perspective on the role of social democratic parties in the United Kingdom, France, Germany, and Sweden.

Harrington, Michael. *Socialism.* New York: Bantam, 1973. Attempts to relate Marxism to the modern world. Favors the democratization of economic, social, and political power. Seeks to distinguish between an authentic and a spurious socialism. Opts for a socialist alternative to communism and the welfare state. See also Harrington's *The Twilight of Capitalism* (New York: Simon & Schuster, 1976) and *The Politics at God's Funeral: The Spiritual Crisis of Western Civilization* (New York: Holt, Rinehart & Winston, 1983).

Lipsey, David, and Leonard, Dick, eds. *The Socialist Agenda: Crosland's Legacy.* London: Jonathan Cape, 1981. Describes the British democratic socialist as half priest and half plumber: concerned with ethical values (equality and poverty) and with techniques of social change and economic modernization (redistributive taxation and nationalization).

Schwartz, Joseph M. *The Permanence of the Political: A Democratic Critique of the Radical Impulse to Transcend Politics.* Princeton, N.J.: Princeton University Press, 1995. Seeks to "liberalize" the radical tradition of democratic socialism and "democratize"

liberalism. Favors a more sensible political democratic socialism that would appreciate compromise and consensus as well as conflict.

Sinder, David. *Is Socialism Doomed?* Oxford: Oxford University Press, 1988. May be profitably read by those who are skeptical of the reforming efforts of communists.

Tilton, Timothy A. *The Political Theory of Swedish Social Democracy.* Oxford: Oxford University Press, 1989. Provides information for those seeking to probe more deeply the Swedish variety of democratic socialism.

SUGGESTIONS FOR FURTHER READING

Bernstein, Eduard. *Evolutionary Socialism.* New York: Schocken, 1961.

Bobbio, Norberto. *Which Socialism?: Marxism, Socialism and Democracy.* Minneapolis: University of Minnesota Press, 1987.

Bronner, Stephen E. *Socialism Unbound.* New York: Routledge, 1990.

Butler, Anthony. *Transformative Politics: The Future of Socialism in Western Europe.* London: Macmillan, 1995.

Christopherson, Thomas R. *The French Socialist in Power, 1981–1986.* Newark: University of Delaware Press, 1991.

Crick, Bernard. *Socialism.* Minneapolis: University of Minnesota Press, 1987.

Dixon, Keith. *The Moral Basis of Democratic Socialism.* London: Routledge & Kegan Paul, 1986.

Dorrien, Gary J. *The Democratic Socialist Vision.* Totowa, N.J.: Rowman & Littlefield, 1986.

Hamilton, Malcolm B. *Democratic Socialism in Britain and Sweden.* New York: St. Martin's, 1989.

Macridis, Roy C. *Modern Political Systems: Europe,* 7th ed. Englewood Cliffs, N.J.: Prentice-Hall, 1990.

Markovits, Andrei S., and Gorski, Philip S. *The German Left: Red, Green and Beyond.* New York: Oxford University Press, 1993.

Markovits, Andrei S., Abraham, David, Goldman, Guido G., Katzenstein, Peter J., Lankowski, Carl F., Maier, Charles J., Riemer, Jeremiah M., and Semmler, Willi. *The Political Economy of West Germany: Modell Deutschland.* New York: Praeger, 1982.

Milner, Henry. *Sweden: Social Democracy in Practice.* New York: Oxford University Press, 1989.

Owen, David. *Market, State, and Community: Theoretical Foundations of Market Socialism.* Oxford: Clarendon Press, 1989.

GLOSSARY TERMS

codetermination
cooperative movement
democratic socialism
Fabians

mixed economy
revisionists
utopia
utopian socialists
welfare state

ALTERNATIVE POLITICAL PHILOSOPHIES AND IDEOLOGIES

IN PART II OF THIS BOOK, we have been exploring the good political life. We have reviewed the perspectives of the great political philosophers on the "great issues" of politics. To investigate such political ideologies as liberal democracy, communism, and democratic socialism, we have focused on the operative ideals of the United States, China, and Great Britain.

In this chapter, we address some challenges to the dominant political ideologies in the democratic and communist worlds. We first turn to a past challenge, fascism, and its most virulent form, nazism. We then turn to a current challenge in what has often been called the Third World: the developing, and often poor, nations in Asia, Africa, and Latin America. Finally, we turn to a future challenge: that posed by a diverse group of political futurists who call for a world order that will enable human beings to live sanely and humanely in the twenty-first century.

Our central question is, *How do fascism, Third World ideology, and the political philosophy of the futurists challenge dominant political ideologies such as liberal democracy, communism, and democratic socialism?*

THE NAZI VARIETY OF FASCISM

Fascism is the general term used to describe a totalitarian or authoritarian political ideology characterized by dictatorial leadership, an oppressive one-party system, glorification of the nation-state and its people, aggressive militarism, and political, economic, and social policies designed (allegedly) to overcome the weaknesses of liberal democracy, the threat of anarchy, and the fear of communism. The term *fascism* first came into prominence when used by the Fascist party, organized by Benito Mussolini, that ruled Italy from 1922 until Mussolini's defeat in World

War II. **Nazism,** as we shall see in this chapter, is the particularly virulent racist, anti-Semitic, militantly aggressive variety of fascism that characterized Germany under Adolf Hitler's dictatorship.

Why study nazism—a dead, discredited political ideology that held power for only twelve years, from 1933 to 1945? There are several reasons. First, nazism had a catastrophic impact on Europe and the world. Hitler's Germany brought on World War II and its enormous costs in death and destruction. The Nazis destroyed German democracy and aggressively attacked neighboring countries. The Nazis barbarically exterminated millions of innocent Jews in the Holocaust. The Nazis threatened to annihilate modern civilization. They opened the door to Soviet Communist power in Eastern Europe. For twelve nightmarish years German power, guided by the insane Nazi ideology, was a mortal enemy of peace, social and political justice, human rights, economic well-being, and human decency.

Second, nazism posed a mortal challenge to liberal democracy, democratic socialism, and communism. For twelve years it destroyed those outlooks in Germany, in all areas under its control, and almost throughout Europe. How could this have come about? And what lessons can be learned from a critical examination of nazism?

Third, a study of nazism may shed light on neofascism and right-wing authoritarianism. Although it does not appear that nazism could regain control of a major state in the contemporary world, many thoughtful, civilized people believed that nazism could not arise in the first place. Elements of fascism, and of nazism, still remain. Neo-Nazis have blatantly attacked and even killed "foreigners" in Germany. Outbursts of anti-Semitism still mar a number of European countries. Moreover, authoritarian regimes on the right side of the political spectrum still prevail in the world. Thus, a study of nazism may illuminate the political ideology of right-wing groups and regimes that play an important role in modern politics.

Historical Roots and Evolution of Nazism

Nazism was not a coherent, comprehensive, rational ideology. There was no political philosopher for the Nazis as there was a Marx for communists or a Locke, Madison, or Mill for liberal democrats or a Bernstein for democratic socialists. Moreover, the Nazis were highly opportunistic and did not hesitate to shift their principles or stance on policies. Nonetheless, key ideas did influence their outlook and behavior, and these ideas have roots and an evolution.

Nazism's roots include racism, anti-Semitism, elitism, totalitarianism, nationalism, socialism, militarism, economic autarky, and the "might makes right" doctrine.

The Racial and Anti-Semitic Roots—Belief in racial superiority is a major root of Nazi ideology. This belief is expressed in several ways and finds its most murderous manifestation in **anti-Semitism.** Johann Gottlieb Fichte (1762–1814) in his *Address to the German People* (1808) preached the superiority of the German people in an effort to awaken their nationalistic instincts. A Frenchman, Count Joseph Arthur Gobineau (1816–1882), argued on behalf of the supremacy of the white race (and of the Teutons within that race). An Englishman, Houston Stewart Chamberlain (1855–1927), conceived the folk-nation, the German nation, "destined to triumph because of its superior genetic gifts."[1] Not only were certain races considered superior (the white race), but other races (the black race or the yellow race) were considered inferior. And, of course, there was a hierarchy within the white race, with Germans at the top and (depending on the writer) groups like the Slavs at the bottom.

Anti-Semitism was an important part of the racial myth, with deep roots in a perverted interpretation of Christian teaching. It was reinforced by the variety of racism that made the so-called Aryan race the pure and superior one, and by social and economic hostility toward a religious group that was different. Such hostility manifested itself in false charges and cruel attacks on Jews.

The Elitist and Leadership Roots—The call for a truthful and righteous leader has, of course, deep roots in the Judeo-Christian tradition and in Greek philosophy. But the Judeo-Christian tradition also warned against false prophets and false messiahs. Although Aristotle personally preferred monarchy (rule by one virtuous man) or aristocracy (rule by the wise few), he rejected Plato's philosopher-kings and opted for polity, or constitutional democracy (see Chapter 5). Nonetheless, the cry for an elite leadership continued to echo in European and German thought. Johann Gottfried Herder (1744–1803) saw the Germans as the ruling elite in Europe. The influential German philosopher Georg Hegel (1770–1831) was impressed by Napoleon and other "world-historical" individuals. Friedrich Nietzsche (1844–1900) looked to a race of supermen. And the Social Darwinists (who applied Darwin's ideas about the struggle for existence to society and politics) envisioned the leader as an example of the survival of the fittest. It is, of course, a mistake to see Nietzsche or Hegel or other elitists as Nazis; often their ideas were misconstrued or misused. Nonetheless, their contributions to the mythology of an elite and of a leader remain part of a falsely aristocratic heritage from which fascism, and especially nazism, drew.

The Totalitarian Roots—The totalitarian state, as approximated in Nazi Germany, became possible only with the advent of modern means of controlling mind and body. Yet the idea of a state that promotes its own engulfing claims against the freedom of the individual has older roots. Although elements of a closed society are found in Plato's *Republic*, it was not until the idea of sovereignty emerged, with the modern nation-state, that the totalitarian state became a theoretical possibility. Modern **totalitarianism** calls for the destruction of all limits on state power. Not God nor religion nor natural law nor the constitution can limit the state's powers. When these limits are destroyed, the totalitarian state becomes a reality, in theory and practice.

Our modern understanding of sovereign power was first crystallized by the Frenchman Jean Bodin (1530–1596), who defined **sovereignty** as supreme power over all, unrestrained by law.[2] Bodin saw in sovereignty a weapon to protect nations against civil war. Englishman Thomas Hobbes, in his *Leviathan* (1651), also saw no theoretical or practical limits on sovereign power. Neither, of course, advocated a modern totalitarian state, but both underscored the cry for order that made the masterful sovereign state so appealing. All those who exalt the state, who fight against an open society, and who would limit reason and freedom make the totalitarian state possible. Some critics note that Hegel contributed to the idea of the all-powerful state. Paul M. Hayes, in his study of fascism, wrote: "Hegel saw the state as an organism free from moral obligation, the enemy of all other states, committed to warfare against other states and subject only to the test of success."

The Nationalist Roots—Nationalism, of course, can be used for good or evil. In the nineteenth century, **nationalism** was mainly a movement for national freedom and independence; it was an effort to achieve political, economic, and social freedom. However, as **ultranationalism,** it could become divorced from freedom. Ultranationalism leads to the denial of freedom for minority ethnic groups within a nation or to aggression against other nations. Those who preach ultranationalist ideas such as "my country right or wrong" help prepare the way for fascism. Clearly, not all nationalists were, or are, fascists, but all fascists must be nationalists. The Nazis fed on national pride and honor. They fed on the resentment that grew out of Germany's defeat in World War I and its national weakness in the 1920s. They fed on the passion to vindicate German strength and respect. They certainly capitalized on nationalism by branding their political enemies as being opposed to the true interests of the German nation. They condemned liberal cosmopolitans as decadent. They castigated communists as belonging to an international conspiracy, subservient to the Soviet Union. They attacked Jews as alien and subversive. The totalitarian nature of the Nazi state rested on belief in the national state as the instrument for achieving totalitarian objectives. The Nazi state also easily incorporated racial ideas of the *Volk,* or people, into its nationalist outlook.

The Socialist Roots—The Nazis called themselves National Socialists. Benito Mussolini (1883–1945) was a socialist before becoming a fascist and Italy's dictator (1922–1945). Sir Oswald Mosley (1896–1980) in England and Marcel Deat (1894–1955) in France were also socialists who later turned to fascism. Jacques Doriot (1898–1945) was a leading member of the French Communist party before leaving it to join the French fascists. Clearly, there was considerable hostility to capitalism among fascists, and this hostility was not confined to renegade socialists.

As early as 1920, the infant Nazi party "included a number of statements of intent that might generally be regarded as impeccably socialist in origin. Among these were the nationalization of major industries and industrial combines, the abolition of unearned income, profiteering, and speculation, the provision of equal opportunity in education and employment, the institution of workers' shops, acknowledgment of the right to work and encouragement of work in the communal interest."[3]

The fact that the Nazis did not deliver on these early party planks is less important than the fact that their initial bias was hostile to big business and its abuses and that the Nazis deliberately sought to appeal to workers. They named their party the National Socialist German Worker's party. When in power, the Nazis, like fascists elsewhere, did not destroy private property, even if they did regulate and control capitalistic enterprises and the economy.

The Militarist Roots—The glorification of the military and of military virtues has clear roots in German history, particularly Prussian history. This glorification placed a halo over war. Thus,

University of Berlin professor of history Heinrich von Treitschke (1834–1896) wrote that although the "superficial observer" saw war as "brutal and inhumane," it was really a "moral force," justified by "the great patriotic idea." The literary philosopher Nietzsche wrote, "Ye have heard men say: Blessed be the peacemakers; but I say unto you: Blessed are the warmakers, for they shall be called, if not the children of Jahwe, the children of Odin, who is greater than Jahwe." And: "Do ye say that a good cause halloweth even war? I say to you a good war halloweth any cause." And the official organ of the German army declared in 1932: "War has become a form of existence with equal rights with peace. Every human and social activity is justified only if it helps prepare for war."

The Autarkic Roots—The economic theories of nazism spring from **autarky,** a doctrine of self-sufficiency that calls for protecting a nation against interfering economic activity by other nations. Autarky favors protectionism rather than free trade. It calls for national regulation to ensure prosperity, access to vital resources, and a strong army. Power must be concentrated in the hands of the state to help it achieve self-sufficiency.

The "Might Makes Right" Doctrine—Long before the Nazis came to power, the ideological forerunners of nazism maintained that "the ordinary concepts of law, natural right and morality could not apply within the organic state." According to Paul M. Hayes, the "search for the heroic leader, militarist glory and economic autarky left no place for individual rights or free will." As we saw in Chapter 5, Machiavelli opened the door for immoral actions in defense of the state. Frederick the Great (1712–1786) frankly expressed the philosophy of *Machpolitik*—the politics of might or power politics. He said that it is "good policy to be . . . perfectly persuaded that we have a right to everything that suits us. . . . I mean by the word *policy* that we must always try to dupe other people. . . . Do not make the mistake of not breaking [alliances] when you believe that your interest requires [such action]. Uphold the maxim that to despoil your neighbours is to deprive them of the means of injuring you."

German historian Heinrich von Treitschke was attracted to Machiavelli's doctrine of the need to sacrifice right and virtue in the interest of national power. Nietzsche, himself no lover of the state and someone who would probably have been disgusted by the Nazis, nonetheless articulated ideas of sacrifice, the will to power, and the rule of the strong that the Nazis found attractive. Oswald Spengler (1880–1936), another German historian, echoed Machiavelli. Spengler wrote that history "knows only the success which turns the law of the stronger into the law of all." The legacy extracted from these writers by the Nazis, according to Hayes, was that no "aggression, no maltreatment, no misrepresentation was invalid if it advanced the cause of force and might" of the nation.

The Operative Ideals of Nazism

Nazism never gave its followers a rational, comprehensive, political ideology. The Nazis were opportunistic and shifted ground in the course of their struggle to gain power, so it is not easy to compile a list of consistent Nazi principles. Yet many of the ideas expressed in Hitler's *Mein Kampf* were put into practice—with catastrophic effect. Thus, we can identify five major operative ideals around which to organize our presentation of Nazi principles and behavior. With modifications and exceptions, these five operative ideals also hold for fascism in general. Nazism's guiding principles include (1) glorification of the authoritarian nation-state, (2) strong dictatorial leadership, (3) racial superiority and anti-Semitism, (4) totalitarian enforcement of conformity, and (5) imperialism, war, and destruction.

The Glorification of the Authoritarian Nation-State— The Nazis articulated a mystical concept of the **nation-state**; for them the German state embodied the good political life. The state expressed the unity, community, power, superiority, virtue, and civilization of the German people. The success of the German nation-state exemplified the survival of the fittest. Only through such a state could the German people find fulfillment. The motto *Deutschland über alles*—"Germany above all else"—expressed this belief.

Mussolini—who led the first major fascist revolt against liberal democracy, democratic socialism, communism, pacifism, and cosmopolitanism—would agree with this assessment, as long as he could substitute Italy for Germany and Italian for German.

Strong Dictatorial Leadership—The Nazis in Germany, like the Fascists in Italy, emphatically endorsed the principle of elite leadership, embodied in a single authoritarian party and culminating in *der Führer,* the Leader. (In Italy, of course, Mussolini was *Il Duce,* the Chief, or the Leader.) This idea illustrates the perverse fulfillment of the great man theory. The Nazis emphasized the importance of the leadership principle (*Führerprinzip*) by which the right goals, principles, direction, and discipline could be achieved. All looked to der Führer, who embodied the rightful will of the nation.

All Germans had to give their obedience to Hitler. The subleadership of the Nazi elite could, in turn, demand obedience from those under their orders. Hitler had articulated these ideas early in *Mein Kampf* ("My Struggle"): "The principle which made the Prussian army in its time into the most wonderful instrument of the German people must some day . . . become the principle of the construction of our whole state conception: authority of every leader downward and responsibility upward." Responsibility "can and may be borne only by one man, and therefore he alone may possess the authority and right to command."

Racial Superiority and Anti-Semitism—The Nazis made racial superiority and anti-Semitism—and their monstrous consequence, genocide—into a fanatical dogma. They had scientific trouble in identifying the Aryans, or Nordics, who were to be the superior people (Volk), but they never doubted that the Jews were inferior. The virulent anti-Semitism of the Nazis was at first translated into a denial of rights. German citizens of Jewish faith and sometimes of Jewish ancestry were dismissed from government jobs, from teaching, and from other professions. Their property was taken away. Their synagogues were destroyed. They were arrested and imprisoned in concentration camps. In time, the anti-Semitic campaign was extended to all countries that came under Nazi control in World War II and resulted in the dreadful "final solution" of the "Jewish question"—the Holocaust and the extermination of 6 million Jews. Other so-called racially inferior groups—gypsies, the mentally ill, "slave laborers" from Slavic countries—were also treated barbarically. The objective of Nazi ideology and policy was a "pure" German people—tall, blond and blue-eyed—who would dominate Europe militarily, politically, economically, and culturally.

Racism was a feature, but not a prominent one, of Italian Fascism; only belatedly, in the late 1930s, did Mussolini attempt to make anti-Semitism a part of the Italian program. In other European fascist regimes, especially those influenced by, or under the control of, the Nazis, anti-Semitism played an important role.

Totalitarian Enforcement of Conformity at Home— To pursue their objective of a dominant German Volk—free of Jewish, communist, liberal, and cosmopolitan "corruptions"—the Nazis required conformity to Nazi political, economic, and social ideology within Germany. The Nazis used both force and craft, carrot and stick in their effort to control key aspects of German life.

Total political domination was a primary objective. Only one political party—the Nazi party—was to operate in Germany. Other parties were abolished. Political opponents were killed, jailed, or driven into exile. Opposing political ideas—in the press, schools, trade unions, the military, and business—were suppressed. Elec-

tions became endorsements of the Führer's will.

Directly or indirectly, the state sought to control the social system and the economic system to buttress its political power. No independent source of political power—in religion, among labor unions, in the military, or in the business community—was tolerated. Hitler signed a Concordat (treaty) with the Catholic Church (never fully honored on either side) which stipulated that, in return for internal religious freedom, the Church would remain silent on political matters. Protestant churches were generally bullied into submission or silence or ineffective resistance. Military support was secured with the bait of great power and glory. German soldiers were required to take a personal oath of loyalty to Hitler. Thus, the independent judgment of German generals and the conscience of ordinary soldiers were severely compromised. The Nazis destroyed or took over the trade unions. Workers lost their bargaining power, particularly the right to strike, and their political independence. In return for job security, they were expected to be loyal and obedient. Industrialists were seduced with the lure of profits from rearmament and economic prosperity. The price they paid for their conformity to Nazi economic plans was, again, a loss of independent political power. Private property was not expropriated but, rather, controlled in the interest of building a self-sufficient economy geared to war. Agriculture received a special status in Nazi propaganda, which helped keep farmers on the land.

The move toward a totalitarian state at home, although never completely realized, was logically in accord with Nazi glorification of the state. It also fulfilled the Nazi demand for dominance in politics and conformity in key social and economic matters. *Gleichschaltung*—freely translated as the totalitarian enforcement of conformity—called for a ruthless policy of exterminating domestic enemies, and it soon manifested itself in foreign affairs.

Imperialism, War, and Destruction—The Nazi commitment to struggle against enemies also found

In 1938 Munich, from left to right, British Prime Minister Neville Chamberlain and French Premier Edouard Daladier meet with fascist dictators Adolf Hitler of Germany and Benito Mussolini of Italy. Also pictured is Count Galeazzo Ciano, foreign minister of Italy. The meeting at Munich became a symbol of Western appeasement of fascism.

expression in Hitler's imperialist policies before and during World War II, policies that brought great destruction to Europe. The Nazis sought revenge for the lands they had lost in World War I (such as Alsace-Lorraine) and "redemption" of ethnic Germans in Austria, Czechoslovakia, and elsewhere. They also sought *Lebensraum*—living space—in the east. Only military might could achieve these objectives, a military might forged by a cleansed, united, and strong German nation under the resolute leadership of the Führer. Fantastic successes included remilitarization of the Rhineland in 1936; *Anschluss* (union) with Austria in 1938; the Munich Pact (1938) and dismemberment of Czechoslovakia in 1939; and the German-Soviet nonaggression pact of 1939. These successes were followed by World War II and incredibly rapid military successes: the defeat of Poland, the overrunning of Holland and Belgium, the capitulation of France, and initial victories in Russia.

At the start, destruction within Germany was minimal. But with the German defeat at Stalingrad in 1942 and Anglo-American bombing of German cities, the tide began to turn. By spring 1945 Germany was in ruins—conquered, divided, and devastated.

The destruction wrought by the Nazis in Poland, Holland, Belgium, France, England, the Soviet Union, and the Balkan states is hard to believe. Even harder to believe is the genocidal murdering of Jews that went on in towns and cities that came under German domination, and the even more systematic extermination that occurred in the Nazi death camps, revealed when the camps were overrun by Allied troops in 1945.[4]

Critique of Nazism

There can be no rational, humane defense of nazism. But we are still puzzled by its operative ideals. How could this Nazi vision of the "good" political life—and the behavior that flowed from this vision—have dominated Germany for even twelve years? This disturbing question forces reflection on the choice (explored in Chapter 4) that Germans made in 1933. Can it happen again? Was nazism unique? Or do the forces and circumstances that produced nazism in Germany—and fascist regimes in Italy and elsewhere—still exist? What lessons in political philosophy and ideology can be drawn from the nightmarish Nazi experience?

Of course, humanity can forthrightly reject the key Nazi operative ideals. Yet intelligent observers have to recognize that the nation-state is very much alive in today's world. So is the demand for strong leadership. So are attitudes of racial superiority and anti-Semitism. And so are imperialism, war, and destruction. They may not retain quite the virulent form they took in nazism, but they are here. How should these ideas be dealt with in today's world? What form will they take in the twenty-first century?

Of course, many people in many nations seek to use the nation-state to achieve freedom and a sense of community. They seek decent, humane, constitutional rulers. They say they fight against attitudes of racial superiority and anti-Semitism and against imperialism, war, and destruction. But what is the actual record? And, in this fight, is the right political philosophy being followed?

Today, Germany (reunited in 1990) and Italy have democratic and constitutional governments. So does Japan, the fascist and militaristic regime that tried in World War II to dominate the Far East. It seems unlikely that fascism or militarism will ever again seriously influence the policies of these countries. Other fascist-like regimes in Spain, Portugal, and Greece—none, of course, as virulent as the Nazi regime in Germany—have been replaced by democratic, constitutional governments. And so Western Europe—strengthened particularly by the European Union—seems not to be seriously threatened by fascism. Also unlikely is a revival of neofascism and militarism in Japan, given its economic prosperity, its close ties to the United States, its democratic and constitutional political system, and its ban on armed forces for offensive purposes.

However, repressive authoritarian regimes are still very much alive in some Middle Eastern, Asian, and African nations. They demonstrate the inability of liberal democracy and of democratic socialism to take hold in unfavorable circumstances. In some countries, right-wing regimes feed on a political or economic crisis and the call for a strong leader. Military leaders sometimes seem to be the only ones capable of maintaining "law and order." Many of these countries have no tradition of constitutional government or respect for political parties and civil rights. This suggests that there may still be breeding grounds for some variety of fascism, if not the seemingly unique, virulent Nazi strain.

But what, more fully, is happening in the developing nations of the Third World, particularly in states that have become independent since World War II? What political ideology

attracts them? The next section explores these questions.

THIRD WORLD IDEOLOGY

The **Third World** comprises many Asian, African, and Latin American nations outside the democratic, constitutional, economically prosperous world of the West and its allies (the United States, Western Europe, Canada, Australia, and Japan) and also outside the Communist world and its allies (China, Cuba, North Korea, Vietnam). Investigation of Third World ideology is important for a number of reasons. First, until approximately the end of World War II, political scientists tended to ignore these countries, even though they contain the bulk of the world's population. The Third World must be studied to overcome Western ignorance and **ethnocentrism**—the belief that one's own race, nation, religion, or culture is superior to all others.

Second, the Third World's struggles for peace, justice, prosperity, and self-government are now, in the perspective of the global community, intimately involved with ours. Their problems, and the political ideologies that guide them, have great relevance for political scientists concerned with the vital interests both of their own nations and of the globe.

Third, it is important to discover how the Third World understands the good political life and how this understanding relates to liberal democracy, communism, and democratic socialism. We need to know how the serious problems faced by many Third World nations (most of which have only come into existence since World War II) have influenced their guiding political ideologies.

In contrast to the democratic and constitutional nations of the West and its allies (which are industrialized; politically, economically, and socially developed; and relatively affluent), and in contrast to such great Communist powers as China, most Third World nations are weak, poor, developing—and sometimes not even developing. Most democratic and Communist nations inhabit the Northern Hemisphere; most developing nations are in the Southern Hemisphere. Many developing nations have been independent only since the end of World War II. This discussion focuses primarily on the relatively new states of the developing world, although many points will also hold for older Third World nations. Although there are great diversities among the new states—even within Asia, Africa, and Latin America—our generalizations about the roots, evolution, and operative ideals of many developing countries will introduce important political outlooks.

The Roots and Evolution of Third World Ideology

The most popular political ideology in most developing countries has its roots in nationalism, democracy, and socialism.[5] Leaders in developing societies often interpret these ideas—especially democracy and socialism—differently than do liberal democrats, democratic socialists, or communists. Yet they use these terms, and so we will attempt to understand what they mean by them. We will also emphasize the importance of two other roots of Third World ideology—pragmatism and the concern for modern development—that are closely linked to nationalism, democracy, and socialism.

Nationalism—Of the five roots of Third World ideology, nationalism is the most important. The early leaders of new states—such as Sukarno of Indonesia, Jawaharlal Nehru of India, Kwame Nkrumah of Ghana, Julius Nyerere of Tanzania, Ho Chi Minh of Vietnam—were dedicated nationalists who wanted their people to be free and independent. Nationalism emerged as a strong response to colonialism and imperialism. India did not want to remain a British colony, nor Vietnam a French colony, nor Indonesia a Dutch colony, nor Angola a Portuguese colony. In their struggle against Western imperialism and domination, leaders of these countries drew not only from Marxism-Leninism but also from those

national and democratic revolutions that shaped the fortunes of the First World: the American Revolution and the French Revolution. At their best, Third World leaders remain staunch nationalists, determined to protect their people against outside domination and exploitation and to help them develop more fully.

Democracy—Democracy is a second powerful influence in the Third World, despite the fact that these countries interpret the concept differently than do liberal democratic countries. Democracy, for them, has been closely linked with the nationalistic movement for freedom, self-rule, and equality. Popular rule for new Third World nations meant rule by the people on their own behalf. Basic rights meant an end to colonial inequality and freedom for the people to protect their own vital interests. Thus, some of the basic ideas of liberal democracy, or of democratic socialism, found a sympathetic hearing in Third World countries, even though such features of liberal democracy as a two-party or multiparty system and a free press were not entirely compatible with conditions in the new states.

Socialism—Socialism, as both a political and an economic idea, has also influenced the Third World. Many leaders of new nations have expressed an ideological commitment to socialism. Julius Nyerere, president of Tanzania for many years, declared: "I believe that no underdeveloped country can afford to be anything but socialist." Such leaders see socialism as a social, economic, and political system designed to give voice and protection to the needs of their people. Most are sympathetic to democratic socialism. They are persuaded that the community's wealth should be employed on behalf of the overwhelming majority of the nation's people, most of whom are workers and farmers. They believe that the people's basic human needs must be met. In the economic domain this means a degree of nationalization. Democratic socialism, however, does not automatically mean a two-party system with a functioning opposition party, or full-scale nationalization, or a welfare state. Whether socialism as an economic system will continue to appeal remains to be seen. Some developing nations seem to be moving away from a rigid commitment to socialism, toward a market economy.

Modern Development—Nationalism, democracy, and socialism are related to a fourth root of ideology in the Third World: the emphasis on modern development. National development can take place only within the framework of the nation-state. The people must be involved in and benefit from such development. And socialism offers the best promise for development. Clearly, the leaders of most of these nations aspire to enter the modern world of literacy and education, better health, helpful machines, improved agriculture and industrialization, economic growth, and more satisfying consumer goods.

Pragmatism—Finally, the new states are influenced by what we might call a philosophy of **pragmatism.** Frequently, they interpret their problems—and nationalism, democracy, socialism, and modern development—in a pragmatic, or practical, manner. Pragmatism might well be the root of a guiding principle: What is good for them is what works well for them in the light of their own conditions. Thus, new state leaders have accepted from developed countries the ideas that work best in their own political circumstances. And they have rejected liberal, socialist, capitalist, or communist ideas that do not work. For example, in the early years of development, many of these leaders held that an individualistic, competitive, capitalist orientation would not fit the scheme of life in their countries. More recently, however, they have had more sympathy for a market economy. Such leaders also held, early on, that a system with competing political parties would not work well either. They were more attracted to a single party expressing a national consensus. Here, too, there has been some modest movement toward politi-

cal pluralism and a competing party system. This pragmatic approach appears to leave ample room for traditional ways—in economics, social organization, and religion—which remain powerful influences in developing nations.

Although attracted to some communist ideas about capitalist imperialism, colonial revolution, and development, most leaders of new Third World nations have not been influenced as much by class conflict as by national conflict. They have won a national revolution against imperialists rather than a proletarian revolution against capitalists. Although sympathetic to much in the Marxist analysis, they are not tuned in to class war, to the dictatorship of the proletariat, or to the withering away of the state. These leaders tend to have more respect for the private sector. They have rejected collectivization of agriculture on the model of the former Soviet Union. They seem to prefer a mixed economy. In some respects they seem to be as much in sympathy with Thomas Jefferson and Jean Jacques Rousseau as with Karl Marx.

Their pragmatic, sometimes eclectic, selection from various influences makes it hazardous to generalize about the roots and evolution of their ideology. Their search for, and incomplete success in finding, a blend of nationalism, democracy, socialism, and modern development makes it difficult to see a coherent set of operative ideals at work. Very often there is a big—and often ugly—gap between ideological aspiration and political and economic reality. But even as we recognize great diversity and frequent contradictions in the political systems of these Third World countries, we can discern some cardinal goals and ideals.

The Operative Ideals of the New Third World Nations

The major goals of the new states, with few exceptions, can be reduced to four, expressed in order of importance: (1) national freedom, independence, and unity; (2) economic development; (3) social advancement; and (4) political democracy—new style. Most leaders profess these goals; not all practice them successfully.

Juacquim Chissano is president of Mozambique, an African country struggling to reconcile nationalism, economic development, social advance, and an African variety of democracy.

National Freedom, Independence, and Unity—The nation's people must be free to govern themselves. There must be no foreign domination—no old-style colonialism or **neocolonialism** (economic and political control by, or dependence on, a former colonial ruler or Big Power). The nation must be truly independent, free of entangling alliances with countries in the Western or Communist worlds. The nation must be united and strong enough to maintain itself as a political entity.

National unity is crucial, Third World leaders believe, because without it nothing else can be accomplished—not national independence or economic development or social advancement or democratic development. The difficulties often facing new states jeopardize national unity. These difficulties may include a people's lack of a historical sense of belonging together; the absence of common language, religion, history, and customs; widespread poverty and illiteracy;

and the divisive influence of caste and tribe. Moreover, the new states often lack the mechanisms that hold a nation together: effective national leadership, political organization, civil servants, economic ties, and national education. These difficulties also help explain why many new states have moved away from liberal democratic or even democratic socialist ideas and toward rule by a strong, charismatic leader, a single party, or a disciplined military junta. Sometimes they even accept (although reluctantly) authoritarian methods to foster primary national values.

Economic Development—Economic development calls for speedy industrial, agricultural, and commercial advances, usually through strong central-government planning of a socialist character. New states react against economic imperialism; they feel that for too long they were a source of cheap resources and cheap labor for their colonial masters. The leaders of these new nations seek to reorder their national economies in the interest of their own people. They lost a lot of time during the period of imperialist domination, and they are in a hurry to develop—to build a more balanced economy that is less dependent on a single crop or resource, to develop a communications and transportation network, to accumulate capital for economic development, and to overcome the social backwardness that inhibits economic development. Again, they must accomplish these objectives without adequately trained administrators, engineers, technicians, teachers, or clerks. Rational planning is necessary to cope with these difficulties and to help new nations achieve economic independence and attend to human needs.

Social Advancement—Social advancement calls for an educational, medical, and cultural revolution to overcome illiteracy, disease, and the fatalistic attitudes of the older, traditional society. New state leaders seek to wipe out the native population's feelings of inferiority, which stem from the colonial power's attitudes of racial, cultural, and social superiority. The new leaders seek a life of greater social freedom, dignity, and moral worth. They often battle not only colonial social prejudices but, in some countries, native ideas of caste and of the inferiority of women. The revolution of rising expectations looms as large in the social field as in the economic field and makes powerful demands on the leadership of new states—demands that sometimes militate against liberal democratic political principles. Elements of the traditional culture compatible with a healthy community must, of course, be encouraged.

Political Democracy—New State Variety—The new state variety of political democracy means, for the most part, government for the people, by strong leaders, through a dominant party or, sometimes, the military. This was not the original dream of most new state leaders. Initially, they aspired toward liberal democratic or democratic socialist models. They were sympathetic to the ideals of an advanced democratic welfare state. At the start, as the embryonic new states advanced toward self-government and independence, they adopted democratic constitutions on the Western model, extended the franchise widely, accepted emerging political parties, and conducted general elections to determine the fate of government. The governing elites favored a radical democratization of their societies.

However, the pressure of circumstances—especially the difficulties of maintaining national unity, achieving economic development, and accomplishing social advances—moved many leaders away from the more liberal democratic model. Constitutional democracy, Western style, ceased to be an operative ideal. A new conception of political democracy emerged. Leaders began to talk about "guided democracy," "basic democracy," and "new state" democracy.

According to proponents of this variety of political democracy, government rules on behalf of the people even if the people do not rule themselves in Western style. The proponents argue that strong leaders will express the will of the people. "New state" democracy will rest on

and support nationalism, economic development, and social advancement. Observers of the pattern note that certain aspects of democracy in the new states are inextricably linked with the powerful attraction of nationalism. Thus, the nationalistic fervor of the new states requires a certain kind of democratization. Some of the people, as they become politically conscious, demand a role in the developing nation-state. New state leaders recognize that the regime needs popular support perhaps more than the people need political rights. Such leaders may argue that the people are not ready for responsible participation. Similarly, as the traditional order breaks up, the reforming leaders must use the masses to help replace the old order with a modern one. Consequently, the leaders exalt the worth of the people, whose energies must be enlisted, and extol their power.

Representative democracy, Western style, thus has not endured as an operative ideal. The prerequisites for liberal democracy were lacking: solid political, economic, and social organizations, and "mass literacy, relatively high living standards, a sizable and stable middle class, a sense of social equality, and a tradition both of tolerance and of individual self-reliance."[6] Liberal democracy was hampered by the absence of, and urgent need for, national unity, social order, political organization, economic modernization, and social advance. More recently, however, there has been a modest movement toward democratic and constitutional government as understood in the West.

Critique of Third World Ideology

How do we assess the operative ideals of these new states? How operative and how ideal are they? Are they feasible? Why did they emerge and how do they compare with, and differ from, those of liberal democracy, communism, and democratic socialism? What difficulties face new state leaders, and what are they willing to pay to reach their goals?

It takes a valiant effort to understand the situation of these new states. In contrast to democratic and communist countries, they are (with some exceptions) often non-Christian, non-Western, and usually nonindustrial. Their peoples are mostly poor, agrarian, illiterate, and traditional. These nations are trying, amidst great difficulty, to compress the complex process of modern development into a few short years.

Not all new states have abandoned the two cardinal principles of liberal democracy and democratic socialism: popular rule and protection of basic rights. For example, India, the largest new state in Asia, retains these principles, despite some government actions that have smacked of dictatorial or authoritarian rule. Democratic elections continue to be held. The once-dominant Congress party has been in and out of power in recent years. Despite some violations, democratic civil liberties have been maintained. Opposition parties function. The nation has by no means adequately achieved its goals—national cohesion, economic development, social advancement, and fuller democracy—but it has survived and demonstrated, often against great odds, that a more democratic version of new state democracy can work.

A question arises, however, with regard to new states that have been less successful than India: Can the high priority that they have placed on national unity, economic development, and social advancement be adapted to their own conception of democracy? Some sympathetic critics argue that this question permits a more positive look at the new states' strong leadership, single-party system, military rule, state intervention, and nonalignment in foreign affairs. Other critics, however, contend that we cannot close our eyes to authoritarian leadership, violations of human rights, and political and economic corruption in the developing states of the world.

Thus, sympathetic critics may see a need for strong leadership, and even **constitutional dictatorship,** a pattern not unknown in the liberal democratic West. Under this pattern, rulers are given extraordinary powers during an emergency, powers to suspend certain liberties. Clearly,

this is a very dangerous idea, but some critics believe it is preferable to a clear-cut military dictatorship or to a fascist dictatorship or to the communist dictatorship of the proletariat, party, Politburo, and leader. For a period of genuine crisis, when the very safety of the new state is at stake, they argue that leaders should try to develop this idea within the framework of the liberal democratic or democratic socialist tradition. Because it is such a dangerous idea, and such a handy justification for tyranny, constitutional dictatorship should be a last resort; it should be limited in time and power, monitored carefully, and terminated if power is abused.

The fact that it may be impossible to limit the abuse of power leaves other less sympathetic critics to conclude that toying with the idea of constitutional dictatorship is a very serious mistake. They argue that too often military dictators' promises of free elections and a return to democratic government are not fulfilled. To legitimize such dictatorships is a serious mistake. These critics seek more acceptable alternatives.

Single-Party System—Some sympathetic critics also argue for the democratic possibilities of the single-party system. They note that restraint on divisive partisan issues and coalitions of various groups are well established in Western democratic and constitutional tradition, particularly during periods of grave national emergency. They emphasize that citizens may be able to participate responsibly and democratically within a single party. Less sympathetic critics, however, have deep reservations about the short-range behavior and long-range consequences of a "democratic" single party. They worry about the absence of real opposition to the leadership, and they are disturbed by its chilling effect on freedom. They also note that one-party rule has often led to political and economic corruption. Finally, they note that one-party rule has not even consistently maintained stability.

Military Rule—Some sympathetic critics also defend military rule, which seems essential in some new states to preserve unity, fight corruption, and advance development. These critics also recognize the armed forces' democratic and organizational potential. Other critics, however, underscore the dangers of military control: undemocratic and inhumane rule, including the physical destruction or torture of a regime's political opponents.

State Intervention—Sympathetic critics argue that a large measure of state intervention seems necessary in the interest of economic and social advances. They urge a democratic socialism that would protect basic freedoms and guard against the abuse of power. They also urge new state planners to guard against economic blunders and inefficient administration. Other critics, however, call attention to the failures of socialism, the possibilities of capitalism and a market economy, and the values of decentralization and local initiatives.

Nonalignment Policy—Some critics endorse the **nonalignment** policy favored by many new states. These critics remind Americans that they, too, benefited from a comparable policy at the beginning of their history. They contend that nonalignment can help reduce tensions in global politics. Nonalignment may even encourage the richer developing nations to increase economic aid to nonaligned nations. Other critics, however, are suspicious of nonalignment. They view it as a deceptive myth that prevents developing nations from seeing the real dangers in international politics—for example, the danger of aggressive Third World neighbors or of Western imperialism. The character of these dangers is being more candidly assessed now that the Cold War has ended and a more just global order is struggling against great odds to be born.

The foregoing arguments—pro and con—suggest the importance of being open to, but still critical of, political possibilities in the new states. But to be open-minded is not to be empty-headed. Political scientists need to be open to new democratic possibilities—and to peace, jus-

tice, and prosperity—but they cannot ignore the dangers of dictatorship, a one-party state, military rule, economic stupidity, civil war, and jingoistic foreign policy.

Political scientists must also be open to the possibility that the leaders of some new states are conceiving a good life that does not perfectly fit the liberal democratic, the democratic socialist, or the communist pattern. These leaders are attempting to do so under great difficulties. They face an enormous gap between aspiration and fulfillment. They lack the prerequisites for effective democratic and constitutional government but are seeking to further their goals of national unity, economic development, social advancement, and new state democracy as best they can. In appraising the emerging political ideologies of the new states, political scientists must be sympathetic to, but constructively critical of, an emerging constitutional democracy. It remains to be seen whether new states in the Third World can reconcile national stability and democratic liberty, can achieve prosperous and efficient economies, and can fulfill their dream of a healthy, literate, and vibrant society. The prospects are daunting.

WHICH POLITICAL PHILOSOPHY FOR THE FUTURE?

As we bring Part II, "Political Philosophy and Ideology," to a close, we must ask, Is there something better than liberal democracy, communism, democratic socialism, fascism, or new state democracy? Political scientists, as philosophers, must stand back from traditional and dominant ideologies and ask some radical questions about the political philosophy best equipped to introduce a better world. It is important to see the political scientist as a political philosopher who can criticize existing systems and propose creative breakthroughs to desirable political communities.

Exploring the outlook of political futurists is important for several persuasive reasons. First, some thoughtful political scientists doubt whether any current political ideology is adequate for the future. They believe that all dominant political outlooks are flawed because of their sometimes blind commitment to ideas such as the sovereign nation-state or the war system or the dominant economic system (whether capitalism or communism) or sexism or racism.

Second, a more radical, more fundamental, assessment of the gaps between political ideals and political realities, between professed principles and actual behavior, may be necessary. Such an assessment is prompted by a political ethic that takes itself seriously, by a concern for empirical truth, and by a determination to avoid foolish, perhaps disastrous, public policies throughout the world.

Third, such exploration is needed to achieve creative breakthroughs on pressing issues of world peace, justice, prosperity, and ecological balance.

It thus makes sense to close this chapter and Part II with a discussion of the futurists. Political philosophy at its best is critical and creative. It offers both diagnosis and prescription and does not shrink from systemic criticism or imaginative reconstruction. Clearly, there is much to criticize around the globe. Weaknesses as well as strengths are apparent in the sovereign nation-state system. Nationalism gone mad is best illustrated in nazism. But, clearly, dangerous nationalism did not perish with the death of the Nazi regime. In many areas of the world a war system, related to a nation-state system, is still at work and threatening people with disaster. Of course, truly vital interests must be defended, but are these vital interests being defined sanely? The national movements for independence, freedom, economic and social advancement—as illustrated dramatically in the new states of the Third World—merit applause and support. But what unhappy consequences may also flow from these new nation-states?

Economic systems—whether communism or socialism or capitalism—are not functioning well enough to provide both economic well-being and freedom. Can they be improved? Political systems that do not safeguard human rights or

advance social and political justice are apparent. Can they be helped? Ecological problems affect all nations on the globe. Has political philosophy become attuned to the new ecological imperatives? A worldwide struggle to enhance the quality of human life continues. But is this important battle being fought hard enough? A political philosophy for the future must address these problems critically and creatively. Whether the political futurists do a proper job in facing up to these problems remains to be seen.

The Roots of Futurist Political Philosophy

Since World War II, the Holocaust, the advent of the atomic bomb, the rise of new and developing states in the Third World, and the recognition of ecological crisis, there has been an absorbing interest in the future of the planet. Can we prevent a Third World War or another genocidal holocaust? Will Third World countries manage to combine cohesiveness and constitutionalism? Can the very biosphere—earth, water, air—that makes human life on earth possible be protected? Troubling questions like these have, in the second half of the twentieth century, stimulated an outpouring of literature on the future of humankind. They are questions that will still dominate thinking and policy in the oncoming twenty-first century.

This literature on the future varies widely. Some writers are interested in the future because they want to save souls. Others want to enhance profits. Still others want to solve specific problems—whether it's finding a cure for cancer or for AIDS or other troubling diseases or ending genocidal ethnic wars, persistent poverty, racism, sexism, or ecological disasters. In the United States, concerns for universal health care, welfare reform, and budget deficits join the list of other problems demanding our attention. Much of the literature has focused on how new inventions and ideas affect economics, employment, and sales; family life and sexual habits; or formal and informal education. Surprisingly, however, there has been little systematic exploration of how to arrive at a desired political future.

A participant at the U.N. Conference on Environment and Development in Rio de Janiero, Brazil, signs the environmental pledge wall. The pledge is a promise to "help make the Earth a secure and hospitable home for present and future generations."

The political futurists, usually social scientists, have attempted to address the what and the how of tomorrow's political world. They are not all traditional political philosophers, but they are asking serious questions in the tradition of political philosophy: Which concept of the good political life should guide future politics? How do political actors behave, and how do their behavior, principles, and institutions relate to the good political life? Which prudent judgments and policies are necessary to narrow the gap between a preferred world order and the present one?

The political futurists pursue a number of objectives:

1. To bring the future of politics and the politics of the future onto center stage in political science.
2. To remind political philosophers that at its best political philosophy has been future-oriented, and that it must continue to deal with coming, as well as current, problems.
3. To strike a better balance between the forces of conservation and the forces of change and to underscore the relation between wise conservation and wise change.
4. To encourage political scientists to develop a more imaginative, more realistic theory of

social change and a comparable theory of social conservation.

5. To do justice to the powerful forces that have shaped the twentieth century and that will crucially affect the twenty-first century. These forces include constitutionalism, democracy, nationalism, capitalism, socialism, federalism, science, technology, universality, liberation, equality, community, ecology, and excellence.

The Outlook of the Political Futurists

Are the political futurists foolishly utopian or wisely realistic? A radical vision of world order dominates the political futurists' thinking. They take the values they endorse—life, peace, democracy, economic well-being, ecological health, and human excellence—seriously and question whether these values can be fulfilled under the principles and institutions of liberal democracy or socialism or communism or the nation-state.

The political futurists' concept of the good political life takes on additional meaning as we examine their criticism of the existing order and the gulf between the existing order and their vision of the good life. They advance a sixfold argument:

1. Too many powerful leaders in the modern world have been afflicted by a strange

attraction to death, destruction, and despair.

2. We are plagued by a war system rooted in a state system in which some powerful sovereign nations possess nuclear weapons capable of mass annihilation and in which rich and poor nations alike spend disproportionate sums on armaments.

3. Most of the world is still ruled by elitist, oligarchic, tyrannical forces convinced that democracy is a dangerous illusion.

4. Poverty, inequality, worker alienation, and imprudent use of economic resources characterize capitalist, socialist, and communist economies in both developed and developing countries.

5. Ecological degradation and imbalance plague the world.

6. Powerful social, economic, political, and ideological forces militate against cultural excellence and a good quality of life.

These six interrelated factors constitute dangers that add up to a global crisis.

The futurists' responses to current problems set forth a plan of action and indicate their understanding of the future political order. They also throw light on the key questions of what, how, and why: What political breakthrough should prevail in the future? How will humanity break through to such a future politics? Why is the breakthrough persuasive? In general, and with variations on some points, the political futurists advocate interlocking breakthroughs to (1) a more prophetic consciousness, (2) a new constitutional world order, (3) a new covenant of democratic power, (4) a more humanistic economics, (5) ecological health via biospheric balance, and (6) social and cultural excellence.

Cardinal Values of the Futurists

We can summarize the philosophy of the political futurists under six main headings corresponding to their cardinal values: life, peace, democracy, economic well-being, ecological health, and human excellence.

Life: The Primary Commitment—Political futurists such as Erich Fromm, Abraham Maslow, and Victor Ferkiss endorse a life-affirming philosophy. In the words of Erich Fromm: "Good is all that serves life, evil is all that serves death. Good is reverence for life, all that enhances life, growth, unfolding. Evil is all that stifles life, narrows it down, cuts it into pieces."[7] The love of life is the foundation for the futurists' other values. It leads them to protest war, tyranny, meaningless work, pollution, and decline in the quality of life. It leads political scientist Victor Ferkiss to state that the "task of social and political philosophy is one of determining which policies and institutions are best able to fulfill" a life-affirming ethics, one concerned with satisfying legitimate human needs.[8]

We can only sample the evidence in support of their argument about death and war. It is disturbing and thought-provoking. Not all practitioners of death and destruction are as explicit as the Spanish fascist general who, in a dramatic encounter with a Spanish philosopher at the University of Salamanca, declared: "Long live death!" and "Down with intelligence!" Yet the record of death and destruction in the twentieth century is undeniable: in numerous wars and civil wars; in Stalin's liquidation of his opponents; in the Holocaust; in the firebombing of London and Dresden and the atomic bombing of Hiroshima and Nagasaki; in the post–World War II period in China, Vietnam, and Cambodia (Kampuchea); in the Middle East, Latin America, and Africa; in Bosnia and other places in today's headlines. In view of this record, it is easy to despair of a more peaceful world order.

Almost without exception the futurists call for a more ethical and global consciousness. They believe that a breakthrough to such a new consciousness is required because civilized life, healthy growth, and mature fulfillment are jeopardized by the dominant nationalistic, undemocratic outlook of today's world. Most see world leadership as able to bring the new consciousness into being. Some trust the people themselves to create the change. All believe that resistance to war, tyranny, poverty, and ecological malaise will facilitate the breakthrough. They concede that a vast educational process is required to achieve a new world order but believe it can succeed. They are sustained by the conviction that the key values of a new consciousness command widespread support. People will choose life over death, democracy over oligarchy, economic well-being over poverty, and ecological health over biospheric degradation.

Peace: Swords into Plowshares—The commitments to life and to peace are inextricably linked. Peace must be understood both positively and negatively. Beyond the prevention of an all-out nuclear war, beyond the more modest task of minimizing large-scale violence, is the positive goal of building a constitutional world order wherein political conflicts that lead to war can be sensibly handled. To Richard Falk, for example, peace means moving away from a "military concept of security" toward nonviolent resolution of conflicts.

Richard Falk and Harold and Margaret Sprout are among those who have criticized the war system and the nation-state system. Falk argues that the war system (because it creates the risk of a major nuclear war) is a serious threat not only to the existence of all countries but to human survival itself. The war system makes national populations into hostages; diverts resources from feeding, educating, and caring for people; prevents people from working together on common and urgent problems; and perpetuates domination by military means. Harold and Margaret Sprout see the nation-state system as a "narrow tribalism," unable to provide security for citizens and unable to cope with pressing problems. Falk agrees. The nation-state system cannot protect against war; it cannot "minimize violence in world affairs"; it does not permit "reasonable progress in attaining social and economic justice"; it cannot cope with poverty or violations of human rights; and it cannot protect the global environment.[9]

Almost all political futurists call for a new

"Let us beat our swords into ploughshares." This statue was donated by the former Soviet Union to the United Nations.

world order that is democratic and constitutional. In such an order, they argue, tasks aimed at furthering peace, resolving conflicts, fostering economic well-being, promoting political and social justice, and achieving ecological balance would be assigned to the political actors best able to handle them—national communities, regional communities, key functional organizations, and a world polity association.

Progress toward this world order would occur in stages. Falk, for example, would build on enhanced domestic consciousness in stage one, experiments toward regional world order in stage two, and a central guidance system in stage three.

Advocates for a new world order would lead in educating people. Groups adversely affected by war, tyranny, poverty, and ecological malaise under the old system would support such leadership. Key interest groups seeking greater peace, freedom, prosperity, and ecological health would also lend support. The dangers of war, famine, pandemic disease, economic collapse, ecological decay, and resource shortages would also encourage pragmatic peoples and nations to try reasonable experiments in world governance. Overcoming the dangers of the modern world will not be easy, but futurists believe that a determined effort can succeed.

Democracy: A New Covenant on Human Needs, Basic Rights, and Popular Management—The political futurists seek to complete the democratic revolution by extending both popular rule and basic rights. More people must participate in crucial decisions affecting their need for a decent life, healthy growth, and self-actualization. Democratic self-management must extend beyond government in the narrow sense to the workshop, to technology, and to other spheres of society. Basic rights must also be interpreted more generously to include satisfying employment, decent housing, good health, quality education, a caring community, and greater ethical, scientific, and cultural fulfillment. The political futurists are particularly concerned with giving the oppressed, the poor, and the needy a greater voice in decisions affecting their lives.

The political futurists see an undemocratic order operating all over the world, in both developed and developing countries. They concede that liberal democratic and democratic socialist governments may have better records than authoritarian regimes on the left or right in protecting popular rule and basic rights. But they maintain that the fuller promise of the democratic revolution is not being fulfilled: small groups in the United States, the entrenched party elite in China, and the Third World ruling elite call the signals in their respective countries. The power and self-interest of the few thus prevail. The iron law of **oligarchy**, which holds that a small group of insiders will inevitably run the show in a large organization, also explains the absence of greater democratic voice in decision making. Entrenched leaders will simply not give up their guiding role. Radical political futurists extend their attack on antidemocratic forces to the workplace, technology, and society itself and criticize "boss control," "aristo-technology," and subordination to societal authority, as well as representative government. L. S. Stavrianos, for example, sees "the present meritocracy of bosses, bureaucrats,

and experts . . . going the way of the early aristocracy of kings, priests, and landlords."[10]

The political futurists thus propose a new compact on democratic power. Such an agreement would move significantly toward satisfying legitimate human needs, protecting human rights, facilitating popular participation, and advancing a more creative political community. Stavrianos, for example, would increase "self-management" in key phases of human life: in government, economics, and technology. He favors more participatory politics to mobilize people in the community on important matters. He advocates greater worker control in the workplace in the interest of freedom, satisfaction, and efficiency. He supports E. F. Schumacher's argument that "small is beautiful," that we "should now give some thought to . . . reforming our technology in the direction of smallness, simplicity and nonviolence." He also anticipates that people will increasingly move away from "self-subordination to authority and toward self-actualization"—the "realization of personal and collective human potential." Stavrianos, a historian, sees these developments as part of a "long historical process of popular awakening" that is now culminating in the "twentieth-century demand for self-management in all phases of life."

Economic Well-Being: The Quest for Economic Justice and Prosperity —In the economic sphere the political futurists' concerns sometimes overlap their desire to extend the meaning of democracy.[11] They attack poverty, inequality, economic authoritarianism, and imprudent economics. They deplore the fact that so many people live under conditions below or barely at the level of survival. They are appalled at the gap between rich and poor. They criticize dehumanization, alienation, and exploitation in the workplace and marketplace. They worry about economic policies that are wasteful, harmful, and short-sighted. They criticize both capitalism and communism as economic systems: capitalism because it perpetuates domination and exploitation, and communism because it fails to give workers real control of their economic lives.

The political futurists anticipate a breakthrough to a more humanistic economics. They argue that economic well-being calls for replacing poverty with ample subsistence—a decent prosperity. Economic justice calls for redistribution to narrow the gap between rich and poor—to help severely deprived minorities in affluent countries and severely deprived majorities in most other countries. Economic democracy calls for greater worker control of the means of production and greater consumer voice in the economic process. Prudent management calls for wise stewardship of resources and wise judgments about economic and social costs, benefits, and trade-offs.

Ecological Health: Respect for the Biosphere The political futurists argue strongly for clean air, pure water, the prudent use of natural resources, and a sensible balance between population and resources. They insist that we must respect not only human needs and rights but also the rights of the natural world. Respect for our planet—which affords us beauty and amenity as well as "ample subsistence"—requires respect for the carrying capacity of the globe.[12]

The political futurists see pollution, the depletion and misuse of scarce resources, and the imbalance of population and resources as threats to life and quality of life—for current and future generations. They worry about the planet being slowly degraded by poisoned water and air, poverty-stricken by the disappearance of vital resources, or dehumanized by populations wildly in excess of resources sufficient to sustain decent life. Ecological malady, they insist, is worldwide. The reasons lie in values, institutions, and behavior that characterize both capitalist and communist societies, developing and developed societies. These patterns are found in societies that are industrial (or would become so), exploitative, materialistic, and hedonistic (pleasure-loving). They are found in societies driven by a mania for growth and oblivious to the reality of finite resources. They are found in societies that believe in the myth of a scientific or technological "fix" for ecological problems.

Ecologically, the political futurists endorse a breakthrough to a **steady-state society.** Such a breakthrough would call for an end to the philosophy of mindless growth and exploitation that characterizes both liberalism and socialism.

Human Excellence: The Fuller Cultivation of a High Quality of Life—Beyond survival, more generous democracy, economic justice and prosperity, and ecological balance, the political futurists look to fulfillment in artistic, cultural, intellectual, scientific, and spiritual endeavors. The brilliant flowering of human culture— in religion and ethics, politics and economics, lit-erature and the arts, the physical and biological sciences, philosophy and history, education, and sports—is a cardinal feature of their vision. War, tyranny, poverty, and ecological imbalance prevent human excellence from receiving the high priority it deserves. The political futurists believe that a cultural renaissance would accompany the breakthroughs to peace, democracy, prosperity, and ecological health. Thus, Victor Ferkiss emphasizes the great adventure of enhancing human development and creativity in a free, pluralistic, and genuinely human community. Richard Falk believes that an adequate vision of the future must be informed by values that require "conditions of social life in each society that promote harmony, joy, and creativity" and that reflect a concern with beauty and the maintenance of privacy and personal dignity. Other value would require that government, science, and technology be humanized, that diversity of lifestyles and of nature be affirmed, and that humane social and political experiments be encouraged. And William Ophuls looks to a future in which people can find fulfillment in artistic, cultural, intellectual, scientific, and spiritual endeavors.

Critique of the Political Futurists

How do we appraise the outlook of the political futurists? Are they naive and foolish utopians preaching a set of attractive but empty values— peace, human rights, economic well-being, and ecological health? Or are they humane and realistic observers seeking to preserve the best and avoid the worst values of liberalism and socialism? Are their values sound but their approach utopian because it does not realistically indicate how to move from the present endangered state to their more sensible future? Do recent events vindicate their vision?

The most perceptive political futurists realize the need to move beyond wishful thinking about a perfectly harmonious politics. They also realize humanity's need for a sensible transition from its current position to where it ought to be. They understand the reality of conflict in politics and hence the need for constitutional mechanisms to deal with inevitable compromises. They recognize the dangers of abuse of power and the need to guard against it in an open, self-correcting political system. What is not clear, however, is whether they have put forth a feasible theory of transition.

The political futurists do not, for example, convincingly show how the forces for world order will be able to overcome the forces of the status quo. Nationalism and the nation-state system are strongly entrenched. Despite the fact that there has been no World War III and that the Cold War is over, the war system itself shows no signs of withering away. Undemocratic rule, poverty, and ecological malaise are widespread. The forces promoting world order are weak.

Criticism of the political futurists must be cautiously approached lest the baby be thrown out with the bathwater. For example, apropos of the effort to democratize politics, economics, technology, and society, the "baby" would be legitimate and necessary leadership by scientific or technocratic leaders, skillful economic managers, wise elected representatives, or genuine "aristocrats" in varying societal endeavors. Apropos of our ecological sins, the "baby" would be freedom to start a business, drive a car, have more than two children, or keep a job in a "dirty" industry. Apropos of efforts to curb the abuses of power of the nation-state, the "baby" would be a valuable political community (the nation) whose citizens share a sense of covenant.

Critics also question the futurists' failure to fully address a number of important problems. For example, how would they guard against abuse of power by a world government with powers to maintain the peace, advance the cause of economic justice, and protect the environment? Will rich and powerful nations agree to global policies that reduce their wealth and power? Will freedom survive the demise of traditional capitalism? How would the futurists deal with conflicts between one democratic community and another? What are the costs, risks, and trade-offs required by their vision of world order?

Although many of the futurists' values are attractive, and their criticism of current society is often cogent, critics argue that they do not make a persuasive case for their proposed breakthroughs to a new world order. But even as we question the futurists' philosophy, we are compelled to think more carefully about the good political life. We are also encouraged to explore those theories of social change and transition that would illuminate ways of achieving that good political life. And, finally, we are stimulated to assess the problems of politics in a world free of the dangers that the political futurists currently see.

CONCLUSION

Fascism—and especially its most virulent variety, nazism—seriously challenged liberal democracy, communism, and democratic socialism. The defeat of fascism and militarism in World War II does not, however, mean that challenges to dominant political philosophies and ideologies have disappeared. Right-wing authoritarian regimes still function in many parts of the world. Militarism continues to rear its ugly head across the globe.

Political philosophers and politicians must

also respond wisely to emerging political ideologies. The struggle of the new states—and of many other countries in the developing Third World—demonstrates the appeal and yet the inadequacy of dominant political ideologies, especially nationalism. The challenge is underscored by the gap in most developing countries between aspiration and reality.

Thus, the question that political philosophers insist on asking becomes ever more compelling: Is there a better political philosophy to guide communities today and in the future? Clearly, there is room for improvement in all dominant political philosophies and ideologies. The futurists' political philosophy raises an attractive vision of politics as a civilizing enterprise. Is this vision foolishly utopian or soundly realistic? The futurists also stimulate political scientists to reconsider their vocation as philosophers and to respond appropriately.

Political scientists must respond critically to the great ethical, empirical, and prudential issues of politics. They must respond critically to the strengths and weaknesses of liberal democracy, communism, democratic socialism, fascism, new state ideology, and other alternative political philosophies. These responses link the task of political scientists as political philosophers to their task as scientific students of empirical phenomena—the task we turn to in Part III. The critical exploration of political philosophy, especially the question of the good political life, helps political scientists clarify values, standards, and problems. Such exploration indicates what is significant and worthwhile, and sets the stage for significant empirical investigation of key problems involving actual public policies. A solid grasp of empirical phenomena, in turn, prepares the political scientist to grapple with problems of wise public policy (Part IV).

Let us turn next, in Chapter 10, to the quest for political science as a science of politics.

ANNOTATED BIBLIOGRAPHY

Auerbach, Bruce E. *Unto the Thousandth Generation: Conceptualizing Intergenerational Justice*. New York: Peter Lang, 1995. Provides a keen investigation of a concept—intergenerational justice—that should be central to the exploration of any future political philosophy. See also Auerbach's Chapter 11, "Intergenerational Justice and the Prophetic Tradition," in Neal Riemer, *Let Justice Roll: Prophetic Challenges in Religion, Politics, and Society* (Lanham, Md.: Rowman & Littlefield, 1996).

Bracher, Karl D. *The German Dictatorship*. New York: Praeger, 1970. Offers an authoritative account of the internal and external Nazi record of domination, aggression, and war.

Clapham, Christopher. *Third World Politics: An Introduction*. Madison: University of Wisconsin Press, 1985. Illuminates Third World ideology by concentrating on problems of survival and management of state, economy, and foreign affairs. Judicious.

Falk, Richard A. *A Study of Future Worlds*. New York: Free Press, 1975. Presents a world order perspective dedicated to peace, social justice, economic well-being, and ecological balance. Critical of the nation-state system, the war system, and dominant ideologies. For an update, see also Falk's *Explorations at the Edge of Time: The Prospects of World Order* (Philadelphia: Temple University Press, 1992) and *Revitalizing International Law* (Ames: Iowa State University Press, 1989).

Goldhagen, Daniel J. *Hitler's Willing Executioners: Ordinary Germans and the Holocaust*. New York: Knopf, 1996. Presents a powerful and provocative account of the murderous role of many ordinary Germans, infected by a diabolical anti-Semitic mindset that characterized so many in Nazi Germany, in the nefarious execution of the Nazis' "final solution."

Holmes, Robert L. *On War and Morality*. Princeton, N.J.: Princeton University Press, 1989. Provides a resource for futurists critical of violence, war, and political realism and favorable to the alternative of nonviolence.

Kershaw, Ian. *The Nazi Dictatorship*, 2nd ed. London: Edward Arnold, 1989. Offers interesting reading in Chapter 2, "The Essence of Nazism: Form of Fascism, Brand of Totalitarianism, or Unique Phenomenon?"

Lutz, Mark A., and Lux, Kenneth. *Humanistic Economics: The New Challenge*. New York: Bootstrap Press, 1988. Highlights the significance of human needs, reasonable rather than rational humans, and democracy in the workplace. A sharp challenge to conventional economics.

McCord, William, with Arline McCord. *Paths to Progress: Bread and Freedom in Developing Societies.* New York: Norton, 1989. Examines socialist, capitalist, and Islamic visions of development. Also highlights a "pragmatic fourth way" as illustrated by the Ivory Coast, Malaysia, and Costa Rica—countries that hold "values emphasizing science, rationality, planning, tolerance, innovation, and a belief that man influences his fate." Will be challenged by pessimists and skeptics.

Mosse, George L. *Crisis of German Ideology: Intellectual Origins of the Third Reich.* New York: Grosset & Dunlap, 1964. Emphasizes that Nazi ideas are deeply embedded in German history. Stresses the unique variety of German fascism, and the primacy of Volk, nature, and race in Nazi ideology.

Ophuls, William. *Ecology and the Politics of Scarcity Revisited: The Unraveling of the American Dream.* San Francisco: Freeman, 1992. Criticizes capitalism and socialism and raises serious questions about American democracy's capability in the new ecological age. Update of a brilliant critique.

Pottenger, John R. *The Political Theory of Liberation Theology: Toward a Reconvergence of Social Values and Social Science.* Albany: State University of New York Press, 1989. Offers a more sympathetic interpretation of liberation theology. See also Pottenger's Chapter 9, "Liberation Theology, Prophetic Politics, and Radical Social Critique: Quo Vadis?" in Neal Riemer, ed., *Let Justice Roll: Prophetic Challenges in Religion, Politics, and Society* (Lanham, Md.: Rowman & Littlefield, 1996).

Riemer, Neal. "Prophetic Politics: On the Political Philosophy of Stavrianos, Ferkiss and Falk," *Alternative Futures 2,* no. 4 (1979): 66–82; "Prophetic Politics and Foreign Policy," *International Interactions 8,* no. 1-2 (1981): 25–39. A pair of critical essays.

Riemer, Neal. *The Future of the Democratic Revolution: Toward a More Prophetic Politics.* New York: Praeger, 1984. Articulates a model of prophetic politics based on commitments to prophetic values, criticism, constitutional action, and futuristic scrutiny and projection.

Riemer, Neal. *Creative Breakthroughs in Politics.* Westport, Conn.: Praeger, 1996. Explores several historical breakthroughs, a contemporary breakthrough in European Union, and a proposed future breakthrough to protection against genocide.

Riemer, Neal, ed. *Let Justice Roll: Prophetic Challenges in Religion, Politics, and Society.* Lanham, Md.: Rowman & Littlefield, 1996. See especially, Chapter 10, "Reinhold Niebuhr, Political Realism, and Prophetic Politics," and Chapter 12, "The Prophetic Mode and Challenge, Creative Breakthroughs, and the Future of Constitutional Democracy."

Sigmund, Paul E., Jr. *Liberation Theology at the Crossroad: Democracy or Revolution?* New York: Oxford, 1990. Throws light on an outlook that has appealed in the Third World, particularly in Latin America.

Weiner, Myron, and Huntington, Samuel, eds. *Understanding Political Development.* Boston: Little, Brown, 1987. Provides helpful perspective on Third World ideology by exploring political change and the development of state and society. Huntington's chapter highlights the problem of conflict or compatibility of developmental goals. Also contains Gabriel Almond's critical review of "The Development of Political Development."

SUGGESTIONS FOR FURTHER READING

Blinkhorn, Martin, ed. *Fascists and Conservatives: The Radical Right and the Establishment in Twentieth-Century Europe.* London: Unwin Hyman, 1990.

Bookchin, Murray. *Remaking Society.* Quebec: Black Rose Books, 1989.

Brandt, Willy. *North-South: A Program for Survival.* Cambridge, Mass.: MIT Press, 1980.

Coates, Joseph F. *What Futurists Believe.* Mt. Airy, Md.: Lomond, 1989.

Dawidowicz, Lucy S. *The War Against the Jews, 1933–1945.* New York: Holt, Rinehart & Winston, 1975.

Diamond, Larry, Linez, Juan J., and Lipset, Seymour Martin, eds. *Democracy in Developing Countries.* Vol. 2, *Africa.* Boulder, Colo.: Lynne Rienner, 1988.

Etzioni, Amitai. *The Moral Dimension: Toward a New Economics.* New York: Free Press, 1988.

Falk, Richard A., Johansen, Robert C., and Kim, Samuel S. *The Constitutional Foundations of World Peace.* Albany: State University of New York Press, 1993.

Hughes, Barry. *World Futures: A Critical Analysis of Alternatives.* Baltimore: Johns Hopkins University Press, 1985.

Jalal, Ayesha. *Democracy and Authoritarianism in South Asia: A Comparative and Historical Perspective.* New York: Cambridge University Press, 1995.

Laqueur, Walter. *Fascism: Past, Present, and Future.* New York: Oxford University Press, 1996.

Milbrath, Lester W. *Envisioning a Sustainable Society*. Albany: State University of New York Press, 1989.

Pirages, Dennis. *Global Technopolitics: the International Politics of Technology and Resources*. Pacific Grove, Calif.: Brooks/Cole, 1989.

Smith, Woodruff D. *The Ideological Origins of Nazi Imperialism*. New York: Oxford University Press, 1986.

Soroos, Marvin. *Beyond Sovereignty: The Challenge of Global Policy*. Columbia: University of South Carolina Press, 1986.

GLOSSARY TERMS

anti-Semitism
autarcky
constitutional dictatorship
ethnocentrism
fascism
nation-state
nationalism
Nazism
neocolonialism
nonalignment
oligarchy
pragmatism
sovereignty
steady-state society
Third World
totalitarianism
ultranationalism

P   A   R   T   T   H   R   E   E

COMPARATIVE AND
WORLD POLITICS

In Part III we move on to the empirical task of political science. The overall question in Part III is, *How far have we come in our search for a fruitful science of politics?*

In seeking to answer that question, Chapter 10 (1) explores the common features of the scientific enterprise as seen by empirical political scientists, and (2) attempts to assess the strengths and weaknesses of the scientific enterprise.

Chapters 11 through 15 empirically investigate three important areas: the political values of political actors; patterns of political cooperation, accommodation, and conflict; and decision making in politics. Chapter 11 is concerned with the gap between professed values and actual values. Chapters 12, 13, and 14 focus on how current political patterns in selected countries and the international community protect security, liberty, justice, and welfare. Chapter 15 explores some models of decision making.

THE SCIENTIFIC ENTERPRISE

THE GUIDING QUESTION in this chapter is, *Which scientific research strategy is most profitable in political science, and why?* This question will require us to define science, to identify the common features of the scientific enterprise, and to assess its strengths and weaknesses. In general, we argue that the appropriate research strategy for political science depends on the character of the problem being investigated. A sensible research strategy thus calls for a fourfold approach: (1) identifying the significant problem, (2) articulating a guiding hypothesis to address the problem, (3) obtaining evidence to test the guiding hypothesis, and (4) validating and explaining the fuller significance of the hypothesis and the findings on which it rests.

The most fruitful research strategy seeks to place scientific work in a theoretical framework that demonstrates how the part relates to the whole. At its best the research will be genuinely comparative. Such a research strategy is oriented toward the future and is as predictive as the subject matter permits. It takes into account the tie between values and scientific research, and the tie between scientific research and practical political action designed to maximize preferred values.

In subsequent chapters in Parts III and IV we will also explore the various ways in which political scientists obtain evidence to support their empirical hypotheses.

SCIENCE AS A CRITICAL AND SYSTEMATIC SEARCH

Most students of the meaning of science emphasize **science** as a critical and systematic search for knowledge. Philosopher of science Jacob Bronowski called science a "search for order within the facts." Science is, he declared, "an activity of putting order into our experience."[1] And the ordering is systematic.

Similarly, philosopher and logician Irving Copi underscored science as a search for systematic relationships of particular events. The scientist, he wrote, "seeks more than a mere record of . . . phenomena; he strives to understand them. To this end he seeks to formulate general laws which state the patterns of all such occurrences and the systematic relationship between them. The scientist is engaged in a search for the natural laws according to which all particular events occur and the fundamental principles which underlie them."[2]

Karl Popper, another philosopher of science, emphasized the quest for truth rather than the possession of absolutely certain knowledge. "The wrong view of science betrays itself in the craving to be right; for it is not his possession of knowledge, or irrefutable truth, that makes the man of science, but his persistent and recklessly critical quest for truth." Science, Popper wrote, "never pursues the illusory aim of making its answers final. . . . Its advance is, rather, towards an infinite yet attainable aim: that of ever discovering new, deeper, and more general problems, and of subjecting our ever tentative answers to ever renewed and ever more rigorous tests."[3]

W. C. Kneale also called attention to the searching and creative character of science. He viewed science as a "search for judgments to which universal assent may be obtained . . . a search that never ends and is never satisfied." The "pursuit of science is the search for knowledge and understanding through the formulation of the laws of nature." Kneale emphasized science as "the making of knowledge and . . . not knowledge itself."[4]

These views of science as a critical and systematic search are perhaps more sophisticated than the view of physicist Percy Bridgman, who held that the scientist is simply someone "doing his damnedest," or the view of philosopher/psychologist William James that the scientist is engaged simply in hard thinking. Yet Bridgman

and James would not disagree on the importance of the continuing search for order, the primacy of problem solving, the fruitful interplay between theory and data, or the value of explanation.

Is there a right approach to scientific searching? Clearly, as Aristotle recognized long ago, there are many methods in the many sciences. And we would be foolish indeed to insist that the method of any one science (say, physics) is necessarily the method that can successfully be used in all sciences, including the social sciences. Abraham Kaplan loved to quote James Conant's view that the historians and philosophers of science performed a public service by emphasizing that there is no such thing as the scientific method. Practitioners of each science must use the methods that best enable them to do their jobs in accord with what Kaplan called the principle of "autonomy of inquiry."[5]

And the social sciences, because they deal with people, may differ from sciences that deal with inanimate objects or nonhuman animals. Social scientists may have a capacity for understanding other human beings that physical scientists do not have. Nonetheless, we can think of **scientific method** in the singular as meaning some pattern of reasoning common to all empirical sciences. Such a pattern of reasoning may hold for the social sciences in general and for political science in particular.

COMMON FEATURES OF THE SCIENTIFIC ENTERPRISE

In their problem solving, in their quest for order, in their search for more comprehensive knowledge to enhance understanding, all scientists use some common methods:

1. Scientists have to identify the problem to be investigated. The problem must be formulated clearly and precisely and must be susceptible to empirical investigation.
2. Scientists try to shape an initial hypothesis to guide their empirical and logical investigation of the problem. They must begin

their search within a rationally circumscribed field and with an organizing idea that enables them to collect data relevant to the problem that puzzles them or calls for additional knowledge.

3. Scientists must obtain and organize their data in order to make the facts coherent and useful.

4. Scientists must test, retest, corroborate, establish, and exploit their tentative hypothesis to clarify their problem, preferably within the framework of a larger theory.

Let us now expand on these four common features.

Problem Identification

Empirical scientists speculate or investigate because they are puzzled or troubled about a problem. The problem, then, creates an initial sensitivity, or primary orientation, that leads to an effort to articulate the trouble, to get at its root. Identification of the problem is the first step in the scientific procedure. It is the first effort to see which questions need to be asked and answered if the problem is to be "solved," the difficulty overcome, the uncertainty cleared up.

Some of the troubling questions in political science are

- Why is there war, or political injustice, or poverty, or ecological imbalance?
- What are the necessary and sufficient conditions of peace, justice, prosperity, and ecological health?
- How do we account for cruelty, intolerance, vulgarity, or mediocrity in social, cultural, and political life?
- What are the necessary and sufficient conditions of excellence in the community?

These are certainly big questions. But they provide a framework for posing and exploring more manageable problems. Thus, political scientists can focus on a specific war, such as World War II, the Vietnam War, or the Gulf War against Iraq, or on a specific peaceful arrangement, such as the Camp David peace accord between Israel and Egypt, the Oslo accords between Israel and the Palestinians, or the Dayton peace accords on Bosnia. Or they can focus on specific instances of injustice, whether Hitler's savage treatment of the Jews, Stalin's liquidation of the kulaks (well-off peasants), or America's mistreatment of minorities. Why certain societies (such as Sweden) score higher on a democratic and constitutional index than others (such as Argentina) could also be explored.

Even these topics may be too big and may have to be formulated more clearly and narrowly. A problem must always be formulated precisely if it is to permit empirical and logical investigation. The problem must also be posed in a context that indicates its relation to what is known and unknown. The problem, as a puzzle, must be tentatively fitted into the larger configuration that will give it meaning. In brief, the problem must be posed in such a way that it cries out for exploration and explanation.

On one hand, it is important not to bite off too big a chunk in trying to identify the problem. If the problem is big, its components should be reduced to manageable size. To bite off too much is to invite intellectual indigestion; on the other hand, to attempt too little is to be condemned to intellectual starvation and triviality.

The ability to formulate a problem calls for curiosity, an appreciation of facts that have no current acceptable explanation, a recognition of a difficulty that demands clarification, an appreciation of a mystery that begs for a solution. This ability is a creative ability. Only when we are able to formulate an answerable question can we make progress in dealing with a problem. As Karl Popper pointed out, "It is we who always formulate the questions to be put to nature; it is we who try again and again to put these questions so as to elicit a clear-cut 'yes' or 'no' (for nature does not give an answer unless pressed for it)."[6]

The significant problem, clearly formulated, provides a focus for worthwhile scientific investigation.

Hypothesis Articulation

Once the problem has been identified, the scientist has a target to shoot at, a goal to achieve. But how is this goal reached?

To start, the researcher needs a point of view or an organizing idea, to indicate which direction to take. This organizing idea constitutes a tentative **hypothesis,** a statement designed to help the investigator explore the problem, fit the puzzle into a larger configuration, and move toward a satisfactory explanation.

The tentative hypothesis guides investigators by sensitizing them to the data relevant to the problems that puzzle them. It sharpens their focus in what they consider to be the proper field of vision, while blurring or obscuring other points of view and data outside their range. It is, therefore, a powerful tool for focusing intelligence, directing vision, and relating data to the problem. If the tentative hypothesis is sound, it is a great aid. Even if it is not sound, it offers a chance to explore and exclude an initially persuasive possibility.

Here are some tentative hypotheses to illustrate the task of articulating a hypothesis:

1. *Problem:* Why did World War II occur? *Tentative hypothesis:* World War II was caused by the aggressive, nationalistic ambition of Germany to dominate Europe and of Japan to dominate Asia. *Alternative tentative hypothesis:* World War II was caused by the stubborn refusal of the Allies—Britain, France, the Soviet Union, and the United States—to allow Germany and Japan a more generous "place in the sun" in Europe and Asia.

2. *Problem:* Why was Stalin's treatment of Russian kulaks so brutal? *Tentative hypothesis:* Stalin believed that communism in the Soviet Union could not be achieved unless farms were taken away from their owners to make way for collectivization; farmers, such as the kulaks, who opposed Stalin's will had to be destroyed or repressed to ensure the triumph of communism. *Alternative hypothesis:* A psychopathic Stalin violated the principles of Soviet communist legality: the fault is not communism's but Stalin's.

3. *Problem:* Why is the United States rich and India poor? *Tentative hypothesis:* A number

What caused World War II? Several hypotheses have been proposed.

of factors account for America's affluence and India's poverty: (a) America has a relatively small population and abundant resources, whereas India has a large population and meager resources; (b) America has been an independent nation since 1776–1787, whereas India, before 1949, was an exploited colony of another country; (c) America has a more favorable geography than India; and (d) America's religious and social system is more attuned to the production of wealth than India's. *Alternative hypothesis:* America profits from capitalistic imperialism; India is a victim of it.

4. *Problem:* What causes ecological imbalance all over the world? *Tentative hypothesis:* A materialistic, hedonistic, egoistic philosophy of growth accounts for worldwide ecological imbalance—growth in population and in gross national product, even at the cost of pollution and a profligate waste of resources. *Alternative tentative hypothesis:* The Martians are to blame for ecological imbalance.

Articulating a useful hypothesis in scientific investigation is vitally important, according to a number of students of science. W. C. Kneale declared that the "all-important act in scientific discovery is the finding of a hypothesis that will survive testing." A hypothesis such as "The Martians are to blame for ecological imbalance" would never survive testing, even if it managed to be formulated. That "World War II was caused by the aggressive, nationalistic ambition of Germany to dominate Europe and of Japan to dominate Asia" may survive testing.

A hypothesis is a point of view designed to address a problem and to make data meaningful and testable. The point of view is crucial because, as the great English biologist Charles Darwin emphasized, "all observation must be for or against some view, if it is to be of service." The hypothesis provides direction and guidance. Undirected, unguided observation is fruitless.

Although there is no textbook rule or clear-cut method for formulating hypotheses, criteria—in addition to that of testability—exist for determining the worth and acceptability of a tentative hypothesis. These criteria include relevance, compatibility with previously well-established hypotheses, predictive or explanatory power, and simplicity. These criteria supplement, but by no means replace, testability. The hypothesis that "America profits from capitalistic imperialism; India is a victim of it" is simple, may be compatible with previous hypotheses, has predictive power, and may be relevant, especially for India; it may not, however, survive testing.

"Hypotheses are nets: only he who casts will catch."[7] But how do we cast and catch?

Before evidence can be gathered, researchers must know as precisely as possible what is being sought. Thus, key terms in the problem and hypothesis must be clearly defined. For example, in our problem and hypothesis about World War II, we would need to know the meaning of "aggressive, nationalistic ambition," and of "dominate." These words must have an operational meaning, so that empirical evidence can be used to confirm or disprove the hypothesis that the "aggressive, nationalistic ambition of Germany to dominate Europe and of Japan to dominate Asia" caused World War II. The word *caused* would also have to be carefully defined. Unless the terms are carefully defined, the hypothesis will be too full of holes or slippery to allow us to cast or catch sensibly.

Reliable Data Collection

The next systematic step is to obtain, organize, and focus the relevant data. The data must be coherent, accurate, and usefully related to the hypothesis and problem. Thus researchers need a scheme for knowing what data to obtain, how to classify them, and what instruments to use to gather them. The scheme, classification, and instruments will depend on the specific problem being investigated.

Data make testing possible. Scientists seek data that will corroborate their hypotheses. Debate still rages on the correct way to test and verify, but it is clear that data are indispensable no matter what procedure follows. The data must be relevant to the hypothesis; they must be able to prove the empirical proposition true or false. The data must be accurate. The data must add up or fit together as a meaningful pattern.

To understand the causes of World War II, for example, we would seek evidence, in word and deed, of Germany and Japan's aggressive, nationalistic ambition; or, alternatively, of the stubborn refusal of Britain, France, the Soviet Union, and the United States to allow Germany and Japan a "place in the sun." To understand Stalin's unjust treatment of his own Russian people, we would seek evidence of his conviction that communism in the Soviet Union could not be achieved without collectivization and that collectivization could not be a voluntary and peaceful process; alternatively, we would look for proof that Stalin acted not in support of communist principles but in opposition to them. To understand prosperity and poverty in the United States and India, we would need evidence concerning population and resources in both countries, the history of each as a colony and as an independent nation, and information on their geography and their religious and social systems. To understand ecological imbalance, we would seek evidence of conscious or unconscious decisions that led to dangerous levels of pollution, population wildly in excess of resources, and profligate waste and misuse of resources. We would need evidence of a "growth mentality."

The data may verify a hypothesis or prove it false. They may also lead an investigator to modify the tentative hypothesis and statement of the problem, or to substitute a new and different hypothesis. This, in turn, would lead to the gathering of additional data to establish or disprove the new hypothesis.

Hypothesis Validation and Scientific Explanation

After testing and critical examination, the tentative hypothesis is either established more firmly or rejected. This step involves **validation** or corroboration to determine a fit between hypothesis and evidence. Does the hypothesis help solve the problem, overcome the difficulty, clear up the uncertainty? The hypothesis must take into account what needs to be accounted for.

After full investigation, for example, do we attribute World War II to the aggressive, nationalistic ambition of Germany and Japan, or to the stubborn refusal of Britain, France, the Soviet Union, and the United States to allow Germany and Japan a "place in the sun," or to some other hypothesis—perhaps the clash of capitalistic and imperialistic rivals, or sunspots? Was communism or Stalin's psychopathic personality and his behavior (in violation of Soviet norms) responsible for the unjust treatment of so many Soviet citizens under his rule? Do prosperity and poverty depend not on a single factor—such as capitalistic imperialism—but on a conjunction of circumstances: population, resources, geography, and economic and social philosophy? Is ecological imbalance understandable only in terms of a materialistic, hedonistic, egotistic philosophy of growth that characterizes the United States as well as China, India as well as Brazil, and Japan as well as Egypt?

The validation of hypotheses is closely linked to scientific explanation. Scientists want to validate an immediate hypothesis (such as about World War II or Stalin's injustices), but they also want to see how the mature hypothesis fits into a larger pattern, a more complete and satisfactory story. Hence we ask, does aggressive, nationalistic ambition also explain World War I? All war? And why does this aggressive ambition exist? Is it rooted in the sovereign nation-state system? Or in the aggressive nature of people? We also want to know whether a rigid ideology might explain injustice in China or Iraq or what was once Yugoslavia, as well as in Stalin's Soviet Union or Hitler's Germany. Or is the deeper explanation to be found in pathological leaders, or a repressive economic system? Similarly, we want to know whether ecological imbalance is rooted in a growth mania characteristic only of modern capitalism and socialism or in a philosophy of mastery as old as recorded civilization.

Explanation is the process of fitting the pieces of the puzzle together. Explanation involves how the pieces of the puzzle relate to each other and also how the immediate problem relates to the larger puzzling configuration. World War II is one major conflagration. How does it fit into the larger pattern of conflict and accommodation? Are sovereign nation-states key factors in major wars? Communism is one ideology. Is there something about rigid ideologies that makes for injustice? Is economic prosperity the result of luck or of design? Is ecological imbalance characteristic only of the modern impulse to dominate nature? As we explore topics such as war, totalitarian ideology, economic prosperity, and economic imbalance, we must ask large questions like these to find a full explanation.

Explanation expands our scientific power enormously, enabling us to connect links in a chain and to extend the chain. This extension involves expanding the hypothesis to gain the maximum value. Explanation may pull together ideas and evidence not previously linked. It may throw unexpected light on additional problems. It can considerably extend the range of knowledge and illuminate further hypotheses. In all these ways explanation clarifies the initial problem and hypothesis.

Let us use the analogy of a mystery story. The explanation of the mystery—what the crime was, who did it, and how—may throw light on other unsolved crimes. In another analogy, solving the mystery of a disease that has strangely afflicted one person will explain the same ailment in others. At the beginning of the search for causes of infectious disease, scientists discovered that certain germs caused chicken cholera and anthrax in animals. With the germ theory, or explanation, accepted, the scientists went on to search for other "germs" responsible for other diseases.

Significant problems in the social sciences—war, injustice, and poverty—are more complicated than most problems in the physical sciences.

Single-factor explanations—for instance, the sovereign nation-state, capitalism, or ideology—are rightly suspect most of the time. And yet bold and seemingly outrageous hypotheses—such as certain Marxist hypotheses—may illuminate problems. And so may hypotheses about the sovereign nation-state, falsely messianic ideologies, and the growth mania that afflicts communist and capitalist countries alike.

Fuller understanding of a hypothesis calls for answers to the "why" and "how" questions. When these questions have been satisfactorily answered, investigators have an explanation. With the explanation, the pieces of the puzzle fit together. The explanation removes the puzzling character of the problem that first called for investigation.

Fruitful hypotheses and explanations solve significant problems and account for a wide range of puzzling circumstances. At the highest and most fruitful level these hypotheses serve as a guiding scientific **theory.** So empirical scientists move from hunch to tentative hypothesis to scientific theory. In this way they try to move from opinion to knowledge, from the less systematic to the more systematic, from scattered knowledge to more reliable architectonic (systematic) understanding. They seek, by their more systematic and critical searching, to expand the boundaries of humanity's understanding as widely as possible. Problem solving is their primary function. Their objective in performing this function is to attain the broadest and most reliable knowledge and understanding.

THE STRENGTHS AND WEAKNESSES OF THE SCIENTIFIC ENTERPRISE

Properly used, the common features of the scientific enterprise can greatly help the scientific investigator in politics. But we should not expect too much of the scientific enterprise, and we need to be aware of certain dangers that may befall the scientific investigator in politics.

Strengths of the Scientific Enterprise

There is value in a systematic, rational, and critical scientific approach. Such an approach seeks to clearly define the empirical problem so that it can be investigated with the help of relevant evidence. There is value in responding to the empirical problem by framing a tentative hypothesis that can be tested. There is value in moving beyond hunch to evidence, beyond opinion to knowledge; there is value in bringing relevant evidence to bear on a tentative hypothesis. And there is value in validating a hypothesis, obtaining a sensible explanation of a "why" or a "how" question, and fitting the pieces of a puzzle together in a more coherent whole.

The scientific enterprise facilitates problem solving. It helps political scientists to be more directed, more economical, more logical, and more searching. It helps them manage their problems.

The scientific enterprise also encourages political scientists to work within a framework of scientific theory that helps them see which variables or factors are significant. The scientific enterprise encourages them to classify, generalize about, and integrate evidence relevant to their problems. Thus, political scientists are helped with their second major task: the empirical task.

Weaknesses of the Scientific Enterprise

Political scientists make a serious mistake, however, if they expect too much of the scientific enterprise and if they succumb to certain dangers that sometimes affect the scientific investigator.

Excessive Expectations—For example, empirical political scientists may think (1) that all problems in politics are empirical, (2) that all empirical problems can be easily solved, (3) that even difficult problems can be solved if enough money and effort are poured into the search for a solution, and (4) that politics is ultimately reducible to physics, or biology, or mathematics.

As we noted in Chapter 3 and emphasized throughout Part II, politics contains ethical problems as well as empirical ones. And, as we stressed in Chapter 3 and will reemphasize in Part IV, politics contains prudential problems as well. We are concerned with questions about the

good political life and wise public policy as well as with strictly empirical questions.

Moreover, not all empirical problems can be easily solved. Many important empirical problems are exceedingly difficult. Solutions to such big problems as "Why war?" or "Why injustice?" or "Why poverty?" are not easily found. The empirical problems that can be successfully dealt with are generally much more modest.

Furthermore, it is not clear that even large expenditures of money and effort can solve difficult empirical problems. Governments in most industrial societies still struggle to achieve economic stability, which involves, for example, the problem of avoiding periodic recessions, maintaining high levels of employment and income without inflation, and taming (as in the United States) budget and trade deficits.

Finally, although political science may wisely borrow some methods from the physical or biological sciences, the fruitfulness of such borrowing is limited. For example, political scientists cannot experiment with political actors in the same controlled way that physicists or chemists can experiment with atoms and molecules, or biologists with bacteria or DNA. Fruitful empirical generalizations are rare in political science. Master generalizations (such as Einstein's $E = mc^2$) do not exist in politics.

Dangers—In addition, a number of dangers face the empirical political scientist. One is the ant complex. This is the danger of what David Easton has called "hyperfactualism"[8]—collecting information for its own sake, as the ant piles up bits of dirt in big mounds. This is the danger of operating without a guiding empirical theory that gives direction and meaning to the collection of data.

A second danger is the spider complex. This is the danger of sterile theoretical speculation, of spinning grand empirical theories divorced from fertile interaction with reality. It is the danger of the armchair theorist who develops grand ideas about empirical reality but is unwilling to relate theory to evidence, to test theory in the real world.

Abraham Kaplan, following Francis Bacon, preferred the bee syndrome to the ant or spider complex. "Bacon himself characterizes the scientist as being neither wholly speculative and like the spider spinning his web from his own substance, nor wholly empirical and like an ant collecting data into a heap, but like the bee feeding on the nectar it gathers, digesting it, and so transmuting it into the purest honey."[9]

A third danger is that of the drunkard's search. Kaplan explained this danger as follows: "There is a story of a drunkard searching under a street lamp for his house key, which he had dropped some distance away. Asked why he didn't look where he had dropped it, he replied, 'It's lighter here!' Much effort, not only in the logic of behavioral science, but also in behavioral science itself, is vitiated, in my opinion, by the principle of the drunkard's search."[10]

A fourth danger is that of the law of the instrument. This is the danger of becoming so fascinated with a newly discovered tool—greatly useful on a particular problem or in a particular area—that one insists on using it on all problems and in all areas. The popularity of the survey method—an instrument of great help in a particular area of research—may illustrate this danger. Survey research greatly illuminates certain problems, particularly in the realm of public opinion, but its usefulness may be nil, or decidedly limited, in studying other important empirical questions, such as why the Soviet Union decided to withdraw offensive missiles from Cuba.

A fifth danger is that of focusing on the **status quo**—currently dominant actors, institutions, or ideas. This danger exists because of the visibility and influence of powerful political actors, institutions, and ideas. It is easier to explore what is familiar. It is more difficult to deal with the invisible or less visible, the unimportant or less powerful. Thus, it is relatively easy for the empirical political scientist to ignore the invisible poor, impotent minorities, and the unorganized. The danger is that preoccupation with the dominant forces of the status quo leads to neglect of other important forces in politics,

forces whose potential is recognized only when a riot occurs or when a revolution overthrows the regime in power. Then empirical political scientists who have been preoccupied with the status quo are surprised by the dramatic development. This danger can also lead the empirical political scientist to ignore the gap between an ethical ideal and political (and social and economic) reality, to neglect the empirical exploration of the process of social change (whether development or decay), and to miss the emerging realities of the future. The failure of almost all political scientists to predict the collapse of the Soviet Union—and the demise of communism in the USSR—is a most dramatic illustration of the danger of focusing on the status quo.

A sixth danger is triviality—that is, choosing to investigate inconsequential problems. Such problems are often chosen because they are easy to handle. The trick in empirical research is to select a meaningful but manageable problem. Striking a balance takes considerable judgment, but guarding against the danger of triviality will help strike that wise balance.

Assessment of the Scientific Enterprise

The dangers we've just discussed warn empirical political scientists that they must use their creative imaginations in a number of ways. They must identify worthwhile and manageable problems. They must search in fruitful areas. They must use appropriate instruments (concept, theory, hypothesis, classification, and data-gathering tools). They must transform the data into "the purest honey." As Aristotle first admonished, they must not ask for, or expect, more scientific precision than the subject matter permits. One model of science—for example, physics—must not be expected to fit in all domains. And empirical political scientists must not be discouraged by different rates of development in the sciences. Many approaches to scientific problems can be explored, but an investigator must always fit the approach to the problem rather than automatically assuming that one approach can solve all problems. Political scientists can carefully assess scientific development to see how it will ease their problem solving and make it bear fruit in various fields.

On balance, the behavioral revolution in political science—which placed great emphasis on the scientific approach—has strengthened empirical political science. When divorced from the status quo bias that has sometimes characterized it, when carried on in a more critical spirit—to address significant problems of war and peace, injustice and justice, poverty and prosperity— the behavioral revolution can show that the quest for a science of politics is compatible with the good political life.

The empirical aspects of political science must be investigated with the best scientific tools available. Investigation is subject to the limitations and constraints imposed by the nature of empirical phenomena in politics. The search can be only as rigorous and objective as the problem permits. The complexity of political phenomena—the multiplicity, interaction, and elusiveness of key variables in politics—makes a scientific effort difficult but not impossible. Human freedom does not make it impossible to study human regularities and even to scientifically attempt to account for creativity, surprises, and departures from regularity.

Science does not require perfect understanding. It does not demand a specific, elegant, hypothetical-deductive model. It does not insist on an architectonic, all-encompassing general theory. It does not invariably stipulate a controlled experiment or even prediction or mathematically precise laws. Science requires only a search for greater understanding, with the help of whatever tools will advance that understanding.

In science, investigators rely on sensory data, but they are not limited to one preconceived empirical model in their efforts to understand political phenomena. Quantification is a tool to be used on significant empirical problems and pushed as far as the subject matter will permit. Empirical political scientists can dream of an architectonic general theory, even though it may

not seem presently attainable, if the quest for such a theory is fruitful and does not discourage more modest, middle-range, empirical theory or more modest generalizations.

Moreover, empirical political research can focus on problems of great ethical importance. Why are some political communities more successful in achieving a peaceful, just, prosperous, constitutional order? Do answers to this question also throw light on peace, justice, prosperity, and democracy in the emergent global community? Although these are big questions, they can be broken down into smaller, more manageable problems—involving, for example, the exploration of certain operative ideals in certain countries, certain patterns of conflict and accommodation, and certain public policy decisions.

Empirical research on the burning practical issues of the day is most important. But political scientists must always realize that fundamental empirical research (which may not seem immediately relevant) may have an important payoff for momentous practical problems. The question of the triviality of empirical research must be raised, but not always because of a concern for immediate practical payoff. The question may be raised out of concern for a genuinely fruitful understanding of politics. So a balance must be struck between a concentration on the practical and the manageable on one hand, and the fundamental and the significant on the other hand. The most fruitful empirical research would be simultaneously fundamental and practical, significant and manageable.

It cannot be successfully argued that empirical political science is intrinsically characterized by conservatism, a fear of popular democracy, and an avoidance of vital political issues, even though some empirical research may reveal these characteristics. However, empirical political scientists who focus only on what is (and ignore what has been, and will or can be) may be status quo oriented. Empirical political scientists who want to do justice to politics as a dynamic activity, and to political actors as both products and shapers of evolution, cannot ignore change.

Within the framework of this critical assessment—unafraid of politics and convinced that politics can be a civilizing activity—empirical political scientists can proudly hold as their motto: "The more science at its best, the better."

CONCLUSION

In this chapter we have argued that an appropriate research strategy depends on the character of the empirical problem to be investigated. This suggests the great importance of clarifying and stating the problem. The significant problem will then suggest to creative and imaginative political scientists which approach to take. There is no rigid, dogmatic formula for the right scientific approach to every empirical problem. Given the diversity of empirical problems, there will be diverse strategies and diverse methods.

Empirical theory of one kind or another will guide empirical political scientists. Their theory may be modest or ambitious. It may rest on an age-old formulation of politics as a struggle for power in which political actors seek to protect their vital interests, or on the pluralist formula of public policy as a result of group pressures. It may rest on a Marxist concept of class struggle, or on a more complex systems theory. To be most fruitful, however, empirical theory must link up with ethical theory and with prudential theory. That is, the search for an empirical science of politics must be related to the quest for the good political life and to wise public policy.

The importance of the empirical exploration of values, of patterns of cooperation, accommodation, and conflict, and of decision-making models will be examined in the succeeding five chapters. These chapters will illustrate in more detail many of the generalizations about the scientific enterprise made in this chapter.

ANNOTATED BIBLIOGRAPHY

Almond, Gabriel A. *A Discipline Divided: Schools and Sects in Political Science.* Newbury Park, Calif.: Sage, 1989. Offers a recent assessment by a keen student of comparative politics. Chapter 1 deals with political science as a science. Critically explores a number of models in political science.

Baer, Michael A., Jewell, Malcolm E., and Sigelman, Lee, eds. *Political Science in America: Oral Histories of the Discipline.* Lexington: University Press of Kentucky, 1991. Presents revealing conversations with Charles Hyneman, E. Pendleton Herring, Belle Zeller, Emmette S. Redford, R. Taylor Cole, Marian D. Irish, C. Herman Pritchett, Gabriel Almond, David Truman, Robert Martin, Robert A. Dahl, Heinz Eulau, David Easton, Austin Ranney, and Warren Miller.

Brecht, Arnold. *Political Theory: The Foundations of Twentieth-Century Political Thought.* Princeton, N.J.: Princeton University Press, 1959. Explores the key features of the scientific enterprise. The author is open, however, to the insights and contributions of other approaches to political science.

Crotty, William, ed. *Political Science: Looking to the Future.* 4 Vols. Vol. 1: *The Theory and Practice of Political Science* (Evanston, Ill.: Northwestern University Press, 1991). See, particularly, the illuminating articles by Donald M. Freeman, "The Making of a Discipline"; J. Donald Moon, "Pluralism and Progress in the Study of Politics"; and Terence Ball, "Whither Political Theory." Vol. 2: *Comparative Politics, Policy, and International Relations.* Vol. 3: *Political Behavior.* Vol. 4: *American Institutions.*

Easton, David. *The Political System: An Inquiry into the State of Political Science.* New York: Knopf, 1953. Presents a highly influential attempt to direct work in political science toward a more self-conscious, systematic, empirical theory. Easton's own follow-up work is found in *A Framework for Political Analysis* (Englewood Cliffs, N.J.: Prentice-Hall, 1965) and *A Systems Analysis of Political Life* (New York: Wiley, 1965). Long on system, framework, and classification; short on rich empirical generalization and theory.

Graham, George J., Jr. *Methodological Foundations for Political Analysis.* Waltham, Mass.: Xerox College Publishing, 1971. Presents the "basic principles of methodology drawn from the philosophy of science literature, as they apply to political science research and analysis." Maintains that scientific and traditional approaches to political science are not incompatible.

Gunnell, John. *Philosophy, Science, and Political Inquiry.* Morristown, N.J.: General Learning Press,

1975. Introduces the student to the controversies surrounding the understanding of empirical/behavioral political science. Disapproves of "doctrines uncritically appropriated from logical positivism and empiricism." Boldly argues on behalf of the "thesis that the logical positivist/empiricist analysis of the logic and epistemology of science is inadequate and that it has no claim to authority whatsoever in the area of social scientific investigation." See also his *Between Philosophy and Politics: The Alienation of Political Theory*. Amherst: University of Massachusetts Press, 1986.

Kuhn, Thomas. *The Structure of Scientific Revolutions,* 2nd ed. Chicago: University of Chicago Press, 1970. Stresses the importance of the new paradigm, or model, that helped scientists break through to a hypothesis that could overcome the puzzles of normal science (the accepted way of understanding). Enormously influential book in the social sciences.

McCoy, Charles, and Playford, John, eds. *Apolitical Politics: A Critique of Behavioralism*. New York: Crowell, 1967. Quarrels with the narrow methodology and restrictive orthodoxy of behavioral political science, whose practitioners betray in their work conservatism, a fear of popular democracy, and an avoidance of vital issues. Written by political scientists who favor a better, more realistic empirical political science.

Popper, Karl R. *The Logic of Scientific Discovery*. London: Hutchinson, 1968. Stresses the critical quest for truth as the distinguishing characteristic of the scientist. For Popper's adverse criticism of the "science" of Plato, Hegel, and Marx, see *The Open Society and Its Enemies* (Princeton: Princeton University Press, 1945).

Ricci, David M. *The Tragedy of Political Science: Politics, Scholarship, and Democracy*. New Haven, Conn.: Yale University Press, 1984. Sees a conflict between science and commitment to the good, wise, democratic life.

Somit, Albert, and Tanenhaus, Joseph. *The Development of Political Science*. Boston: Allyn & Bacon, 1967. Regards the behavioral revolution as the most recent scientific emphasis in a discipline always concerned with science—as well as with education for citizenship and involvement in public policy.

SUGGESTIONS FOR FURTHER READING

Ball, Terence. *Transforming Political Discourse*. New York: Blackwell, 1988.

Ball, Terence, Farr, James, and Hanson, Russell L., eds. *Political Innovation and Conceptual Change*. Cambridge: Cambridge University Press, 1989.

Crick, Bernard. *The American Science of Politics: Its Origins and Conditions*. Berkeley: University of California Press, 1959.

Eulau, Heinz, ed. *Crossroads of Social Science: The ICPSR 25th Anniversary Volume*. New York: Agathon Press, 1989.

Farr, James, Dryzek, John S., and Leonard, Stephen T. *Political Science in History: Research Programs and Political Traditions*. New York: Cambridge University Press, 1995.

Finifter, Ada, ed. *Political Science: The State of the Discipline II*. Washington, D.C.: American Political Science Association, 1993.

Johnson, Nevill. *The Limits of Political Science*. Oxford: Oxford University Press, 1989.

Kariel, Henry S. *Saving Appearances: The Reestablishment of Political Science*. North Scituate, Mass.: Duxbury Press, 1972.

Kavanagh, Dennis. *Political Science and Political Behavior*. Winchester, Mass.: Allen & Unwin, 1983.

Moon, J. Donald. "The Logic of Political Inquiry: A Synthesis of Opposed Perspectives." In Fred I. Greenstein and Nelson W. Polsby, eds., *Political Science: Scope and Theory,* vol. I. Reading, Mass.: Addison-Wesley, 1975.

Murphy, John W. *Post-Modern Social Analysis and Criticism*. Westport, Conn.: Greenwood, 1989.

Weisberg, Herbert F. *Political Science: The Science of Politics*. New York: Agathon Press, 1986.

GLOSSARY TERMS

explanation
hypothesis
science
scientific method
status quo
theory
validation

THE POLITICAL VALUES OF POLITICAL ACTORS

THE FRUITFUL SEARCH for a science of politics begins with significant empirical questions that can be answered in a theoretical, critical, and rewarding way. The focus of our attention in this chapter is, *How do the actual political values of political actors compare with civilized values such as peace, liberty, justice, and welfare?*

Our discussion of political philosophy and ideology in Chapters 5 through 9 has already thrown considerable light on the professed and actual values of political actors. For example, political leaders, political parties, voters, and interest groups in the United States, Great Britain, and France generally share the values of liberal democracy or democratic socialism. Thus, both liberal democrats and democratic socialists share the values of popular, limited, representative government. They share the vision of individual realization within the framework of the common good. Democratic socialists endorse the value of extending democracy in all spheres. They favor public ownership of key aspects of the economy. They advocate a more equitable sharing of the common wealth in a cooperative community and a peaceful world. Their guiding vision is social justice.

Historically, the guiding vision for communist political actors has been Marx's vision of freedom, peace, abundance, humanity, community, and development. They value worker, or popular, control of the means of production and exchange. They have, at least in the past, valued the Communist party as the voice and leader of the proletariat. They endorse the communist principle: From each according to his ability; to each according to his needs.

It is more difficult to characterize the values of political actors in the developing countries, if only because of the enormous number and variety of cultures involved. In many instances, what might be termed hybrid sets of values have emerged, which may borrow from several traditions, indigenous as well as imported. It is probably fair to say, however, that many Third World political actors have strongly endorsed the goals of national freedom and independence, in part as a reaction to the repressive colonial heritage of the nineteenth and twentieth centuries. Further, they appear to endorse economic development and social advancement. Finally, increasing numbers of Third World countries have professed fundamental principles of democracy.

KEY QUESTIONS AND DEFINITIONS

But critical questions must be asked about visions of the good political life and about the operative ideals of political actors in differing political systems. What do their professed values really mean? Are they honored in practice?

Questions About Values

Here we need to expand this chapter's central question on the comparison of actual and civilized values as follows:

1. What is the full meaning of the political values that political actors believe in and practice?
2. What can we say about the struggles between, and harmony among, values?
3. What gap exists between civilized and actual values, between rhetoric and reality?
4. What can we say about the future of political values?

To answer critical questions, political scientists must define key terms.

Some Key Definitions

Political values are important beliefs about the goals, principles, and policies that are worthwhile in public affairs.

A **goal** is an objective. It may be peace, security, and order, or war, domination, and power. It may be liberty, equality, justice, and fraternity,

or slavery, subordination, tyranny, and enmity. The goal may be a fair return on national investment and international respect, or rampant profit and national self-righteousness. The goal may be democratic and constitutional government, or oligarchic or dictatorial/authoritarian rule. It may be economic prosperity for all, or affluence for the few. It may be a healthy environment or a highly productive society that ignores ecological health. The goal may be a creative, robust quality of life, or mediocrity. As necessary, each of these goals must be defined more precisely.

A **principle** is a basic truth or doctrine used as a basis of reasoning or a guide to behavior. It may be peaceful change (reliance on ballots rather than bullets) or violent change (breaking heads). The principle may be freedom of speech for all or freedom only for the elite. Principles actually at work in political communities often illustrate compromises among competing ideas.

A **policy** is a course, or general plan, of action. It may be balance of power, balance of terror, or unilateral disarmament. The policy may be universal suffrage or suffrage limited to rich, well-educated males. The policy may be a progressive income tax or a sales tax. The policy may be public standards for clean air and pure water or a hands-off policy.

Goals, principles, and policies (which sometimes overlap) often function as norms. They help determine whether certain standards are being met. Consequently, they serve as important guideposts in politics. As such, they merit careful study.

The Array of Political Actors

Political actors are the individuals or groups that express and shape public values, struggle for power, and decide issues of public policy. Political communities are political actors. So are governmental leaders who exercise power on behalf of political communities. Governmental, economic, social, and sometimes military elites are political actors as well. Political parties, a wide range of interest groups, and agencies of the mass media—newspapers, television networks, news magazines—are political actors. Individual citizens—letter writers, demonstrators, and voters—are political actors.

Nation-states constitute one important variety of political community. The United Nations is another type of political community. The subdivisions of nation-states—for example, the 50 states of the United States, its 3,043 counties, and its nearly 87,000 local governments—are also political actors. A number of regional and functional organizations, such as the European Union, are political actors. And so, increasingly, are the multinational corporations.

This incredibly large array of political actors has led political scientists to wrestle with what is sometimes referred to as the *level-of-analysis* problem.[1] In attempting to understand international relations, for instance, is it more appropriate to concentrate on *national governments* as the primary actors or on the decision makers who lead the governments? Or should one concentrate on the *international system* itself and its patterns of military, economic, and political interaction between governments, international organizations, and nongovernmental organizations? In other words, must one operate on a global level to really understand what is going on?

Guiding Hypotheses

In our exploration of the values of political actors in this chapter, we limit our analysis to national values, popular (citizen) values, and interest group and class values. A helpful theoretical orientation always advances a sound empirical analysis. Such a theoretical orientation uses a meaningful hypothesis addressed to the empirical questions. Our rough but ready guiding hypothesis is fourfold:

1. The political values of political actors are rooted in their vital needs, fundamental interests, and perceived desires.
2. The struggle over political values is conditioned by differing interpretations of needs, interests, and desires by diverse political

actors and by the historical distribution of power. These factors make for both conflict and consensus in politics.

3. The world of politics often contains serious gaps between professed values and actual behavior. The gaps exist because political actors—nation-states, governing elites, powerful interests, and often citizens themselves—are unable to break out of parochial, rigidly ideological patterns of thought and behavior. Because human resources and capabilities are limited, it is often difficult to narrow these gaps.
4. Although prediction is hazardous, the future will probably include a major constitutional and democratic struggle between broad and narrow values. This struggle will manifest itself in several ways. There will be a contest between broader global or regional human needs and narrower, parochial national interests. There will also be a contest between broad, truly fundamental community interests and narrower, selfish group and individual desires. Finally, there will be a contest between vital individual and local interests and oppressive, centralized interests and desires. This struggle will most certainly require a realistic understanding of vital needs, of compatible fundamental interests, and of modest and prudent desires.

THE VALUES OF NATIONS AS POLITICAL ACTORS

Nations (more accurately, national leaders, ruling elites, or governing parties) generally profess and often seek to protect the *national interest* in foreign affairs and the *public interest* in domestic affairs. They generally interpret the national and public interest in terms of four main values—security, liberty, justice, and welfare—that they take to be the vital needs and fundamental interests of nations.

The **national interest** is frequently endorsed as the standard for statesmanship in a nation's dealings with other nations.² The **public interest** is supposed to be the interest of the entire community, which presumably transcends the selfish interests of individuals or groups. It presumably expresses the best long-range interests of the nation.³

There is considerable historical evidence that many leaders of national governments value survival, security, safety, peace, territorial integrity, defense, prosperity, independence, and power. They value their **liberty**—their capacity to govern themselves, to be in control of their own destiny, and to enjoy the rights, at home and abroad, that make freedom meaningful. They seek a measure of justice at home and, sometimes, abroad. They profess, at least in most nations, to favor equality before the law, due process of law, and an equitable distribution of wealth. They favor the principle of equal treatment of sovereign nations in the world community and respect for international law and procedure. They profess to care about the welfare of their citizens at home and the afflicted abroad. They often favor policies to enhance national economic well-being through growth, production, full employment, decent farm prices, and satisfactory business profits. They support policies to enhance social well-being through literacy, good health and housing, and adequate food and nutrition. They endorse stable institutions and organizations as a way to ensure political well-being.

But—in the critical and truth-seeking tradition of political science—we must probe more deeply. What more specific meaning—indeed as well as in word—do those who exercise power on behalf of nations give to their values? Are such terms as the *national interest* and the *public interest* idealistic myths? Are they cover-ups for naked national power or for dominant elites? Are vital national needs really vital? For whom? Do nations often mistake lustful desires for legitimate interests? And are there serious gaps between civilized (and often professed) values and the actual values revealed in national behavior?

Let us now attempt to probe key national values of the developed, communist, and developing regions of the world. We can, of course, present only a modest part of the evidence that bears on our questions and might sustain our hypothesis. But such evidence may at least suggest the larger empirical task required for a more rewarding understanding of nations' political values.

Security and Peace

The leaders of most nations say they believe in security and peace. Yet the historical record reveals that nations frequently engage in war, often with mutually disastrous results. Figure 11.1 summarizes the global war experience from 1816 to 1992.

For a conflict to classify as a war, at least 1,000 battle deaths must occur. The data clearly indicate that the number of wars has not dramatically increased. This is remarkable, considering the increased number of countries in the world. But before we think things are improving, two observations should be made. First, the thousand-death criterion means that hundreds of violent engagements—border skirmishes, interstate sabotage, acts of state-sponsored terrorism—are not included. Further, although the number of wars over time seems to be holding fairly steady, the number of deaths has increased dramatically in the twentieth century, as revealed in Figures 11.2 and 11.3.

There is a sarcastic adage in international relations that says, "All wars are fought in self-defense." Has each nation engaged only in just wars, defending itself against aggressive opponents and protecting its security against real attack? Or have at least some nations, using the pretext of protecting their vital interests, attacked and jeopardized the security of other, peace-loving nations? Do defense preparations, or war, actually serve to protect a nation's security?

Scholars will quarrel about answers to these questions. Evaluations are difficult because there is no agreement on key terms. For example, there is no common definition of *just war, defen-*

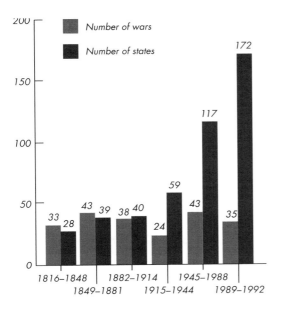

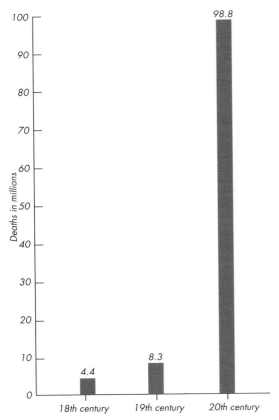

Figure 11.1
The frequency of war, 1816–1992.

Source: Data for 1816 to 1988 generated by Melvin Small and J. David Singer, Correlates of War Project. See Small and Singer, "Patterns in International Warfare, 1816–1990," in Small and Singer, eds., International War: An Anthology, 2nd ed. (Chicago: Dorsey Press, 1989) and J. David Singer, "Peace in the Global System: Displacement, Interregnum, or Transformation?" in Charles W. Kegley, Jr., ed., The Long Post War Peace (New York: HarperCollins, 1991), 56–84. Data for 1989–1992 from Peter Wallenstein and Krill Axell, "Armed Conflict at the End of the Cold War, 1989–1992," Journal of Peace Research 30 (August 1993), 331–346, and U. S. Central Intelligence Agency, The World Factbook, 1993–94 (New York: Brassey's, 1993).

Figure 11.2
Deaths in wars by century.

Source: Ruth Leger Sivard, World Military and Social Expenditures, 1986 (Washington, D.C.: World Priorities, 1986).

Figure 11.3
Increase in war deaths versus increase in world population.

Source: Ruth Leger Sivard, World Military and Social Expenditures, 1986 (Washington, D.C.: World Priorities, 1986).

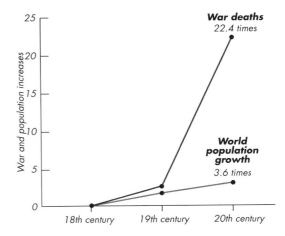

sive war, or aggressive war, or of vital interests or security. Neither is there consensus on the meaning, value, and cost of adequate defense. These problems assume enormous importance as the world passes out of the forty-five-year Cold War between the Soviet and Western blocs. The enormous tension and distrustful atmosphere of the Cold War provided a powerful driving force for the building of conventional and nuclear arsenals in the post–World War II period.

There can, however, be little quarrel about the following points:

1. A serious gap exists between talk of peace and the reality of war.
2. Different nations often hold incompatible conceptions of national security.
3. Sometimes nations counter power with power in order to protect vital national interests.
4. National defense expenditures are huge and distort other priorities.
5. The machinery for peace and peaceful change is inadequate.

Hitler talked of peace but did not hesitate to launch World War II by attacking Poland, then the Low Countries and France, then Britain, and then the Soviet Union. Was Germany's security threatened by those it attacked?

Since its inception in the early twentieth century, the Soviet Union professed to be a peace-loving state that respected the national integrity of its neighbors. Yet in 1956 the Soviets invaded Hungary to put down a revolt against the rigid Communist regime that ruled the country. In 1968 the Soviet Union invaded another Communist neighbor, Czechoslovakia, to turn back an attempt to liberalize the regime there. In late 1979 the Soviet Union invaded Afghanistan, presumably to defend a recently installed Communist regime against alleged internal and external enemies. In these cases the Kremlin's interpretation of the USSR's national security and national interest clashed with its alleged peace-loving and freedom-loving pretensions, and perhaps with the national and security interests of most

people in Hungary, Czechoslovakia, and Afghanistan.

The United States, too, professes to be a peace-loving nation, yet it became involved in a bloody, destructive, expensive war in Vietnam between 1965 and 1973. Was this action in Vietnam, like U.S. military resistance to Germany and Japan in World War II, based on protecting the legitimate security interests of the United States?

Clashing conceptions of national security highlight international relations. In the 1930s Japan's co-prosperity zone in the Far East clashed with the national security interests of China, Britain, France, and the United States and led directly to the Japanese attack on Pearl Harbor on December 7, 1941. In 1956, presumably to protect their strategic security interests, although at Egypt's expense, Britain and France, with Israel's help, seized control of the Suez Canal after Egypt's Nasser had nationalized the waterway. Israel has resisted the establishment of a Palestinian state on the west bank of the Jordan River because of its fears about Arab military forces being close enough to its cities to jeopardize Israel's security. But whose interpretation of national security is correct?

The record of huge military expenditures and the distortion of national priorities is clear, yet nations do not stop the arms race or alter national politics to achieve a more sensible balance of often competing values. Even given the end of the Cold War, it will take time to substantially reduce defense expenditures, and there are no guarantees that funds will be transferred to other needs. Moreover, violent conflict, much of it ethnic and religiously based, has continued after the Cold War, slowing down arms reduction.

This discussion does not necessarily prove that all official government policies on military spending are wrong and that the critics are right. We should, however, be leery of automatically accepting what governments profess. The national value of security and peace is subject to differing interpretations. We should be sensitive to the price that is often paid to achieve national security. And we should be aware of the gap that

United Nations ambulance in devastated city of Vukovar, Croatia, 1992.

so often exists between professed, civilized values and the actual values expressed through behavior.

Liberty, Human Rights, and Democracy

Most nations profess a commitment to liberty, human rights, and democracy. But how do they perform?

One study by Robert Dahl in 1971 attempted to formulate a freedom/democratic index based on the following seven points: (1) freedom to form and join organizations, (2) freedom of expression, (3) the right to vote, (4) the right of political leaders to compete for support, (5) access to alternative sources of information, (6) free and fair elections, and (7) whether institutions for making government policy depend on votes and other expressions of public preferences.[4] Such a study makes it possible to rank nations in order to study their comparative commitment to these values.

Dahl concluded that most developed countries (such as Belgium, Sweden, and the United States) ranked fairly high, whereas most com-

munist countries (such as the Soviet Union and Czechoslovakia) ranked fairly low. Today, most if not all of the East European countries seem well on the way toward democracy and would no doubt rank higher. In the former Soviet Union, the picture is not uniform. The fifteen former Soviet republics range from quite democratic (the Baltic countries) to more authoritarian (Ukraine). In Dahl's study, developing countries ranged from the upper middle range (India) through the middle (Mexico) to low (Saudi Arabia).

Political scientists must continue to investigate the gap between rhetoric and reality. For example, in 1975 the Soviet Union, the United States, and thirty-three other governments signed the Helsinki Pact, which included provisions for respecting human rights. But did the Soviet Union act in accord with its signature? The record reveals that until Mikhail Gorbachev instituted the free exchange of information (*glasnost*) and major democratic reforms in the Soviet Union, peaceful dissent against Soviet policy was punished. Dissenters were imprisoned, confined to mental hospitals, exiled within Russia,

Nelson Mandela speaking in Capetown, South Africa, upon his election as president, May 10, 1994.

and forced into foreign exile. Soviet citizens were not allowed the right of free emigration, and the free flow of information was impeded. Between 1975 and 1987, Soviet behavior was not consistent with the principles professed in the Helsinki Pact.

Historically, the U.S. record on human rights, although considerably better than that of the Soviet Union, has by no means been exemplary. FBI actions at home and CIA actions both abroad and, more disturbingly, at home have been criticized by civil rights groups, the press, congressional committees, and governmental commissions. The FBI made illegal wiretaps particularly in the 1950s and 1960s. In the mid-1960s and early

1970s, the CIA worked covertly in Chile to influence a presidential election and to overthrow a democratic government led by Salvadore Allende.[5]

For over forty years, the Republic of South Africa professed to treat all human beings with respect. But its apartheid laws, mandating a separation of the races and a denial of full citizenship to blacks within South Africa, belied such statements. Only recently, with the end of white minority rule and the election of Nelson Mandela as president in 1994, has South Africa's behavior matched its rhetoric.

A comparable gap between rhetoric and reality exists in many developing countries. The annual

Country Reports on Human Rights Practices by the U.S. State Department, testimony before congressional committees, and documented records of such groups as Amnesty International illustrate this gap. The records of such countries as North Korea, South Korea, Cambodia, Iraq, and Uganda have been shocking. And the record of the People's Republic of China has been horrendous, particularly during the Cultural Revolution in the late 1960s. As political and economic reform movements swept through the communist world in the 1980s, there was considerable hope that basic human rights and principles of democracy would be part of the Chinese reform movement. Tragically, a stated respect for human rights by the Chinese government lost all meaning as hundreds of students were either shot or crushed under the treads of tanks at Tiananmen Square in Beijing in June 1989. A wave of trials, executions, and long imprisonments followed the defeat of the democratic movement.

Most frequently, of course, governments cite national security to justify their violations of liberty, human rights, or democracy.

Justice and Equality

Justice involves balancing liberty, equality, and fraternity. It is perceived in different ways by different nations and by different groups within nations. Developed nations, and the more affluent in all nations, may understand justice in terms of liberty, including the liberty to pursue wealth and protect property. In contrast, communist and developing countries, and the poor in almost all nations, may understand justice in terms of **equality**, particularly as signifying a fair share of the national wealth.

Thus, there are many ways to measure a nation's commitment to justice, understood roughly as "fairness." One way is to examine the division of the national pie—that is, the way in which income is actually distributed within a nation.

Table 11.1 indicates the extent to which overall national income was distributed within a variety of countries, listed by level of development from low to high. The data represent the distribution of total disposable household income accruing to the wealthiest 10 percent of the population in each country.

What is evident from these data is that the higher the development level, the more equitable the distribution of income within the society. However, a number of factors may contribute to the more skewed distribution of income in the developing world. In some cases, consciously designed policies ensure that a small elite retain a higher percentage of wealth. But other factors, such as limited resources, capabilities, and power structures, may also be relevant. Also, the larger pie in more affluent countries permits larger slices to be offered to all parts of the population.

Despite these qualifications, the distribution of shares of the national income and the gap between rich and poor that it reveals do indicate something important about the success of nations in implementing egalitarian policies. Such policies are an important index of social justice. Additional information on welfare and economic well-being also sheds light on justice and equality.

Table 11.1 *Percentage Share of Income Concentrated in the Wealthiest 10% of the Population (countries listed in development rank high to low)*

Country	Share of Income
United States	25.0
Norway	21.2
Netherlands	24.1
Australia	25.8
Spain	21.8
Tunisia	30.7
Philippines	32.1
Bolivia	31.7
Nicaragua	39.8
Kenya	47.9
Tanzania	46.4

Source: World Development Report 1995 (Oxford University Press, published for the World Bank, 1995).

Welfare and Economic Well-Being

Most nations endorse (at least in their rhetoric) the **welfare** and **economic well-being** of their people. But what do the national governing elites mean by welfare and by economic well-being? And how successful are nations in advancing them?

Again, richer, industrial, developed nations have a much easier time satisfying their people's needs for employment, income, food, housing, health, and literacy. The extent of each nation's commitment to these values can, to some extent, be measured by their public expenditures for programs in defense, education, and health. Figure 11.4 summarizes such public expenditures as a percentage of gross national product (GNP).

As the graph makes clear, more-developed countries allocate more for health and education combined than they do for military spending. The opposite is true in the developing world. It is

doubtful that any single factor explains these differences. In developing regions of the world, there is a tendency toward greater domestic political instability and a higher frequency of border and territorial disputes. Also, unfortunately, a significant number of authoritarian leaders seek to preserve their power. These and similar factors lead to inordinate allocations of national funds for military purposes rather than for improving the human condition.

Many methods can be used to assess the value commitments of states. The data presented here suggest that actions as well as words should be considered in any analysis.

POPULAR VALUES

There is considerable evidence that the values of the people who make up political communities are rooted in, and correlated with, a hierarchy of human needs: for sustenance and safety, for belonging and esteem, and for intellectual, aesthetic, and social fulfillment. This proposition is associated with the work of social psychologist Abraham Maslow (mentioned in Chapter 4).

Human Needs

Ronald Inglehart (who subjected Maslow's hypothesis to a partial test) explains:

Maslow argues that people act to fulfill a number of different needs, which are pursued in hierarchical order according to their relative urgency for survival. Top priority is given to the satisfaction of physiological needs as long as they are in short supply. The need for physical safety comes next; its priority is almost as high as that of the sustenance need, but a hungry man will risk his life to get food. Once an individual has attained physical and economic security he may begin to pursue other, nonmaterial goals. These other goals reflect genuine and normal needs—although people may fail to give them attention when deprived of the sustenance or safety needs. But when at last minimal economic and physical security are present, the needs for love, belonging, and esteem become increasingly important; and later, a set of goals related to intellectual and aesthetic satisfaction looms large. There does not seem to be any clear hierarchy within the last set of needs, which Maslow calls "self-actualization needs." But there is evidence that they become most salient only after an individual has satisfied the material needs and belonging needs.[6]

Figure 11.4
Public expenditures as a percentage of GNP, 1990–1991.

Source: United Nations Development Program, Human Development Report 1995 (New York: UNDP, 1995), p. 206.

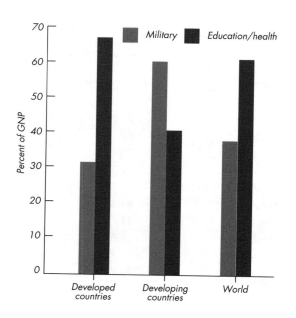

A group of street children in Dacca, Bangladesh, prepare a meal on the pavement.

Maslow's needs. Cantril found that human beings everywhere impose the following eleven demands "on any society or political culture because of their very nature":

1. Human beings seek the "satisfaction of survival needs."
2. They need "a sense of both physical and psychological security to protect gains already made and to assure a beachhead from which further advances can be made."
3. They crave "sufficient order and certainty" in their lives.
4. They "continuously seek to enlarge the range and to enrich the quality of their satisfactions."
5. They "are creatures of hope and are not genetically designed to resign themselves."
6. They "have the capacity to make choices and the desire to exercise this capacity."
7. They "require freedom to exercise the choices they are capable of making."
8. They "want to exercise their own identity and integrity."
9. They "want to experience a sense of their own worthwhileness."
10. They "seek some value or system of beliefs to which they can commit themselves."
11. They "want a sense of surety and confidence that the society of which they are a part holds out a fair degree of hope that their aspirations will be fulfilled."[7]

Marxists strongly endorse the primacy of sustenance needs. Friedrich Engels, Marx's lifelong friend and collaborator, put the Marxist perspective succinctly, if too simply, in his speech at Marx's graveside, when he declared that "mankind must first of all eat, drink, have shelter and clothing, before it can pursue politics, science, art, religion, etc."

Empirical studies conducted over the past twenty-five years and based on public opinion surveys tend to support Maslow's hypothesis. Thus, social psychologist Hadley Cantril in a 1965 study involving such industrialized countries as the United States and West Germany, such Communist countries as Poland and Yugoslavia, and such developing countries as Brazil, Nigeria, India, Egypt, and the Philippines found human "demands" that compare roughly to

Cantril's questions were designed to explore both personal and national hopes and fears. He found that a decent standard of living, a happy family life, and health ranked high among popular hopes. Economic, family, and health concerns ranked high among popular fears. Not surprisingly, war loomed large as a major fear among countries that had experienced war. Similarly, political instability was a major fear among people whose countries had experienced major disorders.

The importance of sustenance needs, understood as aspirations for improved economic conditions, is best captured by responses of people in developing countries. A forty-four-year-old woman in Egypt explains: "My main wishes are to have enough food to eat and enough decent water to drink." A forty-five-year-old housewife in India with a family income of about $80 a month says: "I should like to have a water tap and a water supply in my house. It would also be nice to have electricity." And a forty-year-old housewife living in a small town in Brazil declares: "What I would like would be a sewing machine, some clothes, a cow to give milk to the children. I work and when I am sick I am hardly able to buy food."[8]

Ronald Inglehart surveyed public opinion in 1970, 1971, 1972, 1978, and 1990–1993 to test Maslow's hypothesis in a number of developed countries. In his initial survey, Inglehart attempted to correlate Maslow's hierarchy of needs with certain values, as shown in Figure 11.5.

Inglehart found that, with some exceptions, the "priorities of Western publics correspond to a Maslovian model." The values reflect both "broad societal goals" and "personal goals." His findings seemed to "provide a considerable measure of support for the idea that human needs tend to be hierarchically ordered."[9]

Table 11.2 summarizes some of the evidence for Inglehart's cautious conclusion. He found that "materialists" outnumber the "postmaterialists" by a ratio ranging from 5 to 1 to more than 2 to 1. He also noted that there is some correlation between affluence and more postmaterialist values; that among the youngest age cohorts, the postmaterialists are almost as numerous as the materialists; that the more highly educated and those who place themselves on the political left

Figure 11.5
Values and needs in Western society.
Source: Ronald Inglehart, The Silent Revolution: Changing Values and Political Styles Among Western Publics. Copyright 1977 by Princeton University Press, Fig. 2.1 p. 42, reprinted by permission of Princeton University Press.

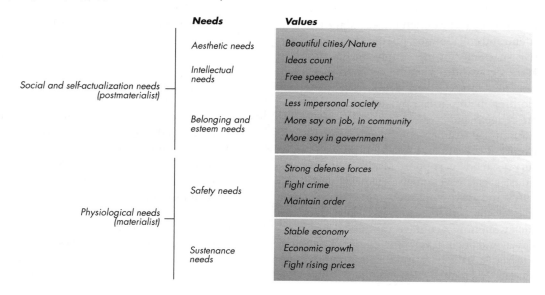

Table 11.2 Goals of Western Publics, 1973[a]

Goal	Belgium %	France %	Luxembourg %	Germany %	Netherlands %	Denmark %	Britain %	Ireland %	Italy %	Mean Nine European States %	United States %
Fight rising prices (E)[b]	52	43	29	44	26	24	50	44	41	39	25
Economic growth (E)	19	18	33	24	14	23	29	29	31	24	16
Fight crime (S)	21	20	9	21	26	21	17	25	37	22	22
Stable economy (E)	12	12	22	39	16	28	25	24	16	22	21
Maintain order (S)	10	21	28	18	18	31	11	16	17	19	20
More say on job (B)	18	13	22	12	24	20	15	20	9	17	16
Less impersonal society (B)	17	28	11	11	26	17	12	8	14	16	12
More say in government (B)	11	9	19	9	14	8	15	15	11	12	16
Protect free speech (A)	17	14	7	11	13	11	11	6	9	11	10
More beautiful cities (A)	15	9	7	4	10	7	6	5	3	7	18[c]
Ideas count (A)	7	11	9	3	10	7	4	3	5	7	8
Strong defense forces (S)	2	3	3	5	4	2	6	6	7	4	16

Source: Ronald Inglehart, The Silent Revolution: Changing Values and Political Styles Among Western Publics. *Copyright ©*
1977 by Princeton University Press. Table 2.6, p. 49, reprinted by permission of Princeton University Press.
[a]Percentage choosing given goals as first and second most important out of twelve.
[b]Letters in parentheses indicate category of the given goal; (E) = Economic, (S) = Safety, (B) = Belonging, (A) = Self-Actualization.
[c]In the United States, the item was "Protect nature from being spoiled and polluted."

rank higher (i.e., are less materialistic) on the materialist/postmaterialist scale. All of Inglehart's follow-up surveys, including the most recent in 1990–1993, revealed a pattern almost identical to that of 1972.[10]

Guides to Public Opinion

Elections and voting statistics, as well as other public opinion surveys, also help to explain popular values, to reveal consensus and conflict in political communities, and to clarify agreements and differences between citizens and their governing leaders.

For example, party positions, electoral outcomes, and public opinion surveys in all Western democracies demonstrate that the main features of the modern welfare state—for example, unemployment compensation, old age pensions, health care, and housing support—are here to stay. Similarly, most Western democracies are clearly committed to maintaining economic sta-

bility (in employment and prices) and to safeguarding law and order.

Even within a political party, however, voters may disagree on specific policies, as Table 11.3 shows. In the United States, Republicans and Democrats differ substantially on the issues of gays in the military and environmental protection. There is moderate disagreement on the death penalty, and there is considerable agreement on support for NAFTA (the North American Free Trade Agreement) and the passage of a balanced budget amendment to the U.S. Constitution.

The Gap Between Popular Values and National Values

It is important to explore the reality of the gap between popular values (the values held by the individuals who make up the nation) and national values (the values of governing leaders, elites, and parties). The normal assumption is

Table 11.3 Opinions Held by Republican, Democratic, and Independent Voters, 1994–95

	Republican (%)	Democratic (%)	Independent (%)
Do you support or oppose the "Don't Ask, Don't Tell" compromise on allowing gays in the military? (1994)			
Support	35	61	49
Oppose	62	36	47
No Opinion	3	3	4
Here are two statements which people sometimes make when discussing the environment and economic growth. Which of these statements comes closer to your own point of view—protection of the environment should be given priority, even at the risk of curbing economic growth; or economic growth should be given priority, even if the environment suffers to some extent? (1995)			
Protection	49	70	60
Economic growth	46	23	28
No opinion	5	7	6
Are you in favor of the death penalty for a person convicted of murder? (1995)			
In favor	89	67	76
Oppose	7	20	13
It depends	4	10	9
No opinion	0	3	2
Do you support or oppose the North American Free Trade Agreement with Canada and Mexico, also known as NAFTA? (1994)			
Support	50	57	50
Oppose	42	33	41
No opinion	8	8	9
Would you support or oppose a constitutional amendment to require a balanced federal budget? (1994)			
Support	75	73	73
Oppose	19	17	20
No Opinion	6	10	7

Source: George Gallup, Jr. The Gallup Poll: Public Opinion 1994, 1995 (Wilmington, Del.: Scholarly Resources, Inc., 1995/96).

that in genuinely democratic countries national and popular values are pretty much in agreement. But is this uniformly the case? In one study, Hadley Cantril compared parliamentarians and the public in six countries: the United States, West Germany, Brazil, Nigeria, India, and the Philippines. He concluded that "the legislators tend to view the nation's problems in rather the same way as does the public," although he noted some differences. For our investigation, it will be helpful to see what such studies have found about popular values versus parliamentarians' values on such issues as security, liberty, justice, and welfare.

On the issue of security, Cantril found that "the problem of maintaining peace on the international front was high among both publics and parliamentarians" in the United States and West Germany and "low among both the public and parliamentarians in all the less-developed countries, which were more concerned with their domestic problems." He also found that "with the exception of Nigeria, parliamentarians in all countries are less concerned than the public with the problem of avoiding war and its devastation." With regard to international stability, unity, and independence, parliamentarians exhibited "a greater sensitivity to efficient, balanced, and stable government." This, Cantril found, was particularly true in all the underdeveloped nations covered in his study.[11]

With regard to liberty, evidence from several sources suggests that parliamentarians in the United States are more respectful of civil liberties than is the public at large.[12] This difference seemingly springs from the greater involvement of parliamentarians, as politicians, in public affairs and from their higher level of education. Similarly, West German legislators were more concerned than the public "about the possible loss of freedom and democracy" in Germany; the same was true of Indian parliamentarians.[13]

As to justice, Cantril found that legislators in the United States seemed "more concerned about domestic problems of social justice" than did the public. For example, U.S. legislators have been

more concerned than the general public about overcoming racial segregation in schools, transportation problems, and the lack of sufficient public facilities. Cantril also found Indian parliamentarians to be more sensitive than the public to such social problems as ridding India of its ancient discriminatory practices.[14]

As we noted earlier regarding welfare, Western democratic publics and legislators have historically agreed about the main outlines of the welfare state, although more recent conservative governments (such as former Prime Minister Margaret Thatcher's government in Britain or former President Ronald Reagan's administration in the United States) have begun movements to cut back or reform, the welfare state. During the summer of 1996, President Bill Clinton, who had campaigned on the pledge to change welfare as we know it and who had previously vetoed two Republican welfare bills as too harsh, finally signed into law sweeping welfare reform legislation that had been largely sponsored by Republican lawmakers. In addition to significant changes in welfare benefits, the law called for greater emphasis being placed on getting welfare recipients off the welfare rolls and back to work. Finally, the federal government began divesting itself of some of its responsibility for welfare and giving greater responsibility to the state governments.

According to Cantril, people in Brazil, Nigeria, and India seemed more concerned with eco-

Political cartoonist Keefe came down hard on 1996 welfare reform legislation.

(© Denver Post)

nomic problems and public health than their legislators. Yet in the same nations, parliamentarians were more aware than the public of the need for greater technological advancement.[15]

Changes in Values over Time

Political scientists may begin with such leads about values. Yet they must go on to compare the stated values with what people and nations have actually done. Political scientists must also recognize that changes occur over time. For example, from 1965 to 1973 American public opinion turned against involvement in the war in Vietnam. Over a longer period, comparable or greater changes have taken place on other issues—changes supercharged with meaning for liberty, justice, and welfare. For example, U.S. values have changed significantly regarding race relations (attitudes toward African Americans), religious relations (attitudes toward Catholics and Jews), gender relations (attitudes toward women), and labor-management relations.

Such changes, in the United States and throughout the world, call attention to the need to monitor popular values over time, in order to guard against stereotypes and to understand the limited validity of public opinion surveys and election statistics.

We have little evidence on public opinion for most communist and developing countries. From 1917 in the Soviet Union and from the late 1940s in Eastern Europe to the recent collapse of communism in these regions, there were no elections involving competing parties to indicate popular responses to governing parties. Due to the lack of electoral history and general chaos in some of the systems, it may still be too early to make anything more than preliminary assessments. The peoples of the former Soviet Union and Eastern Europe are struggling with campaign and electoral processes that they find unfamiliar. Slowly but surely, however, electoral processes are taking hold. The 1996 presidential election in Russia was hotly fought by those who constituted the winning majority in support of Boris Yeltsin and the reform movement and by those who campaigned vigorously on behalf of the losing, but significant, minority who supported Gennadi Zyuganov, the Communist leader.

Recent events in Eastern Europe and the former Soviet Union indicate a profound difference between the long-held values of government officials and values held by the people. For years Communist officials extolled the virtues of the economic systems they led. They publicly justified invasions of Hungary, Czechoslovakia, and Afghanistan. Centrally planned and administered policies were designed to provide adequate food, shelter, and medical care for all citizens. When the Eastern European economies collapsed and the Soviet system faced severe self-criticism under glasnost, the differences between the elite and the people became glaring. To varying degrees, domestic policies in all these states had failed to provide adequate food, housing, and medical care. The people were bitter; they felt betrayed. Hungarians and Czechoslovakians obviously resented the Soviet invasions of 1956 and 1968. It is clear now that many Soviet citizens saw the 1979 invasion of Afghanistan as immoral, destructive, and wasteful, despite years of official pronouncements about its necessity.

INTEREST-GROUP AND CLASS VALUES

Many political scientists are skeptical of national and popular values and of such notions as the national and the public interest. They see politics as a tug-of-war among competing interests. Or, to express it differently, they see public policy as the result of group pressures. Consequently, political scientists emphasize the importance of understanding the values and behavior of powerful **interest groups** in the political community. Interest groups usually comprise members of the public who organize and attempt to shape public policy on issues of concern to them.[16]

Other social scientists, often of a Marxist persuasion, call special attention to the interests held by each of the various classes, especially workers and capitalists. These social scientists emphasize the crucial political role played by

class values. They, too, see key interests struggling for power, struggling to implement their values in laws, administrative policies, and court decisions. But these political scientists identify the key interests as classes. They see bourgeois politics in terms of conflict between the working class and the capitalist class. Communists see politics in communist countries in terms of a classless society. Other social scientists, however, saw conflicts at work even in the former Soviet Union and detected struggles among interest groups there.

What interest-group and class values operate in highly industrialized, communist, and developing countries? How do interests and classes agree and disagree? And is there a gap between actual values and the ideal values often associated with the public interest?

Interest Groups

Almost all modern political communities contain interest groups—economic, religious, ethnic, racial, professional, and reform—seeking to protect their vital needs and fundamental interests. For example, labor unions seek to protect their right to organize and bargain collectively and to obtain full employment at good wages under good working conditions. Business and industrial groups seek to maintain a good profit margin. Farm groups seek higher farm prices.

Religious groups insist on religious freedom and a climate of opinion and public policies compatible with their objectives. Ethnic groups (which are sometimes also sectional groups) seek to preserve their heritage, including their language, customs, and way of life. Racial groups seek protection against an oppressive majority—protection in employment, housing, voting, and education. Professional groups (doctors, lawyers, journalists) seek to protect their independence, integrity, freedom, and profits.

A multitude of reform groups work to advance their special concerns. They fight for or against nuclear plants, for or against gun control, for or against national health insurance. They fight for amnesty for political prisoners.

American students are familiar with many such interest groups: the NRA (National Rifle Association), the AFL-CIO (American Federation of Labor/Congress of Industrial Organizations), NAM (National Association of Manufacturers), the U.S. Chamber of Commerce, the National Council of Churches of Christ, the Anti-Defamation League of B'nai B'rith, the NAACP (National Association for the Advancement of Colored People), the Sierra Club, Planned Parenthood, and the National Right to Life Committee.

Assessing the role that interest groups play in developing countries is difficult, given the wide range of economic and political systems. In older developing nations (such as those in Latin America), interest groups are generally well developed. Trade unions, in particular, have been extremely powerful in places like Chile and Argentina. Catholic liberation theologians and priests working in the rural and poverty-stricken areas of Latin America have become influential in recent decades. In more recently independent countries (such those in Africa), interest groups are present but are not always well developed and possessed of a strong sense of history. They and their values become more apparent in times of political crisis, particularly when their actions produce dramatic change.

Because government, party, and public are so closely tied in communist countries, nongovernmental interest groups have been less visible. Yet students of the communist political systems argue that governing party professionals, security police, military officers, industrial managers, economists, writers, scientists, educators, and jurists function the way that interest groups do in most developed nations, even though these people are very closely tied to the government.[17]

Class Values

In noncommunist countries, are values based on class? Do capitalists in bourgeois societies value private property, profits, and prestige and act to enhance these values? Do workers value control of the means of production and exchange, a democratic political order able to satisfy their vital needs, cooperative production, and equitable enjoyment of community wealth? Do the values of capitalists and workers conflict in bourgeois societies?

Public opinion surveys, election statistics, and other studies throw some light on these questions. The evidence supports some aspects of class analysis but invalidates other aspects. Most European countries are highly class conscious, but the United States tends to identify with the large, all-embracing middle class. Like the United States, Mexico is only moderately class conscious. But workers and lower-paid groups in Britain, Germany, France, and Italy tend to "vote for working-class Labour, Socialist, and Communist parties, while middle-class and professional people are more likely to vote for liberal and conservative parties."[18] Class values are more prominent in countries with strong social democratic parties (such as Britain and Germany). Yet in Britain there are a sizable number of working-class Tories, and in Germany a sizable contingent of workers support the more conservative Christian Democratic party.

The power of class values in European countries was put to one dramatic test in World War I. In general, socialist parties, which expressed class values, had opposed the war because they interpreted it as a capitalist war; they endorsed the brotherhood of workers across national lines. Yet, when push came to shove in 1914, German, French, and English workers forgot their class values of peace and international brotherhood, jumped on the nationalist bandwagons, and supported their countries' war efforts with great patriotism, courage, and sacrifice.

Proponents of class analysis sometimes explain the working class's lack of devotion to class values by invoking Marx's doctrine of "false consciousness." They argue that workers have been brainwashed by dominant capitalist values and have thus acquired bourgeois values that do not serve their vital needs and fundamental interests. Critics of class analysis maintain that workers are not a monolithic class united by their common economic exploitation; although

they will press pragmatically for their vital interests, they do not subscribe to wholesale socialism.

What about capitalists as a class? If workers do not neatly fit into a rigid class scheme, do capitalists? There is abundant evidence—in words, votes, and deeds—that capitalists try to protect the institution of private property, their profits, their power, and their prestige. But it would be a mistake to conclude that all capitalists agree on a common "class line." Although they may all want to protect private property and enterprise and to enhance their profits and influence, they differ about how to achieve those ends.

Moreover, in advanced industrial and democratic countries, capitalists accept a degree of government intervention in the economic sphere that their laissez-faire ancestors would have considered intolerable. Such an acceptance has, of course, resulted from considerable struggle: economic organization and strikes, political organization and reform leadership, and social education. Capitalists have, often reluctantly but sometimes in their own self-interest, accepted democratic reforms designed to satisfy not just the interests of workers but also the interests of small-business owners, farmers, and consumers in general.

CONCLUSION

Our guiding hypothesis helps us understand the political values of political actors. The values of nations, citizens, and interest groups are rooted in their vital needs, fundamental interests, and perceived desires. But we must precisely define such values as security, liberty, justice, and welfare. And we must ask critical questions. Security, liberty, justice, and welfare for whom? At what price?

Agreement about fundamental needs and interests holds all political communities together and enhances politics as a civilizing process. People may not have to agree on all fundamentals (say, on religion and economics), but they must know how to disagree in a civilized way.

There are sharp disagreements within and between political communities on needs, interests, and desires. These disagreements challenge politics as a civilizing process. Can humane and peaceful patterns of accommodation be worked out? Or must conflicts lead to violence, lawlessness, civil war, and international war?

Our investigation of values invites both hopeful and fearful forecasts. When individual values are correlated with a hierarchy of needs, it becomes obvious why such values are firmly grounded in human biology, psychology, and sociology. And also why they cannot be so easily whistled away by governing elites who fear satisfaction of the people's needs as a threat to their own income, power, or status. In all likelihood, sustenance and security needs, which rank high even in more advanced industrial societies, will preserve welfare policies in all political communities.

But our investigation also underscores the tragic folly of policies that force nations to choose between guns and butter—to skew other urgent national priorities in favor of armaments even though their limited resources are badly needed for food, clothing, shelter, and education.

There is evidence that more affluent, better-educated people in all systems are more attuned to the social value of belonging, and to intellectual and artistic values. These postmaterialist attitudes seem to be correlated with a more internationalist set of values. It should be possible for such people to transcend the narrow nationalist commitments so frequently associated with war, as well as the materialist concerns that threaten the environment.

This prospect is less promising, however, in the poorer countries of the developing world, where basic needs are not fulfilled and where nationalism remains a potent, and often valuable, force for social cohesion.

The critical political scientist must ask tough questions about interest groups and classes. If public policy results from powerful group pressures, what does this mean for the peace, liberty, justice, and welfare of the less powerful (such as the poor, minorities, and women)? Will their vital needs and fundamental interests be ne-

glected? Or will changes favorable to them only be slow paced or in small increments?

If the dominant class (the capitalist class in bourgeois society or the working class in communist society) calls the tune on values, what will this mean for peace, liberty, justice, and welfare? Is there a capitalist Establishment? Do working people really call the tune in communist countries?

As we critically explore the values of political actors, we become aware of political well-being in communities around the globe. We understand such well-being as a particular cluster of values: security and peace; liberty, human rights, and democracy; justice and equality; economic and social welfare. We may also ask what accounts for such political well-being. A fuller account requires an exploration of patterns of cooperation, accommodation, and conflict in politics. These patterns within nations are discussed in Chapter 12.

ANNOTATED BIBLIOGRAPHY

Almond, Gabriel A., and Verba, Sidney. *The Civic Culture: Political Attitudes and Democracy in Five Nations*. Boston: Little, Brown, 1965. Explores the cluster of values that sustain an effective and stable democratic policy. For a valuable criticism and update of five countries studied (United States, Britain, Mexico, Italy, and West Germany), see Almond and Verba, eds. *The Civic Culture Revisited* (reprinted by Sage Publications, 1989).

Cantril, Hadley. *The Pattern of Human Concerns*. New Brunswick, N.J.: Rutgers University Press, 1965. Uses global interviews and sample survey techniques to identify popular values. Provides basis for cross-national comparisons. Finds common demands rooted in values of self-preservation, security, order, opportunity for development, and integrity.

Free, Lloyd A., and Cantril, Hadley. *The Political Beliefs of Americans: A Study of Public Opinion*. New Brunswick, N.J.: Rutgers University Press, 1967. Finds that Americans are operational liberals and ideological conservatives whose pragmatism enables the American system to work. Should be compared with Gerald M. Pomper, *The Election of 1992: Reports and Interpretations* (Chatham N.J.: Chatham House, 1993), to see whether Americans have now become both ideologically and operationally conservative.

Holmes, Robert. *On War and Morality*. Princeton, N.J.: Princeton University Press, 1989. Provides a penetrating critique of violence, political realism, the just-war doctrine, and nuclear deterrence. Opts for nonviolence.

Inglehart, Ronald. *The Silent Revolution: Changing Values and Political Styles Among Western Publics*. Princeton, N.J.: Princeton University Press, 1977. Sees the values of Western publics shifting from an overwhelming emphasis on material well-being and physical security toward a greater emphasis on the quality of life. Provides empirical support for Maslow's hierarchy of needs theory. Thought-provoking—but premature? Also see Inglehart's *Culture Shift in Advanced Industrial Societies* (Princeton, N.J.: Princeton University Press, 1990) and Paul R. Anderson and Inglehart's *Value Change in Global Perspective* (Ann Arbor: University of Michigan Press, 1995).

Ketschelt, Herbert. *The Transformation of European Social Democracy*. New York: Cambridge University Press, 1994. Raises significant questions about political values, the influence of class structure, and the nature of economic institutions in contemporary Europe.

Marx, Karl. *The German Ideology: Part I* (Marx and Engels), 1845–1846; *Preface, A Contribution to the Critique of Political Economy*, 1859; *Manifesto of the Communist Party* (Marx and Engels), 1848; *The Eighteenth Brumaire of Louis Bonaparte*, 1842. In Robert C. Tucker, ed., The *Marx-Engels Reader*. New York: Norton, 1972. Provides an introduction to the thesis that the economic foundation of life significantly shapes political values, that capitalistic values predominate in capitalistic society, and that only with a communist revolution and an ultimate communist society can real freedom, peace, community, and development take place.

Maslow, Abraham H. *Toward a Psychology of Being*. Princeton, N.J.: Van Nostrand, 1962; *Motivation and Personality,* 2nd ed. New York: Harper & Row, 1970. Presents Maslow's influential views of the relationship between needs and values and his famous hierarchy of needs. For a keen and penetrating analysis of the concept of human needs, see Patricia Springborg, *The Problem of Human Needs and the Critique of Civilization* (London: Allen & Unwin, 1981).

Mundo, Philip. *Interest Groups: Cases and Characteristics*. Chicago: Nelson-Hall Publishers, 1992. Offers a first-rate analysis of American interest groups using a case study approach.

Parenti, Michael. *Democracy for the Few,* 6th ed. New York: St. Martin's Press, 1994. Provides a refreshing, democratic socialist interpretation of American politics, rhetoric, and reality. Argues that American government represents the privileged few rather than the needy many, that elections, parties, and civil liberties are seldom effective against corporate wealth.

Sivard, Ruth Leger. *World Military and Social Expenditures*. Washington, D.C.: World Priorities, issued annually. Reveals that expenditures and comparable data about national performance tell much more about actual values than does political rhetoric. Invaluable!

Truman, David B. *The Governmental Process*. New York: Knopf, 1951. Presents an influential pluralist interpretation of the government process, highlighting the role of interest groups and, therefore, the significance of their values in politics.

Weiner, Myron, and Huntington, Samuel P., eds. *Understanding Political Development*. Boston: Little, Brown, 1987. Represents an important anthology of articles by noted scholars in the development field. The essays provide critical reassessment of long-held views on development.

Zaller, John. *The Nature and Origins of Mass Opinion*. New York: Cambridge University Press, 1992. Provides a first-rate analysis of the formation of public opinion by one of the preeminent writers in the field of political psychology.

SUGGESTIONS FOR FURTHER READING

Beer, Francis A. *Peace Against War: The Ecology of International Violence*. San Francisco: Freeman, 1981.

Brzezinski, Zbigniew. *The Grand Failure: Communism's Terminal Crisis*. New York: Scribner's, 1989.

Camp, Roderic Ai. *Democracy in Latin America: Patterns and Cycles*. Wilmington, Del.: Scholarly Resources/Jaguar Books, 1996.

Dahl, Robert. *Who Governs?* New Haven, Conn.: Yale University Press, 1961.

Dogan, Mattei. *Comparing Pluralist Democracies: Strains on Legitimacy*. Boulder, Colo.: Westview, 1988.

Hayward, Jack, and Page, Edward C., eds. *Governing the New Europe*. Durham, N.C.: Duke University Press, 1995.

Small, Melvin, and Singer, J. David, eds. *International War: An Anthology and Study Guide,* 2nd ed. Homewood, Ill.: Dorsey Press, 1989.

Tocqueville, Alexis de. *Democracy in America.* 2 vols. Edited by Phillips Bradley. New York: Knopf, 1946.

U.S. Department of State. *Country Reports on Human Rights Practices.* Washington: U.S. Government Printing Office, published annually.

GLOSSARY TERMS

class values
economic well-being
equality
goal
interest groups
justice
liberty
national interest
policy
political actors
political values
principle
public interest
welfare

12

NATIONAL POLITICS I: CONSTITUTIONS, VOTERS, INTEREST GROUPS, POLITICAL PARTIES, AND THE MEDIA

IN CHAPTER 11 WE WERE CON-CERNED with the political values of political actors. These values call attention to the purposes of politics, the vital needs and fundamental interests of political actors, and especially such objectives as security, liberty, justice, and welfare. But we did not explore the patterns that political actors work out to satisfy these values. These patterns will be the subject of our inquiry in this chapter and in Chapter 13.

As we noted in Chapter 11, political actors do not always agree on their needs, interests, and desires. They interpret security, liberty, justice, and welfare in different ways. They often disagree about public policy. They struggle for power to determine who gets what, when, where, and how. These facts of political life prompt political scientists to ask: How then, in the absence of unanimity as a regular condition in politics, do political actors achieve their values? How do they cooperate for common ends, work out **accommodation** among competing interests, and handle conflicts when accommodation fails?

Political actors must *cooperate,* because if they do not, politics and effective government on behalf of civilizing purposes is impossible. Political actors must also *accommodate competing interests,* because if they do not, priorities cannot be established nor decisions made. Moreover, political actors must *handle conflicts* prudently lest the political community be torn apart by strife too difficult to moderate or overcome.

Accommodation must involve both governmental and nongovernmental actors. Because government is one major instrument to help citizens achieve their purposes, citizens must make sure that government does what they want it to do. And because government is so powerful, citizens must make sure that it does not abuse its power—that it remains subject to their control.

These ethical and empirical considerations point toward the significant empirical problem we explore in this and the following chapter: *Given that politics is a struggle for purpose and power, which political patterns further cooperation, advance accommodation, and handle conflicts in domestic politics?* This is a big problem that we can only modestly answer here. We can only suggest an approach and briefly illustrate an argument on behalf of successful patterns of accommodation.

SUCCESSFUL PATTERNS FOR COOPERATION, ACCOMMODATION, AND CONFLICT RESOLUTION

We define success in terms of maximizing willing cooperation, humane accommodation, and peaceful resolution of conflicts, as well as in terms of the ability to maximize security, liberty, justice, and welfare.

Although we cannot definitively resolve this important but complex problem, we may use our key question to explore patterns of politics in industrialized democratic countries, communist countries, and the developing world. Our guiding hypothesis in Chapters 12 and 13 can be briefly put as follows: Successful patterns for furthering cooperation, advancing accommodation, and handling conflicts in politics require (1) agreement on certain constitutional fundamentals; (2) meaningful opportunities for expressing needs, interests, and desires; (3) sound mechanisms for selecting priorities; (4) acceptable ways of legitimizing public policy choices; (5) effective governance; and (6) regular and effective controls on government. Let us briefly clarify each of these six points.

1. Agreement on certain constitutional fundamentals facilitates consensus and trust. Without a certain amount of consensus, no political community can carry on its business. Without a certain amount of trust, orderly procedures for discussion and deci-

sion would be impossible. Agreement on fundamentals involves accepted rules of the constitutional game (on voting; freedom of speech, press, and assembly; majority decision; due process of law) that enable political actors to civilize the struggle for power. Some political cultures are more effective at reaching agreement on fundamentals by making it easier to educate and socialize citizens in sound rules of the political game.

2. Meaningful opportunities for expressing needs, interests, and desires direct us to **interest articulation.** Political actors must be able to express themselves, to articulate their needs, interests, and desires. They may do so in a number of ways: by voting, speaking out in public forums, working for a political party, joining interest and pressure groups, using the mass media, and contacting their elected representatives. Such opportunities facilitate cooperation and accommodation in responsive political systems. Those who take advantage of such opportunities are often more knowledgeable about politics than nonparticipants; they are also usually more highly educated and self-confident.

3. Sound mechanisms for selecting priorities involve what some call **interest aggregation,** by which political actors build support for certain proposals and not for others. Some needs and interests are more important than others. Political actors usually find it necessary to work with others to advance the ideas that they believe merit support. Political leaders and parties play key roles in building support for political priorities, but they do not have a monopoly on this enterprise.

4. To be concerned with acceptable ways of legitimizing public policy choices is to be concerned with articulating, and agreeing on, principles and mechanisms of political obligation. Why do people obey those who make law and execute public policy? Why

do they accept, or agree to go along with, the political actors who (or principles, laws, rules, and regulations that) make claims on their obedience? Why, for example, in the United States do citizens accept the result of an election, a law passed by Congress, a decision of the Supreme Court, a presidential initiative in foreign affairs? Why do people go along with a majority decision? Without agreement on ideas and ways to obtain approval of the exercise of political power, the struggle for power could easily get out of hand. Cooperative advancement in politics would quickly disappear, and lawlessness, disorder, and civil war would ensue.

5. Effective governance calls for a government that can maintain freedom, law, and order; raise and spend revenue on behalf of agreed-on public purposes; and ensure necessary services and benefits. If government cannot modestly fulfill its own objectives—say, of security, liberty, justice, and welfare—it is in deep trouble. Political patterns cannot succeed unless they advance effective governance.

6. There must be regular and effective controls on government. Constitutional mechanisms must exist to ensure that government is a wise and limited servant and not a tyrannical and authoritarian master.

We will explore our hypothesis (which throws a great deal of light on the meaning of political health) by focusing on the constitutional framework of politics and on such nongovernmental actors as citizens, interest and pressure groups, the media, and political parties. In Chapter 13 we will turn to governmental actors: legislatures, executives, bureaucracies, and the courts. Throughout our analysis, and especially in our conclusion in Chapter 13, we will be concerned with whether the political patterns we have examined are voluntary (or imposed), humane (or barbaric), peaceful (or violent). And we will also

be especially concerned with the benefits and costs of the patterns we examine.

THE CONSTITUTIONAL FRAMEWORK OF POLITICS

We shall focus in this section on how the **constitutional framework** contributes to successful patterns of political accommodation. We will first discuss the broader constitutional ethos of politics, which some observers also call the political culture. Then we will explain and emphasize the importance of the constitutional agreement on fundamentals. Finally, we will call attention to a number of constitutional features that illustrate the diversity of actual political patterns in today's world.

The Broader Constitutional Ethos, or Political Culture

We are using **constitutional** here in a broad sense, referring to more than the strictly political constitution, which may be defined as the written or unwritten set of rules about who governs, how, to what ends, and with what results. The broader constitution refers to the larger historical, cultural, economic, and social ethos that suffuses the political community. It refers to the distinguishing attitudes, habits, and behavior patterns that characterize a political community. For example, the ethos, or **political culture**, may be peaceful or warlike, tolerant or intolerant, concerned or unconcerned; it may be altruistic or selfish, trustful or suspicious, cooperative or competitive. The ethos of a political community may be spiritual or materialistic, cosmopolitan or parochial. The dominant ethos may be genuinely egalitarian or racist and sexist. The people may be cultured, literate, and active in politics, or they may be uncultured, uneducated, and uninvolved. A political community's constitutional ethos is significantly influenced by the larger environment, as we saw in Chapter 4. That larger environment decisively affects political goals, principles, policies, and behavior.

A nation's historical experience and memory clearly shape its political constitution, as do its language, religion, literature, art, and social mores. Economics (how people earn a living) and geography (especially the prevalence and distribution of resources) also influence the constitutional ethos. Science and technology influence how political business is conducted. These influences in the broader culture dictate certain patterns of cooperation and accommodation, and they set in motion certain conflicts, which politics must moderate or resolve. Thus, key aspects of the nation's broadly defined culture vitally affect successful accommodation in politics.

Some examples may help illustrate the importance of the political culture. For example, in the United States the reality of a nation half slave and half free led to political trouble. The acceptance of slavery in the southern states and the development of an industrial and agricultural economy based on free labor in the northern and western states created tension and conflict between South and North and West. The outcome was a dreadful civil war—the worst fate that can afflict domestic politics. But although slavery in the United States made for conflict, the fact that Americans have been a people of plenty—and have lived in a spacious land of abundant resources—has undoubtedly taken the edge off class conflict and made it easier to achieve accommodation in politics.

Great Britain's long and successful constitutional and parliamentary history—after a civil war in the seventeenth century—has enabled liberty and authority to be reconciled and programs of socialist reform to be inaugurated in a nation still living under a monarch and still possessing the democratic anachronism of a House of Lords. The British sense of fair play makes it possible, moreover, for the people to accept the principle of parliamentary supremacy without worrying that Parliament will use its supreme power to abuse human freedom.

Centuries of czarist despotism had a decided effect on Soviet politics. Czarist despotism unquestionably stimulated cruel and conspiratorial responses by the Russian Bolsheviks as they sought to overthrow this despotism and build a heroic communist society. For generations Russia lacked a tradition of natural law (or higher law), meaningful representative government, and effective local democracy. Finally, in the late 1980s and early 1990s, forces arose to challenge the centralized power of the Soviet Communist party. But even in 1996 during the post–Communist era, the Russian government under Boris Yeltsin struggles to preserve new democratic patterns. As economic frustration grows in Russia, forces of authoritarianism threaten its fragile representative institutions.

In India, religious, social, geographic, and economic differences have made cooperation and accommodation in politics most difficult. Even though after World War II old British India was divided into a primarily Muslim Pakistan and a primarily Hindu India, these religious divisions have caused great tension in modern India. Kashmir, which is populated largely by Muslims, remains an Indian state and a source of chronic conflict. In the fall of 1993, religious differences led to violent clashes and urban bombing campaigns that swept India. Caste differences—with Brahmins at the top and untouchables at the bottom of the social and economic scale—also militate against cooperation in the spirit of equality. India's religious and social system makes reform urgent and yet extraordinarily difficult. On the other hand, Mohandas Gandhi's philosophy of nonviolence and democracy has encouraged peaceful resolution of disputes and the maintenance of traditions such as village industry—much to the dismay of those Indian revolutionaries who believe that the country will not become free and prosperous without a radical, even violent, revolution to usher in a new social and economic system.

The broader constitutional framework—a nation's broader culture—thus makes an important contribution to successful (or unsuccessful) patterns of political accommodation. Indeed, the other factors that we examine—expression of needs and interests, selection of priorities, legitimation of public choices, effective governance, and controls on government—flow from the broader constitutional framework. This will become clearer as we consider the more strictly constitutional agreement on fundamentals.

Constitutional Agreement on Fundamentals

The constitutional framework is important because it provides the fundamental agreement—and therefore the trust—without which politics cannot advance as a civilizing process. It provides sound rules for the political game.

This agreement on fundamentals does not require agreement on all aspects of life. All citizens need not belong to the same religion or speak the same language. They do not have to have the same economic, political, or social views. Homogeneous (similar) values may contribute to political trust, but heterogeneous (diverse) values do not necessarily lead to civil war. What is crucial is that there is enough agreement on enough fundamentals, or on any fundamental issue, to hold the political community together. And there must also be agreement on how to disagree.

Thus, Americans may be Protestants, Catholics, Jews, Muslims, atheists, or agnostics. They may be capitalists, socialists, or believers in some variety of a mixed economy. They may be Democrats or Republicans or members of a third, fourth, or fifth political party. They may like Beethoven or the Beatles or Bruce Springsteen. They may believe that virtue resides only in the breast of the farmer or that culture is only to be found in big cities, perhaps only in New York and San Francisco. They may speak English or Spanish or one of a number of other languages. They may disagree sharply on the welfare state or on how to cope with inflation or on how to deal with Russia. They may strongly differ on policies involving abortion or taxation or disarmament. Yet they may still be able to work out successful patterns of accommodation because they agree on the basic principles of the American Constitution: government based on the consent of the governed; free elections; freedom of speech, press, assembly, and religion; equal justice under the law; and majority rule.

Diversity, then, need not lead to failure in coping with the struggle for power. Diversity does not automatically make cooperation and accommodation impossible. However, learning to cope with diversity is the key to successful accommodation.

Different nations have different constitutional frameworks and different conceptions of what is fundamental. We will spell out one model, the Western democratic model, which has been called **polyarchy** (rule by the many), and briefly contrast it to the communist model of party dominance. Polyarchy is prominent in the highly developed industrialized countries; party dominance characterizes what is left of the communist world. Variations of these models, as well as dictatorship and monarchy, are found in the developing world.

Polyarchy—The democratic or polyarchal constitutional framework requires citizens and governments to agree on the following fundamentals:

1. Citizens and governments must agree to strive for the common good. Although preached more than practiced, this fundamental principle (as understood in terms of security, liberty, justice, and welfare) clarifies the purposes of politics. It requires citizens and the government to cooperate to achieve these purposes. Conflicts must respect these values, safeguard vital human needs, and protect fundamental interests.

2. Citizens and governments must also agree on certain bounds for political maneuvers, ruling out patterns of politics such as slavery, genocide, class liquidation, and religious persecution—practices considered evil by most civilized people. Accommodation must be based on an open, not a closed, society.

3. Citizens and governments must agree that an important area for accommodation lies outside the public sphere. They must agree, therefore, on a large private sphere in which individuals and groups may work out their

problems by themselves, so long as life, liberty, and law are respected and so long as private accommodation does not violate the common good.

4. Citizens and governments must agree on the reality of human diversity and human fallibility as well as on the imperative of searching for patterns of accommodation that are helpful if not fully perfect. They must therefore be skeptical about claims that a universal harmony of interests makes for the flawless resolution of conflicts. To avoid the imposition of tyrannical or totalitarian truths, they must insist on free expression and free acceptance.

5. Citizens and governments must also agree about the need for judicious balance. Often, sensible accommodation calls for striking a balance between contending claims, interests, and units of government—the claims, for example, of producers and consumers; the interests of workers, farmers, and industrialists; and the action of central and local government.

6. Citizens and governments must agree that balancing, harmonizing, and adjusting the purposes and powers of political actors call for various skills and functions at many levels. This process requires diverse contributions to successful accommodation—hence, pluralism and polyarchy.

7. Citizens and governments must agree on how to secure willing obedience to the process of accommodation. This ensures legitimacy—acceptance of key decisions and public policies. In polyarchies legitimacy is enhanced by widely accepted ideas such as free and competitive elections, the protection of basic rights, opposition political parties, due process of law, and limited government.

Although countries following the polyarchal, or Western democratic, model may agree on fundamentals, they do not have to have identical political systems. For example, both the British and United States systems are demo-

cratic. Yet the British may choose parliamentary supremacy, cabinet government, strong party government, and quasi-unitary government (terms that will be clarified shortly), whereas Americans may opt for separation of powers, presidential government, weak party government, and federalism.

Party Dominance—In contrast to the polyarchal model of Western democracies, we offer the traditional Leninist communist model of **party dominance.** This model also calls for agreement on certain fundamentals. For example, communist nations must accept the ideology of Marxism-Leninism. They all must accept the leading role of the Communist party.

Clearly, there are more differences than similarities between the Western democratic models and the communist model; the differences and similarities will emerge more clearly in the following pages. Here one major point can be made. If many political actors—the electorate, media, interest groups, parties, legislatures, executives, bureaucrats, and courts—play important roles at one or more levels in working out the pattern of accommodation we call polyarchy, the Communist party until recently played the crucial and decisive role at almost all levels in working out the Soviet pattern of accommodation, and it still does in some Asian communist countries.

It is difficult to generalize about a dominant pattern of accommodation in the developing world because of its great diversity. Constitutional frameworks in the developing world range from the political dictatorship of a strong leader through military or party dominance through polyarchic patterns to chaos. To illustrate this diversity, we will draw examples from a number of countries. But first we must clarify a number of special constitutional features that help us understand domestic politics.

SPECIAL CONSTITUTIONAL FEATURES

This section presents some constitutional features that are especially relevant to conflict and accommodation in politics.

Limited or Unlimited Government

Joseph Stalin's Soviet and Adolf Hitler's German governments exercised almost unlimited domestic power. Today, there are, to be sure, some highly repressive governments, such as those in Iraq and North Korea. But no political system is as fully totalitarian as those found in Stalin's and Hitler's regimes under which the government was free to exercise almost unlimited power in every sector of the society—education, the economy, the arts, and the private lives of citizens. As noted in Chapters 6 and 7, liberal democratic and democratic socialist governments (which follow the polyarchal pattern) insist that government power be limited. Democratic socialists allow somewhat more government power than do liberal democrats. But both groups maintain that the government powers in communist nations (although somewhat limited in theory) have been expanded too far. They agree, too, that authoritarian governments of the left or right still make a mockery of the concept of **limited government**; such governments violate human freedom with impunity.

Representative Government or Direct Democracy

Although governments in the highly developed industrial countries usually depend on the consent of the governed, the people exercise their power through elected representatives—for example, through a president and members of Congress in the United States. **Direct democracy**—in which the people make laws firsthand—is rare in the United States. It exists primarily at the state or local level, as in the New England town meeting, or when the people vote to amend a state constitution or on other cardinal issues of public policy. Other developed systems occasionally permit the whole nation to vote on a major issue—for example, the British people's vote on whether to join the European Common Market. Despite these exceptions, most of the business of government is carried on by representatives rather than directly by the people.

Theoretically, a **representative government** prevails in all communist countries. But in practice, Communist parties, not the people's representatives, have exercised overwhelming power. This was certainly true in the Soviet Union and remains true in Asian communist countries such as the People's Republic of China and Vietnam. Whether the conversion to market economies in the Asian communist countries will bring parallel democratic political reform is still an open question. So far, the People's Republic of China, Vietnam, and North Korea have not been eager to adopt democracy.

Many developing countries have effective representative institutions. In other countries, power is not based on the people's representatives and is certainly not in accord with the consent of the governed. In many developing nations, power is held by a military or political elite (sometimes referred to as a junta) that has seized power by force and rules without benefit of electoral legitimacy. The predominance of authoritarianism in the developing world may stem from several factors, depending on the region, its history, and its culture. For instance, there is ample evidence that the peoples of Central America aspire to democratic forms of government. One longstanding democracy is Costa Rica. But for long periods, powerful families such as the Somozas in Nicaragua from 1937 to 1979 and military strongmen such as Manuel Noriega in Panama from 1988 to 1989 have dominated the political life of many of these countries. Patterns of imposed authority left over from Spanish colonial rule and a long history of military involvement in politics sustain these trends.

Democracy has had a difficult time in many Asian countries. Even highly developed countries such as South Korea have until recently been authoritarian. Singapore, one of the most dynamic economic actors in Asia, remains politically authoritarian. Parliamentary democracy has had a rocky, unstable, and limited existence in Indonesia. After its inception in 1950, the Indonesian parliamentary system experienced seventeen governments in five years. While the current president, General Suharto, has been elected six times since 1968, he in fact rules with an iron fist through a powerful government party. According to Nathan Keyfitz of Harvard, one must understand the various strains of Asian culture—the value placed on order, unity, and concentration of power and the fear of chaos—to understand these difficulties. In Indonesia a key strain is a very strong Hindu-Javanese tradition.[1]

In Africa there have been many democratic experiments. Richard Sklar posits five different forms—liberal democracy, guided democracy, participatory democracy, social democracy, and cosociational democracy—and proposes a sixth: developmental democracy.[2] But democracy in Africa is fragile, as Sklar so eloquently points out: "Democracy in Africa is widely approved but everywhere in doubt. Democratic dreams are the incandescent particles of current history which gleam brightly in the sunlight of liberation only to fade beneath the lengthening shadow of grim economic realities."[3]

Disease, poverty, and hunger, along with deep-seated tribal animosities throughout Africa, make the creation of democratic traditions very difficult.

Separation or Connection of Powers

To ensure greater safety amidst the struggle for power, a nation's constitutional framework may, in addition to limiting power, also require that power be held by different hands. Thus, in the United States power is divided among three branches of government—legislative, executive, and judicial—according to the principle of **separation of powers.** Constitutionally, Congress must enact all legislation. The president may sign or veto the legislation, but Congress may, by a two-thirds vote, override the president's veto. For good measure, the U.S. Congress consists of a Senate and a House of Representatives, and both branches must agree on legislation before it can be enacted. Moreover, the U.S. Supreme Court is independent of both the legislature and executive branches. The Supreme Court may de-clare an act of Congress unconstitutional or hold that a presidential action violates a valid law.

Of course, the Founding Fathers did not intend that separation of powers would paralyze government. They expected separation of powers to ensure wise governance. The American system thus rests on the premise of cooperation and accommodation. Deadlocks may occur, however, when the president and Congress share different political philosophies. Such deadlocks make for either sensible compromise or ineffectual government. The possibilities of conflict in a system of separation of powers have increased the importance of strong and responsible parties to unite Congress and the president in a common program endorsed by the people.

By way of contrast, political power in the British government rests in a prime minister and a cabinet responsible to a majority in the House of Commons. Here we have a **connection of powers,** not a separation. Unlike the American president, who is elected for a four-year term independently of members of Congress, the British prime minister (formally selected by the monarch) is usually the person who commands a majority of votes in the House of Commons. The House of Commons and the cabinet are thus connected. British prime ministers lead the government because they have been empowered by a majority in Commons. Losing that majority seriously jeopardizes their ability to remain in power.

The British Parliament must formally enact legislation, but such legislation usually originates in the cabinet. Theoretically, the British Parliament consists of two branches: the House of Commons and the House of Lords. Constitutionally, however, all effective power resides in Commons. The British also have an independent system of courts. But British courts, in contrast to their American counterparts, have no power to declare an act of Parliament unconstitutional. Consequently, deadlock between the executive and the legislature is impossible in the British system. If the prime minister and the cabinet do not command a majority in Commons, the prime minister must either resign in favor of someone who will command such a majority or call for

Effective power in the United Kingdom rests in the House of Commons.

new elections that will produce a new majority in Commons and a prime minister who again has the confidence of that majority.

The Soviet Union historically followed a different path: a connection between the Communist party and the official Soviet government. From the revolution to the reform movement of the 1980s, the principal government officials (the prime minister), the executive decision-making council (the Council of Ministers), and the primary legislative body (Supreme Soviet) were all creatures of the Communist party. Through its Politburo, Central Committee, and Secretariat, the party defined government policy and made all major personnel appointments. The Soviet system thus did not even entertain the possibility (as in the American system) of conflict among its executive, legislative, and judicial branches, or the possibility (as in the British system) of a loyal opposition party contending with the government of the day. Similarly, in the People's Republic of China we see a system of "interlocking membership"—that is, a system in which the Chinese Communist party (CCP) holds political power and, through its governing apparatus, insures that virtually all the chief governmental positions are held by party members.

The 1990s seem to be bringing on a wave of democratic experiments in the developing world. For instance, by 1993 all twelve South American republics had free governments for the first time. But many developing countries do not illustrate the American principle of separation of powers. Some (such as India) are close to the British principle of connection of powers, with a prime minister responsible to a majority in the legislature. Others (such as Mexico) have an independently elected president who rules without effective interference from an elected legislature or an independent judiciary. Nigeria has a long tradition of an independent judiciary, even through periods of military rule. But these examples appear more the exception than the rule. Regarding the Asian cultural emphasis on unity and order, Keyfitz observes: "A division of constitutional responsibility between government, parliament, and the courts would be a dispersal of power, a sign that the community was breaking up."[4]

The American Founding Fathers favored separation of powers because they believed (as James Madison expressed in No. 47 Federalist) that "the accumulation of all powers, legislative, executive, and judiciary, in the same hands, whether of one, a few, or many, and whether hereditary, self-appointed, or elective, may justly be pronounced the very definition of tyranny." But Madison understood the foolishness of absolute separation and appreciated the need for governmental connections to advance "unity and amity." Similarly, the British have understood that a connection of powers—with the prime minister responsible to a majority in Commons and a loyal opposition party monitoring the party in power—can advance effective and responsible government without sacrificing freedom. Americans and the British would, however, seriously question a connection of powers that gives a single party or ruler all power. That would, indeed, be tyranny.

Federalism or Unitary Government

Every large and complicated political community must include cooperation between the center and the circumference—that is, between the national political community and its component parts. There must also be accommodation between the central government and local governments. And conflicts that arise between various levels of government must be handled sagaciously. How does a federal system contribute to successful accommodation? How is the problem of decentralization handled in a unitary political system as compared to a federal system? How is it possible to keep government close to the people?

Federalism, as in the United States, is one attempt to reconcile local liberty and national authority. It is one attempt to allow the people living in the fifty states (and serviced by innumerable local governments) to handle their own state and local problems while giving the central government (in which they also have a voice) power to handle nationwide concerns.

A federal system achieves this accommodation by demarcating national and state jurisdictions and powers, by indicating which powers the national government and the state governments may exercise concurrently, and by denying them certain powers (see Figure 12.1).

Figure 12.1
A simplified version of a federal system, United States style.

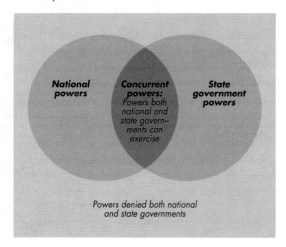

Federalism is generally a response to large size and diversity, as in the United States, Canada, and India. It is designed to balance necessary central authority on behalf of the nation with local liberty and self-government. Federalism attempts to strike a balance between empire and anarchy.

The United States—A classic federal system exists in the United States. Here the central, or national, government holds broad but carefully enumerated powers: to handle matters of national concern such as defense, foreign relations, taxation, spending for the general welfare, and regulation of interstate and foreign commerce. Some powers (foreign relations and interstate and foreign commerce) are exclusive powers that only the central government can exercise. Other powers (such as taxation and spending) may also be exercised by the states and at the local level. All powers neither delegated to the central government nor logically implied as belonging to it (such as provisions for schools, clean water, and police and fire protection) come under the jurisdiction of state or local governments. Certain powers are denied to both the central government and state governments (such as the power to deny a person life, liberty, or property without due process of law).

Theoretically, federalism makes it possible for political actors in state and local governments to express their needs and interests. They can determine their local priorities—for example, where they want to locate their schools, or what speed limit to impose on traffic. In this way citizens can keep a closer eye on their local government and make sure that it is acceptable to them and effective in addressing their concerns. In addition, a federal system keeps the central government from absorbing all power.

In fact, in the United States federalism has had a mixed record in advancing the security, liberty, justice, and welfare of all the people. For decades, some state governments discriminated against African Americans, after having kept them in slavery before the Civil War. Some state governments have not adequately helped the poor or protected the rights of women. And sometimes they have lacked the resources or the will to deal with key problems involving the security, liberty, justice, or welfare of their people.

The failures of state government have often led to a call for national action to protect African Americans, farmers, working people, consumers, and women. In addition, national action has often been taken in the interest of alleviating inequities between poor and rich states and of providing financial resources for cities.

The successes of state and local government must, however, also be acknowledged. State and local governments enhance democracy by keeping government close to the people. People can more easily participate in such governments; they can take initiatives and exercise greater local responsibility. They can respond more quickly to problems. In general, the federal division of powers encourages experimentation, with the opportunity to cancel bad experiments without great losses and to duplicate good experiments nationwide after success at the state level. Thus, a great deal of reform legislation involving, for example, wages and hours, collective bargain-

ing, unemployment compensation, and health care—was pioneered in progressive states.

France and Japan—By way of contrast with federalism in the United States, France and Japan have a **unitary form of government.** In unitary governments all power emanates from the center from Paris or Tokyo. National power includes not only the power to make war or regulate the economy but also the power to shape the educational curriculum of all public schools, so that, in France, for example, on any given day in the public school system all children are reading the same books. In France the prefect is the national government's chief administrator in each of the country's ninety-five departments (geographical and administrative units). Elected assemblies in the departments and communes (local governmental units) lack significant power. The national government thus carries out policy at the local level; locally elected officials are pretty much restricted to municipal questions and to bargaining with Paris and the prefect. But the logic of decentralization is strong. The Socialist Mitterrand government, elected in 1981 and ending with his death in 1995, promised to move toward giving greater power to local governments.

Great Britain—Great Britain, or the United Kingdom (England, Scotland, Wales, and Northern Ireland), illustrates a pattern between a federal and a unitary form of government, although leaning toward the unitary. Traditionally, all power emanated from London—and the British Parliament. But Northern Ireland had its own parliament before the bloody conflict between Irish Catholics seeking union with Ireland and Protestants insisting on keeping their tie with the British Crown. Moreover, the Scots and the Welsh have been given opportunities to vote on having their own governments within the framework of the British Constitution. Thus, because of the unique historical composition of the United Kingdom, the centuries-old tradition of local government, and the complexities of the modern welfare state, Britain has seen a great deal of devolution and increased local control. For example, many national policies are carried out by local units of government. British municipalities govern themselves in local matters, much as do American municipalities. And efforts have been made to maximize the voice that the Scots, Welsh, and Irish have in their own geographical domains.

West Germany—Before German reunification, West Germany illustrated another variation on federalism. From one point of view the German states (called Laender) seem to play a prominent role in the German government. Thus, Germany's constitution (the Basic Law) was drafted by delegations from the parliaments of the Laender and was ratified by them. The second house of the German federal legislature in Bonn—the Bundesrat—consists of delegates from the Laender; they are not separately elected by the people as in elections to the U.S. Senate. Moreover, votes in the Bundesrat are cast by Laender delegations as a unit and according to instructions from the Laender governments.

But from another point of view, the central government in Bonn clearly has more power

than the U.S. national government, and the Bundesrat is not as powerful as the U.S. Senate. Bonn controls defense, foreign affairs, and the economy, and it has generous concurrent jurisdiction in most other matters. And even though the Laender have the usual residual powers over education, police, and local government, the cost of Laender programs—for example, higher education—has led to federal involvement and greater control. Of the two branches of the German government, the Bundestag (whose members are separately elected by the people) is more influential than the Bundesrat. The German Laender are responsible for the administration of federal law, which makes them look like tools of the central government but which also gives them a power to sabotage federal policies by not cooperating.

Canada—The continuing trials and tribulations of federal Canada demonstrate that striking the right balance between central authority and provincial liberty (whether in Quebec or Alberta) is quite difficult. The Canadian experience points up both the advantages and disadvantages of federalism as a means of cooperation, accommodation, and resolution of conflicts. The

Separatists in Quebec lost their bid for independence in a national vote in Canada in 1990.

Canadian experience also raises difficult questions. Should the French-speaking people of Quebec (who are a majority in that province) be able to secede from Canada or be granted special privileges not granted to other provinces if they are unhappy as a minority in an English-speaking Canada? Should the people of oil-rich Alberta be able to keep most of their wealth for themselves, or does a federal union require sharing that wealth?

Soviet Union—Federalism seems to be a response to size and ethnicity. Thus it should be no surprise that the Soviet Union—large as it was and comprising as many nationalities as it did—should (theoretically) have been a federal state. Actually, the Communist party in Moscow historically decided all basic policies. Theoretically, the states that made up the Soviet Union could secede; in reality, it was unthinkable. One has only to look at Lithuania's attempted secession in 1989–1990 to appreciate the difficulty of breaking away. Moscow virtually sealed the small Baltic republic off, shutting off access to food, gas, and other elements of its economic lifeline. Yet the Lithuanian case proved a portent of the future.

For the remainder of 1990 and into 1991, other republics of the Soviet Union began breaking away from Moscow's control. As the process of fragmentation gained momentum, conservative Communist officials attempted a coup in August of 1991 and failed. For many, this last-ditch attempt to maintain a unitary state under the Communist party sealed the fate of the Soviet Union. In short order, Boris Yeltsin became president of the Russian Republic; the old Soviet Union became a loose federation of former republics—the Commonwealth of Independent States (CIS). But as of 1996, the CIS is hardly a paragon of federal unity. Many of the republics have completely severed their ties with the Commonwealth; at least two (Armenia and Azerbaijan) waged a vicious war with each other; Moldavia's population is divided over the issue of uniting with Romania or remaining in the CIS; and the

predominantly Muslim republics of South Asia are fiercely independent and establishing ties with the Islamic world to their south.

Developing Nations—The experience of federalism in the developing world is difficult to chart. For example, Mexico and Nigeria are formally federal. They illustrate federalism's response to large size. In Mexico, which has a popularly elected president, power has remained with the president and the central government. Nigeria's effort to maintain a federal union led to a bloody civil war in the late 1960s. The largely Muslim people of the north and the largely Christian people of the east and south could not get along. The future success of some federal pattern in Nigeria will depend on overcoming the suspicions that separate the Muslim Hausa-Fulani and the Christian Ibo.

India is, relatively speaking, one of the most successful federal countries in the developing world. Again, its federal system was largely dictated by its size and ethnic and historical divisions. Indian nationalism, the strength of the Congress party, and the leadership of Jawaharlal Nehru as prime minister in the 1950s and 1960s helped make India's federal system work. India's system is quite different from that of the United States. Indian states are much weaker. The central government can abolish a state or alter its boundaries. It can appoint a governor or take over a state in an emergency. The states, as in Germany, carry out the central government's policies; regional language differences make it practical for the government in Delhi to use the administrative machinery of the states to carry out federal policies.

Not all large countries are federal; China, for example, is not. Meanwhile, a number of small countries (including Switzerland and Austria) are federal. Nevertheless, three characteristics of states make them good candidates for federalism: large size, diverse ethnic and linguistic groups, and a historical tradition of local self-government. In responding to these factors, federal systems can provide ways to reconcile central authority and local liberty. Successful reconciliation may, however, depend on combining a sense of nationalism with a respect for diversity—a combination difficult to work out at any time.

Majority Rule

Space does not permit a more definitive treatment of all constitutional techniques of accommodation in politics. Yet it is important to treat at least one additional method—majority rule—that has figured prominently in the developed countries, that is partially used in communist countries, and that plays absolutely no role in purely authoritarian systems. We define **majority rule** as the power of one-half of the members, plus one, of any decision-making group to bind the remainder of that group to a decision.

Should heads be counted or broken? This question underlines the key issue: Will political actors rely on discourse and votes, or on edicts and force in dealing with the struggle for purpose and power? And how many heads are to be counted? In reaching decisions, what percentage of ballots are relied on to identify the winning candidate or policy?

In addressing these questions, nations in the highly developed industrial North have generally followed John Locke, James Madison, and Abraham Lincoln. They have generally used majority rule to make electoral and legislative decisions. They have accepted the force of Lincoln's argument in his First Inaugural Address: "Unanimity is impossible; the role of a minority as a permanent arrangement is wholly inadmissible; so that, rejecting the majority principle, anarchy or despotism in some form is all that is left." Lincoln, of course, had the Southern states in mind. He knew that one consequence of the rejection of majority rule in his nation would be civil war.

Locke argued that it was both fair and practical to rely on majority rule. Madison endorsed majority rule as a central principle of republican government—government by the people. Majority rule ensures popular and effective

government. It avoids the difficulty of having to achieve unanimity on all issues, a difficulty that could lead to a dangerous breakdown in government and thus to either impotence or anarchy.

Majority rule also avoids the unrepublican consequences of relying on a minority whose power is based on force, birth, or wealth. Such minority power lacks legitimacy—the consent of the governed. Minority decisions would not command the will, respect, and peaceful obedience of a population whose support is necessary to ensure political stability and governmental effectiveness. Often minorities lack the force necessary to execute their decisions or to make them stick. As both Locke and Madison perceived, these consequences would engender popular disrespect for law and undermine the resolution of conflicts by peaceful and orderly processes. Furthermore, the difficulty of ascertaining which minority is to rule would produce troublesome conflicts among rich and poor, educated and ignorant, white and black.

Majority rule is thus an expression of popular rule. In the industrialized world it has generally worked well to enable the people to rule, and it has not proved incompatible with the protection of minority rights. This is true largely because the constitutional rules of the game in the highly developed nations also require protection of basic rights for all—majority and minority. Historically, majority rule has facilitated orderly decision making. Winners have been able to act; losers have abided by the results of the ballot box. Decisions made by majority rule—whether in elections or in the legislative body—have been accepted as legitimate. In the process of resolving disputes by majority rule, a great deal of accommodation goes on. To achieve a majority, conflicting demands must be adjusted to work out sane compromises. This process makes for helpful moderation and desirable reconciliation.

Majority Rule in Developed Nations—The functioning of majority rule in the United States and Britain has not produced "majority tyranny." One discerning historian, Henry Steele Commager, has written, apropos of the United States, that there is no "persuasive evidence from our own long and complex historical experience that majorities are given to contempt for constitutional limitations or minority rights. . . . They have not taxed wealth out of existence; they have not been hostile to education or to science. The pulpit, the press, the school, the forum, are as free here as anywhere in the world—with the possible exception of that other great majority-rule country, Britain."[5]

Majority rule works well in pluralist societies with a substantial middle class, in moderate societies that have been able to avoid extremist politics, and in fluid societies where majorities shift and change on issues. Because electoral and (more noticeably in the United States) legislative majorities are not static, groups having a majority for one candidate or issue may be with the minority on other decisions. This overlapping of rulers and ruled, of majority and minority, fosters confidence in the majority process. It increases trust among citizens, interests, and party members. This trust encourages the minority to accept the majority's decision and to work for peaceful change. The majority, knowing that it may well be in the minority on a subsequent vote, is encouraged to respect the minority's rights.

The widespread use of majority rule can also be illustrated in the choice of party leaders in Britain and in runoff elections in France and in many American states. It may also be seen operating in the decisions of the U.S. Supreme Court. Thus, in Britain the leader of the Conservative party in the House of Commons is selected by a majority vote of the party's parliamentary caucus. When the Conservative party has a majority in Commons, this vote effectively determines the prime minister, insofar as the monarch asks the leader of the majority party to become prime minister. The leader of the Labour party was, until recently, also selected by a majority decision of the party caucus in Commons. Now this power is shared with trade unions and local party organizations. But the party leader is still chosen by majority vote.

In France and in some American states a runoff election is held when a candidate for president or governor does not receive a majority of votes in the first election. This practice guards against having an official elected by a **plurality** of votes— that is, the highest number cast but below 50 percent. The second election ensures that the winner has the electoral support of a majority of those voting.

The practice of majority rule is also at work in judicial decision making. Thus, the U.S. Supreme Court operates on the basis of majority decisions, as do many multimember courts throughout the United States. Five out of nine votes (when all nine justices are on the bench) are required for the Supreme Court to reach a decision. Although a steady diet of 5 to 4 decisions will raise questions about the Court's judgment, the majority decision is, nonetheless, accepted. As in the electoral process, the Court's minority may look forward to victory at another time.

In assessing majority rule as an accommodating technique in countries such as the United States, we should note several qualifications or reservations.

Electoral decisions are often made by a plurality (that is, by the highest number cast for a given candidate) rather than by a majority. This may happen, for example, in a race among three or more candidates for a U.S. House or Senate seat, where there are no runoff elections. Indeed, President Bill Clinton was elected by a plurality in 1992, by virtue of a three-way race between himself, George Bush, and Ross Perot.

In the United States (to emphasize another qualification), the Constitution dictates a two-thirds vote or a three-fourths vote on certain matters. Thus, Congress needs a two-thirds vote to overturn a presidential veto. Options available for proposing a constitutional amendment are by two-thirds vote in both houses of the U.S. Congress or the call for a constitutional convention by two-thirds of the state legislatures. Proposed amendments are ratified by a three-fourths vote of state legislatures.

Some political scientists look beyond the facade of formal decision making (such as in a specific election or a specific vote by a legislative body) to the question of who really rules in a democracy. They emphasize different varieties of rule by minorities.

For example, some political scientists argue that minorities really rule in the United States. Thus, Robert Dahl, although rejecting the reality of rule by a power elite, maintains that "on matters of specific policy the majority rarely rules." Rather, he argues, different minorities rule on different issues. He insists that in the United States "the relevant question is the extent to which minorities in a society will frustrate the ambitions of one another with the passive acquiescence or indifference of a majority of adults or voters."[6]

Finally, critics on the left deny that true majority rule prevails in the United States. Unlike Dahl, however, they note the reality of rule by a power elite—a cohesive and dominant minority that they also call the military-industrial complex. They insist that the formal facade of majority rule in elections and in legislative bodies conceals the fact of rule by such a pervasive power elite.

These points are most important as they direct attention to the actual operation of popular rule and the extent to which the needs and interests of the great bulk of the people—especially their security, liberty, justice, and welfare—receive attention in the accommodation process. Patterns of accommodation fail unless these needs and interests are advanced.

Majority Rule in Developing Countries—Majority rule faces difficulties in the developing countries because it presupposes trust among citizens, respect for elections, and leadership responsive to the popular will. When these elements are lacking, as they are in many developing countries, majority rule cannot function. Citizens will fight each other; elections will be set aside; military leaders will rule by force. Yet some developing countries have successfully used majority rule in their elections. The 1980s saw remarkable advances in the propensity of Latin American nations to use the electoral process for selecting leaders.

When elections are honest and accurately reflect popular sentiment, political accommodation is enhanced because elected officials can point to majority support. Party leaders elected only by plurality can expect difficulties in governing unless they can put together a cohesive coalition of parties.

Majority Rule in Communist Countries—Majority rule is not completely unknown in the commu-

After ten years of civil war, elections were held in El Salvador in 1994.

nist world. True, under the Soviet political system, majority rule was virtually nonexistent in most country-wide elections. But at the upper levels of the party, there was some recognition of majority rule. Under Lenin, the Soviet Union's first great leader, there was considerable discussion in the Politburo and the Central Committee—the top decision-making organs of the Communist party—and disputes were resolved by majority decision in the absence of consensus. All members of the Politburo and Central Committee were then required to abide by the decision reached. This was the principle of democratic centralism. Such practices within the top echelons of the party tended to disappear under Stalin's tyrannical rule.

With Stalin's death, majority decisions were once more resumed in the Politburo and in the Central Committee. On at least one occasion when Stalin's successor, Nikita Khrushchev, was outvoted in the Politburo, he took the decision to the parent body, the Central Committee, and won a majority victory. Later, Khrushchev was ousted from power by an adverse decision of the Central Committee. So at least the top decision-making organs of the Soviet Union perceived the value of majority rule.

THE ROLE OF NONGOVERNMENTAL ACTORS

How do nongovernmental actors contribute to successful patterns of accommodation? Citizens, interest groups, political parties, and the media play a significant role in expressing vital needs and interests in developing countries. All these nongovernmental actors, but especially parties, play an important part in guiding public policy. In varying ways, all nongovernmental actors help legitimize public policy choices. Similarly, these actors, especially political parties, make effective governance possible and help keep government under control.

The Role of Citizens

In highly developed countries such as the United States and Great Britain, citizens express vital

needs and interests in many ways. They talk about corporate downsizing or the budget deficit or nuclear proliferation. They worry about crime and drugs and affordable housing. They complain about high taxes. They attend meetings about environmental pollution or the location of a new school. They write to government officials about budget cuts. They sign petitions about human rights. They may also join an interest group that supports their position on business or labor or agriculture. They may also participate actively in a political party. And, of course, they vote. Many analysts believe that a vote for Bill Clinton in 1996 was, at least in part, a vote to protect major government programs such as Medicare from severe cutbacks from a conservative Republican-controlled Congress.

Citizens also modestly select priorities. They do so, for example, when (with the help of political parties and elections) they give a very general direction to policy by voting Labour or Conservative in Britain or Democratic or Republican in the United States. Thus, a vote for Bill Clinton in 1992 was a vote for "Change!" and for reviving the economy.

Citizens also legitimate public policy choices and enhance and control government in a number of ways. For example, they show approval of government policy in Britain when at election time they return the government in power. They register disapproval when they vote to turn the "rascals" out. In the United States, citizens may bring pressure on their state legislators to approve or reject a proposed constitutional amendment such as the Equal Rights Amendment to give equal rights to women. American citizens may directly support or reject an amendment to a state constitution, and they have frequent opportunities to vote directly on propositions involving gambling or bonds for education or new jails. In contrast to traditional British constitutional practice, British citizens voted in a national referendum to join the European Common Market.

Citizens' willing obedience to law or public policy enables government to do its job. Their refusal to pay taxes, to support an unpopular war, or to abide by a hated policy could cripple government. Their opposition, although now generally lawful and peaceful, has sometimes been lawless and violent. In the United States, for example, Prohibition failed because too many people—whether a real majority or a very large minority—wanted to drink beer and liquor. In another example, President Lyndon Johnson's decision not to run for reelection in 1968 and the subsequent decision to pull out of Vietnam were attributable to the growing public hostility to American involvement in that tragic war.

Citizens can exercise control over government in ways other than by throwing or (threatening to throw) the "rascals" out of office in the election process. They can also exercise control through public opinion, interest groups, and legal action. Public opinion cautions government when government seeks to overturn a popular policy or when it oversteps its bounds. For example, public opinion polls, by indicating the popularity of key features of the welfare state, may dissuade a conservative government from tampering with the social security system. Polls may also indicate support for welfare reform or fiscal responsibility, thus encouraging a government to reduce the federal deficit or crack down on "welfare chiselers." Interest groups may protest or support governmental policies. For example, environmentalists may protest government efforts to weaken enforcement of pure air and water legislation; pacifists may protest escalating arms expenditures. Citizens can also take legal action to check governmental abuse of power. For instance, individual citizens may sue the government if it engages in illegal wiretapping or violates other civil liberties.

In these varying ways, then, citizens act to further (or deny) cooperation with the government. They may facilitate (or resist) the resolution of conflicts. We should neither exaggerate nor deprecate the role of citizens in a system based on the consent of the governed.

In communist systems, because power is concentrated in the party elite, citizens have had

less opportunity to express their needs and interests. But even in these systems, if living conditions get bad enough, popular movements may emerge and have an impact. During the 1980s in Communist Poland, citizen support for Solidarity, the independent Polish labor union, unquestionably alerted the government to public displeasure over its labor, economic, and political practices. The Polish people applauded the words of one Solidarity leader who told the deputy prime minister: "We don t want to live in a country where unity is forced by a police stick!"[7] The police stick was, however, very evident when the Polish government imposed martial law in December 1981 and at least temporarily squelched the free expression of public opinion. But the seeds of revolution had been sown, and nine years later a leader of Solidarity, Lech Walesa, was elected president of Poland.

Most nations, including communist and even authoritarian governments, would undoubtedly prefer willing cooperation from their citizens. Authoritarian nations cannot deny that there are limits to the use of force and terror to mandate cooperation. Clearly, cooperation is more compatible with security, liberty, justice, and welfare than is the police stick.

In comparison with citizens in the industrialized world, citizens in developing countries have generally played a less important role in politics. But their role is slowly changing as more democratic and constitutional patterns emerge and mature. Some authoritarian governments in the developing world must either listen to their people or face the consequences of electoral defeat or revolutionary overthrow. Three specific examples of authoritarian governments overthrown by the force of "people power" are the 1979 Sandinista revolution against Nicaraguan strongman Anastasio Somoza Debayle; the 1981 Iranian revolution led by the Ayatollah Khomeini to oust the shah of Iran; and the popularly supported removal of Ferdinand Marcos in the Philippines that put Corazon Aquino in power in 1986. People power does not guarantee that authoritarian systems will necessarily become democratic. In Iran, an Islamic republic replaced the monarchy of the shah and proved to be anything but democratic.

The Role of Interest and Pressure Groups

All political communities include interest and pressure groups. (See Table 12.1 for a classification.) Such groups are, however, more numerous, freer, and more powerful in developed nations such as the United States and Britain than in communist countries. These groups contribution to political accommodation is a source of controversy.

Interest Groups in Developed Countries—In the United States and Britain **interest groups** clearly express their own needs and concerns by providing information, tendering advice, and exerting pressure. They operate through the media, within political parties, before legislative committees, and in the offices of the bureaucracy. They are not bashful in speaking up on behalf of their constituencies or in spending money to advance their concerns. They represent industrialists, farmers, trade unionists, and a wide range of other professional, ethnic, religious, and reform groups. Unquestionably, they constitute a major source of demands on government.

Thus, for example, workers in the U.S. electronics industry would like to limit the number of Japanese television sets and stereos entering the American market. Furniture workers in North and South Carolina would like to limit the importation of finished furniture. Ranchers oppose the importation of foreign beef. The housing industry would always like to see interest rates come down. Consumers, however, would like cheaper electronics, food, furniture, and housing. Environmentalists would like the government to impose tighter controls on air-polluting factories and cars, strip mining, clear cutting of timber, chemical dumps, super oil tankers, and offshore oil drilling. Industries and unions oppose overstrict regulations that threaten profits and jobs. And so the battles rage.

By the very nature of their self-interested concerns, most interest groups do not hold the

Table 12.1 *Classification of Interest Groups*

Type	Interests Represented
I. Economic	Manufacturers, retailers, workers, farmers
II. Professional	Doctors, lawyers, educators, journalists
III. Religious	Catholics, Muslims, Protestants, Jews
IV. Racial	African Americans, Asians, Hispanics, whites
V. Reform	Pacifists, prohibitionists, anti-vivisectionists, environmentalists, pro-choice, anti-abortion, pro–gun control, anti–gun control
VI. Ethnic	Welsh, Basques, Kurds, French-Canadians
VII. Cultural	Friends of opera, art, music, architecture

broad public good as a high priority. They are not normally in business to unite interests or to reconcile a wide range of claims. They may make it either easier or more difficult for others (political parties, legislatures, or executives) to assess priorities. They make it easier by presenting accurate information and sound advice; they make it more difficult if they distort their positions and obscure more vital needs and fundamental interests. Yet the priorities of powerful interest groups often prevail in politics, particularly if their pressure, money, organizational skills, and political friends are influential, and particularly if they have built legislative coalitions (as in the U.S. Congress) or are in a very strong position in a political party (as, for example, the British Trade Union Congress in the Labour party).

Only in a few developed nations (such as Holland and Austria) do interest groups have an official constitutional role in approving—and therefore legitimizing—some aspects of policy. Nonetheless, very often interest groups' approval of policy provides an informal, extralegal, but important blessing in democratic and developed countries. This approval contributes significantly to effective governance. Disapproval, on the other hand, may nullify governmental policy.

For example, the historic effectiveness of governmental efforts in the United States, Great Britain, France, Brazil, Argentina, Israel, and many other countries to control inflation through either voluntary or compulsory wage and price controls depends on the willingness of unions to forgo wage increases above a certain percentage and of industries to forgo price increases above a certain percentage. Massive disobedience would nullify even compulsory controls.

Interest groups are often better able to prevent action than to accomplish it. For example, in 1969, by withholding their approval of a Labour government proposal for a new industrial relations act, British trade unions effectively vetoed the proposal in the British cabinet. And in 1971 when a Conservative government passed such an act, the unions refused to cooperate with it, and

it was subsequently repealed by a Labour government.[8] In the United States, the National Rifle Association has prevented meaningful national gun control legislation for decades, and the American Association of Retired Persons has thwarted efforts by budget-minded legislators to limit or cut Social Security and Medicare benefits.

The political "veto" that powerful interest groups have over legislation that would adversely affect them cannot always block it. Sometimes when governments take actions that are disliked by key interest groups, the actions are nonetheless effective, particularly if there is widespread support within the country as a whole. For example, in the United States, the National Labor Relations Act of 1935 (the Wagner Act, which required employers to recognize as collective bargaining agents unions that had the support of a majority of workers) was unpopular with many industrialists and their major organizations (such as the National Association of Manufacturers). Yet the public supported the principle of giving a majority of workers, through their unions, the opportunity to bargain collectively and peacefully with their employers; this would advance industrial democracy and avert labor strife. Despite management's opposition to the Wagner Act, and its legal actions to nullify the act's administration, the law was passed.

It is nevertheless much more likely that controversial legislation will be effective if, before passage, government obtains the support, or at least the acquiescence, of opposing interest groups and if, after passage, skillful administrators consider the valid criticisms of opposing interests.

This analysis suggests how interest groups can exercise control over government by seeking to protect their own interests. They do so by watching for ill-advised use of government power affecting them. They naturally scream about policies that adversely affect their profits, wages, prices, and benefits. Reform groups, in particular, play a watchdog role. They are on the alert for violations of civil liberties (the American Civil Liberties Union), good ecological principles (the Sierra Club), safety and quality in

Peaceful demonstrations (this was a pro-choice rally in Buffalo, New York) represent one way in which interest groups make their position known.

consumer goods (Ralph Nader), government integrity (Common Cause), and, at least from their perspective, moral transgressions (the Christian Coalition). They may challenge government—legally, in the courts; politically, in Congress; or administratively, in the bureaucracy.

Interest Groups in Communist Countries—Interest groups in communist countries, particularly in the most authoritarian systems, have historically played little if any role. To be sure, the Soviet Union of the 1970s and 1980s contained a large number of political dissent groups. Intellectuals, scientists, religious leaders, and writers were all part of this movement. Enormous resources were poured into the Soviet internal security system to keep these groups under some control and ensure the Communist party's monopoly of power. With the advent of major democratic reforms under Mikhail Gorbachev in the late 1980s, interest groups achieved greater legitimacy and ultimately hastened the collapse of the communist system.

Interest Groups in Developing Countries—The role of interest groups in the developing regions of the world varies widely. In authoritarian or military regimes, free and independent interest groups

have little power or effect. The interests that capture headlines by challenging the government are exceptions.

In India and other democratic developing countries, business, labor, student, and religious groups have played an important role in influencing government. Indian industrial and business groups (which help to fund what was until recently the dominant Congress party) keep the Congress party from moving too far to the left. Student and labor strikes and religious campaigns have been used to oppose unpopular government policies or authoritarian tendencies. Such actions have several times required the government to rule by emergency decree—not the most desirable or successful pattern of accommodation in a democratic society.

Business and industrial groups in Mexico also tend to influence the government to adopt more conservative policies or at least to resist more radical ones. Such groups favor economic growth as the way to achieve prosperity and a better life. Students in Mexico and many Latin American countries (as well as India) have often pressed for reforms, usually in the interest of farmers and workers, and other egalitarian objectives. One dramatic failure of peaceful accommodation occurred on the eve of the 1968 Summer Olympics in Mexico City, when hundreds of National University students died in an ugly clash with police. This kind of violent confrontation between student activists and government authorities has been repeated in many of the developing countries of Asia, Latin America, Africa, and the Middle East.

The Role of Political Parties

As they respond to public opinion, help the electorate, manage interest groups, and carry on the business of government, **political parties** are the unsung heroes in the process of furthering cooperation, advancing accommodation, and handling conflicts. Modern politics is impossible without political parties. They are indispensable in the democratic states of the developed world; they make liberal democratic and democratic socialist governments work. So, too, is the Communist party the cornerstone of the political process in the communist world. And some critics contend that good party organization is the key to success for developing nations. They maintain that the lack of such organization accounts, to a large extent, for the difficulties facing many developing countries: absence of cohesion; disorder; inadequate integration of people, interests, and government; and ineffective and uncontrolled government.

Interest Groups Versus Political Parties—Here a comparison of a major political party and an interest group in the developed world may be illuminating. Like the political party, the interest group wants to obtain, wield, and enjoy the fruits of power. But the interest group desires power not usually for the sake of mastery or prestige, but for the sake of advancing its group, economic, and social purpose. The interest group tends, therefore, to be concerned with more specific matters than the political party. For example, it may favor or oppose higher prices for domestic oil, higher wages, or farm price supports. It may oppose or support gun control. It may work hard for or against pollution control or public housing or comprehensive health in-

surance. It may concentrate on banning abortion or on making "freedom of choice" effective. The interest group generally does not put up candidates for public office as does the party. In contrast to the political party, most interest groups do not usually have a permanent organization concerned primarily with electing or defeating candidates for public office and with marshaling support in the legislature on a wide range of issues. Unlike the political party, the interest group has little or no responsibility to the electorate for the victory or defeat of its favored candidate.

The party, on the other hand, plays a formal as well as an informal part in elections. Its motivation is not necessarily angelic. But its operation, in accord with its abilities, makes it an extremely valuable broker in the process of accommodation. Its generally broader perspective, its greater sensitivity to votes and to public opinion, and its accommodating disposition are all interrelated. The party functions both formally and informally. It enables the electorate to translate its ultimate authority into general public direction, links public opinion and public policy between elections, mediates among a wide range of interest groups, and gives the people's representatives an instrument by which government may go forward. In its own self-interest, it usually functions as a prudent organ in the process of democratic and constitutional accommodation.

Party Platforms and Priorities—In developed nations the party expresses vital needs and fundamental interests as it responds to public opinion and shapes public priorities. Parties winnow and sift from a wide range of demands by citizens and interests and try to incorporate the most important into a more coherent party program. Establishing priorities constitutes a kind of preliminary legitimation. Effectiveness in delivering on party platforms depends on discipline and the character of the party system.

These generalizations can be dramatically illustrated in Great Britain and the United States. For example, the British Labour party fought for several decades for a socialist Britain. Its 1945 party manifesto *Let Us Face the Future* "had been debated and approved at its party conference and was packed with pledges that had been accumulating over the years and that were derived from many different groups within the movement."[9] When the Labour party won a parliamentary majority in 1945, it proceeded to fulfill its pledges. Prime Minister Clement Attlee's Labour government nationalized the Bank of England (1946), electricity (1946), coal (1946), civil aviation (1946), transportation (1947), gas (1948), and iron and steel (1949). It established the British welfare state with the National Health Service Act of 1946, the National Insurance Act of 1946 (sickness, unemployment, and retirement benefits; maternity grants; widow's pensions; death grants), and the Housing Acts of 1946 and 1949 (low-cost housing). Its Agricultural Act of 1947 gave farmers "assured markets and guaranteed prices."

Three decades later, in 1979, Margaret Thatcher became prime minister when her Conservative party won a parliamentary majority. In contrast to her Labour party counterparts, Thatcher promised a policy of nonintervention in industry and encouragement of private enterprise while reducing expenditures in central and local government. Over the next eight years, the Conservatives made good on their promises. By 1988 the government had sold to private interest all or part of its holdings in petroleum, gas, civil aviation, airports, shipbuilding, aircraft engine manufacturing, weapons, buses, freight and telecommunications, and seed development and plant breeding, and had privatized the Trustee Savings Banks. The steel industry also became private, as did the water and electric industries and the bus network in Scotland.

American parties, although not as disciplined and coherent as British parties because of separation of powers and federalism, have often responded to a call for reform by the public and key interest groups. For example, the election of Franklin D. Roosevelt, a Democratic president, and large Democratic majorities in the House of

Representatives and the Senate resulted in a flood of important legislation: the Agricultural Adjustment Act (1933), the National Labor Relations Act (1933), the Tennessee Valley Authority Act (1933), the Social Security Act (1935), and the Fair Labor Standards Act (1938). These measures responded to farmers calling for stable farm prices; advocates calling for better public power, flood control, and recreation; labor unions' appeal for collective bargaining; and workers' demands for unemployment compensation, old-age pensions, a floor under wages, and a forty-hour work week.

It can hardly be said that Roosevelt's New Deal program was reversed during the Republican administrations of Dwight D. Eisenhower (1952–1960), Richard Nixon (1968–1972), or Nixon and Gerald Ford (1972–1976). Nevertheless, the administrations of Republican Ronald Reagan (1980–1988) did introduce a significant conservative movement away from the tradition of government intervention, support, and regulation. Ronald Reagan based his presidential campaign on a promise of deregulation, cuts in spending on social programs, and significant increases in defense spending. The Reagan administration oversaw deregulation of several key industries, most notably the commercial airline system. Social welfare programs such as Head Start, a preschool program for inner-city children, were cut. Tough, uncompromising stands were taken against federal employees, such as the federally supervised air traffic controllers, who tried to organize and strike. And consistent with his Republican party platform, President Reagan proposed and supervised an enormous military buildup, the largest peacetime military strengthening in U.S. history.

In 1992 the Democrats under Bill Clinton returned to the White House after a twelve-year absence during the Reagan and Bush years. The early days of the Clinton administration clearly signaled several shifts in policy direction. The new Democratic administration almost immediately passed legislation requiring employers to provide unpaid leaves of absence for employees during family emergencies. A gag order on abortion counseling in federally funded clinics—an order implemented during the previous Republican administration that had opposed abortion—was lifted. And finally, the new president struggled to lift the ban on gays and lesbians in the U.S. military, a ban supported by the Republicans while in power. The successful 1996 presidential campaign of Bill Clinton indicated that his second administration, while still seeing a role for the national government, would nevertheless move toward the more moderate center of American politics.

Party Coalitions—Political parties provide a mechanism for building coalitions. They rally divergent groups and interests on behalf of common programs. In so doing, they work against narrow and extremist positions. They tie sometimes differing interests and groups together on unifying issues. Thus, they build support for proposals that the party, if successful in elections, may then transform into legislation.

The effectiveness of that transformation depends on parliamentary majorities in cabinet governments such as the British and on single-party control of both Congress and the presidency in the United States. Generally, government is more effective when one of the two major parties has (alone or in coalition with a minor party) a clear majority, as in Britain or West Germany. In multiparty systems, as in Italy, the lack of a strong party with a clear-cut majority makes for instability, with governments falling as coalitions come apart. Some multiparty systems, however, with strong, astute leaders in a trusting relationship with the top party leaders, can—as in Belgium or the Netherlands—sometimes achieve effective government. But as we shall see in the next few paragraphs, a nation with a two-party system may have trouble enacting a coherent national program.

In the United States the principles of separation of powers and of federalism make for a very loosely structured two-party system and, often, deadlock in the national government. Federalism contributes to such a system by creating a number of independent power sources—national, state, and local. Separation of powers reinforces the loose party structure by affirming the inde-

America's two main political parties gain the spotlight every four years at their national presidential nominating conventions.

pendence of the president and members of Congress in their respective spheres. The two major American parties, Democratic and Republican, thus emerge as coalitions built around presidential candidates, national party committees, Democratic and Republican members of Congress (or aspirants to congressional seats), state and local parties, officeholders, candidates, rank-and-file partisans, and other key interests seeking a payoff for their support.

Nationally, each party coalition attempts to forge some unity every four years to elect a president, gain majority control in Congress, and enact a party program. It is, however, difficult to achieve unity and carry out a national party program, because national interests (most often addressed by the presidential candidates) do not always coincide with regional, state, and local interests. Members of Congress, those seeking election to Congress, and state and local politicians (such as governors and mayors) are often preoccupied with their own elections and with state and local concerns. They are not passionately committed to a national party program. Moreover, the U.S. electoral system, rooted in federalism, does not ensure that the president and a majority in Congress will be of the same political party. Additionally, separation of powers ensures the independence of members of Congress in their own sphere of power, which often translates into conflict with the president. Thus, the absence of a cohesive and responsible national party system—with deep and disciplined roots in the country—and the constitutional independence of nationally elected officials frequently create governmental deadlock in Washington.

This deadlock may exist even when the president's party controls both houses of Congress. There is no danger of the government falling in the United States if the executive (president) and legislature (Congress) disagree. Representatives and presidents are elected for fixed terms. The president is not responsible to a majority in the Congress, as the British cabinet is responsible to a majority in the House of Commons. In the United States deadlock does not threaten new elections and thus encourage agreement between members of Congress and the president.

Nonetheless, the loose coalitions known as the Democratic and Republican parties in the United States may still make government effective. They may be coherent and responsible on some issues. The president's party in Congress may support him or her on some issues, particularly when the president can use the considerable powers of public opinion, patronage, veto, and political clout to induce recalcitrant representatives to support the executive position.

Political Parties in Developed Countries—Competing political parties in developed countries also help to maintain a measure of government control. The opposition political party may selectively challenge the party in power on both policy and performance and may continuously express criticisms that well up from the electorate or from interest groups.

In parliamentary systems like the British, the opposition party may call for a vote of confidence in the House of Commons whenever it has reason to believe that the existing government no longer commands a majority. And, of course, the opposition party is always looking ahead to the next mandated election (the House of Commons can sit for no longer than five years without an election). The opposition party hopes that its criticisms of the existing government will lead to the government's ouster in such new elections.

In the United States, with its staggered elections for the House of Representatives (every two years), for the president (every four years), and for one-third of the Senate (every six years), the minority party still hopes to use its criticism of the majority party to gain control of Congress or the White House. During the first two years of the Clinton administration, the Democratically controlled House of Representatives was under increasingly heavy attack from the Republican right wing. So effective was the criticism that the Republicans seized control of the House in the mid-term elections of 1994 and were able to hold the majority in both houses of Congress in the 1996 elections.

The loyal opposition (as the opposing, or minority, party is called in Britain) is, without doubt, a marvelous contribution to responsible and peaceful accommodation. Such accommodation clearly rests on the consent of the governed and encourages a humane and civilized politics. This pattern of accommodation ensures a smooth and peaceful transition from one government to the next and, in this way, enormously enhances effective governance and responsible control of government.

Political Parties in Communist Countries—In communist systems, the Communist party plays the decisive role in furthering cooperation, advancing accommodation, and handling conflicts. The party dominates the political process. Through its executive body, the Politburo, the party has historically monopolized the task of establishing priorities on important matters. Its judgment on priorities is final. It functions to coordinate the thoughts and actions of other political actors: citizens, interests, the media, even government. Party decisions establish the legitimacy of public policies. The Politburo places its stamp of approval on all key measures. The party's organs, which parallel those of government, can thus supervise key measures. The party emerges as the real political power in the modern communist state. For all these reasons, the party cannot really be considered as "nongovernmental"; for all intents and purposes, the Communist party *is* the government.

Political Parties in Developing Countries—In the developing world political parties play widely varied roles. Some parties—for example, the Congress party in India—operate in the same ways as strong parties in the industrial nations. In a number of developing systems a single party dominates the political scene. In Mexico, for instance, the PRI (or Institutional Revolutionary party) has, until recently, fully dominated the political scene. Despite its power, the PRI ac-

cepts opposition political parties, and under its rule Mexico has protected basic freedoms and preserved private property. In other developing systems such as Iraq and Libya, the governing party functions as the instrument of a dominant, often authoritarian, leader. In such countries civil liberties for an opposition party are minimal or nonexistent. Former President Ferdinand E. Marcos of the Philippines was another illustration of an authoritarian ruler who used a political party, called the New Society Movement, to maintain his power. Marcos came to power in 1966 and imposed martial law in 1972—to save the republic, he said. Marcos (and his party) were ousted from power in 1986 through a broad-based popular movement led by Corazon Aquino.

The case of the ruling Mexican party is particularly instructive. The PRI, originally founded in 1929, has dominated Mexican politics for over fifty years. It has co-opted the popular Mexican revolution. It has taken over key sectors of the Mexican economy, bureaucracy, and society and used them to maintain popular and interest-group support and to ensure the success of popularly elected and powerful presidents. Thus the party has a labor sector, a farmer or peasant sector, and a popular sector composed of government bureaucrats, professional people, businesspeople, small landowners, and the military. Clergy and major business organizations may not belong to the popular sector.

Some scholars maintain that the PRI has succeeded admirably in stabilizing Mexican politics and in ending the regimen of coups and assassinations. They emphasize how the PRI has tried to satisfy labor, peasant, and business interests, how it has tried to accommodate both Marxist socialists and advocates of free enterprise.[10] More recently, however, other critics have challenged the PRI's ability to secure cooperation, advance accommodation, and handle conflicts. They have highlighted corruption and undemocratic practices within the PRI. They especially note that the PRI is dominated by a small group of insiders. Although they concede that the PRI has prevented disorders and military coups like those in other Latin American countries, ensured peaceful elections, and given Mexico strong leadership, they nonetheless advocate a more democratic and honest political system.

The PRI's somewhat authoritarian character clearly troubles democratic critics. Serious charges of election fraud followed the congressional elections of 1985, the gubernatorial elections of 1986, and the presidential, gubernatorial, and municipal elections of 1988. The cumulative effect of these scandals contributed to the emergence and strengthening of opposition party coalitions: the PMS (Partido Mexicano Socialista), the FDN (Frente Democratico Nacional), and the PAN (People's Action Party). In the 1988 elections, for the first time ever, the opposition secured seats in the Senate, and the PRI suffered clear defeats in the Federal District and in at least three other states. For a while it looked as though meaningful party opposition would become a reality in Mexico, but throughout 1989, 1990, 1991, and 1992, President Salinas instituted widespread economic reforms in the form of free-market economic policies and government divestment programs. These dynamic changes dramatically stimulated and improved the Mexican economy and, to some extent, reduced the momentum of the parties arrayed against the PRI. As of 1996, the PRI remains the dominant party in Mexican politics, despite the rather severe ups and downs of the Mexican economy, a troublesome rebellion in the very poor southern province of Chiapas, and increasing party competition. Perhaps the most significant developments are the unprecedented degree of dissent recently manifest within the PRI and some opposition gains in state and local elections.

Many developing countries, however, lack strong two-party or one-party systems. Thus, the task of political accommodation is inadequately performed: Integration does not take place, priorities are not articulated, legitimate legislation and administration are not accomplished. And often, in the absence of effective government, a military

junta or a military leader steps in to maintain order and move the economy forward. Most often, the military represents the political right; sometimes it attempts to balance left and right. Even its temporary presence, however, is a sign that civilian patterns of political accommodation are malfunctioning. Needless to say, effective and regular control by such military regimes is minimal. Their usual promise of elections and a return to civilian government is a unilateral promise that may or may not be fulfilled.

The Role of the Media

By the media we mean agencies of communication such as newspapers, magazines, radio, and television. Depending on the country involved, the media play an important role in expressing needs and interests, in sharpening priorities, in legitimizing government, in strengthening government's effectiveness, and in guarding against the abuse of power. Where the media are free and independent, as in the democratic countries of the developed world, their capacity for expression and their ability to influence government is greater than in the communist world or in many developing countries, where newspapers, radio, and television are often under party or government control. These media play a vital role in securing approved and effective governance in all countries.

In the United States and Great Britain, for example, the agencies of mass communication attempt, with varying degrees of success, to give citizens "an account of the day's events in a context which gives them meaning"; to provide "a forum for the exchange of comment and criticism"; to project "the opinions and attitudes of the groups in the society"; and in general, to reach "every member of the society by the currents of information, thought and feeling" that the media supply.[11]

Through editorials, feature columns, or programs, the media may also, directly or indirectly, express judgments on public priorities and build public support on behalf of policies or candidates. They thus illuminate public discussion and choice, for example, on how to reduce the national deficit, enhance employment, curb nuclear proliferation, fight pollution, improve education, or deal with the AIDS crisis.

Sometimes media can contribute to the enactment of policy. Such may have been the case in the American humanitarian intervention into Somalia in 1992. Many analysts believe that a major factor in the decision to intervene was the constant barrage of images of war-torn Somalia projected on American television screens—starving children, bodies in the streets of Mogadishu, harried and frightened international relief workers. Dubbed the "CNN effect," these images generated considerable sympathy for the plight of innocent Somalians and contributed to the pressure brought on President George Bush to do something to relieve the situation.[12]

Both before and after the enactment of public policies, the media serve to legitimize such policies by their editorial approval or disapproval. Media support or opposition, depending on its intensity and the extent to which it reflects public opinion or key interest groups, may strengthen or weaken government. This holds particularly for controversial issues: for example, the British decision to send its military forces to retake the Falkland (Malvinas) Islands after they had been invaded by Argentina in 1982, the American involvement in the Vietnam war from 1960 to 1975, deregulation of U.S. airlines by the Reagan administration, and various policies attempting to deal with a troubling national deficit.

The media have often played a vital role in guarding against the abuse of governmental power. They have zealously protected freedom of the press against censorship and other violations. They have taken strong stands on behalf of freedom of speech, assembly, and religion. They have sought to make government, especially in the United States, function in "daylight" by opposing government secrecy (except in very limited cases). They have sought to expose what happened in important matters—as in the Pentagon Papers case—even at the risk of challenging

government contentions that national security mandated such secrecy.[13]

Constantly on the lookout for government illegalities (as in the Watergate case during the Nixon administration, the Iran-Contra affair and the Housing and Urban Development scandal during the Reagan years, and the "filegate" and Whitewater controversies during the first Clinton term), wasteful spending, shady government transactions, and adverse effects of governmental policy (as in the dumping of radioactive materials), the media play an important role in keeping government honest. But sometimes the price paid for a free and independent press in Western democratic countries is distortion, narrowness, and sensationalism, which the best members of the press deplore.

In the communist political systems, the media have generally functioned as organs of the party or government to test party and governmental priorities, legitimize policies, and enhance the government's effectiveness. They do not generally function as watchdogs in the Western democratic sense. They do, however, inform the people of the party line, reprimand those who deviate from this line, and exhort the people to support party and government. They have fundamentally been instruments of party and government in achieving accommodation.

In developing countries, the role of the media, especially the print media, is mixed. In some countries, such as India, the press functions pretty much as does the press in developed nations. In other countries, the press serves as an organ of the government or ruling party or ruling military junta, much as the press in traditional communist nations. In still other developing countries, the press occasionally plays a courageous and dangerous role: expressing needs, interests, and criticism—in news stories or editorials—contrary to the approved line of the dominant government. The newspaper *La Prensa* in Nicaragua is a good example of this kind of courage. For years it criticized the ruling Somoza family for its policies. After the Sandinista revolution (which *La Prensa* supported) succeeded, the paper continued to criticize what it perceived to be the ill-advised and sometimes authoritarian policies of the Sandinista ruling council.

However, the full independence of newspapers in even such professed democratic countries as Mexico and India can be threatened. In the mid-1970s the press in both countries incurred governmental displeasure and retribution for positions critical of the incumbent regimes. In both cases, elections freed the press to once again criticize the government.

CONCLUSION

Our analysis in this chapter suggests the rich variety of constitutional frameworks in domestic politics. Our analysis also underscores the importance of citizens, interest and pressure groups, political parties, and the media in securing willing cooperation, humane accommodation, and peaceful resolution.

Before we can more fully assess our tentative hypothesis about patterns of accommodation, we must consider the role of governmental actors, especially legislatures, executives, bureaucracies, courts, and other political elites. In Chapter 13 we will turn to that examination and to questions about who governs, how, to what ends, and with what results.

ANNOTATED BIBLIOGRAPHY

Almond, Gabriel, and Powell, G. Bingham, Jr., eds. *Comparative Politics Today: A World View,* 5th ed. Boston: Little, Brown, 1991. Examines Britain, France, West Germany, the Soviet Union, China, Mexico, and Tanzania within a framework of system, process, and policy. Focuses on political socialization, political recruitment, interest articulation, interest aggregation, and policymaking.

Brand, Jack. *British Parliamentary Parties: Policy and Power.* London: Oxford University Press, 1992. Offers a thorough and readable analysis of the British government by a Scottish political scientist.

Brzezinski, Zbigniew. *The Grand Failure: Communism's Terminal Crisis.* New York: Scribner's, 1989. Chronicles and analyzes the fall of communism in the late 1980s. Written by the former national security adviser under President Jimmy Carter and Columbia University academic.

Clapham, Christopher. *Third World Politics: An Introduction.* Madison: University of Wisconsin Press, 1985. Provides lucid and informative overview of Third World politics. Places particular emphasis on the fragility of Western political institutions and processes as applied in developing countries.

Clawson, Dan, Neustadt, Alan, and Scott, Denise. *Money Talks: Corporate PACs and Political Influence.* New York: Basic Books, 1993. Presents a first-rate analysis of how corporations, through the use of political action committees (PACs) influence the political process, particularly through the tax code and other forms of legislation, not in roll call votes.

Coleman, Fred. *The Decline and Fall of the Soviet Empire: Forty Years that Shook the World, from Stalin to Yeltsin.* New York: St. Martin's, 1996. Puts Coleman's fourteen years of journalistic experience in Moscow to good use. The primary assertion seems to be that the Soviet Union was always much weaker and more insecure than United States officials ever knew.

Elazar, Daniel J. *Federal Systems of the World,* 2nd ed. New York: Stockton Press, 1994. Fine comparative study by one who is sympathetic to federalism and its contributions to cooperation and accommodation.

Macridis, Roy C., and Brown, Bernard E., eds. *Comparative Politics: Notes and Readings,* 8th ed. Pacific Grove, Calif.: Brooks/Cole, 1991. Touches on virtually all of the important issues in comparative politics, including methodology, democracy, authoritarianism, the concept of the state, communism, institutions, political change, and much more.

Miller, Judith. *God Has 99 Names: Reporting from a Militant Middle East.* New York: Simon & Schuster, 1996. Provides a very fine analysis of the Islamization of politics in the Middle East, written by the former Cairo bureau chief of the *New York Times.*

Mundo, Philip. *Interest Groups: Cases and Characteristics.* Chicago: Nelson-Publishers, 1992. Offers a first-rate analysis of American interest groups using a case study approach.

Parenti, Michael. *Democracy for the Few,* 6th ed. New York: St. Martin's, 1994. Criticizes the actual performance of liberal democratic patterns.

Riemer, Neal. *The Revival of Democratic Theory.* New York: Appleton-Century-Crofts, 1962. Sees democratic and constitutional accommodation as a response to the problem of conflicting potentialities in politics. Emphasizes the case for majority rule as a technique of public decision making.

Rothberg, Robert, and Weiss, Thomas G. *From Massacres to Genocide: The Media, Public Policy and Humanitarian Crises.* Washington: Brookings, 1996. Contains essays on how media coverage shapes foreign policy and distorts perceptions of the Third World.

SUGGESTIONS FOR FURTHER READING

Birnbaum, Jeffrey H. *The Lobbyists: How Influence Peddlers Get Their Way in Washington.* New York: Times Books/Random House, 1993.

Frank, Reuven. *Out of Thin Air: The Brief, Wonderful Life of Network News.* New York: Simon & Schuster, 1991.

Fuentes, Carlos. *A New Time for Mexico.* New York: Farrar, Straus & Giroux, 1996.

Meyer, Michael J., and Parent, William A., eds. *The Constitution of Rights: Human Dignity and American Values.* Ithaca: Cornell University Press, 1992.

Neuman, Johanna. *Lights, Camera, War: Is Media Technology Driving International Politics?* New York: St. Martin's, 1996.

Riemer, Neal. *James Madison.* Washington, D.C.: Congressional Quarterly Press, 1986.

Salmore, Stephen A., and Salmore, Barbara G. *Candidates, Parties, and Campaigns: Electoral Politics in America,* 2nd ed. Washington, D.C.: Congressional Quarterly Press, 1989.

Smith, Tony. *Thinking Like a Communist: The State and Legitimacy in the Soviet Union, China, and Cuba.* New York: Norton, 1987.

Verba, Sidney, and Orren, Gary R. *Equality in America: The View from the Top.* Cambridge: Harvard University Press, 1987.

Wasserstrom, Jeffrey N., and Perry, Elizabeth J., eds. *Popular Protest and Political Culture in Modern China.* Boulder, Colo.: Westview Press, 1994.

Wiarda, Howard J., ed. *New Directions in Comparative Politics.* Boulder, Colo.: Westview Press, 1991.

GLOSSARY TERMS

accommodation
connection of powers
constitutional
constitutional framework
direct democracy
federalism
interest aggregation
interest articulation
interest group
limited government
majority rule
party dominance
plurality
political culture
political party
polyarchy
representative government
separation of powers
unitary form of government

NATIONAL POLITICS II: LEGISLATURES, EXECUTIVES, BUREAUCRACIES, AND THE COURTS

THIS CHAPTER focuses on the role of governmental actors in working out political patterns of cooperation and accommodation and in handling conflicts. We remain concerned with how these patterns contribute to security, liberty, justice, and welfare. Our analysis still rests on the premise that unanimity rarely, if ever, exists in the political community. Citizens often disagree; interests frequently conflict. In most countries the media are not of one mind and parties compete. No invisible hand functions to ensure that the organs of government—legislatures, executives, courts, and bureaucratic departments—work in perfect harmony. How, then, do governmental actors function in the struggle for power that is politics? How voluntary, humane, and peaceful are the patterns they work out?

Governmental actors perform their roles within a constitutional framework of politics, which establishes the rules of the political game. If our guiding hypothesis set up in Chapter 12 is correct, governmental patterns will succeed if they rest on (1) agreement on certain constitutional fundamentals; (2) meaningful opportunities for the expression of needs, interests, and desires; (3) sound mechanisms for the selection of priorities; (4) acceptable ways for legitimizing public policy choices; (5) effective governance; and (6) regular and effective controls on government.

The political constitution is concerned with who rules, how, to what ends, and with what results. Critical political scientists must not only investigate these matters but must also pointedly ask who benefits and who suffers as political actors cooperate and compete. Governmental actors are in business to manage the struggle for power. Successful patterns must neither be so severe that they destroy the freedom of conflicting interests and parties nor be so ineffectual that they are unable to prevent the ultimate terror within a political community: civil war.

In our exploration we will contrast a governmental system from the developed world, drawn largely from the United States or Great Britain, with patterns in communist systems and several examples from the developing regions of the world.

THE ROLE OF LEGISLATURES

Legislatures in developed democratic countries have four main, but interrelated, functions: a **representative function,** a **forensic function,** a **legislative function,** and a **supervisory function.** In performing these functions legislatures fulfill most conditions of successful accommodation.

The Representative Function

Legislatures give voice to the political, economic, social, and geographic interests of the political community. American legislators are likely to be "politicos," attempting to balance the interests of constituency, pressure group, party, and nation. British legislators are likely to be "partisans," hewing to the party line on key issues. But because voters are generally interested in only a few subjects, congressional representatives are often freed from their role as "delegates" who do what the dominant interests in the constituency want done. They are often free to function as "trustees," deciding issues by judging what they think is best for the nation. Similarly, members of Parliament (M.P.'s) may vote as "delegates" on nonparty issues and as "trustees" on fairly rare matters of conscience. In general, legislators translate key segments of public opinion—and the interests of majority voters, interest groups, and parties—into tangible public policy.

Terms of office vary from country to country in the developed regions of the world. Terms are designed to keep government reasonably close to the people, although few developed nations adhere to a motto popular at the time of the founding of the American republic: "Where yearly elections end, there tyranny begins." In the United States, the term of office for members of the House of Representatives and of the Senate is fixed in the Constitution. Members of the House are elected by voters in congressional districts for a term of two years. Members of the Senate are elected by a statewide constituency for a term of six years. As we noted in Chapter 12, one-third of the Senate is elected at a time. This feature keeps sentiment in the Senate close to current opinion in the states.

In Great Britain, members of the House of Commons may, if an election is not called earlier, serve for five years. Parliament cannot sit longer than five years without a new election. More often than not, however, new elections are called before the end of the five-year period. If the prime minister and cabinet lose their majority in the House of Commons, they can resign or call for new elections.

The second house of the British Parliament, the House of Lords, provides an interesting contrast to the U.S. Senate. The U.S. Senate is one of the most powerful second legislative organs in the world. Its influence, in both domestic and

The Capitol in Washington, D.C., is home to the House of Representatives and the Senate.

foreign affairs, is significant. No law can be enacted without its approval. The president must seek the Senate's **advice and consent** on treaties and key appointments. It has often provided leadership on legislative programs. In comparison, the British House of Lords is not an elected body but consists of the hereditary peerage and other lords appointed by the government. The hereditary peerage represents Britain's aristocracy of birth. Peers appointed by the government represent an aristocracy of intellect, experience, and accomplishment. The powers of the House of Lords are minimal; for example, it may momentarily delay but not permanently defeat legislation that the British cabinet and the House of Commons wish to enact.

Interestingly, the highest judicial body in the British legal system comprises members of the House of Lords with legal or judicial experience, who are known as the "law lords." The law lords constitute a kind of British "supreme court," but they lack power to declare an act of Parliament unconstitutional. Freed of electoral pressures, the House of Lords is theoretically able to represent the interests of the British nation as a whole. In fact, its majority political position is generally conservative, reflecting the interests of hereditary birth-rights and wealth.

The Forensic Function

Legislatures provide a forum for debate and formal decision making. Thus, they facilitate the examination of the views of contending parties. Because key decisions in Britain are made in the cabinet, debate in the House of Commons rarely alters the outcome of legislation. Debate may, however, clarify the parties' positions on key issues and thus educate the public to some extent. In the United States—given the greater independence of Congress—the House and the Senate provide a hearing for the folks back home and for a host of economic, religious, and social interests. They provide—especially through the congressional committee structure—a channel for information and an arena for the articulation of grievances, ideas, and pressures. They pro-

vide an opportunity to measure the intensity of the feelings of voters and interests. They provide an arena for a modest amount of deliberation.

The claims and priorities of contending interests can be examined in the legislature. This provides an opportunity (not always effectively used) for confrontation and compromise. Here legislators and party leaders (who may also be legislators) may face each other. In the American system especially, legislators, key interests, and members of the executive branch may meet at committee hearings. Issues may be clarified, positions reaffirmed, policies defended and attacked. Through this process, a great deal of accommodation takes place in the American political system.

The Legislative Function

Legislatures also have the formal responsibility for making law. Figure 13.1 illustrates the cooperation required to enact a bill into law in the United States.

In passing laws legislatures not only express interests and shape priorities; they also place the stamp of legitimacy on public policy. In the United States the president's signature is required before a bill can become a law. If the president chooses not to sign—if he vetoes a bill—a two-thirds vote in both the House and the Senate can override the veto. Duly enacted legislation constitutes formal legitimacy; such legitimacy in turn makes for effective governance. Although in Britain the cabinet shapes basic policy, Parliament must still officially enact legislation. Parliamentary approval embodies the final act of sovereign legitimacy.

Historically, in both the United States and Britain, legislative control of the purse—the power to provide money for the support of government—has provided a major control on government. Here, the legislative and supervisory functions overlap. In the United States the power of Congress to raise and spend money exerts a powerful control over the executive. Money, which must be lawfully raised and spent, crucially affects the exercise of political power.

Figure 13.1
A simplified version of how a bill becomes a law.
Source: Adapted from Congressional Quarterly Almanac, vol. XXXI (Washington, D.C.: Congressional Quarterly, Inc.), 1975, p. 24.

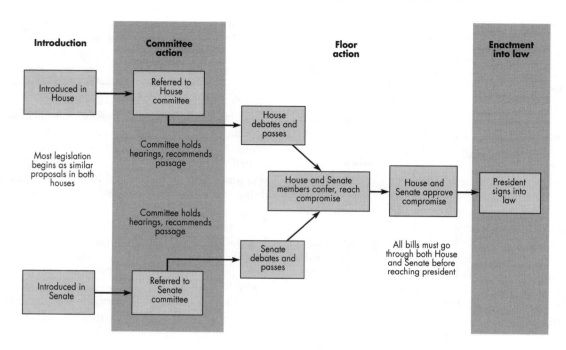

To grant money is to make the exercise of power possible; to withhold funds is to limit power.

Today in Britain, because the cabinet is really the executive arm of a parliamentary majority, legislative control of the purse is no longer a real safeguard against the executive, the way it was when the British monarch was the executive and when government was not responsible to a parliamentary majority. Nevertheless, the budget, which the House of Commons must formally approve, remains a powerful instrument to control the content and direction of public policy.

The Supervisory Function

Legislatures also supervise the work of the executive and the bureaucracy. For example, the U.S. Congress regularly reviews the work of the administration, particularly when money bills are being considered and often when new legisla-

tion has been proposed. Congressional committees have an extensive investigatory power that they often use to evaluate, and thus control, the functioning of the bureaucracy. Debates in the House and the Senate also provide opportunities for the people's representatives—particularly members of the opposition party—to criticize governmental policy. The Senate's agency in giving advice and consent on treaties and other key appointments enables senators to scrutinize policy and personnel. Moreover, the House may impeach (bring charges against) and the Senate may try officials, including even the president of the United States, for "treason, bribery, or other high crimes and misdemeanors."

In Britain the "watchdog" role falls primarily to the opposition party—Her Majesty's **loyal opposition**—whose task it is to criticize, expose weaknesses, and insist on good performance from the party in power. This task is often performed during the question hour in the House of Commons when the prime minister, or other cabinet officers, may be queried about the conduct of British policy. Parliament may also investigate key problems or government scandals. This is often done through royal commissions, which are really investigatory committees.

Let us now look briefly at the prominence of these functions in communist systems and in the developing world.

Legislative Functions in Communist and Developing Countries

In communist systems, legislatures have historically played a modest role. Representation is formal but ineffective. The primary purpose for the existence of legislative bodies is to "rubber stamp" policies as they emanate from the Politburo. Real supervision of government by the legislature is unheard of. Nevertheless, elaborate procedures are followed to elect representatives and hold endless meetings. In the People's Republic of China the key legislative unit is the National People's Congress, consisting of 2,970 deputies. They are indirectly elected for five years by the provincial congresses, autonomous regions, municipalities directly under the Central Government, and the People's Liberation Army (PLA). A Standing Committee elected by the Congress is in permanent session. But again, real legislative as well as executive functions power resides with the Communist party.

Legislatures in the developing world vary widely. Some are ineffective; others have modest powers. The legislature in India behaves in a parliamentary fashion. Legislatures in other developing countries are dominated by a single party (as in Mexico) or an authoritarian leader (as in Indonesia). In many developing countries the representative, forensic, legislative, and supervisory functions remain relatively weak.

THE ROLE OF EXECUTIVES

Modern executives in developed countries dominate the political process. They plan, initiate, and implement overall governmental policy. They are indispensable in the process of articulating vital national needs and fundamental interests. Without executive leadership, developed nations would lack both a national vision and the ability to pull the country together on behalf of national priorities. Executives serve to enunciate and gain approval for policies. Their resourcefulness and vigor enable modern governments to do their jobs. They also act to control the very bureaucracy they head. In performing their tasks they must obtain widespread cooperation from among legislators, key interests, and citizens in general. They must also work out innumerable accommodations among contending forces and prudently deal with difficult conflicts.

Before examining the important roles of executives, let us recall the way they are chosen and their relation to their respective legislatures. We will again use the United States and Great Britain to illustrate presidential and parliamentary patterns of cooperation, accommodation, and conflict.

How Executives Are Chosen and Their Relation to Legislatures

The American president is elected for a four-year term and may now be reelected only once. The president is chosen (indirectly, through the electoral college) by the people of the states. Presidential candidates for both the Democratic and Republican parties are chosen by their respective party's national conventions. Members of Congress are also elected independently and for fixed terms. It should be noted, however, that in the early 1990s a widespread movement to impose Congressional term limits swept the United States. A number of states passed referendums limiting the number of terms that can be served in succession. However, there is a constitutional question as to whether states have the right to limit the terms of federal legislators. Most experts agree that the issue is headed for the courts for resolution.

Congress must formally enact legislation. The president's signature is required for legislation, unless Congress can override a presidential veto. Constitutionally, presidents cannot force Congress to follow their will, and if neither the Senate nor the House can muster a two-thirds vote to override a presidential veto, Congress is unable to enact legislation. The president and Congress must cooperate to avoid deadlock.

In the British parliamentary scheme, the executive is the cabinet, headed by a prime minister. The prime minister is a member of Parliament who has been elected as party leader by the majority party's caucus in the House of Commons. Other members of the cabinet are leaders of the majority party (generally members of the House of Commons) selected by the prime minister and reflecting support within the dominant party. In 1981 the Labour party changed its traditional way of electing its leader. Now Labour party M.P.'s share this power with trade unions and local party organizations. The prime minister is first among equals in the cabinet. Although in U.S. cabinet sessions the president's decision prevails (since cabinet members have no authority to override the president as chief executive), in the British cabinet the principle of collective responsibility prevails. The prime minister is powerful and often decisive, yet he or she must have the cabinet's support (or at least its majority) to continue functioning.

The British cabinet as a group bears responsibility for key decisions. Cabinet members hold key ministerial posts and are responsible for the day-to-day operation of the government. Cabinet members may, of course, resign to take the heat for bad decisions, as British Foreign Secretary Lord Carrington did in 1982 after the Argentine invasion of the Falkland (Malvinas) Islands; they may also resign if they are unable to support a decision favored by a majority of the cabinet. Conflict between the cabinet and the majority party in Parliament is impossible insofar as the cabinet is the majority party's instrument to plan, initiate, and implement policy. The cabinet is thus a forceful and cohesive executive, depending on majority support in Commons to govern responsibly and vigorously. Yet the cabinet leads Parliament. If the cabinet should lose a majority in the House of Commons, the prime minister can ask for new elections to permit the British electorate to speak and return a new Parliament with a clear party majority (and thus a prime minister and a cabinet with authority).

American presidents have a more difficult job of achieving cooperation with the legislature than their British counterparts. The fact that the president and members of the House and Senate are independently elected makes it possible for the president to be of one party and for one or both branches of Congress to be dominated by another party. In 1988, for example, when President Bush assumed his duties, he faced a Democratic House and a Democratic Senate. During President Clinton's first term, the Republicans seized control of both the House and Senate in 1994. Two years later, Bill Clinton was reelected, but both houses of Congress remained in Republican hands.

If deadlock occurs between president and Congress, the American people cannot resolve the conflict in new elections. The president remains in office for the full four-year term; members of the House occupy their seats for their two-year terms, and senators for six years. It is also possible for the president's party to lose (or gain) control of the House and Senate during his or her tenure in office. Because of separation of power, there is no effective constitutional reason forcing a president and Congress to agree on a common program. And America's relatively weak party system does not build a strong bridge between the legislative and executive branches. Thus, conflict between the American president and the Congress is frequent, stormy, and often disruptive. This was recently evident in 1995 when disagreements over the federal budget between President Clinton and the House of Representatives led by Speaker of the House Newt Gingrich resulted in a temporary shutdown of the federal government.

A strong and resourceful president is needed to work out patterns of cooperation. We will shortly examine the resources the president may draw on to achieve cooperation and leadership.

The Roles of the U.S. President

Figure 13.2 calls attention to the multiple roles the American president plays. Most of these roles are also played by leaders of other developed countries. In a number of such countries, however, the role of ceremonial chief of state (such as the British monarch and the president of the Republic of Italy or Germany) is separate from the real head of government. The sources of the U.S. president's powers are to be found in the U.S. Constitution, in historical custom and tradition, and in court decisions. For example, the

Figure 13.2
The American president's multiple hats.

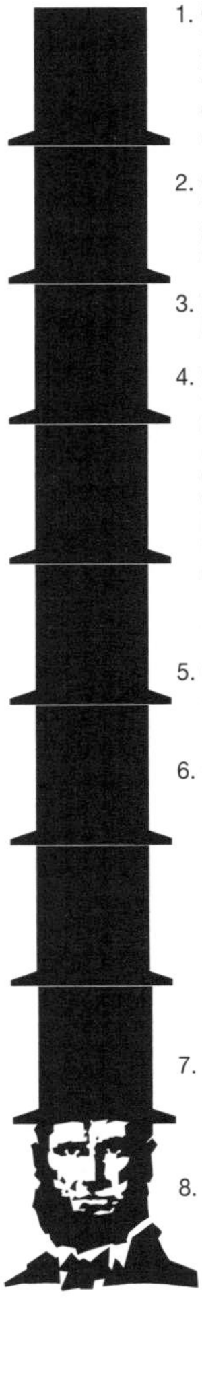

1. **Chief Executive and Administrator**
   "The executive Power shall be vested in a President of the United States of America."
   "He...shall take care that the Laws be faithfully executed." (U.S. Constitution, Article II, Sections 1 and 3)

2. **Commander-in-Chief**
   "The President shall be Commander-in-Chief to the Army and Navy of the United States." (U.S. Constitution, Article II, Section 2)

3. **Party Chief**
   Based on historical custom and tradition.

4. **Chief Legislative Braintruster**
   "He shall from time to time give the Congress Information of the State of the Union, and recommend to their Consideration such Measures as he shall judge necessary and expedient." (U.S. Constitution, Article II, Section 3)
   Power to veto legislation. (U.S. Constitution, Article I, Section 7)
   Custom and tradition.
   Power of patronage. (U.S. Constitution, Article II, Section 2)

5. **Chief National Spokesperson**
   Spokesperson on the "State of the Union."
   Historical custom and tradition.

6. **Chief Diplomat**
   Chief Diplomat. (U.S. Constitution, Article II, Section 1)
   "He shall have Power, by and with the Advice and Consent of the Senate, to make treaties, provided two thirds of the Senators present concur." (U.S. Constitution, Article II, Section 1)
   Leader of Cabinet—including the Department of State. (U.S. Constitution, Article II, Section 2)
   Power to appoint ambassadors. (U.S. Constitution, Article II, Section 2)

7. **Chief Popular Leader**
   Election, indirectly through the electoral college, by the people. (U.S. Constitution, Article II, Section 1)
   Historical custom and tradition.

8. **Ceremonial Chief of State**
   U.S. Constitution (implied). Custom and tradition.

president's role as party chief is not laid down in the Constitution; it emerged in the course of American history. The president's powers have evolved over time and largely in response to national problems that called for strong executive leadership. Similarly, the increased powers of all modern executives have developed to permit them to cope with increased demands of the modern world.

The American president's powers have, to a great extent, increased as a result of modern war and economic crises. To preserve the Union, President Abraham Lincoln had to take extraordinary actions. Without congressional sanction he called for troops, suspended the writ of habeas corpus in parts of Maryland, and imposed martial law on a wide range of civilians. Similarly, to participate in World Wars I and II, Presidents Woodrow Wilson and Franklin D. Roosevelt had to expand the powers of the presidency, often within the framework of very broad legislation passed by Congress. In the Great Depression of the 1930s, Roosevelt boldly assumed a leadership role in initiating legislation and a host of programs to create jobs, lift prices, protect bank depositors, and stimulate the economy.

The problems of the welfare state, whose creation began in Roosevelt's time, remain today. They are, moreover, worldwide problems that underscore the demand for strong leadership to advance security, liberty, justice, and welfare. Indeed, modern executives all over the world face what two scholars (Harold and Margaret Sprout) have called "the statesman's dilemma," which they define as the "dilemma of rising demands and insufficient resources."[1] These problems challenge modern executives and require the critical political scientist to ask if executives can (without abusing their power) plan, initiate, and implement governmental policy successfully.

Planning Public Policy

Modern executives plan on behalf of the nation. Much more so than legislatures, executives possess and use those resources that permit them to plan effectively. These resources include

1. Comprehensiveness, or an ability to see the whole problem as a national problem
2. Foresight, or the ability to look ahead and anticipate dangers and opportunities for proposed policies
3. Access to relevant and significant information made available by their command of the bureaucracy
4. The capacity for broad coordination, the ability to pull together diverse interests on behalf of common programs
5. The ability to act with speed and energy

These ingredients of successful planning do not belong simply to the person who is the American president, the British prime minister, or the German premier; they belong, rather, to the executive office. Moreover, these resources do not inevitably lead to decisions that enhance security, liberty, justice, and welfare. They do, however, increase the chances for sensible planning.

Initiating Public Policy

Modern executives have also been called on to use their formidable powers to initiate governmental policy. The American president, for example, has become the nation's chief legislator as well as its chief executive. The president can base legislative initiative on his or her constitutional power to recommend "necessary and expedient" measures to Congress. The president can also use numerous other powers to mobilize support for legislative priorities. For example, veto power can be used to oppose and defeat legislation that the president does not favor, assuming that the veto will not be overridden by a two-thirds vote in Congress. The president can also use the power to make appointments—the power of patronage—to encourage legislators to support his or her policies. Moreover, as head of the party, the president can draw on party support on behalf of programs. Party regulars know

that loyalty can bring them money and support in their reelection campaigns. In addition, both as a popular leader and as a figure who can command television and radio to address the nation, a president can mobilize public opinion on behalf of his or her policies. In all these ways, then, a president can push for legislation.

Policy also arises within the governmental bureaucracy. Because legislation cannot possibly cover all detailed matters, power increasingly is given to the president as head of the administration to interpret general legislation. Thus, as chief administrator, the president initiates policy in the course of administering the law.

In performing this role as initiator of public policy, the president is in a strategic position to accommodate a wide range of political actors—voters, interest groups, party members, legislators, and bureaucrats. A skillful president who has sound policies makes American democracy work well. When a president is inept and has flawed policies, the nation suffers. Sympathetic observers of President Lyndon Johnson's domestic programs point to his successes in promoting three civil rights bills, inaugurating the "War on Poverty," and improving health care legislation. But critics of his foreign policy fault him for involving the American nation in a disastrous war in Vietnam (without an official declaration of war by Congress) and for contributing to inflation by refusing to raise taxes while fighting that war. President Richard Nixon was hailed for his progressive policy in establishing links to the People's Republic of China after twenty-one years of hostility and virtually no contact between the two nations. Within three years of these policies, Nixon was forced from office in the wake of the Watergate scandal.

President Ronald Reagan is given much credit for lifting the morale of the American public and controlling spiraling inflation. During his later presidency and after he left office, however, he came under severe criticism for allowing the national deficit to grow to enormous levels, partly through gigantic military expenditures; failing to monitor and stop a disgraceful scandal at the Department of Housing and Urban Development; failing to recognize and prevent the Savings and Loan scandal, which will cost the American taxpayers billions of dollars for years to come; and allowing the Iran-Contra affair.

Finally, we might note that President George Bush was given high marks by many for the skill with which he built the Desert Storm political and military coalition to retake Kuwait after Iraq's invasion in 1990. Yet, in 1992 he was denied reelection primarily because Americans believed he had mishandled the nation's economy. Conversely, President Bill Clinton, Bush's successor, was given a vote of confidence through his reelection in 1996. After a disastrous attempt to completely redesign the nation's health care system during his first two years in office, Clinton rallied and was able to achieve a number of successes, including passage of the Brady bill controlling handguns, family leave legislation, a deficit reduction bill, a modest increase in the minimum wage, a peace accord ending the Bosnian conflict, and restoration of democracy in Haiti.

The British cabinet, headed by a strong prime minister, carries the initiative by making policy. Conflicts between divergent interests in the governing party are usually hammered out within or between governmental ministries and then brought to the cabinet for discussion and decision. The cabinet then assumes responsibility for enactment of agreed-on policy in the House of Commons.

The British prime minister, like the American president, also uses a number of powers (prestige, ability to influence public opinion, patronage, leadership in the party, and bestowal of benefits) to sustain policy initiatives. In contrast to the American president, the British prime minister can rely on strong party discipline and the threat of new elections to carry policy initiatives. If the majority party does not support the prime minister, the cabinet may fall and a new election may be required; majority members of Parliament may lose in the new elections. Thus there is pressure for party members to stick together in support of their party and the prime minister.

Bill Clinton began his second term as U.S. President in January 1997.

Pressures work both ways. The cabinet cannot be out of tune with either the majority party or popular sentiment. In using the office's powers, the prime minister has enormous opportunities to achieve cooperation, advance accommodation, and deal with conflicts in the struggle for power. Again, however, a weak prime minister with weak defective policies may squander any opportunities.

Implementing Public Policy

Executives, traditionally, are in charge of implementing policy and managing the great bureaucracy. The American president is constitutionally required to "take care that the laws be faithfully executed." The president is the nation's number-one diplomat. The president is commander-in-chief of the armed forces. In performing these tasks, the president cannot assume that things will get done automatically. Legislation is not self-executing. Orders do not necessarily get carried out. The president, through his or her cabinet and aids, must follow up on policy. Politics inevitably impinges on administration. Members of Congress are especially concerned with policies that affect their home districts or home states. Forces within the cabinet or the administration may not see eye-to-eye on key issues. In view of these considerations, the president must enlist the support of cabinet members, key aides, key bureaucrats, public opinion, affected interests, and members of Congress in carrying out administrative duties. In this process—in building and maintaining support, in putting out fires—the president achieves accommodation and also facilitates government performance.

Policy cannot be implemented without legislative, party, electoral, and interest-group support. If such support fails, policies can be jeopardized. Hence, as chief executives plan, initiate, and implement public policy, they must constantly attend to the bases of their political power.

A comparable concern for political support and accommodation is evident in the British cabinet as it carries out public policy. The cabinet is in trouble, for example, if inflation and unemployment rise too high, if public opinion turns against the European Union, or if an unpopular tax is proposed. The cabinet must look to the interests whose votes and money sustain it. Thus a Labour party cabinet cannot neglect the trade unions and the policies they favor; and a Conservative party cabinet cannot neglect industrial, business, and farming interests. The party in power must look to its parliamentary majority, paying attention not only to its leading figures but also to its back-benchers or lesser-known members. Without the support of the parliamentary majority, the cabinet falls and, consequently, loses the ability to deliver on its policies. And, of course, when the party in power has a slim parliamentary majority—and depends

for that majority on one or more splinter parties—it must accommodate the members of those parties on vital matters or lose power.

Despite the resourcefulness of the American president or the British prime minister, it is not clear that they are always equal to the tremendous responsibilities that they are asked to shoulder. Striking the right balance remains the challenge. If they do too much, they may be accused of being "imperial"; if they do too little, they are derided as impotent. They do demonstrate, however, the value of peaceful succession based on broad electoral support.

Executive Functions in Communist and Developing Countries

Let us now turn to executives in the communist and developing worlds to see what role they play in planning, initiating, and implementing policy.

In discussing any communist system, we must distinguish between the formal government executive (generally the prime minister and Council of Ministers) and the real executive (the Communist party general secretary and Politburo). The distinction can be tempered with the knowledge that more often than not there is a high degree of "interlocking membership" in the Council and Politburo. In other words, many of the highest-ranking government executive officials are also members of the Politburo and/or Central Committee.

A further consideration in analyzing executive power in communist systems is the fact that historically they have been vulnerable to what might be called "personalist" tendencies: one person rising to extraordinary power, often transcending the highest party organs. Certainly, Josef Stalin epitomized this tendency in the Soviet Union from 1924 until his death in 1953. In the People's Republic of China, Mao Zedong wielded tremendous power for over two decades after the Communists came to power in 1949. Though not as charismatic, Mao's successor, Deng Xioping, wielded enormous personal power for many years, even without holding any official government position!

Despite severe health problems, Boris Yeltsin, President of the Russian Republic, struggles to maintain the momentum for politicol and economic reform in his country.

In general, leaders of developing countries play enormously important roles in implementing public policy. For a variety of reasons, the executive branch of government has tended to be even more import than in the developed world. Planning and implementing of public policy has commonly been in the hands of a strong leader (Saddam Hussein of Iraq, 1979–present; Muammar al-Qaddafi of Libya, 1969–present), a military junta (Argentina, 1976–1983), or a civilian authoritarian figure (Papa "Doc" Duvalier of Haiti, 1957–1971). This has been particularly true in developing regions that do not have strong legislative traditions or where political and economic circumstances have required a particularly strong hand.

In other developing nations, however, the chief executives are freely elected by the people (as in Mexico) or freely chosen by a majority in the legislature (as in India).

The executive pattern in Mexico illustrates an ingenious combination of selection, election, and power.[2] The outgoing president designates his personal choice as the dominant party's choice for popular election. The party dutifully ratifies the president's choice as the person to carry the party's banner in the next election. This candidate then runs for a single six-year term. The new

Mexican president (thus designated, ratified, and elected) consequently has a powerful persona, with a party and an electoral mandate to provide strong executive leadership. He chooses a cabinet, and they assume a dominant role in planning, initiating, and implementing public policy.

Mexican presidents are close to being popularly elected dictators, but their power vanishes when their six-year term of office is ended. They cannot be reelected. In office, however, they are extraordinarily powerful. The legislature (dominated by the president's party) may debate policies, but presidents usually get what they ask for. The dominant party, the Institutional Revolutionary Party (PRI), is their vehicle for accomplishing their purposes. However, it should be noted that in recent years opposition parties, most specifically the People's Action Party (PAN), have made some significant gains in state and municipal elections.

In addition to the single six-year term of office, certain conventions may also regulate the Mexican president's exercise of power. For example, presidents must pay at least lip service to Mexico's revolutionary tradition. They cannot antagonize key interests in the party and in the country: peasant farmers, workers, business and industry. They cannot too flagrantly offend intellectuals, students, and the Church. The recent tradition of civilian leadership inhibits military dictatorship, and the limited power and size of the armed forces further discourages military rule by an ambitious president or military junta.

Although increasing numbers of developing countries, particularly in South America, have adopted free elections to select their leadership, an unfortunately large number of executives in developing states are authoritarian or military dictatorships. Conflict is often handled by jailing opponents, and cooperation proceeds on the executive's terms only. Accommodation consists in going along with the dominant ruler or junta.

THE ROLE OF BUREAUCRACIES

Space does not permit us to fully discuss the role of bureaucracy in the process of accommodation. Yet, despite frequent and often disturbing complaints about how bureaucrats interfere with security, liberty, justice, and welfare, it would be a mistake to ignore their important role in enabling legislatures, and especially executives, to carry out governmental responsibilities. Indeed, some observers see the top civil servants (often nameless and faceless) as the key policymakers in government. Clearly, government would come to a standstill without a responsible and capable bureaucracy.

Rational, Efficient, Impartial Administration

Max Weber, an influential German social scientist and perceptive student of bureaucracy, was one of the first political observers to note the importance of **bureaucracy** and to delineate the characteristics of the bureaucratic style: rational, efficient, and impartial. Such governance, contrary to our common pejorative understanding of bureaucracy, was a great advance over government that was often irrational (having no coherent rhyme or reason for policies), inefficient (unable to keep accurate records, collect taxes, and perform services), and based on favoritism and bribes rather than on merit and honesty. Rational, efficient, and impartial treatment of citizens—based on sensible procedures, good record keeping and follow-up, and even-handed behavior—contributes to successful accommodation in the political community.

Of course, government bureaucrats can also be impersonal, inflexible, tangled in "red tape," overbearing, inconsiderate, and unhelpful. This type of behavior—too frequent in every bureaucracy—gives the word its bad name. It is thus easy to associate bureaucracy with government out of control—with abuses of power, rude and offensive behavior, waste, and overregulation. The greater the power of government over our lives, the greater a chance there is for bureaucratic abuse of that power. And there is considerable evidence, in all governments, to support charges against the bureaucracy.

Carrying Out Public Policy

Yet there is a more positive side to bureaucracy. The bureaucracy is government in action; it consists of all the departments or ministries, agencies, officials, and commissions required to carry out public policy. It plans, initiates, and implements on behalf of presidents, prime ministers, and premiers. In doing so the bureaucracy responds to interest groups affected by legislation and regulation, often working out compromises between different interests and the general public. The bureaucracy provides information to executives and legislatures, to the press, and to the public. Lower-level officials may inform senior officials of what is workable. In administering the law honestly and competently, civil servants contribute to approved and effective governance. They may also check on, and work to control, the abuse of power within their domain. There can be little doubt that a well-trained, well-organized, and honest bureaucracy makes an invaluable contribution to modern government. On the other hand, a defective bureaucracy is a prime source of political malaise. Thus, the training and quality of the bureaucracy is vitally important.

In Great Britain, Japan, France, and the United States, for example, top civil servants (another name for bureaucrats) are usually trained at the best universities. Their entrance into government service is usually based on examination, so they constitute a **meritocracy.** Top civil servants are usually highly intelligent, competent, and honest. In government service they usually acquire considerable expertise and are thus usually well equipped to help executives plan, initiate, and carry out policy. They tend, however, to be committed to the established way of doing business and frequently need to be prodded by innovative executives to try new ways of working. In the past, and to some extent today, top civil servants have constituted a bureaucratic aristocracy not always in tune with democratic politics. However, they have increasingly become sympathetic to the democratic process, especially in developed countries.

Ensuring Governmental Stability and Continuity

A nation's dependence on its bureaucracy may be more readily understood if we look to those countries where government at the top level is unstable, where prime ministers and cabinets come and go—for example, Italy. Despite frequent changes of top leadership, the business of government goes on, largely because the permanent civil service is stable. The bureaucracy continues to collect taxes, dispense benefits, and maintain law and order.

This stability characterizes the civil service in almost all the developed world and is crucial to effective government. New administrations in Britain, for example, can count on knowledgeable civil servants to carry on while the new cabinet is "tooling up" and on impartial civil servants to assist them devise and execute new programs. By thus ensuring continuity of administration, the permanent bureaucracy makes a most valuable contribution to the transition from one government to the next, and also to public trust in orderly government. In the United States, the number of top administrators who come and go is greater when the party in power changes; even so, a core of permanent civil servants near the top remains to ensure vital help. There is, of course, a penalty to pay for this stability—namely, orientation to the status quo. Bureaucrats have a strong tendency to do things today as they did yesterday. On the other hand, many civil servants welcome a change in administration and the opportunity to innovate and reform.

Bureaucratic Functions in Communist and Developing Countries

Communist bureaucracies are in essential respects, similar to those in the developed world. Their powers, however, are greater than those of civil servants in the Western world simply because the powers of the government embrace more areas. Government managers control all major economic enterprises (coal mines and steel mills, automobile plants, collective farms, hospitals, and department stores), in addition to collecting taxes, issuing passports, and regulating foreign trade. As systems such as those in the People's Republic of China and Vietnam move toward a free-market economy while trying to maintain Communist party control, we might expect a weakening of the traditionally strong communist bureaucracy.

Communist bureaucracies seem more pragmatic and less ideological than the Communist parties. This trait often enhances its accommodating disposition and willingness to face facts and be guided by scientific rather than by ideological considerations. But Communist party control of top-level bureaucrats has historically inhibited the ability of professionals in governmental posts—economists, engineers, agronomists, and biologists—to take an independent line, even when they think a policy is wrong.

With a few exceptions, bureaucracies in most developing countries are weak. The number of qualified personnel—at both the top and the bottom of the system—varies tremendously. Two key factors in determining the strength of the bureaucracy are the numbers of years of independence and the extent to which colonial powers left a bureaucratic infrastructure when independence was achieved. Corruption, by no means absent from developed and communist countries, plagues many bureaucracies in the developing world.

A weak bureaucracy means a weak and ineffective government. Such a government in a developing country often means that crucial tasks vitally affecting the lives of citizens are not performed or are performed poorly. Children may not receive schooling. Pure water may not be available in the villages. Peace and order may be nonexistent.

Some developing countries have, however, fared better than others. India inherited a reasonably good civil service from British rule, and this has undoubtedly strengthened the Indian government's ability to cope with its serious problems. Without such a well-trained administrative structure in place at the time of independence, India would have had much more difficulty carrying on the business of government. By way of contrast, Zaire (the former Belgian Congo) did not fare as well, largely because Belgian rulers did little to train native civil servants and to prepare Zaire for independence and self-rule. One dreadful result, partly attributable to the lack of a strong bureaucracy able to hold the nation together and govern it effectively, was the devastating civil war that followed independence in 1960.

THE ROLE OF THE COURTS

The role of the courts in the political process varies greatly from nation to nation. Courts are more powerful in developing nations than in communist countries. They are weaker in developing nations than in developed nations, although the variety of developing countries makes generalization hazardous. When they function at their best, courts clearly advance politics as a civilizing process by protecting human rights against the abuses of power and by safeguarding other key constitutional rules. Courts uphold valid law when it is challenged and provide a peaceful forum in which citizens can settle innumerable disputes. Thus the courts enable political actors to express their needs and interests; they affirm priorities; they legitimize legislation and administration; they advance effective governance; and they control the abuse of power.

Safeguarding Human Rights and Other Roles of Constitutional Politics

United States federal courts, for example, protect against federal or state government violation of the basic political and nonpolitical freedoms that ensure the proper functioning of the democratic and constitutional process. The federal courts safeguard the **Bill of Rights**—a great source of protection of the vital needs and fundamental interests of citizens and groups. The courts guard a host of crucial rights. Some of these rights—such as the "privilege of the **writ of habeas corpus**"—are found in the body of the U.S. Constitution. This famous right protects the people against illegal detention or imprisonment. A prisoner must be brought before a court at a stated time and place so that the court may determine whether the prisoner is being lawfully held in jail. Other rights are found in the first ten amendments to the Constitution (popularly known as the Bill of Rights) and in other crucial amendments. For example:

Amendment I: Congress shall make no law respecting an establishment of religion, or prohibiting the free exercise thereof; or abridging the freedom of speech, or of the press, or the right of people peaceably to assemble, and to petition the Government for a redress of grievances.

Amendment IV: The right of the people to be secure in their persons, houses, papers, and effects, against unreasonable searches and seizures, shall not be violated, and no Warrants shall issue, but upon probable cause, supported by Oath or affirmation, and particularly describing the place to be searched, and the persons or things to be seized.

Amendment V: No person shall be . . . deprived of life, liberty, or property, without due process of law; nor shall private property be taken for public use, without just compensation.

Amendment VI: In all criminal prosecutions, the accused shall enjoy the right to a speedy and public trial, by an impartial jury of the State and district wherein the crime shall have been committed, which district shall have been previously ascertained by law, and to be informed of the nature and cause of the accusation; to be confronted with the Witnesses against him; to have compulsory process for obtaining Witnesses in his favor, and to have the Assistance of Counsel for his defense.

Amendment VIII: Excessive bail shall not be required, nor excessive fines imposed, nor cruel and unusual punishments inflicted.

Amendment XIII: Neither slavery nor involuntary servitude, except as a punishment for crime whereof the party shall have been duly convicted, shall exist within the United States, or any place subject to their jurisdiction.

Amendment XIV: All persons born or naturalized in the United States, and subject to the jurisdiction thereof, are citizens of the United States and of the State wherein they reside. No State shall make or enforce any law which shall abridge the privileges or immunities of citizens of the United States; nor shall any State deprive any person of life, liberty, or property, without due process of law; nor deny to any person within its jurisdiction the equal protection of the laws.

Amendment XV: The right of citizens of the United States to vote shall not be denied or abridged by the United States or by any State on account of race, color, or previous condition of servitude.

Amendment XIX: The right of citizens of the United States to vote shall not be denied or abridged by the United States or by any State on account of sex.

Amendment XXVI: The right of citizens of the United States, who are eighteen years of age or older, to vote shall not be denied or abridged by the United States or by any State on account of age.

Both federal and state courts protect these rights as well as other rights enacted by Congress and state legislatures. It is difficult to overestimate the value of such protections for democratic and peaceful accommodation. Citizens know that they need not resort to force and violence to ensure their rights. They know, too, that the electoral process is available as a way to protect their interests. In safeguarding civil liberties and other basic constitutional rules, the courts ensure agreement on fundamentals that are essential to the success of democratic and constitutional government.

The position of the U.S. Supreme Court is unique in the developed world because of the American principles of separation of powers, judicial review, and federalism. These principles make the Supreme Court one of the most powerful judicial bodies in the world. Under the principle of the **separation of powers,** the Supreme Court may thus protect its own, independent, and separate status—its own powers and integrity—under the U.S. Constitution. Under the principle of **judicial review,** the Supreme Court may declare an act of Congress unconstitutional. And finally, under the principle of **federalism,** the Supreme Court also maintains the federal division of powers between the national government and the fifty state governments.

Federal courthouse in San Antonio, Texas.

The Supreme Court and the other federal courts umpire the federal system. They do so under rules established in the Constitution and interpreted by the Congress, president, and courts. Such umpiring is designed to maintain a harmonious and indestructible union of co-operative and indestructible states. Usually, the federal courts have acted to protect this inter-pretation of the federal system—and thus the respective powers of nation and state. They guard against state encroachment on federal power by declaring acts of state legislators and governors that violate the Constitution or federal law to be unconstitutional or unlawful. But, if the fed-eral government encroaches on state govern-ments—particularly in ways that threaten their very existence—the Supreme Court has the power, exercised only rarely, to invalidate na-tional legislation that violates the rights and powers given to states. In umpiring the federal system, the federal courts guard against serious conflicts between the nation and the states or among the states. When this umpiring is suc-cessful, cooperation and accommodation occur. When rulings are ignored, serious troubles be-fall American federalism. The most serious and calamitous of these troubles was the American Civil War.

British courts also protect civil liberties and the rules of the British Constitution. They do so under Parliament's legislation, which is the su-preme law, and no court can declare otherwise. The highest British court—composed of the "law lords" of the House of Lords—has no power to declare an act of Parliament unconstitutional. This, however, does not mean that civil liberties are violated at will in Britain. The largely unwrit-ten British Constitution, acts of Parliament, and the British legal tradition ensure that basic hu-man rights are protected. It would be unthinkable for the British Parliament to violate the privilege of the writ of habeas corpus (which had its origin in British history) or to deny British citizens the freedoms of religion, speech, press, assembly, or due process of law. British courts thus operate to maintain basic liberties under law. They do not

hesitate to rule against British officials who act beyond the law.

Upholding Valid Law and Administration Under Challenge

In the United States, for example, the courts also play a vital role in legitimizing economic and social public policy under challenge. In a gov-ernment of limited powers, the Supreme Court serves as a court of last resort in legal actions to test whether Congress has exceeded its powers in passing certain legislation or whether the president has exceeded his or her power in executing duties. In upholding national policy the Supreme Court gives it a stamp of final constitutional approval. This clearly enhances effective governance by definitively ruling on whether or not the government can, for example, enact social security legislation, regulate labor-management relations, control the banking system, and subsidize farmers.

In an earlier period, the Supreme Court struck down both state and federal legislation—for example, those laws designed to cope with child labor, business monopolies, unfair trade prac-tices, depressed agricultural prices, and lower wages and industrial prices. Most observers of the Supreme Court now generally agree that these Court actions prevented state legislatures and Congress from attending to problems that needed to be addressed. These actions hurt the nation's ability to adjust to the realities of an increasingly industrial, urban, and interdepen-dent society and to achieve social reforms essential to a healthy life in modern society. They inter-fered with the power of voters—acting through their elected representatives—to satisfy basic needs and address fundamental interests.

Now, however, the courts rarely overturn na-tional economic and social policy; moreover, they have given state legislatures greater free-dom to address their problems. Only in the field of civil liberties does the Supreme Court main-tain its more activist role. Two such issues that the Court has been wrestling with recently are the rights of the accused in criminal cases and the right to abortion. The courts may still keep an eye on the bureaucratic actions in the economic and social fields that are **ultra vires**—that is, beyond the law. In other words the courts may uphold national policy but insist that government stay within the law in administrating such policy. In this fashion, the Supreme Court enables the president and Congress to respond to national needs and interests, yet still controls overzealous administration.

British courts may also scrutinize governmental actions in appropriate cases to ensure that governmental action follows the law. They may also raise questions about the meaning of a law passed by Parliament. But once Parliament's position on a law is clear, British courts must respect that law. Thus they also function to legitimize legislation and to guard against overzealous administration.

Adjudicating Disputes Under the Law

Just as elections enable citizens to decide contests by counting heads instead of breaking them, so the courts enable individuals, groups, corporations, states, and local units of government to rely on judicial procedures instead of force and violence to resolve conflicts. Here we concentrate not on disputes between the individual or group and government, but on those quarrels involving private citizens, groups, or corporations. Unquestionably, these disputes involve most of the work of U.S. state, county, and municipal courts. These disputes may involve, for example, the law of contracts or the law of torts. A **tort** is a wrongful act, injury, or damage (not involving a breach of contract) for which a civil action can be brought. A **contract** is an agreement, usually written, and enforceable by law, between two or more people to do something. We call attention to the courts' role in handling these disputes to underscore both the existence of a mechanism to deal with conflicts and the cultural habit of resort to the law. Although it is not without its weaknesses, the legal system (when it functions at its best and is respected) provides a valuable means for fur-

thering cooperation, advancing accommodation, and peacefully resolving disputes. Effective judicial systems exist in virtually all developed countries.

Courts in Communist and Developing Countries

Courts in the communist and developing countries do not generally contribute as significantly to political accommodation as they do in developed countries. Communist courts, in contrast to the U.S. courts, have no power to invalidate legislative acts. They function to see that the law is obeyed, not to safeguard human rights as they are understood in Western democracies.

Like legislatures, executives, and bureaucracies, the judicial systems of the developing world vary considerably. In some countries, they are strong enough to challenge the chief executive. For example, in India in 1973 a lower court found Prime Minister Indira Gandhi guilty of minor electoral offenses and disqualified her from holding office for six years, even though the court's decision, pending appeal to the Indian Supreme Court, was suspended for six months. In many developing countries, particularly those under authoritarian regimes, the courts are powerless to protect citizens against false arrest, illegal imprisonment, and arbitrary punishment. The courts in many developing countries have a long way to go to advance security, liberty, justice, and welfare for their citizens.

ASSESSMENT OF THE PATTERNS OF GOVERNANCE

What has the brief, and admittedly sketchy, analysis in Chapters 12 and 13 taught us? It should have given us a clearer picture of successful patterns of furthering cooperation, advancing accommodation, and handling conflicts. How voluntary, humane, and peaceful are these patterns? Do they maximize security, liberty, justice, and welfare? Which patterns are most successful, and why? What are their costs and benefits? We will try to answer these questions as we examine how our guiding hypothesis holds up.

According to our guiding hypothesis, successful patterns for dealing with the struggle for power in politics rest on (1) agreement on certain constitutional fundamentals, (2) meaningful opportunities for the expression of needs and fundamental interests, (3) sound mechanisms for selecting priorities from among competing interests, (4) acceptable ways for legitimizing public policy choices, (5) effective governance, and (6) regular and effective controls on government.

Our conclusions must be tentative, given that we have been able to review only a small sample of relevant evidence and given our heavy reliance on evidence from highly developed democratic countries, particularly the United States. Moreover, our conclusions on the relationship between political patterns and cardinal national objectives (security, liberty, justice, and welfare) must be treated cautiously because we did not explore this correlation fully. Nonetheless, although we focused more on institutions and process than on policy results, we need not feel inhibited in asking some key questions regarding the adequacy of these patterns to advance substantive governmental ends.

Agreement on Fundamentals

It seems reasonably clear that the constitutional frameworks and the nongovernmental actors of most developed countries have been more successful than their communist and developing world counterparts in working out voluntary, humane, and peaceful patterns of accommodation in domestic politics.

All countries strive for agreement on fundamentals. In important respects, however, they differ on which fundamentals are crucial. In developed countries such as the United States and Britain, successful agreement rests on a historic consensus on popular, or majority, rule and basic rights. These fundamentals call for free elections, representative government, open discourse, opposition parties, and peaceful change. Although communist systems in places like China and Vietnam have emphasized fundamentals,

the ideas of communist ideology such as public ownership of the means of production and exchange, and the leading role of the Communist party, it seems reasonable to assume that some of these fundamentals are changing. In the People's Republic of China, for instance, new free-market mechanisms will undoubtedly alter adherence to the traditional communist value of public ownership.

In the developing world, high value is placed on national freedom, independence, cohesion, economic development, and social advancement. But here, too, the winds of change appear to be blowing in some countries where individual freedom and internal democracy are acquiring greater appeal. In a number of South American nations, for example, basic democratic values, such as free and open elections, are becoming highly cherished.

But, the critical political scientist must look beyond the rhetoric of agreement on fundamentals to the reality of their operation. He or she must also ask about the costs as well as the benefits of such agreement. For example, in the United States, African Americans, women, and the poor have often been excluded from elections and still have not been fully granted what are presumably the right of all Americans: genuine equality of opportunity and protection against discrimination. In communist systems, public ownership (understood as true worker control of the means of production) is questionable, given the history of party and bureaucratic control of the economy. In the developing world, national cohesion may turn out to be rule by a dictator (as in Iraq and Libya). Economic development may (as in Brazil) widen the rift between rich and poor. Social advancement may take the form of genocide, as with the Khmer Rouge in Kampuchea (Cambodia) from 1975 to 1978.

The strengths and weaknesses of fundamental principles in all three worlds—developed, communist, and developing—must be critically assessed. Thus, American federalism can enhance liberty, democracy, and effective government, particularly when the nation and the fifty states cooperate. But, federalism frustrates these objectives when certain American states violate civil liberties or tolerate plutocratic tendencies, or when both the nation and the states fail to respond to problems such as protection of the environment. Anticolonialism in the developing world can mean a sensible endeavor to get out from the domination of an imperial power, or it can become a blind opposition to all Western influence.

Human Needs and National Priorities

And how do patterns in the three worlds deal with human needs and national priorities? **Polyarchies**—the prevalent mode of democratic government in virtually all developed nations—tend to offer more meaningful opportunities for the expression of vital needs and fundamental interests than are found in communist and developing countries. Yet here, too, critical political scientists cannot be complacent. In the United States, for example, a number of minority groups—African Americans, native Americans, Hispanics—do not yet (despite some significant advances) have a strong voice in American politics. And women are still shut out of many aspects of life.

Mechanisms are at hand in developed countries—in elections, parties, legislatures, and executive leadership—to select priorities. But how wise are the priorities? Critics argue that the United States, despite recent defense cuts, spends much too much money on arms without enhancing American security. They note, too, that the United States has not been able to use its polyarchic system to cope successfully with an enormous federal deficit. They also wonder whether, throughout the developed world, the right voices are being heard and the right priorities established on ecological questions.

Comparable, perhaps even more severe, criticism can be leveled at the Communist party of the former Soviet Union. The collapse of the communist system in the U.S.S.R. tends to support critics' contention that the party's historic dominance prevented it from making wise judgments on priorities that would more genuinely

enhance security, liberty, justice, and welfare for Soviet citizens. For instance, disproportionately high spending on the military and Cold War foreign ventures seriously hampered the government's ability to ensure adequate housing, food, consumer goods, and medical care throughout the Soviet Union.

In many developing countries, citizens, interest groups, and the media cannot always articulate their needs and interests effectively. Developing countries may also lack effective means for selecting wise priorities: a stable party system, a functioning legislature, and responsible executive leadership. Their task is often compounded by factors that militate against effective social and political organization and sound decisions—poverty, illiteracy, and serious class and ethnic divisions. In too many developing nations armaments may win out over education, health care, and housing. Economic growth that benefits an affluent minority may win out over distributive justice—that is, greater equity for the poor.

Legitimacy and Effective Governance

Although by no means perfectly responsive to popular needs (particularly those of the "least free"), most developed nations have worked out effective patterns (through electoral and legislative majorities) for legitimizing public policy choices. Yet the fuller effectiveness of their governments is mixed. Most developed nations have made considerable progress through the welfare state. Yet in affluent and supposedly progressive countries such as the United States, poverty has not been eradicated, women have not achieved full equality in either theory or practice, and often ethnic minorities are still not treated as first-class citizens. Homelessness still plagues too many American citizens, and unemployment is a critical problem in the United States and Britain. Pollution remains a major concern in all modern industrial societies.

Moreover, if a healthy government means a government able to ensure peace abroad, we must take a critical look at the war record of developed nations. Although no world war has occurred since 1945, a number of developed nations have been engaged in armed conflicts. France fought wars in Vietnam and Algeria to try to prevent the breakup of her colonial empire. The United States fought in Korea and Vietnam to block the spread of communism in Asia. Britain remains embroiled in an intractable dispute in Northern Ireland and fought a brief war in the Falkland (Malvinas) Islands. Most of these conflicts have produced considerable domestic turmoil. Ironically, among the major powers, only Japan and Germany—aggressor nations in World War II—have not been involved in war since World War II ended in 1945.

In communist systems, such as China's, public policy choices have been legitimized through the dominance of the Communist party and ratification by the National People's Congress. From the Western democratic point of view, this legitimacy would be more convincing if it were clear that the Chinese people truly endorsed the Communist party's perspective.

The legitimacy and effectiveness of many developing governments is in serious doubt. Governments backed by military rule can claim no popular legitimacy. Those ruled by strong political leaders or single parties on the basis of questionable elections may also be challenged. Only time will tell if the wave of democratic reform sweeping parts of the developing world (such as South America), can be sustained. Poverty, corruption, disease, famine, excessive military spending, and political instability challenge the critical political scientist to explore why the necessary and sufficient conditions of voluntary, humane, and peaceful accommodation are absent in too many developing countries.

Regular and Effective Controls

Regular and effective controls on government are strong in most developed nations. Even so, the controls have not always prevented abuse of power. For example, the Watergate case involved top officials of the U.S. executive branch; this case led to the jailing of an attorney general

and key presidential aides and the resignation of President Nixon. Similarly, U.S. involvement in the Vietnam war raised serious questions about the ability of an American president (Johnson) to commit the country to a major war without a declaration of war by Congress. Other abuses of power—for example, by the FBI and the CIA—have also been documented. Most notorious was the abuse of power in the Iran-Contra affair, which led to convictions of the president's national security adviser and a key member of his staff. Ironically, in the very interest of national security, government can violate liberty and justice.

Effective and regular controls on government are weak in communist systems. Political opposition was routinely crushed in the Soviet Union and continues to be repressed in China, as evidenced by the Tiananmen Square demonstrations and their aftermath. Vietnam placed political opponents in "New Economic Zones," which were nothing more than reeducation compounds bearing a strong resemblance to concentration camps.

Controls on government in the developing world vary from country to country. In a few nations, controls are comparable to those in the developed world. At the other extreme, in authoritarian regimes of either the right or the left, peaceful opponents of the regime are killed, imprisoned, tortured, or exiled. In the middle are a number of countries that permit only mild peaceful protest, as voiced by brave dissidents.

CONCLUSION

The challenge to work out successful patterns of accommodation to cope with the struggle for power remains. Even modern developed nations—which have a relatively better record than communist and developing countries—still have plenty of room for improvement. How to make these patterns voluntary, humane, and peaceful is a problem that taxes thoughtful political scientists. How to develop patterns that enhance security, liberty, justice, and welfare is a problem that challenges modern statesmanship.

In our next chapter we turn to the patterns that international political actors seek to develop to achieve cooperation, advance accommodation, and handle conflicts in international politics.

ANNOTATED BIBLIOGRAPHY

Abraham, Henry J. *The Judicial Process,* 6th ed. Oxford: Oxford University Press, 1993. Provides helpful introduction to the American judicial process—federal, state, and local. Also compares American and other judicial systems.

Almond, Gabriel, and Powell, G. Bingham, Jr., eds. *Comparative Politics Today: A World View,* 5th ed. Glenview, Ill.: Scott, Foresman, 1991. Examines Britain, France, West Germany, the Soviet Union, China, Mexico, and Tanzania within a framework of system, process, and policy, focusing on political socialization, political recruitment, interest articulation, interest aggregation, and policymaking.

Baker, Ross. *House and Senate,* 2nd ed. New York: Norton, 1995. Offers a comprehensive and systematic comparison of the two houses of the United States Congress. Very readable.

Hayes, Louis D. *Introduction to Japanese Politics.* St. Paul, Minn.: Paragon House, 1992. Presents a fine introduction to the Japanese political system with emphasis on distinctive features of Japanese social and economic systems and how they help define the Japanese world of politics.

James, Simon. *British Cabinet Government.* London: Routledge, 1992. Provides an excellent brief overview of contemporary British government.

Kingdon, John W. *Agendas, Alternatives, and Public Policies,* 2nd ed. New York: HarperCollins, 1995. Offers a first-rate analysis of the public policy process in America. Winner of the Aaron Wildavsky Award by the American Political Science Association.

Neustadt, Richard E. *Presidential Power: The Politics and the Modern Presidency: The Politics of Leadership from Roosevelt to Reagan.* New York: Free Press, 1989. Analyzes the presidency, emphasizing the importance of the president's persuasive powers. Fast becoming a classic.

Parenti, Michael. *Power and the Powerless.* New York: St. Martin's, 1978. Presents a refreshing antidote to the glorification of the American model. Parenti's perspective is suggested by his conviction that "what we called 'socialist' societies today are in many ways more productive, more secure, and happier places, and therefore less oppressive for the common people than is the United States." Thought provoking, but thesis must be seriously challenged given events in the late 1980s.

Rourke, Frances E. *Bureaucracy, Politics, and Public Policy,* 3rd ed. Glenview, Ill.: Scott, Foresman, 1984. Provides a good introduction to bureaucracy's role in facilitating cooperation, achieving accommodation, and handling conflicts.

Smith, Hedrick. *The Power Game: How Washington Works.* New York: Random House, 1988. Presents a shrewd analysis of power in the nation's capital by the author of the award-winning *The Russians.*

Ulam, Adam. *The Communists: The Story of Power and Lost Illusions, 1948–1991.* New York: Macmillan, 1992. Presents a sweeping analysis of the decline of communism, written by a distinguished Soviet observer.

Wice, Paul. *Lawyers: Judges and the Human Side of Justice.* New York: HarperCollins, 1991. Offers an excellent personal look at those who are in the trenches of the American judicial system. See also Wice's *Chaos in the Courthouse* (New York: Praeger, 1985).

Will, George. *Restoration: Congress, Term Limits, and the Recovery of Deliberative Democracy.* New York: Free Press, 1992. Calls for major congressional reform, by one of America's leading conservative journalists and political observers.

SUGGESTIONS FOR FURTHER READING

Blondel, Jean, and Muller-Rommelo, Ferdinand, eds. *Cabinets in Western Europe.* New York: St. Martin's, 1989.

Burke, John P. *The Institutional Presidency.* Baltimore: Johns Hopkins Press, 1992.

Clifford, Clark, with Richard Holbrooke. *Counsel to the President: A Memoir.* New York: Random House, 1991.

Cox, Archibald. *The Court and the Constitution.* Boston: Houghton Mifflin, 1987.

Cronin, Thomas E., ed. *Inventing the American Presidency. Studies in Government and Public Policy.* Lawrence: University Press of Kansas, 1989.

Fisher, Louis. *Politics of Shared Power,* 2nd ed. Washington, D.C.: Congressional Quarterly Press, 1987.

Goldman, Sheldon. *American Court Systems: Readings in Judicial Process and Behavior,* 3rd ed. New York: Longman, 1989.

278

PART THREE COMPARATIVE AND WORLD POLITICS

Schwart, Bernard. *A History of the Supreme Court.* New York, Oxford University Press, 1993.

Wice, Paul. *Miranda v. Arizona.* Danbury, Conn.: Franklin Watts, 1996.

Woodward, Bob, and Armstrong, Scott. *The Brethren: Inside the Supreme Court.* New York: Simon & Schuster, 1979.

GLOSSARY TERMS

advice and consent
Bill of Rights
bureaucracy
contracts
federalism
forensic function

judicial review
legislative function
loyal opposition
meritocracy
polyarchy
representative function
separation of powers
supervisory function
torts
ultra vires
writ of habeas corpus

INTERNATIONAL POLITICS AND THE GLOBAL COMMUNITY

IN CHAPTERS 12 AND 13 we argued that successful patterns of domestic accommodation rest on agreement about fundamentals, opportunities for expressing vital needs and interests, sound mechanisms for selecting priorities, acceptable ways for legitimizing public policy choices, effective governance, and regular and effective controls on government.

Are these the same conditions required for success in furthering cooperation, humane accommodation, and peaceful resolution of conflicts in international politics? Will these conditions maximize security, liberty, justice, and welfare in the global community? Or are there vital differences between domestic and international politics?

These questions may guide our inquiry and help us formulate the significant empirical problem investigated in this chapter:

- What agreement on fundamentals, if any, exists among nations? (Among friends and among foes?) And what accounts for the sharp disagreements on fundamentals?
- Are the vital needs and fundamental interests of nations, and of peoples within nations, accurately expressed? What facilitates and what blocks that expression?
- How do nation-states and other international actors determine which issues should receive priority?
- Are there regular and effective controls on the international conduct of nations?

This framework of questions, borrowed from domestic politics, may not always be relevant on the international level, but it can be refreshing. It may encourage us to see similarities and differences between the two levels.

The foregoing considerations help us formulate our significant empirical problem in this chapter: *Do current international patterns for furthering cooperation, advancing accommodation, and handling conflicts adequately protect the vital needs and fundamental interests of nation-states and of peoples in the global community?*

We can now identify these needs and interests in terms of security and peace; liberty, human rights, and democratic governance; economic, social, and political justice; and human welfare, economic well-being, ecological balance, and a good quality of life.

In this chapter we focus primarily on nation-states' patterns of foreign policy—whether they emphasize a balance of power, nonalignment, domination, or multilateralism to secure their national interests.

POST–WORLD WAR II CHALLENGES

This chapter focuses mostly on the patterns evident since World War II, which was an important dividing line in many respects. To a large extent, this war ushered in a new international world, characterized by (1) the dominance of two superpowers—the United States and the Soviet Union; (2) the advent of the atomic and hydrogen bombs and the globe-girdling missiles, planes, and submarines that deliver these weapons of mass destruction; (3) the breakup of the great colonial empires; (4) the emergence of new nation-states; (5) an economically interdependent global community; (6) a revolution of rising expectations in all parts of the world, developing and developed; and (7) a host of disturbing ecological problems: population growth out of balance with dwindling resources, deterioration of the earth's ozone layer, the fouling of the air in many urban areas, and the pollution of the world's rivers, lakes, and oceans.

The 1990 Iraqi invasion of Kuwait clearly demonstrated that traditional problems like blatant aggression are still with us. But the world is changing, and our focus must extend beyond the characteristics normally associated with the post–World War II international environment. Historical events are transforming much of the post–World War II order into another "new world of poli-

tics." This new world is characterized by (1) the demise of the Soviet Union, and its dangerous fragmentation; (2) the rapid collapse of communist political systems in Eastern Europe; (3) the reunification of Germany; (4) the economic integration of Western Europe; (5) the emergence of Islamic fundamentalism, particularly in the Middle East and South Asia; (6) a dramatic shift from historically authoritarian political systems to democratic systems of government; (7) the prospect of a meaningful reduction in nuclear armaments by the superpowers, concurrent with nuclear proliferation in other parts of the world; (8) an alarming increase in civil wars and regional conflicts, many emerging out of long-standing ethnic, tribal, and religious resentments, and (9) a globalization of the international economic system.

Earlier we asked whether the current international system could adequately protect the vital needs and interests of nation-states and peoples. What do we mean by "adequately protect"? We believe that patterns of international politics should accomplish at least four objectives:

1. They must prevent a mutually devastating and catastrophic World War III and guard against devastating civil wars.
2. They must ensure that people all around the globe live in freedom under governments of their own choice, enjoy basic rights, and govern their own affairs.
3. These patterns must guard against political, economic, and social exploitation of one nation by another.
4. They must ensure that peoples everywhere have food, decent housing, good medical care, and basic schooling; are safeguarded against ecological disaster; and can enjoy their own diverse lifestyles.

Our guiding hypothesis is as follows: *Despite some recent and striking successes in international cooperation, current international patterns do not yet adequately protect the vital needs and fundamental interests of all nations and peoples in the global community.*

CURRENT PATTERNS IN INTERNATIONAL POLITICS: SOME PRELIMINARY CONSIDERATIONS

In this chapter we elaborate on our guiding hypothesis by analyzing the strengths and weaknesses of four patterns of foreign policy: balance of power, nonalignment, domination, and multilateralism as practiced in the United Nations and the European Union. Throughout this discussion we pay close attention to patterns of international conflict as well as to the practice of cooperation and accommodation that does exist in the international community.

The standard of **national interest** adopted by nation-states throughout the world and the distribution and exercise of power are key factors influencing the shape of international relations.

The Standard of National Interest

Patterns in international politics are significantly influenced by national interest. A nation will choose a policy based on balance of power, domination, nonalignment, or multilateralism because it offers assurance of protecting the national interest.

As noted in Chapter 11, the national interest serves as a central concern for leaders in international politics. Leaders must protect the fundamental interests of their nation: its freedom and independence, its safety against foreign aggression or subversion, its prosperity, and the rights and welfare of its people. We have used the four concepts of security, liberty, justice, and welfare to summarize the meaning of the national interest.

Debate rages, however, on the more specific meaning of the national interest. Moreover, what is one nation's interest may not be another's. American involvement in the Vietnam war between 1960 and 1973 illustrates both aspects of this controversy. Some scholars argue that America's national interest was hardly threatened by North Vietnam's effort to take over the whole of Vietnam and unite the country. Others argued that America's national interest was threatened: If South Vietnam fell to the North Vietnam Communists, then—like so many dominoes—every country in Southeast Asia would fall, and the United States would have been dealt a grievous blow by "international communism." Of course, the United States and the North Vietnamese differed on what was in the best interest of Vietnam. The United States sought to contain the spread of communism; the North Vietnamese sought to unify all of Vietnam under the communist banner and rid the country of foreign interests that had caused problems in Vietnam for centuries. Needless to say, the rulers of South Vietnam and the rulers of North Vietnam had conflicting views of national interest. The rulers of South Vietnam argued that the invasion from the north was no noble gesture to unite the country but rather an aggressive seizure of their territory and a violation of their sovereignty.

To a large extent, conflicts in international politics involve conflicting concepts of national interest. The standard of the national interest—and not some global standard of the human interest of all peoples—is nonetheless the primary standard for politicians in international relations.

The Primary Role of Power

Patterns in international politics are also significantly influenced by the distribution and exercise of power. **Power** means the ability of one political actor (say, a nation-state) to get another (say, another nation-state) to do (or not do) something.

Political realists assert that power must be mobilized and used in a balanced system, either to maintain an equilibrium of power between countries or to maintain superiority over an opponent. Similarly, domination cannot be maintained, if it is attempted, without the threat or use of power. Moreover, the nations that during much of the Cold War pursued a policy of *nonalignment* in the struggle between the world's superpowers (the United States and the Soviet Union) often did so because they were preoccupied with exercising their own power domestically or in their region of the world, because they were weak, or because they saw dangers to their national interest in becoming involved in the superpowers' conflicts. Finally, true collective security, in which peace-loving states band together against aggressors in a global organization, requires that peace-loving states use their collective power against aggressive nations that violate the peace or international law. Thus, regardless of the policy they pursue, nations will use power to maintain national conceptions of security, liberty, justice, and welfare.

Power can be exercised in many ways. It can be military might. It can also be charismatic persuasion—the personal appeal of a gifted leader. Power can be economic threat or benefit: an economic stick or an economic carrot. Power can be political skill: that of the experienced diplomat. Power can be public opinion: the views of masses of people. Power can be prestige: the influence of the respected. Power can be rooted in law: the influence of legitimate authority. Thus, power can be military, psychological, economic, political, sociological, legal, or ethical. It is neutral; only its particular use and abuse makes it good or evil.

But another desire also operates in international politics—a desire for mutual benefit. This frequently leads to cooperation, accommodation, and the peaceful resolution of disputes without any military might, economic threat, or political sanctions. Thus, nations cooperate on a wide range of practical matters—global communications, ocean and air safety, health, and international postal service—without the threat of coercive power.

Nonetheless, when mutual benefits are not obvious, or when disagreements seriously threaten national interests, the exercise of political, economic, and military muscle will be more likely.

THE BALANCE OF POWER

For most of the post–World War II era, balance of power has been the most prominent pattern of international politics among the Great Powers. This pattern has dominated the international scene because conditions were not favorable for other patterns (nonalignment, domination, or multilateralism).

Balance of power has many meanings, although most are variations on the same theme. At its core is the idea that peace is assured when nations' military powers are distributed so that no one state (or combination of states) is strong enough to threaten other states with its military strength. Simply put, peace is achieved through equilibrium. Classic balance-of-power systems are based on the European experience during the seventeenth, eighteenth, and nineteenth centuries. As depicted in Figure 14.1, the system generally had multiple actors: five, six, or seven states. During most of the post–World War II period, balance of power has been applied to the Cold War bipolar relationship between the United States and the Soviet Union. Another form of balance would be **hegemonic,** in which one power tends to be an overwhelming stabilizing force.

Given the difficulty, if not the impossibility, of living alone in the world today, isolation and noninvolvement in international politics are rare, and even nonalignment has had only limited success. Worldwide domination by a single nation-state now seems out of the question. Domination, understood as old-fashioned imperialism, has been rapidly disappearing with the breakup of the old colonial empires of Britain, France, Holland, Belgium, and Portugal. Only regional domination—such as that of Eastern Europe by the Soviet Union from 1947 to 1989, or of Central America by the United States off and on since early in the twentieth century—seems feasible. But even regional domination seem impractical. Although **multilateralism**—a commitment to international organizations and political and economic integration—is on the increase, the world is not abandoning the basic principles of balance of power.

The Cold War Balance of Power

For forty-five years (1945–1990), the bipolar balance-of-power system was best illustrated by the United States (and its allies) and the Soviet

Figure 14.1
Balance-of-power configurations.

Multipolar

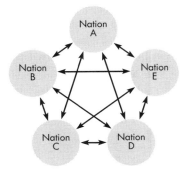

Bipolar

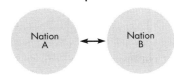

Hegemonic

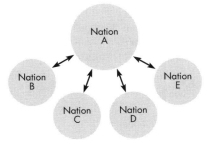

Union (and its allies). In its own interests, each superpower sought at least equality, and preferably superiority, of power. Each side was heavily armed. Both the United States and the Soviet Union maintained an arsenal of nuclear weapons designed, so each superpower said, to deter an attack by the other. These arsenals still exist, but both parties have been considerably reducing their overall military capability.

The United States and Its Allies—Crucial to the U.S. balance-of-power policy was its alliance

system. The heart of the system was the North Atlantic Treaty Organization (NATO, originated in 1949), which affirmed that the

parties agree that an armed attack against one or more of them in Europe or North America shall be considered an attack against them all; and consequently they agree, that if such an armed attack occurs, each of them in exercise of the right of individual or collective self-defense recognized by Article 51 of the Charter of the United Nations, will assist the party or parties so attacked by taking forthwith, individually and in concert with the other parties, such action as it deems necessary, including the use of armed force, to restore and maintain the security of the North Atlantic Area.[1]

In 1996 NATO's members included the United States, the United Kingdom, Canada, Norway, Denmark, France, the Netherlands, Luxembourg, Belgium, West Germany, Italy, Greece, Turkey, Iceland, Spain, and Portugal. France withdrew from NATO's integrated military command in 1966 but still maintains membership in the alliance.

During much of the Cold War, NATO's success depended on more than an apparent military threat to Western Europe. Members of NATO also agreed on certain cultural, political, and economic fundamentals. These fundamentals, and the cooperation and accommodation they make possible, are expressed in the NATO treaty. The treaty's preamble declares that the

parties "are determined to safeguard the freedom, common heritage and civilization of their peoples, founded on the principles of democracy, individual liberty and the rule of law." And Article 2 affirms that the parties will contribute toward the further development of peaceful and friendly interrelations by strengthening their free institutions, by bringing about a better understanding of the principles upon which these institutions are founded, and by promoting conditions of stability and well-being. They will seek to eliminate conflict in their international economic policies and will encourage economic collaboration between any or all of them.[2]

In the early 1990s NATO began a crucial self-examination in response to the collapse of communism in the Soviet Union and Eastern Europe—and, most important, in response to the demise of the Communist bloc's Warsaw Pact as a viable opposition to NATO. In light of a drastically reduced threat from the East, what should be NATO's role in the future? Should it remain the primary mechanism for European security? Should it substantially reduce its forces? Should it become more political instead of strictly defensive? Should it expand its membership to the east European countries? to the new independent states emerging out of the former Soviet Union? Should it extend its reach beyond Europe to protect vital interests in other parts of the world (such as oil in the Middle East)?

Even before all these questions were answered, a partial step toward expansion of NATO took place in 1994. Known as Partners For Peace (PFP), it offered the opportunity for a number of states to establish a consultative relationship with NATO on both political and security matters. As of 1996 the following states had entered into the PFP program: Albania, Armenia, Azerbaijan, Belarus, Bulgaria, Czech Republic, Estonia, Georgia, Hungary, Kazakistan, Kyrghyz Republic, Latvia, Lithuania, Moldavia, Poland, Romania, Russia, Slovakia, Slovenia, Macedonia, Turkmenistan, Ukraine, and Uzbekistan. Whether many of these countries will eventually be asked to become full members of the NATO alliance is a question undergoing intense debate.

Returning to the Cold War era, elsewhere in the world the United States sought to protect its national interests. It extended its protective arm against external aggression over Latin America with the Rio Pact, joined with Australia and New Zealand in the ANZUS Pact, and signed bilateral security treaties with Japan and the Philippines. The Southeast Asia Treaty Organization (SEATO), another Cold War security arrangement, dissolved at the end of the Vietnam War in 1975. ANZUS was crippled in 1986, when New Zealand objected to American nuclear warships in its ports.

The Soviet Union and Its Allies—In the Warsaw Pact, the Soviet Union allied with Eastern European countries as a counterweight to NATO. The relationship between the Soviet Union and its European allies, however, clearly rested on a more coercive relationship than that in NATO.

The Soviet Union did not hesitate—as its invasions of Hungary (1956) and Czechoslovakia (1968) made clear—to intervene in its allies' internal affairs to ensure reliable Communist governments. In protecting its own national interests (presumably threatened by a united Germany, rearmed and allied with the West), the Soviet Union perpetuated the division of Germany and utilized a rearmed East Germany as one of its Warsaw Pact allies, just as the United States, since 1955, had utilized a rearmed West Germany as its ally. Austria, a buffer state between East and West, was permitted to regain its sovereign independence on the condition that it remain neutral in world affairs.

For most of the post–World War II period, the Soviet Union supported national liberation movements in Asia and Africa, opposed American political and economic "imperialism," favored peaceful coexistence with and nonalignment for developing nations, and in general sought to diminish the power of the United States and its allies. By the end of the 1980s, however, the Soviet Union began to reorder its priorities. Enormous resources had been expended in Cold War efforts around the world at the expense of the Soviet economy. Under Mikhail Gorbachev, the Soviets began to dramatically reduce their commitments. They withdrew their military forces from Afghanistan and cut their military and developmental assistance to Cuba, Ethiopia, Nicaragua, Vietnam, Angola, and other client states in the developing world.

Results of the Cold War

How did the post–World War II balance-of-power system function? Did it adequately protect the vital needs and fundamental interests of nation-states and of peoples in the global community? Did it further willing cooperation and peaceful resolution of disputes? Did it enhance security, liberty, justice, and welfare? We have no easy answers to these questions, but some replies are possible.

World War III did not erupt. The Soviet Union did not invade Western Europe or attack the

United States. The United States did not attack the Soviet Union or seek to upset any Communist government in Eastern Europe. The mutual fear of a nuclear war, or even a conventional war that might escalate into a nuclear war, preserved the post–World War II settlement in Europe.

American economic aid through the Marshall Plan contributed enormously to Western Europe's recovery. And, stimulated by the Marshall Plan, Western European countries banded together in the European Economic Community to overcome former disastrous economic and political rivalries (particularly the Franco-German rivalry). Fear of the Soviet Union and the communization of Eastern Europe served to unite historic enemies (West Germany, France, and Britain) and to keep them in military, political, and economic concert with the United States, primarily through NATO and the European Economic Community. Up to a point, these relationships enhanced security, liberty, justice, and welfare for all the contracting parties.

Yet a heavily armed Western Europe, possessing nuclear weapons, created much anxiety. If deterrence failed and NATO used nuclear weapons to stop a conventional Soviet attack on Western Europe, the outcome would have been catastrophic.

It is now clear that the Soviet Union's allies (more accurately, the peoples of Eastern Europe under Communist governments) greatly resented their domination by the Soviet Union in the Warsaw Pact or in Comecon, the communist equivalent of the European Economic Community (later to be renamed the European Union). Certainly the Hungarian Revolution in 1956, the attempted liberalization of the Czech Communist government in 1968, and the Solidarity movement in Poland suggested unhappiness with Soviet domination and no great sympathy with the Brezhnev Doctrine, which asserted the Soviet Union's responsibility to intervene in a Communist country to prevent overthrow or liberalization.

The dramatic events of 1989, which overturned Communist party rule in most of Eastern Europe and destroyed the Berlin Wall, confirmed long-held suspicions that most citizens in Eastern Europe were highly dissatisfied with their subjugation.

But what about cooperation, accommodation, and peaceful resolution of disputes between the Soviet Union and the United States? And between East and West? During the late 1960s and early 1970s a policy of **detente** (relaxation of tensions) modestly relieved the worst aspects

A banner in front of the Berlin Wall in 1989 reflects the end of the Cold War. It says: "For Berlin without a wall. In a Germany without tanks. In a Europe without borders."

of the Cold War. The United States and the Soviet Union did agree to (1) stop testing nuclear weapons in the atmosphere; (2) not place nuclear weapons in space; (3) sign a Nuclear Non-Proliferation Treaty; (4) limit the arms race as outlined in the Strategic Arms Limitation Talks; (5) install a hot line between Moscow and Washington (so the two powers could instantly communicate about urgent matters); (6) eliminate all Intermediate Range Nuclear Forces (INF), about 4 percent of the nuclear weapons in their combined arsenals; and (7) limit chemical and biological weapons.

Periods of relative calm and progress were, however, interrupted by crisis. Chapter 4 discussed the 1962 Cuban missile crisis, when the Soviets installed nuclear-tipped missiles on the island country just ninety miles from Florida. Another crisis occurred in late 1979, when the Soviets invaded Afghanistan; the Soviet Union's prolonged military presence there adversely affected detente. One casualty of the deterioration of Soviet-American relations after that invasion was SALT II, a second treaty to limit strategic arms. Both governments had agreed on Salt II, but it did not go to the U.S. Senate for "advice and consent" because it would certainly have failed. Only later was another set of talks— START (Strategic Arms Reduction Talks)—begun in an attempt to reduce arms.

The nations of East and West also agreed that some Jews could emigrate from the Soviet Union and that some citizens of East Germany could immigrate to West Berlin and West Germany. In the Helsinki accords on human rights, the West accepted the status quo in Eastern Europe in exchange for human rights concessions from the Soviets. During the 1970s and early 1980s, before Gorbachev's rise to power, the degree of Soviet compliance with these agreements aroused considerable controversy in the United States.

Costs of the Cold War

It does appear that the balance of power—understood as the balance of terror—at least prevented

a World War III fought with nuclear weapons. But only at a very high cost:

1. Steady, huge expenditures on military armaments (when such monies might have been better spent on domestic needs or to aid the poor in developing countries)
2. The continuing anguish of the balance of terror: the possibility that through deliberate choice, miscalculation, or accident the world could be plunged into nuclear catastrophe
3. Periodic crises (whether the Berlin blockade or the Cuban missile crisis) that threatened to bring on World War III
4. The Soviet domination of Eastern Europe and its adverse effects on the security, liberty, justice, and welfare of the people of Eastern Europe
5. The Red Scare in America during the Joseph McCarthy period of the 1950s, and its adverse effects on civil liberties
6. A war fought by the United States (primarily) and the United Nations to resist Communist North Korean aggression against South Korea
7. Strenuous U.S. efforts to shore up anticommunist regimes around the world, even at the price of accepting right-wing or authoritarian regimes that suppress human rights or stifle peaceful domestic reform
8. Persistent Soviet efforts to support national liberation movements all over the globe, to weaken Western influence, and to support nonaligned nations in the Third World
9. A war fought first by the French and then by the United States in Indochina to prevent a Vietnamese Communist victory and, presumably, a Communist victory in all Southeast Asia

These are only a few examples of the costs of the struggle for power that involved the United States and its allies and the Soviet Union and other Communist regimes.

The uncertainty and instability of the balance

of power is also underscored by the Chinese Communist victory on mainland China in 1949 and by the conflict between Communist China and Communist Russia, which resulted in a number of violent border clashes between 1960 and 1985.

The Aftermath of the Cold War

The end of the Cold War raises a critical question about the balance of power. Is the international system realigning itself into a new balance-of-power configuration? No crystal ball can answer this question, but several developments in recent years give some clues.

First, the Cold War balance of power no longer exists. The Warsaw Pact was disbanded in 1991. NATO has lost its primary reason for existence—the possible invasion of Western Europe by the forces of the Soviet Union and its Warsaw Pact allies.

Second, the United States, although still enormously powerful, has lost much of its dominance in the system.[3] New centers of power (Western Europe and Japan) have risen to challenge what was certainly an economic hegemony by the United States during the immediate post–World War II years.

Third, although the major powers still maintain enormous nuclear and conventional military establishments, the world increasingly defines power in more economic terms. A new balance between enormous regional economic actors—individual states or regional organizations—may be emerging. This pattern will become clearer later in this chapter.

Fourth, the concept of military balance of power is certainly not extinct. But security arrangements will probably operate at a regional level rather than a global level.

NONALIGNMENT

Nonalignment is a policy adopted by many nation-states in the developing world, primarily in Asia, Africa, the Middle East, and occasionally in Europe (the former Yugoslavia) and Latin America. The heart of nonalignment was a refusal to participate in the struggle between the two superpowers during the Cold War years. Nonalignment was strongly rooted in the desire of new states (recently emancipated from colonial rule) and of older states (seeking to avert imperialist domination) to affirm their national freedom and independence and to advance their political, economic, and social development. The policy was designed to protect their security, liberty, justice, and welfare in a world made more difficult by the Cold War rivalry between the United States and the Soviet Union. Nonalignment does not require a superpower balance of power; it can be practiced by states in a multipolar world or at a regional level. Nonalignment requires states, in their interest, to avoid entangling commitments.

This is not necessarily a policy of isolation or abstention from world affairs. Nor does it mean, as does the concept of neutralism, that these countries refuse to express preferences in conflict situations. Quite the contrary; nonaligned nations feel a positive responsibility to protect their national freedom and independence, to support efforts to eliminate colonialism and imperialism, to guard against the dangers of a hot war that will engulf them along with all other nations, and to actively fight for economic and social advancement, especially in the developing world.

Nonalignment is designed, then, to advance these objectives through a cooperative exercise of power by nonaligned nations. It is designed to protect them against Big Power encroachments, to gain aid from larger and richer nations, and to reduce the dangers of a catastrophic World War III.

In general, nonaligned nations endorse such principles as (1) respect for each others' territorial integrity and sovereignty, (2) nonaggression, (3) noninterference in internal affairs, (4) equality and mutual benefits, and (5) peaceful coexistence.[4] At least, these are their professed principles.

But what can be said about their actual practices? Let us consider two leaders in the nonaligned

movement: India and Egypt. Their foreign policies illustrate the pragmatic methods they use to
advance their national interests within a framework of global peace.

Two Examples: India and Egypt

India has no military alliances with any nation,
yet it remains a member of the British Commonwealth. India has fought hard to establish the
principles of peaceful coexistence and to reduce
the dangers of nuclear war. Yet India has gone to
war with neighboring Pakistan over the disputed
province of Kashmir, has fought in a border
dispute with China, and has invaded and absorbed the Portuguese colony of Goa on the
Indian subcontinent. India also played a decisive
military role in enabling Bangladesh, formerly
part of Pakistan, to achieve independence. Although very concerned about nuclear war, India
maintains a peaceful nuclear capability. During
the Cold War, India received economic aid from
both the Soviet Union and the United States.
India has been an outspoken critic of Western
imperialism and colonialism and was a rather
soft-spoken critic of the Soviet invasions of Hungary and Afghanistan. India has played an
important role in supplying military contingents
for U.N. peacekeeping forces.

Egypt, too, during the Cold War, steered clear
of formal alliance with either the Soviet Union or
the United States, although under the leadership
of Gamal Abdel Nasser it had close military ties
to the Soviet Union. Nasser's successor, Anwar
el-Sadat, had close military ties to the United
States, as does current president Hosni Mubarak.
In the past Egypt received economic and military
aid from both the Soviet Union and the United
States. Nonalignment has not prevented Egypt
from fighting and then making peace with Israel
(in the Camp David accords). Similarly, Egypt
has both cooperated with and quarreled with its
Arab neighbors.

As these examples illustrate, the nonaligned
nations are by no means homogeneous in their
outlook and behavior. They generally agree on
protecting their national interest, opposing co-

lonialism and imperialism, favoring nuclear disarmament, reducing the danger of war between
the superpowers, encouraging economic aid from
the more affluent North, and condemning racism. However, during the most intense Cold
War years, the nonaligned nations frequently
split on issues that divided the Soviet Union and
the United States: some supported the United
States, some supported the Soviet Union, and
some abstained. But often their seemingly pro-
Soviet stance was really a pro–developing nation
stance shared by the Soviet Union.

Other differences and diversities are also apparent: some nonaligned nations are extraordinarily affluent (Saudi Arabia and other oil-
producing states), and some are impoverished;
some are giants in size and population (India),
others are tiny island republics (Seychelles).

Strengths and Weaknesses of Nonalignment

How, then, has the pattern of nonalignment
worked to advance the security, liberty, justice,
and welfare of the nonaligned states of the Third
World? Accurate generalizations that will stand
the test of time are hazardous, but a few observations will probably hold up.

On the positive side, nonalignment has probably (1) significantly advanced the cause of
decolonization and protected the freedom, independence, and self-respect of most developing
states; (2) reduced severe East-West tensions
and confrontations by preventing a massive,
formalized polarization of most of the world's
nations into giant alliances; (3) speeded up economic aid from affluent nations, particularly
from the United States and the Soviet Union, and
(4) reduced certain superpower threats against
older states (Yugoslavia and Egypt).

On the other hand, the policy of nonalign-
ment (1) was not the major factor in preventing
World War III; (2) was not able to prevent
Soviet domination of Eastern Europe (and in-
vasions of Hungary, Czechoslovakia, and
Afghanistan); (3) did not prevent a number of
regional conflicts between nonaligned nations
(India-Pakistan, Iran-Iraq, Vietnam-Cambodia,

Ethiopia-Somalia) or between developing nations and Western nations (the Korean and Vietnam wars), or other disputes (Israel and Arab states, South Africa); and (4) did not encourage developing nations to cut back on spending for armaments and instead use scarce monies for domestic needs.

The fate of nonalignment in the post–Cold War world will depend a great deal on global and regional power realignments. Obviously, the primary condition that gave rise to the movement—superpower rivalry—no longer exists. But it is far too early to tell if the policy is still useful for many countries in the international system.

DOMINATION

Domination is the policy of exercising direct or indirect control over others. Domination may take the form of imperial conquest, colonization or the exertion of political and economic power. In World War II, Germany and Japan made imperial conquests. In the nineteenth and twentieth centuries, imperial colonization was practiced by Great Britain, France, Holland, Belgium, Spain, Portugal, and to a more limited degree the United States and certain Asian, African, and Latin American countries. Another variety of domination is illustrated by Soviet control in Eastern Europe from 1947 to 1989.

Despite charge and countercharge in the Cold War, probably neither the United States nor the Soviet Union wanted, or had the power, to dominate the globe. Charges of regional domination are somewhat more persuasive and will have to be examined more fully.

Domination is, of course, a question of degree. Critics of the Soviet Union, building on communist rhetoric of worldwide triumph, argued that the Soviets sought to dominate the world in the post–World War II era. The Soviet Union would achieve this objective in one or more ways: (1) by direct aggression or takeover (as in the absorption of Latvia, Lithuania, and Estonia in 1939); (2) with the help of local Communists, fortified by the Red Army, as in Eastern Europe; (3) through peaceful means, as in France and Italy, where Communists could poll large numbers of votes; (4) through subversion wherever it was to their advantage; (5) by encouraging decolonization of the Western imperial regimes, supporting nationalism in the new states and elsewhere, and subsequently taking control in Third World countries when Communist power and the time were ripe.

Similarly, communist and some noncommunist critics of the United States alleged that the U.S. plans to dominate the world through a capitalist conspiracy, using capitalist puppets to do the bidding of "imperialistic" U.S. masters.

Both conspiratorial theories (although grounded here and there in the realities of the Soviet or American struggle for power) are farfetched. Global domination by the United States, the USSR, or any other power is a practical impossibility. This is probably even more true now that the world seems to be moving toward greater nuclear and economic multipolarity.

Not farfetched, however, are varying degrees of regional domination or significant influence. The Soviet Union dominated Eastern Europe for over forty years. The United States exercised almost overwhelming influence, particularly economic, over Western Europe, Japan, Latin America, South Korea, and Formosa (Taiwan) for nearly fifteen years after World War II.

But even regional domination is increasingly difficult in a world characterized by the rise of new major powers. Within the Communist world, the Soviet Union reigned supreme until China emerged in the 1950s. In 1989 the Soviets felt that, in view of their collapsing domestic economy, they could no longer afford the high cost of dominating Eastern Europe.

Although the United States continues to wield great influence in Western Europe, Japan, Latin America, and other countries, it can no longer dominate these nations even if it wanted to do so. Increasingly, the United States must cooperate with its partners as equals, even though it can still limit some of their initiatives. But even this limited power is being eroded by the economic integration of Europe, which will create one gigantic economic actor that is far less vulnerable to U.S. influence.

Increasingly, old-fashioned domination will not work. Nationalism, restive peoples, the spirit of freedom, the pragmatic recognition of who rules and who benefits under various patterns of domination and influence all tend to undermine any pattern of domination and cause it to be replaced by more willing cooperation, humane accommodation, and peaceful resolution of disputes.

MULTILATERALISM

The final pattern of behavior we will examine is multilateralism. **Multilateralism** involves groups of countries collectively solving problems and conflicts, usually through formal international organizations. These organizations may be global, such as the United Nations, or regional, such as the Organization of African Unity and the Organization of American States. They may be both regional and economic, such as the European Union, or resource based, such as the Organization of Petroleum Exporting Countries. Multilateralism is most often practiced through the day-to-day operations of international organizations. It can also be conducted through special conferences on any number of issues, ranging from arms control to AIDS, pollution of the world's oceans, women's rights, and terrorism.

The basic motivation for a strong commitment to multilateralism remains the same, regardless of the problems being dealt with. Decision makers believe that their country's interests will best be protected or advanced through the collective efforts of governments. It is increasingly difficult for individual countries (or even two countries) to deal with the wide range of problems confronting the international system. Terrorism is a transnational phenomenon; the use of torture is increasingly viewed as a problem of humankind, not just individual countries. Water and air pollution do not recognize national borders; neither do the deadly viruses

that cause AIDS. As a community of nations, the world is becoming increasingly interdependent. Although other patterns—balance of power, nonalignment, domination—have not been abandoned in the international system, multilateralism is increasingly seen as a viable technique for advancing the security, liberty, justice, and welfare of states.

We will examine three variations of multilateralism: the work of the United Nations, the economic integration of Europe, and the concept of international regimes.

The United Nations in Theory and Practice

It would be a mistake either to overestimate or to ignore the rhetoric, purposes, and principles of the U.N. Charter, but they cannot substitute for a critical analysis of U.N. behavior. As we examine the United Nations (founded in 1945), we must consider its aspirations and ideals, but we must also look candidly at the realities of fulfillment— what the U.N. actually does. The preamble to the Charter contains an inspiring vision of peoples in nations "determined to save succeeding generations from the scourge of war . . . to reaffirm faith in fundamental human rights . . . to promote social progress and better standards of life in larger freedom . . . to practice tolerance and live together in peace with one another as good neighbors . . . to unite our strength to maintain international peace and security."[5]

Article 1 elaborates on that vision in spelling out the purposes of the United Nations:

1. To maintain international peace and security, and to that end: to take effective collective measures for the prevention and removal of threats to the peace, and for the suppression of acts of aggression or other breaches of the peace, and to bring about by peaceful means, and in conformity with the principles of justice and international law, adjustment or settlement of international disputes or situations which might lead to a breach of the peace;

2. To develop friendly relations among nations based on respect for the principle of equal rights and self-determination of peoples, and to take other appropriate measures to strengthen universal peace;

3. To achieve international cooperation in solving international problems of an economic, social, cultural,

The United Nations celebrated its fiftieth anniversary in 1995 with this special lighting of the Secretariat building in New York.

or humanitarian character, and in promoting and encouraging respect for human rights and for fundamental freedoms for all without distinction as to race, sex, language, or religion; and

4. To be a center for harmonizing the actions of nations in the attainment of these common ends.

Article 2 lists some of the important principles that guide the United Nations. These guidelines include "the principle of the sovereign equality of all its Members"; a commitment to settle "international disputes by peaceful means in such a manner that international peace and security, and justice, are not endangered"; a commitment to "refrain from the threat or use of force against the territorial integrity or political independence of any state"; a recognition that nothing "contained in the present Charter shall authorize the United Nations to intervene in matters which are essentially within the domestic jurisdiction of any state." Theoretically, membership in the United Nations is "open to all . . . peace-loving states."

The key U.N. organs are a General Assembly, a Security Council, an Economic and Social Council, a Trusteeship Council (no longer very important), an International Court of Justice, and a Secretariat. These organs and their functions are outlined in Figure 14.2.

But how has the United Nations functioned in practice, and in the context of rivalry between the world's two great superpowers, the end of the U.S. monopoly of nuclear weapons, the breakup of Western colonial empires, and the startling emergence of a host of new nations in Africa, Asia, and the Middle East, and now the complex problems characteristic of the post–Cold War era?

The United Nations has experimented with a number of approaches to peace—its primary concern—and to related concerns such as human rights, economic and social progress, and self-determination of peoples. Seven such approaches can be discerned: (1) collective security, (2) peaceful settlement, (3) disarmament, (4) preventive diplomacy (peacekeeping), (5) the "grand debate," (6) trusteeship and anticolonialism, and (7) functionalism. We use these approaches to explain and illustrate the functioning of the United Nations.[6]

Collective Security—**Collective security** is a policy that envisages that all peace-loving nations, including the most powerful, will band together to maintain international peace and law and that they will use their collective strength to deter or punish aggressors who would violate international peace and law.

The United Nations was a move in the direction of collective security, but only if the Great Powers that had banded together to defeat fascism and aggression in World War II could remain united. Given the veto that the superpowers had in the Security Council, genuine collective security was clearly not possible. In a conflict situation, the Americans and the Soviets invariably found themselves on opposite sides, making it virtually impossible to adopt meaningful resolutions.

Figure 14.2 The basic organizations of the United Nations.

General Assembly

Includes all U.N. members

Meets annually. Sessions last 3 to 4 months

May discuss any matter within scope of charter

May make recommendations on any matter within scope of charter unless item is on Security Council agenda

Two-thirds vote required on all important matters

Elects nonpermanent members of Security Council and Trusteeship Council, and all members of Economic and Social Council and International Court of Justice

Elects new members to U.N. on recommendation of Security Council

Approves U.N. budget

Supervises work of Economic and Social Council and Trusteeship Council; receives annual reports from Security Council and all other U.N. organs

Security Council

Has 15 members:

5 permanent (U.S., United Kingdom, France, Russia, China)

10 nonpermanent (elected for 2-year term by General Assembly)

Meets any time it is necessary

Has primary responsibility for maintaining peace

Determines the existence of a threat to peace, or act of aggression, and decides what measures shall be taken to restore peace

All nonprocedural decisions require 9 votes, including the 5 permanent members (veto provision)

Decisions are binding on all U.N. members

International Court of Justice

Located at The Hague, Netherlands

Consists of 15 judges, elected by General Assembly and Security Council for 9-year terms

May arbitrate any dispute states are willing to submit to it

Has no compulsory jurisdiction, except over certain legal disputes that states may have voluntarily agreed to submit to compulsory arbitration

Trusteeship Council

Designed to help a number of territories that were not self-governing at the close of World War II, such as colonies and League of Nations mandates; these areas are designated Trust Territories with Trustee countries named to help in the transition to independence

Membership originally consisted of Trustee countries and the permanent members of the Security Council

This council has almost worked itself out of a job since most of the Trust Territories have achieved independence, with the exception of the Trust Territories of the Pacific

Economic and Social Council

Has 54 members, 18 of whom are selected each year by General Assembly for 3 years

Makes studies and reports regarding international economic, social, cultural, educational, health, and related matters, including human rights; may make recommendations on these matters to General Assembly

Meets usually twice a year for 4 to 6 weeks

Majority vote required for its decisions

Much of its work is done through commissions, such as Human Rights, Narcotics, Regional Economic

Coordinates work of U.N. Specialized Agencies, such as World Health Organization (WHO), Food and Agriculture Organization (FAO), World Bank, International Monetary Fund (IMF), International Labor Organization (ILO)

Secretariat

Headed by Secretary-General, who is chief administrative officer of U.N.

Secretary-General makes annual report to General Assembly on work of U.N.

He or she may also bring to attention of Security Council any matter thought to endanger peace and security

Staff of Secretariat are international civil servants, not delegates from national governments; they provide services and assistance for all U.N. organs

Main Secretariat Headquarters is in New York; has field offices throughout the world

The United Nations Security Council is the center of attention for collective security.

Other factors have operated in conjunction with the veto to make genuine collective security impossible. These factors included the absence of clear standards of peace and aggression, and the U.N.'s failure to develop an international "police force" for use against aggressors.

In only one major instance has the United Nations been able to act militarily when a major power (the Soviet Union) opposed such action. The United Nations voted to prevent a North Korean military takeover of South Korea. The vote was possible only because the Soviet Union was absent from the Security Council. Moreover, a powerful police action became possible only because the United States was willing to deploy U.S. manpower and military arms. When the Soviet Union returned to the Security Council and began to exercise its veto, further U.N. action in Korea became possible only when the General Assembly passed the Uniting for Peace Resolution. This resolution allowed the General Assembly, by a two-thirds vote, to authorize action and invite volunteer nations to participate.

The outcome of the Korean War was only a partial success for the United Nations. The North Koreans were prevented from taking over South Korea by force of arms. But Korea remains divided. The intervention of Communist China (not then a U.N. member) to prevent the total defeat of the North Koreans, in addition to Soviet opposition to the U.N. police action, suggest why genuine collective security will not be easy when one or more Great Powers are opposed.

Two additional instances of collective action are worth noting, although neither involved the use of military force. In 1966 the Security Council imposed limited economic sanctions on Rhodesia after Prime Minister Ian Smith declared independence from Britain in order to maintain white minority rule in that African country. In 1968 the sanctions were extended to full sanctions: Rhodesian ferrous chrome was not to be purchased by the world's nations, nor were critical resources, particularly oil, to be shipped to Rhodesia. Some oil and gasoline reached Rhodesia, however, from South Africa and from Mozambique (then controlled by Portugal). The other instance of nonmilitary collective punishment was the arms embargo imposed by the Security Council against South Africa in 1977. Evidence clearly indicates that several countries violated this collective action.

Finally, by 1991 no less than twelve Security Council resolutions were passed condemning Iraq for its invasion of Kuwait, establishing a worldwide economic embargo against Iraq, authorizing military action to enforce the embargo and, if necessary, to force Iraq to withdraw from Kuwait. Many observers considered this operation to be a major watershed for the United Nations, since the sanctions and military action were authorized under Chapter 7 of the U.N. Charter, the document's collective security provision. The Iraqi invasion constituted the first major post–Cold War international crisis, and for the first time in United Nations history, the collective security machinery operated precisely the way it was designed. By early 1991, a U.S.-led coalition of military forces had successfully forced Iraq to withdraw from Kuwait. The coalition's ground campaign, which had been preceded by an intensive strategic bombing assault, lasted only one hundred hours.

The U.N. military action against Iraq was followed up with missions to provide relief and security for the Kurdish minority population, which was being viciously repressed by Saddam Hussein. Finally, the United Nations authorized teams of scientists and weapons experts to seek out and destroy Iraq's nuclear, chemical, and biological weapons research facilities and arsenals. As of the end of 1996, those teams are still active in Iraq.

Despite these actions directed at Iraq, the U.N.'s appeal to collective security for handling breaches of peace has been disappointing.

This burning oil well and destroyed Iraqi tank in March 1991 are results of the Desert Storm operation to defeat Iraq's attempt to take over Kuwait.

Peaceful Settlement—**Peaceful settlement** uses inherited techniques such as influence, inquiry, mediation, and conciliation. Here the United Nations—whether through the General Assembly, the Security Council, the secretary-general, or the International Court of Justice—functions as a third party in the dispute. But success depends on the disputants' willingness to allow the United Nations to work out a peaceful settlement. The techniques may work for unnecessary and essentially avoidable wars but not for the gravest threats to world peace and order.

The United Nations has attempted to facilitate peaceful settlement in a host of cases: Greece, Palestine, Indonesia, Kashmir, Afghanistan, Iran and Iraq, and most recently the Balkan conflict involving Serbia, Croatia, and Bosnia-Herzegovina. The record is mixed. Peace came to Greece in the late 1940s less because of U.N. actions aimed at stopping military aid for Greek Communists seeking to overthrow the government than because of U.S. military support for Greece under the Truman Doctrine and because of Yugoslavia's break with Moscow. The U.N.'s efforts to achieve a peaceful partition of Palestine in 1947 did not succeed. War between Israel and its Arab neighbors broke out, and the region has suffered through a seemingly endless cycle of violence. But the United Nations has facilitated a number of cease-fires and monitored them (as discussed later in this chapter). The United Nations played an important role in ending hostilities between Indonesia and the Netherlands and in gaining Indonesian independence. In Kashmir, where Moslems claiming allegiance to Pakistan and Hindus loyal to India have slaughtered each other for decades, the United Nations has helped restrain more open and serious conflict but has not been able to achieve a final solution. The most promising developments took place when the United Nations negotiated the withdrawal of Soviet forces from Afghanistan and when it effected a cease-fire in the war between Iran and Iraq (1980–1988); these two efforts are widely considered major successes. In sum, the U.N. has encountered mixed results in its efforts toward peaceful settlement. It has certainly helped make violence less intense and less contagious than it might otherwise have been.

Disarmament—The theory of **disarmament** rests on achieving peace by significantly reducing armaments. The United Nations has attempted to advance the cause of disarmament without success. Neither the Great Powers nor the smaller powers have been willing to disarm. Mutual distrust prevented any agreement on nuclear weapons immediately after World War II, when the United States held most atomic weapons; comparable mistrust prevented real disarmament after the Soviet Union gained nuclear weapons. The U.N.'s debates on disarmament have not overcome this mistrust or come up with a foolproof disarmament plan. The United Nations will probably not prevent war by sponsoring disarmament conferences. But by using its many approaches to peace and by encouraging nations to cooperate against the underlying causes of war, the United Nations may help reduce the burden of excessive arms. International order may have to precede significant disarmament.

Preventive Diplomacy—Dag Hammarskjold, Secretary-General of the United Nations from 1953 to his untimely death in 1961, was a major architect of **preventive diplomacy.** Hammarskjold understood preventive diplomacy as action by the United Nations to help smaller powers settle disputes peacefully, before they escalated and involved the United States and the Soviet Union in a dangerous confrontation. Such U.N. intervention was designed to keep the superpowers out of conflicts in areas outside their crucial spheres of influence. The Middle Eastern crisis of 1956 and the Congo crisis of 1960 illustrate preventive diplomacy at work. In 1956 a U.N. emergency force was put into the field and maintained peace between Israel and Egypt until 1967, when the force was withdrawn at Egyptian President Nasser's request. Additional U.N. operations were established in the Middle East in the Sinai between Israel and Egypt in 1973 (U.N.

Emergency Force II), on the Golan Heights between Israel and Syria in 1974 (U.N. Disengagement Observer Force), and in Lebanon in 1978 (U.N. Interim Force in Lebanon).

Similarly, in 1960 Hammarskjold used a U.N. operation in the Congo to enable that nation to survive the political, military, and social troubles that threatened to tear it apart. The United Nations performed a host of vital services to keep the Congo afloat. But above all the U.N. kept the United States and the Soviet Union out of the conflict.

A list of current U.N. **peacekeeping** operations is provided in Figure 14.3. Preventive diplomacy can work only if the immediate parties to the dispute will accept the U.N. peacekeeping role and if the major powers on the Security Council go along with this role. Preventive diplomacy will not work, or will not work well, if one of the major powers with a Security Council veto opposes U.N. action. Moreover, preventive diplomacy requires the smaller powers to cooperate by providing the peacekeeping force. If they are unable or unwilling to do so, the United Nations would lack an emergency police force. These ifs suggest both the possibilities and limitations of preventive diplomacy.

Grand Debate—By serving as an international forum for the **grand debate**—where problems can be brought up, discussed, and analyzed, where diplomats can meet and test ideas, where the strength of policies can be measured—the United Nations can modestly advance the cause of peace and other U.N. objectives. Through the constitutional processes of debate and voting, major issues facing the global community can be aired: the danger of nuclear holocaust; the struggle for national independence and healthy growth (particularly among developing countries); conflicting ideas about domination, imperialism, and national self-determination; and ways to overcome poverty, ill health, illiteracy, and violations of human rights. Through discussion, standards of international conduct can be articulated, policy propositions advanced,

Figure 14.3
Current United Nations peacekeeping operations.

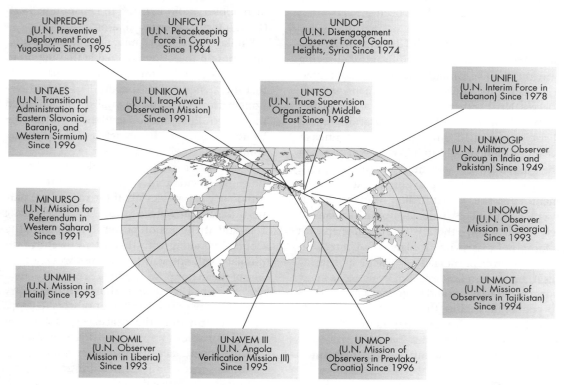

and education furthered. Global consciousness can be raised.

On the other hand, we should not expect too much from such an international forum. Talk is not always salutary: it may exaggerate and intensify mistrust. And U.N. resolutions are no substitute for peaceful settlement. Some minorities may feel beleaguered by the barrage of hostile U.N. resolutions (Israel is a good case in point), whereas developing nations (a big majority in the U.N. General Assembly) may decline to censure a favored nation for its aggression, domination, or violation of human rights.

Inis Claude's judgment about the contribution of the grand debate is very perceptive:

> The grand debate is no panacea. It does not alter the fact that the ultimate responsibility for determining the course of world affairs is vested in a multitude of states, and particularly in two great powers. Nevertheless, it has

a significance which cannot be gainsaid. . . . Debate alone will not eliminate disorder. But human experience suggests that the kind of order for which decent men yearn cannot be established and maintained except by means which involve the processes of deliberation.[7]

Trusteeship—**Trusteeship** involves the idea that a developed nation, most often a colonial power, should look after dependent people and prepare them for independence and self-governance. **Anticolonialism** involves the movement of the colonies or former colonies to become and remain independent nation-states able to govern themselves and achieve economic, social, and political progress. The United Nations was entrusted with supervising the system of trusteeship and other non-self-governing territories that, a few years after the close of World War II, involved only eleven territories in Africa and some

Pacific islands. The United Nations fulfilled its supervisory responsibility reasonably well, although it took forty-five years for the League of Nations Mandate Territory of Namibia (formerly Southwest Africa) to achieve independence because of South Africa's refusal to withdraw.

During the 1950s, 1960s, and 1970s, the General Assembly functioned as a powerful organ in the process of anticolonialism. The General Assembly emphatically declared that all peoples have a supreme right to national self-determination. Especially since the advent of many new nations after World War II, the General Assembly consistently tried to protect dependent peoples in their battles with colonial powers. In many ways, the United Nations moved from being antifascist (at its inception) to anticommunist (in the early days of the Cold War) to anticolonialist.

The United Nations was an important but not primary cause of the gradual elimination of European empires. The U.N.'s 1960 Declaration on the Granting of Independence to Colonial Countries and Peoples illustrates its position and influence. The anticolonial battle within the United Nations illustrates that its founders did not fully appreciate the power of anticolonialist sentiment and did not realize that people in the colonies would insist on speedy emancipation, even at the risk of violence and being unprepared for national independence. The new states' needs—for cohesion and economic and social development—put pressure on the United Nations for help. The United Nations has modestly tried to help these nations, many of whom were perhaps born prematurely. Its success in overcoming the history of Western imperialism remains to be seen.

Functionalism—**Functionalism** is based on the premise that the barriers to cooperation and peaceful resolution of disputes can best be overcome when peoples and nations work together to meet common needs and advance mutual interests. These needs and interests involve practical problems such as trade and shipping, health and literacy, agriculture and fishing, aviation and broadcasting, and nuclear research and development and are primarily nonpolitical.[8] These common needs and interests—involving the laborer, farmer, businessperson, child, expectant mother, doctor, scientist, aviator, engineer, fisher, meteorologist, and broadcaster—are delineated by the specialized agencies of the United Nations. Their very names indicate the functions that unite people across national borders, solve mutual problems, and thus help overcome the divisive consequences of national sovereignty.

Some of the better known U.N. specialized agencies include:

1. International Labor Organization (ILO). The ILO seeks to improve labor conditions and labor welfare around the globe.
2. Food and Agriculture Organization (FAO). The FAO, through advice and research on problems of production, aridity, forestry, and fisheries, seeks to increase the quantity and quality of foods and forests.
3. U.N. Educational, Scientific and Cultural Organization (UNESCO). This organization helps governments promote basic education in the developing areas of the world and seeks to enhance educational, scientific, and cultural endeavors around the globe.
4. International Civil Aviation Organization (ICAO). The ICAO deals with air safety, general flight rules, standardization of communication, and cooperation in search and rescue operations.
5. International Bank for Reconstruction and Development (World Bank). The World Bank makes loans, especially to Third World countries, to aid economic development and stability.
6. International Monetary Fund (IMF). The IMF encourages governments to collaborate on problems involving balance of payments, foreign exchange, debt rescheduling, and currency reevaluation. It offers help to member governments in financial trouble.

7. World Health Organization (WHO). The WHO helps governments improve their health services, fight epidemics, study diseases, advance mental health, and develop standards of nutrition, sanitation, housing, and recreation.

Other specialized agencies include the International Maritime Organization, World Intellectual Property Organization, International Fund for Agricultural Development, U.N. Industrial Development Organization, the General Agreement on Tariffs and Trade (GATT), the Universal Postal Union, the International Telecommunications Union, and the World Meteorological Organization.

Through the General Assembly and the Economic and Social Council, the United Nations has created a number of programs and organizations that report directly to the Assembly or the Economic and Social Council. These organizations include the United Nations Development Program, the United Nations Children's Emergency Fund (UNICEF), the World Food Council, and the United Nations Environmental Program.

All these organizations, often known as functional agencies, contribute to peace by getting at what some consider the root causes of war: poverty, illiteracy, disease, and distrust. Some of the work of these agencies and programs is very impressive. The United Nations has eradicated smallpox, immunized millions of children, and funded more than 4,000 projects, including schools, health clinics, communications systems, and food preservation and processing facilities. The organization has played an important role in world weather forecasting and has cut illegal opium production by 50 percent in Southeast Asia. It has taken the lead in the global fight against AIDS and in efforts to preserve the earth's ozone layer. The successes are heartening, but it is by no means clear that these programs have dealt with the real political problems that create national rivalry, conflict, and war. Still, without the work of the United Nations and its agencies, distress among peoples

would probably be greater, and tensions more likely to erupt into conflict.

Assessing the U.N.—How do we assess the U.N.'s contribution to security, liberty, justice, and welfare for the peoples of the globe? Although the balance of terror between the United States and the Soviet Union was most responsible for preventing a nuclear World War III, the United Nations has underscored the mutually disastrous consequences of such a war and has kept the superpowers apart in certain potentially explosive arenas (the Middle East, South Asia, and the Congo) but not in others (Berlin or Cuba). The United Nations was able, under extraordinary circumstances, to prevent North Korea from conquering South Korea, but it was unable to bring peace to Vietnam. The United Nations has not been able to prevent war in a number of cases (such as the Israeli-Arab, India-Pakistan, and Bosnian conflicts), but its peacekeeping activities have sometimes helped mitigate a grave crisis. In some instances, as in Indonesia or Kashmir, the U.N.'s good offices have either brought peace or cooled off an actual conflict.

The United Nations has probably spurred movements for national independence in the Third World, but it was ineffective in preventing Soviet domination of Eastern Europe or U.S. interference in Chile and elsewhere. It has raised a standard of human rights throughout the world, but this did little to prevent violations in the Soviet Union, South Africa, Argentina, Cambodia (Kampuchea), or elsewhere.

Through its functional agencies, the United Nations has greatly contributed to the battle against poverty, disease, and illiteracy, particularly in many developing countries. These activities are promising but still inadequate, and they do not yet grapple with or dissolve the political rivalries that have led to war.

Regional Integration: The European Union
Space does not permit us to explore the many and varied regional organizations in the world

today. But special attention must be given to at least one that illustrates the functional approach to peace and economic prosperity, and perhaps ultimately to political union: the European Union (EU). After a brief examination of the EU we will make some observations on the extraordinary 1992 movement leading toward the complete economic integration of Western Europe.

The European Union was built on a foundation created after World War II by the Marshall Plan, a plan that required Europe to organize for economic cooperation and development. The EU was also built on the European Coal and Steel Community of 1952, which was designed to tie France and West Germany together economically. In the Treaty of Rome (1957) the six "inner" nations of Western Europe (France, Belgium, the Netherlands, Luxembourg, Italy, and West Germany) moved on to establish the European Economic Community (EEC). These six nations sought to establish an internal Common Market among themselves and a common tariff toward other countries. They sought to abolish "obstacles to the free movement of persons, services, and capital." They sought to inaugurate common agricultural and transport policies. They hoped to improve employment and raise the standard of living in the six nations. In 1994 the European Coal and Steel Community, the European Economic Community, and the European Atomic Energy Community (Euratom) collectively adopted the designation of the **European Union.**

The rationale of the European Union (whose current full membership is depicted in Figure 14.4) builds on that of the Coal and Steel Community: to overcome devastating political rivalries (which had led to three wars between France and Germany between 1870 and 1939) by integrating the economies of the separate countries in bonds of mutual interest and prosperity so that war would be unthinkable.

The Coal and Steel Community, which exists under the umbrella of the EU, has been a remarkable economic success. Its executive organ (the High Authority) constitutes Europe's first genu-

Figure 14.4
The European Union.

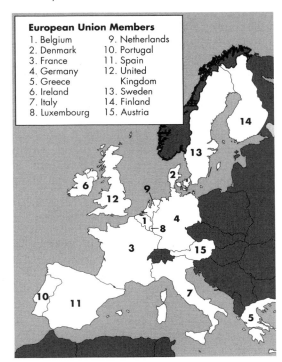

European Union Members

1. Belgium
2. Denmark
3. France
4. Germany
5. Greece
6. Ireland
7. Italy
8. Luxembourg
9. Netherlands
10. Portugal
11. Spain
12. United Kingdom
13. Sweden
14. Finland
15. Austria

inely supranational executive: Its decisions are not subject to veto by its members' governments.

In the economic sphere, despite difficulties in such areas as agricultural policy, the European Economic Community (again, under the umbrella of the EU) has also helped its member countries. It has raised the level of living in all member nations. One measure of its success is the fact that nations other than the inner six have sought to join and share its benefits. For instance in 1973, Great Britain joined the European Economic Community.

The European Economic Community illustrates a remarkable success in the economic sphere and holds promise for a larger political success. Although it has not entirely overcome important nationalistic suspicions and rivalries, it has significantly reduced conflict between France and Germany and has enhanced economic strength and relative prosperity in Western Europe.

Building on the success of the European Coal and Steel Community, the European Atomic Energy Community, and the European Economic Community, the twelve countries of Western Europe (Belgium, Denmark, France, Germany, Greece, Ireland, Italy, Luxembourg, the Netherlands, Portugal, Spain, and the United Kingdom) signed the Single European Act (SEA) in 1986. In doing so they committed themselves to complete economic integration by the end of 1992. This unified market would have a gross national product exceeding $4 trillion, which exceeds the approximate combined total of $3 trillion for Japan, South Korea, Taiwan, Hong Kong, and Singapore.

As of 1996, the 1992 target was not fully met, nor is European economic integration complete. To be sure, tremendous progress along this path has been made. But what would it mean for the West European countries to become a single economic actor? If the total integration envisioned in 1986 were to take place, goods, services, people, and capital will move with complete freedom between the EEC member-nations. Safety and technical standards for all vehicles, telecommunications, food additives, measuring instruments, loading equipment, emissions, and the like will agree. Food labeling will be standardized. Bidding for services will be open throughout the EEC. Banking, financial services, broadcasting, tourism, and passenger transport will have common regulations. Capital and stocks will be freely transferred between the members, and common rules will be established for consumer protection. In all, over 300 separate agreements on standards and guidelines for economic transactions are being negotiated and must be signed. Put simply, people, money, goods, and services will move as easily within the European community as within the United States.

What is the objective of this enormous undertaking? As Dennis Swann of the United Kingdom put it:

The short answer is that the elimination of barriers to trade and the boost to competition will have an eco-

nomic pay-off. Costs will fall due to the fuller exploitation of economies of scale in a truly European market. Efficiency will also improve as prices and costs move down under the pressure exerted by more competitive markets. More economic patterns of resource allocation will result as underlying comparative advantages are allowed to exert their full potential. Hopefully, increased competition will stimulate a more rapid rate of innovation. In the period up to the end of 1992 this could add 4.5 percent to EC Gross Domestic Product and create 1.8 million new jobs.[9]

Aside from the Single European Act's enormous economic implications, an intriguing issue is the extent to which it will contribute to Europe's political integration. Over the years, the political arm of the European Union, the European Parliament, has increased in prestige. Some believe that by the turn of the twentieth century, a high percentage, perhaps 80 percent, of domestic legislation will emerge from the Parliament. This alarms those who cherish their national sovereignty, and it may well be an exaggeration. There is little doubt, however, that if the Single European Act succeeds in economic integration, an enormous step will have been taken toward meaningful political integration in Europe.

International Regimes

The international system is often viewed as a system in anarchy—no world constitution, no enforcement power, no authoritative coordinating body. But for all the "anarchy," there appears to be an incredible amount of cooperation. One means of approaching what may in fact be "ordered anarchy" is the concept of international regimes. International regimes are normally treated in the field of international economics, where the greatest progress toward multilateralism has been made. Our discussion will highlight their importance to international politics. Because the concept of regimes is relatively new, there has been considerable latitude in defining it.[10] We define **international regimes** as rules, practices, and institutions in a particular functional area (such as environment, trade, human rights) that evolve and are accepted over time by countries in the international system.

The international trade regime is one of the

best known. The institutional core of this regime is, of course, the World Trade Organization (WTO), formerly known as the General Agreement on Tariffs and Trade (GATT). Around this institution (which began only as a set of negotiations), additional institutions have been formed (such as the U.N. Conference on Trade and Development). Rounds of trade negotiations have taken place; guidelines have been agreed on. Regional trade associations such as the European Economic Community and the European Free Trade Association have been born. Principles have been generally agreed on, such as the principle of *most-favored nation,* which states that the tariff preferences granted to one nation must be granted to all others exporting the same product. Taken together, these institutions, agreements, norms, and practices constitute the international trade regime.

The number of possible international regimes seems almost limitless—monetary, human rights, environmental, disaster relief, and so on. The underlying and most important assumption of regime theory is, of course, that regimes make a difference in the behavior of individual states.

Countries are inclined to abide by regime values and practices because it is in their self-interest to do so.

Systematic study of regimes has just begun. But such study affords an opportunity to view the world in a more organized fashion. This study also helps explain multilateral, integrative processes beyond a mere regional level.

THE MULTINATIONAL CORPORATION

Our treatment of the patterns of international behavior has focused on nation-states and their organizations. But the international system also includes a variety of other actors, from terrorist groups (the Japanese Red Army, Hammas) to international academic societies (the International Studies Association) and human rights organizations (Amnesty International). Of all these organizations, the most powerful over the past several decades has been the **multinational corporation (MNC)**. To illustrate the power of MNCs, Table 14.1 indicates that the total combined production of only five large corporations exceeds the total combined production of fifty-six countries.

Table 14.1 The Economic Power of Multinational Corporations

Combined Production (in millions of dollars) $505,508	Combined GDP[a] (in millions of dollars) $501,800			
General Motors	Mozambique	Cote d'Ivoire	Mauritania	Niger
Royal Dutch Shell	Somalia	Papua New Guinea	Egypt	Benin
Exxon	Bhutan	Peru	Senegal	Kenya
Ford	Bangladesh	Tunisia	Dominican Rep.	Togo
IBM	Uganda	Tanzania	Cameroon	Guinea
	Sierra Leone	Nepal	Ecuador	Lesotho
	Rwanda	Lao PDR	El Salvador	Bolivia
	Burkina Faso	Burundi	Jordan	Guatemala
	Pakistan	Madagascar	Jamaica	Morocco
	C. Africa R.	Nigeria	Ethiopia	Syria
	Sri Lanka	Rwanda	Chad	Congo
	Honduras	Haiti	Malawi	Paraguay
	Zimbabwe	Ghana	Zaire	Colombia
	Philippines	Zambia	Mali	Chile

Source: *Fortune Magazine,* July 29, 1991, p. 245; World Bank, *World Development Report 1992* (New York: Oxford University Press, 1992, published for the United Nations, World Bank).

[a]GDP, or gross domestic product, is the total output of goods and services for final use produced within a country.

The multinational corporation has been both extravagantly praised and blamed. It has been praised for its vision of a global market, its recognition of international economic interdependence, its ability to get things done, and its contribution to profits and economic development. On the other hand, it has been blamed for exploiting peoples and nations, interfering in the internal affairs of nations, and holding back human development.

The MNC's importance in the global economy is clear. But how does it affect security, liberty, justice, and welfare around the globe? Does it contribute to voluntary cooperation, humane accommodation, and peaceful resolution of conflicts?

Despite its global economic perspective, the multinational corporation lacks the political vision and power to resolve political conflicts or to promote liberty, justice, or welfare in the global community. Its primary business is, after all, to make profits for its stockholders. To the extent that profit making is compatible with the security, liberty, justice, and welfare of the peoples in the communities in which it does business, the multinational corporation may enhance these objectives, but they are not its primary objectives. Moreover, profit making may, in fact, lead the MNC to act contrary to those objectives. In addition, the multinational corporation is not a political organ; it is a private, elitist organization. And multinational corporations have often meddled in countries to the detriment of their independence and integrity and to the detriment of their poorer people. Chile is a good case in point. There is reliable evidence to support the charge that U.S. corporate actions (International Telephone and Telegraph, to be specific), in league with the Central Intelligence Agency, tried to prevent the democratic election of Salvador Allende Gossens in 1970.

Multinational corporations may play an important role in enhancing global prosperity, but nations will have to pass laws to guard against their abuses. Their activities will also have to be coordinated with larger developmental purposes, and their vision broadened to include the creation of a global mass market based on the fulfillment of human needs. Because multinational corporations are not philanthropic organizations and are not responsible political organizations, it may be asking too much to expect that these qualifications will be fulfilled.

THE SPECIAL ROLE OF DIPLOMACY

All patterns of accommodation in international politics and the global community call for diplomacy. **Diplomacy** is the art and skill of conducting relations between nations or between parties in politics; diplomacy may also be defined as the means, through discussion and negotiation, of achieving one side's objectives without violence and with a minimum of adverse consequences for the other side.

We single out diplomacy for special attention to underscore the requirements for statesmanship in the patterns we have discussed: the balance of power, nonalignment, domination, and multilateralism. In concentrating on these patterns we must not forget the human beings entrusted with defining and employing them.

Diplomacy evolved as a means for enabling nations to talk to one another about their common problems. Such talk permitted them to exchange information, make proposals, and negotiate. They could try to achieve their goals without recourse to war.

Because their tasks were held to be highly important, diplomats were given immunity—guarantees of safe conduct to, from, and at the site of negotiations. Out of this grew the principle of the safety and integrity of diplomatic embassies. The results of diplomatic negotiations were often recorded, frequently as treaties, and regarded with respect. Over time, diplomats acquired an ability to use language that minimized hostility, respected national differences, and consequently facilitated discourse and settlement.

Diplomats and statesmen also acquired skill in bargaining, persuading, and compromising. They recognized the value of flexibility and accommodation. They became adept at employing "carrots" and "sticks." Using these skills, they were often able to facilitate agreement.

Diplomacy, of course, can be used to enlighten or to deceive. Diplomatic negotiation can lead to peaceful settlement or to war. At its best, diplomacy seeks to maximize mutual security, liberty, justice, and welfare. To function at its best, diplomacy must be attuned to vital needs and fundamental interests. It must also recognize the realities of modern politics, particularly the catastrophic possibilities of modern war, the mutual suspicions of nations, and nations' increasing interdependence. And diplomats must also exercise prudent judgment.

Most diplomats follow, certainly in theory and often in practice, such commonsense maxims of diplomacy as the following:

• To make a fine choice yet decline to pay for it is folly.
• Fashioning your methods in the light of your ends is prudence.
• To believe you are more generous than you really are is hazardous.
• Asking only for immediate and tangible rewards is short-sighted.
• Safety lies in acting on the truth of the matter rather than the imagination of it.
• To talk as well as you perform makes sense.[11]

But how well have these maxims been applied since World War II? The record is mixed. Diplomatic negotiation has not achieved a peaceful united Korea. It has not brought full peace to Cambodia, which is troubled by the memory of civil war and a possible return of the violent and dreaded Khmer Rouge. A complete peaceful settlement still eludes the parties in the Israeli-Arab dispute. However, a significant advance did take place with the signing of the 1974 Camp David peace accords and testifies to a bold initiative by President Anwar el-Sadat of Egypt, a courageous response by Prime Minister Menachem Begin of Israel, and the persistent efforts of U.S. President Jimmy Carter. Similarly, the 1993 Oslo agreement between Israel and the Palestinians opens up the possibility of peace between long-contending parties in a land still troubled by outbursts of violence.

Diplomacy also gained success (as well as failure) in the process by which Western colonial powers and leaders in a host of new states—India, Pakistan, and Burma, for example—worked to achieve independence with a minimum of violence. Decolonization has not, of course, been an entirely peaceful process, as disputes in Indonesia, Vietnam, Algeria, the Congo, and Angola testify. Yet farsighted and prudent diplomats have frequently eased this remarkable birth of new nations. The transition to majority rule in Zimbabwe (formerly Rhodesia) in 1980, after years of conflict and white minority rule, is certainly a tribute to diplomats such as former British Foreign Secretary Lord Carrington. Similarly, although there was some violent struggle in Namibia (formerly Southwest Africa), it finally achieved independence in 1990, after years of arduous diplomatic activity. In 1996 at Wright Patterson Air Force Base in Dayton, Ohio, the United States, backed by the deployment of a powerful NATO peacekeeping force (IFOR), undertook an extraordinary set of very difficult negotiations with the principal protagonists of the Bosnian conflict—the Bosnian Muslims, Bosnian Serbs, Serbia, and Croatia—and succeeded in hammering out a settlement to the war. Whether the peace will hold remains to be seen. However, given the deep regional hatreds and the ferocity of the Bosnian war, to have gotten the parties together to talk, much less to agree on ending the war, is widely conceded to be a major diplomatic achievement.

Prudent diplomacy must also be given credit for East-West agreements aimed at a ban on nuclear weapons in space, a nuclear nonproliferation treaty, a Strategic Arms Limitation Treaty (SALT I), an Intermediate Nuclear Force Treaty, and the Strategic Arms Reduction Treaty (START). These diplomatic efforts must be mentioned even as we recognize the failure of more comprehensive and genuine disarmament efforts.

Similarly, prudent diplomacy must be credited with reestablishing American/Chinese relations and seating the People's Republic of China at the United Nations (1971). These developments—like other successful diplomatic efforts—advanced the vital interests of the nations involved. Yet it took courage and skill to achieve them. Successful efforts most often highlight the value of a diplomacy divested of the crusading spirit, a foreign policy understood in terms of farsighted national interest, and a prudent willingness to compromise on nonvital issues. Wise and patient diplomacy offers the possibility, not always seized, of a more genuine peace through accommodation.

ASSESSMENT OF THE PATTERNS

And so we return to our tentative guiding hypothesis that, despite some successes, current international patterns do not yet adequately protect the vital needs and fundamental interests of all nations and peoples. The global community lacks agreement on fundamentals, except perhaps about the horrors of an all-out nuclear war. Although the United Nations has emerged as a forum for vital needs and interests, establishing priorities, and legitimizing decisions, it was not intended to be, and does not function as, a global government. Other patterns of politics—such as working through alliances in the balance of power or through nonalignment—have achieved only partial success.

The balance of power probably prevented an American-Soviet war—a mutually devastating World War III fought with nuclear weapons. Yet the peace so secured for forty-five years was fragile and was purchased at a heavy price. This was the price of armaments, the domination of Eastern Europe for virtually that entire period, and conflicts in Berlin and Cuba that threatened to escalate into World War III. There was also the price of a worldwide struggle for power that was intertwined with drives for national independence and unity and that turned much of the developing world into a violent battleground. Thus, it cannot be said that the vital needs and fundamental interests of Americans or Russians—

or of other peoples and nations—were protected without enormous cost and risk.

In 1996, with the end of the Cold War, the world may have taken a step back from the nuclear abyss. But although the United States and the former Soviet Union have stepped back, there is still the disturbing possibility of widespread proliferation of these terrible weapons of mass destruction. As long as these weapons remain in arsenals of the United States, Russia, the Ukraine, the People's Republic of China, Israel, France, the United Kingdom, and India, and as long as countries like Pakistan, Iraq, and North Korea seek to acquire them, the possibility that sections of the world will turn into nuclear battlefields is real.

The disturbing image of millions of people dead, cities destroyed, ecological systems irreparably damaged, and widespread genetic harm to all species makes people ask how much protection the balance of terror offers. Neither security nor liberty nor justice nor welfare can be safeguarded for any country as long as nuclear holocaust remains a grim possibility.

Will wise diplomacy, in all nations and in all regional and global organizations, be dedicated to preventing this possibility from becoming an actuality? No one can say for sure. But as long as countries insist on arming themselves with weapons of mass destruction, and as long as delivery systems keep an eye on enemy targets, the possibility of nuclear holocaust must be faced.

The patterns of international politics worked out by many Third World nations must also be critically scrutinized. Nations that practice nonalignment still try to avoid entanglement in the major alliances and polarizing conflicts that plague the world. But during much of the Cold War, even though developing nations gave lip service to peaceful coexistence and genuine neutrality in East-West conflicts, they did not always honor those standards in fact. This was particularly true when alleged vital interests of a Third World country were threatened by regional dispute. Moreover, nonalignment has not successfully advanced the cause of disarmament among Third World nations, and this failure adversely affects welfare and economic and social justice in such countries.

So our assessment of balance of power and nonalignment does not offer great hope. Does multilateralism offer more hope—and less risk? Our answer is a qualified yes. The United Nations has set laudable standards for peace, liberty, and economic and social justice and, through its varied approaches to peace, has achieved modest success in a number of cases. It defeated military aggression in two important instances (Korea, and Iraq's invasion of Kuwait). The United Nations has promoted peace in Indonesia and Kashmir and has kept the superpowers from confronting each other in the Congo, the Middle East, Cyprus, and parts of South Asia. The United Nations has helped dozens of Third World countries advance from colonies to independent nations and has helped them fight disease, illiteracy, and famine. It has aided the economic development of many new states. It has provided a valuable forum for airing global problems and has played an increasingly important role in such places as Iran, Iraq, Afghanistan, Angola, Cambodia, Namibia, and Central America.

Despite these modest successes, the United Nations did not deal effectively with East-West tensions or facilitate political accommodation that might lead to real peace and disarmament in the world.

The European Union has taken significant steps to overcome historic military struggles among its members and to advance mutual economic and political union. It remains to be seen if its very promising results can be successfully extended to the rest of Europe.

Economic integration as currently practiced, we must note, suffers from its inherently limited approach. This limited approach promotes small successes—for example, a common market in a given region—but has been unable to solve larger economic and political problems, including the maldistribution of wealth, global environmental degradation, and massive violations of human rights. Whether the further evolution of international regimes will begin to solve these problems is open to conjecture.

What of the promise and peril of the multinational corporation? The multinational corporation, although sometimes praised for a global vision that transcends narrow national interests, remains devoted primarily to profits, not to people and politics. It lacks the economic or political motivation or the power to unite diverse interests and peoples for mutual prosperity (including that of the least free). The multinational corporation lacks the ability to forge a political community that can grapple successfully with world tensions.

CONCLUSION

The end of the Cold War has brought enormous change to the international system. With major shifts in the distribution of power, forces of both integration and fragmentation are clearly evident. It remains to be seen how the international community will respond to these unfolding forces.

With the qualification that some forces of multilateralism—an enhanced United Nations, greater economic integration, and the continuing evolution of global regimes—have had salutary consequences, we must nevertheless conclude that current international patterns do not adequately protect the vital needs and fundamental interests of all peoples and nations. Can we do better? We will return to this question in Part IV. In the meantime, we can benefit from a fuller consideration of models and patterns of political decision making.

ANNOTATED BIBLIOGRAPHY

Allison, Graham T., ed. *Rethinking America's Security: Beyond the Cold War to New World Order.* Boston: Norton, 1992. Presents a first-rate collection of essays discussing the post–Cold War world.

Barber, Benjamin. *Jihad vs. McWorld.* New York: Times Books, 1995. Thought-provokingly, book posits conflict between two powerful forces: an integrative capitalist global economy and the return of a fragmentary ethnic and religious movements.

Barston, R. P. *Modern Diplomacy.* New York: Longmans, 1988. Posits that modern diplomacy has undergone a number of major changes in recent years: (1) a broadening perspective beyond the narrow confines of political issues, (2) an increase in the number of people practicing diplomacy, and (3) major shifts in the content and methods of diplomacy.

Bennett, A Leroy. *International Organizations: Principles and Issues,* 6th ed. Englewood Cliffs, N.J.: Prentice-Hall, 1994. Presents useful information on the United Nations: its organization, processes, and history.

Craig, Gordon A., and George, Alexander L. *Force and Statecraft,* 3rd ed. New York: Oxford University Press, 1995. Describes the evolution of the international system from the emergence of the modern state to the present. An excellent survey of the lessons of diplomatic history.

Dougherty, James E., and Pfaltzgraff, Robert I. *Contending Theories of International Relations,* 3rd ed. New York: Harper & Row, 1990. Provides a comprehensive, well-organized, and lucid survey of major theories of international relations.

Keohane, Robert. *Local Commons and Global Interdependence: Heterogeneity and Cooperation in Two Domains.* Beverly Hills: Sage, 1995. Offers thoughtful discourse on the rapidly changing international post–Cold War environment.

Krasner, Stephen D., ed. *International Regimes.* Ithaca, N.Y.: Cornell University Press, 1983. Although regime theory has fallen a bit out of favor, nevertheless stands as a benchmark collection of articles.

Mingst, Karen A., and Karns, Margaret P. *The United Nations in the Post–Cold War Era.* Boulder, Colo.: Westview, 1995. Presents a timely and well-received treatise on the problems plaguing the United Nations in the 1990s and offers recommendations for addressing those concerns.

Morgenthau, Hans J. *Politics Among Nations: The Struggle for Power and Peace,* 6th rev. ed. Kenneth Thompson, ed. New York: McGraw, 1985. Articulates the position of the most influential realist in international politics. Morgenthau strongly defended the standard of an enlightened national interest.

Poulsen, Thomas. *Nations and States: A Geographic Background to World Affairs.* Englewood Cliffs, N.J.: Prentice-Hall, 1995. Offers an excellent introduction to the basic tenets of political geography.

Riemer, Neal. *Creative Breakthroughs in Politics.* Westport, Conn: Praeger, 1996. See Chapter 6, "European Union: Beyond War, Economic Malaise, and Political Turmoil via Transnational Integration."

Stoessinger, John G. *Nations in Darkness: China, Russia and America,* 5th ed. New York: McGraw-Hill, 1990. Provides a highly readable analysis of how perception has influenced relations between the United States, China, and Russia.

Waltz, Kenneth. *Man, the State, and War: A Theoretical Analysis.* New York: Columbia University Press, 1959. Presents classic statement on the cause of war.

SUGGESTIONS FOR FURTHER READING

Gilpin, Robert. *The Political Economy of International Relations.* Princeton, N.J.: Princeton University Press, 1987.

Keohane, Robert O., ed. *Neorealism and Its Critics.* New York: Columbia University Press, 1986.

Riemer, Neal, Simon, Douglas W., Messmer, William, Rhone, Richard, Rodes, Robert, Bull, Vivian, and Chatfield, Donald. *New Thinking and Developments in International Politics: Opportunities and Dangers.* Lanham, Md.: University Press of America, 1991.

Spanier, John. *Games Nations Play,* 7th ed. Washington, D.C.: Congressional Quarterly Press, 1990.

Thompson, Kenneth W. *Masters of International Thought: Major Twentieth-Century Theorists and the World Crisis.* Baton Rouge: Louisiana State University Press, 1980.

GLOSSARY TERMS

anticolonialism
balance of power
collective security
detente
diplomacy
disarmament
domination
European Union
functionalism
grand debate
hegemonic
international regimes
multilateralism
multilanational corporation (MNC)
national interest
nonalignment
peaceful settlement
peacekeeping
power
preventive diplomacy
trusteeship

DECISION MAKING IN POLITICS

So far in our search for a science of politics we have explored (1) the political values of political actors and (2) domestic and international patterns of cooperation, accommodation, and conflict. In doing so, we have already shed some light on decision making and public policy. In Chapter 11, for example, we explored the gap between professed values and the values actually embodied in public policy. We were, moreover, concerned with the reasons for this gap; these reasons require that we consider the logic of public policy decisions and especially the key question: Why are decisions made as they are?

In Chapters 12 and 13 we touched on the role of voters, interest groups, the media, political parties, and governmental actors in working out patterns of cooperation, accommodation, and conflict. These patterns also involve decision making and throw light on the question of how and why political actors make decisions.

In Chapter 14 we explored patterns in international politics and some of the reasons for decisions within the framework of foreign policies such as the balance of power.

Chapters 11 through 14 also built on our introduction to decision making in Chapter 1, "Games Politicians Play," and Chapter 2, "Politics and Choice." These games and choices throw considerable light on the who, what, how, and why of politics.

Similar light on these questions was provided by our discussion of political philosophy and ideology in Part II. For example, in our treatment of liberal democracy, communism, and democratic socialism, we focused on a number of elements that affect both decision making and public policy: cardinal values, political principles, assessments of the struggle for power,

307

and competing alternatives. And in our summaries of the great political philosophers, we focused on the problems that gave rise to their responses and on their ethical, empirical, and prudential "proximate solutions."

We have thus already touched on a number of ingredients crucial to decision making and public policy. We can now attempt, somewhat more systematically, to organize our understanding of decision making in politics.

We are searching for a science of decision making in politics—a most difficult task. As social scientists, we are intrigued by significant empirical problems in the domain of decision making. For example, at varying levels, and in varying political contexts, what values, what understanding of political phenomena, and what grasp of public policy alternatives actually influence decision making? How adequate is the machinery available to decision makers? What are the consequences of our public policy decisions?

In this chapter we may not be able to deal with all these questions, but we can make a start. We will leave a fuller treatment of the great issues to Part IV. Here, however, we can address a key question: *Which guiding model best illuminates our scientific exploration of decision making in politics?*

Our tentative hypothesis is this: To do justice to decision making in politics, among all actors and at all levels, we have to synthesize at least five decision-making models. A **model** is a simplified version of what goes on in the real world; it highlights the important elements in the subject of interest. The first part of this chapter focuses on five decision-making models: (1) the rational actor, (2) the political actor, (3) the organizational actor, (4) the elitist actor, and (5) the idiosyncratic actor. These models are not mutually exclusive. Some elements may be found in more than one model. But the models emphasize the importance of different factors in, and different approaches to, decision making.

The final section in this chapter will address several important queries: Is one model more

helpful than another in explaining decision making? Does one model make more sense in domestic politics and another in international politics? Does one model do a better job of explaining decision making in democratic and developed countries, another in communist countries, still a third in developing countries? Is it possible to integrate all five models in one masterful synthesis?

THE RATIONAL ACTOR MODEL

In the rational actor model of decision making, decision makers seek to accomplish four tasks:

1. They consciously seek to identify the problem that confronts them. They especially want to understand the problem in terms of its relevance to, or effect on, their values, purposes, and goals. They are particularly concerned with protecting the national interest.
2. They try to take into account the key factors in the political (and general) environment that bear on the problem—factors that may facilitate or limit their efforts to fulfill their goals.
3. They endeavor to critically examine alternative courses of action designed, in the light of political realities, to address the problem and thus to maximize their values.
4. They try to make a choice that will wisely maximize benefits and minimize costs.

Problem Identification

Problems can often best be identified if they are put in question form. Thus, in the 1996 American presidential election, the key problem facing voters was, Which presidential candidate should I vote for and why? Or, Which candidate, supporting which set of policies, will best advance the national interest? A rational president and rational members of Congress must ask, Which policies will enable the nation to protect its vital interests? to obtain an adequate defense? to achieve a balance between income and expenditures? to stimulate employment at good wages? to achieve more comprehensive health coverage? to encourage economic investment and enterprise? to complete the process of humane welfare reform? to enhance education, fight crime, and protect social security?

And how are sometimes conflicting equities to be balanced? Are both budget and tax cuts an option? Cutting the budget may help the nation balance income and expenditures, but it reduces government income and may harm people who depend on expenditures for social services. A big defense budget may conflict with a balanced budget. As a champion of liberty, should the United States vigorously safeguard international human rights? If so, where? and at what price? How does the government balance respect for environmental standards against the adverse effect these standards may have on profitability and jobs? In all such matters, rational decision makers pose the general problem and then seek to refine it. As they identify the relevant issues, conflicts, and difficulties, they are better able to formulate the exact problem.

Other countries face comparable problems that tax their decision-making ability. Can Russia balance the introduction of free-market practices with adequate protection of vital social services? How can a host of countries—France, Germany, Britain, Sweden—retain generous welfare benefits and still balance their budgets? What policies will bring peace to Israel and its neighbors?

Political problems—involving, as they always do, people, power, and passion—are innumerable, disturbing, and challenging. They are intimately related to such values as national security, human liberty, social justice, and economic welfare. The task is to understand the problem clearly in terms of the values that decision makers deem most worthy.

The Environment of Politics

Problems do not occur in a vacuum. They emerge out of an often troublesome environment that shapes their character. What do people or interests or nations want? Which factors influence what political actors can do or get? These factors—including information, money, support, time, geography, and military, economic, and political power—may either facilitate or limit responses to political problems.

It is difficult to make decisions when not all the facts are known and when future consequences of current actions cannot be accurately measured.

How to deal with a bothersome deficit has perplexed U.S. presidents. Excessive deficits penalize future generations. They harm the economy by siphoning money away from capital markets. It would seem that some combination of budget cuts and increased revenue should be instituted. But what combination? As a president addresses this complicated issue, it becomes obvious that there are no easy answers. How much should the federal budget be cut, and where—defense? social programs? What are the immediate and long-term consequences of cutting defense or major social welfare programs?

A variety of factors complicate the ability to answer these questions. These factors may involve, for example, a sudden military or economic crisis in international affairs, midterm congressional or presidential elections, or major natural disasters.

Similarly, other factors bearing on problems such as arms control, human rights, poverty, and ecological health must also be understood. For example, the breakup of the Soviet Union complicates the control of atomic weapons. In the political communities that were once Yugoslavia, war and "ethnic cleansing" have produced a bitter legacy (of death, forced migration, rape, and hatred) that now challenges the attempt to reconstruct a Bosnia composed of distrustful Muslims, Christian Serbs, and Croats who once lived together in harmony. Another example is the modern world's taste for oil and automobiles, which pollute the air and, when big oil spills at sea occur, the world's oceans and shorelines.

Clearly, leaders will be better equipped to pose alternatives and make wise choices as they increase their understanding of the relevant factors in politics.

Alternative Possibilities

Rational political actors attempt to state, and critically examine, the strengths and weaknesses of alternative courses of action. Thus, in the American presidential election of 1996, rational voters sought to assess the pros and cons of the policies of Bill Clinton and Robert Dole. Presumably, by weighing favorable and unfavorable arguments on an ethical, personal, political, and economic scale, they could arrive at a sensible judgment.

Comparable calculations enter into the decision-making process in the national government. According to some critics, the American government can achieve economic prosperity by encouraging freer trade and investment in edu-

In 1996 the American public weighed the pros and cons of the two major presidential candidates to come to a decision on how to vote.

cation and technology. It can reduce the federal deficit by cutting the defense budget, certain entitlement programs, and bureaucratic fat and by selectively raising certain taxes (such as those on the wealthy or on gasoline). Other critics, however, may have a different view of how to create economic prosperity, increase employment, or achieve a leaner government. They may want to leave the economy to its own laws; they may be loath to cut the military budget; they may strongly oppose new taxes; and they would more deeply cut key entitlement programs such as social security, medicare, and welfare.

In protecting international human rights, presidents can rely primarily on "quiet diplomacy," publicity, political pressure, or economic sanctions, reserving military action for rare and carefully selected cases, involving just humanitarian intercession. In choosing their course of action, they consider the likely consequences of the policy as it relates to their values—protecting national security, safeguarding human rights, and enhancing the moral reputation of the United States. They will, of course, also consider the costs and benefits of their course of action.

Other nations and decision makers presumably act in a comparably rational manner as they examine the strengths and weaknesses of alternative policies.

Wise Judgment

According to the rational actor model, choices will be reached after careful balancing of costs and benefits to ensure that preferred values will be maximized. Thus, the voter decides that, on balance, Candidate X is preferable to Candidate Y. Congress concludes that Policy A is preferable to Policy B in dealing with economic growth, job creation, the budget deficit, tax cuts, health care, welfare reform, the environment, or civil rights.

The rational actor model thus assumes that decision makers are *conscious, careful, calculating* people who face problems sensibly. They know exactly what their values, purposes, and goals are and what is at stake in the problem that confronts them. They are, or try to become, cognizant of the key environmental factors that bear on their problem. They are able to set forth and debate alternative courses of action. And they have the ability, after careful analysis of costs and benefits, to make a wise judgment that, in light of their values, will maximize benefits and minimize costs.

But is this the way decisions are really made? Or do other models suggest a different answer?

THE POLITICAL ACTOR MODEL

According to the political actor model:

1. Decision makers are involved in a struggle for power, and decisions emerge from that struggle for power.
2. Decision making involves numerous political actors with diverse values, purposes, and goals; diverse interests; and diverse perceptions of relevant political realities, alternatives, costs, and benefits.
3. Decision making necessitates bargaining, accommodation, and consensus and controversy, conflict, bluff, threat, even deceit.
4. Reaching the key decision in politics is most often the result of bargaining among political interests.

Politics as a Struggle for Power

According to the political actor model, decision making is not essentially rational deliberation, as depicted in the rational actor model. In this second model, decision making does not involve well-thought-out values, careful understanding of environmental factors, orderly presentation of selected alternatives, or deliberate choices best designed to maximize preferred values or advance the national interest. Rather, decision making involves a struggle for purpose and power among a number of political actors, some more powerful or influential or strategically placed than others. This struggle calls for bargaining, negotiating, and compromising. The great Greek political philosophers Plato and Aristotle saw politics as a struggle for power. So did Karl Marx. Twentieth-century students of American politics have also

seen politics in this light. Thus, a keen student of congressional decision making, Bertram Gross, titled one of his books *The Legislative Struggle*. Another scholar, Roger Hilsman, talked about the foreign policy of President John F. Kennedy as "a story of battles." Hans J. Morgenthau subtitled his book *Politics Among Nations* "The Struggle for Power and Peace."

The Plurality and Diversity of Players, Values, and Interests

According to Graham T. Allison, in this model decisions are not made by a "unitary actor but rather [by] many actors as players." These players "focus not on a single strategic issue but on many diverse intranational problems." They "act in terms of no consistent set of strategic objectives but rather according to various conceptions of national, organizational, and personal goals." They "make government decisions not by a single, rational choice but by the pulling and hauling that is politics."[1]

Not even the president of the United States is a monolithic commander who can simply order an action and see it effectively carried out. President Truman's comment in contemplating Eisenhower's taking over the presidency is very apt: "He'll sit here and he'll say 'Do this! Do that!' And nothing will happen. Poor Ike—it won't be a bit like the army."

Allison gives us a helpful summary of the many players involved in what he calls "the national security game":

For example, in the U.S. government the players include *chiefs*: The president, the secretaries of state, defense, and treasury, the director of the CIA, the Joint Chiefs of Staff, and since 1961, the special assistant for national security affairs; *staffers*: the immediate staff of each Chief; *indians*: the political appointees and permanent government officials within each of the departments and agencies; and *ad hoc players*: actors in the wider governmental game (especially "congressional influentials"), members of the press, spokesmen for important interest groups (especially the "bipartisan foreign policy establishment" in and out of Congress), and surrogates for each of these groups. Other members of the Congress, press, interest groups, and public form concentric circles around the central arena—circles that demarcate limits within which the game is played.[2]

This model emphasizes the many diverse goals and values that must be reconciled in decision making, the many competing people associated with key alternatives, and the power of key actors. Advocates of this model maintain that the power of key political actors is as important to the final decision as the attractiveness of their goals or the persuasiveness of their arguments.

The Crucial Role of Bargaining

Decisions are not made calmly by isolated, rational players pursuing a priestlike dedication to a clear-cut national interest. Rather, they are made amidst conflict and controversy by political actors who bargain and negotiate, bluff and threaten. Political actors may compromise, sidestep, or paper over conflicts. They may iron out or ignore disagreements. They may threaten or seek to seduce their opponents.

Moreover, decision making in politics is characterized much more by incremental (step-by-step) "muddling through" than by deliberate, rational choices in accord with a well-thought-out plan or grand design. What seems a coherent policy may really be hundreds of diverse bargains.

According to advocates of this model, bargaining characterizes all of politics. We may be able to recognize bargaining more clearly in the Congress, but it also characterizes the presidency. And it is also a prominent, if neglected, feature of the Supreme Court. Moreover, bargaining goes on among voters and, certainly, among interest groups.

Decisions as "Political Results"

Decisions are not, then, coolly calculated to maximize preferred values or to satisfy abstract standards such as the public interest or national interest. Rather, they are the result of conflicts among political actors with competing interests. A prominent school of political scientists, whose point of view is illustrated by the influential work of David Truman, has emphasized this aspect of decision making in national politics. Similarly, Gabriel Almond and other keen students of international politics have maintained

that American foreign policy must also be perceived as a result of pluralist politics.

Graham Allison sums up this view of decision making as the outcome of the pulling and hauling of key political actors and interests as follows:

> The decisions and actions of governments are intranational political resultants in the sense that what happens is not chosen as a solution to a problem but rather results from compromise, conflict, and confusion of officials with diverse interests and unequal influence; political in the sense that the activity from which decision and actions emerge is best characterized as bargaining along regularized channels among individual members of the government.[3]

However persuasive the political actor model is, it does not exhaust the range of empirical possibilities. We now turn to a third model.

THE ORGANIZATIONAL ACTOR MODEL

The organizational actor model affirms the organization's crucial role in decision making:

1. The model stresses the importance of the organization's vital interests, standard operating procedures, and capabilities.
2. It emphasizes how the organization sees problems, obtains information, shapes alternatives, assesses costs and benefits, and makes choices.
3. It stresses the organization's important role in political bargaining, accommodation, and consensus. These points are interrelated. We analyze them separately to underscore their importance.

Organizational Interests, Procedures, and Capabilities

Organizations, both inside and outside government, seek to protect their vital interests. Inevitably, they favor decisions that enhance those interests. For example, almost all government agencies—whether the Department of Defense or the Department of Health and Human Services—seek adequate budgets; without them, they say, they cannot fulfill their missions. They argue vigorously that they need money to defend the nation, improve education, increase good housing, and the like. Similarly, they oppose policies that adversely affect their interests. This same logic of protection holds for organizations outside government (such as organizations of industrialists, farmers, or workers) that are vitally interested in certain policies and decisions.

Government organizations make decisions in the very process of carrying out decisions; their operating procedures are therefore highly important. **Standard operating procedures** determine governmental priorities, speed of response, and how services are delivered. For example, these procedures may determine whose income tax return is audited and how thoroughly, whose safety regulations are inspected and how carefully, whose civil rights are protected, and in what way the military responds to suspicious "hostile" missiles, planes, and ships.

The capability of government organizations also affects decision making and public policy. Their perspective is most often partial and incomplete, their approach limited and cautious. They do best in handling familiar routines. They seek solutions that are "good enough" rather than solutions that maximize benefits. For example, armies are always better at fighting the last war than the next war. Bureaucracies, in general, find safety in familiar process; they avoid uncertainty. Consequently, they often lack imagination, the ability to deal with new circumstances, and the courage to break through to new choices.

How Organizational Life Affects Decision Making

Organizations view problems from their own special angle. For example, those in the military worry less about the nation's overkill capacity, the impact of the arms race on social priorities, and the deficit than about their ability to defend the nation against actual and potential dangers. The Department of the Treasury worries about inflation; the Department of Labor about unemployment. These limited perspectives inevitably affect organizations' understanding of problems.

These perspectives also clearly influence an organization's understanding of relevant information and significant alternatives, its assessment of costs and benefits, and thus its final decision. Depending on one's perspective, this may be helpful or harmful. Thus, even within an organization such as the State Department, the section concerned with human rights will see things differently than the unit concerned with safeguarding national security. The human rights people will wish to protect human rights around the globe and will more readily endorse publicizing violations and imposing sanctions against offending countries. They will see protecting international human rights as advancing, not harming, national security. Thus, they will opt for a more vigorous, outspoken human rights policy.

In general, organizations are not farsighted, creative, or flexible. America's failure to be prepared for the Japanese attack on Pearl Harbor on December 7, 1941, is a case in point. The U.S. Navy did not carry out long-distance reconnaissance of Japanese activities around Pearl Harbor. The U.S. Army, which had focused on the threat of subversive activity, was woefully unprepared for the actual Japanese air attack. Central coordination of navy and army intelligence did not exist.

An organization's lack of creative long-term planning, and even imaginative short-term problem solving, is often explained by its dedication to its own "life"—its concern for its own budget, personnel, and territory. The struggle of organizations to protect their central concern leads to our next point.

Organizational Bargaining

Organizations are important actors in political bargaining. They are concerned with who gets what (money), who does what (leadership and personnel), and where power is exercised (territory). Thus, they are driven by monetary, leadership, and territorial imperatives. Conflicts on these matters within and between organizations significantly influence decisions about dealing with other countries, fighting illegal drugs, coping with the AIDS epidemic, and a host of other issues. Here, of course, the political actor model and the organizational actor model overlap.

The State Department and the Defense Department may not see eye to eye on disarmament. The Coast Guard, the FBI, the Drug Enforcement Agency, the U.S. Air Force, and the U.S. Navy may disagree on how to handle the War on Drugs. The Department of Health and Human Services may have a different strategy on AIDS than the Centers for Disease Control in Atlanta or the Office of Management and Budget.

In working out any given policy—say, America's response to Chinese human rights violations (whether in Tibet, or in the 1989 massacre of dissident students in China's Tiananmen Square), to Chinese threats to Taiwan, or to Chinese violations of copyright agreements—opposing interests have to be satisfied. And in this process considerable bargaining goes on. For example, the State Department would have to be persuaded that America's response would not jeopardize its hopes for long-term diplomatic relations. The Department of Commerce would have to be persuaded that economic sanctions

against the People's Republic of China are worth the cost to American business and balance of payments. The Defense Department would be concerned that U.S. strategic interests are safeguarded.

THE ELITIST ACTOR MODEL

The elitist actor model affirms that

1. Elites make the really significant decisions in politics.
2. They do so to protect their own self-interest and power.

So to understand political decision making, we must identify these elites as well as the vested interests and economic, political, and social power they seek to guard. Students of the elitist actor model believe they are more realistic than political scientists who are tuned in to the other models. Elite theorists are persuaded that they are asking the really important questions in politics: Who really rules? Who really benefits?

The Pervasiveness of Elite Rule

Proponents maintain that basic decisions in politics and government—as in all large organizations—are always made by a small, self-interested, knowledgeable, and active group of insiders: the **elite**. Proponents of this model recognize an "iron law of oligarchy."[4] The very nature of large organizations—and government is certainly a large organization—makes this law of elite rule inevitable. There may, of course, be a rotation of such elites—that is, leadership may change from time to time or even from issue to issue—but there will always be an elite in charge of decision making.

This view asserts that decision making cannot really be democratic. It takes interest, intelligence, money, skill, and time to make decisions, and these qualities are to be found only in a tiny minority: the governing elite. Such elite rule is not restricted to authoritarian or totalitarian regimes—left or right, communist or fascist—or military regimes or old-fashioned aristocratic

Bureaucratic bargaining is the essence of the organizational actor model.

"Now as I see it, in order to get a sound antidrug policy in place, all we have to do is simply coordinate the interests of your various agencies—Office of the President, DEA, ATF, CIA, FBI, FDA, IRS, Defense, Immigration and Naturalization, Health and Human Services, Housing and Urban Development, Education, Commerce, Transportation, Justice, and 50 state law enforcement agencies . . . no problem!"

regimes. It characterizes *all* governments, no matter how democratic they say they are. The United States is no exception.

Thus, in the United States "a small number of persons allocate values for society." These people are "drawn disproportionately from the upper socioeconomic strata of society." Nonelite individuals move only slowly into the governing circle and only after they have "accepted the basic elite consensus." Public policy reflects "the prevailing values of the elite." In the United States these values include belief in private property, free enterprise, limited government, and individual liberty.[5]

Historically, in authoritarian regimes of the far left or far right, a communist or fascist elite has clearly been in charge. In the old Soviet Union or in China today, this elite has been made up of top leaders of the Communist party. In Nazi Germany, the leaders of the Nazi party constituted this elite. In many developing countries a similar pattern of elite rule takes the form of a military junta, a small group of extraordinarily wealthy and powerful families, or a dictator.

Self-Interested Rule

It is important to know not only who rules (and how) but who benefits (and how). Here scientific judgment among students of elitism ceases to be unanimous. Some are hostile to elite rule as being undemocratic and procapitalist; others see elite rule as efficient and wisely aristocratic, even favorable to civil rights and economic well-being.

Marxists argue that a bourgeois elite rules in capitalist countries. This elite does not represent the interests of the overwhelming majority of people, who are workers. Rather, the governing elite—reflecting the dominant influence of capitalism in all aspects of life—represents an interlocking directorate of industrialists, bankers, corporate lawyers, politicians, and high-ranking military officers working hand in glove with the active or passive support of educational, religious, and media leaders. Key policy decisions are designed to protect capitalism, private

property, and corporate profits. Those who benefit from government decisions are the capitalist "haves." Those who suffer under such regimes are the proletarian "have-nots." The exploitation of workers and peasants in most Third World countries, Marxists argue, can be understood in terms of imperialism, colonialism, domination, and dependence.[6]

Other students of elite rule argue that such governance characterizes all authoritarian regimes. Historically, the Politburo—the top leadership of the now defunct Communist party in what was the Soviet Union—may have claimed to rule as representative of the people, but it was actually ruling on behalf of the Communist party elite. Such rule, moreover, perpetuated undemocratic domination, violations of human rights, flawed economic policies (guns instead of butter), and foreign policies contrary to the wishes of the people (interventions in Afghanistan, Czechoslovakia, and Hungary). A similar critique applies to the Communist party in China, North Korea, and Cuba, and to other authoritarian left-wing regimes.

Elite theorists also sharply criticize right-wing regimes as perpetuating military dictatorships and as contemptuous of human rights. These theorists maintain that such regimes often use anticommunism as an excuse for repressing even peaceful opposition and for sustaining a capitalist, or feudal, economic system that exploits workers and peasants and continues the cycle of poverty and repression. Such regimes may benefit a wealthy minority of the native elite and their foreign friends, but they do little or nothing for most of the people.

Still other students of elite rule note that not all elites are intellectually or morally backward. They cite the positive, humanitarian, modernizing role played by many elites. These groups would be Thomas Jefferson's "natural aristocrats," prominent, for example, in shaping a democratic future for the new American Republic. They have carried Europe forward in a wide range of activities, including the rebirth of democratic institutions in post–World War II Germany, the growth of Western European Union, and the end of colonialism. They are also the leaders in modern America who are more responsive than the general public to civil rights for African Americans and greater freedom for women. The motivation of such leaders may spring from genuine humanitarian considerations, or from the calculated, broadly self-interested view that the liberal Establishment must consistently pursue the principle of freedom in order to stay in power.

The leadership role of such enlightened elites, which some scholars consider atypical, leads us to consider yet another form of decision making, the idiosyncratic actor model.

THE IDIOSYNCRATIC ACTOR MODEL

The idiosyncratic actor model stresses the crucial role of the decision maker's unique personality. This model emphasizes both the (1) destructive role and (2) creative role that leadership has in decision making. Given the tremendous impact of leaders such as V. I. Lenin, Joseph Stalin, Adolf Hitler, Franklin Delano Roosevelt, Winston Churchill, Mao Zedong, Charles de Gaulle, Mohandas Gandhi, Martin Luther King, Jr., and Mikhail Gorbachev, the political scientist must pay careful attention to the role of personality in politics.

This model highlights the importance of personal qualities. Such qualities may be neutral (intuition, critical acumen, and speech), positive (charisma and compassion), or negative (demagoguery, ruthlessness, and dogmatism). Historical experience suggests that personal qualities can play either a destructive or a creative part in political decision making.

The Destructive Decision Maker

Joseph Stalin and Adolf Hitler are two frightful examples of the destructive decision maker. Saddam Hussein is a more contemporary example.

Stalin's crafty, ruthless, paranoid leadership transformed the Soviet Union into a modern Communist state. Stalin's continuous purges of enemies on the left and right, his liquidation of the kulaks (prosperous peasants), his decimation of military leaders, and his savage treatment of millions of rank-and-file citizens left the Soviet Union in a weakened condition to repel the brutal Nazi onslaught in June 1941. Yet because of, or in spite of, Stalin's leadership, the Soviet people and armies, with great courage and at great cost, did turn back the invader. But did the Soviet Union's achievements, and the particular shape that communism took under Stalin, result from powerful forces over which Stalin had no control? Or did his personal decisions, rooted in a paranoid personality, shape the character of Soviet communism? These questions cannot be answered definitively. But the damage Stalin did to his own people and others requires a serious investigation of the possibilities. It is particularly important to study the factors that *limit* the exercise of power.

Hitler is another case in point. Would the German state have done what it did—brutally attack its European neighbors, barbarically destroy Europe's Jews—if Hitler had died in 1933? Would Germany's fate have been different if Hitler had trusted his generals more and his intuition less? if Hitler had not been driven by a megalomanic passion, symbolized in the expression *Deutschland über alles?* Again, these questions cannot be answered decisively. But Hitler's personality—his depraved mind, dogmatic convictions, political and military intuitions, and oratorical gifts—made a vital difference.

Saddam Hussein of Iraq must also be considered a destructive decision maker. His brutal murders of those he suspected of domestic disloyalty or political opposition, his repression of Kurds and Shiites in Iraq, his destructive seven-year war against Iran, and his aggression against neighboring Kuwait certainly suggest megalomania, paranoia, cruelty, and irrationality of a terribly destructive kind.

The Creative Decision Maker

Leaders may, however, be charismatic in a positive way. They may possess unique gifts of grace, appeal, and talent that inspire allegiance and that are used to further peace, freedom, and justice. Mohandas Gandhi and Martin Luther King, Jr., illustrate these qualities. Although India's fight for independence and African Americans' struggle for civil rights are complicated, Gandhi's and King's decisions to use nonviolence made an important difference in their campaigns.

Similarly, the eloquent leadership of Franklin Delano Roosevelt and Winston Churchill made a difference. Roosevelt's buoyant personality, pragmatic temper, and sagacious political skills helped the United States cope with its worst depression. Typical of his forceful leadership are the following words, delivered in a radio address on April 7, 1932:

> The country needs and, unless I mistake its temper, the country demands bold, persistent experimentation. It is common sense to take a method and try it. If it fails, admit it frankly and try another. But above all, try something.

And of course there is the famous line from his First Inaugural Address in 1933, as he tried to quiet the fears of a country in the throes of economic disaster: "The only thing we have to fear is fear itself."

Churchill's stubborn courage, memorable words, and special relationship with Roosevelt sustained Britain during its greatest peril in World War II and prepared the way for Allied triumph. Churchill was one of the twentieth century's most eloquent masters of the English language. A sample of his great skill with language is the following passage from his famous speech on Dunkirk, delivered to the House of Commons on June 4, 1940:

> We shall not flag or fail. We shall go on to the end. We shall fight in France, we shall fight on the seas and oceans, we shall fight with growing confidence and growing strength in the air, we shall defend our island, whatever the cost may be, we shall fight on the beaches, we shall fight on the landing grounds, we shall fight in the fields and streets, we shall fight in the hills; we shall never surrender.

Churchill was not without humor—but humor with a point, as in the following speech delivered at the Lord Mayor's Day Luncheon on November 10, 1942:

Saddam Hussein is a prime example of a destructive decision maker.

Winston Churchill is a prime example of a creative decision maker.

When I warned [the French] that Britain would fight on alone whatever they did, their generals told their prime minister and his divided cabinet, "In three weeks England will have her neck wrung like a chicken." Some chicken; some neck.

Both men, despite their mistakes, were creative democratic leaders. Their foibles as well as their great talents illustrate the importance of idiosyncratic decision making. For example, Britain's ill-fated and futile attempt in World War II to recapture Crete from the Germans (which resulted in a disastrous loss of British men, ships, and planes) partly resulted from Churchill's persistent belief that the road to victory against Hitler lay through Europe's "soft underbelly." Roosevelt's occasional failure to work out a clear-cut policy can be explained in terms of his inability to silence or dismiss lieutenants who quarreled with each other.

Other examples also illustrate the role of creative leadership. Charles de Gaulle's sense of French *grandeur* (greatness) clarified the constitutional structure of the current French Republic, built as it is on the concept of a strong president. Key French policies—for example, within the European Union or earlier, within the NATO alliance—can also be explained in terms of de Gaulle's insistence on France's need to protect French vital interests. And probably only de Gaulle could have made the difficult decision to grant independence to Algeria, which had been considered a part of greater France.

The idiosyncratic actor model thus points to important personality factors that may sometimes run counter to the rational, political, organizational, and elitist assumptions of the other models. Highlighting the unexpected, which may be either creative or demonic, better equips political scientists to deal with novel elements in decision making.

Whether these varying models can be integrated into one coherent model remains a challenging question for political scientists. Before reflecting on that possibility, we will use the five models to explore decision making in American politics.

DECISION MAKING AT VARIOUS LEVELS IN AMERICAN POLITICS

Let us now consider the role played by the voter, the legislative representative, the president, and the Supreme Court judge in American politics. How do the five models help explain the way they vote?

The Voter

Why do American voters vote the way they do? Do they make rational choices based on enlightened self-interest? Do they follow a party line? Do they go along with the organization—corporation, labor union, or farm bureau—that represents their vital interests? Do they follow an elitist leader? Or are their choices idiosyncratic—based on their personality quirks?

Studies of American voting behavior show that voters are not fully informed, keenly discriminating, totally rational, supremely dedicated to the public interest. Neither, on the other hand, are they vastly ignorant, utterly lacking in powers of analysis, completely irrational, or unaware of how their self-interest relates to the common good.

Let us examine some generalizations about voters in presidential elections. Which model of decision making do these generalizations sustain?

As Table 15.1 (pages 320–321) and other studies suggest, from the mid-1970s to the 1990s Americans tended—generally but not inevitably—to vote for the Democratic presidential candidate if they (1) were working class, (2) had at most a grade school education, (3) were African American or Hispanic, (4) were Jewish, (5) lived in cities, and (6) were in lower-income brackets, and/or (7) considered themselves liberals.[7]

People—again, generally but not inevitably—tended to vote for the Republican presidential candidate if they (1) were business or professional people, (2) had a college education, (3) were white, (4) were Protestant, (5) lived in small towns or rural areas, (6) were in the upper income brackets, and/or (7) considered themselves conservatives.

These correlations could support the rational actor model. For example, working-class, grade school-educated, African American, urban, and lower-income voters could logically perceive that their interests in jobs, housing, medical care, education, and mass transportation are better served by a Democratic president. Similarly, professional, college-educated, white, Protestant, small-town, and upper-income voters could believe that their interests in lower taxes, less regulation, and budget cuts are best served by a Republican president. These conclusions assume that a Democratic president will favor more liberal policies, and a Republican president more conservative policies. Moreover, voters who consider the family's financial situation worse at the time of the election tend to vote against the incumbent president.

Other evidence, however, supports other hypotheses. Despite a general weakening of political allegiances, partisan identification—as Table 15.1 makes very clear—still accounts for a large percentage of the American presidential vote. After heated and sometimes bitter primary battles, the faithful return to the fold and vote for their party's candidate in the final election.

Nonparty organizational loyalty also plays a role in how people vote. This is true particularly

when the organization's single issue—such as abortion, the environment, gun control, social security, or Israel—achieves great importance. Although workers did not overwhelmingly follow the recommendations of trade union leaders in the last couple of decades, many workers who had voted Republican in earlier elections supported their organizational leaders and voted Democratic in 1992 and 1996.

Even the elitist actor model may affect the voter's decision. The voter may be influenced by the leadership qualities of the presidential candidate: character, personality, strength, eloquence, and "class." Candidates may be helped or harmed by perceptions that they are "safe" or "radical"—sympathetic or hostile to the operative ideals of the Establishment. For example, in 1964 Senator Barry Goldwater was perceived as too radical on the right, while in 1972 Senator George McGovern was perceived as too radical on the left. Elitist influence may also be manifested in voters' support for candidates endorsed by an elite voice they respect, such as the *New York Times*.

Finally, voters may make their decisions on idiosyncratic grounds: on the basis of a candidate's character or age, a candidate's personality or sex appeal, or a candidate's stand on a single, sometimes odd, issue. In the 1996 presidential election some of these factors hurt and some helped both Bill Clinton and Robert Dole.

Thus, a number of factors—rational, political, organizational, elitist, and idiosyncratic—help explain a voter's decision.

The Representative

Why do representatives in Congress vote the way they do? Five hypotheses can be entertained. Three correspond to single decision-making models; the other two overlap several models.

The Representative as Trustee —According to this hypothesis, the representative actually matches Edmund Burke's famous portrait: Although the representative lives in "the closest correspondence . . . with his constituents," he does not

"AND NOW I APPEAL TO YOU NON-VOTERS. ACCORDING TO THE LATEST POLLS, I HAVE A SUBSTANTIAL LEAD. PLEASE DO NOT SPOIL THIS BY SURPRISING US AND COMING OUT TO VOTE."

Table 15.1 Portrait of the Electorate

% of '96 Total		1976		1980			1984		1988		1992			1996		
		Carter	Ford	Reagan	Carter	Anderson	Reagan	Mondale	Bush	Dukakis	Clinton	Bush	Perot	Clinton	Dole	Perot
48	Total vote	50	48	51	41	7	59	40	53	45	43	38	19	49	41	8
48	Men	50	48	55	36	7	62	37	57	41	41	38	21	43	44	10
52	Women	50	48	47	45	7	56	44	50	49	45	37	17	54	38	7
83	Whites	47	52	56	36	7	64	35	59	40	39	40	20	43	46	9
10	Blacks	83	16	11	85	3	9	90	12	86	83	10	7	84	12	4
5	Hispanics	76	24	33	59	6	37	62	30	69	61	25	14	72	21	6
1	Asians	—	—	—	—	—	—	—	—	—	31	55	15	43	48	8
40	White men	47	51	59	32	7	67	32	63	36	37	40	22	38	49	11
43	White women	46	52	52	39	8	62	38	56	43	41	41	19	48	43	8
5	Black men	80	19	14	82	3	12	85	15	81	78	13	9	78	15	5
5	Black women	86	14	9	88	3	7	93	9	90	87	8	5	89	8	2
66	Married	—	—	—	—	—	62	38	57	42	40	41	20	44	46	9
34	Unmarried	—	—	—	—	—	52	47	46	53	51	30	19	57	31	9
17	18–29 years old	51	47	43	44	11	59	40	52	47	43	34	22	53	34	10
33	30–44 years old	49	49	55	36	8	57	42	54	45	41	38	21	48	41	9
26	45–59 years old	47	52	55	39	5	60	40	57	42	41	40	19	48	41	9
24	60 and older	47	52	54	41	4	60	39	50	49	50	38	12	48	44	7
6	Not a high school grad.	—	—	46	51	2	50	50	43	56	54	28	18	59	28	11
24	High school grad.	—	—	51	43	4	60	39	50	49	43	36	21	51	35	13
27	Some college education	—	—	55	35	8	61	38	57	42	41	37	21	48	40	10
43	College grad. or more	—	—	52	35	11	58	41	56	43	44	39	17	47	44	7
26	College grad.	—	—	—	—	—	—	—	62	37	39	41	20	44	46	8
17	Post grad. education	—	—	—	—	—	—	—	50	48	50	36	14	52	40	5
46	White Protestant	41	58	63	31	6	72	27	66	33	33	47	21	36	53	10
29	Catholic	54	44	50	42	7	54	45	52	47	44	35	20	53	37	9
3	Jewish	64	34	39	45	15	31	67	35	64	80	11	9	78	16	3
23	Union household	59	39	44	49	6	46	53	42	57	55	24	21	59	30	9

Family income is															
11	Under $15,000	58	40	43	49	7	45	55	37	62	58	23	19	59	28	11
23	$15,000–29,999	55	43	53	39	7	57	42	49	50	45	35	20	53	36	9
27	$30,000–49,999	48	50	59	32	8	59	40	56	43	41	38	21	48	40	10
39	$50,000–$74,999	36	63	54	26	10	69	33	62	37	39	44	17	44	48	7
18	$75,000–$99,999	—	—	—	—	—	—	30	—	—	36	48	16	41	51	7
9	Over $100,000	—	—	—	—	—	—	—	65	32	—	—	—	38	54	6
Family's financial situation is															
33	Better today	30	70	37	55	7	86	14	—	—	24	61	14	66	26	6
45	Same today	51	49	46	47	7	50	50	—	41	41	42	17	46	45	8
20	Worse today	77	23	66	25	8	15	85	—	60	60	14	25	27	57	13
23	From the East	51	47	47	42	9	53	47	50	49	47	35	18	55	34	9
26	From the Midwest	48	50	51	41	7	58	41	52	47	42	37	21	48	41	10
30	From the South	54	45	52	44	3	64	36	58	41	41	43	16	46	46	7
20	From the West	46	51	53	34	10	61	38	52	46	43	34	23	48	40	8
35	Republicans	9	90	86	9	4	92	7	91	8	10	73	17	13	80	6
26	Independents	43	54	55	30	12	63	36	55	43	38	32	30	43	35	17
39	Democrats	77	22	26	67	6	25	74	17	82	77	10	13	84	10	5
20	Liberals	71	26	25	60	11	28	70	18	81	68	14	18	78	11	7
47	Moderates	51	48	49	42	8	53	47	49	50	47	31	21	57	33	9
33	Conservatives	29	70	73	23	4	82	17	80	19	18	64	18	20	71	8
9	First time voters	—	—	—	—	—	61	38	51	47	46	32	22	54	34	11

Source: New York Times, November 10, 1996. Reprinted by permission.

Notes: Data for 1996 were collected by Voter News Service based on questionnaires completed by 16,627 voters having 300 polling places around the nation on election day. Data for 1992 were collected by Voter Research and Surveys based on surveys conducted by 15,490 voters. Data for 1980 through 1988 were based on surveys conducted by The New York Times and CBS News: 11,645 in 1988; 9,174 in 1984; and 15,201 in 1980. Data for 1972 and 1976 were based on questionnaires completed by CBS News, with 15,300 voters in 1976 and 17,595 in 1972.

Family income categories in 1976: Under $8,000, $8,000–$12,000, $12,001–$20,000, and over $20,000. In 1980: Under $10,000, $10,000–$14,999, $15,000–$24,999, $25,000–$50,000, and over $50,000. In 1984: Under $12,500, $12,500–$24,999, $25,000–$34,999, $35,000–$50,000, and over $50,000. In 1988: Under $12,500, $12,500–$24,999, $25,000–$34,999, $35,000–$49,999, $50,000 and over. In 1992: $15,000–$29,999, $30,000–$49,999, $50,000 and over, and $100,000 and over.

The category of independents includes respondents who indicated they considered themselves "something else" in 1972, 1992, and 1996. "Something else" was not an option the other years. In 1984, first-time voter refers to voters first registered to vote in that year. In 1976 and 1980 the Congressional vote does not include New York and California. Family financial situation is compared to one year ago in 1976 and 1980 and four years ago in 1984, 1992, and 1996; 1976 and 1984 data are from NBC News.

Those who gave no answer are not shown. Dashes indicate that a question was not asked that year.

"sacrifice . . . his unbiased opinion, his mature judgment, his enlightened conscience," to any person. His judgment is "a trust from Providence," exercised after reasonable discussion and deliberation and on behalf of the common good.[8] The representative does not blindly follow the constituents' wishes as an unthinking delegate, or the party's dictates as a robotlike partisan. Here we can detect the rational actor model at work.

Empirical support for this hypothesis has come from a number of sources. In *Profiles in Courage*, John F. Kennedy noted that a number of brave senators did in fact act as trustees in the Burkean sense. They bucked party and constituent pressures and even risked their careers to follow their consciences. They acted on the assumption that the voters selected them because they respected their judgment and ability "to exercise that judgment from a position" where they "could determine what were their own best interests, as part of the nation's interests."[9]

Despite the skepticism of "realistic" political scientists who tend to scoff at the reality of the trustee (or Burkean) role, political scientists have found empirical support for this hypothesis. For example, John Wahlke, Heinz Eulau, and their colleagues in a classic 1959 study of four states—California, New Jersey, Ohio, and Tennessee—found that 63 percent of the states' legislators defined themselves as trustees. This was in contrast to 14 percent who saw themselves as delegates—following the majority will of their constituents—and 23 percent who saw themselves as "politicos"—attempting to balance the pressures of party, constituents, and conscience.

Wahlke and his colleagues concluded that rather than "being a 'pious formula,' the role orientation of trustee may be a functional necessity."[10] They argued that under modern conditions the trustee orientation is more realistic than it first appears—more realistic, in fact, than the other roles. Their conclusion was based on a number of points. Wahlke, Eulau, and their colleagues emphasized the representative's greater access to facts and information, the difficulty of knowing what constituents want, the conflicting desires of constituents, and constituents' lack of interest in key matters. These points, they noted, emphasize the actual discretion representatives have in following their own good, rational judgment as trustees.

More recent studies also support the conclusion that the representative functions as a trustee. These studies note that the influence of interest groups is exaggerated and emphasize that legislators respect the expertise of colleagues—concerned with the common good—whose grasp of issues may exceed their own.[11]

The Representative as Delegate—According to this hypothesis, representatives are delegates who express the will, and speak the opinion, of the constituents (especially the powerful ones) who elected them to office. This hypothesis is supported in such studies as James MacGregor Burns's *Congress on Trial* (1949), by polls indicating that the public expects their congressional representatives to vote the way the majority in the district feel, and by more rigorously empirical studies of representatives.

Burns, a perceptive observer of American politics, contended that the typical congressional representative is a diplomatic agent for his or her constituency. Members of Congress are realists who vote in harmony with the home folks—especially the well-organized home folks. Always aware of the next election, members avoid or straddle national issues that seriously divide their supporters while being sure to protect local rights. When their party's national platform conflicts with the strongly held interests of their constituents, they do not hesitate to disagree with their party. They feel that they must first represent their district's interests.

To stay in office—a primary concern—Burns's typical member of Congress follows this Machiavellian advice:

(1) vote for the home folks first, especially for those who are well organized; (2) keep on good terms with the local party bosses; (3) stress your protection of your district's interests as a whole against the outside

world; (4) as far as possible do not commit yourself on the important national issues that divide your constituents.[12]

In defending their decisions, such members of Congress, of course, talk of "the importance of following a safe and sane middle way, of the dangers of extremism and centralism, of the need for protecting local rights and interests."

Is Burns's assertion about the constituency's importance still valid? Most studies indicate that constituencies are still critical. One indicator is found in data collected by Glenn R. Parker about the time senators and representatives spend with their constituents. His study reveals that the average number of days spent with constituents increased dramatically from approximately 11 days per year for both types of legislators in 1959 to over 150 days for senators and nearly 250 days for representatives in 1980.[13] John Kingdon's empirical data and more recent studies also clearly support the contention that constituencies greatly influence modern legislators.[14]

The Representative as Partisan—Political scientists who advance this next hypothesis maintain that the representative is a **partisan** who, more often than not, votes with the party on key issues. In strong party systems like the British, this hypothesis is supported with rather overwhelming evidence. But how does it fare in the supposedly weaker party system of the United States?

A brilliant 1952 study by Julius Turner, *Party and Constituency: Pressure on Congress*, spoke to this question, although the study was more an attempt to measure party cohesion in Congress than to determine whether members are, or see themselves as, party persons. Turner's study underscores the significant partisan role of the representative. While conceding the great pressure of constituencies, Turner argued that "the great majority of congressmen . . . yield . . . especially to the pressures of party in casting their votes." Turner wrote:

While it is true that American discipline falls short of that achieved in some European democracies, and is less effective than party discipline in the McKinley era in the United States, evidence of great party influence can still be found. Party pressure seems to be more effective than any other pressure on congressional voting, and is discernible on nearly nine-tenths of the roll calls examined . . ..[15]

Turner's evidence thus emphasized the organizational actor model—here, the party organization. Are Turner's conclusions valid today? The answer is mixed. Data gathered by Patricia A. Hurley indicate an overall decline in party votes and party unity in the House of Representatives over an extended period (Table 15.2A).

Data from the U.S. Senate reveal a similar decline in party votes but much less of a decline in party unity (Table 15.2B). In a seeming reversal of these trends, party voting and unity increased in the early 1980s (Table 15.2C).

Obviously, party-based voting coalitions arise for a number of reasons—not just because of party identification. Leadership, the nature of the issue before the legislature, the size of party majorities in the House and Senate, and the party in the White House all contribute to a representative's propensity to vote with or against the party. After the Republican party gained control of both the U.S. House of Representatives and the U.S. Senate in the mid-term elections of 1994, there was a significant increase in partisan voting—particularly in the House of Representatives. It remains to be seen how partisan voting will play out after the 1996 presidential election.

The Representative as Politician—Our next hypothesis illustrates well the political actor model. Supporters of this hypothesis argue that the representative is, in fact, a politician who, depending on political circumstances, juggles several roles in response to diverse and shifting interests and pressures. Representatives are sometimes trustees, sometimes delegates, sometimes partisans, depending on the political conditions that affect their decisions. But always they are politicians, sensitive to the bargaining and balancing that is central to political decision making.

Table 15.2 Party Voting and Party Unity in the U.S. Congress

Period	Average Party Votes (%)	Average Party Unity	
		Democratic (%)	Republican (%)
A. House of Representatives			
1891–1911	68.2	86.8	88.5
1911–1941	56.3	83.0	85.4
1941–1968	49.5	79.3	82.1
1969–1986	40.4	75.9	76.3
B. Senate			
1933–1937	62.4	n.a.	n.a.
1938–1954	56.3	n.a.	n.a.
1955–1961	44.3	78.6	78.5
1962–1969	39.8	75.0	76.3
1970–1986	43.5	74.9	75.3
C. Selected Votes in the House and Senate in the 1980s			
House			
1981	74.4	70.2	81.1
1982	76.0	70.4	76.3
1983	92.8	79.7	84.8
1984	85.1	75.4	91.9
1985	91.5	76.5	83.4
Senate			
1981	75.6	69.6	79.5
1982	71.4	76.7	76.6
1983	80.5	76.3	76.8
1984	84.8	74.6	81.9
1985	84.0	77.9	81.8

Source: Patricia A. Hurley, "Parties and Coalitions in Congress," in Congressional Politics, Christopher J. Deering (Chicago: Dorsey Press, 1989), pp. 117, 122, 131.

Note: A party vote is one in which a majority of members of one party vote in opposition to a majority of members of the other party. The party unity score assesses the extent of party agreement and is simply the percentage of members voting together.

George Galloway, a keen and knowledgeable student of Congress, insisted that a member of Congress is neither purely the spineless agent of constituents nor the godlike trustee of the public interest. Members lead and follow. On most issues they legitimately compromise with party and constituency because they are political animals with an eye on the next election. As Galloway put it:

The desires of [the congressman's] constituents, of his party, and of this or that pressure group all enter into his decision on matters of major importance. The influence of these factors varies from member to member and measure to measure.[16]

Several studies of state legislators also support the hypothesis that the representative is a politician. In his study of Wisconsin legislators, Wilder Crane concluded:

Whether they say they are trustees voting on the merits of bills, delegates voting in accordance with demands of districts or interest groups, or partisans voting in accordance with perceived positions of their political party, they are actually all politicos, who vote on differing bases depending on the issues confronting them.[17]

Crane's conclusion was reinforced by his own service in the Wisconsin legislature in 1957–1958.

Similarly, Frank Sorauf, in his prize-winning study *Party and Representation* (involving the Pennsylvania legislature), concluded that the average legislator balances constituency, party, and personal judgment and makes tentative and cautious choices on the issues in light of these demands:

> The average legislator appears, then, to make no firm commitment to constituency, party, or self. Their demands on him and their sanctions over him shift from issue to issue. Both the shifting political demands and the finely balanced equities of choice force him to choose only tentatively and cautiously, one issue at a time.[18]

Other students of the legislative process, such as perceptive journalist Elizabeth Drew, have a more cynical view of the legislator as politician.[19] Special interest groups can generate enormous amounts of money to support ever more expensive election campaigns. This situation seems to have become worse during the 1980s and 1990s, leading to the assertion that American legislators are captives of special interests and not responsive to the people, or to their political parties.

The Representative as Idiosyncratic Legislator— There is also evidence to support the view that representatives often vote on a purely personal basis, which may reflect their own preferences, biases, institutions, or quirks.[20] They may support a personal friend or oppose a foe. They may, as in Senator Edward Kennedy's case, strongly favor gun control because of the tragic loss of family members. They may support disarmament because of a loved one's death in war, or human rights because of a memory of the Holocaust, or environmental controls because of a love of nature.

These views on representation address the *why* question—why representatives reach the decisions they do. Rational and elitist factors enter into the trustee role. Political and rational factors influence the delegate role. The interests, procedures, and capabilities of the party—as an organization—shape the representative's role as a partisan. The political actor model almost completely explains the role of the representa-

tive as a politician. And idiosyncratic elements do enter into the representative's judgment on at least some issues.

In turning next to consider decision making in the White House and on the Supreme Court, we will explore the *how* (as well as the *why*) of decision making.

The Chief Executive

How do presidents make decisions, and why? A pluralist interpretation—drawing on all five of our models—may be the most helpful. We take our leading example from *The Essence of Decision*, Graham Allison's in-depth study of the Cuban missile crisis.[21]

Superficially, presidential decision making seems to illustrate splendidly all the elements of the rational actor model: problem, environmental factors, alternatives, and choice. The 1962 Cuban missile crisis seems to offer a textbook example.

1. The problem: how safely to get the Russian missiles out of Cuba
2. The environmental factors: the proximity of the missiles (ninety miles from Florida), their range, destructive capability, and effect on the balance of power
3. The alternatives: an invasion of Cuba, a "surgical" air strike, a quarantine (blockade), negotiation with the Russians, an approach to Castro, doing nothing
4. The choice: the quarantine, plus contact with the Russians and support in the Organization of American States (OAS) and at the United Nations

As we saw in Chapter 2, President Kennedy and his team of advisers (ExCom) addressed the problem carefully and prudently. They were disturbed by the military, political, and psychological consequences of the Soviet missiles because they believed the missiles threatened America's national security. The team considered a number of alternatives for safely putting pressure on the Soviet Union to remove the missiles, and they held in reserve the possibility of more drastic military action. ExCom gave the Russians time to respond and to save face (withdraw the missiles in return for a "no invasion of Cuba" promise) while building support for the U.S. position with allies in Europe, other American states, and other nations.

Yet, as Allison demonstrates, the complete dominance of the rational actor model is open to challenge. A good deal of political bargaining went on. The hawks on ExCom pressed for a strong military response: a "surgical" air strike to take out the missiles, if not an invasion; they were also open to conducting a surprise attack. United Nations Ambassador Adlai Stevenson's arguments to rely on diplomacy at the United Nations were not well received. Defense Secretary Robert McNamara's idea of a quarantine (blockade) was not strongly endorsed at first. Attorney General Robert Kennedy took a strong stand against a surprise attack. The do-nothing option was not seriously entertained.

Only slowly did judgment crystalize around the idea of the quarantine as a firm but prudent response, buttressed by the threat of stronger measures, contact with the Russians, and diplomacy at the OAS and the U.N. to obtain support for the American position. Although the president listened carefully to his advisers, although he worked for consensus, it was clear that the quarantine was the decision that he wanted them to agree on. It was also clear that some of the political actors—especially Robert Kennedy and Robert McNamara—were more influential than others such as Secretary of State Dean Rusk or Adlai Stevenson.

The incomplete dominance of the rational actor model is also suggested by other aspects of the crisis: how the United States came to know that the Soviet Union had put armed missiles in Cuba; why the Soviet Union acted the way it did; how the quarantine worked. The procedures of U.S. military intelligence account for the late discovery of the missiles in Cuba, which intensified the urgency of the decision-making process. Soviet military organization—and differences in procedures between Soviet intel-

ligence and Soviet military—help explain how the Americans could identify the sites once the missiles had been secretly introduced into Cuba. The Soviet intelligence organization took great pains to conceal the introduction of the missiles. But the Soviet military, following installation procedures, did little to conceal the sites. The American blockade did not run its normal course according to the navy's standard operating procedures. President Kennedy insisted on retaining personal control of the operation; he did not want World War III started by an American submarine commander following routine blockade procedure and sinking a Russian vessel. These examples illustrate the triumph of rational decision making over organization procedures. They also illustrate how President Kennedy's awareness of the way mobilization imperatives led to World War I put him on guard against such dangers.

The Cuban missile crisis also underscores the elitist character of decision making. There was no public referendum on the president's decision. A very small group of men advised him. And the final decision was made by the president himself.

Finally, idiosyncratic elements are also apparent in the president's decision. For example, the president's tendency to reject a do-nothing approach was probably reinforced by his need to demonstrate toughness (especially in light of a presumed Russian impression of him as weak, after an earlier meeting with Khrushchev in Vienna). Robert Kennedy's opposition to a surprise attack on Cuba was based on his strong conviction that, after Pearl Harbor, the world would not forgive such an attack. The hawkish posture of Secretary of State Dean Rusk and the dovish posture of Adlai Stevenson may also be considered idiosyncratic.

In-depth examination of other presidential decisions would also support a pluralist interpretation. Presidents rationally seek to maximize goals, but they often have to accept something less than ideal. They engage in negotiating, bargaining, and compromising. They strive for

The White House, home of the American executive.

consensus among divergent political actors. They are influenced by the bureaucratic organizations on which they rely for an understanding of key problems, relevant information, selected alternatives, and recommended choices—choices with the greatest benefits and the least costs. Very few people may actually participate in key decisions designed to protect the national interest as understood by the Establishment. And idiosyncratic factors play a role. The ingredients of these models are not neatly isolated from one another; they often interweave and overlap.

Let us now turn to the decision-making process on the U.S. Supreme Court to test the five models of decision making.

The Supreme Court Justice

Superficially, the judicial process seems to be a model of rational decision making:

1. Judges begin with a legal problem that calls for a resolution.
2. They seek to understand the problem in its context, which means that they must understand both the facts of the case and relevant precedents (previous court decisions).
3. They then argue alternative approaches to the problem.
4. Finally, they vote and by majority decision reach a choice, with one justice being selected to write the majority opinion (and set forth the reasoning that led to that opinion), and with opportunity for concurring or dissenting justices to set forth their differing logic.

For example, does separate-but-equal education in Topeka, Kansas (and other states), violate the equal protection clause of the Fourteenth Amendment to the U.S. Constitution, which declares that no state shall deprive a citizen of the equal protection of the laws? The facts proved that African Americans were being educated in separate schools. The key legal precedent held that separate-but-equal education does not inherently violate the equal protection clause. Arguments centered on whether the Court should reverse that precedent. Finally, the Court unanimously decided that separate-but-equal schools are inherently unequal and constitute a violation of the equal protection clause of the Fourteenth Amendment.[22]

Thus, judges, in a highly rational manner, attempt to face problems, facts, precedents, alternatives, and choices. They seek to maximize the values enshrined in the Constitution. They address the relevant factors in the judicial environment. They seriously consider the pros and cons of alternative arguments. And they finally arrive at a reasoned judgment that balances, as necessary, costs and benefits.

But is the judicial process quite as neat and pat as this discussion suggests? Most observers of the Supreme Court think not. The Court's problem is not always so clear-cut; often several formulations of the key problem compete for selection. Similarly, the facts and the meaning of the pertinent precedents are not always clear-cut; judges often interpret the facts and precedents differently. They may quarrel about the relevance of precedents. Moreover, different judges will find differing responses to the agreed-on problem logical and compelling. Thus, there may be concurring opinions that set forth different reasons for the same conclusion, or dissenting opinions that set forth reasons for different conclusions.

Do our other decision-making models help explain these differences among well-educated, intelligent, and rational judges who are dedicated to the values of the Constitution? Let us look next at the political actor model as it illuminates judicial decision making.

Students of politics would be naive indeed if they ignored the fact that judges are often appointed because they reflect a particular political ideology. To put it bluntly, liberal presidents normally appoint liberal judges to the Court, and conservative presidents usually appoint conservative judges. Although judges may be remarkably independent once they accept their lifetime posts, they usually bring to the Court a socioeconomic background and political and judicial ideology that influence their judicial opinions. For example, they may be more or less sympathetic to the power of the president, of Congress, or of the states; or to civil rights, business, labor, and the environment.

Justices cannot be oblivious of the struggle for power in politics and of the Court's role in that struggle. They cannot overlook the diverse values and interests of those who struggle for power: labor and management; president and Congress; the federal government and the states; farmers, consumers, Hispanics, African Americans, and women. They cannot be removed from the bargaining, accommodation, and consensus of politics.

For example, in unanimously declaring that "separate but equal" was unconstitutional in 1954, the Court made an important political statement against racial discrimination. Over the course of the Supreme Court's history, majorities on the Court have reflected diverse views on key political questions in the struggle for power. They have, for example, upheld national power, protected slavery, been sympathetic to state regulation, defended corporations, overturned an income tax, aided farmers, secured labor's right to organize and bargain collectively, safeguarded social security, expanded the rights of defendants, and advanced the civil rights of African Americans. In these diverse matters, justices have also made political statements and participated in the struggle for power in American politics. Given the diversity and complexity of this struggle, concurring and dissenting opinions on the Court should not be a surprise.

But it would be a mistake to think of the Court as the same kind of political actor as Congress or the president. The Court, as an organization, has a life and logic of its own. Here the organization process model may throw additional light on judicial decision making.

The Court has its own vital interests to protect. These are clearly spelled out in its constitutional power, the "judicial power" of Article III, Section 2 of the Constitution, and its historically affirmed and sanctioned power to declare an act of Congress unconstitutional. The Court will protect its independence and integrity against congressional or presidential onslaughts. It will try to avoid "mistakes" or "self-inflicted wounds" that weaken its prestige, such as upholding slavery, striking down an income tax, limiting the ability of either Congress or the states to regulate corporations, or upholding racial discrimination. Chief Justice Charles Evan Hughes, in the midst of the nation's efforts to cope with the Great Depression of the 1930s and to adjust to the realities of what later would be called the welfare state, worked very hard (especially on Justice Owen Roberts, a "swing" member of the Court) to build a bare majority of at least five to sustain key New Deal legislation. Justice Roberts's switch in 1937 from the conservative to the liberal side of the Court has been facetiously called "the switch in time that saved nine." The Court might have lost some of its powers if it had persisted in striking down vital New Deal legislation.

The Court's standard operating procedures also significantly influence its decision making. These procedures, or rules, greatly influence which cases the Court will or will not take. For example, the Court will not take a case unless a real controversy between real adversaries exists under the Constitution. The Court will not take a case unless it involves "the protection or enforcement of valuable legal rights, or the punishment, prevention, or redress of wrongs directly concerning the party or parties bringing the justiciable suit," to quote Henry Abraham, a longtime observer of the Court.[23] Legal procedure requires the party or parties in a suit to have "standing," that is, the right to be recognized in a court of law.

The Court's standard operating procedures also dictate that the Court not render *advisory opinions*—that is, opinions rendered in the absence of a real legal controversy properly before the Court. Decisions can be made only on live issues. The Court also insists that all remedies in lower courts be exhausted before review by the Supreme Court. The Court normally avoids clearly political questions by insisting that they are properly handled by legislative bodies. In dealing with an act of Congress, the Court normally

presumes that the act is constitutional; this means that challengers will have to demonstrate very clearly why they think the act is unconstitutional. The Court normally will also decide cases before it on the narrowest basis—avoiding, for example, constitutional questions if the case can be decided on other grounds. The Court generally avoids passing judgment on the wisdom of governmental action. In many ways, then, the Court's operating procedures condition its decision making.

The elitist actor and idiosyncratic actor models may also throw light on judicial decision making. Members of the Supreme Court are clearly an elitist group of nine persons. In a split decision the majority may comprise only five. Before Sandra Day O'Connor was appointed in 1981, no woman had served on the Supreme Court. As of 1996, only two African Americans, Thurgood Marshall and Clarence Thomas, had ever been so appointed. Does the Court go its independent way, regardless of legislative, executive, and public opinion? Or do the Court's decisions reflect the views of voters and their representatives? The historical record is mixed. For example, in the post–Civil War period, the Court's defense of corporate interests was often not in tune with majority sentiment as reflected in state or federal legislation. In the 1950s the Court's record on civil rights was perhaps in advance of national sentiment as measured by state and federal legislatures. In general, the Court has protected the following values: private property, free enterprise, limited government, and individual liberty.

Idiosyncratic factors may also influence judicial decisions. Judges are not bloodless, emotionless creatures; they are not legal computers. They love and hate with passion. They may be judicial activists, open to governmental reform and judicial initiatives in politics, the economy, and society, and vigorously committed to civil rights and environmental protection. Or, despite their personal liberal or conservative views, they may be committed to a philosophy of judicial restraint, allowing Congress to take the initiative in matters of social policy. They may be pragmatic or dogmatic as well as liberal or conservative in their decision making. The personality of the chief justice is particularly important because it is his or her task to keep the Court together, to assign judges to write decisions, and in general to assure the Court's healthy functioning. Powerful chief justices, such as John Marshall, have made a difference. Political or ideological leadership, whether from a Charles Evans Hughes or an Earl Warren or a William Rehnquist, has been important.

TOWARD A THEORY OF COMPARATIVE DECISION MAKING

Let us now reflect on the five decision-making models and our brief explanation of some decision makers in American politics. We will be particularly interested in how widely these models apply to decision making in other countries and in international organizations such as the United Nations. We are also curious about whether these five models can be combined into a coherent and helpful synthesis. We would like to know how decision-making patterns can help satisfy human needs.

Some tentative, exploratory propositions may help the critical student move toward a more substantial theory of worldwide decision making.

First, all political decisions contain rational, political, organizational, elitist, and idiosyncratic elements. The political scientist's task is to precisely identify these elements and to assess their actual influence in decision making.

Second, although a pluralist decision-making model is more helpful than any one of the models outlined in this chapter, a synthesis of all five models is too difficult to obtain at this time.

Third, only more modest generalizations about aspects of decision making are possible at this stage in the history of political science. For example:

- The rational actor model is an ideal that is rarely approximated in the real world of politics.

- The political struggle for power is universal, and bargaining is widespread in all political communities. Political bargaining is more prominent in the countries lacking strong party systems or effective legislative majorities. Constituents have more influence in the United States than in Britain and more influence in Britain than in China.

- Organizational influences are worldwide, but they are potent in liberal democracies such as the United States and in the social democracies of the industrial world. Organizations are also potent in the communist world and in some developing countries because of the power of bureaucracy and the primacy of party in communist countries and because of the prominence of the military in many developing countries. In developing countries where the bureaucracy, party, and military are weak, such impact is lacking.

- Elite rule is worldwide, but the elites may be authoritarian or subject to varying degrees of democratic control. Elites normally seek to protect the status quo (whether capitalism, communism, democracy, or authoritarianism), but there may also be revolutionary, reactionary, and reform elite groups seeking to alter the status quo.

- Idiosyncratic actors do make a difference in politics. We have just barely begun to understand the role of the creative (or destructive) idiosyncratic decision makers.

Finally, certain decision-making models are more helpful in explaining foreign policy decisions than domestic decisions. In most countries the foreign policy decision-making process tends to be concentrated in the executive. There are several reasons for this: (1) executives tend to control the instruments of foreign policy; (2) they tend to have more resources for gathering and processing information about foreign affairs; and (3) because countries must "speak with one voice," executives—whether prime ministers, presidents, dictators, or kings—speak for the country as a whole. For these reasons, rational actor, organizational, elitist, and idiosyncratic models tend to be more influential. Domestic decision making is a bit more diffuse, and more political factors affect the process.

CONCLUSION

Thus, we see how decision making in politics may be illuminated by exploring a number of key empirical models: (1) the rational actor model; (2) the political actor model; (3) the organizational actor model; (4) the elitist actor model; and (5) the idiosyncratic actor model. These five models enable us profitably to examine actual decision-making processes in American politics and to ask about the relevance of these models in decision making in other countries and in international politics. With more empirical work in this vital area of decision making it may be possible to move beyond modest generalizations to a more ambitious synthesis of key models.

Beyond decision-making models, other important questions must be asked. Who benefits, and who suffers, as a result of policy decisions? Is there any relationship between certain decision-making processes and values such as peace, liberty, justice, and economic well-being? Can the decision-making process be improved to enhance these values?

The four chapters of Part IV—"Political Judgment and Public Policy"—provide a fuller opportunity to discuss these questions. We will pose and explore some of the big issues of public policy—troublesome problems that engage our capacity for prudent judgment. We will set forth key aspects of the record on these problems and explore policies relevant to war and peace in the modern world, the battle on behalf of the "least free," the struggle for economic well-being, and the imperative of ecological health.

ANNOTATED BIBLIOGRAPHY

Allison, Graham T. *Essence of Decision: Explaining the Cuban Missile Crisis.* Boston: Little, Brown, 1972. Uses three models (the rational actor, organizational process, and governmental politics) to throw light on decision making in general and the Cuban crisis in particular. Brilliant!

Anderson, Charles. *Statecraft: An Introduction to Political Choice and Judgment.* New York: Wiley, 1977. Focuses on the art of making public decisions. Examines the points of view of the policymaker, the activist, and the revolutionary. Emphasizes goals and strategy and practical programs and political organization.

Bachrach, Peter. *The Theory of Democratic Elitism.* Boston: Little, Brown, 1980. Analyzes and criticizes the theory that an elite makes decisions in democratic politics. An eye-opener for naive pluralists.

Burns, James M. *Roosevelt: The Lion and the Fox.* New York: Harcourt Brace Jovanovich, 1956. An in-depth study of FDR. Illuminates the rich context of presidential decision making. Compare to Arthur M. Schlesinger, Jr.'s work on John F. Kennedy, *A Thousand Days* (Boston: Houghton Mifflin, 1965) and Garry Wills's *Nixon: The Crisis of the Self-Made Man* (Boston: Houghton Mifflin, 1970). Comparison makes more reliable generalizations possible.

Janis, Irving. *Groupthink: Psychological Studies of Policy Decisions,* 2nd ed. 2 vols. New York: Houghton Mifflin, 1982. Provides an excellent study of how advisers can fall all over each other to please the decision maker and achieve consensus without genuine debate. Both good and bad decisions are reviewed: Bay of Pigs, Marshall Plan, Vietnam, and more. See also Janis's *Crucial Decisions: Leadership in Policymaking and Crisis Management* (New York: Free Press, 1989).

Kingdon, John. *Congressmen's Voting Decisions,* 3rd ed. Ann Arbor: University of Michigan Press, 1991. Offers a critical weighing and blending of statistical data and information generated by personal interviews. See also Kingdon's perceptive *Agendas, Alternatives, and Public Policies,* 2nd ed. New York: HarperCollins, 1995.

Mills, C. Wright. *The Power Elite.* New York: Galaxy, 1959. Presents a vision of an interrelated political, industrial, financial, educational, and military elite making key decisions in capitalistic America. Provocative, controversial.

Monroe, Kristen Renwick. "The Theory of Rational Action: What Is It? How Useful Is It for Political Science?" In William Crotty, ed., *Political Science: Looking to the Future.* Vol. 1: *The Theory and Practice of Political Science.* Evanston, Ill.: Northwestern University Press, 1991. Argues that recognition of self-interest must be balanced by human needs for sociability. Would not neglect emotional or intuitive strategies that lead to successful outcomes, and would recognize that political actors have multiple identities. An excellent summary and critique.

Monroe, Kristen Renwick, ed. *The Economic Approach to Politics*. New York: HarperCollins, 1991. A splendid critical collection. See especially Anthony Downs on "Social Values and Democracy" and Harry Eckstein on "Rationality and Frustration in Political Behavior."

Neustadt, Richard E. *Presidential Power and the Modern President: The Politics of Leadership from Roosevelt to Reagan*. New York: Free Press, 1990. Underscores the importance of presidential personality and the constraints on, as well as opportunities for, presidential leadership. Full of valuable insights.

Parenti, Michael. *Democracy for the Few*. New York: St. Martin's Press, 1994. Sees decision making in the United States as dominated by capitalist values, institutions, and political actors. Offers sharp criticism of the dominant liberal democratic elite.

Pomper, Gerald M., et. al. *The Election of 1996: Reports and Interpretations*. Chatham, N.J.: Chatham House, 1997. Investigates voter decisions in the Clinton/Dole race. A helpful summary. See also the brilliant reporting of Theodore H. White in his several studies of *The Making of the President* (New York: Atheneum). White covers presidential elections in 1960, 1964, 1968, 1972, 1976.

Riemer, Neal, ed. *The Representative: Trustee? Delegate? Partisan? Politico?* Lexington, Mass.: D.C. Heath, 1967. Explores four hypotheses about the representative's decision making.

Simon, Herbert. *Models of Bounded Rationality*, vols. 1 and 2. Cambridge: MIT Press, 1982. Emphasizes the importance of goals, self-interest, conscious choice, the individual as basic actor, preference orderings, choice of alternative with highest expected utility, and appreciation of consequences. Recognizes decision makers' limitations and uncertainties. Highlights importance of "satisficing"— seeking a satisfactory, or good, outcome (if not an optimal outcome). See also Simon's *Reason in Human Affairs* (Stanford, Calif.: Stanford University Press, 1983).

Truman, David. *The Governmental Process: Political Interests and Public Opinion*, 2nd ed. New York: Knopf, 1993. Sees public policy as a result of group pressures. One of the best accounts of pluralistic politics.

SUGGESTIONS FOR FURTHER READING

Barber, James D. *Presidential Character: Predicting Performance in the White House*, 4th ed. Englewood Cliffs, N.J.: Prentice-Hall, 1992.

Dahl, Robert A. *Who Governs?* New Haven, Conn.: Yale University Press, 1967.

Graff, Henry F. *The Tuesday Cabinet: Deliberation and Decision on Peace and War Under Lyndon B. Johnson*. Englewood Cliffs, N.J.: Prentice-Hall, 1970.

Greenstein, Fred I. *Leadership in the Modern Presidency*. Cambridge: Harvard University Press, 1989.

Halberstam, David. *The Best and the Brightest*. New York: Random House, 1972.

Kaplan, Mark. *Decision Theory in Philosophy*. New York: Cambridge University Press, 1995.

Korany, Bahgat. *How Foreign Policy Decisions Are Made in the Third World*. Boulder, Colo.: Westview, 1986.

Sorauf, Frank. *Money in American Elections*. Glenview, Ill.: Scott, Foresman, 1988.

Wice, Paul. *Chaos in the Courthouse*. New York: Praeger, 1985.

Wice, Paul. *Judges and Lawyers: The Human Side of Justice*. New York: HarperCollins, 1991.

Wicker, Tom. *JFK and LBJ: The Influence of Personality on Politics*. New York: Morrow, 1968.

Wilson, James Q. *Bureaucracy: What Government Agencies Do and Why They Do It*. New York: Basic Books, 1991.

GLOSSARY TERMS

elite
model
partisan
politician
standard operating procedures
trustee role

P   A   R   T   F   O   U   R

POLITICAL
JUDGMENT AND
PUBLIC POLICY

In Part IV we turn to our third major concern in political science: the development of political wisdom in the public policy arena. The overall problem that we shall address is, *How can we sharpen our prudent judgment on key issues of public policy?*

We shall attempt, by critically examining key issues of public policy, to explore the prudential component of political science, the component concerned with wise judgment. In dealing with such issues as war and peace in the modern world (Chapter 16), the battle on behalf of the least free (Chapter 17), the struggle for economic well-being (Chapter 18), and the imperative of ecological health (Chapter 19), we will encourage you to study political judgment and public policy in light of what you have learned about political philosophy in Part II and about a science of politics in Part III.

You will be encouraged to articulate and examine the guiding ethical values that are so crucial to political philosophy and ideology. You will also be asked to assess empirical findings relevant to a science of politics. Prudent judgments—wise judgments—draw on such critically understood ethical values and empirical realities. They demand that political actors clearly understand their purposes and the possibilities of the real world. Prudent judgments also demand that political actors balance a number of equities in deciding issues of public policy.

Chapters 16, 17, 18, and 19 should thus engage your judgment on a number of important and controversial problems of the day, the decade, and the future. These issues also reflect what we have termed the "new world of politics." Momentous changes in the communist world raise the possibility of major progress in reducing the onerous historical burden of the arms race. But the world is not yet fully relieved of the terrors of conventional war and nuclear catastrophe. Democratic movements in various parts of the world give us hope for a significant improvement in human rights. But our euphoria must be tempered with the reality that arbitrary imprisonment, torture, and political murder are still all too prevalent. In many countries of the world, great progress has been made in raising standards of living. But millions upon millions of people still live in abject poverty. Finally, environmental degradation, which not too many years ago was perceived as a national or regional problem, is now obviously global, as we confront the possibility of drastically damaging earth's fragile biosphere. These chapters will invite you to explore creative break-throughs in the new world of politics.

In addressing momentous issues of public policy, we shall first explore ethical and empirical factors. Second, we shall identify alternative approaches to the problems, paying special attention to their strengths and weaknesses. Third, after highlighting some of the important ethical, empirical, and prudential considerations, we shall invite you to set forth and defend your own "proximate solutions."

WAR AND PEACE IN THE MODERN WORLD

THE SPECIFIC QUESTION to be explored in Chapter 16 is, *What creative breakthroughs can help us achieve a more peaceful world order?* First, we must define some of the key words in our chapter title and in our statement of the problem.

By **war** we mean military activity, or armed violence, carried out in a systematic and organized way by nation-states (or organized groups that aspire to become nation-states) against other nation-states to impose their will.[1]

By **peace** we mean the absence of war. Positively, peace is a condition of harmony between nation-states (or organized groups that aspire to become nation-states) that enables them to cooperatively, lawfully, and voluntarily (through discussion, voting, mediation, conciliation, and arbitration) work out conflicts and deal with disputes.[2]

By **modern world** we mean a world characterized by (1) the sovereign nation-state system, in which nations possess supreme power to make decisions affecting their destiny, (2) a war system in which nations threaten to use their military might to safeguard their national security and other vital interests, and (3) conditions of political, economic, and ecological interaction and interdependence.

By **creative breakthroughs** we mean in this chapter ethical, empirical, and prudential changes to promote a more peaceful world order: a higher ethical consciousness of global community, a new or more penetrating scientific understanding of the causes of war, and wiser judgments about how to overcome war and its disastrous consequences.

By a **more peaceful world order** we do not mean the end of all conflict, competition, and tension. Rather, we mean eliminating catastrophic world wars, regional wars, civil wars, and wars of national liberation. We mean minimizing the level of armed conflict. We also mean making significant arms control and disarmament possible. In essence, we envision a world in which major disputes (between and within nations) are settled without resort to violence and bloodshed, in which dangerous international tensions are considerably reduced, and in which world energies and monies are used to meet human needs for food, housing, medical care, education, community, and social and cultural development.

As we address the possibility of creative breakthroughs to this more peaceful world, we must be particularly sensitive to the difficult task of social change. This is the task of working out a cogent theory to tell us how to get from where we are to where we would like to be. Although it is wise to be skeptical about quick and easy solutions to political problems—especially the problem of social change—as political scientists we must strive for breakthroughs.

KEY ETHICAL AND EMPIRICAL FACTORS

This section presents several key factors that affect war and peace in the modern world. These factors include the threat of nuclear war, the consequences of conventional war, the arms race, the sovereign nation-state system, the shifting balance of power, and the weaknesses of the United Nations.

The Mortal Threat of Nuclear War

As of this writing (the end of 1996), the world seems to have stepped back from the edge of the nuclear abyss. The immediate threat of a major nuclear exchange between the United States and the former Soviet Union has lessened. In 1993 the United States and Russia signed the START II (Strategic Arms Reduction Treaty II) agreement under which both countries pledged to eliminate land-based missiles with multiple warheads and overall to cut their nuclear strategic warhead inventories by roughly two-thirds shortly after the turn of the century.[3] Thus, the Cold War

tension that fueled the nuclear arms race has now subsided.

But these bilateral steps are tempered by other grim realities. The threat of nuclear war is far from over. The American and Russian arsenals still contain thousands of strategic nuclear warheads. The United Kingdom, France, China, India, and Israel are also capable of making nuclear war. And several developing countries, including Iran, Iraq, and Pakistan, are actively pursuing the means to produce nuclear warheads. With the collapse of the Soviet Union there is great concern over the disposition of thousands of tactical nuclear weapons spread throughout the former republics of the USSR. There is further a fear that fissionable material and nuclear know-how could be sold to countries outside the former Soviet Union. As long as nuclear weapons exist in large numbers and international conflicts continue, the possibility of nuclear war remains.

The continuing danger of **nuclear proliferation** and conflict suggests the immediate and pressing need for a more peaceful world order. In a worst-case scenario, all-out nuclear war would destroy the only globe that human beings know. The biological destruction of the species *Homo sapiens* would be a real possibility.

But even if humanity is not literally wiped out in the event of a nuclear war, the devastation wrought by a more limited nuclear exchange of several hundred large warheads in a regional or global war is almost too horrible to contemplate. Assuming urban centers would be prime targets, nuclear warheads would burn everything and everyone within a radius of ten to twenty miles. Millions more would suffer grave wounds and would, subsequently and rapidly, perish. Additional millions—burned or mutilated—would suffer a lingering death from their wounds or radiation sickness. The wounded would overrun hospitals, and doctors would be unable to care for them. The networks of modern life—communication, business, factories, agriculture, government, and social life—would unravel. Survivors would face the psychological trauma of

Charred remains of a boy found about 2,500 feet from the center of the atomic bomb explosion at Nagasaki, Japan, August 10, 1945.

loss of loved ones, the dangers to unborn children, and unknown genetic mutations.

For a number of years, this was our concept of nuclear destruction. In 1983 another horror was added to our understanding: **nuclear winter.** Gwynne Dyer describes it:

> A major nuclear exchange . . . would cover at least the Northern Hemisphere, and perhaps the entire planet with a pall of smoke and dust that would plunge the surface into virtual darkness . . . and cause a drop of up to 40 degrees centigrade [72 degrees Fahrenheit] in the continental interiors (which would be far below the freezing point in any season) for a similar period. . . . The cold and the dark may persist worldwide for half a year, killing off entire species of animals and plants already gravely weakened by high doses of radioactivity.[4]

The data about the destructive power and accuracy of weapons are chilling. The weapons in the world's nuclear arsenal have nearly 2,000 times the power of all the conventional weapons detonated in three major wars of this century: World War II, Korea, and Vietnam.[5] Nuclear weapons stockpiles have become truly grotesque: collectively, they contain more than a thousand times the explosive energy used in all wars since the introduction of gunpowder six centuries ago.

One modern nuclear submarine like the Poseidon or Trident has enough power to destroy every city in the former Soviet Union with a population of 150,000 or more. Contemporary missiles carry their warheads 6,000 miles in thirty minutes and drop them a few hundred feet from their targets.

Nuclear physicist Robert Oppenheimer's description of the atmosphere at Los Alamos, New Mexico, during the first detonation of the atomic bomb that he helped develop, is thought-provoking:

> We knew the world would not be the same. A few people laughed. A few people cried. Most people were silent. I remembered the line from the Hindu scripture—the Bhagavad-gita. Vishnu is trying to persuade the prince that he should do his duty and to impress him, takes on his multi-armed form and says, "Now I am become Death, the destroyer of worlds." I suppose we all felt that, one way or another.[6]

The Disastrous Consequences of Conventional Wars

The record of conventional wars in the twentieth century is one of massive deaths, injuries, and dreadful human suffering. The human, monetary, social, and physical costs of these wars have been devastating.

Human Costs—World Wars I and II alone killed over 60 million people (Tables 16.1 and 16.2; the figures for Japan include those killed at Hiroshima and Nagasaki). In addition, over 21 million soldiers and civilians have been killed in conventional wars since the end of World War II. Internal wars have contributed to these totals. For example, between 1960 and 1990, internal wars killed an estimated 700,000 Chinese, 500,000 Indonesians, 2,000,000 Nigerians, 600,000 Ugandans, 500,000 Ethiopians, 415,000 Mozambiqueans, 105,000 Iraqis, and 138,000 Guatemalans.[7] The consequences of war also include the wounded; for example, roughly two times as many were wounded as killed in World War II.

The following statistics from World War II offer a glimpse of war's immense fatalities: one out of every 22 Soviet citizens was killed, one out of every 25 Germans, one out of every 46 Japanese, one out of every 150 British, and one out of

Table 16.1 Casualties Among Major Participants in World War I

Country[a]	Total Mobilized	Killed or Died of Wounds	Civilians Killed or Died from Injuries (estimate)	Total Killed or Died
Austria-Hungary	7,800,000	1,200,000	180,000	1,380,000
Belgium	267,000	14,000	90,000	104,000
Bulgaria	560,000	87,000	n.a.[b]	87,000+
France	8,410,000	1,363,000	150,000	1,513,000
Germany	11,000,000	1,774,000	225,000	1,999,000
British Empire	8,904,000	908,000	9,000	917,000
Italy	5,615,000	460,000	300,000	760,000
Rumania	750,000	336,000	170,000	506,000
Russia	12,000,000	1,700,000	n.a.[b]	1,700,000+
Serbia	707,000	125,000	n.a.[b]	125,000+
Turkey	2,850,000	325,000	250,000	575,000
United States	4,355,000	126,000	n.a.[b]	126,000+
Total	63,218,000	8,418,000	1,374,000+	9,792,000+

Source: David Wood, Conflict in the Twentieth Century, p. 24. Reprinted by permission of The International Institute for Strategic Studies.

[a]This list excludes non-European belligerents (such as China, Japan, Thailand, and Latin American countries) and certain smaller European belligerents (such as Greece, Luxembourg, and Portugal) that played a relatively minor role in the war.

[b]n.a. No figures available.

every 500 Americans. For a more graphic image of the number of soldiers killed or missing in World War II, picture a parade lasting over twelve weeks (89 days), with a row of ten soldiers passing the reviewing stand every five seconds, day and night.

Civilian casualties in World War II were considerably higher than in World War I, about twice the number of military deaths. Civilian casualties would probably be even greater in a major nuclear war.

In addition to directly killing and wounding people, wars also bring death, injury, and suffering from starvation or malnutrition; the ravages of disease; violations of liberty and justice; the plight of refugees; and ecological damage.

For example, the Holocaust—the Nazi destruction of 6 million Jews in Europe—could not have happened without World War II. The creation of "slave laborers"—people forced to work for the Nazi war machine—would have been impossible in peacetime. The displacement and dislocation of whole peoples (by the Nazis, the Russians, and also the Americans, in the case of Japanese Americans) was another consequence of World War II.

Monetary Costs—Reliable estimates put the monetary costs of World War II at more than $1.3 trillion. To conceive the war's astronomical cost, imagine spending approximately $12 million a week, year in and year out, from the birth of Jesus to 1980.[8] The costs of war in terms of battle casualties, dollar expenditures, victims of the Holocaust, and refugees only partially outline its disastrous consequences. A recitation of numbers cannot recapture the brutal inhumanity of war and especially its violence to the human spirit. To understand these consequences, we must turn to literature and art.

Political Costs—War also produces unsettling political effects. For example, it seems quite likely that World War I opened the door to

Table 16.2 Casualties Among Major Participants in World War II

Country	Total Mobilized	Killed or Died of Wounds	Civilians Killed or Died from Injuries (estimate)	Total Killed or Died
Australia	1,000,000	27,000	nil	27,000
Britain	5,896,000	557,000	61,000	618,000
Canada	1,041,000	32,000	nil[b]	32,000
China	17,251,000	2,220,000	20,000,000	22,220,000
France	5,000,000	202,000	108,000	310,000
Germany	10,200,000	3,250,000	500,000	3,750,000
India	2,394,000	36,000	nil	36,000
Italy	3,100,000	149,000	783,000	932,000
Japan	9,700,000	1,507,000	672,000	2,179,000
Poland	1,000,000	64,000	2,000,000	2,064,000
Rumania	1,136,000	520,000	n.a.[c]	520,000
U.S.S.R.	22,000,000	7,500,000	7,500,000	15,000,000
United States	16,113,000	292,000	nil[b]	292,000
Yugoslavia	3,741,000	410,000	1,275,000	1,685,000
Total	99,572,000	16,766,000	32,899,000	49,665,000
Countries not listed above[a]	8,410,000	167,000	1,406,000	1,573,000
Grand Total	107,982,000	16,933,000	34,305,000	51,238,000

Source: Adapted from David Wood, *Conflict in the Twentieth Century,* p. 26, reprinted by permission of The International Institute for Strategic Studies; and Quincy Wright, *A Study of War,* p. 1542, by permission of the University of Chicago Press, copyright 1942, 1965 by the University of Chicago.

[a]Including Belgium, Brazil, Bulgaria, Czechoslovakia, Denmark, Finland, Greece, Hungary, Netherlands, New Zealand, Norway, Philippines, and South Africa.

[b]nil. None or less than 1,000.

[c]n.a. No figures available.

communism in czarist Russia—to Lenin and then to Stalin. World War I also weakened Germany (as it had weakened Russia) and opened the way to Nazism and the triumph of Hitler. Similarly, World War II enabled Stalin to establish communist regimes in most Eastern European countries and to dominate them. America's tragic involvement in Vietnam not only led to terrible devastation in that land but encouraged the murderous Pol Pot regime in neighboring Cambodia (Kampuchea).

Despite the end of the Cold War, the 1990 Iraqi invasion of Kuwait proves that there has been little reduction in conventional wars. Many of today's conflicts originated in bitter and long-standing ethnic tensions (see Figure 16.1). Tribal rivalries in Africa have led to devastating wars in Liberia, Mozambique, Ethiopia, Uganda, Angola, Nigeria, Burundi, and most recently in Rwanda. South Asia has been racked by ethnic violence in India, Sri Lanka, and Iran. In the Middle East, terrible ethnic violence has plagued Iraq, Syria, and Lebanon. And Southeast Asia has not been immune. Ethnic violence is not confined to the developing world. In Europe as well, especially in multicultural societies such as Yugoslavia and the former Soviet Union, the potential for widespread violence is ever present. Areas of the former Soviet Union have recently been racked by protests and violent conflict,

Figure 16.1
Ethnic- and religious-based conflicts, 1990–1996.

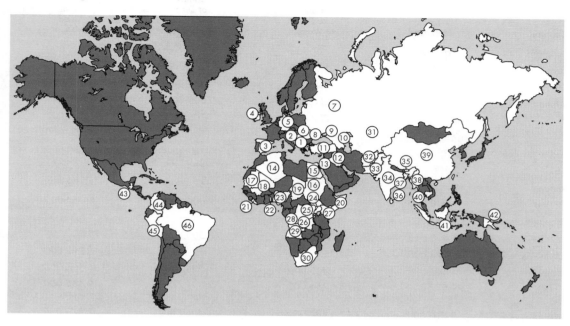

1	BOSNIA-HERZEGOVINA: Serbs vs. Muslims.	
2	CROATIA: Croatian separatist movement.	
3	SPAIN: Basque nationalist movement.	
4	BRITAIN: War in Northern Ireland.	
5	GERMANY: Right-wing Neo-Nazis vs. foreign workers.	
6	ROMANIA: Ethnic Hungarians want autonomy.	
7	RUSSIA: Chechenyan, Ingushetian, Ossetian autonomy.	
8	MOLDAVIA: Romanian majority seeks unification to Romania.	
9	GEORGIA: Georgian Muslim independence.	
10	AZERBAIJAN: Armenians vs. Azerbaijanis.	
11	TURKEY: Kurdish separatists.	
12	IRAQ: Kurds in north/Shiites in south.	
13	ISRAEL: Palestinian independence movement.	
14	ALGERIA: Islamic militants.	
15	EGYPT: Islamic militants.	
16	SUDAN: Arab Muslims vs. Christians in south.	

17 MAURITANIA: Arab government vs. black minority.
18 MALI: Ethnic Tuaregs fight for sovereignty.
19 CHAD: Zakawa vs. Gurane tribes.
20 SOMALIA: Clan anarchy.
21 LIBERIA: Gio and Mano fight the Krahns.
22 TOGO: Kabiye tribe vs. Ewe tribe.
23 NIGERIA: Muslim Hausas vs. Christian Yorubas.
24 UGANDA: Baganda and Banyarwanda vs. Acholi and Langi.
25 RWANDA: Hutu vs. Tutsi tribes.
26 BURUNDI: Hutu vs. Tutsi tribes.
27 KENYA: Intensive tribal warfare.
28 ZAIRE: Rebels vs. President Mobutu.
29 ANGOLA: Civil war. Government vs. UNITA.
30 SOUTH AFRICA: White vs. black and Xhosa vs. Zulu.
31 TAJIKISTAN: Tajik Muslims vs. Communists.
32 AFGHANISTAN: Civil war between rival Muslim armies.

33 PAKISTAN: Sindh and Northwest Frontier secessionists.
34 INDIA: Hindu vs. Muslim and Sikh vs. Hindu.
35 BHUTAN: Nepalese vs. government.
36 SRI LANKA: Hindu Tamils vs. Buddhist Sinhalese.
37 BANGLADESH: Muslim vs. Buddhist.
38 MYANMAR: Karen and other separatists. Muslim persecution.
39 CHINA: Tibetan rebellion and revolt by Turkic Muslims.
40 CAMBODIA: Khmer Rouge vs. noncommunists.
41 INDONESIA: East Timor civil war and Sumatran separatists.
42 PAPUA NEW GUINEA: Bouganville rebels.
43 GUATEMALA: Government vs. leftists. Indian repression.
44 COLOMBIA: Indians, Marxists, drug lords vs. government.
45 PERU: Shining Path Maoist guerillas vs. government.
46 BRAZIL: Amazon Indian tribes fight for homeland.

most notably in the province of Nagorno-Karabakh, where the struggle has been between Christian Armenians and Muslim Azerbaijanis. And finally, over the past couple of years, a particularly brutal civil conflict has broken out in Chechnya within the Russian Republic itself, where rebel secessionist forces continue to hold off the Russian Army.

The Onerous Burden of Arms Expenditures

World War III, fought with nuclear weapons, is a potential. Conventional warfare has been a grim reality. Another oppressive reality is the high levels of global expenditures on armaments. Economically, politically, and socially, the global quest for weapons is expensive.

While global expenditures for arms have declined recently, primarily because of the collapse of the Soviet Union and cuts in U.S. defense expenditures, they remain formidable. In 1993 the total global expenditure reached roughly $778 billion.[9]

The costs of weapons—both nuclear and conventional—are staggering. During the 1960s and 1970s America's frontline fighter planes cost between $2 million and $4 million each. By the 1990s, a mainstay fighter plane in the American inventory, such as the F-16 Falcon, cost between $18 million and $31 million depending on the model and various modification packages. The Lockheed Martin F-117 Nighthawk stealth attack aircraft runs an astounding $43 million a plane.[10] Nor are strategic weapons systems exactly cheap. The estimated cost of producing the Trident II missile was roughly $40 billion and B-2 bombers run $2.3 billion each.[11]

Although people tend to think of arms expenditures in terms of powerful and technically sophisticated weapons systems, the fact is that the world's military establishments are labor-intensive. The number of people in the military and closely related fields is staggering. At the end of 1994 there were an estimated 22 million people in the world's regular forces.[12] To that figure can be added tens of millions of paramilitaries, reserve forces, and civilians who work in defense research, production, or related activities.

Patterns in international arms trading are disturbing. During the 1980s, global arms transfers from Russia, France, the United Kingdom, West Germany, and China declined.[13] As the Cold War ended, Russian arms transfers in particular plummeted, although in recent years, the Russians have begun selling an enormous quantity of their conventional weapon systems in order to obtain hard currency. As the Russian arms sales initially plummeted, the United States and countries such as Italy, Czechoslovakia, Spain, Canada, Belgium, the Netherlands, and Sweden increased their arms sales slightly, picking up the slack. Developing countries have also increased their exports of arms, growing from roughly 4 percent of the market in 1979 to 10 percent by 1989.[14] A most important development here is the extent to which developing countries have begun to manufacture their own weapons systems. Brazil, Chile, China, North Korea, Pakistan, and South Korea, for instance, are actively pushing their way into the major leagues of weapons development, manufacturing, and sales. Twelve developing countries now produce combat aircraft; thirteen produce trainers and cargo planes; twelve produce major combat vessels; eleven produce armored vehicles of some kind; and ten produce artillery systems.[15] No less than nine developing countries—Argentina, Brazil, Egypt, India, Iran, Iraq, Libya, North Korea, Pakistan, and South Korea—either unilaterally or in consortium with a second country, produce some form of ballistic missile system.[16] Seventeen of the forty-one countries that sold weapons to either Iran or Iraq during their decade-long war in the 1980s were developing countries.

Perhaps the most distressing aspect of the arms race is that everywhere it drains resources away from basic human needs: for constructive jobs; for food, clothing, housing, education, and medical care; and for social and cultural development. As Ruth Sivard notes, "In the 1980s, two governments in three have spent more to defend their citizens against military attack than against the everyday hazards of disease, accidents, and ill health; one in three has spent more on military power than on education and health care combined."[17]

Spending in the arms race hurts the battle against inflation and national debt; militates against healthy economic growth; and wastes valuable money, personnel, and resources. In rich and poor countries throughout the world, governments neglect basic human needs in favor of military might and the technology of destruction.

The Dangers of the Sovereign Nation-State System

The threat of nuclear war, the disastrous consequences of conventional wars, and the burden of arms expenditures are all intimately tied up with the sovereign nation-state system. Robert Holmes makes this point as part of a scathing attack on the state system in his highly regarded book On *War and Morality*.[18] Holmes notes:

> The threat of nuclear annihilation grows out of the workings of an international system in which, if many realists are correct, the promotion of national interest is the governing norm. And if, as many of them would also have it, national interest ought to be the guiding norm (either of some or of all nations), then we need some accounting of how such a judgment is justified in light of the apparent consequences of its implementation. If one places the highest value upon the survival of the state, and if that survival is jeopardized by the pursuit of national interest, it would seem that pursuit should be abandoned.[19]

Continuing this line of reasoning in relation to the magnitude of the Holocaust against European Jews, Holmes states:

> The underlying issue is whether there are any limits— moral as well as legal—to what a government may justifiably do to try to preserve the state. . . . If a government considers it acceptable that millions should die under these circumstances, why should it shrink from killing a fraction of that number—say six million, to think the unthinkable for a moment—if by doing it could remove no less a perceived threat to national security?[20]

The nation-state system requires countries— for example, the United States, the People's Republic of China, and Israel—to protect their national interests by relying on their own arms. No peaceful appeal to a supranational authority or global law is required in the event of serious conflicts between nations. Nothing prohibits a nation's ultimate resort to war to protect its vital interests. The United States, Russia, Britain, France, China, and Israel have interpreted their own vital national interests as requiring stockpiles of nuclear weapons and the capability to deliver them. Nations such as Iran, Iraq, and Pakistan, which some believe have also tried to acquire nuclear weapons, may have reached the same judgment. These nation-state interpretations feed an arms race and increase the threat of nuclear war.

National rivalries have also played a major role in triggering conventional wars. Wars existed before the modern nation-state system took shape with the Peace of Westphalia in 1648. But they have become broader and more savage with the development of modern nationalism—and, paradoxically, with the advance of democracy, science, and socialism. Nationalistic rivalries have had devastating consequences in the twentieth century. Nationalistic conflicts helped produce World War I. The nationalistic and militaristic ambitions of Germany and Japan primarily caused World War II.

Since World War II, wars for national liberation have also been fought. The great nation-states of Western Europe did not usually relinquish their colonial empires—for example, in Asia and Africa—peacefully. They often fought to protect what they considered their vital national interests in preserving their empires, whether in India, Malaysia, Indonesia, Indochina, Algeria, or the Congo. Sometimes the colonial powers granted independence with reasonable speed and grace, as the British did in India after partitioning the subcontinent between Pakistan and India. In other instances—the French in Indochina and Algeria, for example—nation-states fought bitter and bloody battles against "native" peoples who felt justified in resorting to arms to gain national independence and freedom.

The great Western nation-states are not the only ones to go to war because of rivalry. Wars between India and Pakistan, Israel and its Arab neighbors, Iran and Iraq, Ethiopia and Somalia, Vietnam and Cambodia, and Peru and Chile indicate that nationalistic rivalries also cause war among less powerful countries. Whether small or large, weak or powerful, the sovereign nation-state defers to no higher law or court to settle disputes affecting its vital national interests.

The imperative of self-defense leads nation-states to arm themselves, and thus begins the spiral of the arms race. Nation after nation seeks protection in more arms and more sophisticated (and expensive) weapons—and, if it can manage, even nuclear arms. So the war system seems locked in a deadly embrace with the sovereign nation-state system.

The Uncertainties of a Shifting Balance of Power

Nations seek security not only in self-defense but also in alliances; they seek a posture of strength through the balance of power. As we saw in Chapter 14, the **balance of power** is designed to prevent domination—whether of a continent or a globe—that would actually or potentially threaten a nation's (or a group of nations') vital interests. The balance required to protect such vital interests can be either (1) an equilibrium, or equality, of power, or (2) a favorable or superior power relationship (that is, possessing more power than an opponent, or being able to inflict unacceptable damage). Both equilibrium and superiority of power are designed to deter aggression that would upset the existing power relationship and damage the vital national interests of those attacked.

But the bipolar distribution of power has collapsed. The Warsaw Pact no longer exists, and NATO is in the throes of self-examination. Although the United States is still very powerful, it is no longer quite the hegemonic power it was for perhaps the fifteen years following World War II. Russia and other republics of the former Soviet Union suffer from severe internal economic troubles and so have clearly moved away from extensive foreign ventures. Emerging global powers such as Japan and Germany base their strength far more on economic prowess than on military prowess.

And yet, certain vestiges of the bipolar balance of power remain and are of great concern. Enormous nuclear and conventional weapons arsenals still exist, leaving a feeling of insecurity. This sense of insecurity remains because nuclear war is a possibility. So far the balance of power (understood as the balance of terror) has prevented the outbreak of World War III, but what might happen tomorrow? The United States, for example, remains nervous about Soviet nuclear forces, particularly tactical weapons spread throughout a territory that has, in fact, badly fragmented. Will the Russian government in Moscow retain control of all these weapons? Will reactionary, revolutionary, or secessionist forces seize them? Will a unified Germany constitute a threat to Russia, particularly without the East European buffer zone? These and other questions haunt the world as the international balance of power shifts.

Will a new military balance of power emerge in the future? Will China dramatically increase her military power, particularly nuclear power? Can the United States and Russia extricate themselves from balance-of-power politics if other nuclear powers emerge? These questions are relevant not only because of the insecurities that characterize balance-of-power politics but also because of the enormous costs: the price of armaments to maintain the balance, the jockeying for power in various regions of the world, the propensity to intervene militarily in other countries, and the danger of crises such as the Berlin blockade or missiles in Cuba.

The United Nations and a Changing Balance of Power

If the balance of power (which has prevented World War III, albeit with questionable stability and at a high cost) is in fact changing, is there another system to keep the world from merely reconfiguring a military balance? Can the United Nations provide such a system? Despite modest successes, the United Nations has not advanced genuine collective security. It has not been able to dispel the mortal threat of nuclear war. It has not succeeded in averting a number of conventional wars, and it has not successfully moved the world toward disarmament. Put simply, the United Nations has not been able to cope with the dangers of war posed by the sovereign nation-state system.

Will the end of the Cold War allow an invigorated United Nations to fulfill the objectives of its Charter? The international response to the Iraqi invasion of Kuwait relied heavily on the U.N.'s collective security machinery by imposing an economic embargo on Iraq and authorizing the Desert Storm military response. Despite success in this case, it is too early to tell whether the U.N.'s collective security will routinely be used to deal with international conflicts. Certainly, the lack of an effective United Nations response to Serbian aggression and ethnic cleansing in Bosnia-Herzegovina raises doubts. We therefore turn to other possibilities for creative breakthroughs to a more peaceful world.

ALTERNATIVE APPROACHES TO A MORE PEACEFUL WORLD

In this section we consider six approaches to a more peaceful world order: (1) a new balance of power, (2) an invigorated United Nations, (3) global economic integration, (4) functionalism, (5) disarmament and a new global order, and (6) nonviolence. These alternatives do not exhaust all the possibilities and they may sometimes overlap. They do illustrate the strengths and weaknesses of key approaches. While reading this section, consider whether they are truly "creative breakthroughs."

Peace Through a New Balance of Power

This first approach is based on the assumption that foreign policy must realistically accept the struggle for power in world affairs generally and between Great Powers specifically. Great Powers will seek to exert and extend their influence on behalf of their vital national interests. Only power can balance power; only strength can deter or defeat aggression. Current trends in the international system indicate that a new balance of power, while based on the power versus power equation, would differ in some ways from the system that characterized the Cold War.

First, a new balance of power would probably be multipolar rather than bipolar. The United States, Japan, Germany, Russia, China, and perhaps some regional units such as Western Europe, Latin America, or Southeast Asia might constitute a new balance-of-power system. Whether all of these actors would have nuclear weapons is uncertain. No doubt all would be capable of arming themselves with such weapons if they chose.

Second, it is likely that a new balance would place greater emphasis on economic power (though military might would certainly not be abandoned). Apropos of this new power configuration is a comment by former Prime Minister Margaret Thatcher at the end of the 1990 Economic Summit in Houston, Texas. Mrs. Thatcher noted that a new balance of power had been formed in the world, but, rather than being based on bullets and bombs, the new balance was created with dollars, yen, pounds, and marks.

A new multipolar balance of power might preserve the peace if three conditions were to prevail: (1) if all members of the system have sufficient countervailing military power (in nuclear or conventional arms) to deter attack by any other member of the system; (2) if all members of the system have adequate economic and political power to defeat nonmilitary threats by any other member of the system; and (3) if all members of the system have the political skill, via the diplomacy of accommodation and creative statesmanship, to avoid mistaken judgments about vital interests, to pursue detente (relaxation of tensions), and to build the conditions of international security, human rights, economic prosperity, and social justice that will make free peoples immune to authoritarian rule.

Such a policy is both desirable and feasible, but it will call for strong, astute, and farsighted statesmanship. It is desirable because it guards the member nations' vital interests, particularly peace and national freedom. The policy provides time to work, step-by-step, toward arms control, real disarmament, worldwide democracy and constitutionalism, and economic well-being.

Peace through a new balance of power is feasible because this policy did work at the bipolar level to prevent World War III. It safeguarded the freedom of Western Europe and Berlin. It was also compatible with modest efforts to achieve detente and the ban on nuclear weapons in space, the prohibition against testing atomic weapons in the atmosphere, the Washington-Moscow hot line, SALT I and II, and the Intermediate Nuclear Force Treaty (INF). The balance of terror, although not ideal—based as it is on the recognition of mutually assured destruction in the event of a Soviet-American nuclear exchange—did prevent World War III. It made the United States and the Soviet Union careful about taking actions that would threaten each other's vital interests. It restrained aspects of Soviet-American rivalry that might have gotten out of hand and escalated into the nuclear war that neither party wanted.

Keen statesmanship is necessary if this policy is to work. Members of the balance-of-power system must not be tempted to make a preemptive nuclear first strike. All sides must interpret their national interests sensibly and not be motivated by misguided ambitions to save the world. Amidst the military, political, and ideological rivalry that so often characterizes the Great Powers, accommodation must be sought, and opportunities for advancing a just world order must be pursued.

The weaknesses of this policy must, however, be recognized:

1. A policy of strength calls for armaments, and this call figured in the arms race during the Cold War years.

2. Even overwhelming strength does not always enable major actors in the system to deter aggression. For example, the old Cold War bipolar balance did not dissuade a less powerful actor such as North Korea from attempting to seize South Korea. Nor were the North Vietnamese deterred from attempting to unify Vietnam—first through peaceful means (nationwide elections) and then through internal subversion, guerrilla warfare, and military intervention. In Vietnam (in contrast to Korea, where the United States intervened with the U.N.'s blessing), American arms did not prevent the Communists from taking over the whole country.

3. It is not always easy to identify vital national interests. Was American involvement in Vietnam dictated by vital American interests? Would a Communist Vietnam really have upset the American/Soviet balance of power?

4. Following the old adage, "Those who possess a gun will eventually use it," a balance-of-power policy based to any degree on military strength increases the probability that at some point power will be used for purposes other than deterrence.

5. The balance-of-power mentality may make it extremely difficult to avoid the paranoia that, for example, sometimes characterized the Cold War in the 1950s.

6. A multipolar balance is more complex than a bipolar balance system; because there are more major actors, assessing the power of each relative to the others is far more difficult.

7. A new emphasis on economic power does not guarantee a lower probability of military confrontation. An economic balance of power can get out of hand. Rather than an arms race, member states might engage in trade wars, using protectionist methods (high tariffs, quotas, and so on) to counteract the economic power of actors they view as threatening. Of course, economic warfare can lead to military warfare if decision

makers believe that vital national interests are threatened.

But what are some other alternatives for a more peaceful world order?

United Nations Third-Party Activities and Collective Security

The ending of the Cold War has profoundly affected the United Nations. This is most evident in the Security Council's ability to agree on a variety of issues that had previously sustained frequent vetoes by either the United States or the Soviet Union. The impact is also reflected in the major powers' propensity to give the organization more genuine power. This raises the possibility of a more vigorous and effective role for the United Nations as a third-party actor or a counterforce to aggression in international conflicts.

Third-Party Activity—It should be possible to build on the U.N.'s current third-party activities through a resourceful secretary-general, supported by a Security Council fulfilling its role under the charter and by a General Assembly equally dedicated to maintaining international peace and security.[21]

Third-party activities cover "a wide range of essentially ad hoc techniques: good offices, conciliation, investigation, mediation, arbitration, observation, truce supervision, interposition [in the case of the United Nations, placing U.N. forces between the fighting parties]."[22] The third party does not participate directly in the conflict but seeks to help both sides resolve the situation. The third party does not coerce; it persuades.

The third-party approach thus relies on the essentially persuasive means of Chapter VI of the charter, "Pacific Settlement of Disputes," rather than on the essentially coercive means of Chapter VII, "Action with Respect to Threats to the Peace, Breaches of the Peace, and Acts of Aggression." That is, third-party intervention looks to such means as "negotiation, enquiry, mediation, conciliation, arbitration, judicial settlement, re-

sort to regional agencies or arrangements, or other peaceful means."[23] It does not rely on economic, diplomatic, and military sanctions. The third party helps opponents work out their disputes peacefully or extricate themselves from military conflicts. For example, the third party may simply help opponents talk to each other. The third party may dramatize the dangers in failing to reach an accord. The third party may dissolve fears by inspecting danger spots and verifying the absence of aggressive forces. The third party may provide a neutral buffer between military forces.

This approach to peace recognizes the facts of international politics. It recognizes that the United Nations is not, and was not intended to be, a true collective security organization, in which the overwhelmingly powerful peaceful nations use their collective strength (through diplomatic boycott, economic pressure, or military force) to deter and punish an aggressive state that dares violate the peace. This approach recognizes that during the Cold War years, veto power made it impossible for the Security Council to act coercively against a Great Power that was accused of or guilty of aggression and made it extremely difficult, if not impossible, to act against an aggressive ally of a Great Power. This approach recognizes that even with the end of the Cold War, it may be difficult for U.N. members to agree that collective action against aggression should be taken. The United Nations' failure to halt ethnic cleansing in the former Yugoslavia is a case in point. The best the Security Council could muster was a rather ineffective peacekeeping force, UNPROFOR, which operated from 1992 to 1995. The ethnic cleansing and warfare was not really brought under control until the fall of 1995 when a powerful non-U.N., United States/NATO–led force, IFOR, was deployed in Bosnia to oversee the Dayton Accords, which had been brokered by the United States, not the United Nations.

The persuasive peacekeeping activities of the United Nations were pioneered by Dag Hammarskjold, secretary-general from 1953 to 1961,

A United Nations peacekeeper from Venezuela stands guard at a camp where Nicaraguan forces surrendered their weapons to ONUCA as part of the overall peace process in Central America.

and they have characterized the bulk of the Security Council's work. These tasks are also prominent in the General Assembly.

The Role of the Secretary-General—According to the U.N. Charter, the secretary-general, who is appointed by the General Assembly on the recommendation of the Security Council, is the chief administrative officer of the United Nations and has a vital concern for matters that threaten international peace and security. The secretary-general, in the spirit of Dag Hammarskjold, is expected to exert bold leadership to save succeeding generations from the scourge of war and to encourage nations to live together peacefully. The secretary-general must pursue a key purpose of the United Nations: to prevent and remove threats to peace and to bring about peaceful, just, and lawful settlement of international disputes.

Building on the creative initiatives of predecessors, the secretary-general can resourcefully expand his or her role to deal with Great Power disputes and with disputes that could escalate to involve the Great Powers.

Under favorable conditions—namely, having the trust and support of the major power—the secretary-general is well equipped to perform important third-party functions. The secretary-general position is impartial, respected, trusted, knowledgeable, skillful, creative, and capable. He or she has legitimacy as the chief executive officer of the United Nations. He or she can act with speed and dispatch, possesses important resources, and can be given additional resources by means of a "crisis staff," located in a well-enhanced crisis center.

The Role of the Security Council—Clearly, the secretary-general's position will be strengthened when the Security Council itself is committed to third-party activity. According to a keen analysis by Richard Rhone, between 1946 and 1978, the heart of the Cold War years, 77 percent of Security Council resolutions in response to questions involving peace and security were essentially "persuasive"—that is, in accord with a third-party model. This is in contrast to 14 percent of such resolutions that were essentially "coercive" (the kinds of sanctions anticipated by Chapter VII of the U.N. Charter), and also in contrast to 9 percent that were essentially "administrative." Rhone concludes that the Security Council is "primarily an agent of third-party activity."[24]

Such Security Council support for third-party activity provides a legitimate base for the secretary-general's third-party role. If a permanent member's veto deadlocks the Security Council, the General Assembly can reinforce the secretary-general and thus provide legitimacy for the secretary-general's third-party initiatives.

Strengths and Weaknesses of Third-Party Activity—United Nations third-party efforts at the end of the Cold War and beginning of the post–Cold War era were impressive. United Nations personnel helped negotiate and observe the Soviet withdrawal from Afghanistan. Third-party efforts helped work out difficulties between Afghanistan and Pakistan. The secretary-general arranged a cease-fire between Iran and Iraq after their terrible war of attrition; the United Nations also polices the cease-fire. United Nations observers oversaw the Nicaraguan elections of 1990, and a team was sent to Angola to monitor the withdrawal of Cuban troops. Finally, a U.N. group was established to administer elections in Namibia and to smooth the way to independence. These developments highlight the brightened prospects of the United Nations at the end of the Cold War.

But the third-party process has not been without problems. For instance, in Angola, following successful U.N.-supervised elections in 1992, the country plunged into renewed civil war. Moreover, as mentioned earlier, the U.N. proved incapable of stopping Serbian aggression and ethnic cleansing in Bosnia-Herzegovina.

So, despite some success, this third-party approach is not a panacea. In appraising the U.N.'s third-party role as a creative breakthrough, we can identify at least eight weaknesses:

1. Third-party intervention will not work if the parties to the dispute do not consent to such intervention, and in some cases they will not.
2. The veto of a Security Council resolution on third-party activity may weaken the secretary-general's role.
3. The secretary-general and the Security Council may disagree.

4. Because of the time it takes for the Security Council (or the General Assembly) to act, the secretary-general may have to risk speedy action in a controversial case, which may create difficulties.
5. The office of secretary-general may not always be held by a creative, resourceful, and sagacious person
6. Even with the best intentions—and the fullest support in the Security Council or General Assembly—third-party activities may not work.
7. Adequate financial and other resources (including a crisis center, a crisis staff, and a U.N. police force) may not be available.
8. Third-party peacekeeping usually attacks the symptoms, not the causes, of conflicts; it does not address the fundamental causes of war.

In addition, it should be noted that the United Nations is having difficulty wrestling with conflicts that some have referred to as being in the gray area, where neither traditional peacekeeping nor collective security measures seem appropriate. These conflicts—like those in Haiti, Bosnia, and Rwanda—found initial U.N. intervention occurring while the violence still raged. Further, these conflicts were basically internal, not classic cases of aggression by one nation against another. In these cases, the Secretary-General's neutrality was highly susceptible to compromise since he was forced, almost by the nature of the conflict itself, to take sides. Whether the United Nations becomes more adept at dealing with these kinds of conflagrations remains to be seen. At the very least, a great deal will depend on the support of the major powers on the Security Council.[25]

Collective Security—The inability of the United Nations to make full use of collective security during the Cold War was treated extensively in Chapter 14. But the end of the Cold War may have made the collective punishment of aggressors under Chapter VII of the United Nations

Charter more feasible. After all, the two super-powers are no longer squared off against each other in the Security Council. But two recent conflicts indicate that it is far too early for a definitive prediction about the future of **collective security.**

Iraq's 1991 invasion of Kuwait led to more than a dozen Security Council resolutions condemning the aggressor and levying sanctions. A worldwide economic embargo against Iraq was established, with military force authorized to enforce it. Ultimately, direct military force was authorized to expel Iraq from Kuwait. Desert Storm was carried out under these resolutions. Later, authorization was granted for United Nations teams to enter Iraq to find and destroy its stockpiles of and production facilities for weapons of mass destruction—nuclear, chemical, and biological. But it should also be noted that few conflicts in the international arena so *clearly* threaten the national security interests of so many countries as the Iraqi actions did. For the United States, the European community, and Japan, the seizure of the Kuwaiti oil fields and the threat to the Saudi oil fields was unacceptable. For many of the Arab states, Saddam Hussein's actions were a clear sign that he was a potential threat to their security.

Nevertheless, the collective actions against Iraq might be a cause for optimism. But as already noted, the United Nations' response to the tragedy in the former state of Yugoslavia was anything but heartening. Serbian aggression against the people of Croatia and Bosnia-Herzegovina remained unchecked until U.S./NATO action in 1995. In this case, the threat to national security interests was not so clear.

At best it seems doubtful whether United Nations collective security will be an effective instrument for peace on any consistent basis, even with the end of the Cold War. The major obstacle to collective security is no longer an ideologically based veto in the Security Council. The main obstacle now appears to be the international community's lack of will and resources to use the instrument with any degree of consistency.

What, then, in addition to a new balance of power, strengthened third-party activities by the United Nations, or collective security, might lead to a more peaceful world order?

Global Economic Integration

Some scholars contend that global **economic integration,** which is well under way, works powerfully against the basic norms of the nation-

Serbian soldiers after taking the town of Srebrenica. Muslim refugees were driven from the town. Ethnic cleansing was not halted until a NATO force led by the United States, IFOR, was deployed into Bosnia.

state system. Extensive patterns of global integration have developed in the last twenty years. Seyom Brown notes,

> As many as 20,000 corporations have subsidiaries in two or more countries, amounting to some 100,000 firms around the world that are controlled from corporate headquarters in a foreign country. These transnational firms are estimated to be responsible for marketing at least three-fourths of all the world's goods and services that traverse national borders.[26]

Karlheinz Kaske, chief executive of Siemens, the German electronics firm, asserts, "It is no exaggeration to say that international business is racing ahead, leaving international politics trailing in its wake."[27]

Strengths—Governments increasingly participate in the integration process. As described in some detail in Chapter 14, the European Union seeks to thoroughly integrate the economies of Western Europe. The United States and Canada signed a free trade agreement in 1990, and a new free trade treaty between the United States, Canada, and Mexico (the North American Free Trade Agreement, or NAFTA) was ratified in 1993. Other regional economic units exist in Southeast Asia, Africa, and South America.

The question, however, is not whether powerful economic integrative forces are operating in the international system and leading to greater interdependence. Obviously they are. The question is: Do they constitute a basis for a new world order that is better equipped to mitigate violent conflict, ensure adequate standards of living for the world's population, and guarantee fundamental human rights?

A certain logic argues that economic integration helps reduce international conflict. In its simplest (indeed, probably oversimplified) form, widespread economic integration mean that many countries have economic investments in other countries. Therefore, it is in the interest of all countries to ensure that each other's economies thrive. To injure or destroy another economy is to risk injuring or perhaps destroying one's own economy. If economic integration becomes elaborate enough, warfare will be perceived as benefiting

no one. As Charles Kegley, Jr. and Eugene Wittkopf put it:

> global interdependence may draw the world's diverse components together in pursuit of mutual survival and welfare. Awareness of the common destiny of all, alongside the inability of sovereign states to address many shared problems through unilateral national action, may energize efforts to put aside national competition. Conflict will recede, according to this reasoning, as few states can afford to disentangle themselves from the interdependent ties that bind them together in the common fate on which their welfare depends. From this perspective, then, we should welcome the continued tightening of interstate linkages, for they strengthen the seams that bind together the fragile tapestry of international relations.[28]

Finally, as the integrative process becomes more complex, the need for multilateral diplomacy increases. Group deliberation and decision making about how to manage this complex system becomes imperative.

Weaknesses—Does global economic integration provide the basis for a new world order? Most international relations scholars and practitioners would probably agree that economic integration is a positive force in international affairs. But it is not without its problems:

1. It is not at all clear that economic integration can either confront or overcome some of the most intractable problems in international affairs: ethnic, religious, cultural, and territorial tensions and disputes.

2. Multinational corporations and financial institutions provide much of the impetus behind economic integration, and despite international efforts to establish guidelines of behavior, there are still serious questions about their accountability.

3. Despite the promise of such dramatic patterns as the European Union (which holds out the hope of genuine global integration), critics worry about the limited perspective of such regional organizations. The critics contend that in periods of scarce resources or generally bad economic times, these trade zones could adopt some less-desirable traits

of nation-states, such as protectionism and self-righteousness. Regional associations would be characterized by the same blind loyalties that we have seen in nation-states. Moreover, globally oriented integrationists, such as the functionalists, contend that regional associations still do not address humanity's fundamental problems—disease, food production and distribution, shelter, poverty, environmental quality—from the necessary global perspective.

Peace Through Functionalism

Those who endorse peace through **functionalism** affirm that human beings will move toward world peace if functional organizations can better meet common needs and advance mutual interests. With increased powers, funds, and activities, and by grappling with common problems, these organizations can build a trusting global community. The common problems involve providing decent jobs and increased productivity for workers, farmers, and fishermen; providing better health care for children, mothers, and workers; building decent housing; developing effective transportation; providing good schools; developing freer trade, access to raw materials, credit, and markets; performing scientific research; curtailing crime; limiting pollution; and encouraging cultural development and creative uses of leisure. In solving such basic problems, some of the underlying causes of war—distrust, fear, poverty, illiteracy, and disease—will be dealt with. In dealing pragmatically with these problems, humanity can transcend the limitations of national sovereignty and build a workable global system.

David Mitrany has made one of the most cogent arguments on behalf of the functional approach. Here we present and, as necessary, modify and update the analysis in his influential book, *A Working Peace System: An Argument for the Functional Development of International Organization.*[29]

Background—The fundamental problem of the present age, according to Mitrany's initial formulation, is to determine how to achieve a new international system. This system must be able to prevent aggression and to organize peace and peaceful change. Without destroying the valuable diversity and freedom of nations, the system must be able to unify a badly divided world. The new world order must also successfully address the world's mounting insistence on social and economic betterment. National loyalties have tended to divide people politically in the modern world, even if they have frequently increased human freedom within the nation-state. On the other hand, the demand for social and economic betterment and the fact of economic interdependence have increasingly bound people together, even if they have also created tensions between the rich and poor in all countries and between countries.

Logically, unity might be obtained by conquest or by consent, immediately or over a long period, by revolution or by reform. The new world order might result in a centralized world state or a federal state or a global order. The new world order might be pursued according to a formal, constitutional blueprint or by informal, practical pursuit of urgent needs.

On the basis of these considerations, Mitrany reformulated the problem as follows: *How is it possible to stimulate a voluntary and progressive evolution of world society that will preserve the valuable aspects of nationality and yet satisfy the legitimate needs of humankind?*

Mitrany was impressed by the difficulties of the formal, constitutional approach to peace through a new kind of international system. He did not believe that current nations, divided as they are and functioning within the framework of a balance-of-power system, will put aside their differences and agree at some constitutional convention to establish a global world order.

Similarly, he did not believe that the United Nations could do the job required, because it leaves untouched the identity and policy of the sovereign nation-states that compose it; it is too loose an organization to achieve unity in diversity.

Theoretically, a federal system of international organization provides the cohesion lacking in a league of sovereign nations, but, in Mitrany's opinion, the basic community of interest needed for such a federal state does not yet exist worldwide. A federal system would have to operate within the limits of a region or within the framework of an ideological union. However, such a regional or ideological union would be defective because it could divide the world into several potentially competing units.

And so, after rejecting unity via conquest or the other alternatives, Mitrany outlined his case for the functional approach.

The Case for Functionalism—The primary advantage of the functional approach, according to Mitrany, is that it would "overlay political divisions with a spreading web of international activities and agencies, in which and through which the interests and life of all nations would be gradually integrated."[30] International government, he argued, can be effective only when it coexists with practical international activities. The starting point for a system of peace must be common needs, with momentary disregard for the presence of jealously sovereign nation-states and the absence of a larger political or ideological unity. The proper approach must be experimental and practical, free of insistence on formal blueprints and constitutional requirements.

Mitrany would use the functional approach to deal with the problem of national sovereignty and nations' insistence on protecting their vital interests through military power. As peoples and nations work together to meet practical and pressing problems—involving trade and shipping, health and literacy, agriculture and fishing, aviation and broadcasting, scientific research and development—sovereignty would be gradually transferred, in the work involved, from the participating nations to the agencies performing the agreed-on job. "By entrusting an authority with a certain task," Mitrany wrote, "carrying with it command over the requisite powers and means, a slice of sovereignty is transferred from the old authority to the new; and the accumulation of such partial transfers in time brings about a translation of the true seat of authority."[31]

In this way, too, Mitrany maintained, the tough questions of peaceful change, sovereign borders, and vital national interests would be given a new perspective.

Peaceful change must come about internationally as it does nationally. We can make changes of frontiers unnecessary by making frontiers meaningless through the continuous development of common activities and interests across them. A change of frontier is bound to disturb the social life of the groups concerned, no matter whether it comes about peacefully or forcibly. The purpose of peaceful change can only be to prevent such disturbance; indeed, one might say that the true task of peaceful change is to remove the need and the wish for changes of frontiers. The functional approach may be justifiably expected to do precisely that: It would increase positive and constructive common work, common habits and interests, thus making frontier lines meaningless by overlaying them with a natural growth of common activities and common administrative agencies.[32]

The functional approach would bypass the thorny questions of sovereignty, legal equality, and national prestige. The keys to what nation does what would be (1) common interests or common problems, (2) the nature of the task, and (3) capability. Thus nations with common interests or problems would work together— say, on railroad or transportation problems in Europe or North America or Africa. Geography—not politics or ideology—would indicate the broad, continental lines of organization. The nature of some tasks—say, aviation or broadcasting, especially with the advent of satellites— might dictate organization on a universal scale. Nations would be involved in tasks that match their capabilities, and the principle of natural selection would operate to determine which nation would have which role in which task. No nation would be arbitrarily excluded from a task that it was interested in and could handle. Seagoing nations (such as Britain, Japan, Norway, or Greece) would have a major role in shipping and fishing. Mountainous countries, or other nations with the appropriate water and terrain (such as Switzerland, the United States, Egypt, or India), would cooperate to produce hydroelectric power. Countries with lots of sun (such as Israel or Libya) would cooperate to manage solar power.

The Problem of Security—Mitrany recognized the special problem of security in a peaceful world order. He believed that security is first among the essential functions that must eventually be transferred to a new international organization: "There can be no real transfer of sovereignty until defense is entrusted to a common authority, because national means of defense are also means of offense and also of possible resistance to that common authority." He recognized that the problem of security, a political problem, is crucial, "for on its being solved effectively the successful working of the other [functional] activities will depend." He saw security as an important function that cannot be considered in isolation from other functions. Security is indispensable to the peaceful growth of an international society but, interestingly, cannot produce that growth by itself.

Mitrany believed that, in addition to developing the conditions that must underpin the eventual world community, functional agencies can play an important role in advancing the crucial function of security. For example, they might watch over and check activities that lead to aggressive warfare, whether nuclear or conventional, including mobilization of soldiers, deployment of armaments, uses of transport, and accumulation of strategic materials. In conventional wars these agencies might even check those threatening aggression by withholding vital services from the potential aggressors.

Fulfilling the Vision—Mitrany was thus persuaded that the functional approach, if followed, could "grow in time into a rounded political system." The system would, of course, grow gradually by natural selection and evolution, tested and accepted by experience. It would have a cohesiveness based on mutual service and a strength rooted in free growth and successful accomplishment. Functional integration would pave the way for political integration. A functional international society, socially interdependent and economically united, would prepare for a more complete political federation, in which people could turn from preoccupation with the prevention of aggression and war and focus their attention on the "real tasks of our common society—the conquest of poverty and of disease and ignorance."

The specialized agencies of the United Nations illustrate the functional approach in operation today. The European Union also illustrate regional functionalism at work. With increased powers, funds, and activities, such specialized agencies could move toward fulfilling Mitrany's vision.

Weaknesses—What are the weaknesses in the purely functional approach to a more peaceful world order?

1. It does not deal with the immediately pressing problems of nation-state rivalry that threaten to break out into armed conflict.
2. It does not move the world immediately away from the mortal threat of nuclear war.
3. It has not yet been demonstrated that the functional approach will lead nations to slowly give up dangerous aspects of their sovereign power.
4. It is not clear how the functional approach, further down the road, will help transfer national means of defense to a common global authority.
5. It is not clear that economic, social, and scientific successes in dealing with poverty, disease, ignorance, and other problems are strong enough to overcome nations' sover-

eign pride, parochialism, and prejudice, or elites' desire to maintain their privileges.

On this final note of criticism, we should mention a vision in the intellectual tradition of functionalism yet different in one important respect. This is **neofunctionalism**.[33] Mitrany's vision of functionalism was essentially non-political: the world must work around the political flashpoints that divide the human race. The neofunctionalists believe that human beings cannot avoid the political problems that divide them. Nor can they ignore the power of nationalism and of national elites. In recognition of this, cooperation and integration must take place at the political level and not be confined to merely economic, technical, and humanitarian levels. Political union is as important as nonpolitical union.

But are more radical approaches realistic?

A New Global Order and a Security System Based on Disarmament Now

Advocates of a new global order take sharp issue with the balance-of-power model and its continued reliance on the sovereign nation-state system. They are sympathetic to third-party activities through the United Nations but seek a more effective global security system, one that will move toward real **disarmament** and not hesitate to establish an effective force to maintain the peace. They are also sympathetic to the functional approach but believe that problems of security and global organization must be addressed now.

An articulate spokesman for this approach to a new global order is Richard A. Falk.[34] Falk's values are peace, social and political justice, economic well-being, and ecological balance. Here we will focus on his argument for a breakthrough to a more peaceful world order.[35]

How It Would Work—Falk calls his central guidance system the World Polity Association. Its principal policymaking organ would be a World Assembly that "will set world standards and render binding decisions by achieving a four-fifths majority vote within each of its three chambers [Assembly of Governments, Assembly of Peoples, Assembly of Organization and Association] having two hundred votes apiece." The World Assembly could also make recommendations by a two-thirds vote of its three chambers. The Council of Principals would function as the main executive body of the World Polity Association (see Figure 16.2). The World Security System—our concern here—would focus on minimizing large-scale violence.

The Central Committee of the World Security System—comprising the directors of the World Security Forces, the World Disarmament Service, and the World Grievance System—would "coordinate activities directly related to war prevention."

Thus, the World Security Forces would maintain international peace under all possible circumstances. This organization would operate as a police force rather than as an army. It would emphasize nonviolent strategies of policing and regard violence as a last resort. It would work closely with regional security forces, would use early-warning procedures against violators of the peace, and would use minimum-violence weapons and tactics.

The "permanent constabulary" of the World Security Forces, Falk holds, "might be a police force of 200,000, or even less, supplemented by regional constabulary establishments of 50,000 to 75,000 and by much larger standby militia forces specially trained under national auspices for emergency international service." The constabulary "might undertake most, if not all, of its functions without benefit of arms."

The World Disarmament Service would "supervise the agreed-upon process of disarmament, . . . report violations immediately to the World Security Forces and the Council of Principals, and . . . verify compliance with the terms of the disarmament arrangement so as to maintain confidence." The "goal of disarmament will be to eliminate national military establishments." The World Disarmament Service would stress non-

Figure 16.2
Central guidance in Falk's World Order Preference Model: The World Polity Association.

Source: Reprinted with permission of Macmillan Publishing Co., Inc. From A Study of Future Worlds by Richard A. Falk. Copyright 1975 Institute for World Order, New York.

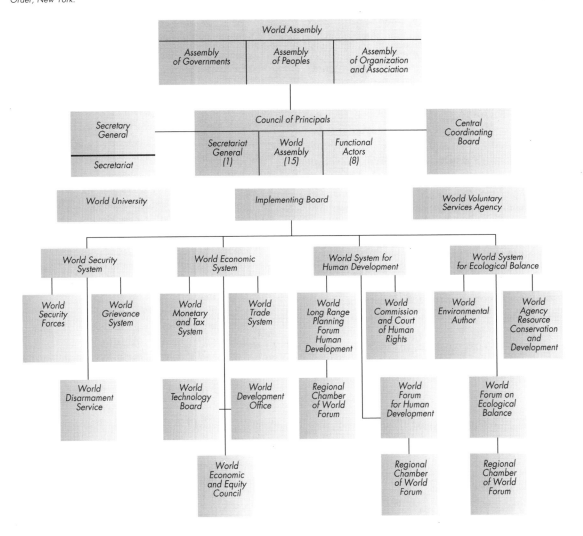

violent, conciliatory resolution of actual or potential violations.

The World Grievance System would rely strongly on "mediational procedures and flexible solutions" and on regional decentralized approaches. Its Central Commission would review grievances, through hearings and fact-finding, and would recommend a mode of settlement via private or public (global) conciliation or mediation. Implementation would be left to the Implementing Board and the World Security Forces. Again, voluntary, noncoercive resolution would be stressed.

Gradual Stages—In perhaps his best known work, *A Study of Future Worlds,* Falk opts for a strategy of "drastic gradualism" to move toward his preferred world order. He would work by stages: (1) enhancing domestic desires for such an order, (2) experimenting with regional world order, and finally (3) constructing a central guidance mechanism.

Writing in 1975, Falk anticipated "notable progress toward minimizing collective violence" during stage one of his scenario. But he "did not expect any dramatic transfers of police and peace-making capabilities to the United Nations, regional organizations or some new international institution" to occur in this first stage. He did not expect an end to regional wars. Arms development, especially of nuclear weapons, would still be troubling. Even though the "objective status of the war system" would not change in this period, a new mood would make it possible to dismantle the system later. Even in stage two, the war system would not be dismantled, but governments would be less disposed to use military capabilities to solve national problems. The war system would continue to erode until stage three, when dismantling would occur.

Weaknesses—What weaknesses do critics see in the new global order and security system that figures so prominently in the thinking of scholars like Falk?

1. It is by no means clear that nations trust each other enough to undertake bold plans for disarmament. Indeed, despite the success of the START agreements between the United States and Russia, the trend for nuclear proliferation seems to move in the opposite direction.
2. Nations remain too dedicated to their sovereign powers to move toward a new world organization with expanded powers of world security.
3. It is naive to assume that security, disarmament, and grievances can be resolved nonviolently. The world security system will have to use force to enforce its will, and so this system substitutes war between a

global organization and delinquent member nations for war between sovereign nation-states.
4. Freedom itself, as currently understood by nation-states, could be jeopardized by a powerful global organization with a monopoly on weapons in a substantially disarmed world.

Peace Through Nonviolent Civilian Defense

Advocates of peace through nonviolent civilian defense maintain that a breakthrough to a more peaceful world order can be achieved only if **nonviolence** is seriously considered. "Now, more than ever, we need to question some of our basic assumptions about defense, security, and peace, and to examine possible new policies that might help achieve those goals." So writes Gene Sharp in his book *Exploring Nonviolent Alternatives.*[36]

Sharp is extremely critical of the "dangers and limitations of modern military means" and of "traditional answers to the problem of political conflict." Thus, he argues that military power "today often exists without real capacity to defend . . . the people and society relying upon it. . . . Often it only threatens mutual annihilation."

Another proponent of nonviolent defense, Robert Holmes, seriously questions the basic function and efficiency of violence. He writes:

> Destructive force does not automatically add up to social power . . . Moreover, beyond a certain point increments in the capacity for violence cease to yield increases in power. Beyond that point, in fact, power may decrease, however much destructive force one commands. The United States discovered this in Vietnam . . . The Soviets did the same in Afghanistan.[37]

Sharp notes that although conflict is unavoidable, traditional means of dealing with conflict are inadequate and may be disastrous. These traditional means, according to Sharp, include (1) removal of causes; (2) increased understanding of the opponent; (3) compromise; (4) negotiation, conciliation, and arbitration; (5) democratic institutions; (6) world government; (7) violent revolution; (8) war; (9) avoidance of

Mohandas Gandhi preached nonviolent resistance.

provocation; and (10) apathy and impotence. Although some of these means may have merit, they are still insufficient. For example, there is not always time to remove the causes of conflict, including war; current conflicts must be dealt with immediately. Understanding does not automatically reduce conflicts; indeed, it may sometimes heighten them. Some compromises are morally and politically dangerous; they may not achieve acceptable results. Democratic institutions are frequently nonexistent, incomplete, or inadequate. World government is, at best, a long way off; it may not be achieved peacefully, and even if it is, it may turn out to be dangerous.

So, Sharp maintains, nonviolence must be examined seriously "as a possible full replacement for violence." Sharp defines *nonviolent action* as "those methods of protest, noncooperation and intervention in which the actionists, without employing physical violence, refuse to do

certain things which they are expected, or required, to do; or do certain things which they are not expected, or are forbidden, to do." Nonviolent protest, noncooperation, or intervention seeks to bring about change by conversion, accommodation (political, economic, or social), and nonviolent coercion.

But can nonviolent action, as a substitute for military armaments, ensure defense, security, and peace? Sharp believes that nonviolent civilian defense is not only desirable but feasible. He maintains that nonviolent action can both deter and defeat aggressors.

The Case for Nonviolence—Sharp argues that nonviolent civilian defense would actually discourage nuclear attack by eliminating the national lightning rod of nuclear weapons. "Fear of nuclear attack, then, or fear of military defeat in a major conventional war, may be a strong reason for launching a nuclear attack on the enemy. Civilian defense, which can only be used for defensive purposes, would remove that motive, and hence, if not cancel out the danger, at least greatly reduce it." Consequently, there is much less "likelihood of a nuclear attack against a country employing only civilian defense as a deterrent." Moreover, nonviolent civilian defense would deter conventional aggression because the aggressor would know that resistance would take the form of effective nonviolent protest, noncooperation, and intervention.

If aggression did occur, nonviolent civilian defense would defeat it. The invader would "encounter a population well prepared to fight for its freedom with methods that, precisely because they are nonviolent, will be especially insidious and dangerous to the invader." For example, the entry of enemy troops can be resisted by obstructing the docks, refusing to operate railroads, or blocking highways and airports with thousands of abandoned automobiles. Strikes, boycotts, empty streets, shuttered windows, and noncooperation in general would give the aggressor an empty victory. "Civilian defense aims to defeat military aggression by using resistance by the civilian population as a whole to make it impossible for the enemy to establish and maintain political control over the country. . . . The citizens would prevent enemy control of the country by massive and selective refusal to cooperate and to obey, supporting instead the legal government and its call to resist."

According to Sharp's philosophy of nonviolent civilian defense, police would refuse to arrest patriotic opponents of the invader. Teachers would refuse to use invader propaganda in the schools. Workers and managers would strike and obstruct to prevent the enemy from exploiting the country. Clergy would extol refusal to help the invader. Politicians, civil servants, and judges would defy the enemy's order, thus denying the use of the community's legal machinery. Underground newspapers and radio stations would support the cause of nonviolent resistance and report only the truth. In these ways, Sharp maintains, nonviolent action would deny the aggressor the obedience needed to make aggression successful.

Nonviolent civilian defense, Sharp concedes, involves risks, dangers, costs, and discipline. But it averts a nuclear catastrophe. The injuries and deaths that may result from enemy actions are "likely to be much fewer than in military struggles." People remain alive to fight in a nonviolent way for their freedom. Nonviolent defense is not easy. It takes considerable training and commitment.

Robert Holmes elaborates on this point by noting that "nonviolence is no guarantee against bloodshed. No system has such a guarantee. But the use of violence not only allows situations to develop in which bloodshed is inevitable; it entails the shedding of blood."[38]

Sharp recognizes the need for *transarmament,* which is a changeover from military defense to civilian defense. Thus, "for a significant period, civilian defense preparations would be carried out alongside military measures, until the latter can be phased out as no longer needed." Education, specialized training, civilian defense specialists, civilian defense games and maneuvers, and considerable preparation are all needed

to help a nation achieve nonviolent civilian defense.

At its best, then, nonviolent civilian defense would deter and defeat aggression—reducing the level of violence, inhibiting invaders, resisting tyrants, and enhancing peace and freedom. Although not inexpensive, it would permit significant savings. It would make possible "a step-by-step removal of war from the international scene" and thus increase world security. Developed and, especially, developing countries would have more money to deal with unmet human needs. Civilian defense "would very likely become a potent force around the world for liberalizing or overthrowing tyrannical regimes." It would give people greater control over their own destinies. Indeed, "increased confidence in civilian defense and liberation by nonviolent action could produce a chain reaction in the progressive abolition of both war and tyranny."[39]

At worst—the failure of nonviolent civilian defense—people would still be alive and capable of struggling to overcome aggression and tyranny (in contrast to the aftermath of a major nuclear war).

Weaknesses—Critics point to a number of weaknesses in the nonviolent approach.

1. Given the nature of people and nations, critics say, it is utopian to assume that the nonviolent option can be relied on. Unless there is a miraculous transformation of human nature and of nations, the adoption of nonviolence invites surrender and domination by one's rivals.

2. Although nonviolent civilian defense might make a nuclear attack unnecessary, it is not at all clear that nonviolent civilian defense can prevent hostile domination.

3. The notion that it is better to live under an authoritarian regime than not to live at all is cowardly and unacceptable.[40]

4. Although nonviolent civilian defense might work with humane, civilized, and reasonable opponents, there is no surety that it

would work, at acceptable costs, with brutal barbarians or ideological fanatics.

TOWARD CREATIVE BREAKTHROUGHS TO A PEACEFUL WORLD ORDER

Which approach makes the most sense? How do we appraise the costs and benefits of each? Which alternative is most desirable and most feasible? To further debate these matters—and to facilitate a prudent choice—we will review each approach we have considered, pose the key questions that must be answered, and present sample responses, pro and con.

Multipolar Balance of Power

Is a new multipolar balance-of-power policy (based on positions of both military and economic strength) the most sensible way to maintain peace in the modern world and simultaneously protect America's vital interests?

Some scholars argue that such a policy is the only realistic one, given the continued existence of significant numbers of nuclear weapons in the world's arsenals and the trends toward nuclear proliferation. They insist that although the cost of such a policy is high, it is worth following because it protects the security and freedom of the United States and other free, peace-loving societies. Advocates minimize the risk of either conventional or nuclear war by underscoring the improbability that any country would launch an aggressive attack in view of the terrible damage it would suffer if it did so. They maintain that such a policy, which requires strengthening both nuclear and conventional forces, will in time permit arms control and real disarmament. They hold that the realities of international politics make it necessary to accept the present nation-state system, the struggle for power, and some variation of the balance of power.

Critics of the positions-of-strength policy call attention to the catastrophic consequences of nuclear war and urge the development of a better policy. They emphasize both the dangers and costs of current policy. They maintain that detente—a real relaxation of tension—is impossible in any balance-of-power policy that calls for a military buildup and thus another suicidal arms race. They call for a modification of the present bankrupt nation-state system.

Third-Party Activity and Collective Security

To what extent can a policy based on the strengthened third-party or collective security activities of the United Nations be relied on?

Defenders of third-party activity are encouraged by the end of the Cold War. They contend that this option is based on a realistic recognition of what the United Nations can in fact do. They argue that a strengthened secretary-general can serve as a resourceful global leader on behalf of peace. With a properly equipped staff, the secretary-general can persuade parties in conflict to use negotiation, conciliation, arbitration, and judicial settlement to resolve their disputes. This approach can work especially if the Security Council vigorously backs this third-party role. Defenders of collective security are further heartened by the collective sanctions taken by the United Nations against Iraq after its invasion of Kuwait.

Opponents argue that third-party activity does not get at the root causes of war; it deals with symptoms, not causes. It does not seriously address major conflicts of interest and rivalries of other nation-states, North-South tensions, and the internal suppression of peoples. Such an option cannot deal successfully with the problem of disarmament. Moreover, they maintain, such a policy relies too heavily on one person (the secretary-general) and on a sometimes irresponsible General Assembly. As for collective security, there is a deep suspicion that even with the end of the Cold War, member states of the United Nations will find it difficult to muster both the will and the resources to effectively counter aggression.

Global Economic Integration

Does global economic integration provide the basis for a peaceful world order?

Advocates of economic integration assert that complex economic interdependence makes for

Kuwait oil fields were set afire by retreating Iraqis as Operation Desert Storm reversed Saddam Hussein's aggression.

peace by encouraging rational actors to reject the unacceptable costs of violent conflict. Further, economic integration seriously challenges the forces of nationalism and sovereignty, which have stood as barriers to international cooperation and world unity.

Critics note that economic integration, while perhaps a positive force, does not address many fundamental issues that divide peoples (such as territorial disputes and racial, ethnic, and cultural hostility). Further, economic integration depends too much on the policies of multinational corporations and private international financial institutions that are profit-motivated and not always accountable for their actions.

Functionalism

How effective is the functional approach to peaceful world order?

Supporters of functionalism argue that pragmatic success with common problems in a host of fields is the only way to build trust among peoples in the global community. They insist that in time such successes can overcome nationalistic suspicion and rivalry and lead to a global order that will also attend to security. This process may be slow, but it will pay off in

the long run as mutual benefits build mutual trust. In this process, moreover, it is possible for peoples to address the root causes of war in very practical ways.

Skeptics doubt whether nationalism—and nation-states' determination to rely on their own power to protect their vital interests—can be overcome when nations work together on common problems involving health, agriculture, broadcasting, or postal service. They emphasize that smaller successes in these areas will founder on the rock of superpower rivalry and nation-state tensions. Even if nations cooperate on certain tasks, they will not be able to do so when it comes to the crucial function of security. Moreover, critics insist that the current explosive global situation does not allow enough time for the building of functional networks.

Global Security System

Is a dependable peace possible only if it is founded on a global security system that has made radical disarmament a central policy?

Advocates of this option emphasize the bankruptcy of the current nation-state system and especially the danger of reliance on nuclear arms to achieve national security. They call for bold steps to reduce and eventually eliminate nuclear weapons and then to reduce other weapons of mass destruction and establish a global security system with the authority to maintain peace. Their global authority would operate in a democratic and constitutional fashion.

Skeptics doubt both the desirability and the feasibility of this approach, which they believe is naive and utopian. They point out that it is not possible to raise national consciousness, mobilize regional interests, and transform global institutions quickly enough to build a more durable world order. And skeptics are not persuaded that the theory of transition shows clearly and realistically how we can move from where the world is now to where it should be. They do not believe that a new central guidance system can be built and trusted, especially one with crucial powers in the domain of security. National suspicions of "the other side" are too strong to allow radical disarmament. Skeptics also point out that freedom might be jeopardized in a world in which the United States has been disarmed.

Nonviolence

Is nonviolence the policy that must be adopted to build a more peaceful world order?

Advocates of this position hold that the world must turn away from violence before it consumes the planet. Nonviolence protects the integrity of human life and can achieve peace and resist aggressors through protest, noncooperation, and peaceful intervention. This policy recognizes the reality of conflict but would deal with it through conversion; political, economic, and social accommodation; and nonviolent coercion. These methods would lower the level of violence and still permit people to resist aggressors and advance the cause of freedom. By moving away from war, violence, and arms, a policy of nonviolence would free money and human energy to address the unmet needs of the world's peoples.

Opponents argue that nonviolence is neither desirable nor feasible. They insist that neither Americans nor Russians—nor French, Chinese, Israelis, Indians, British, or Argentines—are willing to rely on nonviolent civilian defense as a dependable way to deter or defeat aggression. Opponents hold that the costs of this policy—for example, the loss of freedom under an aggressive occupying power—are too great to warrant trying to implement it. Any probable benefits—such as the end of nuclear war—are not worth the inherent risk to national security. People are not yet ethical enough or strong enough to succeed with this policy. To adopt it would be to invite the triumph of the militarily powerful.

To reach a judgment on a sane and prudent policy, you must work through the pros and cons of these alternative policies. In doing so, you must clarify your values and ethical priorities. You must understand and assess the relevant empirical realities (past and present) and also make some predictions about the future. You must appraise, as wisely as possible, the strengths and weaknesses, costs and benefits of alternative approaches, and compare alternative policies. This requires difficult and prudent calculations. Finally, you must make a choice.

CONCLUSION

We can now see more clearly the importance—and difficulty—of judging wisely on issues of war and peace. A mere dedication to peace does not produce wise judgments on how to achieve it. Similarly, recognition of the dangers of war does not automatically offer a wise choice about how to secure peace. Costs and benefits are often perceived differently by political scientists, citizens, and policymakers. Yet people must make judgments. They must choose. The failure to judge and choose is itself a judgment and a choice.

Judgment and choice are creative acts. They call for critical acumen, for powers of analysis and synthesis, for balancing and weighing values, facts, and alternatives. Judgment and choice call for courage because they are not free of doubts, difficulties, ambiguities, and uncertainties.

The widely varying policy options presented in this chapter were chosen to stimulate the imagination and to make choices more ethical, more realistic, and more prudential. The radical alternatives were deliberately introduced to provoke thought and to make readers reconsider ethical priorities, reexamine realities, and reassess wise choices. Only this kind of intellectual endeavor can lead to genuinely creative breakthroughs.

We turn next, in Chapter 17, to the possibility of creative breakthroughs in the battle for the "least free."

ANNOTATED BIBLIOGRAPHY

Brown, Seyom. *New Forces, Old Forces and the Future of World Politics*. Glenview, Ill.: Scott, Foresman, 1994. An excellent text with well-thought-out projections. See also Brown's *The Causes and Prevention of War* (New York: St. Martin's Press, 1987) and *International Relations in a Changing Global System: Toward a Theory of the World Policy* (Boulder, Colo.: Westview Press, 1992).

Cordesman, Anthony H., and Wagner, Abraham R. *The Lessons of Modern War*, Vol. 4: *The Gulf War*. Boulder, Colo.: Westview Press, 1996. Covers the Arab-Israeli conflict from 1973 through 1989. Fourth in a series that also covers the Afghan and Falkland wars. Very thorough, it is more a reference work than a good read, but is loaded with useful information.

Dawidowicz, Lucy S. *The War Against the Jews 1933–1945*. New York: Bantam, 1986. Provides a scholarly but chilling account of the Holocaust.

Erlich, Paul, Sagan, Carl, Kennedy, Donald, and Roberts, Walter Orr. *The Cold and the Dark: The World After Nuclear War*. New York: Norton, 1984. Seminal work that describes the horrors of nuclear winter.

Falk, Richard A. *A Study of Future Worlds*. New York: Free Press, 1975. Focuses on world order alternatives. Seeks to address the extremely difficult problem of transition from the present world order to a new order. Also see Falk's *Explorations at the Edge of Time: The Prospects for World Order* (Philadelphia: Temple University Press, 1992).

Gurr, Ted Robert, and Harff, Barbara. *Ethnic Conflict in World Politics*. Boulder, Colo.: Westview Press, 1994. Presents a first-rate study on the wave of ethnic conflict emerging after the end of the Cold War. Central thesis is that ethnic hostilities are often triggered as much by international factors as by domestic influences.

Holmes, Robert L. *On War and Morality*. Princeton: Princeton University Press, 1989. One of the finest books in years on the ethics of war. Contains a powerful argument against the realist school and against "just war" theory, and an equally compelling argument for nonviolence.

James, Alan. *Peacekeeping in International Politics*. New York: St. Martin's Press, 1991. Offers an extraordinarily thorough and well-organized history and analysis of major peacekeeping efforts going back to the 1920s and ending with Lebanon in 1984. Maps are included.

Karnow, Stanley. *Vietnam: A History*. New York: Viking Penguin, 1991. Considered the best overall history of the Vietnam war. Companion to the award winning PBS thirteen-part series.

Lund, Michael S. *Preventing Violent Conflicts: A Strategy for Preventive Diplomacy*. Washington, D.C.: U.S. Institute of Peace Press, 1996. Produced by a U.S. State Department commission task force, explores the role of "preventive diplomacy," which attempts to head off conflicts before they start.

Mitrany, David. *A Working Peace System: An Argument for the Functional Development of International Organization*, 4th ed. London: National Peace Council, 1946. Still offers one of the most persuasive arguments for developing an international organization and a functional approach to peace.

Sharp, Gene. *Exploring Nonviolent Alternatives*. Boston: Porter Sargent, 1971. Sets forth the nonviolent approach that makes the hair on the realist's head stand up straight. Is the world ready for this approach? Can the world endure without it? Also see Sharp's *Civilian-Based Defense: A Post-Military Weapon Defense* (Princeton, N.J.: Princeton University Press, 1990).

Sivard, Ruth Leger. *World Military and Social Expenditures*. Washington, D.C.: World Priorities, Annual. Should be on every political scientist's annual reading list.

Small, Melvin, and Singer, J. David. *International War: An Anthology*, 2nd ed. Chicago: Brooks/Cole, 1989. Provides a first-rate collection of essays on the nature and causes of war. Contains everything from excerpts from Steven Crane's *The Red Badge of Courage*, to Small's and Singer's empirical studies of war, to essays on just war, to proposals for preventing war. Excellent!

Waltz, Kenneth. *Man, the State, and War: A Theoretical Analysis.* New York: Columbia University Press, 1965. A classic statement on the cause of war.

SUGGESTIONS FOR FURTHER READING

Blainey, Geoffry. *The Causes of War*, 3rd ed. New York: Free Press, 1988.

Blight, James G., and Welch, David A. *On the Brink: Americans and Soviets Reexamine the Cuban Missile Crisis.* New York: Hill and Wang, 1989.

Brecher, Michael, and Wilkenfeld, Jonathan. *Crisis, Conflict and Instability.* New York: Pergamon Press, 1993.

Falk, Richard A, Johansen, Robert C., and Kim, Samuel S. *The Constitutional Foundations of World Peace.* Albany: State University of New York Press, 1993.

Halperin, Morton H., Scheffer, David J., and Small, Patricia L. *Self-Determination in the New World Order.* Washington D.C.: Carnegie Endowment for International Peace, 1992.

Johnson, James T., and Weigel, George. *Just War and the Gulf War.* Washington, D.C.: Ethics and Public Policy Center, 1991.

Krasner, Stephen D., ed. *International Regimes.* Ithaca, N.Y.: Cornell University Press, 1983.

Mayall, James, ed. *The New Interventionism: United Nations Experience in Cambodia, Former Yugoslavia, and Somalia.* New York: Cambridge University Press, 1996.

Ruggie, John. *Winning the Peace: America and World Order in the New Era.* New York: Columbia University Press, 1996.

Shawcross, William. *Sideshow: Kissinger, Nixon and the Destruction of Cambodia.* New York: Simon & Schuster, 1979.

Simon, Douglas W., and Rhone, Richard. "The United Nations and Conflict Management in the Post–Cold War World," *The Harvard Journal of World Affairs*, Fall 1995.

Stoessinger, John C. *Why Nations Go to War*, 6th ed. New York: St. Martin's Press, 1992.

Thompson, William R. *On Global War: Historical-Structural Approaches to World Politics.* Columbia: University of South Carolina Press, 1988.

Walzer, Michael. *Just and Unjust Wars: A Moral Argument with Historical Illustrations*, 2nd ed. New York: Basic Books, 1992.

GLOSSARY TERMS

balance of power
collective security
creative breakthroughs
disarmament
economic integration
functionalism
modern world
more peaceful world order
neofunctionalism
nonviolence
nuclear proliferation
nuclear winter
peace
third-party activities
war

THE BATTLE ON BEHALF OF THE LEAST FREE

THE ISSUES INVOLVING POLITICAL JUDGMENT and public policy that we are considering in Part IV of this book cannot easily be separated from one another. Peace, human rights, and economic well-being, for example, are inextricably connected. War is perhaps the greatest enemy of human rights, and peace is its greatest friend. War is the great destroyer of human life and a great threat to democratic governance. Human rights and economic well-being also overlap; human rights have come to include economic necessities essential to life such as food, clothing, and shelter. Moreover, peace, human rights, and economic well-being are related to ecological health. War contributes to ecological malaise and wastes natural resources. Certain limited conceptions of freedom and economic life—for example, the freedom to pollute or to waste natural resources—may also injure the environment and the economy.

Yet there is value in singling out a concern for human rights—especially for the "least free"—as a separate problem for analysis. Consequently, in this chapter we consider the question, *What creative breakthroughs can help humanity achieve greater freedom for the least free?* We focus on the **least free**—the powerless, the deprived, and the maltreated, who are often the poor, racial minorities, women, and the politically oppressed—because their status challenges the commitment to democratic, constitutional, and humane values. We are concerned with the problems involved in making human rights meaningful in the modern world, especially for the least free.

Our format will be similar to that adopted in Chapter 16. After clarifying the problem, we will set forth some factors that prompt exploration of the problem. We will then present some alternative approaches to securing greater freedom for the least free. Finally, we will invite you to reach a wise judgment on public policy and, if possible, to move toward a creative breakthrough in the field of human rights.

CLARIFYING THE PROBLEM

We have suggested that the treatment of the least free is a litmus test for democratic, constitutional, and humane politics.

By **freedom** we mean power over one's own destiny. Negatively, freedom means the absence of arbitrary restraints that limit the power to pursue one's destiny. Positively, freedom is the presence of opportunities that enable individuals and groups to fulfill their own peaceful and creative potentialities.

Because we feature **human rights,** a concept closely allied to freedom and sometimes used as a synonym for freedom, let us define this term. Human rights include

1. *The right to be free of violations of the integrity of the person.* Such violations include torture; cruel, inhuman, or degrading treatment or punishment; and arbitrary arrest or imprisonment. They also include denial of fair public trial, and invasion of the home.
2. *The right to the fulfillment of such vital needs as food, shelter, health care, and education.*
3. *The right to enjoy civil and political liberties: freedom of thought, religion, assembly, and speech; freedom of the press; freedom of movement both within and outside one's country; and freedom to take part in government.*[1]

Other definitions of human rights would also explicitly include the right to be free of racial or sexual discrimination and the right of the majority to determine their own national destiny.

These are working definitions; there is no universal agreement on these terms. Some scholars interpret human rights narrowly, limiting them to civil and political rights that are understood as *legal claims* that can be upheld by legal remedies. Thus, for example, if the government deprives you of freedom of speech,

through the courts you can stop such a violation. Others prefer to interpret human rights more broadly to include economic (and even social and cultural) rights that are understood as *moral, political, and legal obligations* that governments are pledged to advance. Thus, in many countries government has a moral obligation to help the destitute, a political obligation to find jobs for the unemployed, and a legal obligation to educate children. A government's capacity to fulfill its legal, political, and moral obligations, however, may depend on the nation's economic development. And, of course, a government's capacity to fulfill legal claims will depend on its constitutional commitments and its political state of health.[2]

Historically, liberal democracies in the West have been primarily concerned with civil and political rights. But with the advent of the welfare state and the advance of democratic socialism, economic, social, and cultural rights have also become prominent. Governments in Communist countries and in some developing countries of the Third World have also emphasized economic, social, and cultural rights. Whether such rights are actually protected is, however, a troubling question. Some Third World countries stress the primacy of national self-determination and the need to end racism. Sometimes these governments underscore their priorities by noting that freedom of speech for starving people is not very meaningful. Arguments over priorities—and the relationship of one right to another right—are central to the battle for human rights.

Other queries are also important. What should and what can the international community do when nations, which should be primarily responsible for protecting human rights within their borders, fail to safeguard such rights? What should and what can human rights advocates within delinquent nations do? What should and what can sympathetic nations do to advance the cause of human rights? What should and what can be the role of the United Nations? of nongovernmental organizations concerned with human rights? Should persuasive or coercive strategies be relied on? What about quiet diplomacy or **sanctions**? This chapter seeks to address such vital questions.

But before we can sensibly explore alternative approaches to this problem, it will be helpful to set forth some key factors that have led to the problem.

KEY ETHICAL AND EMPIRICAL FACTORS IN HUMAN RIGHTS

The least free have always been in need of protection. In the twentieth century, however, ethical consciousness has been raised to a new level of sensitivity because of widespread and flagrant violations of human rights. These massive violations dramatically seized public attention when Allied troops overran Hitler's concentration camps and the dreadful reality of the **Holocaust** was revealed. Other outrageous violations of human rights became public knowledge after Nikita Khrushchev's "secret" speech in which he exposed Stalin's crimes. After World War II, Third World peoples' fight for freedom from colonial masters called attention to imperial exploitation and racism. Until 1989 the Soviet Union's domination of adjacent countries in Eastern Europe illustrated another pattern of imperial control. Racial discrimination in the United States, long a troubling problem, became even more troubling in a post–World War II America that had just defeated a racist Nazi regime and sought to assume political and moral leadership in a world more nonwhite than white. The feminist movement exposed the reality of **sexism**—in the United States and the world. And authoritarian governments of the right and left continued to persecute, imprison, and degrade peaceful dissidents.

Let us now investigate some of the key factors, both historical and contemporary, that have made the problem of human rights so pressing in world politics. Because Chapter 18 is devoted to "The Struggle for Economic Well-Being," we will leave a fuller treatment of poverty for that chapter.

The Dreadful Reality of Genocide

The dreadful reality of Hitler's death camps—the ultimate step in what the Nazis called "the Final Solution of the Jewish Question" strongly influenced the writing of the U.N.'s Universal Declaration of Human Rights in 1948. The shocking stories of the Nazi concentration camps were dramatically revealed when Allied armies broke into Germany and the countries it dominated and liberated the survivors of the Nazi death factories. At Auschwitz, 2,000,000 had been murdered; at Majdanek, 1,380,000; at Treblinka, 800,000; at Belzec, 600,000; at Chelmno, 340,000; at Sobibor, 250,000.[3] The full extent of the slaughter and of the systematic campaign of mass murder was not immediately apparent but emerged at the post–World War II Nuremberg trials of war criminals, and in subsequent investigations. The evidence—in confessions, eyewitness accounts, Nazi records, and pictures of tyranny and terror—of crimes against innocent civilians is incontrovertible and led world opinion to resolve "never again!"

The crimes of Hitler and his supporters against Jews started with prejudice; were stimulated by propaganda; advanced through political, social, and economic persecution; and finally ended in

A sculpture from Dachau concentration camp memorializes the victims of the Holocaust.

mass murder (see Table 17.1). World opinion came to realize that the crimes against Jews by the Nazis and their supporters were inextricably connected with Nazi violations of the human rights of civilian Germans, Poles, Czechs, French, Russians, and other Europeans.

It is difficult to grasp the campaign of extermination carried out by many ordinary Germans in "police battalions" in Nazi-occupied lands. It is equally difficult to comprehend the living hell-on-earth of the Nazi concentration camps—the horror, brutality, starvation, degradation, and murder. Again and again, survivors could only

say: Unless you have lived through it yourself, you could never understand. All the photographs and documents in the world, even seeing the piles of corpses with your own eyes, would never explain what it was like.

In 1948, and in response to these Nazi crimes, the U.N. General Assembly adopted the *Convention on the Prevention and Punishment of the Crime of Genocide;* this convention went into force in 1951. **Genocide** is defined as

any of the following acts committed with the intent to destroy, in whole or in part, a national, ethnic, racial, or religious group, as such:

Table 17.1 Estimated Number of Jews Killed in the Final Solution

Country	Estimated Pre-Final Solution Population	Estimated Jewish Population Annihilated	
		(no.)	(%)
Poland	3,300,00	3,000,000	90
Baltic countries	253,000	228,000	90
Germany/Austria	240,000	210,000	90
Protectorate	90,000	80,000	89
Slovakia	90,000	75,000	83
Greece	70,000	54,000	77
The Netherlands	140,000	105,000	75
Hungary	650,000	450,000	70
SSR White Russia	375,000	245,000	65
SSR Ukraine[a]	1,500,000	900,000	60
Belgium	65,000	40,000	60
Yugoslavia	43,000	26,000	60
Romania	600,000	300,000	50
Norway	1,800	900	50
France	350,000	90,000	26
Bulgaria	64,000	14,000	22
Italy	40,000	8,000	20
Luxembourg	5,000	1,000	20
Russia (RSFSR)[a]	975,000	107,000	11
Denmark	8,000	-	-
Finland	2,000	-	-
Total	8,861,800	5,933,900	67

Source: From The War Against the Jews by Lucy S. Dawidowicz. Copyright © 1975 by Lucy S. Dawidowicz. Reprinted by permission of Henry Holt and Company, Inc.

[a]The Germans did not occupy all the territory of this republic. SSR stands for Soviet Socialist Republic, RSFSR for Russian Soviet Federated Socialist Republic.

a. Killing members of the group;
b. Causing either bodily or mental harm to members of the group;
c. Deliberately inflicting on the group conditions of life calculated to bring about its physical destruction in whole or in part;
d. Imposing measures intended to prevent births within the group;
e. Forcibly transferring children of the group to another group.[4]

The Genocide Convention makes a number of actions punishable: genocide itself, the conspiracy to commit it, incitement to commit it, the attempt to commit it, and complicity in it. Genocide is held to be a matter of international concern, a crime under international law.

But has genocide occurred since World War II? Although nothing quite comparable to the Holocaust has occurred, the actions of the Pol Pot (Khmer Rouge) regime in Cambodia (Kampuchea) can be described as genocidal. "While in power from 1975 to 1979, the Khmer Rouge (Cambodian Communists) compiled one of the worst records of human rights violations in history as a result of a thorough and brutal attempt at restructuring Cambodian society. More than 1 million people, out of a total population of 7 million, were killed or died under the Khmer Rouge's genocidal regime."[5]

Other dreadful attacks on national, ethnic, racial, and religious groups can also be identified; they are close to if not identical with genocide. For example, the Ibo, a tribe within Nigeria, were severely attacked in the civil war that raged there. Kurds were savagely murdered and suppressed in Saddam Hussein's Iraq. Moslems in Bosnia-Herzegovina were subject to horrible "ethnic cleansing" in the warfare that followed the 1991 breakup of Yugoslavia. And genocidal attacks characterized the fighting between Hutus and Tutsis in Rwanda, Africa, in 1995–1996.

The Struggle to Achieve National Self-Determination

Although neither the U.N. Charter nor the Universal Declaration of Human Rights emphasizes it, the principle of **national self-determination**

of peoples (found in the charter but not in the Universal Declaration) has become an international human right. The principle gained importance as former colonies of West European powers in Asia, Africa, and elsewhere achieved independence and joined the United Nations, and as other colonies fought for national freedom.

Thus, in 1960 the U.N. General Assembly adopted the Declaration on the Granting of Independence to Colonial Countries and Peoples. The General Assembly declared that "the subjection of peoples to alien subjugation, domination, and exploitation constitutes a denial of fundamental human rights, is contrary to the Charter of the United Nations and is an impediment to the promotion of world peace and cooperation."

Finally, the United Nations adopted two key covenants that went into force in 1976: the International Covenant on Civil and Political Rights and the International Covenant on Economic, Social, and Cultural Rights. Article 1 of each covenant declared: "All peoples have the right of self-determination. By virtue of that right they freely determine their political status and freely pursue their economic, social and cultural development."

The establishment of this right to national self-determination in the international community constitutes a great victory on behalf of people struggling against colonial rule and imperialistic exploitation. Before so many new nations emerged in Asia and Africa, citizens of most countries now in the United Nations did not control their political destinies. They were ruled by others— the British, the French, the Dutch, the Portuguese. These subject people were not citizens of an independent political community, able to govern their own affairs through free elections and in accordance with the will of the majority. Moreover, they were often exploited economically by their colonial and imperial rulers. They did not control their own natural resources. They were often treated as second-class citizens in their own lands and were discriminated against socially as well as politically and economically.

Since 1945 the struggle for national self-determination has been remarkably successful. Only a relatively few—national and very complicated—struggles remain to be resolved. For example, the Palestinians are still struggling to establish a national state in the Middle East. By late 1996, and as a result of the 1993 Oslo peace accords between Israel and the Palestinian Liberation Authority (PLO), significant steps have been taken to achieve self-determination and peace with security. It remains, however, to be seen how the election of Benjamin Netanyahu, as Prime Minister of Israel, replacing Shimon Peres (who had, with Yitzhak Rabin, shaped the Oslo accords), will affect progress for a national state for the Palestinians. Some Kurds have national ambitions that conflict with their current status in Iraq, Turkey, Iran, and Syria; and Chechnya's nationalism conflicts with Russia's.

Nations that have achieved independence must be asked how meaningful this right of national self-determination is. Although legally free and independent, many of the new nations are not politically stable, economically viable, or socially cohesive and are thus unable to use the right of national self-determination effectively. They remain vulnerable. Their freedom may be more myth than reality. Students of nationalism wonder if old or new developing nations can really achieve political, economic, and social health.

Similarly, the countries of Eastern Europe—Poland, Hungary, Bulgaria, and Romania—that were released in 1989 from the grip of the Soviet Union and of imposed Communist regimes have yet to demonstrate their more complete political health. The breakup of Yugoslavia into component national states has been marred by savage warfare, which bodes ill for carrying the principle of national self-determination too far.

The Ugly Persistence of Racism

Racism has been an ugly reality in the history of humankind. Racism is rooted in the idea that some races are superior or inferior to other races. This judgment becomes a basis for **discrimination** against the race alleged to be inferior. Such discrimination may be legal, political, economic, or social. Racism has promoted human slavery, separate treatment, and prejudice in the United States and around the globe. **Apartheid**—the system of separate treatment of the races—was only recently (1989–1994) legally dismantled in South Africa.

Lest Americans feel too self-righteous about the history of apartheid in South Africa, they must remember that slavery in the United States ended only in 1865. Moreover, despite the Thir-

Legal apartheid in South Africa—strict separation of the races—finally came to an end in 1989–1994. In 1996 South Africa adopted a remarkably democratic constitution.

teenth, Fourteenth, and Fifteenth amendments to the Constitution (amendments designed to protect the civil rights of African Americans), blacks in America suffered notorious discrimination. **"Separate but equal"** remained an approved constitutional doctrine from 1896 to 1954. This doctrine held that equality was not violated if African Americans were required to use separate facilities in transportation, education, and other public facilities. After 1938, it is true, the U.S. Supreme Court looked realistically at so-called separate-but-equal facilities and struck down separate treatment in a number of cases. Yet only in *Brown v. Board of Education* (1954) did the Court declare that "in the field of public education the doctrine of 'separate but equal' has no place" because "separate educational facilities are inherently unequal." Effective laws to protect voting rights of African Americans were not passed until 1964. Even today, racial prejudice mars American society.

Slavery, involuntary servitude, and forced labor have remained problems in the twentieth century. Ethiopia outlawed slavery only in 1942; Kuwait did so only in 1949; Qatar, in 1952. Moreover, both Yemen and Saudi Arabia refuse to report to the United Nations about slavery in their territories. Less than two decades ago, one observer of human rights reported that "some two to four million people still live in slavery or involuntary servitude. Some are plain chattel slaves. Some are serfs, doomed to remain in that status for life. Some are in debt bondage. Some are, in a formal sense, adopted children. Some are wives, bought by their husbands and classified as property."[6]

As might be expected, apartheid has been anathema to African and Asian nations. The U.N. Charter, the Universal Declaration of Human Rights, and the two International Covenants on Human Rights prohibit discrimination on the grounds of race or color. In other conventions the United Nations has ruled against discrimination in employment (1958) and in education (1960). And in 1965 the General Assembly adopted the International Convention on the Elimination

of All Forms of Racial Discrimination. Parties to the convention not only condemn racial discrimination but agree to eliminate it in all its forms. Parties to the convention also declare that disseminating ideas based on racial superiority or hatred or inciting racial discrimination is punishable by law. They also agree to "declare illegal and prohibit organizations" that "promote and incite racial discrimination" and to "recognize participation in such organizations . . . as an offense punishable by law."[7]

Left-Wing and Right-Wing Human Rights Violations

Some might argue that horrors like the Nazis' genocide and Stalin's destruction of the kulaks (well-to-do peasants) and other real or imagined opponents are things of the past. Stalin, Hitler, Mussolini, and Franco—the dictators of the left or right, communist or fascist—are dead. The worst of Western imperialism and colonialism is behind us. Even racism, which lingers in a number of countries around the globe, has few public defenders.

Although the world has come a long way in articulating standards of human rights, some observers contend that persistent and flagrant human rights violations are still widespread. They occur in Communist countries such as China, North Korea, Vietnam, and Cuba. They also occur in a number of right-wing authoritarian regimes in the Middle East, Africa, Asia, and Latin America. Even nations that rank higher on a democratic and constitutional index—the United States, nations of Western Europe, Israel—are not entirely immune.

Despite a significant improvement through 1996, especially in formerly Communist regimes in Eastern Europe and in once authoritarian regimes in South America, even today there "are probably more countries where fundamental rights and civil liberties are systematically violated than there are countries where they are effectively protected."[8] These violations (documented in the annual reports of Amnesty International, Freedom House, and the U.S. State Department's

Country Reports on Human Rights Practices) include systematic torture, imprisonment, and killing of political opponents, as well as denial of freedom of speech, press, and association.

According to Freedom House, the countries with the worst records on political rights and civil liberties include Afghanistan, Burma, China, Cuba, Iraq, Equatorial Guinea, North Korea, Sudan, Syria, and Vietnam[9] (see Table 17.2).

It is also important to emphasize the reciprocal connection between freedom and human development (understood in terms of life expectancy, educational attainment, and income). Economically better-off countries generally also have a large measure of freedom. "There appears to be a link between a country's per capita income and the extent of its democratic free-

dom," even though some rich nations may not rank high on a freedom index, and some poor nations may enjoy a high level of political freedom. "People now see freedom as an essential element in human development, not as an optional extra. . . . Political freedom and human development do seem to move in tandem."[10]

Although violations are widespread and flagrant, there is a positive side to the human rights record in the last few years. Mikhail Gorbachev's highly significant decision to allow the countries of Eastern Europe to pursue their own destiny, free of Soviet domination, signaled the end of the human rights violations that had kept these countries among the least free. The decline of authoritarian regimes in South America—for example, in Argentina and Nicaragua—signaled

Table 17.2 A Sample of Countries Ranked from Most Free to Least Free

Free	2	3.5	5	6.5
1	Argentina	El Salvador	Angola	Laos
Australia	Chile	India	Armenia	Saudi Arabia
Austria	Hungary	Senegal	Congo	
Canada	Israel		Egypt	
Costa Rica	Poland	4	Lebanon	7
Denmark		Algeria	Morocco	Afghanistan
Ireland	2.5	Guatemala	Mozambique	Burma
Italy	Bolivia	Jordan	Romania	(Myanmar)
Portugal	Brazil	Mexico	Tunisia	China
Spain	Ecuador	Peru		Cuba
Sweden	Honduras		5.5	Equatorial
United States	Korea, South	4.5	Indonesia	Guinea
	Venezuela	Nigeria	Iran	Haiti
1.5	Zambia	Pakistan	Kuwait	Iraq
France		Sri Lanka	Niger	Korea, North
Germany	**Partly Free**	Zimbabwe	Zaire	Libya
Greece	3			Sudan
Japan	Colombia		**Not Free**	Syria
United Kingdom	Nicaragua		6	Vietnam
Uruguay	Paraguay		Cambodia	
	Philippines		Chad	
	Russia		Ghana	
	Turkey		Kenya	

Source: Adapted from R. Bruce McColm, ed., Freedom in the World: Political Rights and Civil Liberties 1991–1992 (New York: Freedom House, 1992), pp. 572–573. Freedom House now distinguishes between political rights and civil liberties. In Table 17.2, we have averaged their numerical evaluations. Freedom House gives a ranking of "Free" to countries that range from 1 to 2.5, "Partly Free" to countries that range from 3 to 5.5; and "Not Free" to countries that range from 6 to 7.

another triumph of human rights. Similarly, the end of apartheid in South Africa constituted a most significant advance for human rights. Overall, never before have so many organizations and individuals worked so hard on behalf of human rights.

A number of factors have altered public opinion on human rights issues: (1) the U.N. Charter itself, (2) the 1948 U.N. Universal Declaration of Human Rights, (3) the two 1966 U.N. Covenants on Human Rights, (4) various resolutions of the General Assembly, (5) the papal encyclical *Pacem in Terris*, (6) the Vatican Commission on Justice and Peace, (7) declarations of other churches, (8) the statutes of regional organizations in Europe and in America, (9) the provisions of many national constitutions, (10) Amnesty International (working to protect prisoners of conscience and abolish torture), (11) the International Commission of Jurists (promoting the rule of law and the right to a fair trial), (12) the International Institute of Human Rights, (13) President Jimmy Carter's human rights initiatives, and (14) the Final Act of the Helsinki Conference.[11]

Offenses Against Women: Women's Rights as Human Rights

The rights of one-half the human race continue to be violated on a massive scale around the globe. This is true despite the pronouncements of national constitutions in developed and developing nations and despite the eloquent prohibitions against sexual discrimination in key U.N. documents.

The Preamble of the U.N. Charter endorses the principle of "equal rights of men and women." Article 1, paragraph 3, declares that one purpose of the United Nations is to promote "respect for human rights and for fundamental freedoms for all without distinction as to race, sex, language, or religion." The same language—"without distinction as to . . . sex"—appears again in Articles 13, 55, and 62. Similar, and even more explicit, guarantees are found in the International Covenant on Civil and Political Rights. These rights relate to such matters as marriage, voting, and

public affairs and to protection against sexual discrimination. Both documents affirm that marriage must be entered into with the free "consent of the intending spouses." The International Covenant on Economic, Social and Cultural Rights affirms the principle of "equal remuneration for work of equal value," equal opportunity in promotion (Article 7), the "right of everyone to education" (Article 13), and the "right of everyone" (Article 15) to "take part in cultural life." These provisions build on earlier agreements on the rights of women, and they anticipated the 1967 Declaration on the Elimination of Discrimination Against Women.

The 1967 declaration holds that discrimination against women is fundamentally unjust and an offense to human dignity. It calls for appropriate measures to abolish discriminatory laws and customs. The document contains several provisions to protect women's status in the family; women's right to acquire, use, and inherit property; and the right to legal equality. It calls for measures to end prostitution and to give women equal rights with men in education and in economic and social life. It also proposes measures to prevent women from losing their jobs in the event of marriage and to offer paid maternity leave and necessary childcare facilities.

The language of the 1967 declaration—and of documents from subsequent conferences—is impressive. But what about the reality? The reality of equal rights for women around the globe shows some progress but remains disappointing. Some women are still enslaved or bought by their husbands and classified as property. Certain marriages, including child marriages, are still arranged in Southeast Asia. The traffic in women for purposes of prostitution still exists.

Patriarchy—the belief in male superiority (and female inferiority)—dominates worldwide and is evident even in communist and socialist countries, which took the ideological lead in moving toward equality of the sexes. The persisting impact of the "patriarchal heritage" is disturbing:

Discriminatory practices persist in most places and archaic laws continue to dictate women's subordinate

*Sri Lankan Prime Minister Mrs.
Sirimavo Bandaranaike is one
of a growing number of
women leading governments.*

position in family and society. Women in every country, Western and non-Western, industrialized and rural, modern and pre-modern, are underutilized in terms of their numbers, denied access to positions of prestige and power, and expected to find their primary fulfillment as mothers and wives.[12]

The double standard of morality (one moral code for men, another for women) that the patriarchal heritage often perpetuates is revealed by the following list of practices:

• Adultery (for men only)
• Prostitution (most often, for women only)
• Infanticide (girl children only)
• Child marriage (brides even younger than grooms)
• Arranged marriages (veto power to men)
• Illegitimacy (children as property of men)
• Wife-selling and wife beating
• Slavery in marriage (divorce available only to men)
• Prohibitions against birth control and abortion.[13]

Other practices, emphasizing the double standard actually at work in the world, can also be identified:

• Double duty (women work outside the home and care for the children and home)
• Unequal pay for equal work
• Greater numbers of illiterate women than illiterate men in the world
• Male dominance in policymaking in politics, the corporate world, labor unions, the mass media, and universities
• No pay for wives for housework
• Female workers in lower-level jobs
• The "Kinder, Kirche, Kuche" role for women: children, church, kitchen (cooking)

Especially disturbing is the fact that women are "victims" of crimes of violence in "a culture that degrades them" as sex objects and promotes pornography for profit. Women are poorer than men. Minority women—blacks, Hispanic Americans, Native Americans, and Asian Americans—"must overcome the double burden of discrimination based on race and sex." Women have lacked "effective political and economic power." Too often they have had "only minor and insignificant roles in making, interpreting and enforcing our laws, in running our political

"How can I discriminate against women when I don't even hire them?"

parties, unions, schools and institutions, in directing the media, in governing our country, in deciding issues of war or peace."[14]

A 1991 U.N. study, *The World's Women 1970–1990,* found that although women had made some gains (in low-level positions) in the last two decades, they still lagged far behind men in power, policymaking and decision making, wealth, and opportunity. Moreover, illiteracy among women actually rose between 1970 and 1990. Some gains among urban women were seen in health, education, economic, social, and political participation, but inequalities still characterize rural women and Asian women.

ALTERNATIVE APPROACHES TO FREEDOM AND HUMAN RIGHTS FOR THE LEAST FREE

This section is concerned with who does what and how. Table 17.3 identifies the key political actors (most of whom we will discuss in this chapter) and the options that confront them. These options are not mutually exclusive. We focus primarily on the United States, the United Nations, key nongovernmental organizations, and the least free themselves, and on the possibilities of a new global organization and order.

Here are some of the key questions that these alternative approaches will explore. Should policy emphasize persuasion, legal redress, or coercion? What mixture of persuasion, legal redress, and coercion makes the most sense? How fast or slow can actors move? Will significant protection require moderate reform or drastic revolution? What political, economic, and social considerations influence what key actors should or can do? What are the strengths and weaknesses of alternative policies, strategies, and tactics?

Securing Human Rights Through the Efforts of the United States

Jack Donnelly, a keen student of human rights, argues convincingly that "the fate of human rights—their implementation, abridgment, protection, violation, enforcement, denial, or enjoyment—is largely a matter of national, not

---

Table 17.3 *Political Actors and Options in the Field of Human Rights*

Political Actors	Political Options
Nations (e.g., the United States)	Persuasion *Advocacy of dissidents* *Quiet diplomacy*
Regional Organizations (e.g., European Commission on and Court of Human Rights)	*Investigation and publicity*
United Nations Nongovernmental Organizations (e.g., Amnesty International)	Legal redress *Judicial proceedings*
The Least Free Themselves (e.g., blacks, political dissidents, the poor, women)	Sanctions *Political sanctions* *Economic sanctions*
A New Global Organization	*Military sanctions*

international, action." He emphasizes that the "international human rights obligations of states are implemented, if at all, through national action." He notes that true "protection against human rights violations rests on fundamental national political changes." He warns, however, about the dangers of paternalistic humanitarian intervention by nations and notes that harm as well as help can result from such intervention, especially when undertaken in the interest of security, economic, or ideological considerations. Although Donnelly is strongly persuaded of the "moral universality of human rights" and of the importance of authoritative international norms, he maintains that human rights can be best realized through national action.[15] With this perspective in mind, let us consider how one nation, the United States, might act to protect and promote human rights.

The United States can play its role domestically (by respecting human rights at home) and internationally (by promoting the cause of human rights abroad). But what policies should the United States use to protect international human rights?

We consider four options. The United States could (1) do little or nothing with regard to both friend and foe; (2) adopt a cautious, go-slow policy of quiet diplomacy toward friends and a more vocal and public criticism of foes; (3) push more openly and vigorously, yet prudently via both publicity and sanctions, with regard to allies and adversaries; (4) go all out in its attacks on violators of human rights and in its efforts to protect those rights.

Currently, the do-nothing and all-out policies are not practical options for the United States. The choice seems to be between the cautious option of quiet diplomacy and the vigorous option of publicity and sanctions.

America's concern for the international protection of human rights did not become central until the 1970s. The U.N.'s Universal Declaration of Human Rights was a significant response to the horrible violations during World War II, especially by the Nazis. The United States and the other major Allied powers had not done what needed to be done to prevent Hitler's aggressions, particularly his genocidal actions against European Jewry. The Universal Declaration was a belated "never again." Yet the advent of the Cold War—American-Soviet rivalry—cast a cloud over evenhanded American efforts to protect human rights. Human rights took a backseat to national security. In addition, fears of communism limited more forthright American human rights leadership and support. In the early 1970s, however, fed by evidence of substantial violations all over the world, especially in South America, the U.S. Congress passed important human rights legislation.

Congress passed laws to prohibit economic and military aid to governments brutalizing their populations. Country reports on human rights practices were required. Countries that denied or restricted their citizens' right to emigrate were denied most-favored-nation treatment. American representatives on international lending agencies were also required to vote against loans for countries that grossly violated internationally recognized human rights.

President Jimmy Carter in his inaugural address in 1977 declared that the U.S. commitment to human rights must be "absolute" and a "central concern" of American foreign policy. He supported the establishment of human rights machinery in the executive branch, as well as congressional initiatives to interpret that commitment and concern.

Legislative mandates and executive actions, however, permit a great deal of executive discretion. Thus, the president is reasonably free to choose either the quiet diplomacy option or the publicity and sanctions option. What are the arguments, pro and con, for each of these options?

Those who argue on behalf of quiet diplomacy have maintained that a sound foreign policy must give top priority to national security, to the important distinction between "foes" and "friends," and to the effectiveness of results. That is, advancing human rights must be balanced against protecting the nation's security interests. The United States may have to go easy publicly on authoritarian allies who violate human rights. There are times when it is wiser not to cut off their military or economic aid but to seek privately to improve their human rights record.

In the case of "foes"—for example, Communist countries—such public reticence may not be in order. Normally, Americans should be free to explore human rights violations by communist countries. But sometimes U.S. foreign policy objectives may suggest that quiet diplomacy be used even with such Communist nations as China, in order to maintain good political and economic relations with a powerful state on the Asian mainland.

Quiet diplomacy—action or pressure behind the scenes—enables an offending country to save face. Publicity or sanctions may harm national security by injuring an ally or by destabilizing an anti-Communist country. Rigid adherence to abstract moral standards in foreign policy is dangerous. A more modest, less crusading policy is much more sensible.

Those who argue on behalf of a more evenhanded policy of prudent diplomacy, publicity, and sanctions maintain that there is a better way of balancing what is desirable with what is possible. There is a better way of accommodating the United States to a world in which so many nation-states are controlled by some form of authoritarian regime. Americans can adopt a more pro–human rights stance in foreign policy while keeping in mind the limits of U.S. power and wisdom. Although the Carter administration may not have been as vigorous and evenhanded on human rights issues as some would have liked, former Secretary of State Cyrus Vance outlined a wide-ranging and prudential course of action that commands attention.

Vance suggested that the United States could act on its own or with and through the United Nations. The United States could also work through regional organizations such as the Inter-American Commission on Human Rights.

Vance contended that the means available to the United States "range from quiet diplomacy in its many forms through public pronouncements to withholding of assistance." He further stated: "Whenever possible, we will use positive steps of encouragement and inducement. Our strong support will go to countries that are working to improve the human condition. We will always try to act in concert with other countries through international bodies."

The rationale for the Carter human rights policy was clear. According to Vance: "We seek these goals because they are right, and because we, too, will benefit. Our own well-being, and even our security, are enhanced in a world that shares common freedoms and in which prosperity and economic justice create the conditions for peace. And let us remember that we always risk paying a serious price when we become identified with repression." Vance insisted that it is possible to act forthrightly, and yet realistically, on human rights. A realistic position would explore violations carefully, consider the prospects of effective action, and avoid self-righteousness.[16]

Vance's prudential guidelines are subject to interpretation. They could be endorsed by conservative defenders of the quiet diplomacy option as well as by liberal advocates of publicity and sanctions. Although the Carter administration's position was closer to publicity and sanctions than to quiet diplomacy (the preferred option of the Reagan and Bush administrations), liberal critics have argued that there was more rhetoric than reality in the Carter years. They point out that U.S. policy singled out the Soviet Union and left-wing regimes for criticism. They note that although the United States did cut aid to repressive regimes in Argentina, Uruguay, and Ethiopia, it did not recommend cuts for South Korea, the Philippines, or Iran under the Shah.

Similarly, critics note that the Reagan and Bush administrations did not cut off aid to Iraq or El Salvador—countries with dreadful records on human rights. In those authoritarian regimes, America's alleged security interests conflicted with its human rights concerns. Such critics favor an all-out policy. They would avoid the hypocrisy of going easy on national security friends while leaning heavily on national security foes and on little countries that can be scolded with impunity.

Human rights advocates also note that the Clinton administration, although characterized by good intentions and by positive actions in such countries as Haiti, was nevertheless slow in responding to dreadful violations of human rights in Bosnia and other troubled areas of the world. Realists, however, emphasize that even major powers such as the United States must carefully calculate whether humanitarian intervention on behalf of human rights is not only in the national interest but achievable at an acceptable cost.

Thus, it is clear that wise judgment is called for both in articulating and interpreting policy. It is relatively easy to say that decisions call for "informed and careful judgment." It is much more difficult to recognize a genuinely creative breakthrough in human rights policy and action. These same difficulties of judgment face decision makers at the United Nations.

Securing Human Rights Through the United Nations

Another approach to protecting human rights, not necessarily in conflict with national policy, would emphasize working through the United Nations. This argument builds on the U.N.'s forthright commitment to human rights. The United Nations exemplifies what is called an international human rights regime.[17]

In many respects the United Nations has done a remarkable job of articulating common principles, and thus a common standard, for human rights worldwide. Wise and effective implementation is now the U.N.'s major problem. A host of U.N. organizations are actively concerned with human rights. These include the General Assembly, which, according to the U.N. Charter, is to assist "in the realization of human rights and fundamental freedom for all without distinction as to race, sex, language, or religion"; the Secu-

rity Council, which may be involved if human rights violations endanger international peace and security; the secretary-general; and the Economic and Social Council, which can "make recommendations for the purpose of promoting respect for, and observance of, human rights and fundamental freedoms for all." Most recently, the U.N. established a High Commissioner for Human Rights who should be able to work with the U.N. Commission on Human Rights and other U.N. groups.

But what can these organizations do now to advance human rights principles? What powers do they have to fulfill the U.N. standard? Which policy options might become open in the future?

In general, the United Nations has articulated standards and convinced nations to endorse them. The United Nations invites compliance reports from parties to its human rights conventions. It receives complaints about violations of human rights from governments, nongovernmental organizations, and sometimes individuals. The United Nations may investigate complaints and report on violations—specifically, those revealing "a gross and consistent pattern of violations of human rights." It may exercise quiet diplomacy or invoke sanctions of one kind or another.

In the first two decades of its existence, "the only systematic activities of the United Nations with regard to the monitoring and protection of individual human rights"[18] related to the trust territories and non-self-governing territories. Beginning in 1967, however, U.N. organs became more active. They investigated violations in South Africa, Southwest Africa (Namibia), Rhodesia (Zimbabwe), Chile (after the coup that overthrew Allende in 1973), Argentina, Cyprus, Cambodia (Kampuchea), and El Salvador.

Yet the U.N.'s power to safeguard human rights is constrained—by its limited authority, its reluctance to interfere in the internal affairs of its members (particularly powerful ones), its machinery, its politicization (vulnerability to the political demands of a majority of members), and the stubborn defiance of nations that violate human rights.

Available Options—In view of these considerations, which policy options are available to the United Nations? One option might concentrate on what the United Nations has done best—articulate standards—and would use the techniques of quiet diplomacy; if that fails, it would use tactful publicity to gain adherence to U.N. standards. Without rejecting the efforts of the first option, a second option might focus more sharply on verifying consistent patterns of gross violations (through independent U.N. investigation as necessary) and on "pitiless publicity" and compliance reports to ensure respect for human rights. A third option might build on the first two options but place primary emphasis on developing legal machinery to ascertain and confirm rights violations under international law and to fashion wise legal, political, and economic remedies.

Each option has strengths and weaknesses. The creative breakthrough called for in the United Nations may involve a synthesis in tune with international realities. Clearly, it is important to move toward a global consensus on human rights standards. But what does consensus mean? Agreement on words? or fulfillment of principles?

Clearly, rhetorical consensus on standards is one thing; operative respect is another. Nations may pay lip service to rights but ignore them in practice. Quiet diplomacy is certainly a legitimate means and may work, but often it is a code for procrastination. Tact and tactful publicity are often sensible, but sometimes they enable nations to give precedence to alleged national security interests over ethical human rights obligations. Thus, in the past nations soft-pedaled human rights violations by their friends. And the United Nations did the same.

Verification through U.N. investigation and "pitiless publicity" also run into objections. Nations object to interference in their internal affairs and cite the U.N. Charter in their defense. Investigative visits depend on the consent of the alleged violator of human rights. "Pitiless publicity" may be counterproductive; it may anger the nation whose practices the U.N. is seeking to alter. Compliance reports depend on the good faith of the nation submitting them; no nation guilty of gross human rights violations would willingly incriminate itself.

Given the persistence of the sovereign nation-state system, U.N. member-nations will resist any really effective legal machinery and remedies to protect human rights. The United Nations has generally been loath, or unable, to invoke sanctions, a matter that falls within the powers of the Security Council, where each permanent member can veto action. In one important exception—Rhodesia (now Zimbabwe)—the Great Powers agreed to invoke sanctions. The agreement rested on the fact that the situation there threatened peace. Majorities in the General Assembly can be more easily mustered for resolutions against unpopular members—South Africa and its former practice of apartheid has been the best example—but these resolutions lack the teeth of the Security Council's diplomatic, political, economic, and military sanctions. Now that the end of the Cold War has made Great Power agreement easier, the Security Council is more likely to invoke sanctions in clear-cut cases, especially when aggressors seek to wipe out the very existence of a previously independent nation (as was the case with the Iraqis' invasion and attempted annexation of Kuwait). In more complicated cases—such as the protection of human rights in Bosnia-Herzegovina—economic sanctions may not be sufficient to protect against ethnic cleansing, and military sanctions may be difficult to achieve or enforce.

Global Human Rights Regime—How, then, should and can the United Nations best proceed in protecting human rights? What creative breakthrough might be envisaged, for example, to cope with the agonizing problem of genocide, perhaps the most egregious violation of human rights? One bold thought experiment envisages the establishment of a Global Human Rights Regime, under the auspices of the United Nations, that would (1) significantly strengthen global human rights institutions, (2) be guided by a cogent theory of prudent prevention, (3) use an operative theory of effective staged implementation, and (4) draw on a wise theory of just humanitarian intervention.[19]

1. The strengthened institutions would include, for example, the recently established U.N. High Commissioner for Human Rights, along with the U.N. Commission on Human Rights, working closely with an invigorated U.N. Security Council. These entities would provide executive leadership for a Global Human Rights Regime. Additional institutions would include, for example, a U.N. Human Rights Monitoring Agency, a U.N. Human Rights Protection Force, and a U.N. Human Rights Court—to provide, respectively, watchful eyes, effective muscle, and judicial scrutiny in cases of potential or actual genocide.

2. A cogent theory of prudent prevention (designed to prevent genocide rather than to have to cope with it after it has occurred) would rest on three cardinal principles: the need to develop mature constitutional democracies worldwide; the need to develop the philosophy and practice of deterrence of genocide; and the need to develop the philosophy and practice of preemptive action (in the event that deterrence does not work).

3. An operative theory of wisely staged implementation is also imperative. First, such a policy would call for really effective machinery for monitoring/investigating/reporting on potential or actual genocide. Such a policy would, second, require that the power of publicity be used to deter genocidal violations—where there is a clear and present danger of the eruption of genocide—and to solidify global support for just humanitarian intercession to stop genocide in progress. Third, effective remedies—political, judicial, economic, and military sanctions—must be on hand, to be prudently chosen and used to stop geno-

cide. To have any chance of success, such remedies must have the support of U.N. members willing and able to implement decisions of the U.N. Security Council. Finally, there is a crucial need to work out the problem of what might be called "human rights consolidation"—namely, what it takes to ensure that human rights will continue to be respected after initial efforts at prevention or intercession have been successful.

4. There is, additionally, a need to articulate a cogent theory of just humanitarian intercession. Such a guiding theory might include the following principles: intervention only by an appropriate authority (such as the U.N. Security Council); just cause (such as to prevent or stop genocide); last resort (military intervention only after other pacific means—political, economic, judicial sanctions—have been tried and found wanting); prudent appraisal (of benefits and costs of intercession); expectation of reasonable chance of success (immediate success in preventing or stopping aggression); use of humane and proportionate means; and careful calculation of a long-run reasonable chance of success (to ensure ongoing protection of human rights).

A tall order? Yes! Impossible? No! But how probable?

Political realists are skeptical of the thought experiment outlined above. They argue that little can be done—that the world lacks adequate policy, machinery, and will, that these deficiencies will not be overcome in the foreseeable future, that the costs of intercession and protection are too high, that the United Nations is ill-equipped to handle the tasks outlined, that even well-intentioned nations (looking to their own vital interests) will not cooperate with the U.N., and that it is unwise, dangerous, and unlawful to meddle in the internal, domestic affairs of sovereign nation-states. The reasons for this skepticism must be understood, but it would be tragic, indeed, if the United Nations were to prove unable to bring a halt to genocide.

Securing Human Rights Through Nongovernmental Organizations

Numerous nongovernmental organizations have done splendid work to protect human rights. They include Amnesty International (founded in 1961), the International Committee of the Red Cross (founded in 1863), the International League for Human Rights (founded in 1952), and the International Committee of Jurists (founded in 1942). Amnesty International works to secure the release of prisoners of conscience and, in recent years, to abolish torture and capital punishment. The Red Cross deals with prisoners of war and, more recently, political prisoners. The International League for Human Rights drafts human rights standards for the United Nations, forms civil liberties unions around the globe, protects political dissidents and religious minorities, and guards against the extermination of South American Indians. The International Commission of Jurists seeks to preserve the worldwide rule of law, particularly the right to a fair trial.

Other such nongovernmental organizations (NGOs) also crusade for human rights. Church, scientific, and professional groups have been involved. The Catholic Church has been in the forefront of the battle for human rights in Latin America, stimulated by Vatican II (meetings of the Catholic leadership to discuss key religious and social issues) and the establishment of the Pontifical Commission on Justice and Peace.[20] For Protestants, the World Council of Churches and the (American) National Council of Churches have also made rights a priority. In 1976 the American Association for the Advancement of Science formed a human rights clearinghouse to look after scientific freedom and responsibility. P.E.N. International works on behalf of freedom of expression and champions writers, artists, and intellectuals whose work arouses hostility. Jewish organizations have also worked hard for human rights. In addition, groups such as Hu-

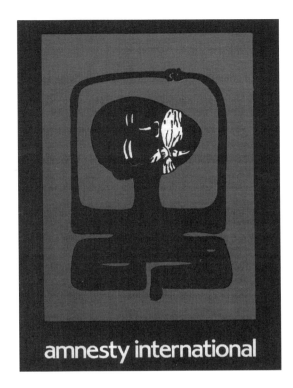

man Rights Watch and Africa Watch perform extremely valuable monitoring roles.

In their early strategy and tactics, the NGOs took a threefold approach. They worked to influence the United Nations to draft international human rights standards. They targeted governments. They adopted a humanitarian response to those whose rights had been violated.

The current option emphasizes the importance of implementing existing standards. Now NGOs, particularly the religious groups, are concerned with the "ecumenical search for a just society" and with "societal change and institutional transformation." These organizations have adopted a more critical attitude toward repressive regimes. The NGOs focus on the United Nations, individual countries (especially the United States), and regional groups, as well as on the World Bank, the International Monetary Fund, and even multinational corporations.

The NGOs are quite strong, particularly in their current role. They can often obtain reliable information about human rights violations and bring it before the United Nations (the U.N. Commission on Human Rights) or a national government (a congressional committee or the State Department). They have made publicity a powerful weapon in the battle for human rights. Because NGOs have no vested national, political, or economic interests to protect, their reports tend to be believed, and they help shape public opinion. Given their singleminded devotion to human rights, they are not compromised by questions of politics or by the balancing of security and rights in their efforts to report on, and obtain relief for, those who suffer human rights violations. The NGO activities often involve hundreds of thousands of people directly. Their consultative status with the United Nations allows NGOs to engage in private diplomacy, and they can directly approach offending governments to seek information about and redress for violations of human rights. Their activities have raised global consciousness, made governments more hesitant to violate rights, secured the release of persons unjustly imprisoned, and mitigated the punishment of others.

But the NGOs also have weaknesses. Their limited personnel and finances inevitably constrain their ability to monitor human rights. Their primary power is the power of publicity, the appeal to conscience; they cannot invoke political, economic, or military sanctions. Often NGOs can act only after violations have occurred. Their scope is often limited to a concern for political prisoners or torture or a fair trial. They have no power to deal with the underlying causes of consistent and gross violations.

Nevertheless, NGOs have great potential for achieving the global consensus that must underlie the constitutional protection of human rights around the world.

Securing Human Rights Through the Efforts of the Least Free Themselves

What role will the least free play in their own emancipation? Some scholars are persuaded that human rights for the least free cannot be achieved

without significant transformation in the global community or without major reform or radical revolution within the countries that now violate their own subjects' human rights. These changes would be initiated by the victims of genocide, colonialism, racism, political repression, sexism, and poverty. For example, to guard against another Holocaust, Jews need a nation-state of their own (Israel) as a homeland for persecuted Jews everywhere. Jews need a strong haven against genocide; they need a nation with the power to make "never again" a reality. Jews who prefer to remain citizens of other countries must actively defend their constitutional rights and must vigorously support the freedom of their co-religionists in Israel and elsewhere in the world.

Similarly, people battling to make national self-determination a reality must be prepared to press (peacefully, if possible) either to achieve or to sustain such self-determination.

Efforts to advance freedom in historically repressive regimes—for example, the former Soviet Union, the Philippines, El Salvador, Argentina, and South Korea—have been challenging but not entirely futile. It seems almost impossible for citizens to effect significant change in the countries that rank among the worst human rights offenders. China, Cuba, and North Korea share this dubious distinction among Communist countries, and Burma, Iran, Iraq, and Syria among developing nations. But the winds of freedom seem to be blowing in the world, and people living in oppressive regimes can take heart from the limited but significant progress of human rights in South Africa, the new Russia, Eastern Europe, and certain countries in Africa, Asia, and Latin America.

Specifically, what can the people in these countries do to protect their human rights? Will strategies vary for different regimes, depending on whether they are totalitarian or authoritarian? Will tactics that enable U.S. citizens to cope with violations of civil liberties work in China, Iraq, Vietnam, or El Salvador? These questions are not easily answered, but they call attention to the important and difficult work of the least free and their allies around the globe. A process of liberalization did overturn an authoritarian Soviet Union; countries in South America are now free of military rule; and some repressive regimes (such as the Marcos regime in the Philippines) have been overthrown with the help of "people power."

It is also important to realize that philosophies such as liberation theology—rooted in a particular interpretation of Christianity and drawing on Marxist social analysis—can help people struggling to improve their human rights. **Liberation theology** interprets Christianity as a gospel of freedom and justice for the oppressed. It also uses a Marxist analysis to highlight capitalism and imperialism as sources of economic, political, and social oppression. Critics still ask which understanding of liberation theology is to be chosen by the least free with this religious commitment. They also wonder how effective liberation theology will be in both theory and practice.[21]

And how can women battle sexism? Perspective is helpful here. Sexism is not genocide. Women do not seek a nation of their own. Although there are some similarities between sexism and racism—especially the notion that women and blacks are inferior—the maltreatment of blacks has been more horrendous than that of white women. Nevertheless, discrimination against women is global and persistent and gross. What strategies and tactics can women use to overcome discrimination and to make equality genuinely meaningful? Some critics argue that women in democratic countries can use the ballot to advance their cause. But they are skeptical about the use of the ballot in authoritarian societies.

Efforts of the poor to overcome poverty are treated in Chapter 18. To the extent that blacks or women or persecuted political dissidents are poor, the strategies will be similar.

One basic policy choice is between peaceful and violent means. Another basic choice is between incremental, constitutional reform and radical, extralegal revolution. Combinations of these choices are, of course, theoretically possible. One variety of "revolution" might be peaceful;

radical constitutional reform is also possible. In making their choices, the least free have to face the most difficult task of judgment—the balancing of costs and benefits. Violence, for example, leads to the loss of life; a militant revolution often calls for a sacrifice of liberty. It is extraordinarily difficult to balance the human rights sacrificed and the lives lost under a repressive regime against the human rights and lives saved by a revolutionary regime of the least free. And there is always the danger that a revolution will simply replace one repressive regime with another. Similarly, it is unusually difficult to balance the sacrifices to human rights of slower, incremental, constitutional, peaceful reform against the gains of speedy, wholesale, extralegal, violent revolution. The choices are agonizing. A top priority of any strategy by the least free should be to avoid, or minimize, any sacrifices of human rights or lives.

Other tasks in the battle of the least free are less agonizing. For example, the least free have to realize their plight and position. They must achieve self-identity and self-reliance. They must also organize to enhance their collective strength. They need to reach out to allies and form coalitions to maximize their strength. And they need to realistically assess the strengths and weaknesses of the institutions that oppress them. At the right time, they must focus their power to extend their freedom.

This is easier said than done. Yet there are success stories to juxtapose against the failures and the incomplete successes. Racism is by no means completely absent in the United States; yet the United States, in a remarkable civil rights "revolution"—aided by the Supreme Court and sparked by African Americans under the leadership of Martin Luther King, Jr.—significantly defeated the separate-but-equal doctrine and has taken major steps to overcome racial discrimination. The Holocaust was a dreadful reality, yet the state of Israel was reborn and lives. The Kurds of Iraq still live under a repressive regime, yet racist Rhodesia, which was ruled by a minority of whites, has become Zimbabwe and follows

majority rule. De facto apartheid may linger in
South Africa, yet it is legally dead. Authoritarian
regimes persist in some Asian, African, and Latin
American nations, yet Spain, Portugal, and Greece
have emerged from the cloud of fascist or authoritarian governments. The Chinese government
brutally repressed a peaceful student protest in
Tiananmen Square, yet a Communist regime is
no longer in power in Russia, and the peoples of
Eastern Europe are now free to govern themselves. Sexism pervades the modern world, with
women enslaved, prostituted, battered, and denied education, the vote, and equal pay for equal
work; but in some countries women have made
signal gains in education, politics, and social life.
Poverty persists, but, as we will see more clearly
in Chapter 18, the poor and their allies are
stirring throughout the world.

Securing Human Rights Through a New World Organization and World Order

In our search for creative breakthroughs for the
least free, it is helpful to examine challenges to
the underlying premises of the political actors
we have considered and to seek bolder visions of
human rights. Some critics especially condemn
the limitations arising from national sovereignty.
They bemoan the fact that national security
considerations often compromise human rights.
They demand more evenhanded concern for,
and action on behalf of, human rights in almost
all nations and in the United Nations. They
support nongovernmental organizations but understand their limited powers. These critics believe
that the framework of a global order is required
to speed up the liberation of the least free and to
minimize the costs of bold action. Richard A.
Falk speaks for such a world order.[22]

Falk's understanding of human rights does
not differ significantly from that explored in this
chapter. He, too, would prevent genocide; drastically modify racist regimes; outlaw all forms
of torture and cruelty; move toward equality
of treatment for different races, sexes, ages,
religions, tribes, and political groups; and ensure rights of self-expression and meaningful

participation.

Falk believes that the current sovereign nation-state system cannot provide and sustain
minimum standards for protecting human rights.
Decent nation-states have been unable to oppose
the abhorrent domestic policies of "outlaw" nations. In the past, and too often in the present,
the principle of national sovereignty has given a
nation too great a power to violate human rights.

Falk maintains that progress in protecting
human rights is closely linked to progress in
overcoming the war system. With real movement toward a peaceful world, nations and regional
groups can move more effectively to safeguard
human rights. In Falk's view, when a Central
Guidance System for the globe is established, it
will include a World Commission and Court of
Human Rights. The World Commission of Human Rights would receive all complaints and
would have real power to investigate them. The
commission would have power to make findings
and recommendations. Initially, it would look to
national or domestic remedies for redress, but
the commission would watch violations until
real satisfaction was obtained.

If nations failed to implement the commission's
decisions within a stated period, redress would
be found in the World Court of Human Rights.
The court would seek a "consent decree" to
uphold the human rights claim, and it would
assure maximum publicity to guard fulfillment
of the claim. The success of such a commission
and court requires, Falk concedes, great strengthening of the commitment to human rights in all
political communities.

Falk does not elaborate on the problem of
enforcement. That is, what happens when a
nation persistently violates human rights? Assuming failures at the national and regional
levels, some critics wonder whether his new
global organization would be able to enforce its
decisions via appropriate financial fines, police
power, and diplomatic, economic, political, or
military sanctions. These critics argue that unless the current mentality of nation-states changes
considerably, Falk's World Commission and

World Court of Human Rights will not be created. Some critics also note that if nation-states do change, such a commission and court may not be necessary. They argue that voluntary domestic settlement and global publicity are desirable, but then they contend that there is a realistic need to move beyond modest implementation to face the occasional need for force to make the court's judgments stick.

These criticisms highlight the strengths and weaknesses of Falk's world order approach. They also indicate the importance of national and regional developments to prepare the way for more effective global protection of human rights. In some respects Falk's scheme resembles the European approach. In 1950 fifteen European states adopted the European Convention on Human Rights, which set up a European Commission on Human Rights and a European Court of Human Rights. States may complain to the commission about violations by other states. Under certain circumstances, any person, nongovernment organization, or group of individuals may petition for redress. The commission determines whether a complaint or petition is admissible, seeks a friendly settlement, and may render a judgment on whether human rights have been violated. Either the commission or the accused state may refer a case to the European Court of Human Rights. If this does not happen, the Committee of Ministers of the Council of Europe may decide the case by a two-thirds vote, and its decision is binding. Although the European commission and court have handled only a few cases, they have been quite successful. Their decisions have been accepted and influential.

Some critics, however, argue that this approach will not work without the kind of consensus on human rights that has recently prevailed among West European countries. These critics do not, for example, believe it would work in Latin America, Africa, or Asia.

Nevertheless, it may be that Falk is more realistic about protecting human rights than his critics think. Global standards may influence regional and national standards, and vice versa.

Protection for human rights is best achieved at the domestic level, but regional organizations can pressure a delinquent nation. And a global organization may help when regional and national communities fail.

TOWARD CREATIVE BREAKTHROUGHS FOR THE LEAST FREE

Which of the preceding approaches makes the most sense? How do we appraise the costs and benefits of each? Which alternative is most desirable and most feasible? To make it easier to debate these issues and to choose wisely, we will review each approach, pose key questions, and present sample responses pro and con.

The United States

Should the United States rely primarily on quiet diplomacy toward offending "friends"? Or should it criticize friend and foe alike and not hesitate to invoke sanctions to punish human rights offenders?

Supporters of quiet diplomacy emphasize that U.S. national security interests, and not abstract morality, must guide foreign policy. Thus, American leaders must be tactful and not publicly scold those who support U.S. foreign policy, even as the leaders privately try to encourage such nations to respect human rights. Proponents argue that it may harm U.S. vital interests to cut off military or economic aid to regimes that help America in foreign affairs. Moreover, proponents note that former right-wing authoritarian regimes (as in Spain or Portugal) have been replaced by more democratic governments, whereas left-wing communist regimes (at least in the past) have held out a less promising prospect for significant change.[23]

Supporters of a stronger, more evenhanded position on human rights argue that the United States cannot adhere to a double standard. America must exert its influence to protect human rights against authoritarian governments of the left or right. Quiet diplomacy has its uses, but the United States must be prepared to use political, economic, and legal sanctions as well. If, ultimately, America is to move toward respect for human rights under international law, there can be only one standard of law for all violators.

The United Nations

Should the United Nations be resigned to mere articulation, and rhetorical acceptance, of human rights standards in the international community? Or should the United Nations develop a Global Human Rights Regime, with strengthened institutions, guided by policies of prudent prevention, staged implementation (via monitoring, publicity, sanctions—political, economic, judicial, military), and just humanitarian intercession, and thus become able to cope successfully with such egregious human rights violations as genocide?

One school of thought argues that the United Nations has an important job to do in articulating standards for the global community. These standards shape the consensus that will make international freedom a reality. At this time, the United Nations cannot go beyond this important task without meddling in nations' internal affairs. Perhaps in the future the United Nations will acquire real power to investigate violations of human rights and to fashion effective remedies.

Another school of thought favors developing wise and effective remedies now. Proponents of

this school would not only strengthen U.N. power to investigate complaints; they would also establish really effective machinery to protect human rights after persistent and gross violations have been verified. If necessary, the U.N. Charter should allow, in such cases as genocide, just humanitarian intercession. In time, the range of protection for human rights can extend beyond such egregious violations of human rights to cover other serious, persistent, and systemic violations of human rights.

Nongovernmental Organizations

Can the nongovernmental organization stop human rights violations as well as publicize them?

Political scientists who are impressed by the NGOs argue that their careful work in documenting and publicizing violations has helped protect human rights by making violating governments take notice. The NGOs cannot perform miracles, but they make actual or potential offenders think carefully about their practices. In fact, they may prevent violations that would otherwise have occurred, and they have secured the release of at least some victims.

Others, who applaud the limited good that NGOs do, emphasize their weaknesses. They note, for example, that although the NGOs can

In 1990 the United Nations articulated standards on the Rights of the Child. It remains to be seen, however, whether the U.N. can implement these rights in a meaningful way in stressful situations around the globe.

organize influential and even mass memberships in the United States and Western Europe, they cannot do so in China, Iraq, Iran, Libya, or North Korea. The NGOs do good work, but their effectiveness is limited. And even their limited effectiveness would diminish if they turned their attention from publicizing specific violations to a broader concern for the underlying causes of political, social, and economic injustice.

The Least Free Themselves

Can the least free themselves achieve self-consciousness, mobilize effectively, gain allies, and transform their condition by using the strategy of incremental, constitutional, peaceful reform? Or must they turn to violent revolution?

Supporters of reform believe that it is important to establish, and then build on, institutions of freedom in all countries. They concede that the battle will be easier in countries having a constitutional tradition and will be more difficult in authoritarian nations. But they state that reform will be less costly and more beneficial if it is achieved by peaceful means than if it results from violent revolution.

Supporters of a more militant policy point out that those who keep the least free powerless will not easily permit peaceful, constitutional change. Repression will continue until power is mobilized to overturn it. Because those who now oppress the least free use explicit violence, violence may be necessary to defeat them. The degree of militancy will depend on the character of the oppressor, and different strategies may be required for different categories of the least free—for example, by blacks or women or political dissidents—as they confront different types of repressive regimes.

New World Order

Can an order be devised that will permit human rights violations to be overcome or dealt with at national, regional, and global levels?

Supporters of a new world order maintain that protecting human rights calls for moving beyond the historical principle of national sovereignty. Nations can no longer have complete authority to violate the rights of their citizens. When nations grossly, persistently, and systematically violate their citizens' rights, there must be recourse to a higher constitutional authority (either at the regional or global level) to protect human rights. There must be an effective constitutional mechanism for receiving complaints of violations, investigating such violations, and protecting victims. Proponents argue that the rule of law can be slowly extended throughout the global community.

Critics note the persistence of jealous national sovereignty and argue that a new world order is a utopian dream. The world is not even ready for modest efforts by the United Nations to protect human rights; it is certainly not ready for a more ambitious global order. Given the strength of the nation-state system, it is unlikely that a new global order will succeed in invoking legal, political, or police powers to protect human rights if voluntary consent or publicity fails. No feasible strategy of transition to a new global order is in sight.

CONCLUSION

If politics is viewed as a civilizing process, creative breakthroughs to policies that can enhance the freedom and human rights of the least free must be explored. Thus, political scientists must understand the values, behavior, and judgments that make such breakthroughs possible.

Ethically, a civilizing politics must give top priority to helping the least free and to opposing the worst evils: nuclear war, official genocide, brutalizing racism, savage torture, and inhumane sexism. Systematic, persistent, and gross violations of human rights must be opposed and ended. A civilizing politics should prefer lawful, constitutional, nonviolent means to protect human rights.

Empirically, we recognize that the global community has articulated splendid standards for human rights. But too many countries fail to honor these standards. And the United Nations has not succeeded in protecting those rights.

Beginning in the 1970s the United States adopted policies to protect internationally recognized human rights, but whether this more vigorous approach will prevail remains to be seen. Nongovernmental organizations such as Amnesty International have done a fine job of publicizing violations, but their power is limited. The least free face serious handicaps in their efforts to protect themselves. Too often, nation-states and international organizations give precedence to national security and political considerations over human rights. In the global community, however, a theory of just, legitimate humanitarian intercession intervention is developing. The views considered in this chapter include a wide range of options, ranging from quiet diplomacy through publicity and legal redress to political, economic, and police sanctions. At this time, however, legal machinery and constitutional enforcement to protect human rights are embryonic.[24]

Prudentially, those concerned with protecting human rights continue to struggle toward a wise calculus of costs and benefits. They struggle to maximize protection of human rights at minimal costs in life, violence, and freedom itself. They also struggle to work out a theory of transition. They struggle to work out wise strategies and tactics: the right rate of advance, the proper balancing of equities, sensible mixture of "carrot and stick," statesmanlike respect for national sensibilities, supportive international law and public opinion, effective constitutional machinery, and creative statesmanship. These efforts tax the keenest judgment of civil rights advocates.

The next chapter focuses on economic well-being, an important ingredient of human rights that merits a separate chapter. We will focus primarily on developing nations.

ANNOTATED BIBLIOGRAPHY

Donnelly, Jack. *Universal Human Rights in Theory and Practice*. Ithaca, N.Y.: Cornell University Press, 1989. Argues on behalf of human rights as universal moral rights. Emphasizes the connection between human rights and Western liberalism. Rebuts various relativist challenges. Favors priority of national action in implementing human rights. A very persuasive analysis.

Donnelly, Jack, and Howard, Rhoda E., eds. *International Handbook of Human Rights*. Westport, Conn.: Greenwood Press, 1987. A valuable resource book!

Falk, Richard A. *A Study of Future Worlds*. New York: Free Press, 1975. Presents the realization of fundamental human rights and of conditions of political justice as one of Falk's four ethical goals. See also Falk's *Explorations at the Edge of Time: The Prospects for World Order* (Philadelphia: Temple University Press, 1992).

Felice, William F. *Taking Rights Seriously: The Importance of Collective Human Rights*. Albany: State University of New York Press, 1996. Maintains that the protection of human dignity calls for expanding our understanding of human rights to include rights of groups, peoples, and collectivities.

Formicola, Jo Renee. *The Catholic Church and Human Rights: Its Role in the Formulation of U.S. Policy 1945–1980*. New York: Garland, 1988. Provides an illuminating study of the movement of the American Catholic Church from complacency and a limited concern for human rights to renewed concern and effective involvement in helping shape a more humane and moral American foreign policy, especially in Latin America.

Howard, Rhoda E. *Human Rights and the Search for Community*. Boulder, Colo.: Westview, 1995. Favors a conception of rights that embraces economic as well as civil and political rights.

Human Rights Quarterly. For scholarly, up-to-date analyses and accounts. Interdisciplinary. Invaluable.

Human Rights Watch. *Human Rights Watch World Report 1996*. New York: Human Rights Watch, 1996. Annually describes and analyzes significant human rights developments in sixty-five nations.

Mowrer, Glen A. J. *Human Rights and American Foreign Policy: The Carter and Reagan Experiences*. Westport, Conn.: Greenwood Press, 1987. Offers a critical and illuminating comparison by a keen observer.

Riemer, Neal. *Creative Breakthroughs in Politics*. Westport, Conn.: Praeger, 1996. Explores "Protection Against Genocide: Toward a Global Human Rights Regime" in Chapter 7. Argues on behalf of strengthened U.N. institutions, policies of prudent prevention, staged implementation, and just humanitarian intercession.

Solzhenitsyn, Aleksandr. *The First Circle*. New York: Harper & Row, 1968; *Cancer Ward,* New York: Farrar, Strauss & Giroux, 1969; *The Gulag Archipelago,* New York: Harper & Row, 1974. Present revelations of life in the Soviet slave labor camps. Grim. Solzhenitsyn's novels, based on his own experiences, make scholarly accounts of the great Soviet purge and domestic terror more vivid.

Strozier, Charles B., and Flynn, Michael, eds. *Genocide, War, and Human Survival.* Lanham, Md.: Rowman and Littlefield, 1996. See especially Chapter 11 by Richard Falk, "Meeting the Challenge of Genocide in Bosnia: Reconciling Moral Imperatives with Political Constraints," and Chapter 12 by Saul Mendlovitz and John Fousek, "The Prevention and Punishment of the Crime of Genocide."

Teson, Fernando R. *Humanitarian Intervention: An Inquiry into Law and Morality.* Dobbs Ferry, N.Y.: Transnational Publishers, 1988. Explores a politically difficult problem. The temptation to intervene is morally attractive yet can be dangerous and counterproductive. Makes a strong case for just humanitarian intervention.

United Nations Department of International Economic and Social Affairs, et al. *The World's Women, 1970–1990: Trends and Statistics.* New York: United Nations, 1991. An invaluable source. Reports some progress but still a big gender gap on such matters as education, pay, public life and leadership, and health care.

United Nations Development Program. *Human Development Report 1996.* New York: Oxford University Press, 1996. Recognizes the intimate connection between freedom and human development. See also the 1992 report's Chapter 2, "Political Freedom and Human Development," which includes a "political freedom index," and the 1991 report, which featured a "human freedom index."

U.S. Department of State. *Country Reports on Human Rights Practices.* Washington, D.C.: Government Printing Office, yearly. The State Department's annual report to Congress. Informative, measured. Should be supplemented by reports of other nongovernmental organizations such as Amnesty International.

SUGGESTIONS FOR FURTHER READING

Arat, Zehra A. *Democracy and Human Rights in Developing Countries.* Bouldler, Colo.: Lynne Rienner, 1991.

European Commission on Human Rights. *Stocktaking on the European Convention on Human Rights.* Strasbourg: European Commission on Human Rights, 1984.

Farer, Tom J., ed. *Toward a Humanitarian Diplomacy: A Primer for Policy.* New York: New York University Press, 1980.

Forsythe, David P. *Human Rights and World Politics.* Lincoln: University of Nebraska Press, 1983.

Goldhagen, Daniel J. *Hitler's Willing Executioners: Ordinary Germans and the Holocaust.* New York: Knopf, 1996.

Hoffman, Stanley. *The Ethics and Politics of Humanitarian Intervention.* Notre Dame, Ind.: University of Notre Dame Press, 1996.

Holleman, Warren L. *The Human Rights Movement: Western Values and Theological Perspectives.* New York: Praeger, 1987.

Hollenbach, David. *Justice, Peace, and Human Rights: American Catholic Social Ethics in a Pluralistic World.* New York: Crossroad, 1988.

Human Rights Watch, Women's Rights Project. *The Human Rights Watch Global Report on Women's Human Rights.* New York: Human Rights Watch, 1995.

Kuper, Leo. *Genocide: Its Political Use in the Twentieth Century.* New Haven, Conn.: Yale University Press, 1981.

Kuper, Leo. *The Prevention of Genocide.* New Haven, Conn.: Yale University Press, 1985.

Milne, A. J. M. *Human Rights and Human Diversity: An Essay in the Philosophy of Human Rights.* Albany: State University of New York Press, 1986.

Monshipourri, Mahmood. *Democratization, Liberalization, and Human Rights in the Third World.* Boulder, Colo.: Lynne Rienner, 1995.

Nichols, Bruce, and Loescher, Gil, eds. *The Moral Nation and U.S. Foreign Policy.* Notre Dame: University of Notre Dame Press, 1989.

Nickel, James W. *Making Sense of Human Rights: Philosophical Reflections on the Universal Declaration of Human Rights.* Berkeley: University of California Press, 1987.

Pottenger, John R. *The Political Theory of Liberation Theology: Toward a Reconvergence of Social Values and Social Science.* Albany: State University of New York Press, 1989.

Pottenger, John R. "Liberation Theology, Prophetic Politics, and Radical Social Critique," Chapter 9 in Neal Riemer, ed., *Let Justice Roll: Prophetic Chal-*

lenges in Religion, Politics, and Society. Lanham, Md.: Rowman and Littlefield, 1996.

Shapiro, Ian. *The Evolution of Human Rights in Liberal Theory.* Cambridge: Cambridge University Press, 1986.

Sigmund, Paul E. *Liberation Theology at the Crossroad: Democracy or Revolution?* New York: Oxford University Press, 1990.

Simpson, Christopher. *The Splendid Blond Beast: Money, Law, and Genocide in the Twentieth Century.* New York: Common Courage, 1995.

Tolley, Howard J. *The United Nations Commission on Human Rights.* Boulder, Colo.: Westview Press, 1987.

United Nations, Department of Public Information. *The United Nations and the Advancement of Women, 1945–1995.* New York: United Nations, 1995.

Vincent, R. J. *Foreign Policy and Human Rights.* Cambridge: Cambridge University Press, 1986.

Vincent, R. J. *Human Rights and International Relations.* Cambridge: Cambridge University Press, 1986.

Weiss, Thomas G., and Collins, Cindy. *Humanitarian Challenges and Intervention: World Politics and the Dilemmas of Help.* Boulder, Colo.: Westview Press, 1996.

GLOSSARY TERMS

apartheid
discrimination
freedom
genocide
Holocaust
human rights
least free
liberation theology
national self-determination
patriarchy
racism
sanctions
separate but equal
sexism

THE STRUGGLE FOR ECONOMIC WELL-BEING

As noted in Chapter 17, many people consider economic well-being to be a basic human right—the right to fulfill vital needs for food, shelter, health care, and education. Because this right is so important, it deserves its own chapter.

Economic well-being is closely related not only to human rights and freedom but also to peace and ecological health. War is a threat to economic well-being. During a war, nations attack each other's soldiers and each other's economic systems—factories, transportation, and sources of strategic raw materials. Modern wars destroy food and housing along with guns, tanks, planes, ships, and munitions. In addition, the arms race uses up valuable resources (capital, labor, scientific skill, organizational ability) that could be better used to fight poverty, disease, illiteracy, and inadequate housing.

As we will see more clearly in Chapter 19, economic well-being and ecological health are also closely connected. For example, economic well-being calls for a sensible balance between population and resources, and both pollution and the imprudent use of resources affect the quality of economic and social life. We will touch on these ecological problems in this chapter, but we defer a fuller discussion to Chapter 19.

This chapter focuses on the following problem: *What creative breakthroughs can promote greater economic well-being?* In responding to this problem, we focus primarily on the world's poor, especially in developing nations and particularly those who live in the least-developed countries (LDCs). But we cannot forget the pockets of poverty and the problems of unemployment, homelessness, inflation, and industrial stagnation that continue to plague the developed world. The interrelatedness of the world economy means that healthy economies in the industrial North benefit the developing areas. Similarly, we cannot close our eyes to economic performance and social well-being in the communist world. The post–World War II record of the Soviet Union, China, Vietnam, Cuba, and the former communist countries of East Europe was at best mixed and at worst disastrous.

DEFINING ECONOMIC WELL-BEING

By **economic well-being** we mean a level of income, food, health care, education, shelter, and quality of life that satisfies minimum standards of life and decency and permits full growth and development.

Economic well-being contrasts with poverty. **Poverty** is that level of income, food, health care, education, shelter, and quality of life that is below minimum standards of life and decency. Poverty usually precludes full growth and development. People in poverty are undernourished. They may die in periods of famine. They are vulnerable to disease. They are often illiterate. They live in substandard housing, are ill-clad, and are poorly equipped to move up the economic and social ladder. They are most often unemployed or are underemployed and poorly

paid. They usually do not participate in politics.

Geographically, most of the poor live in the South—the Southern Hemisphere or the southern part of the Northern Hemisphere. Most of the world's affluent nations are in the Northern Hemisphere. Hence the terms *North* and *South*. The poorest nations and peoples are in Sub-Sahara Africa and South Asia. The poor are also to be found in significant numbers in the Arab countries, Southeast Asia, and Central America. The richest nations are in North America and Europe and include Japan and Australia. There are also several dynamic and relatively prosperous Asian economies, known as the **newly industrialized economies** (NICs); they include South Korea, Taiwan, Hong Kong, Singapore, and increasingly Thailand.

In exploring the struggle for economic well-being, we will set forth the ethical and empirical factors that prompt exploration of the problem. These factors are grim and sobering. They underscore the absence of the political, economic, and social resources that people need in order to cope with economic malaise. They pose troubling ethical and prudential questions—involving the calculus of costs and benefits—for policymakers seeking wise and humane choices.

Poverty grips large sections of the developing world, particularly in South Asia and Africa.

After examining these ethical and empirical factors, we will consider some major alternatives facing policymakers in the United States and the West, in the developing countries, and in Communist China. These alternatives present a number of broad options that involve varieties of capitalism, communism, and democratic socialism. We will consider options that favor the nation-state and the current economic world order as well as options that look toward a different world order.

Finally, we will challenge readers to devise their own solutions on the basis of their critical analysis.

KEY ETHICAL AND EMPIRICAL FACTORS

The approach that will guide our analysis here was summed up by Cyrus Vance in 1977. Vance, then U.S. secretary of state, declared the importance of "increased attention to the basic human needs of all the peoples of the world." He stated: "We need more focus on that part of the world population that lacks essential food, water, shelter, and health care, as well as employment and education. We must direct our efforts to meet more effectively the needs of the poorest peoples in the developing world."[1] Vance maintained that such a focus would benefit not only the poor people involved but also the United States and the entire globe.

The Persistence of Poverty

Between 1980 and 1996, fifteen countries in the developing world experienced dramatic economic growth and improved living conditions for their 1.5 billion people. Unfortunately, during this same period, one hundred developing countries experienced economic decline or stagnation, reducing the incomes of roughly 1.6 billion people, over a quarter of the world's population.[2] Despite the marked success of a few developing countries, the persistence of poverty in a large number of countries remains a major global problem.

What characterizes such poverty? Poor people endure a minimal income, an inadequate diet, and substandard conditions of health and housing. They lack the basic necessities of life. Most are illiterate. They are permanently insecure. They are unemployed or underemployed. They have high birth rates and high infant death rates. They suffer from preventable disease. They live shorter lives than people in more affluent countries. Table 18.1 demonstrates this gap by comparing a variety of countries at differing development levels.

Table 18.1 Comparisons Between Poorer and Richer Countries

Nation	Per Capita GNP ($)	Adult Illiteracy (%)	Infant Mortality (per 1,000)	Life Expectancy (years)
Bangladesh	220	65	106	56
Kenya	270	31	61	58
China	490	27	30	69
Indonesia	740	23	56	63
Philippines	850	10	42	67
Mexico	3,610	13	35	71
Greece	7,390	7	10	78
Spain	13,590	5	7	78
United States	24,740	<5	9	76
Switzerland	35,760	<5	6	78

Source: World Bank, World Development Report 1995 (New York: Oxford University Press, 1995).

Where do the poor live? As Figure 18.1 indicates, the largest concentrations of people within the sixty **least-developed countries (LDCs)** are to be found in East and South Asia, with enormous numbers of poor in China, India, and Pakistan. Sub-Saharan Africa has by far the largest number of LDCs with 34 and holds nearly 15 percent of the population of all LDCs.

The prospects for overcoming poverty are at worst gloomy and at best mixed. The developing world achieved an average annual GNP growth rate of 4.6 percent between 1980 and 1993. In overall terms, that may not be considered a bad performance. The problem is, as indicated earlier, the growth has been terribly uneven. For instance, among the LDCs, the growth rate was only 2.7 percent, and in Sub-Saharan Africa it was a near catastrophic 1.5 percent.[3] Compounding the problem in many of the regions are soaring population growth rates, resulting in many countries struggling to merely achieve and maintain a subsistence living for large numbers of their citizens.

This picture of poverty is made even more disturbing when we realize that there are significant pockets of poverty in affluent countries. For example, as much as 10 percent of the population of some affluent countries live in poverty. As many as 25 million people in the United States live below the American poverty line. Of course, these people are much better off than many of the poor in developing countries. Yet poverty in the midst of affluence, like affluence in the midst of the developing world's terrible poverty, should sensitize critical students to probe for reasons and solutions.

In discussing poverty, we have inevitably touched on unemployment, hunger, disease, and illiteracy. Because these factors so clearly militate against economic well-being, it is important to look more closely at each.

The Scourges of Unemployment, Hunger, Ill-Health, Illiteracy, and Poor Housing

People are poor when they lack money, either because they are unemployed, are underemployed, or are not receiving fair pay for their labor. In both the developed and developing worlds, unemployment remains a chronic problem, mirroring economic ill-health. That ill-health is reflected in industrial stagnation, sectional depression, economic recession, low agricultural productivity and rates of growth, and inadequate use of human and material resources. Economic troubles in the developed world hinder economic well-being in the developing world.

Unemployment is particularly acute in many developing countries. Table 18.2 shows some stark contrasts in unemployment rates between developed and developing countries.

Hunger remains an agonizing problem for the world's poor, despite the fact that world food stocks are reasonably high. The food problem is largely one of inadequate purchasing power and inadequate and inequitable distribution. Whatever the reason, the problem is gigantic. In the developing world, 800 million people do not get enough food and roughly 500 million are malnourished.[4]

Figure 18.1
Population distribution within the sixty least-developed countries.

Source: Based on data extracted from the World Bank, World Development Report 1995 (Oxford University Press, published for the World Bank, 1995).

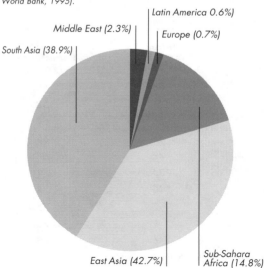

Latin America 0.6%)

Middle East (2.3%)

Europe (0.7%)

South Asia (38.9%)

East Asia (42.7%)

Sub-Sahara Africa (14.8%)

Table 18.2 Comparative Unemployment, 1994

Nations	Percentage Unemployment
Developed countries*	
United States	6.1
Japan	2.5
Austria	6.5
Republic of Korea	2.4
France	8.0
Developing countries	
Algeria	23.8
Barbados	21.9
Morocco	16.0
Sri Lanka	13.6
Panama	13.8

Source: International Labour Office, Yearbook of Labour Statistics, 54th issue. (Geneva, 1995), pp. 407–469.

*Countries are ranked by GNP/Capita.

Hunger and malnutrition are not absent from rich developed countries. For example, malnourishment has been particularly severe among the elderly in the United States, although great progress has recently been made in dealing with this problem. Unemployed women with dependent children also seem to suffer inordinately from malnourishment in richer countries.

People need either money to buy food or the ability to produce their own food. Poorer nations unable to grow food must be able to import it for reasonable prices. To increase their own production, they require fertilizers and appropriate farm equipment. Most experts agree that many developing countries would benefit significantly from agrarian reform, understood as more equitable distribution of land and income. They would also benefit from adequate transportation and educational services to ensure that nutritional food is locally available at reasonable cost. Finally, in periods of famine, many developing nations desperately need shipments of food from richer, food-exporting countries.

In the developing world, poverty and hunger, the lack of clean water and effective sanitation, the absence of immunization pro-

Despite the fact that world food stocks are high, roughly 500 million suffer from malnutrition.

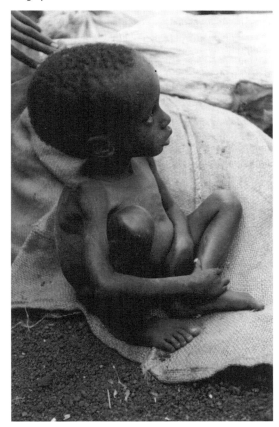

grams, and the shortage of trained health workers all contribute to high infant and child mortality, to a host of debilitating diseases, and to shorter life expectancy.

Statistics reflecting the grim reality of poverty are disturbing. In the developing countries, 12 million children die every year before they reach the age of five. Nearly 1.2 billion people are without safe water.[5] Worldwide, 18 million people have been infected with HIV, 2.5 million have died of AIDs, and every day 6,000 new infections occur—one every 15 seconds. What makes these global statistics so tragic for the world's poor is that 90 percent of all new HIV infections are in developing countries.[6]

The plight of women in the poorest countries of the world is particularly bad. Females in the developing countries receive only about half the higher education of males. In poor households they often shoulder a much greater workload than men and have considerably fewer chances to earn money. The latter problem has, ironically, gotten worse in developing areas where modern technology has led to even lower female employment.

These data point dramatically to a need for action. For example, the World Health Organization contends that infant mortality in developing nations could be reduced by one-third simply by providing clean water and decent nutrition. Obviously, immunization programs and better health services could save millions of lives.

One area where significant progress has been made is in wiping out illiteracy. Between 1970 and 1993, the literacy rate in developing countries increased from 43 percent of those over 15 to 61 percent. Twenty-five developing countries now enjoy literacy rates in excess of 90 percent. But there are still disquieting figures

such as in Sub-Saharan Africa with only a 55 percent literacy rate and South Asia with 49 percent.[7] Further, as Figure 18.2 demonstrates, throughout the developing world troubling percentages of school-age youth are not enrolled in schools.

Poor housing also militates against economic well-being. And poor housing—inadequate space, sanitation, and protection—is the lot of millions, particularly in poor developing nations. Reliable statistics on housing are difficult to obtain, but the plight of the world's poor in rural areas and urban slums is familiar to experienced world travelers. In many crowded cities in the developing world (and, indeed, even in New York, Chicago, and Los Angeles) some poor people sleep in the streets. The loans that the World Bank has made to rehabilitate slums and build low-cost housing testify to the inadequacy of current housing.

The Unsettling Reality of Inequality

No treatment of the struggle for economic well-being can ignore the persistence of inequality

---

Figure 18.2
School-age population in secondary schools, 1993.

Source: UNESCO, *UNESCO Statistics Yearbook 1995 (Bertram Press, published for UNESCO, 1995)*, pp. 2-26/27.

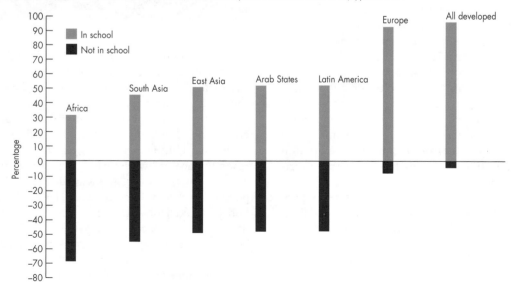

(1) between rich and poor nations and (2) within both rich and poor nations. Global and national inequalities are less disturbing when the economic pie is big enough so that everyone can at least satisfy basic needs. But when the shares are incompatible with economic well-being—especially when millions live in poverty—the question of inequality becomes a disturbing political issue.

Despite gains by some developing nations, and the wealth achieved by a few oil-producing nations, a big gap still remains between developed and developing countries. Developing nations gain too little and their populations grow too fast for them to close that gap. Figure 18.3 dramatically illustrates the maldistribution of wealth on the planet. The richest fifth of the world's population receives 82.7 percent of total world income. Most distressing is that this gap is getting wider. As the U.N.'s *Human Development Report 1996* points out,

- Of the $23 trillion global GDP [gross development product] in 1993, $18 trillion was in the industrial countries—only $5 trillion in the developing countries, even though they have nearly 80 percent of the world's people.
- The poorest 20 percent of the world's people saw their share of global income decline from 2.3 percent to 1.4 percent in the past 30 years. Meanwhile, the share of the richest 20 percent rose from 70 percent to 85 percent. That doubled the ratio of the shares of the richest and the poorest—from 30:1 to 61:1.
- The assets of the world's 358 billionaires exceed the combined annual incomes of countries with 45 percent of the world's people.
- The gap in per capita income between the industrial and developing worlds tripled, from $5,700 in 1960 to $15,400 in 1993.[8]

There are wide differences within regions. In the Middle East, Egypt has a per capita GNP of $660, while in the United Arab Emirates it is $21,430. In Asia, Japan has a per capita GNP of $31,490; the Philippines, $850. In Africa differences range from $90 in Mozambique to $1,190 in Swaziland.[9] Clearly, countries such as Japan and the United Arab Emirates raise the per capita figures for their regions considerably. Without them, the figures would be considerably lower.

There are also big gaps between rich and poor within many nations, particularly in the developing world. It is quite common for the richest fifth of a developing country to command 60 percent or more of the national income, while the poorest fifth has only 3 to 5 percent of such income. In general, wealth is more equitably distributed in communist countries, although in virtually every system a privileged class based on Communist party membership has emerged. In the United States a disturbing trend in the 1980s was the gradual erosion of the middle class and the division of wealth between rich and poor.[10] Between 1970 and 1993, the American **working poor,** defined by an income of below $20,000, increased from 39 percent to 45 percent. The middle class, defined by an income between $20,000 and $75,000, decreased from 57 percent to 47 percent.[11] It remains to be seen whether this pattern continues in the future.

Figure 18.3
The inequality of global income.

Source: United Nations Development Program, Human Development Report 1992 (New York: Oxford University Press, 1992).

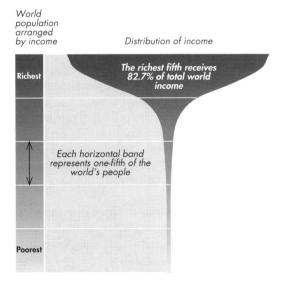

World population arranged by income

Distribution of income

Richest

The richest fifth receives 82.7% of total world income

Each horizontal band represents one-fifth of the world's people

Poorest

The Difficulties of Lifting the Level of Economic Well-Being

Enormous difficulties face poor nations in addition to the ones that we have already discussed. Political instability has characterized most of the developing nations, old or new. For example, the Congo, Sudan, Liberia, Rwanda, Burundi, and Nigeria have been plagued by civil war. Many countries have been affected by coups and revolutions, including Pakistan in Asia, Ghana in Africa, and Brazil in Latin America. Political and revolutionary turmoil has swept Vietnam and neighboring countries in Southeast Asia; Indonesia; the Philippines; Chile, Bolivia, Argentina, and most recently in Mexico in Latin America; Kenya and Zimbabwe in Africa as they fought for independence and rule by the black majority; and Lebanon, Syria, Iraq, and Iran in the Middle East.

Few of these countries have had democratic, cohesive political leadership. Most often they have been ruled by an army strongman or a military junta. One party has dominated in Egypt, Ethiopia, Iraq, North and South Korea, Pakistan, Chile, Bolivia, Argentina, and Libya.

Other prerequisites for political stability are lacking in many developing nations: an honest and effective bureaucracy, schools, transportation facilities, health services, and trained workers. For example, the Belgians left few educated Congolese behind when the Congo became independent.

Adverse trade and financial conditions also affect most developing nations. Many such nations suffer economically because they are highly dependent on the export of key commodities—coffee, tea, rubber, or copper—whose prices fluctuate and thus may not produce steady, reliable income. Compounding the problem, prices for raw materials such as wood, minerals, petroleum, and grains generally increase more slowly than prices for processed or manufactured goods. To protect domestic sectors of their economies, developed nations frequently place extraordinarily high tariffs on manufactured or processed goods from developing countries, which

makes these products noncompetitive. Because of these adverse trade conditions and the net outflow of capital, most developing countries carry alarmingly high debt levels, making it difficult to find new capital for investment and expansion of their economies.

Many people, particularly in the developing world, believe that these conditions are merely carryovers from the era of European **colonialism** during the nineteenth and twentieth centuries. The European colonial powers—Britain, Holland, Germany, Italy, Belgium, and France—did not have the economic well-being of the native people as their prime objective. Colonial powers were interested in profits and their own national security, not in developing balanced economies. Because colonial powers did not care about social justice, they perpetuated patterns of domination and dependence. In the eyes of many scholars, those same patterns exist today in the form of **neoimperialism.**

Population growth, in relation to resources, is also troublesome. Most of the world's major population increases take place in the developing world. Such population growth, particularly in poor countries, "compounds the task of providing food, jobs, shelter, education and health services, of mitigating absolute poverty, and of meeting the colossal financial and administrative needs of rapid urbanization."[12]

These poorer countries desperately need developmental financing to help them meet their needs for food production, industrialization, energy development, transport, communications, education, and health care. They need aid, credit, and investment. Such help would provide the jobs and income necessary to combat poverty, would increase their self-sufficiency, and would enable them to participate more fully in world trade.

The Agonizing Calculus of Costs and Benefits

The benefits in the struggle for economic well-being are reasonably clear: bringing an end to degrading poverty, providing jobs and decent income, ensuring adequate food and good health, advancing literacy, and sharing the common wealth more fairly. But at what costs—as reflected in which policies—may those benefits be obtained?

Debate rages about whether the poor developing nations can lift themselves by their own efforts, with enough speed, and at acceptable costs. Controversy has also surrounded the role of capitalism and communism in the struggle to achieve greater economic well-being. Students of economic development wonder whether the wealthy nations of the North are willing to endorse low-cost credits and economic aid for developing nations. Students of politics ask whether developed nations can cut back on large military expenditures that drain their resources and make them less willing to invest in developing areas.

Developing nations might follow a communist, totalitarian, and egalitarian model. They might also opt for a capitalist, authoritarian, and nonegalitarian model such as Brazil used for most of the 1970s and 1980s. Or they might ask whether a liberal capitalist or democratic socialist path is possible. They might even think about a new world order. We now turn to some possible approaches and their strengths and weaknesses.

ALTERNATIVE APPROACHES TO ECONOMIC WELL-BEING

Which policies adopted by which political actors will bring about economic well-being? First, we will examine a liberal capitalist and liberal democratic option that the United States might adopt. We will then present the strengths and weaknesses of the Chinese communist and Brazilian capitalist models of development. Then we will consider a democratic socialist model. All of these models presuppose the continued functioning of the sovereign nation-state system. Finally, we will examine a more radical option that looks to significant changes in traditional ideas of national sovereignty and world economic order. We present these models to stimulate thought about how to achieve economic well-

being, particularly for the poor in developing countries. Numerous variations on each model are possible.

Economic Well-Being Through Liberal Capitalism and Liberal Democracy

It is impossible in a few pages to present the liberal capitalistic and democratic model for achieving economic well-being. There is no agreement on such a model. There are disputes about wise and effective policy. Thus, we present just one approach in the liberal capitalistic and democratic tradition.

In general, supporters of this model maintain that the way to overcome poverty and related ills is to increase the size of the economic pie (agricultural and industrial production) and to encourage a more equitable distribution of income and services. Robert McNamara, longtime president of the World Bank, held that "the basic problem of poverty and growth in the developing world can be stated very simply. . . . The growth is not equitably reaching the poor. And the poor are not significantly contributing to growth. Development strategies, therefore, need to be reshaped in order to help the poor become more productive."[13]

Strategy—A threefold strategy is required. First, poor people and nations must help themselves. Second, richer nations such as the United States must help developing nations in a variety of ways. Third, private enterprise (including multinational or transnational corporations) must assist in crucial ways. Working together, these forces can contribute to balanced growth and equitable distribution within a framework of freedom.

Developing nations need a stable and reasonably efficient political and administrative structure that can encourage greater agricultural and industrial productivity and thus increase profits, jobs, and income. They require a social, educational, and medical infrastructure (transport, communications, schools, and health services) to deliver basic services (decent housing, clean

water, and literacy) in the interest of basic human needs. As necessary, these nations also
have to undertake agrarian or social reform to
give poor people a greater stake in their productivity and a decent share in the common
wealth. Such reform must include conscious
decisions to bring population and resources into
a better balance and to avoid spending valuable money and resources on excessive military
armaments.

The United States and other rich Western
nations can play an important role by extending
credit and aid, stabilizing prices of commodities
from developing nations at a reasonably remu-
nerative level, and allowing trade to flow freely.
They can also help by ensuring lower food prices
and by working toward a global energy policy to
make oil (or energy substitutes) available at fair
prices. These wealthy nations must encourage
the kind of self-help outlined in the preceding
paragraph. The vital interests of the United States
cannot really be secure in a world containing so
much poverty and discontent.

Moreover, by adopting a more enlightened
view of economic well-being in developing nations, private enterprise can see that sensible
profits and the battle against poverty are not
incompatible. Increased productivity, trade, and
a vast new army of consumers can be linked to
reasonable profits and to the satisfaction of basic
human needs. Thus, wise private investment
and credit can aid in the struggle for economic
well-being. Multinational (or transnational) corporations, operating under sensible rules to ensure
that productivity, technology, and profits re-
dound to benefit the poor in the host country,
can also help overcome poverty.

Evaluation—The strengths of this option are considerable. It emphasizes peaceful, evolutionary
development within a democratic and constitutional framework. It emphasizes the value of
political, economic, and social freedom. It taps
people's interest in their own improvement. It
connects the self-interest in reasonable profits to
the satisfaction of human needs.

The option's weaknesses, however, must be
seriously considered. It may not be speedy enough.
Or fundamental enough. Or equitable enough.
In brief, it may take too long to increase the size
and shares of the pie. It may not overcome the
economic and social inequities of the developing
country. Moreover, this option may presume too
much wisdom and self-control on the part of the
people and leadership of developing nations. It
may also presume too much enlightened self-
interest and long-range perspective on the part
of affluent nations. This option may overestimate the intelligence of capitalist entrepreneurs
both inside and outside the developing country.
Finally, its critics say, this option fails to come to
grips with old-fashioned capitalistic exploitation or economic imperialism. Through unfair
trade practices, developed countries may retard
economic development that would benefit the
poor people of the developing countries and may
resist protective controls on international business corporations.

How desirable and how feasible is the liberal
capitalistic and democratic alternative? How do
we assess, more exactly, its costs and benefits?
Without actual testing of this model, it is difficult to judge. But we may look to the past
performance of the United States, of other liberal
capitalistic and democratic nations, and of countries in the developing world for clues. Past
behavior does not dictate the future, but it may
help the prudent policymaker judge the chance
for significant change.

Economic Well-Being Through Egalitarian Communism

A number of communist models might guide the
struggle for economic well-being in developing
nations. There is a Soviet model, a Chinese
model, a Vietnam model, and a Cuban model.
Because conditions in most developing countries are closer to those in China than to those in
the former Soviet Union, we will look to China in
sketching our model. But we must realize that
the Chinese model has changed since the People's
Republic of China was established in 1949.

The Chinese Model—At first, roughly from 1949 until 1957, China followed the Soviet model of development, emphasizing heavy industry and rapid industrialization. The Maoist model—which featured the unsettling Great Leap Forward and the Cultural Revolution—dominated from 1958 to 1976. It emphasized all-around industrial and agricultural development: self-reliance and communes in the countryside; mass mobilization and heroic labor to increase productivity; the primacy of politics and party to guide the revolution; and decentralization to stimulate local initiatives.

The post-Mao model, which began with Mao's death in 1976 and continues to the present, is attempting, without sacrificing some Maoist emphases, to achieve the **four modernizations:** in agriculture, industry, national defense, and science and technology. These modernizations require a number of crucial balances; we will discuss five of them:

1. The post-Mao model seeks to balance egalitarianism and excellence. That is, without giving up the effort to satisfy the basic needs of all, the Chinese are attempting to enable those with expertise to address specialized problems in industry, agriculture, science, and education.
2. The post-Mao model attempts to balance central direction and local initiative. Here, without squelching local originality and effort, the Chinese are trying to follow a national plan of development.
3. China today seeks to balance party control and order on one hand and greater freedom and legality on the other. Without party control, the Chinese leadership believes, there can be no coherent development, yet people need to be free of oppressive control if they are to contribute their best to national development.[14]
4. The current Chinese model strives to balance the old Maoist emphasis on self-reliance with a modern reliance on foreign trade, credits, and investment. The current lead-

ership recognizes that China needs scientific, technological, and economic help from countries such as the United States and Japan, yet China strives to be as self-reliant as possible as it develops modern capability in a number of fields.
5. The Chinese are attempting to balance public ownership of land and small private agricultural plots. They recognize that the small plots can significantly enhance agricultural productivity, yet they do not want to completely relinquish the principle of communal ownership and operation. The model of egalitarian communism that we will sketch reflects this recent attempted balance. This balance still embraces three major emphases in the Chinese revolutionary tradition: nationalism, the creation of a new political order and society, and socioeconomic development. These emphases are also meaningful in other developing areas.[15]

In 1980 the Chinese leadership decided to slow down the four modernizations but not abandon them. In 1986 priority was given to reform and expansion of the open-door policy—that is, the encouragement of foreign investment. This involved decentralizing the economic system and relinquishing the state monopoly on foreign trade. In addition six "special economic zones" were established to encourage foreign investment and trade. Finally, major reforms were begun in banking, pricing, labor law, and agriculture.

The Chinese model presupposes an armed communist revolution by which working people (for the most part peasants) seize power under the leadership of the Communist party. This revolution overthrows capitalism and the bourgeoisie and establishes public ownership of the major means of production (including agriculture), distribution, transportation, communications, most retail establishments, education, and health services. A single party, the Communist party, directs the life of the nation. Economic

Though the People's Republic of China still maintains a communist form of government, the shift toward a market economic has brought Western-style businesses such as this McDonald's in Schenzhen, Guandong Province.

development calls for agricultural and industrial growth, a strong national defense, satisfaction of basic human needs, and familiarity with advances in science and technology. Agricultural production is essential to feed a large population. Both agricultural and industrial productivity are required to produce the wealth that makes food, health care, housing, and education possible; raises per capita income; reinforces science and technology; and enhances national security. Equitable distribution of resources is mandated; this distribution is adequate although austere. Wise balances must be struck between central direction (and the danger of a rigid bureaucracy) and decentralization that facilitates self-reliance and participation, as well as between national self-reliance and involvement in the world economy.

Success of the Model—This model holds out the promise of significantly improving the economic well-being of the developing nations that choose it. If China is typical, the basic human needs of most of the world's people can be met. China has steadily increased per capita GNP—from $162 in 1952 to $490 in 1993 (in 1993 U.S. dollars).

The welfare of a majority of Chinese living today has significantly advanced. Eighty-one percent of school-age children are in school. China's literacy rate is 80 percent. Life expectancy went from 47.1 years in 1960 to 68.6 years in 1993, and the infant mortality rate dropped from 150 per 1,000 births in 1960 to 44 per 1,000 in 1993.[16]

China's industrial growth has been impressive, though its agriculture has grown only modestly. The gross national product grew from $92 billion in 1952 to $577.4 billion in 1993.[17] Between 1980 and 1993, the GNP increased at an estimated annual rate of 9.6 percent, one of the highest growth rates in the world, and during this same period, the GNP per capita increased in real terms at an average rate of 8.2 percent per year.[18]

China has also been able to slow its growth in birth rate, with the help of family planning, easily accessible abortion, and bonuses for small families. It is true that the population of China has grown enormously. There were 570 million people in China in 1952, there were 983 million in 1977, and there are 1.2 billion today. On a positive note, the rate of population growth has slowed. Between 1970 and 1980 the annual population growth rate was 1.8 percent. Between 1980 and 1993 the growth rate fell to 1.4 percent, and the growth rate from 1993 to 2000 has been projected at 0.9 percent.[19] If other developing countries follow the Chinese model to slow population growth but still cannot increase agricultural production, the pressure of population against food, although not catastrophic, will remain a serious problem. In an austere economy food may be adequate but not abundant; production may remain vulnerable to plague, drought, and famine.

Evaluation—The strengths of the communist model are appealing, in promise if not fully in performance. Life has improved for the vast majority. Starvation is overcome. Abject poverty ceases. People have better nutrition, health, and housing. Literacy spreads. The great gulf between rich and poor disappears. Foreign exploitation ends, and so does domestic capitalistic exploitation. The economy—especially industry—grows rapidly and holds out hope for larger shares of a bigger pie. Income is distributed more fairly. But this rosy picture, particularly China's favorable balance of trade, must be tempered with the understanding that the economy, while certainly not capitalist, has been shifting increasingly towards free market reforms. While great progress in human welfare was made during China's more pure communist phase of development, a disturbing trend has emerged, particularly in the 1990s. Parts of China, in particular the coastal provinces of Jiangsu, Zhejiang, Fujian, and Guangdong, have benefited enormously from a shift from being strict communist economic systems to being free enterprise market economies. The benefits for these regions has been remarkable, but that success has caused increasing economic disparity with the poorer, interior provinces of China.

Putting aside this latest development, the grave weaknesses of the communist regime itself must be faced. One weakness is the continuing high cost of the communist revolution, which includes destruction of the regime's opponents, the terrorization of those who do not follow the leaders' or party's current line, and authoritarian control of speech, press, and culture. These costs include the regime's willingness to sacrifice millions in one generation for gains to be achieved in the next. Communist regimes also have to worry about bureaucratic centralization of power and failures of the master plan. Above all, communist systems do not rely on individual incentives as a prime motivator, and some critics argue there are few if any other incentives to work harder, produce more, or innovate. Without individual incentives, people tend to do only what is necessary, to play it safe, to be more concerned with security than production. The most graphic example of the limitations of this kind of system can be seen in the Soviet economy, which by 1990 was near collapse.

Economic Well-Being Through Illiberal Capitalism and Right-Wing Authoritarianism

There may be many varieties of what we call **illiberal capitalism.** This is capitalism that emphasizes capital growth at the expense of, or in disregard of, economic and social justice. Variations on this model may be found in Chile (under Augustus Pinochet from 1973 to 1989), the Philippines (under Ferdinand Marcos from 1972 to 1986), South Korea (under a variety of military strongmen), Indonesia (under General Suharto), and Singapore (under Lee Kwan Yew, who, while elected the country's first prime minister in 1965, nevertheless ruled the island country for decades with an iron hand).

This option rests on the assumption that economic growth, an enlarged GNP, and capitalist profitability precede, and create the conditions for, greater economic and social justice. Wealth must be created before it can be equitably distributed. And there must be a favorable environment for those who can create wealth—the capitalist entrepreneurs.

Right-wing authoritarianism complements illiberal capitalism in the sense that economic growth requires political, economic, and social stability. Left-wing agitation is not allowed to get out of hand. Strikes are not permitted in essential industries. Adverse criticism of the nation's rulers, if it goes too far, may be subject to punishment. When national security is at issue, civil liberties may be jeopardized.

Directly or indirectly, the military have influenced a number of right-wing regimes in countries such as Brazil, South Korea, Chile, and the Philippines. In recent Brazilian history, for example, a military coup ousted the democratically elected government of President Joao Goulart in 1964. In 1979 General Joao Baptista de Oliveira Figueiredo was sworn in as president after winning a two-party contest in late 1978 and promising a return to liberalization and democracy. In 1985 General Figueiredo's government was replaced by an elected civilian government, which ruled with a fragile coalition. In 1988 a new, substantially liberalized constitution was approved.

In illiberal capitalist and right-wing authoritarian systems, the government encourages a high rate of growth in the gross national product. The state plans, regulates, and directs the economy to accomplish this purpose. The state may even own and operate basic industries crucial to capitalistic growth. The state must be willing, if necessary, to impose wage controls in the fight against inflation. It must be willing to make the poor wait, to defer the satisfaction of basic economic needs. Leaders of the regime seek to advance the nation's economic growth, military strength, and security. They will cooperate with, but try to avoid overdependence on, other rich capitalistic countries and multinational corporations.

This variety of illiberal capitalism seeks a big enough pie to ensure, in time, larger shares for all. Then, presumably, the people's basic needs for greater economic well-being can be satisfied.

The Brazilian Model—Brazil's record from 1964 to 1985 illustrates this model's pattern, its key results, and its continuing problems. During the essentially authoritarian regime from 1964 to 1985, the military or military-backed civilian leadership worked closely with capitalist entrepreneurs, the upper urban bourgeoisie, and technocratic civil servants. They sought to maintain economic and political order and thus make possible the "economic miracle."

From 1967 to 1974, Brazil's economy grew at impressively high rates. For example, Brazil's GDP (gross domestic product) rose an average of 11.3 percent per year during this period. Between 1975 and 1980, the annual growth rate was 6.5 percent, the slowdown partly due to the OPEC oil crisis. Despite recent problems, significant economic growth—the so-called Brazilian miracle—did occur. Investment poured into Brazil.[20] Although the rate of growth has slowed, Brazil's GNP (in U.S. dollars) climbed from $125.6 billion in 1976 to $250.6 billion in 1986. And per capita GNP rose from $1,088 in 1976 to $1,809 in 1986.[21]

At the end of this period of illiberal capitalism, were the people of Brazil any better off than the people of Latin America in general? Using 1986 as the base year for comparison, we note the following. Only 78 percent of Brazil's people were literate compared with 80 percent for all of Latin America. Life expectancy in Brazil was 65 years; for all of Latin America it stood at 66 years. Brazil's annual infant mortality rate was 63 deaths per thousand live births; for Latin America it was 56 deaths per thousand live births. Gross national product per capita for Brazil was $1,809; for Latin America overall it was $1,872.[22] In 1986 a substantial percentage of the population still lived in poverty in both country and city. Finally, there was a severe maldistribution of wealth. In 1984, twenty years after the beginning of the illiberal capitalist period, 10 percent of the population controlled nearly 50 percent of Brazil's household income.[23]

There is little doubt Brazil did achieve an economic miracle of aggregate growth. But how this growth affected human welfare is debatable.

Evaluation—The Brazilian experience helps explain the strengths and weaknesses of this model. Rapid economic growth can occur, particularly in capital-intensive industries. As a result of the groundwork laid during the period of illiberal capitalism, Brazil now produces consumer products—automobiles, refrigerators, and television sets—for its affluent minority. The hope is that sooner or later the larger economic pie—the increased gross national product—will benefit more people, including the poor.

The Brazilian model, like the Chinese one, requires current sacrifice for future gain. Economic and social justice—especially for the poor—is postponed. Although a new constitution has been adopted to reduce the power of the president, abolish censorship, and generally expand civil liberties, it remains to be seen whether wealth can be more fairly distributed.

Brazil's twenty-one-year authoritarian experience was relatively mild in comparison with the illegal arrests, imprisonment, and torture that characterize other right-wing regimes. In Brazil's case, as in other right-wing regimes, the ruling elite maintained that its economic and political policies were necessary but temporary. But one must ask: How necessary? How temporary?

In evaluating the model of illiberal capitalism, students must balance benefits and costs. How can gains in economic growth be balanced against inequitable distribution and loss of freedom? Will the Brazilian model work in other develop-ing countries that lack Brazil's affluent 15 million citizens, whose purchases may spur capital-intensive industry while 85 million citizens endure poverty? Are variations on the Brazilian model possible—for example, variations that do not postpone equitable distribution? variations that more speedily meet basic needs? variations that do not require even temporary authoritarian political rule?

Economic Well-Being Through Democratic Socialism

This next option, democratic socialism, rejects communism, liberal democratic capitalism, and right-wing authoritarian capitalism. It assumes the possibility of public ownership of key economic and social services. Agriculture may be communal and genuinely democratic (say, on the model of the Israeli kibbutz), or it may be private. Other aspects of the economy—small business and service industries—remain in private hands. This option assumes, moreover, a two-party or multiparty system, political competition, and civil liberties. It assumes central guidance in areas essential for satisfying human needs (education, health, or housing) that will not be met by the private sector.

Consequently, the democratic socialist state will not hesitate to nationalize monopolies or regulate fundamental industries (banking, rail-

The Israeli kibbutz or communal farm is an example of democratic socialism.

roads, and key services) to ensure sensible growth, equitable distribution, and key services in the interest of the majority. Top priority is given to employment, minimal levels of income, literacy, health care, and housing. Because of widespread rural poverty in the developing world, there must be substantial agrarian reform, development of cooperatives, attention to labor-intensive production, and balanced industrial growth. Better urban planning is also necessary to ensure decent housing, sanitation, and transportation. Education is crucial to both rural and urban development.

There are few, if any, genuinely successful democratic socialist governments in the developing world. Chile (before the overthrow of Allende) attempted to use this model, as did Sri Lanka (Ceylon) under an earlier democratic socialist government. Tanzania represents a left-wing version (featuring a one-party state and communal farming). Other developing nations may profess a commitment to democratic socialism, although in practice they are often undemocratic and largely capitalistic; so far, they have not overcome poverty or reduced gross inequities.

Democratic socialist governments seek to maintain both freedom and equality. The difficulties that most developing nations face hamper this attempt. Those on the right complain that freedom and egalitarianism breed disorder. Those on the left complain that excessive concern for freedom inhibits egalitarian policy.

Yet it is possible for people in relatively poor countries with a democratic socialist commitment to improve their lives. For example, according to Morris David Morros, "Sri Lanka provides the most dramatic example of a country that has been able to achieve remarkable life-quality results at startlingly low levels of income."[24] Sri Lanka has made these advances despite a fairly low per capita income of $179 in the early 1970s. Literacy increased from 57.8 percent in 1946 to 90 percent in 1993. Life expectancy increased from 48.5 to 72 years in that same period, and infant mortality (per thousand live births) dropped from 141 to 17.[25]

The democratic socialist model for the developing world requires family planning and population control to prevent imbalance between population and resources. Balanced agricultural and industrial growth is also important. Low or modest expenditures for national security are most helpful; resources can thus be used for healthy economic growth and attendance to basic human needs.

The strengths of the democratic socialist option lie in its commitment to meeting basic human needs as quickly as possible and within a framework of freedom. However, given its commitment, democratic socialism may be vulnerable to attacks from the right or left. The right is frightened by socialism and democracy, by the commitment to more equitable distribution and to freedom. In Chile, Allende's democratic socialist government was overthrown by a right-wing military coup in 1971. The left believes that democratic socialist governments cannot restructure society in a more egalitarian way. In 1971 the extreme left mounted an unsuccessful armed rebellion against the government of Mrs. Sirimavo Bandaranaike in Sri Lanka. Both right and left believe (but for different reasons) that democratic socialist governments lack strength and are too easy on leftists and rightists, respectively. The left holds that democratic socialist governments lack the courage to wipe out capitalistic domination. The right maintains that democratic and socialist governments frighten away private investment by threatening profits and are too soft on communists.

Economic Well-Being Through a New World Order

The foregoing models presuppose the continuation of the existing sovereign nation-state system. The final option that we consider anticipates some fundamental changes in this system, in the war system related to it, and in the world economic system. These changes involve some radical revisions in policy.

World order advocates are a diverse breed; there is no one party line on which all agree. In general, however, they affirm the values of peace, human rights, freedom, democracy, economic well-being, and ecological health. They often criticize the sovereign nation-state because it does not fulfill these values. Too often, the sovereign nation-state creates conditions that lead to war and an arms race, to the severe deprivation (and even "violence") that is poverty, and to economic policies that perpetuate exploitation, inequitable distribution, and dependence. World order advocates maintain that nation-state policies are incompatible with democracy and freedom and that such policies ignore human needs in striving for economic growth.

In the interest of greater economic well-being (and other goals), world order advocates seek to move political communities away from war and militarism, economic nationalism, and poverty, and to close the gap between rich and poor. They agree that "governments that do not meet the needs of the citizenry for food, shelter, health, clothing, and education, and yet insist on submissiveness are practicing violence against deprived sectors of their own populations."[26]

World order advocates seek not only to satisfy elementary needs by eliminating poverty but also to improve the quality of life. As Richard Falk points out, they would reduce "disparities in per capita income between and within national societies." Furthermore, they would reduce "economic patterns of exploitation and dependence." And, finally, they would reduce "waste" and allocate more resources for "beneficial purposes."

But what specific policies can accomplish these general goals? Resources can be more fairly distributed in several ways. For example, trade must be adjusted to help producers of primary products in the developing countries. Capital development would have to be subsidized. The world money market and multinational corporations would have to be regulated in the interest of developing nations and global economic health.

The worst effects of economic nationalism and the gap between rich and poor may be countered by shifting control of economic policy to regional and global agencies. In Falk's view, for example, a more just world economic system will require "adequate central guidance" to guard against "the dangers of monetary crises, trade wars, protectionist policies, cartelizing tendencies, and drastic price fluctuations."

Falk argues that a new political philosophy is necessary because none "of the current world ideologies have yet devised satisfactory solutions for the formidable problems of distribution of goods and services, the elimination of waste through manipulation of consumer taste, the conservation of scarce resources, the promotion of aesthetic forms of industrial development, and the need to make work more satisfying for the worker."

Falk proposes a global organization (he calls it the World Polity Association) that would use its revenue to significantly reduce poverty, equalize individual and group living standards, and improve the environment. Falk's organization would raise money for these purposes in strikingly new ways: (1) from licenses granted for withdrawing minerals from the oceans, (2) from a graduated progressive tax on governments and other units of global organization, and (3) from a direct personal tax on incomes above a certain level.

He looks to a steady-state world economy that would emphasize fairness and quality of life rather than blind, wasteful, inequitable economic growth. He believes that such policies would substantially reduce abject poverty everywhere and implement humane and egalitarian trends throughout the world.

Falk is attracted to the idea of minimum and maximum needs thresholds for various groups within the world economic structure. "These needs would include food, housing, clothing, medical treatment, educational and cultural opportunity." He argues that a minimum need threshold might "be established on a planetary basis" but would be "adjusted for climate and possibly for preferred lifestyle." The maximum threshold would involve only material goods—

that is, size of house, number of cars, boats, planes, and level of income. In this fashion, Falk would discourage wasteful or destructive forms of material growth in the interest of first satisfying basic needs. Falk would also establish a 10:1 wealth ratio between rich and poor nations. To provide a safeguard against famine, Falk favors Norman Borlaug's call for an international granary whose supplies could be tapped to avoid starvation in emergencies.

But how is this policy and machinery to be put in place? Falk's general answer is consciousness raising (largely at the national level), mobilization of key interests and forces (with the help of regional and global agencies already in existence), and, eventually, regional and global transformation.

In some respects this approach to economic well-being is attractive. A more comprehensive global attack on poverty and related economic ills makes great sense. But critics deem most of these proposals, such as a progressive income tax to support global development, too radical. They also challenge the feasibility of seriously modifying national powers; they doubt that nation-states will accept a global central guidance system with authority to do what needs to be done. In brief, they believe the world order option is unrealistic.

TOWARD CREATIVE BREAKTHROUGHS TO ECONOMIC WELL-BEING

Which of the approaches we have examined—or which combination of approaches—makes the most sense? How do we appraise their costs and benefits? To help you debate these questions—and reach a prudent choice—we will review each alternative and pose some key questions.

Liberal Capitalism and Liberal Democracy

Are capitalists enlightened enough to see the need, within the framework of liberal democracy, to relate growth and profits to the elimination of poverty?

Some scholars believe the answer is yes. They argue that liberal capitalistic and democratic forces can work together to increase the size of the economic pie and to insist on a more equitable distribution of wealth and services to satisfy basic human needs. With the right policies and the support of the developed world, the job can be done. Leadership elites, dominant economic forces, and the poor in developing countries can work together to address their key problems. They can develop stable political organizations and crucial administrative and economic skills. They can strike a sensible balance between agricultural and industrial development. And they can deliver food, health care, housing, and literacy. Richer nations, such as the United States, will see their self-interest served by extending a helping hand. The United States will recognize the value of extending credit and aid to developing nations, stabilizing commodity prices, ensuring free trade, encouraging abundant and inexpensive food supplies, and supporting mutually advantageous investment and trade. Moreover, such peaceful development can occur speedily and with due regard to economic and social justice.

Critics of liberal capitalism and democracy challenge this optimistic answer. They maintain that capitalists are motivated by a concern for profits, not for economic and social justice. Since capitalists have a vested interest in short-run payoff rather than long-run development, they will be unwilling to adopt those policies necessary to overcome poverty. Critics contend that liberal democratic capitalists are financially too tied in to the dominant system of exploitation to respond to the claims of the least free.

Egalitarian Communism

Is the cost of violent communist revolution and the fundamental restructuring that this entails, especially in terms of lives lost and freedoms violated, justified by the hoped-for results: elimination of abject poverty, gross inequities of income, hunger, poor housing, and illiteracy?

Those who answer yes maintain that the benefits outweigh the costs. Improving the economic well-being of the overwhelming majority of people in a developing nation is well worth the loss of freedom to exploiting capitalists and their friends. Proponents also suggest that a more humane communism than that of the Soviet Union or China is possible.

Opponents of a communist pattern of development question not only the cost of violent revolution but also the temporary character of the dictatorship of the proletariat—the period between the initial revolution and the ultimate triumph of mature communism. They emphasize the costs of revolution: bloodshed, rigid one-party rule, social regimentation, bureaucratic centralism, economic inefficiency, and austerity. They do not believe that the coercive power of the communist state will wither away over time. Finally, they caution that the absence of individual incentive seriously hinders a society's ability to increase production and to innovate.

Illiberal Capitalism and Right-Wing Authoritarianism

Can significant economic growth really take place only under a right-wing authoritarian regime that chooses capitalistic growth at the expense of political, economic, and social justice?

Defenders of this model are firmly convinced that the economic pie must be considerably increased before the basic human needs of the poor can be satisfied. They believe that postponing political, social, and economic justice is a necessary but temporary sacrifice. They concede that capitalist economic growth may immediately favor the affluent minority, but they emphasize that all citizens benefit a little from a larger gross national product and that eventually the less well-off will benefit much more than they would under communism. Proponents also maintain that right-wing regimes offer greater opportunity for political liberalization than left-wing regimes do.

Opponents reject the argument that freedom and economic justice must be sacrificed to economic growth, even temporarily. They believe that this pattern perpetuates an exploiting capitalistic class. They see no convincing evidence

that the gap between rich and poor is disappearing in countries that follow this model or that political liberalization is really occurring.

Democratic Socialism

Despite good intentions, can democratic socialists have their cake (economic well-being) and eat it, too (maintain civil liberties)?

Supporters argue that this model is the only one that makes sense in developing countries. They argue that democratic socialism is the only policy that can strike the right balance between liberty and equality and between economic growth and satisfaction of basic needs. A certain amount of central planning is required to direct a nation's resources, increase production, and tackle problems such as hunger, disease, and illiteracy. Moreover, only a government truly respectful of people's liberties and needs can enlist their energies in a successful program of development.

Skeptics stress the enormous difficulties facing even the best-intentioned democratic socialist government: poverty, populations out of balance with resources, erratic commodity prices, the high price of imported oil, and the lack of requisite skills and institutions. They fear that even moderate socialism (especially the nationalization of key industries) will kill the goose (of capitalism) that lays the golden egg (greater wealth for all). Because of their extravagant expectations and inadequate resources, democratic socialist governments may not be able to deliver on even their modest promises; such governments may succumb to enemies on the far left or right.

New World Order

Is a new world order really desirable and feasible?

Advocates of a new world order remain convinced that global economic well-being cannot be achieved unless a global perspective is adopted. That perspective, they insist, although it builds on some national and regional endeavors, also requires a number of global initiatives that transcend the selfish interests of nation-states. Such global initiatives call for a better price for commodities produced in developing countries, aid to spur production and development in those countries, and other measures to attack poverty. They believe these initiatives require a redistribution of global income.

Opponents see these scenarios as utopian and point out that they provide no realistic theory of transition: How does the world get from where it is now to the level of economic well-being the world order people would like to attain? Opponents reject ideas such as a global progressive income tax as unfeasible. They doubt whether nations can move to the kind of steady-state economy that would stress the satisfaction of human needs and that would avoid wasteful and destructive growth. They scoff, for example, at the idea that rich nations would give up their current standards of living to enable any significant redistribution of wealth on the planet.

These questions and responses underscore the challenge facing those who seek to promote sensible public policy for greater economic well-being. These questions emphasize the need for creative breakthroughs in political theory and practice.

CONCLUSION

The need for a creative breakthrough to greater economic well-being, particularly for the world's poor, is clear and present. The persistence of poverty, unemployment, hunger, ill health, illiteracy, poor housing, and inequality is well documented. What is not clear is how to overcome these agonizing problems and how to deal with the troublesome task of balancing costs and benefits in proposed policies.

All of the alternatives that we have examined contain difficulties. The problem facing the decision maker is to select the alternative that will quickly maximize benefits for the world's poor at acceptable costs to those in developing and developed countries.

Policies for economic well-being must be worked out by most developing nations (where most of the poor live) in the light of severe problems. Most developing nations lack the prerequisites for significant and humane development. They often have no democratic and constitutional consensus. They do not enjoy political stability. They are short on effective party and administrative organization, trained personnel, good transportation, and schools. They face enormous obstacles in the very evils they seek to overcome: low incomes, malnutrition, disease, illiteracy, and inadequate housing.

Scholars concerned with advancing global economic well-being must also question the foresight, will, and judgment of the richer nations of the developed world. Too often such nations seem unable to adopt a long-range policy to help the world's poor; too often their policies are foolishly motivated by short-range interests that are frequently identified with national security. The richer nations seem unable to speed up the process of economic development for the poorer developing nations. Their assistance is not always in tune with freedom and humane treatment for the poor. Moreover, the domestic policies of rich nations such as the United States do not offer attractive models for economic well-being.

Models for the developing world based on China or Brazil are not attractive either. Minimal economic well-being in a totalitarian state is not appealing. Nor is lopsided and unjust economic growth in a right-wing authoritarian regime. Both models call for current sacrifices to achieve future gains.

A democratic socialist model and a more genuinely liberal capitalist and democratic option are more attractive, as is the world order option, but are they fully attractive? And how feasible are they?

Ethically, we political scientists recognize the need for sane and humane policies to deal with the empirical realities of economic malaise, but we find it hard to make prudent decisions that can help balance acceptable costs and clear-cut benefits on the road to greater economic well-being. Ethically, our consciences compel us to search for creative breakthroughs. Empirically, we appreciate the difficulties of achieving greater economic well-being, particularly for the world's poor, but we have not yet developed empirical explanations that would help us, prudentially, overcome economic malaise rapidly and satisfactorily.

In our next chapter we will concentrate on the imperative of ecological health, an issue vitally related to economic well-being.

ANNOTATED BIBLIOGRAPHY

Blake, David H., and Walters, Robert S. *The Politics of Global Economic Relations*, 4th ed. Englewood Cliffs, N.J.: Prentice-Hall, 1992. Provides a readable survey of major international theories and problems, with excellent treatment of various explanations for problems in the developing world.

Falk, Richard. *On Humane Governance: Toward a New Global Politics*. University Park: Pennsylvania State University Press, 1995. To an extent, updates Falk's classic and best known work, *A Study of Future Worlds* (see below). Calls for a people-centered politics that would lead to a decline in poverty, violence, pollution, and human rights abuses.

Falk, Richard. *A Study of Future Worlds*. New York: Free Press, 1975. Probably Falk's best known work. Economic well-being is one of Falk's four world order goals. Goals are easier to articulate than to achieve, even with his proposed world order machinery.

Haggard, Stephan. *Pathways from the Periphery: The Politics of Growth in the Newly Industrializing Countries*. Ithaca: Cornell University Press, 1990. Presents a fine set of essays emphasizing political analyses of various economic strategies of East Asian industrializing countries.

Harrison, Paul. *Inside the Third World: The Anatomy of Poverty*, 2nd ed. New York: Penguin Books, 1987. Offers perhaps the best overview of poverty in the developing regions of the world. Includes many personal stories of people in the grips of poverty.

Heilbroner, Robert. *The Human Prospect: Updated and Reconsidered for the 1990s*, rev. 2nd ed. New York: Norton, 1990. Emphasizes the difficulties facing developing nations and the grim alternative of a strong government (which may not be democratic) if disaster is to be averted.

Lairson, Thomas D. and Skidmore, David. *International Political Economy: The Struggle for Power and Wealth*. New York: Harcourt Brace Jovanovich, 1993. Provides superb coverage of the history,

theory, and policy of international economic relations. Includes several excellent chapters on the plight of Third World states.

Sivard, Ruth Leger. *World Military and Social Expenditures*. Washington D.C.: World Priorities. An excellent annual record.

United Nations Development Program. *Human Development Report 1996*. New York: Oxford University Press, 1996. Presents a valuable analysis of the human condition in the world. Combines both economic indicators and assessment of political welfare.

Weisband, Edward, ed. *Poverty Amidst Plenty: World Political Economy and Distributive Justice*. Boulder, Colo.: Westview Press, 1989. Provides an excellent set of articles that raise critical ethical questions about the distribution of wealth in the world.

White, Gordon. *Riding the Tiger: The Politics of Economic Reform in Post-Mao China*. Stanford Calif.: Stanford University Press, 1993. Presents a first-rate analysis of those forces that brought about the remarkable economic changes in China since the late 1970s.

World Bank. *World Development Report*. New York: Oxford University Press. Presents an excellent and authoritative annual world development picture. Contains invaluable statistical tables.

SUGGESTIONS FOR FURTHER READING

Apter, David. *Rethinking Development: Modernization, Dependency, and Postmodern Politics*. Beverly Hills: Sage Publications, 1987.

Bhagwati, Jagdish N. *Essays in Developmental Economics*. 2 vols. Vol. 1: *Wealth and Poverty*. Vol. 2: *Dependence and Interdependence*. Cambridge, Mass.: MIT Press, 1985.

Brugge, Bill and Reglar, Stephane. *Politics, Economy, and Society in Contemporary China*. Palo Alto, Calif.: Stanford University Press, 1994.

Feinberb, Richard E., and Kallab, Valeriana, eds. *Adjustment Crisis in the Third World*. Washington, D.C.: Overseas Development Council, 1984.

George, Susan. *A Fate Worse Than Debt: The World Financial Crisis and the Poor*. New York: Grove Press, 1989.

Kahler, Miles, ed. *The Politics of International Debt*. Ithaca, N.Y.: Cornell University Press, 1986.

Mead, Lawrence M. *The New Politics of Poverty: The Nonworking Poor in America*. New York: Basic Books, 1992.

Royal Society of London and the U.S. National Academy of Sciences. *Population Growth, Resource Consumption, and a Sustainable World.* London and Washington, D.C.: Royal Society and U.S. National Academy of Sciences, 1992.

Wilson, William Julius. *When Work Disappears: The World of the New Urban Poor.* New York: Knopf, 1996.

Wynia, Gary W. *The Politics of Latin American Development,* 3rd ed. Cambridge: Cambridge University Press, 1990.

GLOSSARY TERMS

colonialism
economic well-being
four modernizations
illiberal capitalism
least-developed countries (LDCs)
neoimperialism
newly industrialized economies
poverty
working poor

THE IMPERATIVE OF ECOLOGICAL HEALTH

ECOLOGICAL MALAISE, or environmental illness, has emerged as a major concern in world politics. It is perhaps less dramatic than the possibility of catastrophic nuclear war. Moreover, the harmful consequences of ecological illness may seem more remote than the deaths through starvation or torture that result from abject poverty or ruthless tyranny. Yet ecological imbalance has consequences as bad as those of poverty or human rights violations; indeed, it may be even more dangerous than modern warfare.

At its worst, ecological ill-health threatens humankind's biological existence. It affects both developed and developing nations. The depletion and waste of resources, population growth wildly in excess of available food, land, water, and energy, global warming and destruction of the earth's ozone layer—these are all real threats to hopes for a better tomorrow. In particular, ecological dangers may prevent developing nations from overcoming poverty and from lifting their level of well-being.

In examining the imperative of ecological health, we see again the linkage between the values of peace, human rights, and economic well-being that we have been considering in Part IV of this book. For example, war not only destroys human beings, it also destroys the countryside, poisons the air, and wastes vital resources. Economic well-being is vitally related to stable population, adequate resources, and clean air and water. Human rights are violated if people starve to death because population outruns food supply, or if they have no clean air to breathe or clean water to drink.

Threats to ecological health are thus challenges to political actors and to politics as a civilizing enterprise. In the interests of biological existence, societal growth and development, and the cultural quality of life, political actors must understand and respond to threats to ecological health. Hence our problem: *What creative breakthroughs can help humanity achieve ecological health?*

Ecological problems cannot be considered apart from political philosophy and practical politics. The philosophies of liberal democracy, democratic socialism, communism, and right-wing regimes are based on ideas of growth and abundance that are intimately related to the world's ecological difficulties. Thus, the ecological challenge is also a challenge to the world's prominent political philosophies and to the ideas and institutions that stem from them. In brief, the ecological crisis suggests (at least to some critics) that both capitalism and communism may have fatal flaws. Liberal democracy and democratic socialism may also be in trouble because some of their key ideas (individualism, freedom, social justice) may be jeopardized by the ecological crisis and responses to it. Thus, a number of political problems may have to be rethought as the world examines and responds to the ecological crisis.

But what is the meaning of **ecology,** particularly of human ecology? Ecology is concerned with the relationship between organisms and their environment. Human ecology deals with the relationship between people and their larger physical, biological, social, economic, and political environment.

For human beings, ecological health is the relationship between people and their larger environment that eases their biological existence and permits a superior quality of life. Ecological health means clean air, pure water, the prudent use of natural resources, and a sensible balance between population and resources. It means respect for the planet, a partnership between people and resources. Ecological health calls for people to manage their "household"—the household of the human race—in a caring way.

Let us consider some of the key factors that prompt our critical exploration of ecological health. Then we will consider some leading approaches to ecological health, and finally we will encourage you to make wise judgments that may move the world toward creative policy breakthroughs on ecological health.

KEY ETHICAL AND EMPIRICAL FACTORS

Our search for key factors in ecological health is part of a search for a sound ecological philosophy to guide humankind toward sane public policy judgments. We have to reconsider whether, and to what extent, traditional political and economic philosophies are adequate. We have to ask how political scientists can respond to a number of factors that bear on ecological health. Although controversy rages between ecological pessimists and optimists about responses to these factors, the challenges are generally recognized by all.

Many people see the depletion of the earth's ozone layer, global warming, depletion and misuse of scarce and nonrenewable resources, air and water pollution, and the imbalance of population and resources as the five major threats to life and the quality of life. They threaten not only those currently living but their unborn children and grandchildren. These are direct ecological threats, present and future, to the biosphere, and indirect political threats to human freedom. Humankind could be overwhelmed by an ecological catastrophe brought on by a major nuclear war, or over time the planet could be slowly degraded by poisoned water and air, and the inhabitants could be rendered poverty-stricken by the disappearance of vital nonrenewable resources or could be dehumanized by populations wildly in excess of the resources necessary to sustain decent living. Efforts to cope with these ecological difficulties could accentuate selfish nationalism and international tensions between have and have-not nations or could intensify class conflicts between rich and poor within both developed and developing nations. Even though the crisis may be more apparent in the most modern, industrial societies, it is really global.

The Depletion of the Ozone Layer

In the mid-1980s scientists confirmed long-held suspicions that something dreadful was happening to the thin **ozone layer** that encircles the earth's stratosphere: the planet's ozone shield was dissipating. The most observable phenomenon was a 1.2 million-square-mile hole above Antarctica.

Ozone is important because it protects the earth from the full force of the sun's ultraviolet rays. As Will Steger and Jon Bowermaster put it in their book *Saving the Earth*:

> The problem with ozone loss is that it increases the amount of one form of ultraviolet light—UV-B—that reaches the Earth. Each 1 percent drop of ozone allows 2 percent more UV-B to reach the ground. This, in turn, increases the potential for skin cancer by 3 to 6 percent. If ozone depletion continues at the current rate, and if CFC [chlorofluorocarbon] usage continues unabated, the EPA [Environmental Protection Agency] predicts more than 60 million additional cases of skin cancer and about one million additional deaths among Americans born by the year 2075.[1]

Loss of ozone may also increase people's vulnerability to infectious diseases through suppression of the immune response. Further, ozone depletion will disrupt the food chain. Field studies of soybeans have demonstrated that ozone depletion of up to 25 percent could decrease crop yields by over 20 percent.[2] The death of microscopic organisms in the world's oceans will seriously endanger other marine life. Finally, climate may be dramatically affected. Ozone depletion will cause a cooling of the stratosphere, perhaps altering global wind patterns.[3]

The cause for this potential ecological disaster is the continuing release of chlorofluorocarbons (CFCs) and bromine from chemicals called halons (fire-extinguishing agents). The CFCs are used as sterilizing agents in the production of plastic foam products, and in aerosols. Figure 19.1 indicates worldwide CFC production from 1950 to 1995. The year of highest production was 1989 after enormous increases in the mid-1970s.[4] The greatest responsibility for reversing the ozone crisis clearly rests with the world's developed

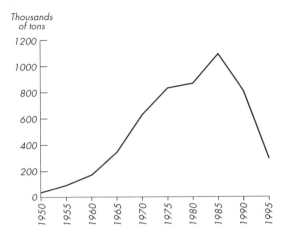

Figure 19.1
World CFC production.

Source: Based on data from Worldwatch Institute, *Vital Signs 1996* (New York: Norton, 1996), p. 69.

nations, which produce roughly 70 percent of the world's total CFCs.

Not all international environmental problems generate responsible international political action. The depletion of the ozone layer may be an exception. Because the threat to life on earth is so dramatic, the international community has moved quickly in its attempt to rectify the problem. In 1987 twenty-four nations and the European Economic Community signed the Montreal Protocol on Substances That Deplete the Ozone Layer. Most of the major producers and consumers of CFCs and halon signed the agreement. The protocol freezes world production and by 1999 would reduce overall consumption by 50 percent. Starting in 1992, halon production is subject to a freeze based on 1986 levels. Since the Montreal signing, the ozone layer has been found to be disappearing at a rate far faster than expected. In response to this development, parties to the Montreal Protocol agreed to a 100 percent ban for developed nations by the year 2000, with a 10-year time lag for developing nations. This agreement included new chemicals that have only recently been recognized as contributors to ozone depletion. Such chemicals include carbon tetrachloride.

The London Amendment to the Montreal Protocol was ratified in May 1992 and went into force in August of the same year.[5]

The Greenhouse Effect

A more controversial, yet no less serious problem is the warming of the planet, or the **greenhouse effect,** resulting from the trapping of the earth's heat in the atmosphere by heat-absorbing gases such as carbon dioxide, CFCs, methane, nitrous oxide, and ozone. Coal burning, vehicle emissions, and large-scale clearing of tropical forests all add to increased carbon dioxide levels in the atmosphere. The situation is getting worse: Annual emissions of carbon into the atmosphere increased from 2,543 million tons in 1960 to 6,056 million tons in 1995. Concentrations of carbon dioxide during that same period went from 315.9 parts per million to 360.7 parts per million. [6]

Although there is a growing consensus in the scientific community that the greenhouse effect is real, there is by no means unanimity. One reason is that the greenhouse effect, unlike the hole in the ozone layer, is not clearly observable. Many of the greenhouse predictions have come from complex computer models. Nor is there agreement on whether a global disaster will result or nature will intervene and compensate for the abuse of the planet.

Believers in the greenhouse effect have little doubt about what is happening and what the impact will be. Steger and Bowermaster note, "Current models predict that the average global temperatures will rise by several degrees Fahrenheit within the next century. By comparison, world temperatures rose just 1 degree in the past 100 years."[7] Figure 19.2 records the average annual global temperatures from 1950 to 1995 noted at five-year intervals. It is thought that the overall rise—some 0.5 °C—is at least partially due to greenhouse warming. It is worth noting that the average global temperature in 1995 reached 15.39 °C, breaking the high mark set in 1990 of 15.38.[8]

Such **global warming** could dramatically affect climate patterns. It would alter crop yields and water supplies, raise sea levels, and flood coastal and low-lying cities. If temperatures were to increase from 3 to 16 °F (2 to 9 °C) by the middle of the twenty-first century, sea levels could rise an average of 2 inches per decade.[9] Fresh-water supplies would be threatened. Fishing yields would decline because of slower ocean currents. Warmer oceans would cause more frequent, stronger hurricanes and typhoons.

The greenhouse effect raises serious questions for policymakers throughout the world. How much longer can fossil fuels be relied on as the primary source of energy in the industrial North?

Heavy air pollution, as seen near this vulcanizing plant Copsa Mica, Romania, is a contributor to the greenhouse effect.

Figure 19.2
Global average temperature, 1950–1995.

Source: Goddard Institute for Space Studies, "Table of Global Mean
Monthly, Annual, and Seasonal Land-Ocean Temperature Index, 1950–
Present," posted at http://www.giss.nasa.gov/Data/GISTEMP, January
1996.

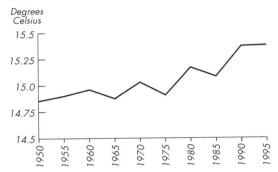

Will developing nations, as they become more industrialized, use more fossil fuels? Can realistic alternatives—hydropower, wind power, geothermal power, solar power, biomass power—be found? How would a drastic reduction in the use of fossil fuels affect the world economy? Can the destruction of the world's great rain forests in places like Brazil be allowed to continue?

At the **Earth Summit** held in Rio de Janeiro, Brazil, in June 1992, a Convention on Climate Change was drafted to propose international action to prevent carbon dioxide and other greenhouse gases from building up in the atmosphere to levels that could cause damaging climate changes. The major problem with the treaty is that it contains no specific emission targets. Nevertheless, it does establish financial aid for developing countries, as well as institutions to review and update commitments.[10]

The Problem of Scarce Resources and Population Imbalance

The problem of scarce resources includes the depletion of nonrenewable resources, the waste of renewable resources, and population growth in excess of resources.

The Depletion of Valuable Nonrenewable Resources— Today people throughout the world are coming to realize that humanity has been living in a kind

of cornucopian dream world. Only now is that dream being replaced by the reality of a scarcity that has, by and large, been the lot of much of humankind during most of *Homo sapiens'* tenure on earth. The idea of seeming endless abundance is relatively new and is associated with the discovery (dated to 1492) by Western peoples of "virgin" and abundant lands and resources in the Americas, Asia, and Africa. Until quite recently, science and technology seemed to hold out the hope of limitless development of resources.

The impression of seemingly limitless air and water nourished the impression of bountiful lands and resources. Given abundant nature and scientific genius, many Westerners concluded that they could overcome scarcity. With hard work and the opportunity to accumulate capital, human beings could produce abundantly and overcome the traditional hardships of nature. Per capita income could grow enormously. Abundant energy sources—whether human labor, water power, coal, or oil—could make production and growth zoom. It seemed as though Malthusian fears—of population growing in excess of food supply unless checked by war, disease, famine, or birth control—had finally been laid to rest.

Liberals and capitalists shared these high hopes with democratic socialists and communists. All assumed that the economy—rightly directed— could produce abundantly and (given the right political and social direction) enhance freedom and justice.

In the period dominated by the idea of growth and progress, few saw that the earth was finite and limited, that exponential growth—unless checked or controlled—might seriously threaten the carrying capacity of the globe.[11] Humanity might be producing too many people, whose increasing appetites might mean running out of the resources necessary to sustain their lives. Some natural resources such as oil are not renewable; once used up, they are gone forever. Resources such as coal might be plentiful, but even they will not last forever. Moreover, such **nonrenewable resources** will be depleted even faster if current practices of consumption continue. And these are the practices on which current economic growth and lifestyle depend. Thus, the supplies of key nonrenewable resources can be exhausted at exponential rates.

And as nonrenewable resources decline, their prices will increase. As key energy sources (such as oil) become excessively expensive and are depleted, a major ingredient of modern growth and life will be denied. Which energy source will then run the modern industrial plant? What will automobiles run on? What about the jobs of auto makers? What will happen to the system of highways?

The Waste and Imprudent Use of Renewable Resources—Wasteful and imprudent use of **renewable resources** can also produce terrible consequences. The land could become exhausted, wasted, and ruthlessly exploited. Trees could be recklessly cut down and not replanted. Water and air could be poisoned.

This picture of the imprudent use of renewable resources has been dramatically captured by Garrett Hardin's metaphor of the **tragedy of the commons.**[12] The commons is the communal grazing plot. If all farmers seek to exploit the free grazing of their herds on the communal plot, the grass will soon be gone and will be incapable of renewal, and all the farmers will lose. Tragically, individual farmers are unable to abstain from overgrazing because selfish competitors will graze while they abstain. Here, immediate self-interest seems to triumph over long-range concern. In the end the grass is destroyed, the commons ceases to benefit anyone, and all farmers and animals suffer.

The global degradation of land is alarmingly illustrated by what has become known as deforestation, brought on by man's seemingly unquenchable need for wood and wood products. Forests once covered in excess of 40 percent of the earth's land surface. Today, forests constitute only 27 percent of the land area. Between 1980 and 1990, the earth lost an annual average of nearly 10 million hectares of forested land, an area about the size of South Korea.[13]

Oceanic and freshwater fish are also overexploited; in time this could significantly reduce fishing catches. Other renewable sources, whether clean air or water, are threatened just as overgrazing threatens the commons. The tragedy of the commons is now a global tragedy.

The United States—so richly endowed with natural resources—illustrates the waste. Americans have recklessly destroyed much of their timber. They have overused the soil, thinking they could perpetually move on to rich virgin soil. Americans have been, and still are, terribly wasteful of water. They have not taken conservation, soil management, and recycling seriously. In 1993 the United States had 752 registered motor vehicles for every 1,000 resident population, more than any country in the world.[14]

So unless Americans can discover new and currently unknown resources or employ science to find substitutes for current resources, they face ecological scarcity. As shortages loom, prices are bound to inflate, living standards are bound to suffer, and inequalities will persist. The waste of scarce resources hurts the current generation but may deal an even more devastating blow to posterity. Today's recklessness may doom future generations to a lack of adequate food, clothing, shelter, energy, clean air, and pure water. Poverty may be intensified; the hope of overcoming it in developing areas will be dashed. Tension between the relatively rich and poor will increase and with it, perhaps, conflict and repressive measures to perpetuate the inequalities no longer relieved by a bigger "pie."

People thus confront the risk of human survival on a finite and destroyable planet with limited resources, to borrow the language of William Ophuls.[15] The exploitation of nature's scarce resources compounds the problem. Human beings have failed to work rationally with nature for ends that respect both people and resources. Wise limits have been overstepped.

If scarcity persists, it may lead to serious inequality, oppression, and conflict, jeopardizing democracy and freedom.

The Danger of Population Growth Wildly in Excess of Resources—Our mania for growth is also reflected in the population explosion. As we saw in Chapter 4, Figure 4.2 and Table 4.1, world population began a steep climb starting with the Industrial Revolution (at the end of the eighteenth century) and continuing with revolutions in transportation, medicine, and agriculture in the nineteenth and twentieth centuries. The world's population doubled between 1850 and 1950, moving up from about 1 billion to 2 billion, and it promises to reach over 6 billion by the year 2000.

Even though population growth has slowed in many developed and industrial countries (to an average annual increase of 0.6 percent), the overall picture remains disturbing, largely because of the increase in poor countries (where the average annual increase is 2.1 percent). Pakistan's population is expected to rise from 136 million in 1994 to 236 million in 2015 and 381 million in 2050. Nigeria will increase from 108 million in 1994 to 190 million in 2015 and 338 million by 2050.[16]

We must keep in mind that the trouble comes from population growth in excess of resources: food, energy, water, nonrenewable resources, space, and heat.[17] Globally, there may not be enough food to sustain the growing population. Estimates by the United Nations indicate that perhaps sixty countries will experience serious food shortages by the year 2000.[18] Countries with high growth rates may also have to double industrial and agricultural production to keep up with population—an almost impossible feat.

High agricultural output fueled optimism between 1950 and 1984—a period of unprecedented increases in world grain production. The period from 1985 to 1995, however, sharply reversed this pattern. Several factors contributed to the decline: monsoon-generated crop failure in India in 1987; North American and Chinese droughts in 1988; a failed Indonesian resettlement program to alleviate land hunger; general land degradation in Mexico; lack of mechanized grain production in many labor-intensive countries; and the conversion of large areas of agricultural land in many developing countries to the purposes of housing and manufacturing.[19]

There is, however, some hope for a better balance. Since 1965 the worldwide birth rate has declined somewhat. But the death rate has been declining for a longer period (Figure 19.3). Because more people are living longer, the birth rate must decline faster to promote ecological hope.

This grim picture raises critical questions. What will happen in the year 2015 when world population has reached 7.5 billion, with 6.2 billion in the less developed regions? Population, of course, may stabilize; but the task of feeding even 7.5 billion (particularly in poorer countries) will be tremendous. And if population does not stabilize, there may be as many as 10 billion people on earth by the middle of the twenty-first century. Feeding these people will be almost impossible. There will simply be too many people for the globe's carrying capacity. And clearly, scarce resources accentuate the problem. Because of limited land and water, little help from the sea, diminishing agricultural returns from currently cultivated lands, and other limits, some students of the problem doubt that 10 billion can be fed.

Figure 19.3
Global birth rates and death rates.

Source: Lester Brown, Christopher Flavin, and Sandra Postel, "Outlining a Global Action Plan," a Worldwatch Institute Report on Progress Toward a Sustainable Society, State of the World 1989 (New York: Norton, 1989), p. 190.

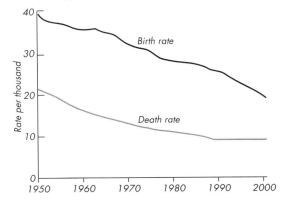

Of course, it may be possible to expand necessary resources and to limit population through family planning. The prospects here are bleakest in the most vulnerable segments of the globe: the poorest regions of South Asia, Southeast Asia, and Africa. The greatest successes will probably occur in countries with richer resources and the lowest birth rates.

Other "solutions" for the imbalance of population and resources are possible: war, famine, and disease. But the war solution (killing off millions of human beings) is no more satisfying than Dean Swift's "solution" of cannibalism for Irish overpopulation and famine.

The Catastrophes of Pollution—Modern war, especially nuclear war, has had a devastating effect on ecological health. Radiation poisoning, which killed one out of every five who died at Hiroshima, has also taken lives in the peacetime testing of nuclear weapons, and it remains a hazard in all nuclear plants and waste dumps. We must consider both the actual and potential dangers of modern war. In Vietnam, as William Ophuls has observed, the United States military "devastated millions of acres of farms and forest with saturation bombing and giant earth-moving machinery."[20] The broadcast use of herbicides—notably Agent Orange—to destroy the cover for North Vietnamese soldiers damaged the countryside and probably caused severe health problems for American soldiers and Vietnamese civilians.

War is a poisonous business. Herbicides, nuclear bombs, and conventional firebombs have been added to more traditional ecocidal weapons such as scorched earth and salted lands. A substantial number of nuclear explosions "would poison world ecosystems and gene pools for untold generations and probably disrupt the structure of the atmosphere enough to cause mass extinctions," Ophuls has noted. In his view, "war has been rightly called the ultimate pollutant of planet earth."[21]

Nuclear weapons can create pollution nightmares even when they have not been used. After the Cold War, the United States began to close many of its nuclear warhead production sites. In 1992 the public learned that many of those sites had become ecological disasters. Nuclear waste had been carelessly discarded, polluting the ground and water supplies in surrounding areas. It may take decades to clean up these facilities, and costs may run to hundreds of billions of dollars.

Wholesale, massive pollution has also accompanied modern industrialization and agriculture. Industrial cities suffer from smog. Acid rain may fall hundreds or thousands of miles from a factory or coal-burning energy plant onto landscapes where it injures lakes, streams, buildings, and antiquities. Factories dump pollutants into rivers or seeping landfills and threaten people and fish. Automobiles are among the worst polluters, filling the air with noxious fumes, including lead. The pollution of rivers, oceans, and air by factory smoke, industrial chemicals, and agricultural pesticides threatens people, animals, and fish. Shorelines are desecrated when millions of gallons of oil spill from ships like the Exxon *Valdez*. How long can the earth sustain this kind of injury? How long will people endure it?

Insults to the environment are found in every industrial society. Europe, which is densely populated and highly industrial, faces pollution problems worse than those in the United States. The Baltic and Mediterranean seas and the Rhine River are heavily contaminated. Oil spills have plagued European shores. Acid rain falls on Scandinavia. Ironically, Japan's very economic success has contributed to its severe pollution problem. An illustration of this problem was the tragedy in Minamata Bay in the early 1950s. Mercury poisoning from industrial sources may have caused the death of over 600 people and severe illness, including paralysis, of approximately 1,300 more.

In 1989 as the cloak of secrecy surrounding much of Eastern Europe was lifted, it became painfully clear that the industrialized communist countries were not immune from ecological problems and damage. Areas of Poland, Roma-

Enormous garbage deposits like these outside Cairo, Egypt, are a serious global pollutant.

nia, and Bulgaria turned out to be ecological disaster zones. The Soviet Union was no better able to deal with insults to the environment than the United States or other capitalistic countries. Some of the most treasured natural assets of the former Soviet Union, such as Lake Baikal, are polluted beyond imagination.

The Reality or Myth of the Scientific and Technological Fix

The depletion of nonrenewable resources and the waste of renewable resources are facts. The imbalance of population and resources is a clear and present danger in certain poor developing countries. Pollution is an ugly reality. But there is disagreement about whether science and technology can save the earth from the perils of the ecological crisis. Can science and technology overcome the energy shortage, find new re-

sources, increase the food supply, and limit population growth?

Some scholars firmly believe in such breakthroughs and argue that economic growth and modern lifestyles can be maintained, that humankind can triumph over scarcity, stabilize the population, and conquer pollution. Others insist, however, that a technological fix cannot be counted on to deal with these problems. They insist that there are decided limits to what scientists can do to save the earth. In 1992, the U.S. National Academy of Sciences and the Royal Society of London stated the following in a joint report: "If current predictions of population growth prove accurate and patterns of human activity on the planet remain unchanged, science and technology may not be able to prevent either irreversible degradation of the environment or continued poverty for much of the world."[22]

Critics of technological solutions point to alarming costs involved in scientific efforts to cope with scarcity, population, and pollution. For example, nuclear power, science's answer to fossil fuel use, is expensive and potentially dangerous. The partial meltdown at the Three Mile Island reactor in Pennsylvania in 1979 and, more alarming, the reactor explosion at Chernobyl in the Soviet Union in 1986 clearly demonstrate that serious accidents at nuclear power plants can happen and can release harmful radiation. The disposal of radioactive waste remains a troubling problem. The widespread use of nuclear power complicates the problem of the proliferation of nuclear weapons.

Alternative sources of clean energy such as solar power are not easily and inexpensively obtained. Hydroelectric power is a possibility only for countries fortunate enough to be able to tap the potential of falling water. Geothermal power, which is comparatively benign but not entirely pollution-free, is by no means universally available. Only wild optimists anticipate that geothermal energy will constitute more than 20 percent of the world's future energy supply.

The loss of cheap, abundant energy is particularly damaging to the dream of a technological

"AND NOW SOME MORE OFFICIAL INFORMATION ON THE ACCIDENT AT CHERNOBYL"

©1986 HERBLOCK 5/6/86

solution, since so much industrial and agricultural productivity relies on such energy. Cheap energy, for example, has fueled growth and affluence in many industrial, developed nations. The green revolution that significantly increased the food supply now requires increasingly expensive fertilizer (itself dependent on oil) for success.

The most serious advocates of technological breakthrough believe a milestone was reached with the discovery, by University of Houston professor Paul Chu, of a compound that is a near-perfect conductor of electricity at high temperatures—the superconductor. **Superconductivity** is the process of transmitting energy with limited or no loss of energy. The potential of this technology is revolutionary. As Robert Hazen described it, "Powerful and efficient lightweight magnets and motors, compact computers faster than any now in existence, magnetically levitated bullet trains able to travel hundreds of miles per hour, money-saving power transmission cables linked to safe, remote nuclear and

solar generators, long-term energy storage systems, and a multitude of other devices are all possible in theory."[23]

Hazen continued: "Superconducting motors could be smaller and more powerful than conventional designs. Battery-powered automobiles with light, efficient superconducting electric motors could revolutionize society and its dependence on fossil fuels."[24]

Even with remarkable discoveries like superconductivity, skeptics conclude that there are decided limits on how far science and technology can go in overcoming the fundamental problems of scarcity, the imbalance of population and resources, and pollution.

On the other hand, the optimists, although conceding some limits, affirm that science and good political and economic management can usher in the reign of both plenty and prosperity.

The more pessimistic and optimistic analyses will be considered again later, when we discuss alternatives.

The Challenges of Ecological Politics

The challenges that face policymakers depend on the fundamental diagnosis of the ecological plight. If ecological scarcity, the imbalance of population and resources, and pollution are realities—and cannot be offset by a natural leveling-off process or by science and technology—a number of key questions must be faced.

Can peoples and nations adjust to the idea of (at least relative) scarcity, which undercuts the modern belief in growth and requires a new lifestyle of prudent ecological balance? Can people adjust to the idea that population growth must slow or stop because it imperils resources? Can people accept the idea that pollution threatens the quality of life on earth?

These ecological challenges are also political challenges. They challenge liberalism and socialism, capitalism and communism, nationalism and internationalism. They challenge democratic and constitutional government.

Is economic laissez faire—with individuals, businesses, and corporations relatively free to produce, consume, and trade as they please—tolerable any longer? Or must government—in recognition of the dangers of scarcity, of the population explosion, and of pollution and in pursuit of a common ecological good—act to safeguard the globe? Will ecological philosopher-kings have to coerce selfish and thoughtless people to save them and the globe? Can democracy endure under these conditions?

Socialists and communists have also built a political, economic, and social philosophy on the premise of productive growth and abundance. But even if the people own the means of production and exchange, can they avoid the consequences of scarcity, population growth, and pollution? Will communist regimes have to be more coercive in order to ration scarce resources, control population, and curtail pollution?

Can developing nations fulfill their dreams of overcoming poverty and achieving democratic development if they cannot fulfill plans for economic growth? Will the need to adopt some form of ecological balance—to husband resources, to limit population growth—doom their aspirations for a better life? And what setbacks will occur if the richer nations cannot extend needed help to the developing nations?

These questions point toward difficult judgments on public policy. If the ecological optimists are correct, these questions will not be so troubling. If a world of abundance can still be counted on, if population growth will stabilize, if pollution can be overcome, the ecological future will be brighter. There may still be some worries, but given the genius of modern science and technology and sound political decisions, perhaps the scenario of the doomsday prophets can be avoided.

ALTERNATIVE APPROACHES TO ECOLOGICAL HEALTH

It is, of course, entirely possible to adopt a do-nothing, hedonistic, or piggish approach to ecological health. One could ignore ecological problems, assuming they will go away. One could also adopt the hedonistic philosophy of "Eat, drink, and be merry, for tomorrow we die."

Or the leaders of currently rich and powerful nations could try to perpetuate their dominance by continuing to exploit the poor. They could try to isolate themselves from growing scarcities, booming populations, and growing pollution. Although all these responses are possible—and, indeed, likely in some nations—we shall presuppose a more rational and ethical response.

Liberal Conservation, Family Planning, and Environmental Protection

Those who adopt the liberal conservation approach maintain that modest liberal reform can do the job. They emphasize the feasibility of conserving scarce resources, limiting family size, and safeguarding the environment. They point to actual policies and developments in countries such as the United States to highlight the possibilities of reform. And they indicate that much more can be done.

During the 1970s and 1980s, a number of steps were taken to conserve energy in the United States, such as the 55-mile-per-hour speed limit; smaller, gas-efficient cars; lower temperatures in heated buildings; and less joyriding. Unfortunately, the mid-1990s witnessed a reversal of a number of these steps. On a more positive note, efforts to recycle such materials as paper, aluminum, glass, and other valuable resources enjoy considerable popularity, but could be increased even more.

Water and land can be used more prudently. Educational programs successfully encourage water conservation. Better farming practices, food control, and reforestation can save soil and trees.

The conservation of nonrenewable resources and the prudent care and replacement of renewable resources can go a long way toward achieving ecological balance. Most of these actions can be done voluntarily, but in some instances democratic government may have to intervene on behalf of the common good.

Family planning is easier in the developed world, where the higher level of well-being reduces the pressure for large families and where education, literacy, and the relative emancipation of women encourage birth control. But the industrialized nations can encourage family planning in other nations through education about birth control, better programs of health and welfare, and efforts to improve economic well-being. Such measures may limit the need for more radical and controversial means of limiting population. These include vasectomy (the operation that prevents passage of the sperm from the testes to the penis), tubal ligation (the cutting and tying off of the fallopian tubes), and free abortions on demand.

Environmental protection can also work. Legislation to protect against flagrant polluters already exists and makes sense. Resources must be protected against those who would pollute the air, water, and land. It is not too much to ask chemical companies to safely dispose of contaminating wastes. It is not too much to insist that factories and power plants release fewer pollutants through their smokestacks. It is not too much to ask strip miners to restore the earth after they have removed the coal.

The strengths of this reform alternative are many. There can be little argument about the need for conservation, family planning, and environmental protection—especially when they are undertaken voluntarily. When good habits are widespread, they contribute enormously to ecological health. Even democratically agreed-on, wise regulation on behalf of these objectives is desirable. And sometimes, especially where the common good is involved, people may legitimately be "forced to be free."

But are reforms that build on existing policies enough? Here we uncover some of the weaknesses of this alternative. Critics maintain that these reforms do not come to grips with the radical problems of scarcity, overpopulation, and pollution. These critics maintain that current conservation only postpones the day of reckoning and that current reforms have not seriously addressed the problem of useless, wasteful, destructive production. They say that these reforms do not address the scandalous fact that the developed countries use a disproportionate share of the world's resources to maintain their high standard of living. Moreover, these reforms cannot balance population and resources in the poorer countries or cut pollution in any significant way. They gravely doubt that current measures can work fast enough to ensure ecological health. They believe that the reformist approach makes too many compromises, such as accepting pollution to avoid the loss of industrial jobs, and succumbing to the mania for growth to maintain prosperity.

These considerations suggest to some that bolder and more radical policies are in order.

Scientific and Technological Advances and Sound Political Management

Scholars such as Herman Kahn and Julian Simon affirm a guarded optimism about ecological health.[25] Kahn and his colleagues at the Hudson Institute set forth their views in 1976 in the widely read book *The Next 200 Years: A Scenario for America and the World.* Although published two decades ago, it remains perhaps the most compelling work of the guarded optimists. These scholars are apostles of growth and opponents of the doomsday critics. They maintain that scarcity can be overcome, population growth limited, and pollution satisfactorily reduced, if not eliminated. People can do all of this without sacrificing their high standard of living and without requiring the poorer, developing nations to abandon hopes for greater economic well-being. Table 19.1 summarizes the way these guarded optimists see themselves and their ecological opponents.

Kahn and his associates argue that problems involving population, economic growth, energy, raw materials, food, and pollution are solvable in the future. These problems are the temporary problems of a world in transition from poverty to prosperity. They insist that overcrowding, famine, scarce resources, pollution, and poverty are temporary or regional problems, not inevitable evils. They maintain that neither the world nor the United States must suffer from long-term shortages of energy or resources. They believe

Table 19.1 Four Views of Ecological Health

Ecological Health Issue	Convinced Neo-Malthusian	Guarded Pessimist	Guarded Optimist	Technology and Growth Enthusiast
1. Basic world model	Finite pie	Uncertain pie	Growing pie	Unlimited pie
2. Technology and growth	Largely illusory and counterproductive	Mostly diminishing return	Required for progress	Solves almost all problems
3. Management and decision making	Failure is almost certain	Likely failure	Moderately successful	Not a serious problem
4. Resources	Steady depletion	Continued difficulties	Generally sufficient	Economics and technology can provide superb solutions
5. Current growth	Carcinogenic	Large potential for disaster	Probable transition to stability	Desirable and healthy
6. Innovation and discovery	A trap	Increasingly ineffective	Usually effective	Humankind's greatest hope
7. Income gaps and poverty	Destined to tragic conclusions	Increasing and threatening	Declining absolute poverty	Not a real problem
8. Industrial development	A disaster	A step backward	Should continue	Necessary for wealth and progress
9. Quality of life	Ruined	In conflict with much growth	More gains than losses	A meaningless phrase and issue
10. Long-range outlook	Bleak and desperate	Contingent disaster	Contingent success	High optimism and confidence

Source: Adaptation of Table 1, pp. 10–16 in The Next 200 Years by Herman Kahn. Copyright © 1976 by Hudson Institute. By permission of William Morrow and Company.

that industrialism can be compatible with a clean environment. They see populations as becoming stable. Despite some reservations, their diagnosis is fundamentally optimistic, in contrast to the diagnoses of most students of ecology.

Kahn and his colleagues argue that the earth's resources are bountiful enough to sustain high levels of population and economic growth at high standards of living. They project a world population of 15 billion in 2176 and maintain that even if it increased to 30 billion before stabilizing, a generally high standard of living could still prevail. They believe that by 2176 the earth's population will become reasonably stable (Figure 19.4). They assume that the rates of population and economic growth are now historically high but will decline and eventually level off. They concede that there may be suffering in some countries because population will outrun food supplies, but that balance will develop. Indeed, recent data demonstrate that since 1960, birth rates have been declining in the preponderance of the world's countries, both developed and less-developed nations.[26]

Despite their recognition of short-term energy problems, Kahn and his associates are optimistic about the future. With some exceptions attributable to bad luck or poor management, they dismiss concern about energy shortages. They see abundant future energy as the world's best insurance that a very large population (even 15 to 20 billion) can be sustained. The existence of inexhaustible energy sources makes future prospects bright. The development of energy sources other than oil can be relied on. Kahn anticipates that by the middle of the twenty-first century, most of the world's energy will come from eternal sources: solar, geothermal, and nuclear.

Kahn and his fellow researchers are also optimistic about other raw materials, which they believe will be abundant for future generations. They reject the idea of exhausted vital resources. They emphasize the potential of mining the oceans and even of extraterrestrial mining. Recy-

Figure 19.4
Population growth in long-term historical perspective.

Source: After Ronald Freedman and Bernard Berelson, "The Human Population," Scientific American (September 1974), pp. 36–37. Reprinted in Herman Kahn et al., The Next 200 Years, p. 29. Copyright by the Hudson Institute. Used by permission of William Morrow.

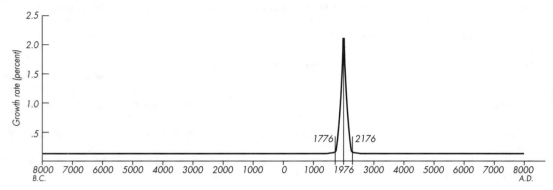

cling, conservation, and substitution can secure vital materials now in short supply.

The guarded optimists are also upbeat about food. They do not see a growing gap between demand and supply. Rather, they see abundant food in the future. Poor weather, natural disasters, bad policies, and inadequate distribution may lead to malnutrition, hunger, and famine in some areas of the world, but there is enough land, water, and fertilizer to sustain the current population. They maintain that good management will ease food problems over time.

As far as the environment is concerned, Kahn and his associates hold that short-term problems can be solved. They place their faith in technology, money, time, and intelligent self-restraint. They believe that by the beginning of the twenty-first century human beings will look back proudly on ecological achievements. There will be clean air to breathe, and even the rivers will have potable water.

They do have serious concerns about the long term, however. They are worried about large-scale nuclear war and other major ecological catastrophes. Yet they endorse science and technology; they prefer to advance prudently rather than to slow down or stop. They believe that the odds are five to one in favor of humanity's successfully solving all its long-term problems.

Kahn and his colleagues are strongly committed to economic growth, but they believe such growth will taper off somewhat over time. Despite some stubborn pockets of poverty, continuing overall economic growth will benefit all. They believe that by the beginning of the twenty-first century, a quarter of the people on earth will live in postindustrial societies and that per capita income will have dramatically increased almost everywhere.

The strengths of this philosophy of guarded optimism are considerable. If true, it provides hope for a future in which science and technology, prudently joined with wise public policies, can cope with scarce natural resources, balance population and resources, and provide a clean environment. Growth and prosperity can continue to progress.

The weaknesses of this alternative are found in its assumptions: that population growth will level off fast enough and be in balance with abundant and deliverable food supplies; that resources and especially energy will be available, at reasonable costs, to keep industrial and agricultural machinery operating; and that pollution can be licked. But if population does not level off, if food supplies do not reach hungry people, if no new natural resources can be found, if the sun, the wind, the rivers and oceans, and the earth cannot be tapped for energy, and if pollution continues and is too expensive to curtail, we human beings will be in deep trouble. Will we have the scientific genius or political will to do all that Kahn and his associates see as essential?

A Sustainable Development Model

In 1987, under the auspices of the United Nations, the World Commission on Environment and Development published *Our Common Future*.[27] The report lays out several clear theses. First, the world is under severe environmental stress. Second, sound ecological management is not incompatible with development. In fact, economic growth can and must continue. The question is, What kind of growth leads to ecological problems and what kind of growth is compatible with sound environmental management? Third, there is a link between environmental protection and world peace. Environmental crises present a threat to national security in two ways. Obviously, the threats to the biosphere, oceans, fresh water, and other resources are a danger to human welfare. Beyond this, arms expenditures siphon off valuable resources that could be used for environmental protection.

The strategy that *Our Common Future* proposes for both development and environmental management is called **sustainable development.** The concept has been widely accepted in United Nations circles and the wider environmental community.[28] As the report notes, sustainable growth contains two key concepts: "the concept of 'needs,' in particular the essential needs of the world's poor, to which overriding priority should be given; and . . . the idea of limitations imposed by the state of technology and social organization on the environment's ability to meet present and future needs."[29]

Sustainable development is really a call for what the commission sees as a more rational and equitable approach to development. Growth in the more industrialized regions of the world has been highly material- and energy-intensive, putting enormous strain on the environment. Similarly, but for different reasons, poverty, as found in the developing regions of the world,

"reduces people's capacity to use resources in a sustainable manner; it intensifies pressure on the environment."[30] High birth rates along with seemingly desperate overuse of land are but two manifestations of this trend.

Sustainable development depends on a two-pronged management approach. First, there must be a high degree of responsible and rational management of growth at the national level. Here, reeducating people to the damage done by short-term, irrational development is crucial. Second, "sustainable development can be secured only through international cooperation and agreed regimes for surveillance, development, and management in the common interest. . . . Without agreed, equitable, and enforceable rules governing the rights and duties of states in respect to global commons, the pressure of demands on finite resources will destroy their ecological integrity over time."[31]

Various regimes—at different stages of development—highlight the possibilities of international cooperation.[32] The oceans are governed under the Law of the Sea Treaty, the International Whaling Commission, and the 1985 Convention on Prevention of Marine Pollution by Dumping of Wastes and Other Matter. Space is regulated via the U.N. Global Environmental Monitoring System and the 1967 Outer Space Treaty, which states that outer space is not subject to national appropriation. Antarctica has been the subject of several agreements, including the 1959 Antarctic Treaty to confine the continent to peaceful uses, the 1964 Agreed Measures for Conservation of Antarctic Fauna and Flora, the 1972 Convention of Conservation of Antarctic Seals, and the 1980 Convention on the Conservation of Antarctic Marine Living Resources. These efforts to build effective regimes for managing earth's ecological welfare are only a start. The future is clearly a multilateral one, and much needs to be done to expand and strengthen these regimes as well as to create new ones.

The sustainable development argument is very appealing. It does not reject the notion of growth. It recognizes that poverty in the developing world must be addressed. It correctly emphasizes the link between national security and environmental degradation. But it does raise some important questions.

In keeping with the tone set by *Our Common Future*, Vice-President Al Gore called for a global Marshall Plan. In his 1992 book *Earth in the Balance*, Gore calls for the United States to lead a dramatic multilateral effort to reestablish global ecological balance.[33] The objectives he advocates, while formidable, parallel the concept of sustainable development:

1. Stabilization of world population
2. Rapid creation and development of environmentally appropriate technologies
3. Economic accounting that assigns appropriate values to the ecological consequences of marketplace choices made by individuals, companies, and nations
4. Negotiation and approval of a new generation of international agreements
5. A cooperative plan for educating the world's citizens about our global environment
6. Establishment, especially in the developing world, of the social and political conditions most likely to build sustainable societies[34]

Will the strategy of sustainable development be effective enough to deal with the magnitude of environmental degradation? Can growth and environmental management coexist? Will developed, industrial societies really jeopardize their living standards by taking a more rational, less materialistic approach? These critical questions raise the possibility that the problems of planet management may require even more radical solutions.

A Steady-State Philosophy

The concept of steady state is closely related to that of sustainable growth, but the emphasis differs. Clearly, economic growth and development is more important to sustainable growth than to a steady state. Advocates of a steady state are convinced that the current ecological crisis is

a deep-seated, ongoing reality and cannot be dealt with through superficial reform and democratic muddling or by relying on a scientific and technological fix. Adopting the minimum, frugal steady state will require radical ecological, political, and economic changes.

William Ophuls has forcefully advanced this argument in *Ecology and the Politics of Scarcity: Prologue to a Political Theory of the Steady State*. He argues that ecological scarcity adversely affects the political system. It seriously challenges policies of liberal reform. Such liberal policies, Ophuls argues, can only briefly postpone the day of reckoning. Our planet's finite character, set against humanity's unchecked exponential growth, materialistic appetites, and indifference to pollution, presages a severe and alarming crisis, for which there is no scientific and technological fix.[35] Figure 19.5 illustrates the crisis in terms of environmental demand versus **carrying capacity,** or the ability of the earth to support human and other life forms. Ophuls estimates that the saturation point will be reached by the year 2036.

Ecological scarcity involves shortages of food and of mineral and energy resources. Human

---

Figure 19.5
Carrying capacity and environmental demand.
Source: William Opuls, Ecology and the Politics of Scarcity, p. 133.
Copyright © 1977 W. H. Freeman and Company.

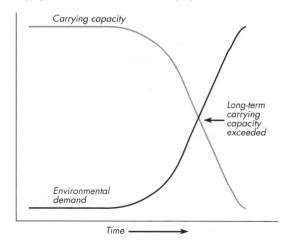

ability to use technology to increase resources is limited. Earth is a finite planet with finite and increasingly costly resources and technology.

The only sane response to the ecological crisis, according to Ophuls, is a **steady-state philosophy.** He defines a steady-state society as "one that has achieved a basic long-term balance between the demands of a population and the environment that supplies its wants."[36] Such a society calls for a healthy biosphere, careful use of resources, wise limitations on consumption, long-term goals to guide short-term choices, and a respect for future generations. Human beings must learn to live within their annual incomes and thus avoid eating up the world's capital. They must manage the earth prudently so that it continues to nourish this generation and future generations.

Ophuls believes that swift action in the right way can achieve transition to a high-level steady state. Otherwise a lower-level steady state may result, or people may even be forced back to a premodern, agrarian way of life (Figure 19.6).

The philosophy of the steady state requires, physically, that human beings tune into the cycle of nature, that they try to replenish what they withdraw. It is vitally important that the human population be maintained within earth's ecological carrying capacity.

We must also consider the sociopolitical characteristics of the steady-state society. Humanity will have to move away from rampant individualism to place a higher priority on community and the common good. The community will need authority to enforce its demands on individuals. Although authority need not be remote, arbitrary, and capricious, and although basic rights will have to be retained in a constitutional system, the right to ecological destruction will have to be curbed. Ophuls anticipates a shift from egalitarian democracy toward political competence and status. He looks to agreed-on governmental values—"aristocratic principles"—favoring the common interests of the steady state. Ideally, a class of Jeffersonian aristocrats, under constitutional restraints, would govern in accord with a steady-state philosophy of virtuous restraint.

Liberal, laissez-faire, muddling-through politics will no longer do. Courageous political decisions will have to be made on behalf of ecological health. Such health will not result from the free play of market forces; such free play has only produced the tragedy of the commons.

Ophuls also sees diversity as a characteristic of the steady-state society. He looks forward to a greater role for small-scale enterprise. He anticipates great opportunities for people at the local level.

The steady-state society will more genuinely embrace the principle of *holism* —the interrelationship of the whole global system. A new, more virtuous and spiritual morality will characterize the steady state philosophy. Ophuls believes that people will cultivate a more mature economy to protect precious resources and the quality of life. Care for the earth will reward humanity with both beauty and amenity as well as ample sustenance. The modern age of thoughtless growth will come to an end.

Ophuls's steady state will offer a happy mean between degrading poverty and wasteful abundance. He insists that the steady state is not stagnation or opposed to all forms of growth. Rather, it seeks a dynamic equilibrium affording ample opportunity for ethical, cultural, and scientific growth. Ophuls is sympathetic to small-scale and self-sufficient enterprises that help individuals control their own economic lives.

Figure 19.6
Three steady-state possibilities.

Source: William Opuls, Ecology and the Politics of Scarcity, p. 133. Copyright © 1977 W. H. Freeman and Company.

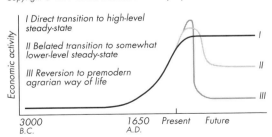

I Direct transition to high-level steady-state

II Belated transition to somewhat lower-level steady-state

III Reversion to premodern agrarian way of life

Economic activity

3000 B.C.   1650 A.D.   Present   Future

Politically, Ophuls favors the Jeffersonian ideal: small, self-governing communities associated with a federal government pursuing clearly defined national purposes. As people turn away from the rape of the globe, from mindless growth, they will find economic, social, and political satisfaction and personal fulfillment.

What can we say of the strengths and weaknesses of this philosophy of the steady state? The vision of a harmonious balance between people and resources is most attractive. So, too, is a world of ample sufficiency that provides generous scope for artistic, intellectual, moral, scientific, and spiritual fulfillment. A philosophical review of materialistic and aggressive appetites (toward other peoples and nations as well as toward the planet) has long been in order. The philosophy of growth and progress needs critical analysis, as does people's often unthinking reliance on science and technology. **Metanoia**—a fundamental transformation of world view—may be required to meet the ecological challenge.

But are the steady-state philosophers correct in their empirical analysis of the ecological crisis? And if they are right, is their prescription desirable and feasible? These questions call attention to possible weaknesses.

Herman Kahn disagrees with Ophuls's empirical analysis. Kahn sees population stabilizing, sees no exhaustion of resources, and believes pollution can be controlled. Kahn insists that Ophuls's extrapolations about exponential growth are misleading. Kahn believes that economic growth will slow in ample time to avert disaster. He also believes that science and technology will ensure abundance and defeat pollution.

But even if Ophuls's analysis is correct, and assuming that the steady-state society is desirable, can such a society be achieved? Critics maintain that people lack the will to cut back to a more frugal existence. People are simply not willing to pay the costs of the steady state: reduced economic growth, more modest lifestyles, and the expenses of pollution control. Furthermore, it is not clear that ecological health on the model of the steady state can be achieved without coercive governmental decisions to limit population, direct economic production, avert the tragedy of the commons, and stop pollution. Other critics find Ophuls's preference for "small is beautiful," "aristocratic principles," decentralization, and less government to be reactionary, authoritarian, and contradictory. These critics insist that the clock cannot be turned back on larger economic and political organizations. They say a central government is needed to ensure the common good; we may need more governmental powers acting on behalf of ecological health rather than fewer.

Benevolent Authoritarianism

Some contemporary critics are convinced that the dangers of ecological ill-health cannot be met in a democratic and constitutional way. They maintain that only benevolent authoritarianism can prevent disaster.[37]

They argue that the masses cannot understand the dangers of ecological disorder and that even if they could, neither they nor the governing elites would be willing to adopt steady-state measures to curb population, protect resources, and stop pollution. Consequently, a benevolent elite (who understand the ecological dangers, who have the common good and posterity in mind, and who have the courage and will to act) must use coercive, authoritarian means to rescue humankind.

Such "medicine" will not be pleasant, but it must be taken. If education and propaganda succeed, people will take the medicine voluntarily. If not, the benevolent authoritarian elite must step in.

Thus, if people can voluntarily—with the aid of bonuses for small families—limit family size through late marriage, abstinence, contraception, sterilization, and sensible abortion, stronger compulsory measures may not be necessary. But if population growth threatens the carrying capacity of the planet, sheer survival may dictate harsher measures. Some worried observers even raise the prospect of *triage*. According to this concept, the peoples of the world would be divided into thirds: one-third will survive with no help; a second can survive with reasonable help; and the final third—considered to be beyond help no matter what is done for them—will be left to die.

Compulsion will be required to conserve the earth's resources and to overcome pollution. Wasteful production will be prohibited. Government will have to allocate scarce resources equitably. Recycling will be compulsory. Automobile travel will be severely curtailed in favor of mass transportation and bicycles and will be heavily taxed. Polluters will also be heavily taxed or, in the worst cases, put out of business.

The benevolent authoritarian government will seek to lower birth rates by lifting the level of economic well-being, education, and social security. And it will go all out to obtain relatively pollution-free energy (such as from solar power) and to use the best scientific and economic knowledge in the interest of ecological health.

This approach appeals to those who believe that a "strong doctor" is needed to restore ecological health. Opponents of benevolent authoritarian government may feel that the medicine is worse than the disease, that ecological health can be regained in ways more compatible with democratic and constitutional government. They worry about the ecological philosopher-kings who will be in charge. They wonder if people have to be "forced to be free" in quite this way. And, of course, those who doubt that there really is such deep ecological trouble will be even less inclined to opt for benevolent authoritarianism.

A New World Order

World order advocates share much of the steady-state philosophy advocated by scholars such as Ophuls. They recognize that human beings are using resources recklessly, that population growth constitutes a major problem, and that the global environment is under serious attack. They share Ophuls's view that the ecological crisis is planetary, that the tragedy of the commons is global, and that ecological scarcity makes building a new world order very difficult.

They also share Ophuls's criticism of nation-states that insist on maintaining their sovereign right to use their resources and shape their national policies as they see it. Finally, they agree with one of Ophuls's key conclusions: that a global authority with coercive power over sovereign states is sometimes necessary to keep them within sound ecological bounds and thus avert a global tragedy of the commons.

World order advocates maintain that partial reform is inadequate. Questions of ecological health cannot be treated without considering related problems of peace, economic well-being, and human rights.

Advocates of world order also distrust the guarded optimism of Kahn and his associates at the Hudson Institute. They are much more disturbed than Kahn about short-term ecological problems and much less sanguine about the long-term future. They may, however, be more sympathetic to science and technology than Ophuls, and more understanding of the tough trade-offs called for in global politics.

True to their commitment to democratic and constitutional philosophy, world order advocates do not endorse benevolent authoritarianism. They generally favor voluntary rather than compulsory solutions. And they are scandalized by extreme solutions such as triage.

Again we will use Richard Falk to outline a world order of ecological health. This perspective builds on Falk's commitment to peace, economic well-being, and human rights.

A basic premise of Falk's thinking is his conviction that "a system of sovereign states is obsolescent in part because of its inability to prevent environmental decay or collapse."[38] Although nations and regions must perform important ecological tasks, central guidance is also required. Ecological problems transcend national and even regional borders. Population pressures are global, as are insults to the environment. Securing adequate resources for all people calls for global action.

Thus, Falk makes maintaining and rehabilitating ecological quality one of his four cardinal values. "Ecological quality as a world order value embraces both the containment of pollution and the conservation of resource stocks."[39] The future must be devoid of dramatic or unperceived ecological disasters. The breakup of a large oil tanker and the collision of a nuclear submarine and a merchant vessel are dramatic disasters, whereas the buildup of DDT in the oceans may go unperceived. In the future nature cannot be raped or neglected. Animal species must not be wiped out. The risks and injuries connected with handling, storing, and disposing of ultrahazardous materials must be minimized or eliminated. Resources must be conserved for the benefit of unborn generations, and the development requirements of poorer countries must be met. Scarce resources must not be used for unproductive, wasteful, and destructive purposes (military arms and consumer advertising). The future must be free of environmental warfare, of malignant modifications of the weather.

Falk's views here are similar to those of Ophuls. But he goes beyond Ophuls in proposing how a world order system might deal with population growth, urbanization, increasing energy consumption, industrial development, and environmental degradation.

Falk would establish a World Environmental Authority to maintain environmental quality (see Figure 19.7). It would deal with pollution, waste disposal, climate change, disaster control, endangered species, oxygen depletion, and polar melting. The World Environmental Authority would provide information, monitor environmental changes, propose standards, report on compliance with standards, respond to disasters, and settle disputes. It would also formulate policies on ecological trade-offs. How, for example, can people's need for work be balanced with the need for clean air and water?

Falk would also establish a World Forum on Ecological Balance, to minimize conflict with economic well-being. Here, too, the jobs-versus-pollution problem might arise. How much economic growth is possible—and at what cost? These are important political, economic, and

ecological questions. The forum would seek to build a consensus on answers. In addition to the central forum, there would be regional chambers of the World Forum.

Falk also advocates a World Agency of Resources, Conservation, and Development Policy. This agency would link resource policy, conservation programs, and development opportunities. When well established, this agency might allocate resources among claimants on the basis of need and equity. The agency would also study future prospects for low-grade ores, underwater mineral deposits, and new sources of energy. It might also assess compliance with global standards on resource use.

A major strength of the world order approach is its recognition that ecological health is a global problem that calls for central guidance—policies, programs, and institutions. Falk is particularly aware of the complex trade-offs that will have to be worked out between, for example, economic growth and environmental protection. He also understands that science and technology can help or harm, integrate or divide. And he sees

Figure 19.7
Richard Falk's World System for Ecological Balance.
Source: Richard Falk, A Study of Future Worlds (New York: Free Press, 1975).

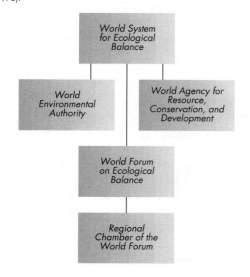

ecological health in the context of a larger global battle to advance peace, economic well-being, and human rights.

How feasible is the world order approach? For example, does Falk really indicate how to control population growth? how to curtail only unnecessary economic growth? how to handle polluters? Can his proposed organizations be established in time? Are forces in the world seriously moving in the direction he outlines?

TOWARD CREATIVE BREAKTHROUGHS TO ECOLOGICAL HEALTH

Which of the alternatives we have so far examined seems most desirable and feasible? This is the question that challenges the wisdom of policymakers. If no one alternative makes sense, perhaps a combination of approaches might be worked out.

Liberal Conservation, Family Planning, and Environmental Protection

Do liberal democratic policymakers really understand the severity of the global ecological crisis, and are they prepared to adopt radical measures and accept the costs required to restore ecological health?

Supporters of this alternative in the United States argue that liberal democrats have become aware of the ecological crisis—as a result, for example, of the OPEC oil crisis of 1973—and are taking steps, especially in the energy field, to make the United States self-reliant or at least less dependent on foreign oil sources. They contend that the United States has acted, such as through the Environmental Protection Agency, to clean up its own industries. Supporters point to America's efforts to feed the world's hungry people and to help developing nations feed themselves and control population growth. America's conservation efforts are perhaps modest, but, with increased education, they can become very effective.

Skeptics seriously doubt that any nation committed to democracy and capitalism can effectively cope with ecological scarcity. Americans, especially affected parties such as industrial polluters, speedy drivers, and wasteful consumers, are

simply not prepared to sacrifice profits, jobs, and convenience for clean air and pure water or to conserve scarce resources. The United States may be able to keep its population and resources in balance, largely because more affluent nations tend to have smaller families and because the United States produces great quantities of food. But U.S. efforts to help stabilize population growth in Southeast Asia, Africa, and Latin America have had little impact. The critics claim that, given capitalism's commitment to blind growth and democracy's commitment to satisfying the current generation, countries such as the United States cannot make the radical change necessary to secure long-range ecological health.

Scientific and Technological Advances and Sound Political Management

What happens if population growth does not level off, if science and technology cannot feed the enormous appetite for resources, and if people are unwilling to pay for pollution control?

Those with confidence in the scientific and political ability to save the human race argue that short-term ecological troubles can be handled while we wait for the future world of prosperity and plenty that science and technology can usher in. They see clear signs that population growth is indeed leveling off. By using both their brains and pocketbooks, people can bring pollution under control.

Critics of the guarded optimistic approach contend that it overestimates science's ability to save the planet. They maintain that it is premature to say that population growth is leveling off. And they do not see people or nations resolving to control pollution. A reliance on science and technology only salves the consciences of the affluent while the poor continue to suffer; this approach creates a false sense of security when it is urgent that people act now to protect the planet.

Sustainable Development Model

Are rational economic development and planetary ecological management really compatible?

Advocates of sustainable growth claim that development in the poorer parts of the world must proceed and that economic growth in the developed world cannot be halted but must be more environmentally sound. Sound national policy must be combined with more international regimes committed to planetary management. To fund national and international efforts, resources now devoted to enormous military establishments must be reallocated.

Is there not an element of "having one's cake and eating it, too" in the sustainable development philosophy? Will developed countries drastically change their energy-intensive and materially driven economies if such change means they must lower their standards of living? Do the international regimes already coming into existence have the power necessary to effectively manage the earth's ecological systems? Will national sovereignty prevent these regimes from gaining more power?

Steady-State Philosophy

Is ecological scarcity an inevitable reality calling unmistakably for limits to cancerous growth and the development of a frugal steady-state society?

Those who believe that the answer is yes point to what they contend are the ecological facts of life. Certain resources are finite—oil is the best example—and once they are gone, they are gone forever. Population has, in fact, been growing too fast. And human beings are guilty of waste and pollution. Unique global developments now call for a major shift in humankind's approach to the globe. That shift calls for a frugal steady-state philosophy.

Critics argue that this perspective is the nightmare of frightened neo-Malthusians who wrongly perceive that the carrying capacity of the earth will soon be exceeded. Even those who are sympathetic to the factual argument doubt that either rich or poor nations will buy the policies called for by a steady-state society. The rich will not give up their high standards of living, and the poor will not abandon their hopes for a comparable standard. The critics see troubles ahead for liberal democratic, democratic socialist, and com-

munist countries—all of whose philosophies have been based on economic growth and abundance. But they do not see a steady-state philosophy emerging triumphantly from this time of troubles.

Benevolent Authoritarianism

Is it really necessary to sacrifice democratic and constitutional government to ensure ecological survival?

Proponents of benevolent authoritarianism maintain that certain democratic freedoms may have to be abandoned to deal with the ecological crisis. A kind of ecological constitutional dictatorship may have to be instituted to handle the coming period of great peril. Strong measures may have to be taken to curb population growth, curtail the reckless use of resources, and develop a new set of ecological habits. The alternative may be mass starvation, an increasing gulf between rich and poor, and other social explosions.

Critics do not believe that the planet is so sick that democratic government must be abandoned. Moreover, they greatly doubt the human ability to identify, or trust, such authoritarian rulers. They maintain that this authoritarian medicine is worse than the disease it seeks to cure.

A New World Order

Does the ecological crisis really call for significant changes in the nation-state system and for global guidance in crucial matters?

Some scholars maintain that the problems of ecological health (and the related problems of peace, economic well-being, and human rights) are genuinely inseparable and can be solved only through a new approach to world order. Global problems must be handled by a worldwide organization. The planet must be perceived as a single ecological entity, and matters affecting all peoples must be governed by global policies. Of course, such policies do not prevent national, regional, and global organizations from working together.

Critics doubt that the policies and institutions of a sane ecological world can be put into place. They argue that it is not possible to bring national self-interest into harmony with a wise global interest. It is premature to believe that national, regional, and global agencies can work together to control population growth, ensure adequate resources, and improve environmental quality.

CONCLUSION

In June of 1992, over 20,000 people representing 172 governments, 1,400 nongovernmental organizations, and hundreds of news media gathered in Rio de Janeiro, Brazil, for the United Nations Conference on Environment and Development, otherwise known as the Earth Summit. Attempts to evaluate this conference illustrate the enormous complexity of global ecological problems and related political difficulties. Some people see the conference as a new beginning, a cause for hope. These people base their optimism on the unprecedented level of participation and the growing scientific consensus on the seriousness of environmental problems. Others do not assess the conference so charitably. True, there was a good deal of consciousness raising. But the fine print of the documents produced— The Rio Declaration, Agenda 21, the Convention on Climate Change, the Convention on Biological Diversity, and the Forests Charter—contains no specific targets or timetables. The documents are filled with good intentions but little more. Can the world's nations find the political will and funding to go beyond Rio to address the ecological dilemmas outlined in this chapter?

Few deny the imperative of ecological health. But, as we have seen, many do disagree about the urgency of short-term problems and on the accuracy of long-term predictions. Some of these disagreements may fade as the future confirms or denies trends and forecasts. There can be little doubt, however, that human beings must work to preserve the planet on which they all live. The form this care must take arouses political dispute. As we have seen, ecological problems require a momentous political response that taxes the human capacity for wise judgment. In responding to the imperative of ecological health, people must rethink their political values; study the empirical realities of ecology, economics, and

politics; consider alternatives and their costs and benefits; and ultimately choose a prudent course of action.

ANNOTATED BIBLIOGRAPHY

Brown, Lester R. *State of the World: A Worldwatch Institute Report on Progress Toward a Sustainable Society.* New York: Norton, published annually. Brown and his researchers cover a variety of global environmental problems in this increasingly influential publication.

Brown, Lester, Flavin, Christopher, and Kane, Hal. *Vital Signs 1996: The Trends That Are Shaping Our Future.* New York: Worldwatch Institute/Norton, 1996. Examines thirty-three key indicators—environmental, economic, military, and social—over periods running from forty to forty-five years and have major impact on the condition of the planet. Extremely valuable use of statistical data, graphs, and charts. An excellent companion to Brown's *State of the World* series.

Committee for the Compilation of Materials on Damage Caused by the Atomic Bomb in Hiroshima and Nagasaki. *Hiroshima and Nagasaki.* New York: Basic Books, 1981. Dramatically underscores the disastrous consequences of nuclear warfare and reminds us that all war is ecologically disastrous.

Ehrlich, Paul, and Ehrlich, Anne. *Population Explosion.* New York: Simon & Schuster, 1990. Builds on and updates Paul Ehrlich's earlier classic, *The Population Bomb.*

Gore, Al. *Earth in the Balance: Ecology and the Human Spirit.* New York: Houghton Mifflin, 1992. Calls for an environmental Marshall Plan to restore global ecological balance.

Hardin, Garrett E. *Exploring New Ethics for Survival.* New York: Viking, 1972. Outlines the philosophy of the author of "The Tragedy of the Commons." Will we have to move toward the benevolent authoritarianism that Hardin sees as necessary to cope with harsh ecological realities?

Kahn, Herman, *The Next 200 Years: A Scenario for America and the World.* New York: Morrow, 1976. Articulates the argument of the guarded optimist who is sympathetic to the technology-and-growth enthusiast and opposed to the guarded pessimist and the convinced neo-Malthusian. Who is right? And what is the price of being wrong? Also see Julian L. Simon and Herman Kahn, eds., *The Resourceful Earth: A Response to Global 2000* (New York: Basil Blackwell, 1984).

436

PART FOUR POLITICAL JUDGMENT AND PUBLIC POLICY

Ophuls, William. *Ecology and the Politics of Scarcity: Prologue to a Political Theory of the Steady State.* San Francisco: Freeman, 1977. Argues that American and democratic values and institutions are grossly maladapted to the era of ecological scarcity. Hope for the U.S. lies in moving toward a politics of the steady state. Also see William Ophuls and A. Stephen Boyan, Jr., *Ecology and the Politics of Scarcity Revisited: The Unraveling of the American Dream* (New York: Freeman, 1992).

Simon, Julian L. *The Ultimate Resource.* Princeton, N.J.: Princeton University Press, 1981. Reinforces the anti-doomsday position. People working (producing wealth) and creating knowledge are the ultimate resource. Vast natural resources remain to be tapped by science and technology. Will, technique, and money can cope with pollution. We can overcome famine. Population alarmists are wrong. See also Julian Simon's, *Population and Development in Poor Countries* (Princeton, N.J.: Princeton University Press, 1992), a compilation of Simon's writing over the 1980s and early 1990s.

Steger, Will, and Bowermaster, Jon. *Saving the Earth: A Citizen's Guide to Environmental Action.* New York: Knopf, 1990. Offers an excellent, well-illustrated summary of the environmental problems plaguing the planet: global warming, ozone depletion, smog, acid rain, rain forest burning, garbage, hazardous waste, ocean pollution, energy consumption, and overpopulation.

Vig, Norman J., and Kraft, Michael E., eds. *Environmental Policy in the 1990s.* Washington, D.C.: Congressional Quarterly Press, 1990. Provides a first-rate collection of essays on domestic and international environmental policy dilemmas.

World Commission on Environment and Development. *Our Common Future.* New York: Oxford University Press, 1987. Lays out the argument for sustainable growth. Influential work presented under the auspices of the United Nations.

SUGGESTIONS FOR FURTHER READING

Auerbach, Bruce E. *Unto the Thousandth Generation: Conceptualizing Intergenerational Justice.* New York: Peter Lang, 1994.

Bates, Albert K. *Climate in Crisis.* Summertown, Tenn.: The Book Publishing Co., 1990.

Carroll, John, ed. *Environmental Diplomacy: The Management and Resolution of Transfrontier Environmental Problems.* Cambridge: Cambridge University Press, 1988.

Conservation Foundation. *State of the Environment: A View Toward the Nineties.* Washington, D.C.: Conservation Foundation, 1987.

Falk, Richard. *Explorations at the Edge of Time: The Prospects for World Order.* Philadelphia: Temple University Press, 1992.

Gribbin, John. *The Hole in the Sky.* New York: Bantam, 1988.

Hazen, Robert M. *The Breakthrough: The Race for the Superconductor.* New York: Summit Books, 1988.

Manes, Christopher. *Green Rage: Radical Environmentalism and the Unmaking of Civilization.* Boston: Little, Brown, 1990.

Meadows, Donella H. *The Global Citizen.* Washington, D.C.: Island Press, 1991.

Revkin, Andrew. *The Burning Season: The Murder of Chico Mendes and the Fight for the Amazon Rain Forest.* Boston: Houghton Mifflin, 1990.

Stone, Christopher. *Earth and Other Ethics: The Case for Moral Pluralism.* New York: Harper & Row, 1987.

Taylor, Robert. *Respect for Nature: A Theory of Environmental Ethics.* Princeton, N.J.: Princeton University Press, 1986.

Wilson, E. O., ed. *Biodiversity.* Washington, D.C.: National Academy of Sciences, 1988.

World Resources Institute. *The Crucial Decade: The 1990s and the Global Environmental Challenge.* Washington, D.C.: World Resources Institute, January 1989.

GLOSSARY TERMS

carrying capacity
Earth Summit
ecology
global warming
greenhouse effect
metanoia
nonrenewable resources
ozone layer
renewable resources
steady-state philosophy
superconductivity
sustainable development
tragedy of the commons

CONCLUSION

In our last chapter we summarize the thesis and argument that have guided us in our exploration of political science and politics, and then focus on the future of the discipline and its central subject matter. We will thus, initially, recapitulate the six cardinal features and key themes that we have explored. We will then highlight some future problems that will confront political scientists in the twenty-first century. Finally, in order to investigate those problems, we will set forth some provocative scenarios that may unfold in the twenty-first century. We invite you to assess the value of these scenarios as ways to stimulate creative responses to the new world of politics.

THE CHALLENGING FUTURE OF POLITICS AND POLITICAL SCIENCE

WE COME, FINALLY, to our last question: *How will the study of politics as a civilizing enterprise be carried on in the twenty-first century?* To answer this final question, we may initially find it helpful to recapitulate the six cardinal and interrelated features that we believe must characterize a sensible approach to political science and to politics in the next century.

SIX CARDINAL IDEAS

Here, succinctly stated, are the six cardinal ideas that must characterize a fruitful political science and a successful politics now and in the future:

1. Political science must focus on four major concerns.
2. Politics must serve as a civilizing enterprise.
3. The concept of political health may helpfully serve as an integrating concept in political science, tying together the ethical, empirical, and prudential concerns of the discipline.
4. Students of political science and politicos must always be keenly aware of the changing nature of politics.
5. The exploration of creative breakthroughs in politics must be given a high priority by political scientists.
6. The very nature of politics requires that political scientists attend to the crucial task of continuous prophetic scrutiny and futuristic projection.

Let us look more closely at each of these featured ideas.

Four Major Concerns

The first cardinal feature of our approach is the proposition that political science has four major concerns: (1) the good political life, (2) a science of politics, (3) wise political judgment, and (4) integration of these three concerns into a unified and coherent field of study. This proposition is the *central thesis* that has guided our inquiry into the nature of political science and the new world of politics.

The *fundamental argument* running throughout the several parts of this book elaborates that central thesis. On the basis of these four concerns, we have argued that political scientists have four tasks to address:

1. At the level of political ethics, they must explore the good political life.
2. At the level of social science, they must investigate significant empirical problems related to politics.
3. At the level of citizen involvement, and in other political capacities, they must develop prudent judgment.
4. At the level of comprehensive theory, they must work out (with the help, possibly, of an integrating concept such as political health) a conceptual framework for integrating the central concerns and major fields of political science.

We have sought to explain the fuller meaning of these tasks throughout this book.

Each task constitutes a challenge to political scientists in the future. And each task also poses significant problems, suggests appropriate methodologies, and underscores the need for fruitful responses.

Politics as a Civilizing Enterprise

A second cardinal feature of our approach is our preference for "politics as a civilizing enterprise"—a preference for values, institutions, behavior, and policies that maximize life, growth, and fulfillment. This, too, must be a major ethical commitment of political scientists in the twenty-first century. *Civilizing values* include security, liberty, justice, and welfare. *Civilizing institutions and behavior patterns* are those that advance voluntary cooperation and accommodation and that resolve conflicts in peaceful and constitutional ways. *Civilizing policies* are those that advance peace, human rights, economic well-being, and ecological balance. To hold this view, however, does not mean that we close our eyes to war, tyranny, poverty, and ecological malaise. Clearly, they decisively affect political health and must therefore be thoroughly under-

Racial harmony is one of the objectives of politics as a civilizing enterprise.

stood if they are to be overcome or, at least, significantly reduced.

Political Health as an Integrating Concept

The values of security, liberty, justice, and welfare—and the policies that advance peace, human rights, economic well-being, and ecological balance—give meaning to a third cardinal feature of our approach: political health. This concept integrates the ethical, empirical, and prudential concerns of political scientists and expands the view of politics as a civilizing enterprise. Healthy political communities live in peace with their neighbors. Their citizens enjoy human rights and economic prosperity and live in harmony with their environment. In the rapidly approaching twenty-first century, political scientists will be challenged to explain the full meaning of these values as goals. They will also have to explain more fully the conditions that make for peace or war, freedom or tyranny, prosperity or poverty, and ecological balance or malaise. Finally, political scientists will be trying—in the light of key ethical values and of the political realities of the new century—to maximize preferred goals and minimize dangers to such goals.

The Changing Nature of Politics

A keen awareness of the ever-changing—and changed—nature of politics is a fourth cardinal feature of our approach. The ability to operate in a changing world will require keen ethical, empirical, and prudential skills. Responding intelligently, for example, to the extraordinary changes that took place in the last four to eight years will test political actors' skills. These changes include, especially, the end of the Cold War and the demise of both Soviet Communism and the Union of Soviet Socialist Republics. The new Russia faces grave dangers as it struggles toward constitutional democracy and economic recovery. These changes also include a United Nations confronting new challenges and opportunities. The breakup of the Soviet Union calls attention to the ominous threat of nuclear proliferation. Ethnic, national, and religious conflicts around the globe—whether in parts of the now defunct Soviet Union, the former Yugoslavia, the Middle East, Africa, or Asia—become more troublesome. The U.S. government faces significant challenges in domestic policy and in foreign affairs. The domestic challenges include, for example, responsible deficit reduction, healthcare coverage for all Americans, and genuine welfare reform. The international challenges include a multipolar world characterized by changing patterns of military, economic, and political power; a modernizing China as the world's remaining great communist power; a prosperous and vital Japan; a Western European community struggling toward fuller union; a temporarily weakened but potentially resurgent Russia; an Islamic world embroiled in religious fundamentalism; and great distress in many countries of the developing world.

Creative Breakthroughs in Politics

The changing—and changed—world of international politics calls attention to a fifth cardinal feature of our approach to political science and politics: the possibility of creative breakthroughs. Such breakthroughs—illustrated, for example, by Roger Williams and the breakthrough to religious liberty or, as described in Chapter 2, by James Madison and the breakthrough to the federal republic in the United States—are rare. Yet creative breakthroughs have occurred in the past, are in process in the present, and most certainly will occur in the future.

For example, the European Union may be considered a contemporary breakthrough in process. Given substantial economic integration and closer political ties in Western Europe, it seems reasonably clear that war in Western Europe is now an impossibility and that the European Union has significantly enhanced economic prosperity and constitutional democracy in Western Europe. Moreover, a future breakthrough to protection against genocide—although seemingly far-fetched to narrow-minded political realists—may become a reality in the twenty-first century. It may be possible for the United

Nations to develop a Global Human Rights Regime—composed of strengthened institutions, guided by a policy of prudent prevention, using a strategy of staged implementation (via political, economic, judicial, and military sanctions), and pursuant to a philosophy of just humanitarian intercession—that can prevent or stop genocide.

Certainly we need to be appropriately skeptical of the conventional wisdom that denies the possibility of momentous changes in politics. Certainly the conventional wisdom did not expect the Soviet Union to relax its grip on Eastern Europe and permit its client states to pursue their own popular and national destinies. Certainly the collapse of Soviet communism and the breakup of the Soviet Union surprised most people, including most Soviet experts. It remains to be seen, of course, whether these momentous changes will in time result, for example, in the emergence of a mature democratic and constitutional Russia. Is it naive or unrealistic or premature to anticipate such a creative breakthrough? It also remains to be seen what will happen in Communist China, in other authoritarian countries, and in many troubled developing nations of the world. Must political scientists, without succumbing to naive utopian thinking, be at least open to favorable changes in such countries that move them toward constitutional democracy and international peace? Political scientists need to be receptive to creative breakthroughs on tough problems that the conventional wisdom deems incapable of solution.

Prophetic Scrutiny and Futuristic Projection
Our concern with creative breakthroughs in politics—past, present, and future—calls attention to a sixth cardinal feature of our approach: the need for continuous prophetic scrutiny and futuristic projection. Political scientists try to learn from the past and to deal with current problems. But they are shortsighted indeed if they do not look into both the immediate and the long-range future. This requires an appreciation of the future effect of values, knowledge

of emerging realities that will transform politics, and perception of the need for wise judgments about potential problems and choices. In this final chapter we will use a number of political scenarios to see what the future may hold and to explore approaches to future problems and choices.

Before we turn to these scenarios, however, it will be helpful to recall the themes we have explored in the several parts of this book and to consider their relevance to the challenging future.

THEMES EXPLORED
Starting with our first four introductory chapters, we have emphasized three interrelated concerns in this book: (1) the good political life and the underlying ethical principles of politics, (2) a science of politics and an understanding of significant empirical phenomena, and (3) wise prudential judgment in the arena of citizenship and public policy.

Political Philosophy and Political Science
In our critical examination of political philosophy and ideology in Part II, we argued that *political philosophy seeks to clarify the purposes of politics, the uses of power, and the wisdom of policies*. The great political philosophers can help all students of political science in these endeavors. They sharpen our critical faculties, which we can then use to understand and appraise discarded, dominant, and future political ideologies.

However, the ethical task of the political scientist, as political philosopher, is concerned with more than a search for the good political life. This task also helps students understand which empirical problems are significant and which hypotheses, data, theories, and explanations are meaningful. In this way political philosophy becomes crucial to fruitful work in empirical political science.

The ethical task of the political scientist is also closely connected to a prudential concern for wise judgment in politics and public policy. What is good in politics provides a standard that helps decision makers explore political goals and ethically defensible means.

The Search for a Science of Politics

Our search for a science of politics in Part III stressed the importance of *focusing on the necessary and sufficient conditions of political health or political well-being.* The common features of most scientific enterprises can help in this search. That is, students of political science can seek to identify significant, and manageable, empirical problems. They can articulate guiding hypotheses. They can use a variety of methods to gather evidence for testing their hypotheses. Finally, they can attempt to validate and explain their empirical findings. Scientific research will be most beneficial if it is consciously related to ethically significant problems (Why peace or war? Why freedom or tyranny? Why prosperity or poverty? Why ecological balance or imbalance?) and if it looks to wise, practical political action. Although the challenge of this approach to a science of politics in the twenty-first century is daunting, it is also most exciting.

Greater understanding of important empirical problems should be given top priority in the search for a science of politics. To be most illuminating, such a science of politics will be genuinely comparative and concerned with fitting problems into a framework of empirical theory. Here the search for the necessary and sufficient conditions of political health or well-being will remain a challenging goal.

Good sense and modest expectations are as appropriate in the search for a science of politics as they are in the quest for the good political life or for wise public policies. Students of political science should avoid the temptation to reduce political science to physics or biology or mathematics. They need all the scientific help they can get, but they must remember that human beings are more than atoms and molecules, that human beings are not guinea pigs, and that finding a political science equivalent of Einstein's famous formula ($E = mc^2$) is probably an impossible dream. Students of political science can

only seek as much precision and predictability as their subject permits. Diverse strategies and methods will be needed to deal with diverse empirical problems. With care, fruitful empirical research on significant problems can go forward. This research will place scientific work in a revealing theoretical framework that clarifies the relationship of the part to the whole. The scientific premise of the authors of this book has been that peace, human rights, economic well-being, and ecological balance are inseparable ingredients of political health or well-being. This premise remains a major aspect of our understanding of the future world of politics.

Political Judgment and Prudent Public Policy

In our exploration of political judgment and public policy in Part IV, we argued that *wise judgment and public policy rest on a clearheaded recognition of sound values and an accurate understanding of political phenomena.* What "can be" (prudent political judgment) differs from what "is" or "has been" or "will be" (empirical understanding) and from what "ought to be" (ethical recommendation). The prudent political judgment, although it must be guided by a conception of the good (especially the common good), may not always be what is absolutely desirable. Moreover, the prudent political judgment, although it must always respect the political realities, may nonetheless differ from what has been, is, or will be.

The virtue of prudence has traditionally been considered under the rubric of political philosophy. By treating prudence in a separate part of this book, we have not meant to deny that traditional consideration but, rather, to emphasize the fuller treatment that prudent judgment and public policy warrant in the discipline of political science. Politics is a practical activity and is concerned with action. To say this, however, is not to denigrate philosophical or ethical contemplation or purely empirical investigation. It is rather to reaffirm, and urge renewed attention to, an old tradition: politics as a practical activity, a civilizing enterprise.

This prudential enterprise, which calls for judgment and action, demands critically examined values, purposes, and goals and, of course, the best understanding of relevant political phenomena. But wise judgment also calls for qualities beyond ethical recommendation and empirical understanding. Wise judgment calls for the critical ability to assess alternative courses of action and to balance costs and benefits. Thus, future political scientists must remain concerned with the creative art of political healing. Political well-being is not only an ideal that political scientists endorse or a theoretical concept that they can investigate empirically. It is also an idea that prompts them to engage in the creative art of political healing. Political scientists can thus put their empirical knowledge to work on behalf of their vision of the good political life. The ethical, empirical, and prudential components come together, and philosophy, science, and public policy join in the discipline of political science.

The interrelation of these components suggests the political scientist's fourth task: theoretical integration. This task will unquestionably receive more attention in the future as political scientists become more sophisticated about the relationship between ethics, social science, and statesmanship and also as they are encouraged to employ a concept such as political health to achieve sound and sensible integration. The concept of political health, we have argued, enables political scientists to (1) focus ethically on the good—the healthy—political life; (2) seek empirically to understand the necessary and sufficient conditions of political health (and political illness); and (3) engage prudentially in the task of political healing. The exploration of theoretical integration should be stimulated by the practical political problems and realities of the future and by the judgments we make to usher in a politically healthier world of politics.

FUTURE PROBLEMS AND THE DISCIPLINE OF POLITICAL SCIENCE

Our major findings point toward the important problems that will emerge in the new world of politics: problems of philosophy and ethics, empirical social science, and wise public policy.

Future Problems and Political Philosophy

Future political problems will require a reassessment of current political philosophies. For example, the possibility of nuclear war and the reality of ecological imbalance require a rethinking of some of the basic principles of political philosophy and some of the basic operative ideals, behavior patterns, and institutions of modern political communities. Some powers of the sovereign nation-state may no longer be tenable, especially the power to engage in all-out nuclear war. This lesson has seemingly been learned by the world's superpowers, and it has dramatically led to the end of the Cold War. But not all nations have abandoned war as an instrument of national policy. Wars, including civil wars, continue to bedevil international politics in too many areas of the world.

The power of the sovereign nation-state to do as it pleases with its own citizens—for example, to grossly and persistently violate their human rights—may also be obsolescent. Unfortunately, not all nation-states or other political actors have given up this power. But there are increasing signs, at the level of global rhetoric and beyond, that such violations (especially genocide) are unacceptable as civilized behavior.

Behavior patterns that produce mass starvation or outrageous pollution may also have to be outlawed. Regrettably, specific policies and actions to effectively accomplish such outlawing remain to be worked out.

Liberal democracies, which have a reasonably good track record on human rights in the closing decade of the twentieth century, still need to rethink their treatment of the least free. Citizens of liberal democracies may need, for example, to reexamine the balance that liberal democracy has struck between liberty and authority, self-interest and the common good, and the weak and the strong. They may have to help liberal democrats overcome their sometimes limited ethical vision, deficient understanding, and timid prudential judgment. For example, African Americans, other ethnic minorities, women, and poor people have not fared so well in the liberal democratic United States. Will they do better in the future?

Similarly, the price in lives and liberties that people in communist states have had to pay must be critically examined. Can communism with a human face (in China or elsewhere) emerge—a communism that is really responsive (in politics as well as in economics) to popular control and human freedom and really dedicated to constitutional change and peaceful coexistence?

Will democratic socialism, which has attempted to combine popular rule with human welfare, kill the goose (of capitalism) that supposedly lays the golden egg (of freedom and economic prosperity)? Or have democratic socialists wisely seen the light and now come to accept a regulated capitalism and a market economy? Democratic socialism may be able to alleviate, but not necessarily overcome, the ills of underemployment, worker alienation, ecological degradation, or cultural malaise that plague many affluent industrial nations of the developed world.

Nazism may have been vanquished, but many of the elements that made it dangerous, indeed virulent, still exist in authoritarian regimes around the world—elements such as dictatorial leaders, a one-party state, militarism, notions of racial or ethnic superiority, violations of human rights, and aggressive behavior. How will such authoritarian regimes be dealt with in the twenty-first century?

Moreover, it is not clear that the poorer, developing nations can achieve their idealistic goals of national unity, economic development, social advancement, and their own variety of democracy. Their struggles to achieve these goals will play a prominent part in the politics of the twenty-first century. But will the developing nations succeed, and at what cost?

In all these matters, political scientists will be challenged to study and appraise developments in political philosophy and ideology and to relate them to empirical political science and public policy.

Future Problems and Empirical Political Science

In their continuing search for a science of politics, political scientists are also challenged to uncover the roots of human values in religion, history, biology, economics, psychology, and sociology. Political scientists are challenged to explore more fully the reasons for the gap—ominous in some respects—between civilized values and actual behavior. Moreover, they need to know more about the conditions for successful cooperation and accommodation in politics and about how various patterns of conflict and accommodation relate to crucial values such as security, liberty, justice, and welfare. The value of a number of decision-making models—involving actors who are rational, political, organizational, elitist, or idiosyncratic—is now recognized, but we do not yet have a synthesis of these models. In addition, decision-making patterns have not yet been correlated with the achievement of key political values. In time, however, there should be a greater understanding of the conditions of political well-being. Political scientists are currently identifying reliable political, economic, and social indicators of political health and are exploring varying hypotheses about political health and illness. In time a more sophisticated empirical theory of political health may lead the way to healing public policies.

Future Problems and Wise Public Policy

The problems of political judgment and public policy are complex and difficult. Here political scientists are challenged to seek creative breakthroughs in politics, a concept that is appropriately a major focus of twenty-first-century politics: creative breakthroughs to the peaceful and constitutional resolution of deadly conflicts, to free and mature democratic and constitutional societies, to economic prosperity worldwide, and to a sound and sane ecological balance.

Political scientists have made good progress in identifying key ethical and empirical factors that prompt the search for a more peaceful world order. These factors include the mortal peril of nuclear war, the disastrous consequences of conventional wars, militarism and the still onerous burden of the arms race, certain dangers of the sovereign nation-state system, the uncertainties of the balance of power, and key weaknesses of the United Nations. Political scientists have also been able to identify most of the alternatives: a new security arrangement, reflecting a new, modified balance of power; a reinvigorated United Nations; functional and economic approaches that enhance prosperity and peace; a new global order and security system; and nonviolent civilian defense.

But political scientists are not so sure about the outcome of these alternatives. For example, the end of the Cold War constitutes a promising breakthrough, but that breakthrough remains to be consolidated. Despite some successes at disarmament, the Great Powers are still heavily armed. Nuclear proliferation remains a deeply troubling possibility. Conventional arms sales continue at an alarming rate. Militarism still rides high in too many countries around the world. Better security arrangements among the Great Powers still must be put in place. Wars continue to erupt in too many areas around the world.

Political scientists also await the achievements of a reinvigorated, post–Cold War United Nations, freer to play a more prominent role in world affairs. Strong U.N. sanctions against Iraq in 1990 were promising; their fuller effectiveness remains to be seen. The Dayton Accords of 1995 finally brought an end to the brutal fighting in Bosnia. But have we have seen a complete end to that bitter dispute and to the brutalities that characterized that ugly war? And can the United Nations really develop an effective global regime capable of preventing or stopping dangerous aggression?

Political scientists continue to debate the feasibility of other alternative policies—such as

Flags of member nations fly at the United Nations.

nonviolent civilian defense—that could foster a more peaceful world order. But is nonviolent civilian defense a realistic or unrealistic alternative?

Similarly, in the battle on behalf of the least free, ethics and science point toward the key factors that students of political science must consider: the dreadful reality of genocide, the struggle to achieve national self-determination, the ugly persistence of racism, and other violations of human rights. Although the United Nations has, for example, articulated splendid global standards for human rights, it is far from working out effective enforcement machinery. How can all nations be convinced to protect human rights? What can nations and organizations that honor human rights do to protect those rights in nations that violate them? Can a sound theory of prudent prevention, appropriate sanctions, and just humanitarian intercession be worked out to protect against genocide? These questions will challenge future political scientists. Of course, the future is made brighter by the death of communism in the former Soviet Union, by freedom for nations in Eastern Europe, by the end of military regimes in South America, and by the attractiveness of constitutional democracy around the globe. Yet the persistence of worldwide violations must temper optimism about a global breakthrough on human rights. Similarly, optimism must be tempered by uncertainties about the evolution of democratic and constitutional processes in Russia, in the other republics of the former Soviet Union, in China, in Iraq, and in a host of other countries with deplorable records on human rights.

In the struggle for economic well-being, most political scientists are quite aware of the persistence of poverty. They understand the scourge of unemployment, hunger, ill health, illiteracy, and poor housing. They have come to appreciate, more and more, the unsettling reality of inequality. They are increasingly conscious of the difficulties of improving the economic lot of the world's poor. They are keenly aware of the onerous burden of debt carried by so many developing countries. They properly agonize over the calculus of costs and benefits. Here, too, no breakthrough to a global reign of prosperity seems imminent. There are serious objections to most of the alternative approaches to greater economic well-being. The urgency of the problem underscores the need for political scientists to break through to a world order that can overcome the dehumanizing consequences of poverty.

Although few deny the imperative of ecological balance, many people disagree about the urgency of the short-term problem and the accuracy of long-term predictions. Nonrenewable resources like oil are finite. And people are also wasting renewable resources. In many areas the population has been growing wildly in excess of resources. Global warming and the loss of a protective ozone shield in the atmosphere warn of future trouble. Pollution remains a disturbing reality. Yet critics differ on whether population growth will stabilize in the future (and how soon) and whether economic growth will stabilize (and at what level). Scientists debate the dangers of global warming and ozone loss. They differ on whether science and technology can rescue humankind from ecological scarcity and pollution at an acceptable cost. Here political scientists are challenged to think through the meaning of a future steady-state society, particularly its consequences for political philosophy, for the traditional economics of growth, and for the quality of life for all of earth's inhabitants.

Now, having recapitulated our argument, we can attempt to see how some futuristic scenarios might illuminate the challenging future of politics and of political science.

SOME PROVOCATIVE SCENARIOS

No one can predict the exact character of future politics. But we are deficient as political scientists if we do not think about the future. If politics is to remain a civilizing enterprise, students of political science need to be concerned about how future developments will affect key values and people's vision of the good political life. Political scientists must be prepared for whatever future unfolds—good or bad.

Let us start with some scenarios that take off from current developments. Then we will move to more futuristic scenarios. We will view these scenarios as "thought experiments" designed to help people get ready for the future.

A Best-Case Scenario

A best-case scenario, based on current developments, presents the fuller consequences of the end of the Cold War. Significant disarmament would occur. The burden of the arms race would be lifted. A democratic polity and a prosperous economy would emerge in Russia and the other republics of the former Soviet Union. Effective constitutional democracies would also triumph in Eastern Europe. A united Western European community would be at peace with its Eastern European neighbors and would gradually include them in an all-embracing European home. The component states and peoples of former Yugoslavia would learn to live together peacefully and in mutual respect. All of Europe would profit from a common, mutually beneficial market. China would move toward a variety of "communism with a human face." North and South Korea would achieve a peaceful reunification under a democratic and constitutional government. Israel and the Palestinians would achieve peace with security, and freedom with prosperity. Sensible rulers would replace Saddam Hussein in Iraq and fundamentalist governments in Iran and Afghanistan. Nations would reap the benefits of a "peace-and-justice" dividend. The United States would eliminate its budget and trade deficits, achieve a strong and prosperous full-employment economy, usher in a sensible national health care plan to cover all people, revitalize its educational system, and free the country of dangerous crime and drugs. Violent revolution or aggressive war as a means of effecting political change would disappear. An invigorated United Nations would fulfill the objectives of its charter. Developing nations would overcome economic malaise and political authoritarianism.

Such a world would still contain sovereign nation-states. There would still be some political and economic rivalry among great and small powers. Countries would debate the extent of arms reduction and the character of the "peace and justice" dividend. Concern about the dangers of nuclear proliferation would continue. Peoples of the developing world would still struggle to overcome pockets of poverty and to deal with the persistent gap between rich and poor nations. People would still argue about how to deal with continuing, if diminished, violations of human rights. And disturbing ecological conditions would remain. In the United States, debate would continue on how to make the new economic, health, educational, and social policies work even better.

The authors of this book cannot confidently predict that this best-case scenario will be fulfilled in the future. The end of the Cold War seems irreversible, but it is by no means clear that all rosy aspects of the scenario will be fulfilled. Russia faces a most difficult battle in achieving a democratic and constitutional polity and a prosperous free market economy. And not all nations of Eastern Europe will achieve politically successful and economically productive societies. Arms reduction seems inevitable, but a generous peace-and-justice dividend is questionable. German unification promises to be successful but not free of painful economic costs and difficult social readjustment. Despite current stumbling, the long-range economic unification of Western Europe will probably occur, although political unification will lag far behind. The Chinese path toward a greater measure of domestic freedom will be halting. The displacement of other authoritarian regimes will not easily occur. The Israelis and Palestinians may hammer out a peace of sorts, but a fully harmonious and prosperous Middle East will still have to confront resistant hardliners. Violent revolution in the developing world may diminish, but violence, poverty, and authoritarian rule will probably still characterize many developing countries. Aggressive war and disruptive civil wars—as in Afghanistan or Chechnya—will continue to plague the world.

The United States will achieve a great measure of economic prosperity, will make some progress in cutting its budget deficit, but will not achieve full employment and will confront the difficult task of keeping but limiting the rising cost of entitlement programs. More modest proposals for universal health care will come, but efforts at full coverage and cost containment will still trouble the health care scene. And the United States will continue to struggle, fitfully, to improve its educational system and to combat crime and drugs. The United Nations will modestly strengthen its war-preventing, rights-protecting, peacekeeping abilities. But it may still have trouble moving from rhetorical resolutions and modest actions to more complete fulfillment of the laudable objectives of its charter.

A Worst-Case Scenario

As they face the future, resourceful political scientists would also be wise to anticipate worst-case scenarios that build on present realities. A worst-case scenario would envisage a resumption of Great Power, East-West rivalry and all of its debilitating consequences. Authoritarian rulers would resume power in Russia. Or a U.S.-China dispute might break out over Taiwan. The arms race would start up again. The danger of escalation to nuclear war would become more real. The proliferation of nuclear weapons (in the possession of Iran, Iraq, North Korea, Israel, Pakistan, India, Libya, Brazil, and Argentina) would increase the risks of local conflicts and could alter the global balance of power. Nuclear terrorism would become a horrible nightmare. Some countries in Eastern Europe would face unbearable tensions and failure. A united Germany seeking the return of former German lands would become a threat to Poland and the Czech Republic, to NATO, and to the movement for European integration. North and South Korea might become embroiled in a military struggle and pull the United States and China into the conflict.

The peace-and-justice dividend would disappear. Poverty and authoritarian rule would characterize almost all developing nations. Moreover, violent revolution, civil war, and aggressive war would return with a vengeance to many areas of the globe. Iraq or Iran would ultimately dominate the Middle East, control world oil prices, and dominate the Islamic world. Islamic religious fundamentalism would topple governments in Egypt, Algeria, Saudi Arabia, and other Islamic countries.

The United States would fail to put its economic, political, and social act together. Its budget and trade deficits would grow menacingly larger. The United States would slide into a persistent recession. Unemployment would rise to 15 to 20 percent. Racial unrest would explode in the

nation's troubled cities. Health care would decline. Housing would deteriorate. Educational reform would fail. Drugs and crime would become rampant. The United Nations would again be rendered impotent to deal with the difficult issues dividing the Great Powers, would become bankrupt, and would be incapable of fulfilling its mission.

Will such a worst-case scenario really materialize? Probably not. But it would be foolish to ignore the underlying realities that might produce such a scenario or at least its key parts. These realities include the persistence of Great Power rivalries and the rivalries of other nations. They also include Russia's difficulties in achieving economic and political reform and thus a stable society, the comparable difficulties facing East European nations trying to overcome the legacy of political and economic authoritarianism, and Chinese nationalist aspirations to regain control of Taiwan. These realities thus include nationalistic and ethnic aspirations and ambitions (whether in Korea, Iraq, Iran, the Middle East), the depth of poverty and authoritarianism in so many developing countries, and the limited capabilities of even the best-intentioned nations.

A more candid assessment of the realities of the U.S. political experience suggests that the United States will probably not continue to slide into economic, political, and social disaster. America's decline has only been relative to its peak position at the end of World War II. The United States remains strong economically. Equally important is the fact that it has historically demonstrated a pragmatic ability to deal with troublesome problems once it perceives that they must be faced. The odds are highly favorable that the United States will control its deficits, shore up its social infrastructure, revitalize its economy, improve its educational system, and in other respects avert a worst-case scenario. So, too, a worst-case scenario will probably not see the United Nations disintegrate as a modest actor in trying to fulfill the laudable purposes of its charter.

Catastrophic Scenarios

Beyond these two scenarios based on current developments, it is possible to anticipate that one or more dreadful catastrophes (such as nuclear war or ecological disaster) might dominate twenty-first-century politics. Nation-states might then be seeking to recover from dreadful wounds. Can they do so within the framework of liberal democracy, or communism, or democratic socialism? Could modern civilization—politically, economically, socially, and culturally—survive such a catastrophe?

In connection with such catastrophic scenarios, students of political science have to face up to several grim alternatives. One alternative is **anarchy**—understood here as lawlessness, the absence of effective government, the prevalence of a brutal dog-eat-dog attitude among survivors. Another alternative would be **authoritarianism** (either benevolent or malevolent), in which the powerful offer protection to the weak at the sacrifice of liberty. This alternative assumes that the demand for security would be so great in a devastated world that survivors would willingly accept strong authoritarianism, law-and-order rule, in the interest of continued survival. A third alternative would be **retrogression**—reversion to a more primitive, preindustrial way of life.

Human powers of recovery and adjustment are great, but they have never been put to the test

of a catastrophe such as all-out nuclear war. Only the bravest optimist could say that civilization as we have known it would survive such a test. People tend to forget that constitutional democracy, in the history of civilization, is very young and has evolved under relatively favorable circumstances. In the event of an all-out nuclear war, the blows to security, liberty, justice, and welfare would be devastating.

These catastrophic scenarios challenge political scientists to avert such outcomes. Although the odds are now probably against an all-out nuclear war in the twenty-first century, the possibility of small-scale nuclear wars cannot be dismissed. And such small-scale nuclear wars, if not the most fearful apocalypse, could trigger comparable pressures toward anarchy, authoritarianism, or retrogression.

Authoritarian scenarios in the absence of a global catastrophe must also be considered. Here, too, malevolent and benevolent authoritarian scenarios can be envisaged.

A Malevolent Authoritarian Scenario

It is possible to envision a twenty-first century in which authoritarian forces of the right or left grow stronger and exert great pressure against the vital center of constitutional democracy. It would be naive to deny that authoritarian forces now exist; it would be equally naive to affirm that they will disappear in the twenty-first century. These forces still operate—and will continue to operate—in communist countries, in some Islamic nations, and elsewhere. Ideological or religious fundamentalism often reinforces these authoritarian regimes. Authoritarian regimes, whether secular or religious, could exert enormous pressure against democratic nations and challenge the march of constitutional democracy.

It does not seem likely, however, that such regimes could threaten the very existence of constitutional democracies. The prospect of a world divided between left and right or an ultimate conflict between these forces is not likely. Nonetheless, the staying power of authoritarian regimes poses serious problems for democratic and constitutional governments and the values on which they rest. Political scientists are, consequently, challenged to ask what can be done to counter authoritarianism throughout the world.

A Benevolent Authoritarian Scenario

Still another authoritarian scenario is possible in the twenty-first century. This is benevolent authoritarianism called into being (prior to a dreadful catastrophe) to cope with building pressures for security, justice, and welfare but at the price of liberty and, ironically, justice. The call for strong law-and-order government arises not only from crime in the cities but from the cry to end war, violations of human rights, poverty, and ecological ill-health. If conditions rapidly deteriorated around the globe, the cry might go up for a benevolent dictator to take charge and save us from ourselves. Such a development might be rationalized through the argument on behalf of a constitutional dictatorship, an institution not unknown in the history of politics when a people's survival is at stake. It is not likely that liberal democracy or democratic socialism could survive under such a benevolent authoritarian regime.

Again, political scientists are challenged to act to prevent the buildup of pressures that might lead to benevolent authoritarianism as a way to avert greater disasters, even if such a prospect is not highly probable. Such actions involve policies to enhance security, justice, welfare, and liberty so as to avert building up a demand for benevolent authoritarian rule.

A Prophetic Planetary Scenario

Grim scenarios are not the only ones that we can envision. It is also possible to see a transition to a twenty-first century characterized by planetary prophetic politics. Here we come to the greatest challenge confronting political scientists as they approach the future: Can ethical, scientific, and prudential resources be used to usher in a world without catastrophic war, flagrant violations of human rights, egregious poverty, or dangerous

ecological malaise? This scenario envisions a world in which conflicts are handled in a democratic and constitutional way, in which prevention would normally make unnecessary political, legal, and military remedies for violations of human rights, in which peoples and communities work together for economic well-being, and in which the steps necessary to ensure ecological health have been taken. This scenario envisions a world in which nations and regional, functional, and global communities cooperate.

The steps necessary to move toward these goals call for numerous creative breakthroughs in politics. Although political scientists would not be the only ones involved in such breakthroughs (humanists, physical and biological scientists, and social scientists from other disciplines will also participate), they will play a leading role. And as creative breakthroughs to a more prophetic politics occur, human beings all over the globe will be able to cultivate that excellent quality of life that is the supreme mark of politics as a civilizing enterprise.

Is such a scenario possible? Yes, because we can envision it. Is it probable? Given our current understanding of political realities, it is not highly probable. But we may be able to take significant strides toward fulfilling key features of this scenario. How far we can go will depend on the creative steps we take now.

CONCLUSION

It is possible to be both bold and prudent in politics. The possibilities of creative human endeavor encourage people to be bold. The limits to human endeavor—the dangers of pride—encourage us to be prudent. Sometimes, however, the prudent course is the bold course, and the bold course is the prudent course. Genuine and effective worldwide arms reduction is both bold and prudent. Establishing global constitutional machinery to protect human rights is also bold and prudent. Similarly, it is audacious and wise to develop programs to advance economic well-being, particularly for poor people in the developing countries. And, finally, it is coura-

Perhaps the ultimate challenge of politics is in seeking harmony among the many races, ethnic groups, and nationalities of the world.

geous and sensible to move globally toward some version of a balanced ecological order.

Politics can be exhilarating as well as depressing. Political science can be as exciting a discipline as our creative minds—focusing on significant ethical, empirical, and prudential problems—can make it.

ANNOTATED BIBLIOGRAPHY

Barber, Benjamin R. *Jihad vs. McWorld: How Globalism and Tribalism Are Reshaping the World.* New York: Ballantine Books, 1996. Argues that vices of parochial tribalism and commercial globalism are threats to a democratic future. Would combine the virtues of a healthier, wealthier world with a sense of democratic community that respects liberty, variety, and difference.

Bronfenbrenner, Urie, et al. *The State of the Americas: This Generation and the Next.* New York: Free Press, 1996. Explores youth, crime and punishment, economic developments, American families, poverty, education. Highlights the impact of current trends on future generations.

Falk, Richard. *On Humane Governance: Toward a New Global Politics.* University Park: Pennsylvania State University Press, 1995. Articulates the views of one of the most perceptive advocates of a global politics that can overcome key weaknesses of the current sovereign nation-state system.

Fukayama, Francis. *The End of History and the Last Man.* New York: Free Press, 1992. Provocatively argues on behalf of the triumph of constitutional democracy and capitalism.

Galbraith, John Kenneth. *The Good Society: The Humane Agenda.* Boston: Houghton Mifflin, 1996. A seasoned economist's assessment of past, present, and future.

Halberstam, David. *The Next Century.* New York: William Morrow, 1991. Examines the unraveling of the former Soviet Union, Japan's economic strength, and challenges facing the U.S.

Kennedy, Paul M. *Preparing for the Twenty-First Century.* New York: Vintage, 1994. Offers the judgment of a thoughtful historian, keenly aware of the rise and fall of great powers, on getting ready for the next century.

McElvane, Robert. *What's Left? A New Democratic Vision for America.* Holbrook, Mass.: Adams Media Corporation, 1996. Focuses on how to overcome poisonous cynicism, collapse of values, and a "winner-take-all" economy of increasing inequality.

Riemer, Neal. *The Future of the Democratic Revolution: Toward a More Prophetic Politics.* New York: Praeger, 1984. Maintains that safeguarding the future of constitutional democracy will require a prophetic politics rooted in prophetic values, using fearless empirical criticism, devoted to sound constitutional action, and acutely aware of the importance of continuous scrutiny and futuristic projection.

Riemer, Neal. *Creative Breakthroughs in Politics.* Lanham, Md.: Rowman and Littlefield, 1996. Contains chapters on the European Union as a contemporary breakthrough in process and on protection against genocide via a newly constituted Global Human Rights Regime.

Toffler, Alvin. *Power Shift: Knowledge, Wealth, and Violence at the Edge of the 21st Century.* New York: Bantam, 1991. Seeks to make sense of the key factors and astonishing changes that will affect us into the 21st century.

United Nations Development Programme. *Human Development Report 1996.* New York: Oxford University Press, 1996. Explores both current patterns and possible futures. Endorses proper links between sound economic growth and sustainable human development, particularly for the poorest of the world's poor.

Yergin, Daniel, and Gustafson, Thane. *Russia 2010 and What It Means for the World.* New York: Vintage, 1995. Explores several scenarios—Russian disintegration, invigoration, or military dictatorship.

SUGGESTIONS FOR FURTHER READING

Ackerman, Bruce. *The Future of the Liberal Revolution.* New York: Macmillan, 1995.

Allison, Graham T., et al. *Avoiding Nuclear Anarchy.* Cambridge, Mass.: MIT Press, 1996.

Anderson, Torben M., et. al. *The Future of the Welfare State.* New York: Blackwell, 1996.

Boulding, Elise, and Boulding, Kenneth E. *Future: Images and Processes.* San Francisco: Sage, 1994.

Brzezinski, Zbigniew. *Out of Control: Global Turmoil on the Eve of the 21st Century.* New York: Simon & Schuster, 1995.

Crotty, William, ed. *Political Science: Looking to the Future.* 4 vols. Evanston, Ill.: Northwestern University Press, 1991.

Forsythe, David. *Human Rights and Peace: International and National Dimensions.* Lincoln: University of Nebraska Press, 1993.

Gardeis, Nathan P., ed. *At Century's End: Great Minds Reflect on Our Times.* La Jolla, Calif.: Alti Publishers, 1995.

Gates, Henry L., and West, Cornel. *The Future of Race.* New York: Knopf, 1996.

Gustavsson, Sverker, and Lewin, Leif, eds. *Future of the Nation-State: Essays on Cultural Pluralism and Political Integration.* New York: Routledge, 1996.

O'Brien, Conor Cruise. *On the Eve of the Millennium: The Future of Democracy Through an Age of Unreason.* New York: Free Press, 1995.

Thurow, Lester C. *Head to Head: The Coming Economic Battle Among Japan, Europe, and America.* New York: Warner, 1993.

Thurow, Lester C. *The Future of Capitalism: How Today's Economic Forces Shape Tomorrow's World.* New York: William Morrow, 1996.

Weldon, Lynn L. *Future: Important Choices.* Boulder: University Press of Colorado, 1995.

Wittkopf, Eugene R. *The Future of American Foreign Policy.* New York: St. Martin, 1993.

GLOSSARY TERMS

anarchy

authoritarianism

retrogression

NOTES

CHAPTER 1

1. The description here and in the following paragraphs is derived from Thucydides, *The Complete Writings of Thucydides: The Peloponnesian War,* trans. Richard Crawley (New York: Random House, Modern Library Edition, 1951), pp. 330–337.
2. U.S. State Department, *Country Reports on Human Rights Practices for 1989* (Washington, D.C.: U.S. Government Printing Office, 1990), p. 792.
3. The following discussion is based on Niccolò Machiavelli, *The Prince,* trans. Luigi Ricci, rev. by E. R. P. Vincent, and *The Discourses,* trans. Christian Detmold (New York: Random House, Modern Library Edition, 1940).
4. Aristophanes, *Lysistrata* in *Aristophanes: the Eleven Comedies* (New York: Liveright, 1943).
5. Henry David Thoreau, "On Civil Disobedience," in *Walden and Other Writings of Henry David Thoreau* (New York: Random House, Modern Library Edition, 1937).
6. Karl Marx illuminates the game of "class conflict"; Alexander Hamilton, that of "stake–in–society"; Dostoevski, that of "miracle, mystery, and authority." See, for example, Marx's *The Communist Manifesto;* Hamilton's state papers; and Dostoevski's "Legend of the Grand Inquisitor" (Book V, Chapter 5, *The Brothers Karamozov*). On Dostoevski, see also Neal Riemer, "Some Reflections on the Grand Inquisitor and Modern Democratic Theory," *Ethics 14,* no. 4 (1954–55), pp. 458–470.

CHAPTER 2

1. The quotations in this paragraph and the following are from *Apology, The Republic and Other Works by Plato,* trans. Benjamin Jowett (Garden City, N.Y.: Anchor Books/Doubleday, 1973), pp. 460–484.
2. Madison defined *faction* as a "number of citizens, whether amounting to a majority or minority of the whole, who are united and actuated by some common impulse or passion, or of interest, adverse to the rights of other citizens, or to the permanent and aggregate interests of the community." *The Federalist* (1787–1788) (Cleveland: World, 1961), p. 57.
3. This section draws freely from Neal Riemer's *James Madison: Creating the American Constitution* (Washington, D.C.: Congressional Quarterly Press, 1986). For a fuller exploration of creative breakthroughs, see Riemer, *Creative Breakthroughs in Politics* (Westport, Conn.: Praeger, 1996).

4. Franz L. Neumann, *Behemoth* (New York: Oxford University Press, 1942), p. 30.
5. For the electoral statistics, see Seymour Martin Lipset, *Political Man: The Social Bases of Politics* (1960; reprint, Garden City, N.Y.: Anchor/Doubleday, 1963), p. 139; and Jeremy Noakes and Geoffrey Pridham, eds., *Documents of Nazism, 1919–1945* (London: Jonathan Cape, 1974), p. 126.
6. Neumann, *Behemoth,* p. 30.
7. Lipset, *Political Man,* pp. 148, 144–145, 147, and 138–148. See also David Schoenbaum, *Hitler's Social Revolution* (New York: Doubleday, 1966; reprint, Anchor Books, 1977), and Noakes and Pridham, *Documents of Nazism.*
8. Lipset, *Political Man.*
9. Seymour Martin Lipset, *Revolution and Counterrevolution* (1968; reprint, Garden City, N.Y.: Anchor/Doubleday, 1970), p. 234.
10. Graham T. Allison, *Essence of Decision: Explaining the Cuban Missile Crisis* (Boston: Little, Brown, 1971), p. 193. The following presentation draws generously on Allison's study and also on the account by Arthur M. Schlesinger, Jr., *A Thousand Days: John F. Kennedy in the White House* (1965; reprint, Greenwich, Conn.: Fawcett Crest, 1967).
11. Schlesinger, *A Thousand Days,* pp. 805–806.

CHAPTER 3

1. The word *empirical* may be unfamiliar to some readers. As used here it means that which is based on experience and observation. The concept is explained more fully on pages 41 and 44. The word *behavioral* refers to those *actions,* or forms of *behavior,* that can be observed, described, and measured.
2. The concept of prudence was first treated systematically in Book VI of Aristotle's *Nichomachean Ethics.* The concept figures prominently in the writings of +St. Thomas Aquinas (particularly I–II, Q. 21, A4, 5, 6 of his *Summa Theological*), Edmund Burke, and James Madison. Charles Merriam, an outstanding American political scientist, devoted a section to "Political Prudence" in his *New Aspects of Political Science* (Chicago: University of Chicago Press, 1939), pp. 163–180. Merriam, p. 163, defined political prudence as follows: "By political prudence I mean the conclusions of experience and reflection regarding the problems of politics—wisdom that does not reach the state of science, yet has its own significance." Leo Strauss was well aware of the concept; see his *What Is Political*

Philosophy? (Glencoe, Ill.: Free Press, 1959), especially pp. 81–82 and 86–87. The concept is also treated prominently in Neal Riemer's *The Revival of Democratic Theory* (New York: Appleton-Century-Crofts, 1962).

3. See, for example, David Braybrooke, *Meeting Needs* (Princeton, N.J.: Princeton University Press, 1987); James Buchanan, *The Economics of Politics* (Lancing, West Sussex: Institute of Economic Affairs, 1978); and Kenneth D. Wald, *Religion and Politics in the United States* (Washington, D.C.: CQ Press, 3rd ed., 1996).

4. For an illustrative reassessment of welfare policy in the United States (as it bears on equality, poverty, and unemployment), see the excellent study of David Raphael Riemer, *The Prisoners of Welfare: Liberating America's Poor from Unemployment and Low Wages* (New York: Praeger, 1988).

5. Karl Deutsch, *The Nerves of Government* (New York: Free Press, 1963), p. 178. For a provocative, sharply adverse critique of American political science's obsession with a narrow view of science and its attachment to, yet ironic neglect of, classic wisdom and democratic ideals, see David M. Ricci, *The Tragedy of Political Science: Politics, Scholarship, and Democracy.* (New Haven, Conn.: Yale University Press, 1984). For a more balanced view, see Gabriel Almond, "Separate Tables: Schools and Sects in Political Science," *PS: Political Science and Politics 21,* no. 4 (Fall 1988), 838–842. Almond contends that mainstream "political science is open to all methods that illuminate the world of politics and public policy."

6. Leo Strauss, "What Is Political Philosophy?" *Journal of Politics 19,* no. 3 (1957): 343–368, and especially 344–345.

7. *Modern Political Analysis* (Englewood Cliffs, N.J.: Prentice–Hall, 1964), pp. 100–107, especially 101.

8. John H. Hallowell, "Political Science Today," *Social Order 11,* no. 2 (1961), 109, 113, 120, 121.

9. Alfred Cobban, "The Decline of Political Theory," *Political Science Quarterly 68,* no. 3 (1963), 321–337, especially 330, 335.

10. David Easton, *A Framework for Political Analysis* (Englewood Cliffs, N.J.: Prentice– Hall, 1965), especially pp. 7, 8, 13ff.

11. Albert Somit and Joseph Tanenhaus, *The Development of American Political Science* (Boston: Allyn & Bacon, 1967), especially pp. 177–179.

12. Christian Bay, "Politics and Pseudopolitics: A Critical Evaluation of Some Behavioral Literature," *American Political Science Review 59,* no. 1 (1965), pp. 39–51, and especially pp. 41 and 51; *The Structure of Freedom* (Stanford: Stanford University Press, 1958).

13. Hans J. Morgenthau, *The Decline of Democratic Politics,* vol. 1 of *Politics in the Twentieth Century* (Chicago: University of Chicago Press, 1962), especially pp. 41, 43, 45, 48, 49.

14. See, again, David Raphael Riemer, *The Prisoners of Welfare.*

15. Neal Riemer, *The Revival of Democratic Theory,* especially pp. 60–65. On prudence and political judgment, see also the fine book by Ronald Beiner, *Political Judgment* (Chicago: University of Chicago Press, 1983).

16. Bertrand de Jouvenal, "Political Science and Prevision," *American Political Science Review 59,* no. 1 (1965), 29–38, especially p. 29.

17. Harold Lasswell, *The Future of Political Science* (New York: Atherton Press, 1963), especially pp. 1, 17–26.

18. David Easton, "The New Revolution in Political Science," *American Political Science Review 63,* no. 4 (1969), 1051–1061, especially p. 1052.

19. See Neal Riemer, *The Future of the Democratic Revolution: Toward a More Prophetic Politics* (New York: Praeger, 1984), especially pp. 236–237; "Political Health as an Integrating Model in Political Systems Theory," *Systems Research 3,* no. 2 (1986): 85–88.

CHAPTER 4

1. Elton Atwater, William Butz, Kent Forster, and Neal Riemer, *World Affairs: Problems and Prospects* (New York: Appleton-Century-Crofts, 1958), pp. 89–90.

2. This discussion follows Abraham Maslow's analysis in *Motivation and Personality* (New York: Harper, 1970).

3. Sir Arthur Keith, *Evolution and Ethics* (New York: Putnam, 1946); quoted in Atwater et al., *World Affairs,* pp. 112–113.

4. Konrad Lorenz, *On Aggression* (New York: Harcourt, Brace and World, 1966); Robert Ardrey, *The Territorial Imperative* (New York: Dell, 1966).

5. Leonard Berkowitz, *Aggression in Social Psychological Analysis* (New York: McGraw-Hill, 1962).

6. Julian S. Huxley, *On Living in a Revolution* (New York: Harper, 1944); quoted in Atwater et al., *World Affairs,* p. 117.

7. Quoted in Atwater et al., p. 114.

8. Quoted in Atwater et al., p. 117.

9. This paragraph and the following two draw on Erich Fromm, *The Anatomy of Human Destructiveness* (New York: Holt, Rinhart & Winston, 1973), pp. 230–232.

10. Gabriel A. Almond and Sidney Verba, *The Civic Culture: Political Attitudes and Democracy in Five Nations* (Boston: Little, Brown, 1965), pp. 312–313.

11. David P. Conradt, "Changing German Political Culture," in *The Civic Culture Revisited,* eds. Gabriel A. Almond and Sidney Verba (Boston: Little, Brown, 1980), pp. 246, 256, 264–265.

CHAPTER 5

1. Plato, *The Republic,* trans. Benjamin Jowett (Garden City, N.Y.: Anchor/Doubleday, 1973).

2. Aristotle, *Politics,* trans. Benjamin Jowett (New York: Random House, Modern Library Edition, 1943), 0pp. 168–169.

3. St. Augustine, *The City of God,* in *Readings in Political Philosophy,* ed. Francis W. Coker (New York: Macmillan, 1946), p. 159.

4. Herbert A. Deane, *The Political and Social Ideas of St. Augustine* (New York: Columbia University Press, 1963), p. 15.

5. St. Thomas Aquinas, *Commentary on the Nicomachean Ethics,* in *Theories of the Political System,* William T. Bluhm (Englewood Cliffs, N.J.: Prentice-Hall, 1965), p. 196.

6. Aquinas, *Summa Theologica* (1265–1273), I-II, 90.4, in *The Basic Writings of St. Thomas Aquinas*, ed. Anton C. Pegis (New York: Random House, 1945), II, p. 747.

7. Niccolò Machiavelli, *Of the Rule of Princes* (1266), quoted in *Readings in Political Philosophy*, ed. Francis W. Coker (New York: Macmillan, 1946), p. 200.

8. See Machiavelli, *The Discourses*, in *The Prince and the Discourses* (New York: Random House, Modern Library Edition, 1940).

9. Thomas Hobbes, *Leviathan* (New York: Dutton, 1943), pp. 64–65.

10. John Locke, *Second Treatise on Civil Government* (1690). A good critical edition is Peter Laslett's *John Locke: Two Treatises of Government* (New York: Cambridge University Press, 1960).

11. Jean Jacques Rousseau, The Social Contract (1762) (New York: Dutton, 1946), p. 1.

12. See, for example, Edmund Burke, *Reform of Representation in the House of Commons* (1782). See also *Reflections on the Revolution in France* (1790) in *Works,* vol. III (Boston: Little, Brown, 1869); *An Appeal from the New to the Old Whigs* (1791); and *On Conciliation with the American Colonies* (1775), in *Orations and Essays* (New York: Appleton, 1900).

13. Burke, *Reflections on the Revolution in France*, p. 359.

14. John Stuart Mill, *Utilitarianism* (New York: Liberal Arts Press, 1957), p. 10.

15. Mill, *Considerations on Representative Government* (1861), in *On Liberty, Representative Government, the Subjection of Women* (London: Oxford University Press, 1946), p. 198.

16. Mill, *On Liberty*, p. 65.

17. Mill, *The Subjection of Women*, in *On Liberty*, p. 427.

18. See Karl Marx, *The Marx-Engels Reader*, ed., Robert C. Tucker (New York: Norton, 1971). See especially *Contributions to the Critique of Hegel's Philosophy of Right* (1844); *Economic and Philosophic Manuscripts* (1944); *Manifesto of the Communist Party* (1848); *Critique of the Gotha Program* (1875); and *The Civil War in France* (1871).

19. For an analysis and appraisal by the senior author of this book, see Neal Riemer, *Karl Marx and Prophetic Politics* (New York: Praeger, 1987).

20. See the bibliography and suggested additional reading for illustrations of the richness and variety of contemporary political philosophy.

21. William T. Bluhm, *Theories of the Political System* (Englewood Cliffs, N.J.: Prentice-Hall, 1965), Preface, vi.

22. Bluhm, *Theories of the Political System*, p. 482.

23. For an analysis and critique of three futurists, see Neal Riemer, "Prophetic Politics: On the Political Philosophy of Stavrianos, Ferkiss and Falk," *Alternative Futures 2*, no. 4 (Fall 1979): 66–82.

CHAPTER 6

1. In this and succeeding sections the senior author has drawn from his work in the field of democratic theory: "Democracy: Merits and Prospects," in Elton Atwater, William Butz, Kent Forster, and Neal Riemer, *World Affairs: Problems and Prospects* (New York: Appleton-

Century-Crofts, 1958); and Riemer, *The Revival of Democratic Theory* (New York: Appleton-Century-Crofts, 1962), *The Democratic Experiment* (Princeton, N.J.: Van Nostrand, 1967), *The Future of the Democratic Revolution: Toward a More Prophetic Politics* (New York: Praeger, 1984), *James Madison: Creating the American Constitution* (Washington, D.C.: Congressional Quarterly Press, 1986), Chapters 10 and 12 of *Let Justice Roll: Prophetic Challenges in Religion, Politics, and Society* (Lanham, Md.: Rowman and Littlefield, 1996), and *Creative Breakthroughs in Politics* (Westport, Conn.: Praeger, 1996).

2. See Neal Riemer, ed., *The Representative: Trustee? Delegate? Partisan? Politico?* (Boston: Heath, 1967).

3. See William S. Maddox and Stuart A. Lilie, *Beyond Liberal and Conservative: Reassessing the Political Spectrum* (Washington, D.C.: Cato Institute, 1984, 1989). For Ted Lowi's classification of traditions of American political thought, see Table 1.3 in his *The End of the Republican Era* (Norman: University of Oklahoma Press, 1995), p. 19. Lowi uses "Left," "Liberal," and "Right" and "Old" in his classification. Thus he identifies "Old Socialism," "Old Liberalism," and "Old Conservatism, " and "Social Democracy," "New Liberalism," and "New Conservatism."

4. As they move left, radicals in the liberal democratic tradition merge into democratic socialism. See, for example, Arnold S. Kaufman, *The Radical Liberal* (New York: Atherton, 1968); Michael Harrington, *Toward a Democratic Left: A Radical Program for a New Majority* (New York: Simon & Schuster, 1967); and Michael Parenti, *Democracy for the Few*, 6th ed. (New York: St. Martin's Press, 1994).

5. Authentic American reactionaries are rare and usually inarticulate in print. They have, however, attracted considerable attention as the "radical right." See Seymour Martin Lipset, *The Politics of Unreason: Rightwing Extremism in America, 1790–1970* (New York: Harper & Row, 1970).

6. For a recent assessment, see Riemer, *The Future of the Democratic Revolution*, Chapter 4, "Liberal Democratic Politics: The Conservative Politics of Pluralistic Balance."

CHAPTER 7

1. For help in understanding the remarkable changes that have occurred in the communist world, see Zbigniew Brzezinski, *The Grand Failure: The Birth and Death of Communism in the Twentieth Century* (New York: Scribner's, 1989), and Adam B. Ulam, *The Communists: The Story of Power and Lost Illusion: 1948–1991* (New York: Scribner's, 1992). See also Neal Riemer, *Karl Marx and Prophetic Politics* (New York: Praeger, 1987).

2. V. I. Lenin, "The Three Sources and Three Component Parts of Marxism" (1913), in *The Lenin Anthology*, ed. Robert C. Tucker (New York: Norton, 1975), pp. 640–644.

3. For a contemporary appraisal, see Riemer, *Karl Marx and Prophetic Politics*. On the deep roots of Marxism, see also Leszek Kolakowski, *The Founders*, vol. 1 of *Main Currents of Marxism* (New York: Oxford

University Press, pp. 408–416. Kolakowski emphasizes a romantic motif, a Faustian-Promethean motif, and a rationalistic, determinist Enlightenment motif.

4. Karl Marx, "Theses on Feuerbach" (1845), *The Marx-Engels Reader*, 2nd ed., ed. Robert C. Tucker (New York: Norton, 1978), p. 145. For the emphasis on action, Marx may also have been indebted to Moses Hess, a German socialist, author, and early journalistic friend, who converted Friedrich Engels (Marx's good friend and frequent collaborator) to communism. On Hess's influence on Marx, see Kolakowski, *The Founders*, pp. 108–110.

5. John Plamenatz, *German Marxism and Russian Communism* (London: Longman's, 1954), p. 308. On Marx and the utopian tradition, see also Frank E. Manuel and Fritzie P. Manuel, *Utopian Thought in the Western World* (Cambridge, Mass.: Belknap Press, Harvard University Press, 1979).

6. See *The Lenin Anthology*, ed. Robert C. Tucker; and also Alfred G. Meyer, *Leninism* (New York Praeger, 1962).

7. The February date is the date according to the Russian calendar, which, until changed, was about a half month behind the Western calendar.

8. Stalin used the words "absolutely necessary" in conversation with Winston Churchill. See Winston Churchill, *The Hinge of Fate* (Boston: Houghton Mifflin, 1950), pp. 498–499.

9. On Mao, see Stuart R. Schram, *The Thought of Mao Tse-tung* (Cambridge: Cambridge University Press, 1989); John Bryan Starr, *Continuing the Revolution: The Political Thought of Mao* (Princeton, N.J.: Princeton University Press, 1979); and Ross Terrill, *China in Our Time* (New York: Simon & Schuster, 1992).

10. James R. Townsend and Brantly Womack, *Politics in China* (Boston: Little Brown, 1986).

11. Karl Marx, *Critique of the Gotha Program*, in *The Marx-Engels Reader*, 2nd ed., ed. Robert C. Tucker (New York: Norton, 1978), p. 531.

12. Marx, "The German Ideology: Part I" (1845–1846), in *The Marx-Engels Reader*, 2nd ed., ed. Robert C. Tucker (New York: Norton, 1978), pp. 155–156.

13. Marx and Engels, *Manifesto of the Communist Party* (1848), in *The Marx-Engels Reader*, 2nd ed., ed. Robert C. Tucker (New York: Norton, 1978), pp. 473–474. For the definitions of *bourgeoisie* and *proleteriat*, see the footnote added by Engels in 1888, in Tucker, *The Marx-Engels Reader*, p. 473.

14. V.I. Lenin, *Imperialism: The Highest Stage of Capitalism* (1917), in *The Lenin Anthology*, ed. Robert C. Tucker (New York: Norton, 1975), p. 244.

15. Marx, "The Possibility of Non-Violent Revolution" (1872), in *The Marx-Engels Reader*, 2nd ed., ed. Robert C. Tucker (New York: Norton, 1978), p. 523.

16. Lenin, *The State and Revolution* (1917), in *The Lenin Anthology*, ed. Robert C. Tucker (New York: Norton, 1975).

17. Joseph Stalin, *Problems of Leninism* (Moscow: Foreign Languages Publishing Company, 1940). See also Leszek Kolakowski, *Main Currents of Marxism*, vol. 3: *The Breakdown* (New York: Oxford University Press, 1978).

18. On Mao, see Stuart R. Schram, *The Thought of Mao Tse-tung* (Cambridge: Cambridge University Press, 1989); John Bryan Starr, *Continuing the Revolution: The Political Thought of Mao* (Princeton, N.J.: Princeton University Press, 1979).

19. Mikhail Gorbachev, *Perestroika: New Thinking for Our Country and the World*. New, updated ed. (New York: Harper & Row, 1988).

20. See Ross Terrill, *China in Our Time* (New York: Simon & Schuster, 1992), and (for the quotation) Roderick MacFarquhar, "Deng's Last Campaign," *The New York Review of Books 39*, no. 21 (December 17, 1992), pp. 22ff.

21. On Eurocommunism, see the work of a Spanish communist leader, Santiago Carrillo, *Eurocommunism and the State* (Westport, Conn.: Hill, 1978).

22. Some defenders of communism may hold that it is a liberating philosophy but that the Soviet Union did not practice communism. This raises the interesting question of the relation of Marx's Marxism to the Soviet Union. Kolakowski, *The Breakdown*, p. 226, writes: "It would be absurd to maintain that Marxism was, so to speak, the efficient cause of present-day Communism; on the other hand, Communism is not a mere 'degeneration' of Marxism but a possible interpretation of it, and even a well-founded one, though primitive and partial in some respects."

23. For a model of the just revolution, and its application to the theory of Marx, see Riemer, *Karl Marx and Prophetic Politics*, pp. 109–120.

24. See Richard N. Hunt, *The Political Ideas of Marx and Engels: II: Classical Marxism* (Pittsburgh: University of Pittsburgh Press, 1984), especially Chapter 7, "The Classless Society as a Polity." See also Frank Cunningham, *Democratic Theory and Socialism* (Cambridge: Cambridge University Press, 1987).

CHAPTER 8

1. Quoted in George H. Sabine, *A History of Political Theory* (New York: Holt, 1937), p. 483.

2. Frank E. Manuel, *The New World of Henri Saint-Simon* (Notre Dame, Ind.: University of Notre Dame Press, 1963), p. 5. On utopian thought in general, see the splendid study by Frank E. Manuel and Fritzie P. Manuel, *Utopian Thought in the Western World* (Cambridge, Mass.: Belknap Press, Harvard University Press, 1979).

3. See Robert Owen's *New View of Society* (1813), quoted in George Lichtheim, *The Origins of Socialism* (New York: Praeger, 1969), p. 114.

4. Lichtheim, *The Origins of Socialism*, p. 34.

5. This account draws on Peter Gay, *The Dilemma of Democratic Socialism: Eduard Bernstein's Challenge to Marx* (New York: Collier-Macmillan, 1962). See also Eduard Bernstein, *Evolutionary Socialism* (New York: Schocken, 1961), and Leszek Kolakowski's account of "Bernstein and Revisionism," in *The Breakdown*, vol. III of *Main Currents of Marxism* (New York: Oxford University Press, 1981).

6. See Donald Drew Egbert and Stow Persons, eds., *Socialism and American Life*, 2 vols. (Princeton, N.J.:

Princeton University Press, 1952), and Bernard K. Johnpoll, *The Impossible Dream: The Rise and Demise of the American Left* (Westport, Conn.: Greenwood Press, 1981).

CHAPTER 9

1. Paul M. Hayes, *Fascism* (New York: Free Press, 1973),p. 23. In our presentation of Nazi roots we follow, with modifications, Hayes's presentation of eight fascist ideas, pp. 19 and 2-118. See also Walter Laqueur, *Fascism: Past, Present, and Future* (New York: Oxford University Press, 1996).

2. For a keen, brief analysis of Bodin's definition of sovereignty ("supreme power over citizens and subjects, unrestrained by law"), see George H. Sabine, *A History of Political Theory* (New York: Holt, 1937), pp. 405–411. See also Jean Bodin, *The Six Bookes of a Commonweale*, trans. and ed. Richard Knolles, with an introduction by Douglas McRae (Cambridge, Mass.: Harvard University Press, 1962).

3. Hayes, *Fascism*, p. 66.

4. For the record of Nazi imperialism, war, and destruction, see Karl D. Bracher, *The German Dictatorship* (New York: Praeger, 1970); William L. Shirer, *The Rise and Fall of the Third Reich* (New York: Simon & Schuster, 1960); Lucy S. Dawidowicz, *The War Against the Jews, 1933–1945* (New York: Holt, Rinehart & Winston, 1975); and Daniel J. Goldhagen, *Hitler's Willing Executioners: Ordinary Germans and the Holocaust* (New York: Knopf, 1996).

5. See Paul E. Sigmund, Jr., ed. *The Ideologies of Developing Nations*, 2nd rev. ed. (New York: Praeger, 1972); Neal Riemer, "Democratic Theory and the New States: The Dilemma of Transition," *Bucknell Review 13*, no. 1 (1965), 1–16; Christopher Clapham, *Third World Politics: An Introduction* (Madison: University of Wisconsin Press, 1985); Myron Weiner and Samuel Huntington, eds., *Understanding Political Development* (Boston: Little, Brown, 1987), especially Huntington's chapter on "The Goals of Development"; Gabriel A. Almond, "The Development of Political Development," in *A Discipline Divided: Schools and Sects in Political Science* (Newbury Park, Calif.: Sage, 1990); William McCord with Arline McCord, *Paths in Progress: Bread and Freedom in Developing Societies* (New York: Norton, 1989); and Rupert Emerson, *From Empire to Nation* (Cambridge, Mass.: Harvard University Press, 1962). The relationship of liberation theology to the struggle for freedom will be more fully considered in Chapter 17.

6. Emerson, *From Empire to Nation*, p. 215.

7. Erich Fromm, *The Anatomy of Human Destructiveness* (New York: Holt, Rinehart & Winston, 1973), pp. 365–366.

8. Victor C. Ferkiss, *The Future of Technological Civilization* (New York: Barziller, 1974), p. 129.

9. See Richard A. Falk, *This Endangered Planet: Prospects and Proposals for Human Survival* (New York: Random House, 1971) and *A Study of Future Worlds* (New York: Free Press, 1975); Richard A. Falk, Robert C.

Johansen, and Samuel S. Kim, *The Constitutional Foundations of World Peace* (Albany: State University of New York Press, 1993); and Harold and Margaret Sprout, *Toward a Politics of the Planet Earth* (New York: Van Nostrand, 1971).

10. L.S. Stavrianos, *The Promise of the Coming Dark Age* (San Francisco: Freeman, 1976).

11. See, for example, Mark A. Lutz and Kenneth Lux, *The Challenge of Humanistic Economics* (Menlo Park, Calif.: Benjamin/Cummings, 1979), and *Humanistic Economics: The New Challenge* (New York: Bookstrap Press, 1988).

12. See, for example, William Ophuls, *Ecology and the Politics of Scarcity: Prologue to a Political Theory of the Steady State* (San Francisco: Freeman, 1977).

CHAPTER 10

1. Jacob Bronowski, *The Common Sense of Science* (New York: Vintage Books, 1960), pp. 130, 100.

2. Irving M. Copi, *Introduction to Logic*, 2nd ed. (New York: Macmillan, 1961), p. 418.

3. Karl R. Popper, *The Logic of Scientific Discovery* (London: Hutchinson, 1968), p. 281.

4. See Kneale's perceptive articles on "Science," and "Scientific Method" in the *Encyclopaedia Britannica*, 14th ed., 1966.

5. See Abraham Kaplan, *The Conduct of Inquiry: Methodology for Behavioral Science* (San Francisco: Chandler, 1964), pp. 1, 27. See also the corollary principle of *autonomy of the conceptual base* (p. 79): "A scientist *may* use whatever concepts he *can* use, whatever ones he finds useful in fact." See, too, the corresponding principle of *autonomy of the theoretical base* (p. 322): "Negatively put, it is that no type of theory defined by general attributes for form or content is in itself more scientific, methodologically more pure. The scientist *may* use whatever theories he *can* use."

6. Popper, *The Logic of Scientific Discovery*, p. 280.

7. Popper, *The Logic of Scientific Discovery*, p. 11.

8. David Easton, *The Political System: An Inquiry Into the State of Political Science* (New York: Knopf, 1953), pp. 66–78.

9. Kaplan, *The Conduct of Inquiry*, p. 308.

10. Kaplan, *The Conduct of Inquiry*, p. 11.

CHAPTER 11

1. J. David Singer, "The Level-of-Analysis Problem in International Relations," in *The International System: Theoretical Essays*, eds. Klaus Knorr and Sidney Verba (Princeton, N.J.: Princeton University Press, 1961), pp. 77–92.

2. See Hans J. Morgenthau, *Politics Among Nations*, 2nd ed. (New York: Knopf, 1954). See also Charles A. Beard, *The Idea of National Interest* (Chicago: Quadrangle Books, 1966). Beard writes that "it may be said that national interest—its maintenance, advancement, and defense by the various means and instrumentalities of political power—is the prime consideration of diplomacy" (p. 21).

3. For clarification of the concept of public interest, see Richard E. Flathman, *The Public Interest: An Essay Concerning the Normative Discourse of Politics* (New York: Wiley, 1966).

4. Robert Dahl, *Polyarchy: Participation and Opposition* (New Haven, Conn.: Yale University Press, 1971).

5. On the CIA, for example, see Senate Committee on Foreign Relations, *CIA Foreign and Domestic Activities*, 94th Congress, 1st session (Washington D.C.: Government Printing Office, 1974). On Chile, see Robert C. Johansen, *The National Interest and the Human Interest: An Analysis of U.S. Foreign Policy* (Princeton, N.J.: Princeton University Press, 1980), Chapter 4, "The United States and Human Rights in Chile," pp. 196–281; the quotation in the text is from page 256. On the FBI, see Senate Select Subcommittee to Study Government Operations with Respect to Intelligence, *Intelligence Activities and the Rights of Americans*, Book II, 94th Congress, 2nd session (Washington, D.C.: Government Printing Office, 1976).

6. Ronald Inglehart, *The Silent Revolution: Changing Values and Political Styles among Western Publics* (Princeton, N.J.: Princeton University Press, 1977), pp. 22–23. For Maslow's own position, see Abraham Maslow, *Toward a Psychology of Being* (Princeton: N.J.: Van Nostrand, 1962), and *Motivation and Personality*, 2nd ed. (New York: Harper & Row, 1970)

7. See Hadley Cantril, *The Pattern of Human Concerns* (New Brunswick, N.J.: Rutgers University Press, 1965), pp. 315–321.

8. Cantril, *The Pattern of Human Concerns*, pp. 205, 208, 211.

9. This language is found in Ronald Inglehart, "The Nature of Value Change in Post-Industrial Societies," in *Politics and the Future of Industrial Societies*, ed. Leon N. Lindberg (New York: David McKay, 1976), pp. 38, 84-85.

10. Ronald Inglehart, *Culture Shift in Advanced Industrial Societies* (Princeton, N.J.: Princeton University Press, 1990), p. 141.

11. Cantril, *The Pattern of Human Concerns*, pp. 286–297.

12. Samuel A. Stouffer, *Communism, Conformity, and Civil Liberties* (Gloucester, Mass.: Peter Smith, 1963)

13. Cantril, *The Pattern of Human Concerns*, pp. 286–290.

14. Cantril, *The Pattern of Human Concerns*, p. 295.

15. Cantril, *The Pattern of Human Concerns*, p. 297.

16. On interest groups, see Philip Mundo, *Interest Groups: Cases and Characteristics* (Chicago: Nelson-Hall Publishers, 1992). Also see Arthur F. Bentley, *The Process of Government* (1908; reprint, Cambridge, Mass.: Harvard University Press, 1967); David B. Truman, *The Governmental Process* (New York: Knopf, 1951); and H. Gordon Skilling and Franklyn Griffiths, eds., *Interest Groups in Soviet Politics* (Princeton, N.J.: Princeton University Press, 1971).

17. Skilling and Griffiths, *Interest Groups in Soviet Politics*, p. 383.

18. See Gabriel A. Almond and G. Bingham Powell, Jr., eds. *Comparative Politics Today*, 2nd ed. (Boston: Little, Brown, 1980), pp. 46, 48, and 49.

CHAPTER 12

1. Nathan Keyfitz. "The Asian Road to Democracy," in *Comparative Politics: Notes and Readings*, 7th ed., eds. Roy C. Macridis and Bernard B. Brown (Pacific Grove, Calif.: Brooks/Cole, 1990), pp. 111–117.

2. Richard Sklar, "Democracy in Africa," in *Comparative Politics: Notes and Readings*, 7th ed., eds. Roy C. Macridis and Bernard B. Brown (Pacific Grove, Calif.: Brooks/Cole, 1990), pp. 101–111.

3. Sklar, "Democracy in Africa," p. 107.

4. Keyfitz, "The Asian Road to Democracy," p. 113.

5. Henry Steele Commager, *Majority Rule and Minority Rights* (New York: Oxford University Press, 1943), pp. 80–81.

6. Robert Dahl, *A Preface to Democratic Theory* (Chicago: University of Chicago Press, 1956), pp. 124, 128, 132, 133.

7. *New York Times*, 13 January 1981, Sec. A, p. 10.

8. Richard Rose, "Politics in England," in *Comparative Politics Today: A World View*, eds. Gabriel A. Almond and G. Bingham Powell, Jr. (Boston: Little, Brown, 1980), p. 177.

9. Samuel H. Beer, "The Modernization of British Politics," in *Patterns of Government*, 3rd ed., Samuel H. Beer et al. (New York: Random House, 1973), p. 276.

10 Robert G. Wesson, *Modern Governments: Three Worlds of Politics* (Englewood Cliffs, N.J.: Prentice-Hall, 1981), p. 277.

11. Commission on Freedom of the Press, Robert Hutchins, Chairman, *A Free and Responsible Press* (Chicago: University of Chicago Press, 1947).

12. See Stephen Hess, *International News and Foreign Correspondents* (Washington, D.C.: Brookings, 1996); Johanna Neumann, *Lights Camera, War: Is Media Technology Driving International Politics?* (New York: St. Martin's, 1966); and Robert I. Rotberg and Thomas G. Weiss, eds., *From Massacres to Genocide: The Media, Public Policy and Humanitarian Crises* (Washington, D.C.: Brookings, 1966).

13. The Pentagon Papers were a secret history commissioned by Secretary of Defense Robert McNamara during the Vietnam war. They were extremely candid in telling the story of how the United States became involved in the war, including distortions and lies told to the American public to justify various Vietnam policies. In 1972, Daniel Ellsberg, a Defense Department employee who had helped write the papers, secretly began feeding them to the *New York Times*.

CHAPTER 13

1. See Harold and Margaret Sprout, "The Dilemma of Rising Demands and Insufficient Resources," *World Politics 20*, no. 4 (1968): 660–693. See also the President's Commission for a National Agenda for the 1980s, which declared that America cannot achieve all of its goals simultaneously and should "face honestly the tradeoffs that inevitably occur when limited resources confront unlimited claims," *New York Times*, 17 January 1981, Sec. 1, p. 1.

2. Robert G. Wesson, *Modern Governments: Three Worlds of Politics*, 2nd ed. (Englewood Cliffs, N.J.: Prentice-Hall, 1985), Chapter 10.

CHAPTER 14

1. Quoted in Elton Atwater, William Butz, Kent Forster, and Neal Riemer, *World Affairs: Problems and Prospects* (New York: Appleton-Century-Crofts, 1958), p. 468. For the full text, see United States Statutes, vol. 63, p. 2241.
2. Atwater et al., *World Affairs*, pp. 467–468.
3. The alleged decline of American power is the subject of a virtual explosion of articles and books. Several of the more important include Paul M. Kennedy, *The Rise and Fall of the Great Powers: Economic Change and Military Conflict from 1500 to 2000* (New York: Random House, 1987); Joseph Nye, Jr., *Bound to Lead: The Changing Nature of American Power* (New York: Basic Books, 1990); David Calleo, *Beyond Hegemony: The Future of the Western Alliance* (New York: Basic Books, 1987); and Clyde V. Prestowitz, *Trading Places: How We Allowed Japan to Take the Lead* (New York: Basic Books, 1988).
4. These principles were first articulated in a Sino-Indian agreement on Tibet on April 29, 1954. See Laurence W. Martin, ed., *Neutralism and Nonalignment: The New States in World Affairs* (New York: Praeger, 1962), p. xv. They were also adopted by the Soviet Union: see the Joint Statement of N. A. Bulganin, N. S. Khrushchev, and J. Nehru, December 13, 1955, in *Report to the Supreme Soviet on the Visit to India, Burma, and Afghanistan* (New York: New Century Publishers, 1956).
5. The Charter of the United Nations. Full texts of the charter can usually be found in the appendixes of most standard textbooks on international organizations or in encyclopedias.
6. Here we follow the excellent analysis in Inis Claude, Jr., *Swords into Plowshares: The Problems and Progress of International Organizations*, 4th ed. (New York: Random House, 1984), pp. 236–365. We draw, too, on Claude's equally keen analysis in *Power and International Relations* (New York: Random House, 1962). The analysis has been historically updated with the help of fine texts such as A. Leroy Bennett, *International Organizations: Principles and Issues*, 6th ed. (Englewood Cliffs, N.J.: Prentice-Hall, 1994).
7. Claude, *Swords into Plowshares*, p. 348.
8. Two of the classic works on functionalism are by David Mitrany, *A Working Peace System* (Chicago: Quadrangle Books, 1966), and Ernst B. Haas, *Beyond the Nation State* (Stanford, Calif.: Stanford University Press, 1964). Here, and in the following section, we have, with appropriate updates, drawn on Neal Riemer's Chapter 14 ("A New World Organization: Man's Eventual Goal?") and Elton Atwater's Chapter 13 ("Can We Count on the United Nations?") in Atwater et al., *World Affairs*, pp. 559–598, 508–558.
9. Dennis Swann, "Europe on the Move to 1992," *Harvard International Review* (Summer 1989), p. 11.

10. For our definition we draw on three sources: Stephen D. Krasner, ed., *International Regimes* (Ithaca, N.Y.: Cornell University Press, 1983); Robert O. Keohane, *International Institutions and State Power* (Boulder, Colo.: Westview Press, 1989); and Barry B. Hughes, *Continuity and Change in World Politics: The Clash of Perspectives* (Englewood Cliffs, N.J.: Prentice-Hall, 1991).
11. These maxims constitute the chapter titles of Dorothy Fosdick's *Common Sense and World Affairs* (New York: Harcourt Brace, 1955).

CHAPTER 15

1. See Graham T. Allison, *Essence of Decision: Explaining the Cuban Missile Crisis* (Boston: Little, Brown, 1971), p. 144.
2. Allison, *Essence of Decision*, pp. 164–165. On this model see also Roger Hilsman, *Strategic Intelligence and National Decisions* (Glencoe, Ill.: Free Press, 1956).
3. Allison, *Essence of Decision*, p. 162.
4. See the work of Robert Michels, *Political Parties* (1915) (New York: Free Press, 1966), who articulated the concept of an "iron law of oligarchy"; C. Wright Mills, *The Power Elite* (New York: Galaxy, 1959); and (for some of the critical literature) David Spitz, *Patterns of Anti-Democratic Thought* (New York: Macmillan, 1949); Peter Bachrach, *The Theory of Democratic Elitism* (Boston: Little, Brown, 1967); David Ricci, *Community Power and Democratic Theory: The Logic of Political Analysis* (New York: Random House, 1971); and Michael Parenti, *Democracy for the Few* (New York: St. Martin's Press, 1994).
5. Thomas R. Dye and L. Harmon Zeigler, *The Irony of Democracy* (Belmont, Calif.: Wadsworth, 1970), p. 6. For a sharper and harsher criticism of elite dominance in American politics, see Parenti, *Democracy for the Few*.
6. For the appeal of Marxist analysis to the clergy in Latin America, see Jose Miguez Bonino, *Doing Theology in a Revolutionary Situation* (Philadelphia: Fortress, 1973).
7. These tendencies are not rigid or fixed for all time and must be examined with care. Clearly, some (or many) business and professional people, college-educated voters, whites, Protestants, small-town and rural residents, and upper-income people vote Democratic. Similarly, some working-class, grade school–educated, African American, Hispanic, Jewish, urban-dwelling, and low-income people vote Republican. Only African Americans maintained their overwhelmingly strong support for the Democratic candidate, Jimmy Carter, in the 1980 election. For the trends over the years 1928–1988, see also Milton C. Cummings and David Wise, *Democracy Under Pressure*, 6th ed. (New York: Harcourt Brace Jovanovich, 1989); for the years 1960–1988, on "Who Likes the Democrats," see James Q. Wilson, *American Government*. 5th ed. (Lexington, Mass.: Heath, 1992), p. 198.
8. Edmund Burke, "Speech to the Electors of Bristol," *The Works of Edmund Burke*, 3rd ed. (Boston: Little, Brown, 1869), II, p. 95. Also quoted in Neal Riemer, ed., *The*

Representative: Trustee? Delegate? Partisan? Politico?
(Lexington, Mass.: Heath, 1967), pp. 2–3.

9. John Fitzgerald Kennedy, *Profiles in Courage* (New
York: Harper, 1956).

10. John C. Wahlke et al., *The Legislative System* (New
York: Wiley, 1962).

11. John W. Kingdon, *Congressmen's Voting Decisions* (New
York: Harper & Row, 1973).

12. James M. Burns, *Congress on Trial* (New York: Harper
& Row, 1949), p. 13.

13. Glenn R. Parker, *Homeward Bound: Explaining Changes
in Congressional Behavior* (Pittsburgh: University of
Pittsburgh Press, 1986), pp. 74–75, 78–79. As
reported in Glenn R. Parker, "Home Styles—Then and
Now," in *Congressional Politics*, ed. Christopher J.
Deering (Chicago: Dorsey Press, 1989), pp. 40–61.

14. Kingdon, *Congressmen's Voting Decisions*, pp. 29-68.

15. Julius Turner, *Party and Constituency: Pressure on
Congress* (Baltimore: Johns Hopkins Press, 1952).

16. George B. Galloway, *Congress at the Crossroads* (New
York: Crowell, 1946), p. 320.

17. Wilder Crane, "The Legislative Struggle in Wisconsin:
Decision Making in the Wisconsin Assembly," doctoral
thesis, 1959; quoted in Neal Riemer, ed., *The
Representative: Trustee? Delegate? Partisan? Politico?*
(Lexington, Mass.: Heath, 1967), p. 84.

18. Frank J. Sorauf, *Party and Representation: Legislative
Politics in Pennsylvania* (New York: Atherton, 1963),
p. 126.

19. Elizabeth Drew, *Politics and Money: The New Road to
Corruption* (New York: Macmillan, 1983). See also
Frank Sorauf, *Money in American Elections* (Glenview,
Ill.: Scott, Foresman, 1988).

20. Wilder Crane, for example, in his doctoral thesis "The
Legislative Struggle in Wisconsin: Decision Making in
the 1957 Wisconsin Assembly," noted that there are
what he called "legislator votes"—votes cast on a
purely personal basis. Also see Riemer, *The Representative*, p. 86. Evidence of idiosyncratic votes calls for an
in-depth study of representatives. Books such as Aage
R. Clausen's *How Congressmen Decide: A Policy Focus*
(New York: St. Martin's, 1973) also throw some light
on such votes.

21. Graham T. Allison, *Essence of Decision: Exploring the
Cuban Missile Crisis* (Boston: Little, Brown, 1971).

22. *Brown v. Board of Education of Topeka, Kansas,* 347 U.S.
483 (1954).

23. Henry Abraham, *The Judicial Process,* 3rd ed. (New
York: Oxford University Press, 1975).

CHAPTER 16

1. Our definition, in contrast to narrower definitions,
includes civil wars and revolutionary wars of national
liberation. Compare Francis A. Beer's definition in
Peace Against War: The Ecology of International Violence
(San Francisco: Freeman, 1981), p. 6: "War . . . is the
presence of direct international violence. . . . Our
definition includes a political condition, the distinction between international and domestic violence. War
is defined to include only violence between states.

Violence within states, between groups or individuals,
is excluded. For example civil war, revolution, class
war, labor war, race war, gang war, range war, street
war are all outside our boundaries unless they are part
of a larger international pattern of violence."

2. Again, our conception of peace speaks to the issue of
civil war and revolutionary wars of national liberation.
In linking war and peace and the nation-state we do
not ignore criminal violence involving individuals or
groups within a nation-state, or troublesome race or
class relations. Such violence is not, however, carried
on in a systematic and organized way by the political
community that has a lawful monopoly on the use of
force and violence, or by those who aspire to achieve
such a monopoly. The fuller meaning of peace will be
addressed in Chapters 17, 18, and 19.

3. It should be noted that while Presidents Clinton and
Yeltsin agreed that the deactivation of warheads called
for by START II would proceed, the legislatures of the
two countries have not, as of 1996, officially ratified
the agreement. In addition, there were some initial
problems with regard to the disposition of strategic
warheads and delivery systems in three of the former
Soviet republics: Kazakhstan, Belorus, and the
Ukraine. Significant progress has been made on this
issue. Most of the nuclear warheads in Kazakhstan and
Belorus have been removed and transported to Russia
for destruction. Compliance with both START I and II
remain a problem with the Ukraine, and intense
negotiation continues in an attempt to resolve the
problem of the nearly 1,600 warheads that remain in
that country as of January 1, 1996. See: James E.
Goodby, Shannon Kile, and Harald Muller, "Nuclear
Arms Control," *SIPRI Yearbook 1995: Armaments,
Disarmament and International Security,* pp. 635–637,
and *Arms Control Today,* November 1995, p. 30.

4. Gwynne Dyer, *War* (New York: Crown, 1985) pp. 201–
202. For complete treatment of the nuclear winter
concept, see Paul Erlich, Carl Sagan, Donald Kennedy,
and Walter Orr Roberts, *The Cold and the Dark: The
World After Nuclear War* (New York: Norton, 1984).

5. Ruth Leger Sivard, *World Military and Social Expenditures 1989* (Washington, D.C.: World Priorities, 1990)
p. 14.

6. As quoted in Dyer, *War,* p. 96.

7. Beer, *Peace Against War,* p. 36; Sivard, *World Military
and Social Expenditures 1989*, p. 22; Kevin Merida,
"Wreckage in Forgotten Lands," *Dallas Morning News,*
6 August 1989, pp. 3M–4M.

8. Total war costs of World War II for the United States
came to $664 billion; of the Korean conflict, $164 billion; of the Vietnam conflict, $352 billion. See Beer,
Peace against War, p. 122. Total war costs take into
account veterans' benefits and interest payments on
war loans. The war costs excluding these items for
World War II, the Korean War, and the Vietnam war
are $288 billion, $54 billion, and $110 billion,
respectively.

9. United Nations Development Program, *Human
Development Report 1996* (New York: Oxford University
Press, 1996), p. 175.

10. *Jane's All The Worlds Aircraft 1995–96* (Surrey, United Kingdom: Jane's Information Group Limited, 1995).

11. Sivard, World *Military and Social Expenditures, 1991*, p. 54 and 1993, p. 56.

12. *Human Development Report 1996*, p. 175.

13. Michael T. Klare, "Deadly Convergence: The Perils of the Arms Trade," *World Policy Journal* (Spring 1989), pp. 146–147.

14. U.S. Arms Control and Disarmament Agency (ACDA), *World Military Expenditures and Arms Transfers, 1992*, p. 15.

15. *SIPRI Yearbook 1989, World Armaments and Disarmament* (New York: Oxford University Press, 1989), pp. 146–147.

16. Theater Ballistic Missile Systems and Capabilities, *Arms Control Today* (March 1996), pp. 29-30.

17. Sivard, *World Military and Social Expenditures, 1989*, p. 7.

18. Robert Holmes, *On War and Morality* (Princeton, N.J.: Princeton University Press, 1989).

19. Holmes, *On War and Morality*, pp. 89–90.

20. Holmes, *On War and Morality*, p. 107.

21. In this section we have relied heavily on Oran R. Young, *The Intermediaries: Third Parties in International Crises* (Princeton, N.J.: Princeton University Press, 1967). We are also especially indebted to our colleague Richard Rhone and his perceptive paper, "What You See Is Not Necessarily What You Get: The Role of the United Nations Security Council" (Jersey City: New Jersey Political Science Association, Spring 1981).

22. Rhone, "What You See," p. 13.

23. This is the language of the U.N. Charter, Chapter VI, Article 33.

24. Rhone, "What You See," especially p. 27, Table 1 on pp. 28–29, and p. 30.

25. For a full analysis of this problem, see Douglas W. Simon and Richard S. Rhone, "The United Nations and Conflict Management in the Post–Cold War World," *The Harvard Journal of World Affairs*, Fall 1995.

26. Seyom Brown, *New Forces, Old Forces, and the Future of World Politics* (Glenview, Ill.: Scott, Foresman, 1989), p. 161. For these data Brown cites the Third Survey of the United Nations Center on Transnational Corporations.

27. Jack Egan, "Business Without Borders," *U.S. News and World Report 16* (July 1990), p. 29.

28. Charles W. Kegley, Jr., and Eugene R. Wittkopf, *World Politics: Trend and Transformation*, 5th ed. (New York: St. Martin's, 1995), p. 553.

29. David Mitrany, *A Working Peace System: An Argument for the Functional Development of International Organization*, 4th ed. (London: National Peace Council, 1946). Mitrany's approach, we must emphasize, does not necessarily disagree with other alternatives presented in this chapter.

30. Mitrany, *A Working Peace System*, p. 14.

31. Mitrany, *A Working Peace System*, p. 9.

32. Mitrany, *A Working Peace System*, pp. 34–35.

33. Perhaps the leading figure in neofunctionalist thinking is Ernst Haas. See *Beyond the Nation-State: Functionalism and International Organization* (Stanford, Calif.:

Stanford University Press, 1964); *The Uniting of Europe: Political, Social, and Economic Forces, 1950–1957* (Stanford, Calif.: Stanford University Press, 1958); *Why We Still Need the United Nations: The Collective Management of International Conflict 1945–1984* (Berkeley: Institute of International Studies, University of California, 1986).

34. Falk is the leading figure in a group of theorists whose work falls under the label World Order Studies. See *A Study of Future Worlds* (New York: Free Press, 1975), *Revitalizing International Law* (Ames: Iowa State University Press, 1989), *The End of World Order* (New York: Holmes and Meier, 1989), and *Explorations at the Edge of Time: The Prospects for World Order* (Philadelphia: Temple University Press, 1992); Falk and Saul Mendlovitz, eds., *Politics and World Order* (San Francisco: Freeman, 1973); Richard A. Falk, Robert C. Johansen, and Samuel S. Kim, *The Constitutional Foundations of World Peace* (Albany: New York Press, 1993); Louis Rene Beres, *People, States, and World Order* (Otsca, Ill.: F. E. Peacock, 1981); and Johan Galtung, ed., *The True Worlds* (New York: Free Press, 1980).

35. All quotations from Falk on the following pages are from *A Study of Future Worlds*.

36. Gene Sharp, *Exploring Nonviolent Alternatives* (Boston: Porter Sargent, 1971). Although we quote here from Sharp's 1971 work, see also Sharp, *Social Power and Political Freedom* (Boston: Porter Sargent, 1980); Robert L. Holmes, *On War and Morality* (Princeton, N.J.: Princeton University Press, 1989); and Mulford Q. Sibley, ed., *The Quiet Battle: Writings on the Theory and Practice on Nonviolent Resistance* (Garden City, N.J.: Doubleday, 1963).

37. Holmes, *On War and Morality*, p. 272.

38. Holmes, *On War and Morality*, p. 274.

39. Sharp, *Exploring Nonviolent Alternatives*, pp. 70–72.

40. The Cold War version of this philosophy was "Better red than dead."

CHAPTER 17

1. This definition comes from Cyrus R. Vance, former Secretary of State, "Law Day Address on Human Rights," in *Human Rights and American Foreign Policy*, eds. Donald P. Kommers and Gilburt D. Loescher (Notre Dame, Ind.: University of Notre Dame Press, 1979), p. 310.

2. For an excellent, balanced, critical account, see Jack Donnelly, *Universal Human Rights in Theory and Practice* (Ithaca, N.Y.: Cornell University Press, 1989).

3. For these estimates of those murdered in Nazi concentration campus and elsewhere, see Lucy S. Dawidowicz, *The War Against the Jews 1933–1945* (New York: Holt, Rinehart & Winston, 1975), p. 149. See also Martin Gilbert, *The Holocaust: A History of the Jews of Europe During the Second World War* (New York: Holt, Rinehart & Winston, 1985), and Daniel J. Goldhagen, *Hitler's Willing Executioners: Ordinary Germans and the Holocaust* (New York: Knopf, 1996).

4. See Vernon Van Dyke, *Human Rights, the United States,*

and World Community (New York: Oxford University Press, 1970), p. 11; and Moshe Y. Sachs, ed., *The United Nations: A Handbook on the United Nations, Its Structure, History, Purposes, Activities and Agencies* (New York: Worldmark Press, 1977), p. 100.

5. U.S. Department of State, *Country Reports on Human Rights Practices for 1989* (Washington, D.C.: Government Printing Office, 1990), p. 792.

6. Van Dyke, *Human Rights,* p. 25.

7. Sachs, *The United Nations,* p. 101; Van Dyke, *Human Rights,* p. 20.

8. A. H. Roberts, "Human Rights: A Global Assessment," in *Human Rights and American Foreign Policy*, eds. Donald P. Kommers and Gilburt D. Loescher (Notre Dame, Ind.: University of Notre Dame Press, 1979), pp. 7–8.

9. R. Bruce McColm, ed., *Freedom in the World: Political Rights and Civil Liberties 1991–1992* (New York: Freedom House, 1992), pp. 572–573. See also Freedom House's 1996 update.

10. See United Nations Development Program, *Human Development Report 1992* (New York: Oxford University Press, 1992), pp. 27, 32. See also the U.N.'s *Human Development Report 1996.*

11. Robertson, *Human Rights,* pp. 25, 23.

12. See Lynne B. Iglitzin, "The Patriarchal Heritage," in eds. Lynne B. Iglitzin and Ruth Ross, *Women in the World: A Comparative Study,* pp. 7–8. For an update, which substantially confirms these conclusions, see United Nations Department of International and Economic Affairs et. al., *The World Women 1970–1990: Trends and Statistics* (New York: United Nations, 1991). See also *The Human Rights Watch Global Report on Women's Human Rights* (New York: Human Rights Watch, 1995).

13. Iglitzin, "The Patriarchal Heritage," p. 14. Here Iglitzin is quoting or citing Carol Andreas, *Sex and Caste in America* (Englewood Cliffs, N.J.: Prentice-Hall, 1971), p. 74.

14. 1977 Declaration of American Women in *The Spirit of Houston: The First National Women's Conference: An Official Report to the President* (Washington, D.C.: National Commission on the Observance of International Women's Year, 1978).

15. Jack Donnelly, *Universal Human Rights,* pp. 250, 252, 258, 264, 269.

16. Cyrus Vance, "Law Day Address on Human Rights," in *Human Rights and Foreign Policy*, eds. Donald P. Kommers and Gilburt D. Loescher, p. 311.

17. "The Universal Declaration and the Covenants provide the norms of what we call 'the global human rights regime,' a system of rules and implementation procedures centered on the United Nations. The principal organs of this regime are the U.N. Commission on Human Rights and the Human Rights Committee." Donnelly, *Universal Human Rights,* p. 206. International regimes are to be understood, writes Donnelly, as "systems of norms and decision-making procedures accepted by states as binding in a particular issue area" (p. 205).

18. As Nigel S. Rodley noted, "Monitoring Human Rights by the U.N. System and Nongovernmental Organizations," in *Human Rights and American Foreign Policy,*

eds. Donald P. Kommers and Gilburt D. Loescher, pp. 152–178.

19. Neal Riemer, *Creative Breakthroughs in Politics* (Lanham, Md.: Rowman and Littlefield, 1996). In addition to the United Nations (a global regime), there are regional human rights regimes—for example, a European regime, an inter-American regime. There are also single-issue human rights regimes that concern themselves with such things as workers' rights, racial discrimination, torture, and women's rights. See Donnelly, *Universal Human Rights,* pp. 213–223.

20. Jo Renee Formicola, *The Catholic Church and Human Rights: Its Role in the Formulation of U.S. Policy 1945–1980* (New York: Garland, 1988).

21. On interpretations of liberation theology, see Jose Miguez Bonino, *Doing Theology in a Revolutionary Situation* (Philadelphia: Fortress Press, 1975); Philip Berryman, *Liberation Theology: The Essential Facts About the Revolutionary Movement in Latin America and Beyond* (New York: Beyer, Stone, 1987); Gustavo Gutierrez, *A Theology of Liberation* (New York: Orbis Books, 1973); John R. Pottenger, *The Political Theory of Liberation Theology: Toward a Reconvergence of Social Values and Social Science* (Albany: State University of New York Press, 1989); Paul E. Sigmund, *Liberation Theology at the Crossroads: Democracy or Revolution* (New York: Oxford University Press, 1990); and John R. Pottenger, "Liberation Theology, Political Realism, and Prophetic Politics," in Neal Riemer, ed., *Let Justice Roll: Prophetic Challenges in Religion, Politics, and Society* (Lanham, Md.: Rowman and Littlefield, 1996).

22. Richard A. Falk, *A Study of Future Worlds* (New York: Free Press, 1975), pp. 23–26. Also see his *Explorations at the Edge of Time: Prospects for World Order* (Philadelphia: Temple University Press, 1992).

23. The demise of the communist Soviet Union and the peaceful replacement of communist regimes in Eastern Europe are points that weaken the argument that left-wing authoritarian regimes can never be peacefully changed.

24. So far, genocide in such places as Cambodia, Rwanda, and Bosnia has gone unpunished by an international criminal tribunal. It remains to be seen whether the international tribunals at the Hague (dealing with Bosnian war crimes and genocide) and in Rwanda (dealing with genocide and war crimes in that distressed country) will establish the credibility of trial and punishment for such crimes.

CHAPTER 18

1. Quoted in Graciela Chichilnisky, "Development Patterns and the International Order," in *Journal of International Affairs 31,* no. 2 (Fall/Winter 1977), p. 275.

2. United Nations Development Program, *Human Development Report 1996* (New York: Oxford University Press, 1996), p. 1.

3. *Human Development Report 1996,* p. 187.

4. *Human Development Report 1996,* p. 20.

5. *Human Development Report 1996,* p. 147.

6. *Human Development Report 1996,* p. 137.

7. *Human Development Report 1996,* p. 22.

8. *Human Development Report 1996*, p. 2.

9. *Human Development Report 1996*, pp. 170–172.

10. This pattern was elaborated on by Kevin Philips in his book *The Politics of Rich and Poor* (New York: Random House, 1990).

11. Donald L. Barlett and James B. Steele, Knight-Rider Tribune News, "America: Who Stole the Dream?" *Daily Record*, 9 September, 1996, p. 1. Data based on analysis of IRS tax return statistics.

12. Willy Brandt, Chairman, Independent Commission on International Development Issues, *North-South: A Program for Survival* (Cambridge, Mass.: MIT Press, 1980), p. 106.

13. Robert S. McNamara, *The Assault on World Poverty* (Baltimore: Johns Hopkins University Press for the World Bank, 1975), p. v.

14. Obviously, in recent years the Chinese leadership has leaned toward party control and order, as the massacre at Tiananmen Square so graphically demonstrated.

15. Our discussion of China has benefited from the keen analysis of James R. Townsend and Brantly Womack, *Politics in China*, 3rd ed. (Boston: Little, Brown, 1986); Gabriel A. Almond and G. Bingham Powell, Jr., *Comparative Politics Today* (Boston: Little, Brown, 1988); and Gordon White, *Riding the Tiger: The Politics of Economic Reform in Post-Mao China* (Stanford, Calif.; Stanford University Press, 1993). Also of great value was the *Europa Yearbook, 1995* (London: Europa Publications, 1995).

16. *Human Development Report 1996*, various statistical tables.

17. *Human Development Report 1996*, p. 186.

18. *Human Development Report 1996*, p. 186.

19. United Nations, *World Development Report 1995* (New York: Oxford University Press, 1995), p. 210.

20. Peter L. Berger, *Pyramids of Sacrifice: Political Ethics and Social Change* (Garden City, N.Y.: Anchor/Doubleday, 1976), p. 155.

21. Ruth Leger Sivard, *World Military and Social Expenditures, 1981* (Leesburg, Va.: World Priorities, 1981), p. 25; Sivard, *World Military Expenditures 1989*, p. 50.

22. Sivard, *World Military and Social Expenditures 1989*, pp. 47–55.

23. The World Bank, *World Development Report 1990: Poverty* (New York: Oxford University Press, 1990), p. 237.

24. Morris David Morris, *Measuring the Condition of the World's Poor* (New York: Pergamon Press, 1979), p. 104.

25. *Human Development Report 1996*, p. 148.

26. This is Richard A. Falk's formulation of a point made by Johan Galtung. See Falk's *A Study of Future Worlds* (New York: Free Press, 1975). All quotations from Falk in the following paragraphs are from that book.

CHAPTER 19

1. Will Steger and Jon Bowermaster, *Saving the Earth: A Citizen's Guide to Environmental Action* (New York: Knopf, 1990), p. 31.

2. Environmental Protection Agency, "CFCs and Stratospheric Ozone" (Office of Public Affairs, Washington, D.C., December 1987, briefing paper).

3. Steger and Bowermaster, *Saving the Earth,* pp. 31–32.

4. Lester Brown, Christopher Flavin, and Hal Kane, *Vital Signs 1996: The Trends That Are Shaping Our Future* (New York: Worldwatch Institute./Norton, 1996), pp. 68–69.

5. Beatrice Lacoste, "Saving Our Ozone Shield," *Our Planet 4,* no. 4, (1992), p. 5.

6. Brown, Flavin, and Kane, *Vital Signs 1996,* p. 65.

7. Steger and Bowermaster, *Saving the Earth,* p. 3.

8. Brown, Flavin, and Kane, *Vital Signs 1996,* p. 15.

9. Robert Morrison, *Global Climate Change* (Washington, D.C.: Congressional Research Service, The Library of Congress, 1989).

10. "The Earth Summit Box Score," *World Wise 3,* no. 2 (1992), p. 1, and "A Summary of the Major Documents Signed at the Earth Summit and the Global Forum," *Environment 34,* no. 8 (October 1992), pp. 12–13.

11. Much of this discussion is based on William Ophuls, *Ecology and the Politics of Scarcity: Prologue to a Political Theory of the Steady State* (San Francisco: Freeman, 1977) and William Ophuls and A. Stephen Boyan, Jr., *Ecology and the Politics of Scarcity Revisited: The Unraveling of the American Dream* (New York: Freeman, 1992).

12. Garrett Hardin, "The Tragedy of the Commons," *Science 162* (13 December, 1968), pp. 1243–1248.

13. Anjali Acharya, "Forest Loss Continues," in Brown, Flavin, and Kane, *Vital Signs 1996,* p. 122.

14. *World Almanac 1996.* (Mahwah, N.J.: Funk & Wagnall, 1996), p. 211.

15. Ophuls, *Ecology and the Politics of Scarcity,* p.11.

16. United Nations. *World Population 1994* (Washington, D.C.: Department of Economic and Social Policy Analysis, Population Division, 1995).

17. These are the six types of resources that Paul and Anne Ehrlich deem essential to the survival of human populations. See their *Population, Resources, Environment* (San Francisco: Freeman, 1972), p. 59. See also Dennis Pirages, *Global Ecopolitics: The New Context for International Relations* (North Scituate, Mass.: Duxbury Press, 1978), especially pp. 14-23.

18. Steger and Bowermaster, *Saving the Earth,* p. 249.

19. Lester Brown, "Reexamining the World Food Prospect," Worldwatch Institute Report on Progress Toward a Sustainable Society, *State of the World 1989* (New York: Norton, 1989) pp. 43–44; "A New Era Unfolds," State *of the World 1993* (New York: Norton, 1993), pp. 11-12; and "World Grain Area Drops," in Brown, Flavin, and Kane, *Vital Signs 1996,* p. 42.

20. Ophuls, *Ecology and the Politics of Scarcity,* p. 215.

21. Ophuls, *Ecology and the Politics of Scarcity,* pp. 214-215.

22. U.S. National Academy of Sciences and Royal Society of London, *Population Growth, Resource Consumption, and a Sustainable World* (London and Washington, D.C., 1992).

23. Robert M. Hazen, *The Breakthrough: The Race for the Superconductor* (New York: Summit Books, 1988), p. 8.

24. Hazen, *The Breakthrough,* p. 257.

25. Herman Kahn, *The Next 200 Years: A Scenario for America and the World* (New York: Morrow, 1976); Julian L. Simon, *The Ultimate Resource* (Princeton, N.J.: Princeton University Press, 1981); Julian L. Simon,

Population and Development in Poor Countries
(Princeton, N.J.: Princeton University Press, 1992).

26. United Nations, *Human Development Report 1996* (New York: Oxford University Press, 1966), pp. 178–179.

27. World Commission on Environment and Development, *Our Common Future* (New York: Oxford University Press, 1987).

28. Three examples of environmental studies adopting a sustainable development model: World Bank, *World Development Report 1992: Development and the Environment* (New York: Oxford University Press, 1992); Worldwatch Institute, *State of the World 1993: A Worldwatch Institute Report on Progress Toward a Sustainable Society* (New York: Norton, 1993); Al Gore, *Earth in the Balance* (New York: Houghton Mifflin, 1992).

29. World Commission, *Our Common Future*, p. 43.

30. World Commission, *Our Common Future*, p. 49.

31. World Commission, *Our Common Future*, p. 261.

32. See Chapter 14 for a definition and discussion of the concept of regimes.

33. Gore, *Earth in the Balance*.

34. Gore, *Earth in the Balance*, pp. 306-307.

35. Ophuls, *Ecology and the Politics of Scarcity*.

36. Ophuls, p. 13.

37. Modern writers who see the need for such an alternative include Garrett Hardin in "The Tragedy of the Commons," and *Exploring New Ethics for Survival* (New York: Viking, 1972); Robert L. Heilbroner, *An Inquiry into the Human Prospect: Updated and Reconsidered for the 1990s* (New York: Norton, 1991); Buckminster R. Fuller, "An Operating Manual for Spaceship Earth," in *Environment and Change: The Next Fifty Years*, ed. William R. Ewald, Jr. (Bloomington: Indiana University Press, 1968); and B. F. Skinner, *Walden Two* (New York: Macmillan, 1948) and *Beyond Freedom and Dignity* (New York: Knopf, 1971). For an analysis of the ecological problem that favors benevolent authoritarianism, see William Ophuls, Chapter 4, "The Politics of Scarcity," in *Ecology and the Politics of Scarcity*.

38. Richard A. Falk, *A Study of Future Worlds* (New York: Free Press, 1975), p. 104.

39. Falk, p. 104.

GLOSSARY

This glossary provides "rough and ready" definitions of key concepts that appear in bold type in the text. For a quick page preference to their location in the book, see the Index.

accommodation Political behavior that seeks a compromise between competing interests. It is marked by cooperation, bargaining, and balloting.

advice and consent What the U.S. Senate must provide on treaties and key appointments by the president.

alienation For Marx, workers' sense of being divorced or estranged from what they produce, from their work activity, from humanity, and from fellow human beings.

anarchy The absence of government, accompanied by lawlessness and the prevalence of a dog-eat-dog attitude among survivors.

anticolonialism The political movement seeking to achieve independence for colonies, thus permitting nation-states to govern themselves.

anti-Semitism Prejudice against or dislike of Jews, often leading to discrimination and persecution.

apartheid South Africa's former legal system of racial discrimination, or separate political, economic, and social life for blacks and whites, designed to perpetuate white supremacy.

arèté The Greek ideal of excellence, which they sought to fulfill in all fields of human activity.

aristocracy Government by the best; rule of those with great wisdom and sense of justice, as understood by Plato and Aristotle.

autarky Doctrine of economic self-sufficiency.

authoritarianism An antidemocratic political stance that favors placing political power in the hands of an elite group or a dictator.

balance of power The view that peace is maintained when power is more evenly distributed among competing nations so that no one state, or combination of states, can be aggressively dominant.

behavioralism An approach to social science that emphasizes empirically observable, discoverable, and explicable patterns of behavior.

Bill of Rights The first ten amendments to the U.S. Constitution, establishing such individual rights as freedom of speech and religion.

bourgeoisie For Marx, the class of modern capitalists, owners of the means of production; generally, the middle class in a capitalist society.

bureaucracy The governmental departments, ministries, agencies, and officials that carry out public policy, ideally in a rational, efficient, impartial, and stable manner.

capitalism An economic system based on private ownership of the means of production and exchange, a market economy, economic competition, free trade, and consumer sovereignty.

carrying capacity The ability of the earth to support human and other life forms.

civic culture The set of attitudes toward citizenship and politics held by those in a particular nation.

civil disobedience The doctrine that a conscientious individual may peacefully, publicly, and selectively disobey a morally outrageous government policy, while being prepared to pay the price for such disobedience.

class The division of people by virtue of their economic, social, and political standing, such as upper class, middle class, and lower class.

class struggle Marx's concept of the conflict between the oppressive capitalist class and the oppressed working class over economic, political, and social power.

class values Basing political values on social class, such as working-class values versus capitalist values.

codetermination A social democratic practice of providing worker representation on the directing board of industrial firms and giving workers a modest voice in setting company policy.

collective security A policy pattern that envisages the banding together of all peace-loving nations, including the most powerful, to maintain international peace and law against aggressors, and the use of collective strength to deter or punish such aggressors.

colonialism The occupation, political control, and economic exploitation of much of the Third World region by European states primarily during the nineteenth and twentieth centuries.

common good The good of all in the community, the public interest, or the best long-range interest of human kind, as opposed to the short-sighted, selfish interest of individuals, groups, or nations.

communes Cooperative economic and government units for both agricultural and nonagricultural work. Instituted by Mao Zedong as a means of accelerating the evolution from capitalism to communism.

communism An economic, political, and social outlook that endorses public ownership of the means of production and exchange, worker control, and satisfaction of human needs in accord with the motto "From each according to his ability, to each according to his needs."

connection of powers Connection of political power among governmental bodies, as opposed to the separation of powers.

conservatives In the American context, those who see themselves as more respectful of traditional values (private property and enterprise, family, church) than liberals.

constitutional Referring to the distinguishing attitudes, habits, and behavior patterns that characterize a political community.

constitutional dictatorship A system of government in which rulers are legally given extraordinary powers to rule during an emergency—powers that could include the suspension of certain liberties.

constitutional framework The larger historical, cultural, economic, and social ethos that suffuses the political community.

contract An agreement, usually written, and enforceable by law, between two or more people to do something.

conversion The peaceful transformation of a political opponent, emphasizing voluntary agreement and free choice. Instruments of conversion include love, conscience, and reason.

cooperative movement Robert Owen's idea of mutually owned stores selling goods for the benefit of their members.

creative breakthrough A significantly fruitful resolution of a major problem—ethical, empirical, or prudential—that conventional wisdom deems insoluble.

democracy Rule by the people, now usually via elected representatives, and under a constitution that provides for the protection of basic rights and majority rule.

democratic socialism Ideology committed to popular constitutional rule and protection of basic rights, as well as to public ownership or social control of key aspects of economic life in the interest of equitable distribution of societal wealth and satisfaction of human needs.

destruction Political behavior, often marked by deadly conflict and war, aimed at the complete annihilation of one's opponent.

detente A relaxation of tensions. In an international context, it characterized the relationship between the United States and the Soviet Union in the late 1960s and early 1970s.

dialectic Hegel's concept of the role of the clash of ideas in producing historical development.

dialectic method A method of getting at the truth by critically examining often clashing ideas, opposing forces, or societal contradictions.

dictatorship Rule by a strong leader with absolute power and unlimited authority. *See also* **constitutional dictatorship.**

dictatorship of the proletariat Forceful socialist rule by the majority of people—workers—in the process of destroying capitalism and bourgeois society and creating the conditions for the advancement of communism.

diplomacy The art and skill of conducting relations between nations or between parties in politics.

direct democracy A form of democracy in which all citizens participate in making laws firsthand, rather than electing representatives to handle that task.

disarmament Reduction in the number of military weapons a nation might possess or use.

discrimination Acting on arbitrary distinctions based on group classification, such as race or gender.

divine law Law revealed by God and found in the scriptures.

domination The policy of exercising direct or indirect control, sometimes despotic, over others.

due process Legal procedures that protect people against arbitrary and unreasonable action by government that would deprive them of life, liberty, and property.

Earth Summit Global environmental conference held in June 1972 in Rio de Janeiro, Brazil.

ecology The relationship between organisms and their environment.

economic integration A process whereby states remove trade and other barriers, engage in increased levels of economic interaction, and thus achieve greater economic unification.

economic well-being A value characterized by economic prosperity, including decent wages, profits, and balanced budgets.

elite A select group, often characterized by superior political, economic, social, or cultural skills or power.

empiricism Concerned with phenomena—with what can be scientifically observed by the senses, such as facts, circumstances, experiences.

Enlightenment An eighteenth-century way of thought, characterized by a belief in freedom, reason, science, and progress.

equality Concept that emphasizes equal political and social rights or the condition of being neither superior nor inferior.

eternal law The reason of God ("God's grand design") by which the universe and all things in it are governed.

ethics Concern with what ought to be, with right or moral standards of judgment and behavior.

ethnocentrism The belief that one's own race, nation, religion, or culture is superior to all others.

Eurocommunism Variety of communism in Western Europe that seeks to combine socialist principles with peaceful parliamentary government and aspects of a market economy.

European Union A largely Western European regional organization, now fifteen nations, formed out of the European Coal and Steel Community, the European Economic Community, and the European Atomic Energy Community. It now includes the European Economic Community, the European Parliament, and the European Court of Justice. The European Union is the premier example of the movement toward international integration.

explanation The process of fitting the pieces of a scientific puzzle together.

extensive republic Madison's term for a federal republic governing a large territory.

Fabians A group of British intellectuals, at work in the late nineteenth and early twentieth centuries, committed to achievement of democratic socialism.

faction A self-interested group that acts in ways inconsistent with the common good.

fascism An authoritarian and militaristic ideology that glorified the state and its often dictatorial leader.

federalism A governmental system that combines central authority for nationwide concerns with state, provincial, or regional authority for local concerns, with certain powers shared by, and certain powers denied to, both levels of government.

four modernizations A post-Mao model for development in the People's Republic of China in the areas of agriculture, industry, national defense, and science and technology.

freedom Power over one's destiny, interpreted negatively as the absence of arbitrary restraints and positively as the presence of those abilities that enable individuals and groups to fulfill their peaceful and creative potentialities.

functionalism Concept in international politics that emphasizes the process of transcending conflicts of national sovereignty by having organizations address specific tasks and problems, thus simultaneously meeting common needs, advancing mutual interests, and contributing to peace, freedom, and prosperity.

general will The idea, associated with Rousseau, that there is a best, long-range, constant view of the public good that should guide a democratic political community.

genocide Systematic mass destruction of a national, ethnic, racial, or religious group.

glasnost The Russian word for openness, popularized by Gorbachev and intended to characterize efforts to achieve a freer society. *See also* **perestroika.**

global warming A theory that posits that because of the emission and trapping of heat-absorbing gases such as carbon dioxide, CFCs, methane, nitrous oxide, and ozone, the temperature of the planet is rising.

goal An objective, purpose, or vision.

grand debate Function of the United Nations whereby problems can be brought up, discussed, and analyzed, ideas can be tested, and the strength of policies can be measured.

greenhouse effect The trapping of heat-absorbing gases within the earth's atmosphere, thereby increasing the temperature of the planet. *See also* **global warming.**

hegemony Political dominance, usually of a given nation-state. In international politics it refers to dominance of a part of the world.

Holocaust The systematic extermination of six million Jews in World War II by the Nazis and their supporters.

human law The application, in specific circumstances, of natural law in earthly affairs.

human needs The biological, physiological, social, and cultural requirements for human survival and development.

human rights Freedom—legal, political, or moral—from government violations of people's integrity; civil and political liberties; and satisfaction of vital human needs such as food, shelter, clothing, health care, and education.

hypothesis A tentative idea, designed to guide investigation, about an approach to or solution of an empirical problem.

illiberal capitalism Capitalism that emphasizes capital growth at the expense of, or in disregard of, economic and social justice.

imperialism Subjugation and control of a country, people, or land by a more powerful state.

interest aggregation A means of selecting priorities in which political actors build support for certain proposals and not for others, usually by working with other like-minded individuals or groups.

interest articulation Expression of political actors' needs, interests, and desires, as by voting, speaking out in public forums, joining political parties or interest groups, and so on.

interest group A public group that organizes in an attempt to shape public policy on issues of special concern to the members.

international regime Norms, practices, and institutions in a particular functional area (such as trade) that have been accepted by parties in international politics.

judicial review The ability of the U.S. Supreme Court to declare an act of Congress unconstitutional.

justice Variously defined as fairness, rightful, a balancing of liberty, equality, and fraternity, and giving persons their due.

laissez-faire Policy of noninterference by government in economic matters.

law A rule established among a community by authority or custom. It may be eternal, natural, human, or divine.

least-developed countries (LDCs) The poorest of the poor developing countries.

least free The powerless, the deprived, and the maltreated, who are often the poor, racial minorities, women, and the politically oppressed.

liberal democracy A philosophy of constitutional government characterized by commitments to popular rule and protection of basic rights.

liberalism A movement for political, economic, social, and cultural freedom.

liberals In the American context, those who see themselves as more tolerant, generous, willing to experiment, and progressive than conservatives.

liberation theology A Christian-based philosophy, influenced by certain Marxist ideas, that interprets Christianity as a gospel of freedom and justice for the oppressed.

libertarians In the American context, those who rather consistently oppose government intervention in economic affairs and favor expansion of personal freedoms.

liberty Freedom from slavery, imprisonment, captivity, or any form of unlawful or arbitrary control; the sum of rights of a free individual or people. *See also* **freedom** and **human rights.**

limited government Placing of limitations on government power, as opposed to authoritarian or totalitarian government.

lion and fox At stake in this "game" of politics, as understood by Machiavelli, are a state's vital interests, which must be protected realistically using both force and craft.

loyal opposition The name given to the opposing or minority party in the United Kingdom.

majority rule The power of one-half of the members, plus one, of any decision-making group to bind the remainder of that group to a decision.

materialism The view that emphasizes the importance of material means of subsistence in shaping life, politics, and civilization, as opposed to the role of ideas.

meritocracy The bureaucratic aristocracy of those in government service.

metanoia Fundamental transformation of a world view.

mixed economy A view that calls for the coexistence of socialism and capitalism in the same economy.

model A simplified version of what goes on in the real world; it highlights the importance of increasing political, economic, and ecological interaction and interdependence.

monarchy According to Aristotle, government by a virtuous ruler.

472 GLOSSARY

more peaceful world order The minimization of the level of armed conflict through the elimination of catastrophic world wars, regional wars, civil wars, and wars of national liberation.

multilateralism Groups of countries working through international organizations, engaged in collective problem solving and problem resolution.

multinational corporations (MNCs) Corporations with ownership and/or operations in more than one country.

nation-state A historical community of people united under a single government with sovereign authority.

national interest The vital concerns—security, liberty, justice, welfare—essential to the independence, protection, prosperity, and power of the nation-state.

national self-determination The right of a people to freely pursue their own political, economic, social, and cultural development.

nationalism A powerful feeling of belonging to a nation held by a group of people who cherished or sought national independence as well as political, economic, and social freedom.

natural law A higher law, known through reason, that provides for individuals and society a standard of good and evil, affirms basic human rights, and emphasizes the criterion of the common good.

nazism The German variety of fascism, characterized by dictatorial and totalitarian rule, aggressive nationalism, anti-Semitism, militarism, and imperialism.

neocolonialism Economic and political control by, or dependence on, a former colonial ruler or Big Power.

neofunctionalism A concept that, like functionalism, emphasizes organizations and activities that meet common needs in economic, technical, and humanitarian areas such as food, public health, and education. But unlike functionalism, it recognizes the power of nationalism and national elites as well as the need to confront political conflicts rather than avoid them.

neoimperialism A pattern of economic dominance perpetuated by the developed countries over the developing countries long after political independence has been achieved.

new world order A future scenario in which various political tasks (resolving conflicts, furthering peace, fostering economic well-being, etc.) would be assigned to the political actors (at the appropriate level, from local to world) best able to handle them, in a democratic and constitutional manner.

newly industrialized economies (NICs) Name given to several dynamic and relatively prosperous Asian economies, including South Korea, Taiwan, Hong Kong, and Singapore.

nonalignment A policy, adopted by many nation-states of the developing world, of nonentanglement in the power struggles and alliances of the superpowers following World War II.

nonrenewable resources Earth resources that cannot be replaced, such as fossil fuel.

nonviolence Resolving conflicts through a variety of peaceful techniques that do not involve the use of physical force or military weapons.

nuclear proliferation The spread of nuclear weapons and/or technology to nation-states or non-state actors that did not previously possess them.

nuclear winter As a result of nuclear war, a pall of smoke and dust encircling the earth, plunging the surface into virtual darkness and resulting in a drastic drop in temperature.

oligarchy Rule by the few rich and lovers of money (Plato); by the few rich and noble (Aristotle); by the self-interested few.

operative ideals Those values that actually inspire political ideologies or guide political systems.

ozone layer The thin layer of ozone that encircles the earth's stratosphere and protects the earth from the full force of the sun's ultraviolet rays.

partisan One who more often than not votes his or her party on key issues.

party dominance A one-party system, as in communist countries.

patriarchy The belief in or practice of male superiority or domination.

peace The absence of war; a condition of harmony between nation-states.

peaceful coexistence Belief that rival nation-states can live together peacefully in a nuclear world, even as they compete peacefully for political, economic, and ideological power.

peaceful settlement The resolution of disputes through nonviolent means such as influence, inquiry, mediation, and conciliation.

peacekeeping The interposition of a multilateral force between conflicting forces to oversee the cessation of hostilities and facilitate negotiations. Mainly, but not exclusively, used by the United Nations.

perestroika A policy of restructuring the Communist political and economic system in the Soviet Union, instituted by Gorbachev.

players Contestants in the game of politics who compete or cooperate in pursuit of certain goals, who exercise power or will, who win or lose.

pluralism Concept that emphasizes the multiple interests at work in the struggle for power in politics.

plurality The highest number of votes cast but below 50 percent.

policy A course or general plan of action to achieve a desired political goal.

polis The Greek city-state.

political actors Individuals or groups that express and shape public values, struggle for power, and decide issues of public policy.

political creativity The vital achievement, in both theory and practice, of a more fruitful ethical, empirical, prudential understanding of politics.

political culture The dominant ethos of a political community.

political health The political, economic, and social well-being of the political community, judged in terms of peace and constitutional change, security, liberty, democratic governance, justice, prosperity, ecological balance, and cultural excellence.

political ideologies The beliefs and practices that guide political actors in real political communities.

political obligation Concept that deals with the reasons people have for obeying, or disobeying, those who demand their allegiance in politics, such as government, law, or the state.

political party An organized group that seeks to play a role in governing a political community by setting an agenda and getting its members elected to office.

political science A field of study characterized by a search for critical understanding of (1) the good political life, (2) significant empirical phenomena, and (3) wise political and policy judgments.

political values Worthwhile ideals, goals, and principles in public affairs.

politician One in politics who, depending on circumstances, seeks to balance the diverse and shifting pressures of constituency, party, interest groups, and conscience in political decision making.

politics A process whereby public values are debated, political actors cooperate and struggle for power, and public policy judgments are made and implemented.

polity Constitutional democracy or, more loosely, political community.

polyarchy Rule by the many in a democratic and constitutional system.

populists In the American context, those who tend to favor government intervention in economic affairs and to oppose expansion of some "liberal" personal freedoms.

positivism A philosophy holding that human beings can know only that which is based on observable, scientific facts, on data derived from experience.

poverty That level of income, food, health care, education, shelter, and quality of life that is below minimum standards of life and decency.

power The ability—political, legal, economic, military, social, moral—of one political actor to get another political actor to do or not do something.

power politics Patterns of politics characterized by the acquisition, preservation, and balancing of power. Most often used to describe the competitive-conflictive behavior of the superpowers (the U.S. and USSR) during the Cold War.

pragmatism Philosophy that emphasizes whatever works best to deal with practical problems in the real world.

prescriptive constitution The successful, tested way of life that is the historical choice of many generations and that embodies the wise principles and institutions of a nation's heritage.

preventive diplomacy Action by the United Nations to help states, often smaller ones, settle disputes peacefully, before they escalate and involve the superpowers.

principle A basic truth, doctrine, or rule used as a basis of reasoning or a guide to behavior.

proletariat The class of modern wage laborers.

prudence Wise, practical judgment, respectful both of sound values and of the limitations and opportunities of social reality.

public interest The interest of the entire community, which transcends the self-interest of individuals or groups and expresses the best long-range interest of the nation.

racism Belief in the superiority or inferiority of a given race, often resulting in discrimination against and maltreatment of members of the allegedly inferior race.

radicals Political activists who are generally very unhappy with the status quo and who seek major changes in modern American society.

reactionaries Those on the right side of the political spectrum who seek to turn the clock back to recapture what for them was a more attractive, old-fashioned past.

regional integration The geographically based movement toward the merging of political and economic systems. Examples include the European Union and the North American Free Trade Agreement.

renewable resources Earth resources that can be replaced, such as forests.

representative government Government in which people exercise their power through elected representatives.

republicanism A political outlook characterized by popular rule, exercised by the electorate's representatives under a constitution that enshrines popular sovereignty and ensures the protection of basic rights.

responsible citizenship The practice of citizens responding sensibly to social, economic, and political tasks and problems.

retrogression Reversion to a more primitive, preindustrial way of life.

revisionists An intellectual tradition, led by the German Eduard Bernstein, that contributed to the development of democratic socialism. It emphasized the importance of a peaceful and parliamentary transition to socialism.

revolution of rising expectations Phrase used to characterize the hopes for a better way of life, especially among peoples in the developing Third World.

rules The agreed on principles and procedures that must be followed if a political game is to retain its identity.

sanctions Penalties, often economic, imposed on states that violate human rights or international law.

science A critical and systematic search for knowledge.

scientific method The approach used in the systematic search for knowledge. It involves identifying the problem, articulating a guiding hypothesis, obtaining evidence to test the hypothesis, and validating and explaining the significance of the hypothesis and the findings on which its rests.

separate but equal A constitutional doctrine in the United States from 1896 to 1954 that held that equality was not violated if blacks were required to use separate facilities in transportation, education, and other public areas, as long as the services were equal.

separation of powers The division of powers into legislative, executive, and judicial in the U.S. government.

sexism Discrimination based on gender.

social contract An agreement involving people uniting to effect a common purpose.

socialism A doctrine of public ownership, or social control, of key aspects of economic life, and public policies to ensure a more equitable distribution of the community's wealth.

sovereignty Supreme power in the nation-state.

stakes The goals that can be gained in victory or lost in defeat in the political game.

standard operating procedures A set of guidelines and procedures used by government organizations in carrying out policy.

status quo the state of affairs as it is or as it was before a recent change.

steady-state society/steady-state philosophy A condition of ecological balance whereby mindless growth and exploitation of the environment would cease.

strike The withdrawal of an indispensable activity by one party against another in order to alter behavior.

superconductivity The process of transmitting energy with limited or no loss of energy.

sustainable development A more rational and equitable approach to development that attempts to balance societal needs against environmental limitations.

theory A set of ideas formulated to explain something, emphasizing how the parts of the phenomena relate to the whole.

third-party activities Conflict-resolution techniques used by the United Nations and other international actors not involved in a given dispute; they include good offices, conciliation, investigation, mediation, arbitration, observation, truce supervision, and interposition.

Third World The often poor, often new, developing nations, most of which are located in the Southern Hemisphere (in Asia, Africa, Latin America, and the Middle East).

timocracy Government by people of honor and ambition.

tort A wrongful act, injury, or damage (not involving a breach of contract) for which a civil action can be brought.

totalitarianism A term used to characterize the complete political, economic, and social control of people and institutions by a dictatorial, single-party regime, driven by a dogmatic ideology, possessing a monopoly of weapons and communications, and in charge of a centrally directed economy and society.

tragedy of the commons Ecological metaphor calling attention to the overuse and eventual destruction of free grazing land.

trustee role Legislators acting on behalf of a higher interest than narrow constituent concerns.

trusteeship Commission from the United Nations to a country to look after a region, territory, or colony until the people of that land are ready for independence and self-government.

tyranny The lawless rule of one man, or an oppressive authoritarian regime.

ultra vires Beyond the law.

ultranationalism Self-righteous nationalistic behavior carried to the extreme and leading to denial of freedom for minority groups or aggression against other nations.

unitary form of government A form of government in which all major power and policy in the country emanates from the central government.

uskornie Russian term denoting the acceleration of reforms in the Soviet communist system under Gorbachev.

utilitarianism Creed whose central principle is utility or usefulness in advancing the greatest good or happiness for the greatest number of people.

utopia The perfect political and social order, characterized by peace, justice, communal life, prosperity, and cultural excellence.

utopian socialism Political philosophy, articulated by eighteenth-century thinkers Henri Claude Saint-Simon, Robert Owen, and Charles Four-ier, which emphasized cooperative, communal living.

validation Corroboration of a hypothesis through gathering and analysis of evidence.

values. *See* **class values; political values.**

war Military activity, or armed violence, carried out in a systematic and organized way by nation-states (or organized groups that aspire to become nation-states) against other nation-states.

welfare Programs in which a state contributes to or provides for its people's needs for employment, income, food, housing, health care, and literacy.

welfare state Society that provides a range of social services designed to ensure adequate income, health care, housing, education, unemployment benefits, retirements benefits, and so on for all who need them.

wipe-out A political game in which one player, insisting on total dominance, encounters resistance and uses brute physical force to destroy an opponent.

working poor In the American context, having an annual income of below $20,000.

writ of habeas corpus A legal document (literally, "produce the body") requiring that a prisoner be brought before a court to determine whether he or she is lawfully being held in jail.

INDEX